ENCYCLOPEDIA OF CONTEMPORARY AMERICAN SOCIAL ISSUES

VOLUME 2
CRIMINAL JUSTICE

Michael Shally-Jensen, Editor

ABC-CLIO

Santa Barbara, California • Denver, Colorado • Oxford, England

Copyright 2011 by ABC-CLIO, LLC

All rights reserved. No part of this publication may be reproduced, stored in a retrieval system, or transmitted, in any form or by any means, electronic, mechanical, photocopying, recording, or otherwise, except for the inclusion of brief quotations in a review, without prior permission in writing from the publisher.

Library of Congress Cataloging-in-Publication Data

Encyclopedia of contemporary American social issues / Michael Shally-Jensen, editor.
    v. ; cm.
    Includes bibliographical references and index.
    Contents: Vol. 1: business and economy — Vol. 2: criminal justice — Vol. 3: family and society — Vol. 4: environment, science, and technology.
    ISBN 978-0-313-39204-7 (set : alk. paper) — ISBN 978-0-313-39205-4 (set ebook)
    1. United States—Social conditions—Encyclopedias.   2. United States—Economic conditions—Encyclopedias.   3. United States—Politics and government—Encyclopedias.
I. Shally-Jensen, Michael.
    HN59.2.E343   2011
    306.0973—dc22   2010041517

ISBN: 978-0-313-39204-7
EISBN: 978-0-313-39205-4

15 14 13 12 11   1 2 3 4 5

This book is also available on the WorldWideWeb as an eBook.
Visit www.abc-clio.com for details.

ABC-CLIO, LLC
130 Cremona Drive, P.O. Box 1911
Santa Barbara, California 93116-1911

This book is printed on acid-free paper ∞

Manufactured in the United States of America

Contents

VOLUME 2: CRIMINAL JUSTICE

VOLUME 3: FAMILY AND SOCIETY

VOLUME 4: ENVIRONMENT, SCIENCE, AND TECHNOLOGY

Preface

The growing prominence of news, information, and commentary of all kinds, and in every medium, has unfortunately not always been matched by a deepening or a widening of consumers' understanding of the issues at hand. In this era of tweets and peeks (information and video clips), of blogging and befogging (electronic opining), people of all stripes are under increased pressure to make snap judgments about matters about which they may know little. The fact that so many of the issues of the day—corporate misdoings, criminal violence, the condition of the schools, environmental disasters—touch the lives of so many Americans suggests that awareness of them at *any* level is a good thing. At some point, however, one needs to move beyond the news feeds and sound bites and begin to appreciate current issues for the complex matters that they are. This is precisely what the *Encyclopedia of Contemporary American Social Issues* is designed to do.

As with other works of its kind, the present encyclopedia is intended to serve as a bridge between the knowledge of experts and the knowledge of those new to the subjects it covers. We present here, then, scholarly research on a broad array of social issues in a format that is accessible and interesting, yet informative. The contributors have taken care with both the quality of their prose and the accuracy of their facts, the aim being to produce entries that are clear, accurate, and thorough. Contributors and editors alike have paid attention to the language of the entries to ensure that they are written in an intelligible style without losing sight of the terms and conventions employed by scholars writing within their disciplines. Thus, readers will find here thoughtful introductions to some of the most pressing issues currently confronting American society.

Scope

The *Encyclopedia of Contemporary American Social Issues* is divided into four volumes: (1) Business and Economy; (2) Criminal Justice; (3) Family and Society; and (4) Environment, Science, and Technology. Within each volume, the entries are arranged in alphabetical order. There are just over 200 entries in the encyclopedia, the essays ranging in length from about 1,500 words to more than 8,000. Each essay discusses a contemporary issue and ends with suggestions for further reading.

The first problem in compiling an encyclopedia of this type, of course, is determining what constitutes a social issue. It would seem a common enough term about whose meaning there is general consensus. Still, the matter bears a quick review. The *American Heritage Dictionary* defines an issue as:

a. a point or matter of discussion, debate, or dispute;

b. a matter of public concern;

c. a misgiving, objection, or complaint;

d. the essential point, crux.

In other words, not only a matter of public debate or discussion but also a point of concern or matter about which there are misgivings or objections. Included in the mix, moreover, is the idea of a neat summary or something boiled down to its essentials.

In the present encyclopedia, readers will find entries reflecting these varied senses of the term *issue*. There are entries, for example, such as "Health Care," "Oil Drilling," and "Gun Control" whose subjects one often hears debated in public forums. On the other hand, there are entries such as "Globalization," "Sprawl," and "Social Justice" whose subjects are rather harder to identify as clear-cut matters for public debate and seem more like general areas of concern. Of course, more than the general public, it is scholars who routinely examine the ins and outs of various subjects; and for scholars there is little doubt that globalization and the like are key issues requiring careful description and analysis. Fortunately for readers of this encyclopedia, included here are the considered opinions of some 170 scholars and professionals from a variety of different fields, all of whom were asked to lay out "the essential points" for lay readers.

No encyclopedia can encompass the complete spectrum of issues within the contemporary United States. The question of what to include and what to omit is one that has vexed us from the start. The best strategy, we found, was to keep constantly in mind the readers who turn to a work like the *Encyclopedia of Contemporary American Social Issues,* whether in a school or college library or in a public library reference center. We recognize that reference works like this serve a range of purposes for the reader, from gleaning facts to preparing a research paper or introducing oneself to a subject in order to appreciate where it fits within the world at large. In the end, as editors who have been around school curricula and have worked in library reference publishing for many years, we followed our own counsel in deciding upon the contents of this work. We do so knowing that we cannot satisfy all readers; we hope, however, that we have satisfied the majority of those in need of the kind of information presented here.

Although the emphasis is on *contemporary* social issues, the entries generally situate their topics in historical context and present arguments from a variety of perspectives. Readers are thus able to gain an understanding of how a particular issue has developed and the efforts that have been made in the past—including in the most recent times—to address it. Thus, perennial issues such as taxes, education, and immigration are examined in their latest permutations, and newer developments such as cloning, identity theft, and media violence are discussed in terms of both their antecedents and the conversations currently surrounding them. If there is any trend to be noted with respect to contemporary American social issues, it might only be that with each step forward comes the likelihood of further steps yet to be negotiated. We get from point A to point B only by making good use of our democratic heritage and anticipating the prospect of multiple voices or multiple intermediary steps. The *Encyclopedia of Contemporary American Social Issues* reflects that fact and advances the idea that it is useful to know where and how a question first arose before attempting to answer it or move it forward in the public agenda.

There is an established tradition in sociology that focuses on "social problems" and the many means by which these problems can be and have been researched and analyzed. Always something of an eclectic enterprise, and drawing on the collective wisdom of social scientists working in a variety of different fields (including criminology, demography, anthropology, policy studies, and political economy), in recent years the social problems tradition has widened its range still further to include questions about the environment, corporations, the media, gender politics, and even science and technology. It is this expanded version of the sociological traditional that the present encyclopedia takes as its animating vision. Encompassed herein are all of the above fields and more. We welcome the expansion and see it as linked to the broader meaning of the term *social issues*.

The four volumes assembled here—Business and Economy; Criminal Justice; Family and Society; and Environment, Science, and Technology—have benefited from work done earlier by others, work hereby democratically brought forward and expanded in scope. Specifically, we have drawn upon a series of books published previously by Greenwood Press and entitled *Battleground*. Key entries from that series have been updated, revised, rewritten, and in some cases replaced through the efforts of either the original authors or experienced editors knowledgeable in the applicable fields. In addition, some two dozen entries appear here for the first time, the aim being to ensure that issues emerging in the last few years receive the attention they deserve. Among this latter group of entries are "Bank Bailouts," "Cybercrime," "Consumer Credit and Household Debt," and "Airport and Aviation Security."

Acknowledgments

It is to the contributors, then, that I, personally, owe the greatest debt of gratitude. Without their patience and understanding, their expertise and professionalism, this work would not have been possible. An associate editor, Debra Schwartz, and development editor Anne Thompson provided invaluable service in the preparation of entries for publication, and the assistance of Scott Fincher in this regard is happily acknowledged as well. Acquisitions editor Sandy Towers, with whom I first worked in conceiving the project, proved a valuable friend and professional asset throughout the process. Also present from the beginning was Holly Heinzer, whom I thank for her support. Many thanks, too, to the production staffs at both ABC-CLIO and Apex CoVantage for their invaluable assistance in helping to refine the text and set up the volumes for publication. I am grateful to Jeff Dixon for handling the graphics.

—*Michael Shally-Jensen*

A

AFRICAN AMERICAN CRIMINAL INJUSTICE

Alexander W. Pisciotta

Although the U.S. criminal justice system has a long and well-documented history of racism, sexism, and discrimination against the poor and powerless, controversies still exist about whether, for example, institutionalized racial discrimination still exists or how a racist past has shaped the lives and mind set of modern African Americans. Black Americans, in particular, have felt the collective wrath and injustice of state coercion from colonial times through the 19th century and well into the 20th century. This entry focuses on the evolution of the intentional and systematic repression aimed at fitting African Americans into their so-called proper place in the economic, political, social, cultural, and legal order.

Background

Crime was not a serious concern during the colonial period. Early settlements in the New World were, as legal historian Lawrence M. Friedman aptly puts it, "tight little islands." Villages were small and isolated. Their populations were religiously, ethnically, socially, and culturally homogeneous—and largely white. The early settlers knew their neighbors intimately and kept them under close surveillance. Colonial criminal justice systems were small, informal, and aimed at correcting the transgressions of misguided neighbors, friends, and relatives. Punishments were based upon the philosophy of re-integrative shaming: public humiliation followed by reintegration into the community. Put simply, the early colonists were their brothers' keepers.

The arrival of the first captive Africans at Jamestown, Virginia, in 1619—possibly as indentured servants, not slaves—was a pivotal event in American history. Africans filled the labor void, providing profits and sparking economic expansion, but they were not willing workers. Resistance was a constant concern. Slaves disobeyed their masters, worked slowly, feigned sickness, destroyed and stole property, poisoned and harmed farm animals, attempted escape, and, in extreme cases, burned buildings, murdered their masters, and plotted revolts. The so-called children of Ham were, quite simply, deviant and dangerous: profitable social dynamite that needed close surveillance and a repressive system of social control.

Laws were the key to combating black resistance. Legislatures passed a variety of colony-specific laws aimed at controlling slave behavior and maximizing profits. South Carolina, a slave state, prohibited slaves from traveling without a pass, owning property, selling goods without a master's written permission, carrying weapons, or meeting in groups. Masters were required to thoroughly inspect cabins every two weeks to look for weapons. White citizens were allowed to stop and question blacks, ask for passes, and even seize inappropriate clothing. Freed slaves were required to leave the state. Laws in Dutch New Netherlands were decidedly less strict. Slaves were allowed to marry, attend church, own property, trade goods, seek an education, join the militia, and even carry weapons. But when the British took over New Netherlands in 1664, the new rulers of New York instituted a much more restrictive set of laws. New York became like South Carolina.

Masters were the first line of defense in monitoring slave behavior, enforcing these laws, and maintaining social order. In most colonies, short of murder, masters generally had a free hand in administering justice without trial. Other colonial law enforcement officers—sheriffs, constables, and night watchmen—also kept slaves and free blacks under close surveillance. When serious crimes were committed (e.g., murder, rape, assault, arson, rebellion), slaves were formally charged in court; in many colonies, however, they were denied even minimal legal rights and faced the prospect of harsh punishment. Punishment and deterrence aimed at instilling terror—not benevolent reintegrative shaming—was the aim of slave discipline.

U.S. political, economic, social, and legal institutions were radically transformed during the first half of the 19th century. Emancipation from England and the ratification of the Constitution and Bill of Rights laid the foundation for the rise of democracy and new state-specific crime-control systems. The publication of *The Wealth of Nations* (1776)—Adam Smith's classic work—and industrialization accompanied the early development and expansion of capitalism in the New World. Exploding immigration produced large cities, especially in the North, and a host of city-related problems, including crime and delinquency. Slavery remained essentially unchanged, however, especially in the South. Repressive laws and crass, unyielding social control were needed to maintain order and preserve profits.

The aims, structure, and character of early-19th-century criminal justice systems were, however, region-specific. Northern states developed formal criminal justice institutions largely aimed at the social control of immigrants, particularly the Irish, who were widely perceived as criminally inclined drunkards. Black criminals were a secondary concern. Southern states relied upon informal surveillance and social control. Slaves merited the closest scrutiny, but free blacks, Northern abolitionists, southern Negro sympathizers, and black and white criminals were all viewed as threats to the southern way of life. In short, the South was under siege.

Northern states responded to their crisis in crime and social disorder by introducing formal police systems. During the 1840s and 1850s, a number of large cities—such as New York, Boston, and Philadelphia—disbanded their ineffective night watch, restricted sheriffs and constables to court duties, and turned policing over to newly created law enforcement agencies. Although these new police departments were largely ineffective—policemen were unqualified, untrained, and corrupt—arrests increased. Courts were expanded to handle the increased volume of cases. Prisons and reformatories were introduced to hold offenders. The demographic profile of prison populations varied by state, but they were usually lower-class, white, urban immigrants and their children—the northern criminal classes.

Southern criminal justice was informal, decentralized, and aimed, first and foremost, at one group: slaves. Southern states expanded the content and harshness of slave codes prior to the Civil War. Masters continued to serve as the first line of policing and social defense. Slave patrols were expanded and more slave catchers were hired. Sheriffs, constables, and newly created police forces, located in larger southern cities, were constantly on the alert for escaped slaves, black and white criminals, and other threatening groups (e.g., abolitionists encouraging escape or revolt). Militias remained on high alert to deal with slave revolts. The laws in many southern states continued to grant all white citizens the authority to stop, question, and arrest free blacks and slaves. For free blacks and slaves, the South was a repressive police state.

Early-19th-century southern courts and systems of punishment were also racially driven. In fact, there were at least four court systems and four sets of legal procedures—white male, white female, black male, and black female—which provided no meaningful rights for members of these groups. Free blacks were often afforded an intermediate status. Black slaves accused of insurrection faced special tribunals that handed out harsh and swift punishments—often death—to prevent future transgressions. A number of southern states opened prisons prior to the Civil War, but they were almost exclusively reserved for white offenders. In the minds of many southerners, even the lowest white criminal was to be spared the humiliation and moral contagion of incarceration with "darkies" and "niggers."

The end of the Civil War and passage of the Thirteenth, Fourteenth, and Fifteenth Amendments to the U.S. Constitution filled freedmen with optimism and hope for equality and justice. Blacks did, indeed, make considerable progress during Reconstruction, but these gains were short-lived. The triumph of the so-called Redeemers—white conservative racists—summarily ended these political, economic, social, and legal gains. The Redeemers were determined to return free blacks to their slave status. Laws and the criminal justice system, coupled with informal means of terror (e.g., lynching), were keys to putting blacks in their proper place and reviving the Old South.

The Redeemers began their calculated assault on black progress and civil liberties by seizing control of the political system. Newly elected white supremacists passed repressive legislation, including vagrancy laws aimed at fostering the sharecropping system. Sheriffs, constables, and newly formed police departments replaced masters, slave patrols, and slave catchers in intimidating former slaves. Black arrest rates soared, courts were overwhelmed with "colored" defendants, and southern prisons took on a new function: race control. After 1865, southern prisons and chain gangs were nearly completely black.

African Americans continued to be regarded as second-class citizens, especially in the South, throughout the first half of the 20th century. "Separate but equal" laws—legitimized by the U.S. Supreme Court's notorious *Plessy v. Ferguson* decision (1896)—kept blacks in a decidedly inferior status: schools and housing developments were rigidly segregated; blacks were excluded from government jobs and segregated in the military; they were isolated in whites-only businesses, including restaurants and movie theaters; and they were relegated to using colored-only water fountains and restroom facilities. Disenfranchisement was widespread; in some southern states, fewer than 5 percent of blacks were registered to vote in the 1950s.

Police forces in the South, and sometimes in the North, were exclusively white. Black faces were rarely seen in courts unless they were defendants. A variety of ruses were employed to exclude blacks from serving on juries. Blacks continued to be disproportionately incarcerated in southern and northern prisons. In many institutions, they were rigidly segregated. Black defendants were far more likely to receive the death penalty, especially for rape, and blacks who murdered whites were much more likely to receive the death penalty than whites who murdered blacks. Simply stated, black victims had less value than white victims in the U.S. criminal justice system.

Crass political, economic, and legal discrimination continued relatively unabated into the 1950s. The 1960s were, however, a pivotal period in U.S. racial and legal history. The rise of the black civil rights movement, women's rights movement, protests against the Vietnam War, and dozens of race riots in cities across the United States raised serious doubts about the veracity and legitimacy of the U.S. government. The promise of freedom, equality, and justice was exposed as sheer hypocrisy, especially for African Americans.

Critics also turned their ire on the U.S. criminal justice system. Television cameras provided graphic accounts of police beating black rioters in the North and civil rights marchers, including children, in the South. The rise of criminal justice and criminology as academic disciplines in the 1960s resulted in an explosion of research highlighting disparities between the promise and practice of the justice system: inadequacies in the public defender system, the discriminatory dimensions of bail, abuses in plea bargaining, discrimination in the hiring and training of minority police, the paucity of minority judges and probation and parole officers, inhumane conditions and racial discrimination in prisons, and racial and class discrimination in sentencing and the application of the death penalty.

The U.S. Supreme Court, particularly under Chief Justice Earl Warren (1953–1968), issued a series of landmark rulings that expanded the legal rights of black and white defendants. Attempts were made to rehabilitate offenders, shut down prisons, and move offenders back to the community. Money was appropriated to improve public defender systems, offer bail to more poor offenders, hire more minority police officers, and divert offenders from the criminal justice system to avoid harmful labels. During this period and into the early 1970s, individual states and the federal government did, indeed, make progress in combating racism, sexism, and discrimination in the United States.

These trends and transformations were, however, short lived. The election of Ronald Reagan as president in 1980 marked the birth of a conservative revolution along with the bankruptcy of rehabilitation. Advocates of the new conservative paradigm argued that criminals were free, rational, and hedonistic actors who needed and deserved punishment. Discussions about racism, sexism, and discrimination—as well as questions raised about the fairness of capitalism and democracy—were dismissed as softhearted and soft-minded liberal drawl. A return to the policies of the past—a get-tough approach on crime and criminals—was the new elixir for crime and deviance.

During the 1980s and 1990s, conservative politicians and crime-control experts—joined, on occasion, by politically astute get-tough liberals, like President Bill Clinton—transformed the criminal justice system: a return to fixed sentencing, "three strikes and you're out" laws, preventive detention for suspected criminals, restrictions on the insanity defense, an end to minority hiring and promotion programs in policing, the increased use of transfers to adult courts for juveniles, boot camps for youthful offenders, electronic monitoring for offenders found guilty of less serious offenses, the opening of new prisons and reformatories, the introduction of "supermax" prisons, an expansion in the use of the death penalty, and a get-tough war on drugs.

Many of these policies have, however, had a decidedly detrimental effect on African Americans, and there is considerable evidence that remnants of racism are still pervasive in the U.S. justice system. Researchers have provided clear and convincing evidence that the death penalty continues to discriminate against the poor and powerless, particularly blacks. Public defender systems remain seriously underfunded, and prosecutors continue to use peremptory challenges to exclude blacks from juries. African Americans are still underrepresented on many police forces, especially in higher ranks. Egregious

INCARCERATION RATES

Since the 1980s the prison and jail population in the United States has increased dramatically; some estimate the increase to be as much as 500 percent. Today there are some 2.2 million people behind bars. The sharp rise in incarceration rates, moreover, is matched by an equally sharp rise in the proportions of African Americans and Latinos entering the nation's prisons and jails. Data from the Bureau of Justice Statistics indicate that African Americans are incarcerated at a rate that is nearly six times (5.6) the rate for whites, while Latinos are incarcerated at a rate that is nearly twice (1.8) the rate for whites.

Race/Ethnic Group	Rate per 100,000
White	412
Hispanic	742
Black	2,290

The national incarceration rate for whites is 412 per 100,000 residents, compared with 742 for Hispanics and 2,290 for African Americans. This means that 2.3 percent of all African Americans are incarcerated, compared with 0.7 percent of Hispanics and 0.4 percent of whites. The combination of age and economic disadvantage is also a key factor. One in nine (11.7 percent) African American males between the ages of 25 and 29 is currently incarcerated, most of them having come from severely disadvantaged neighborhoods (Mauer and King 2007).

cases of police abuse—for example, Rodney King (1991), Abner Louima (1997), and Amadou Diallo (1999)—confirm the suspicion that some law enforcement officers are still racially biased. And the discovery of the "driving while black" (DWB) syndrome in the 1990s provided evidence supporting ongoing African American suspicions and complaints: police officers discriminate against black drivers.

Mandatory sentencing laws and the war on drugs have, however, had a particularly harmful—if not disastrous—effect on African Americans. Racially biased legislation aimed at crack cocaine has resulted in an explosion in black incarceration. Millions of young African American males are currently incarcerated in state and federal correctional institutions or under the control of probation and parole officers. Jerome Miller's thought-provoking analysis of modern crime control reaches a sobering conclusion: the U.S. criminal justice system is engaged in a tragically misguided search-and-destroy mission aimed at young urban black males. Young black males—much like their slave ancestors—continue to comprise the class of dangerous criminals in the United States.

Key Events

Many key events have reflected and shaped the course of African American crime, criminal justice, and social control. Two broad classes of events, however, have played a particularly important role in the treatment of African Americans: black revolts and lynchings.

Revolts

Prior to the Civil War, many defenders of slavery, particularly in the South, argued that Africans needed the guidance of white masters and mistresses. The accursed children of Ham were biologically, psychologically, socially, culturally, and spiritually inferior. Indeed, it would be immoral to leave black Africans to their own vices on the "Dark Continent" (meaning Africa). White masters provided slaves with food, clothes, shelter, and Christian moral instruction. Quite simply, slaves were happy to live in captivity.

Black revolts provide clear and convincing evidence that slaves were not, in fact, content to live in bondage. Herbert Apthecker's classic study of slave revolts—*American Negro Slave Revolts*—documents 250 cases of rebellion in the United States. (Apthecker's [1993, 162] definition includes a number of elements to be counted as rebellion: the act must have included at least 10 slaves; freedom was the primary aim; and contemporary accounts labeled it as an insurrection, revolt, or rebellion. A modified version—including acts containing five rebels—would result in many more revolts.) In fact, many slave masters lived in a state of abject terror. Laws and criminal justice systems in colonial and 19th-century slave societies were, in large part, structured to detect and deal with black rebels, and the penalties were swift and severe.

The 1741 "great negro plot" in New York City, as one example, resulted in a bloody state response: 170 people were put on trial—a performance that was largely devoid of accepted colonial legal procedures. A total of 70 blacks and 7 whites were banished from British North America, 16 blacks and 4 whites were hanged, and 13 blacks were burned at the stake. Revolts led by Gabriel Prosser in Virginia in 1800, Denmark Vesey in South Carolina in 1822, and Nat Turner in Virginia in 1831 were all thwarted, largely owing to black spies. Prosser, Vesey, Turner, and dozens of their black coconspirators were put to death. As in New York City, no efforts were spared in crushing black rebels.

Revolts did not, however, affect only white masters and slave rebels. Whites who did not own slaves also lived in fear, knowing that black revolutionaries would not restrict killing to their masters. Moreover, slave revolts—rumored or real—always had harsh consequences for free blacks and slaves. Masters, slave patrols, sheriffs, and militias invariably launched so-called rebel sweeps to uncover weapons and black revolutionaries. Black revolts also provided abolitionists with a valuable propaganda tool: if slaves were happy living in captivity, why were they revolting?

Lynchings

The liberation of millions of slaves following the Civil War created a panic in the South. Conservative white southerners could not rely upon northern carpetbagger governments to prevent crime and maintain order. A new type of informal social control was employed: lynching.

The historical record is far from complete, but more than 5,000 cases of lynching have been documented, with most occurring in the South between 1880 and 1920. Black men, women, and children were hung, shot, stabbed, burned, dismembered, and put on display—sometimes in public places, like courthouses—in an effort to instill terror and remind blacks of their so-called proper place in the U.S. economic, political, social, cultural, and legal order. The rape or alleged rape of a white woman was one of the primary rationales for lynching, but thousands of blacks were lynched for other so-called offenses, such as stealing a chicken, uttering an insulting remark, making a sarcastic grin, calling to a white girl, talking big, failing to yield the sidewalk, failing to remove a hat, and refusing to remove a military uniform.

"Nigger hunts" and "coon barbecues" were, by design, savage affairs, often witnessed by thousands of spectators. In 1918, Mary Turner, who was eight months pregnant, was hung for threatening to press charges against mob members who lynched her husband. Before she died, her baby was cut from her stomach and stomped to death. A Texas jury convicted Jesse Washington of raping a white woman after four minutes of deliberation. The mob did not wait for sentencing. Washington was dragged from the courtroom, kicked, stabbed, and pummeled with rocks and shovels. At the execution site, he was suspended from a tree limb and doused with oil. His fingers, toes, ears, and penis were cut off. Then he was burned alive. His body was dragged through town by a man on horseback. The lynching of Will Porter in Livermore, Tennessee, in 1911 for shooting a white man was particularly bizarre. The mob took him to a theater, tied him to a chair on the stage, and sold tickets. Those who purchased orchestra tickets got six shots at Porter, balcony seats only one.

Blacks knew that they could not count on government officials to protect them from lynch mobs. Some law enforcement officers showed extraordinary courage in defending their charges. Several were killed or severely injured in the course of doing their job. The historical record indicates, however, that other law enforcement officers willingly handed alleged black criminals over to mobs and, in some cases, coordinated extralegal executions. Lynch-mob members did not wear masks, and photographs were often taken of the lynched as a trophy for the perpetrator. However, police investigations invariably reported that victims were killed by persons unknown or, in extreme cases, that they had committed suicide. A number of southern governors, senators, and congressmen openly advocated lynching, particularly for the crime of violating a white woman, and bragged about their participation in lynching mobs.

Lynching was enormously successful. Well into the 20th century, African Americans lived in fear, knowing that they could be murdered for any reason at any time. Walter White and Thurgood Marshall were both, on several occasions, nearly lynched. If the head of the National Association for the Advancement of Colored People (NAACP) and the nation's first African American Supreme Court justice came close to being murdered, who could be safe from the fury of the white mob?

Important Persons and Legal Decisions

Frederick Douglass (1817–1895), an escaped slave from Maryland, was the foremost intellectual leader and spokesman for African Americans during the 19th century. Douglass was a powerful lecturer for the abolitionist movement and achieved national and international fame with the publication of his autobiography, *Narrative of the Life of Frederick Douglass: An American Slave* (1845). This book—along with two other extended autobiographies and his work as editor of black newspapers (*North Star* and *Frederick Douglass' Paper*)—provided him with a forum to attack slavery and call for basic civil liberties for African Americans.

Douglass's pre–Civil War speeches and writings examined a variety of topics: for example, the kidnapping of blacks from Africa, the horrors of the African passage, the hypocrisy of Christian slave masters, the immorality of breaking up black families, and the failures of the U.S. Constitution and Bill of Rights. Douglass served as an advisor to President Abraham Lincoln and played an instrumental role in the formation of black military units during the Civil War. After the Civil War, Douglass worked for broader political, economic, and legal rights, including the enforcement of voting rights laws and an end to Jim Crow laws and lynching. Douglass's work as an abolitionist, orator, writer, newspaper editor, political activist, and statesman provided 19th-century African Americans with an articulate voice: the herald for freedom and justice.

Sojourner Truth (1797–1883), an escaped slave from New York, and Harriet Tubman (1820–1913), an escaped slave from Maryland, also made important contributions to the battle for justice. Truth, who was illiterate, made her impact as a charismatic speaker. She moved audiences with calls for an end to slavery and, in particular, distinguished herself from Douglass by calling for women's political and legal rights. Tubman, however, was the most courageous black civil rights leader. After escaping in 1849, she made numerous trips back into the South (between 17 and 20, depending upon the source)—knowing that she risked summary execution—and led several hundred slaves to freedom. Harriet Tubman, the legendary symbol of black resistance, was hailed as the Black Moses.

The late-19th- and early-20th-century black civil rights movement was dominated by two leaders who were, in fact, mortal enemies: Booker T. Washington (1856–1915) and W.E.B. Du Bois (1868–1963). Washington was, without question, the most powerful, controversial, complex, and divisive black leader. He was an educator who achieved national fame—especially among whites—by calling on blacks to accept gradual progress toward civil rights and focus on agricultural endeavors and vocational occupations. Du Bois, a brilliant scholar who was Harvard University's first black graduate, ridiculed Washington, called for immediate rights, and urged blacks to seek higher education. Washington used millions of dollars in contributions from white benefactors to build his followers into what northerners called the "Tuskegee Machine." Washington's machine smeared, blacklisted, and spied on Du Bois and other black leaders who opposed his philosophy. While Washington was destroying his opposition, however, he was secretly financing many of their causes, including legal challenges against Jim Crow. Ultimately, Du Bois prevailed. But after a lifetime of extraordinary achievement, including playing an instrumental role in the founding of the NAACP, he became thoroughly disenchanted, renounced his U.S. citizenship, and moved to Ghana, where he died in 1963.

Thurgood Marshall (1908–1993) was the most important champion for black legal justice. He became intimately familiar with racial repression and Jim Crow laws while growing up in Baltimore, Maryland. After graduating from Howard Law School, he became chief legal counsel to the NAACP. Marshall coordinated the NAACP's legal assault on *Plessy v. Ferguson* and Jim Crow laws and actually presented oral arguments in the landmark *Brown v. Board of Education* (1954) case before the U.S. Supreme Court. Marshall went on to become the nation's first African American solicitor general, attorney general, and U.S. Supreme Court justice. He continued to serve as the voice of the poor and powerless, denouncing institutional racism from his seat on the Supreme Court, until declining health forced him to resign in 1991.

Martin Luther King Jr. (1927–1968) has generally been recognized as the father of the modern civil rights movement. King played an instrumental role in the founding of a number of leading civil rights organizations in the 1950s and 1960s. Adopting a Christian–Gandhian model, he coordinated marches and protests and urged his followers to use passive resistance—not violence and riots—to rally world opinion and force an end to racial discrimination. Television coverage of the civil rights movement's most prominent leader and his followers being arrested and handcuffed by police on numerous occasions attracted attention to his cause and shamed the nation. King's brilliant "I Have a Dream" speech, delivered at the March on Washington rally in 1963, has been widely hailed as one of the most important moments in the history of the civil rights movement. King's assassination in Memphis, Tennessee, in 1968 shook the nation, delivering a clear message: Modern white supremacists, much like lynchers of the past, were willing to kill to keep African Americans in their so-called proper place.

Landmark legal decisions also provide important insights into African Americans' ongoing battle for political, economic, social, and legal justice. Key 19th-century decisions leave little doubt that U.S. Supreme Court justices, much like the rest of the country, were torn over the issue of racial equality; however, they opted for repression. In the 1856 Dred Scott decision, the Court ruled that slaves who traveled to free states could not sue for freedom because they were chattel and had no legal standing. Chief Justice Roger Taney explained that slaves were "a subordinate and inferior class of beings, who had been subjugated by the dominant race, and, whether emancipated or not, yet remained subject to their authority, and had no rights or privileges but such as those who held the power and the Government might choose to grant them." In *United States v. Cruikshank* (1875), the Court issued a ruling that had the effect of limiting the federal government's power to intervene in cases of black voter disenfranchisement and lynching. In *Plessy v. Ferguson* (1896), the Court legalized the "separate but equal" doctrine, making blacks inferior citizens well into the 1960s.

Since the late 1960s, the U.S. Supreme Court has, without question, played an instrumental role in dismantling overt legal repression. The Court has, however, demonstrated ambivalence on a number of important issues, including the death penalty. In the 1972 *Furman v. Georgia* decision, the Court ruled that the death penalty was being applied in an arbitrary, capricious, and racist manner and was, as a result, cruel and unusual punishment. In the 1976 *Gregg v. Georgia* decision, the Court reinstated the death penalty, permitting two-stage death penalty proceedings. *McCleskey v. Kemp* (1987), however, reflected the Court's legal and moral ambivalence. The Court conceded, after examining empirical evidence, that Georgia's court system was indeed racist. Nevertheless, they ruled against Warren McCleskey, who was subsequently executed, on the grounds that the statistical evidence did not prove discrimination in this specific case. In future cases, the Court shifted the burden of proof in death penalty cases back to the defendant: each black defendant would have to prove discrimination in his or her particular case, thus posing what was, to be sure, a costly, difficult, and unlikely challenge.

Conclusion

The history of African American crime, criminal justice, and social control is indeed troubling. From colonial times into the 1950s, blacks were subjected to overt and crass political, economic, social, cultural, and legal oppression. The U.S. Constitution and Bill of Rights—along with noble claims of freedom, equality, and justice—clearly did not apply to black Americans.

Much progress has been made. The separate but equal doctrine has been dismantled. Blacks are no longer riding in the backs of trains and buses, attending legally segregated schools, or drinking out of "colored only" water fountains. African Americans are not excluded from law enforcement positions or other government jobs, nor are they denied admission into colleges and universities. They have been afforded, at least on paper, all of the legal rights accorded whites. A trip to almost any court reveals black judges, defense attorneys, prosecutors, and probation officers. African Americans are in charge of police departments in many of the largest U.S. cities, and black wardens can be found at the heads of local, state, and federal correctional institutions across the country.

For conservatives, this progress provides clear and convincing evidence that the American dream has finally been fulfilled. Blacks have overcome the discrimination of the past and are now fully accepted citizens, enjoying the full protection of the state. But liberals remain unconvinced. African Americans, who have experienced generations of systematic repression, are particularly skeptical. The remnants of racism—particularly the explosion in black incarceration and continued disproportionate execution of poor black offenders—raise serious questions about the hidden dimension of race control, resurrecting the specter of the past. History matters. The color of justice in the United States remains, then, a matter of personal perception—a battleground for future generations.

See also **Alternative Treatments for Criminal Offenders; Class Justice; Miscarriages of Justice; Police Brutality; Police Corruption; Prison Construction; Social Justice; War on Drugs**

Further Reading

Apthecker, Herbert, *American Slave Revolts.* New York: International, 1993 [1943].

Barak, Gregg, Paul Leighton, and Jeanne Flavin, *Class, Race, Gender, and Crime: The Social Realities of Justice in America.* Lanham, MD: Rowman & Littlefield, 2007.

Friedman, Lawrence, *Crime and Punishment in American History.* New York: Basic Books, 1993.

Kennedy, Randall, *Race, Crime and the Law.* New York: Pantheon, 1997.

Mann, Coramae, Marjorie S. Zatz, and Nancy Rodriguez, eds., *Images of Color, Images of Crime: A Reader.* New York: Oxford University Press, 2006.

Mauer, Marc, and Ryan S. King, *Uneven Justice: State Rates of Incarceration by Race and Ethnicity.* Washington, DC: Sentencing Project, 2007.

Miller, Jerome G., *Search and Destroy: African-American Males in the Criminal Justice System.* New York: Cambridge University Press, 1996.

Muhammad, Khalil Gibran, *The Condemnation of Blackness: Race, Crime, and the Making of Modern Urban America.* Cambridge, MA: Harvard University Press, 2010.

Provine, Doris Marie, *Unequal under Law: Race in the War on Drugs.* Chicago: University of Chicago Press, 2007.

Russell-Brown, Katheryn, *The Color of Crime,* 2d ed. New York: New York University Press, 2008.

Tonry, Michael, *Malign Neglect: Race, Crime, and Punishment in America.* New York: Oxford University Press, 1995.

Walker, Samuel, Cassia Spohn, and Miriam DeLone, *The Color of Justice: Race, Ethnicity and Crime in America,* 4th ed. Belmont, CA: Wadsworth, 2006.

ALTERNATIVE TREATMENTS FOR CRIMINAL OFFENDERS

DIANNE WILLIAMS AND JESSICA WILLIAMS

The general public, not to mention law enforcement and policy makers, seems to believe that, aside from the death penalty, incarceration is the most severe form of punishment the criminal justice system can impose. In fact, the notion of a continuum of criminal justice sanctions typically places probation on the low end and imprisonment on the high end, with a variety of alternative sanctions falling somewhere in between (Petersen and Palumbo 1997). Unfortunately, the development of a continuum of alternative responses in crime control and the ranking of these alternatives have been developed by legislators and policy makers who had no reliable means of rating the severity of the sanctions imposed, had little or no access to experiential data, and depended primarily on individuals with no firsthand knowledge of the actual impact of the alternatives (Morris and Tonry 1990). As such, the common belief that penal–correctional sanctions must be bound by probation at the one end and imprisonment at the other may not only be misleading in many contexts but also represent the fundamental controversy underlying the development of alternative responses to crime—namely, that there is anything but a consensus on what constitutes an alternative and on what the alternative is alternative to.

In other words, politicians have their notions of severity and leniency, as do criminals, psychologists, penologists, criminologists, and risk-management specialists. There is no agreement between these persons or more generally between those engaged in law enforcement, prosecution, adjudication, and punishment/corrections about which particular alternatives should be used in response to a myriad of offenses. At the same time, over the years, there have been tangible changes in ideologies, theories, and practices associated with society's different responses to crime. As a result, alternatives—or perhaps more accurately, new emphases, some innovative and others not—emerge and develop and become mainstream; then other alternatives to those emerge and develop.

Background

Traditionally, criminal sanctions had four goals: (1) Retribution/punishment, which also connotes the dispensing or receiving of reward or punishment according to what the individual deserves. It implies the payment of a debt to society and thus the expiration of the offense and is codified in the biblical injunction "an eye for an eye." (2) Rehabilitation, which was the major reason for sentencing in the mid-20th century. It is a utilitarian philosophy, defined as the process of restoring an individual (a convict) to a useful and constructive place in society through some form of vocational, correctional, or therapeutic retraining or through relief, financial aid, or other reconstruction measure. (3) Incapacitation, which refers to the deprivation of legal/constitutional freedom and the ability to perform certain civil acts. Its main purpose is to remove offenders from society. (4) Deterrence, with specific and general deterrence based on a utilitarian philosophy that focuses on an understanding of human behavior. It works best when individuals believe they will get caught and punished and when their punishment is severe enough to represent a threat. The concept of restoration, meaning "reparation," or restoring an individual or a community to a state that existed before the crime was committed, was added later on as a fifth goal. The concept of alternatives was developed in an attempt to modify and/or expand the way in which society sanctions criminal acts. Over time, the goals of these sanctions have evolved, which has led to a necessary change in the sanctions themselves.

For example, correctional leaders began to embrace the idea of combining a psychology about personality and human development to probation in the 1940s. They began to emphasize a medical model for probation, and rehabilitation (as opposed to punishment) became the overriding goal. This medical model was popular until the 1960s, when it was replaced by the reintegration model. The main thrust of the reintegration model was to reduce the rate of recidivism by making the prisoner's return to the community easier. The reintegration model assumed that crime was a direct result of poverty, racism, unemployment, unequal opportunities, and other social factors.

The concept of probation underwent yet another change in the late 1970s and remains that way today. The goals of rehabilitation and reintegration have been replaced by what is referred to as *risk management* (Petersilia, Turner, Kahan, and Peterson 1985). The risk-management approach attempts to minimize the probability that any given offender will commit new offenses by applying different degrees of control over the probationer's activity based on the probationer's assessed degree of risk. In essence, the risk-management approach is a combination of the just desserts model (i.e., the severity of the punishment should equal the seriousness of the crime) of criminal sanction and the idea that the community must be safe.

In the 1960s and early 1970s, legislation was also passed to establish financial and programmatic incentives for community corrections. (In 1965, California passed the Probation Subsidy Act. In 1973, Minnesota passed the first comprehensive Community Corrections Act. In 1976, Colorado passed legislation patterned after Minnesota's. In 1978, Oregon passed similar legislation.) The incentives were expected to embrace a wide range of alternatives to incarceration from which judges and other officials could choose. The main goal was to alleviate prison overcrowding, support prisoner reintegration, and reduce rates of recidivism. In 1971, the incarceration rate was 96 per 100,000. By 2003, the rate was 477 per 10,000 (Clear, Cole, and Reisig 2006).

Today, despite research findings demonstrating that offenders perceive the pains of punishment in only one way, policy makers generally categorize alternatives into two categories: (1) low-control alternatives for the less severe crimes or low-risk offenders (e.g., fines or restitution, community service, drug/alcohol treatment, probation, intensive supervision probation, and home confinement) and (2) high-control alternatives for the more serious crimes or high-risk offenders (e.g., boot camp, shock incarceration, and community supervision). Simple probation lies at one end of the continuum (less severe punishment or low-control alternatives) and traditional incarceration at the other end (most severe punishment).

High-control alternatives, although not as severe as incarceration, are seen as the last option before incarceration. On the other hand, studies show that offenders ranked seven alternative sanctions more severely than prison: (1) boot camp, (2) jail, (3) day reporting, (4) intermittent incarceration, (5) halfway house, (6) intensive supervision probation, and (7) electronic monitoring. They viewed prison as more punitive only compared with community service and regular probation (Wood and Grasmick 1999). Regardless of rank in the punishment continuum, the goal of these alternatives is to reintegrate offenders into the community. These alternatives move away from the medical model and, in fact, suggest that the use of prisons should eventually be avoided altogether. In this approach, probation would be the sentence of choice for nonviolent offenders so as to allow them to participate in vocational and educational programs and ultimately make their adjustment to the community easier.

Legal Developments

Approximately two-thirds of adults under the supervision of the criminal justice system live in the general community while on either parole or probation. As discussed throughout this entry, probation is a type of community sentence in which the individual is remanded to some form of community supervision either as punishment for a crime or as a part of a sentence (usually after spending a portion of the sentence in prison). Although there is no right to parole and these individuals are still under the legal control of the correctional system, they, just like those who are incarcerated, still have rights. Therefore, while they are in the community, probationers and parolees enjoy a conditional liberty that is dependent on and regulated by very specific restrictions. These restrictions, by their very nature, may violate the constitutional rights of the probationer/parolee. For example, these individuals are denied the right of free association with prior crime partners or victims. However, because of cases such as *Griffin v. Wisconsin* (1987), parolees are now able to give public speeches and receive publications.

Another legal question arises with respect to probationers and parolees who violate the terms of their probation or parole. The rule of thumb in such cases is that the offender may be sent to prison. Additionally, if the offender commits another crime, his or her probation or parole will likely be revoked. For minor violations (e.g., missing a meeting of Alcoholics Anonymous), the probation/parole officer may decide to how severe the penalty should be. Having said that, the Supreme Court has had to address the issue of due process when revocation is an option.

In the case of *Mempa v. Rhay* (1967), the U.S. Supreme Court determined that a probationer has the right to be represented by counsel in a revocation or sentencing hearing before a deferred prison sentence can be imposed. Additionally, in *Morrissey v. Brewer* (1972), the Court ruled that parolees faced with the possibility of the revocation of parole must be afforded prompt due process before an impartial hearing officer.

Controversial Aspects within the Alternatives

In evaluating the benefits of alternatives, some researchers have noted that "An expanded range of sentencing options gives judges greater latitude to exercise discretion in selecting punishments that more closely fit the circumstances of the crime and the offender" (DiMascio n.d.). They have argued that this type of scheme, if administered effectively, would free up prison cells for violent offenders, whereas less restrictive alternatives would be used to punish nonviolent offenders. Prison overcrowding, the cost of prisons, and the increasing recidivism rates have contributed to the creation of alternatives within the criminal justice system. (Recidivism is the recurrence of a criminal behavior by the offender. Rates of recidivism can be assessed in three ways: by rearrest, reconviction, and reincarceration.) Prisons now account for approximately 80 percent of every correctional dollar spent, and U.S. prisons cost $2.45 billion in 1996. Increasing rates of recidivism seem to be directly related to increasing rates of rearrest, reconviction, and reincarceration, which, in turn, result in the increasing need for prison space. Alternatives to the traditional types of punishment (more specifically imprisonment) within the criminal justice system were the result of a need to change this trend. However, there is a growing body of research suggesting that many offenders actually have a negative perception of alternative sanctions (May, Wood, Mooney, and Minor 2005). In fact, some studies suggest that a significant number of offenders actually believe that serving time in prison is easier than many alternatives; depending on the alternative, up to one-third of offenders refused to participate even if it meant a shorter prison stay (May, Wood, Mooney, and Minor 2005). Some of the reasons given for choosing imprisonment over alternatives include (1) concerns about abuse of power and antagonism by the personnel who run the program and (2) the likelihood that the program would fail, resulting in revocation to prison after time and effort had been invested in the program.

Pretrial Diversion

Pretrial diversion is the first and perhaps most important alternative within the criminal justice system. It allows the defendant to agree to conditions set forth by the prosecutor (e.g., counseling or drug rehabilitation) in exchange for the withdrawal of charges. This concept began because of a belief that the formal processing of people through the criminal justice system was not always the best course of action (Geerken and Hayes 1993). There are three main reasons given for the use of pretrial diversion: (1) many of the crimes committed were caused by offenders with special circumstances, such as vagrancy, alcoholism, emotional distress, and so forth, which cannot be managed effectively within the criminal justice system; (2) formal criminal justice labeling often carries a stigma that actually hurts or cripples attempts at rehabilitation and in the long run can promote an unnecessarily harsh penalty for a relatively minor offense; and (3) the cost of diversion is cheaper than the cost of criminal justice processing.

The concept of diversion is very controversial because some argue that it allows offenders to get off easy. Yet there are also those who argue that the rationale for diversion is sound because incarceration, in effect, does nothing to change the offender's disadvantaged status and the stigma of conviction will ultimately decrease the offender's chances of becoming a productive citizen. Nonetheless, support for diversion seems to wax and wane depending on whether society supports the rehabilitation or incarceration of offenders.

Despite mixed success, critics view pretrial diversion programs negatively as they are applied in expanding the state's authority or widening the net of social control.

In other words, the reach of this alternative correctional program targets or sanctions individuals charged with less serious offenses more seriously than originally intended.

Intensive Supervision Probation

According to the Bureau of Justice Statistics (BJS) *1997 Special Report* (Bonczar and Glaze 1999), approximately 10 percent of all probationers and parolees who participate in alternative sanction programs are under intensive supervision probation. This approach was designed in the 1980s in response to the issue of prison overcrowding. Specifically geared research was conducted to identify a solution, and it was determined that there were a small number of inmates who could, under the right circumstances, be released into the community with minimal risk to the public (Petersilia and Turner 1990). Two hundred inmates were initially selected, but over time the number has risen to well over a thousand participants. Over a four-month period, the inmate must file an application, which must be approved by a three-person screening panel. If approved, a resentence hearing must be held before three judges. If the judges approve the application, the inmate will begin a 90-day trial period of intensive supervision probation. Despite some shortcomings, this program has been extremely helpful in relieving prison overcrowding.

Yet 10 years after its inception, research showed that nearly one-third of nonviolent offenders who were given the option to participate in intensive supervision probation chose prison instead (Petersilia 1990). They felt that the combination of having to work every day, having to submit to random drug tests, and having their privacy invaded was more punitive that serving a prison term. A significant number also indicated that intensive supervision probation had so many conditions attached to it that there was a high probability of violating a condition and being revoked back to prison. These offenders viewed intensive supervision probation as more punitive than imprisonment and equated one year in prison to five years of intensive supervision probation.

Substance Abuse Treatment/Intensive Parole Drug Program (IPDP)

As the title indicates, the Intensive Parole Drug Program (IPDP) is an intensive supervision program for parolees with a history of substance abuse (drugs and alcohol). This program was implemented in certain states as a part of the Department of Corrections' "Stop the Revolving Door" initiative, which has an antirecidivism focus. The program focuses on relapse prevention, intervention strategies, and counseling referrals. Sanctions may include community-based treatment, residential placement, or return to custody with institutional program treatment. Any parolee identified as having a substance abuse problem can be referred (Clear, Cole, and Reisig 2006). Candidates come from a range of programs—from therapeutic community programs to mutual agreement programs or from halfway houses. IPDP is a six-month-minimum program with participants having the option to stay an additional three months. The issue with these types of programs is that although some offenders welcome the opportunity for treatment, they feel that the intrusive nature of the program itself outweighs any possible benefit. As is the case with other programs, offenders who are offered the opportunity to participate frequently decline and choose to serve time instead.

Electronic Monitoring and House Arrest

Electronic monitoring and house arrest are typically used together in conjunction with intensive supervision. House arrest restricts the offender to home except when at school, work, or court-assigned treatment, and electronic monitoring becomes the technological means of securing compliance. Electronic monitoring has been described as the most important penal invention of the 1980s ("The 2002–2003 Electronic Monitoring Survey" 2002). It tries to incorporate some of the goals of criminal justice sanctions yet fits into a category all its own. Electronic monitoring is a "supervision tool that provides information about the offender's presence at, or absence from, his or her residence or other location" (State of Michigan 2006). Although the system does not track offenders' whereabouts like a homing device, it is able to determine if offenders are at home when they should be.

Harvard psychologist Robert Schwitzgebel (Gomme 1995, 489–516) developed the first electronic monitoring device in the mid-1960s. He felt that his invention could provide a humane and inexpensive alternative to custody for many people involved in the justice process. The goal of an electronic monitoring system is to provide community supervision staff with an additional tool to intensely supervise offenders who are not incarcerated. This form of supervision does not support any form of treatment or assistance, but it is more cost-efficient than incarceration, which provides a direct contrast and alternative to incapacitation or imprisonment. Critics of electronic monitoring argue that the concept is self-serving for the manufacturers of the house-arrest equipment. The also argue that there are many rehabilitative-type services and products available but point out that these services are labor-intensive and expensive and would no doubt eat into the corporation's profits.

Boot Camp and Shock Incarceration

Boot camps combine basic elements of both rehabilitation and retribution. They provide rigorous physical activity that many believe to be more beneficial than punitive alternatives. "Boot camps are highly popular residential alternatives (intermediate sanctions) typically used for young offenders which provide for very structured and military-like activities such as strict discipline, physical training and labor, drill, and a regimented schedule of daily activities" (Rush 2004). A sentence of boot camp, also known as shock incarceration, is usually for a relatively short time, approximately three to six months.

The first boot camp programs were implemented in Georgia and Oklahoma in 1983 to help relieve prison and jail crowding. They were first developed in the adult criminal justice system and then expanded to the juvenile justice system (MacKenzie, Wilson, and Kider 2001). Boot camps were created for several reasons. As mentioned previously, one of the main goals of alternatives is to alleviate the overcrowding of prisons. That is, "certain offenders who would normally be sentenced to a prison term (e.g., two to four years) are diverted to a shorter, yet equally punitive and effective, boot camp sentence (e.g., 90 to 180 days)" (Begin 1996).

Deterrence (both specific and general) is inherent in the concept of shock incarceration. The hope is that the shock of incarceration will serve both as a deterrent specific to the criminal and the crime as well as a general deterrent to would-be criminals in the immediate community. Boot camp is considered one of the most demanding alternatives, and the findings on its effectiveness as a deterrent to offenders committing further crimes is mixed at best. Moreover, more often than not, offenders who are offered the opportunity to serve a sentence in boot camp instead of in prison opt to serve prison time because boot camp is seen as being more intrusive than prison.

Day Reporting Centers (DRCs)

Day reporting centers (DRCs) are community-based facilities that provide a strict regimen of supervision and programming for ex-offenders. The 1980s began the era of the use of DRCs in the United States, but this concept actually originated in England as a way of reducing the prison population. The goal of DRCs is to combine high levels of control over offenders so as to meet public safety needs while providing intensive services to address the rehabilitative needs of the offender. Day reporting is an alternative that completely eliminates the cost of jail for these offenders because they do not require housing or confinement.

The rationale behind the implementation of this type of alternative is that sometimes the crime committed does not justify a jail sentence. In fact, it has been argued that some offenders are by nature more responsive to less severe punishment and that they may actually be harmed, more than their crime may merit, by serving a jail term. The use of DRCs would allow offenders to report to a location in a manner similar to reporting to a probation officer. Offenders in this program would be required to account for their activities during the day, including job-searching activities for those participants who are unemployed. Offenders would also be subjected to daily drug and alcohol testing, as would regular offenders. Failure of either of these mandatory tests would result in disqualification from the program.

Day reporting incorporates three of the sanctions that were discussed earlier, and it is in keeping with these that the goals of this type of alternative are formed. As such, the objectives of DRCs are threefold: (1) punishment through restricting clients' activity and requiring community service; (2) incapacitation through intensive supervision, firm enforcement of attendance agreements, and strict adherence to program structure; and (3) rehabilitation through services aimed at "enabling the unable by developing social and survival skills, remedying deficiencies in education, and increasing employability" (Begin 1996).

Daily programming includes but is not limited to educational/vocational training, drug/alcohol treatment, anger management, and conflict resolution. Many of the alternatives are implemented for the purpose of combating the overcrowding and enormous cost of imprisonment. In order to reduce the cost of prisons, the criminal justice system "requires that sanctions be tailored as carefully as possible to ensure that they provide only the supervision or services necessary to achieve their intended goal(s)" (Begin 1996). Alternatives, therefore, present more effective methods of reducing society's total spending on the correctional system in general and the prison population specifically.

The work crew is another option that allows qualifying offenders to work off a portion of their sentence and/or their fine by working on public works projects selected and supervised by participating jurisdictions (Clear 1994). In the end, the amount of work that the offender does for the time period is assessed and deducted from the total sum of time he or she would have spent incarcerated. It is important to note that the difference between the work crew just discussed and work release is that the latter is an option some jurisdictions use to allow individuals to continue to work at their existing jobs according to their established schedule, but they must reside at the jail overnight (Gill 1967). This alternative reduces the cost to correctional institutions for daily services; however, those work release programs that do not have work release centers still require jails to cover the cost of night services.

Residential Community Correctional Facilities (Halfway Houses)

Halfway houses are residential facilities designed to (1) house adult offenders (with at least 70 percent of its residents placed by federal, state, or local authorities), (2) operate independently of the other corrections institution, and (3) permit clients to leave the premises during the day for work, education, or community programs. Additionally, halfway houses are critical in rehabilitating ex-offenders. In addition to providing high levels of surveillance and treatment, the 24-hour residency makes these facilities the community sanction that is closest to the total institutional setting of a prison or jail (halfway between prison and freedom) because, despite the setting, the movements, behavior, and mood of the residents can be continuously monitored.

Halfway houses also provide a safe haven for offenders who have been confined for long periods of time, allowing a smooth transition back into the community. Some offenders who live in halfway houses can actually work and pay rent. They are allowed to leave only to report to jobs, and they must return promptly at the end of the workday. In essence, halfway-house residents have more freedom and responsibility than people in prison but less freedom than ordinary citizens.

A halfway house is a "rehabilitation center where people who have left an institution, such as a hospital or prison, are helped to readjust to the outside world" (Caputo 2004, 72).

Recidivism was a major concern for the criminal justice system, and this form of alternative was supported as a way to combat it. Another purpose of halfway houses is to monitor those offenders just leaving prison to make sure that they are ready to function in society again. It was implemented to also give offenders the opportunity to gradually recondition themselves to the world. The offender is leaving a structured environment in prison, and the halfway house provides a transitioning period for the offender to enter a free public. Thus, halfway-house residents have greater freedom and responsibility than people in prison but less freedom than ordinary citizens (Nelson, Deess, and Allen 1999). Owing to the existence of halfway houses in the community, some safety concerns exist. Such concerns are limited when compared with situations where offenders were released from prison directly into society without any formal supervision.

Another benefit of halfway houses is that an offender must perform community service in the form of manual labor for the government or private, nonprofit organizations without receiving any payment. The courts, on a discretionary basis, determine the number of community service hours an offender must serve.

Fines

Fines are typically used in conjunction with other sanctions, such as probation and incarceration (a typical sentence would be two years' probation and a $500 fine). The biggest complaint about fines as a sanction is the difficulty of collection. A significant number of offenders are poor and simply cannot afford to pay them. On the other hand, judges also complain that well-to-do offenders will be in a better position to meet the financial penalty and less likely to learn the lesson the penalty was intended to teach.

As a result, several states—including Arizona, Connecticut, Iowa, New York, and Washington—have tested an alternate concept referred to as a *day fine*, developed in Sweden and Germany, which imposes a fine based on a fixed percentage of the offender's income. The day fine concept ensures that the financial penalty imposed on the offender will have the same impact regardless of income.

Forfeiture

Forfeiture is the act of seizing personal property (e.g., boats, automobiles, or equipment used to manufacture illegal drugs), real property (e.g., houses), or other assets (e.g., bank accounts) derived from or used in the commission of illegal acts. Forfeiture can take both civil and criminal forms. Under civil law, the property can be seized without an actual finding of guilt. Under criminal law, however, forfeiture is imposed only as part of the sentence for a guilty verdict.

The practice of forfeiture was not actually used after the American Revolution but became more popular with the 1970 passage of the Racketeer Influence and Corrupt Organizations (RICO) Act and the Continuing Criminal Enterprise (CCE) Act. As its popularity grew in usage, congressional amendments were made to streamline implementation in 1984 and 1986 (Spaulding 1989).

Community Service and Restitution

The concepts of community service and restitution are relatively new alternatives. "Community service is a compulsory, free, or donated labor performed by an offender as punishment for a crime" (Inciardi, Martin, and Butzin 2004; Parent and Barnett 2002). "Community service can be arranged for individuals on a case by case basis or organized by correctional agencies as programs" (Inciardi, Martin, and Butzin 2004; Parent and Barnett 2002). Community service provides a chance for offenders to give back to the community for the wrong that they did to society.

The first documented community service program in the United States was implemented in Alameda County, California, in 1966 (Inciardi, Martin, and Butzin 2004; Parent and Barnett 2002). Community service sentencing first began when it was found that many indigent women were forced to go to jail because they could not afford traffic and parking fines. "To avoid the financial costs of incarceration and the individual cost to the offenders [who were often women with families], physical work in the community without compensation was assigned instead" (Inciardi, Martin, and Butzin 2004; Parent and Barnett 2002). This alternative had such outstanding results that it spread nationwide into the 1970s. It was advocated by the idea of "symbolic restitution," whereby offenders, through good deeds in the form of free labors benefiting the community, symbolically repaid society for the harm they had caused (Inciardi, Martin, and Butzin 2004; Parent and Barnett 2002).

Restitution is often viewed as financial compensation, but it can also take the form of community service hours at a community project. Both community service and restitution operate under the assumption that the offender's personal or financial contribution to the victim or the community will compensate for any loss caused by the offender's illegal behavior.

An offender is usually given community service in conjunction with restitution. "Restitution is the payment by the offender of the costs of the victim's losses or injuries and/or damages to the victim" (Department of Health and Human Services 2005, 4). Restitution provides either direct compensation to the victim by the offender, usually with money although sometimes with services (victim restitution), and unpaid compensation given not to the victim but to the larger community (community service). Restitution, as an alternative, is similar to restoration in that both concepts seek to place the victim and/or the community back into the position they were in (whether financial or emotional) before the crime was committed.

Victim restitution programs were adopted in the United States in 1972 with the Minnesota restitution program. It "gave prisoners convicted of property offenses the opportunity to shorten their jail stay, or avoid it altogether, if they went to work and turned over part of their pay as restitution to their victims" (Department of Health and Human Services 2005, 4).

Conclusion

According to policy makers, the concept of alternatives to criminal justice is different from the traditional criminal justice sanctions in four significant ways: (1) It is restorative as opposed to retributive, (2) it uses problem-solving rather than adversarial strategies, (3) the community jurisdiction takes on a more important role than the legal jurisdiction, and (4) the ultimate goal is not to punish the offender but to improve the community through collaborative problem solving. Critics and offenders argue, on the other hand, that the alternatives and community corrections strategies are becoming increasingly punitive despite the emphasis on rehabilitation.

The bottom line is that the offenders are the ones who must evaluate the severity and impact of alternative sanctions. If offenders perceive the alternatives as being too severe, they will choose prison, and the entire concept will serve no purpose. Even offenders receiving identical punishments will react differently to perceived degrees of intrusiveness; some may perceive the punishment as more severe than others, depending on age, race, sex, and prior punishment history (Spelman 1995). According to this research, African American offenders, men, older offenders, unmarried offenders, offenders without children, drug offenders, and repeat offenders rated prison as less punitive than alternatives.

Hence, to ignore these research findings and to disregard the viewpoints of those directly involved—offenders, victims, and community members—is to make policies on the basis of preconceived ideas, biases, and stereotypes.

See also **Domestic Violence Interventions; Social Justice**

Further Reading

Allen, Harry E., ed., *Repairing Communities through Restorative Justice.* Lanham, MD: American Correctional Association, 2002.

Anderson, David, *Sensible Justice: Alternative to Prison.* New York: New Press, 1998.

Begin, P., *Boot Camps: Issues for Consideration.* Ottawa, ON: Research Branch, Library of Parliament, 1996. http://dsp-psd.communication.gc.ca/Pilot/LoPBdP/BP/bp426-e.htm

Bonczar, T., and L. Glaze, "Probation and Parole in the United States 1998." *BJS Bulletin.* Washington DC: U.S. Department of Justice, Office of Justice Programs, 1999.

Caputo, Gail A., *Intermediate Sanctions in Corrections.* Denton: University of North Texas Press, 2004.

Clear, T. R., *Harm in American Penology.* New York: State University of New York Press, 1994.

Clear, T., G. Cole, and M. Reisig, *American Corrections,* 7th ed. Belmont, CA: Wadsworth, 2006.

Clear, Todd R., and David R. Karp, *The Community Justice Ideal: Promoting Safety and Achieving Justice.* Boulder, CO: Westview, 1999.

Department of Health and Human Services, *Combining Substance Abuse Treatment with Inter-mediate Sanctions for Adults in the Criminal Justice System.* Washington, DC: U.S. Government Printing Office, 2005.

DiMascio, W. M., *Seeking Justice: Crime and Punishment in America.* New York: Edna McConnell Clark Foundation, n.d.

Geerken, Michael, and Hennessey D. Hayes, "Probation and Parole: Public Risks and the Future of Incarceration Alternatives." *Criminology* 31, no. 4 (November 1993): 549–564.

Gill, D. R., *Alternatives to the Present Uses of the Jails.* Chapel Hill: Institute of Government, University of North Carolina, 1967.

Gomme, I. M., "From Big House to Big Brother: Confinement in the Future." In *The Canadian Criminal Justice System,* ed. N. Larsen. Toronto: Canadian Scholars' Press, 1995.

Inciardi, James, Steven Martin, and Clifford Butzin, "Five-Year Outcomes of Therapeutic Community Treatment of Drug-Involved Offenders after Release from Prison." *Crime and Delinquency* 50, no. 1 (2004): 94, 102–104.

Jacobson, Michael, *Downsizing Prisons: How to Reduce Crime and End Mass Incarceration.* New York: New York University Press, 2005.

MacKenzie, D. L., D. B. Wilson, and S. Kider, "Effects of Correctional Boot Camps on Offending." *Annals of the American Academy of Political and Social Science* 578 (2001): 126–143.

May, D. C., P. B. Wood, J. L. Mooney, and K. I. Minor, "Predicting Offender-Generated Exchange Rates: Implications for a Theory of Sentence Severity." *Crime and Delinquency* 51 (2005): 373–399.

Morris, N., and M. Tonry, *Between Prison and Probation Intermediate Punishment in a Rational Sentencing System.* New York: Oxford University Press, 1990.

Nelson, Marta, Perry Deess, and Charlotte Allen, *The First Month Out: Post-Incarceration Experiences in New York City.* New York: Vera Institute of Justice, 1999.

Parent, Dale, and Liz Barnett, *Transition from Prison to Community Initiative.* Washington, DC: National Institute of Corrections, 2002. http://www.nicic.org/pubs/2002/017520.pdf

Petersen R. D., and D. J. Palumbo, "The Social Construction of Intermediate Punishments." *Prison Journal* 77 (1997): 77–92.

Petersilia, Joan, "When Probation Becomes More Dreaded than Prison." *Federal Probation* 54 (1990): 23–27.

Petersilia, Joan, and Susan Turner, *Intensive Supervision Probation for High Risk Offenders Findings from Three California Experiments,* R-3936-NIJ/JA. Santa Monica, CA: Rand, 1990.

Petersilia, Joan, Susan Turner, James Kahan, and Joyce Peterson, *Granting Felons Probation: Public Risks and Alternatives.* Santa Monica, CA: Rand, 1985.

Rush, George E., *The Dictionary of Criminal Justice,* 6th ed. New York: McGraw-Hill, 2004.

Spaulding, Karla R., "Hit Them Where It Hurts: RICO Criminal Forfeitures and White-Collar Crime." *Journal of Criminal Law and Criminology* 80 (1989): 197–198.

Spelman, W., "The Severity of Intermediate Sanctions." *Journal of Research in Crime and Delinquency* 32 (1995): 107–135.

State of Michigan, *Electronic Monitoring of Offenders in the Community.* Department of Corrections, 2006. http://www.michigan.gov/corrections/0,1607,7–119–1435–5032—,00.html

"The 2002–2003 Electronic Monitoring Survey." *Journal of Electronic Monitoring* 15, no. 1 (Winter–Spring 2002): 5.

Tucker, Susan, and Eric Cadora, *Ideas for an Open Society: Justice Reinvestment.* New York: Open Society Institute, 2003.

Vass, Anthony A., *Alternatives to Prison: Punishment Custody and the Community.* Newbury Park, CA: Sage, 1990.

Wood, P. B., and H. G. Grasmick, "Toward the Development of Punishment Equivalencies Male and Female Inmates Rate the Severity of Alternative Sanctions Compared to Prison." *Justice Quarterly* 16 (1999): 19–50.

B

BORDER FENCE

Judith Ann Warner

To prevent unauthorized entrants from crossing the U.S.-Mexico border, Congress passed the Secure Fence Act of 2006 to construct either partial or complete fencing. Since 9/11 this project has been referred to as a "border fence." Does the United States have the sovereign right to block off a border with a neighboring country, or does it insult Mexico and violate the rights of people to freely move about the globe? Both Americans and Mexicans residing on the border view it as offensive, and no similar action has been proposed for Canada. Economic migrants from Mexico and from Central and South America have been forced to cross in ever more remote and hazardous regions, which has raised the death toll. The solution for preventing these deaths could be legalizing increased immigration rather than fencing the border. Although fencing could prevent some criminal activity along the border, such as drug trafficking, it might also promote more varied attempts at human smuggling by tunneling, thus overcoming the fence, or coming into the country by sea or air.

Concern has developed about Mexican drug-related violence involving shootouts between traffickers, law enforcement, and the military. The public supports a border fence primarily as a means of stopping unauthorized immigration, and the government advocates it to prevent the entry of terrorists. Increasingly, the prospect that spillover violence could spread from Mexico into the United States may become another motive for blocking the border, by a fence or otherwise.

Background

The U.S.-Mexico border is 1,951 miles long and crosses urban areas, desert, and mountainous regions. Historically, the highest rates of unauthorized entrance have been through the San Diego (California) and El Paso (Texas) urban areas, which suffered increased crime due to the unlawful measures taken to stop the migrants and attempts by bandits to assault and rob migrants during their passage. These are the sites at which the first border fences were built.

Fencing began with the installation of 14 miles of steel wall as a part of Operation Gatekeeper in the Tijuana–San Diego undocumented immigration corridor (Nevins 2002). It was made with steel plates that served as makeshift aircraft runways during the first Iraq War. They are covered with rust in parts and unsightly. In the San Diego region, the 40 miles of primary 10-foot-high fence with horizontal steel corrugation is easy to climb. After the first wall, there is a 10-foot secondary wall that is 15 feet high and more difficult to climb; it is a steel mesh wall sunk in concrete. This appears to be effective, but these walls have been tunneled under.

At Otay Mesa, San Diego, with the use of ground-penetrating radar, a half-mile, 75-foot-deep tunnel with electricity and ventilation was discovered. It led to a Tijuana industrial park and contained bales of marijuana. It is plausible that this tunnel was also used to smuggle people across the border. U.S. Border Patrol (USBP) officials indicate that the San Diego wall was never meant to stop unauthorized entrance but just to slow people down. A fence that caused injury would render the United States subject to liability lawsuits. Tunnels are a drug trafficking escalation in the effort to maintain smuggling routes.

In Arizona, between the U.S. city of Nogales and Ambos Nogales in Mexico, border walls were built in conjunction with Operation Safeguard. Many additional fences have been constructed in Arizona, but they are not as high or secure in remote rural areas, where the USBP considers it easier to apprehend people. In rocky and mountainous areas, there is a simple rail barrier designed to impede cars or trucks but not foot travelers.

Although Operation Gatekeeper and Operation Safeguard were intended to be temporary, they became permanent. The result was displacement of unauthorized entrants and human smugglers to more remote and risky crossing areas (Dunn 2009; Nunez-Nieto and Kim 2008) and an almost complete drop in apprehensions in the urban areas that were fenced. Nevertheless, fences did not stop unauthorized immigration over the long run. Instead, unauthorized crossers choose different and more difficult rural desert areas, which are extremely hazardous.

The Senate confirmed the U.S. House of Representatives Secure Border Fence Bill of 2006 to authorize and partially fund construction of 700 miles of additional double-walled fencing along the U.S.-Mexico border. The sites include two spots in California, most of the Arizona border, and heavily populated areas of Texas and New Mexico. Fourteen known drug-smuggling corridors are included. Michael Chertoff, the first Department of Homeland Security secretary, did not favor a physical fence and wanted to deploy a virtual electronic fence instead. One result of this decision point is that the fence may never be fully extended. The fence does not seal off the entire border and leaves open the question of whether another displacement effect will affect unauthorized immigration, making it more dangerous.

Border fencing has involved up to two layers of secured fencing and physical barriers, parallel roads, and surveillance technology (Nunez-Nieto and Kim 2008). By 2010, U.S. Customs and Border Protection (USCBP, part of the Department of Homeland Security) had extended coverage to 645 miles of fence. The degree of security offered by the fence varies. Often rural fencing is no more than a railing to deter vehicles. Other sections of the border fence located near cities and communities comprise a steel plate wall or two fences that are 15 feet high and run parallel to each other with a track for motor vehicles in between. Individuals or groups crossing the border without authorization trigger motion sensors and alert the U.S. Border Patrol, which polices the fence and crossing locations. On one side of each of the two parallel fences is eight feet of coiled barbed wire, and before the barbed wire are ditches to prevent SUVs and trucks used by human and drug smugglers from crossing. In more remote areas, rail fences have been installed to prevent vehicles from crossing.

Border communities and landowners affected by the border fence project have protested it. The Secure Fence Act of 2006 requires consultation with federal agencies, state and local officials, and local property owners. Nevertheless, former Secretary Chertoff was authorized to waive historic preservation and environmental laws, including the Endangered Species Act, the Clean Water Act, and the Safe Drinking Water Act. On four occasions, DHS has used the waivers. Lawsuits over proposed border walls in south Texas occurred, but in 2008 the U.S. Supreme Court turned down a case against border fencing. DHS paid $50 million to compensate for ecological damage and issues with Native American burial sites. It is possible to develop fencing that will curb floods and restore habitats for endangered species. About $40 million has been spent on restoration. The affected species include ocelots, jaguars, wild pigs (javelinas), and deer.

Early in his term, President Barack Obama expressed a preference for border patrolling and adding surveillance technology in lieu of a fence. The evaluations of the U.S. Government Accountability Office have consistently documented problems with a "virtual fence" known as the Secure Border Initiative network, or SBInet. In spring 2010, current DHS Secretary Janet Napolitano responded by cutting $50 million from a scaled back budget of $574 million to pay for a system of cameras, radar, and sensors that was expected to be operational by 2011 (Archibold 2010). Cost overruns on the Boeing contract, equipment malfunctions such as mistaking blowing trees for migrants, lack of consultation with the USBP, and ineffective assessment of results are considered major issues. By 2010, $1.2 billion had been spent; with only two test sites in Arizona, there was little evidence of effectiveness. In response, Janet Napolitano has frozen funding for SBInet.

The violence of Mexican drug cartels and the possibility that it could spill over into U.S. border communities, a phenomenon labeled "spillover violence," has created a motive for continuing to fence. Originally, Secretary Napolitano was opposed to border fencing; but she now advocates walls and fences as a means of operational control. Napolitano went ahead with the final 60 miles of fencing, estimated to cost $4 million per mile (Reese 2009). In 2010, fencing covered 646 miles of the 1,951-mile U.S.-Mexico border.

Border fencing has been costly to build. Since 2005, $2.4 billion has been spent (Billeaud 2010). Former congressman and 2010 Arizona Senate primary candidate J. D. Hayworth (2009, 3) points out that the original bill calls for double-layer fencing, but only 200 miles are of this more expensive type. Smugglers have overcome single-layer fencing and vehicle barriers with hacksaws, blowtorches, and portable ramps (Billeaud 2010). Migrants may simply use ladders.

Supporters of Border Fencing

Proponents of an extended border fence argue that it is needed for three reasons: (1) to reduce unauthorized immigration, (2) to block drug smugglers and others, and (3) to prevent terrorists from entering through the so-called back door. A border fence is seen as a tool that, with accompanying technology, will allow the USBP to improve enforcement. A 2010 Rasmussen phone survey indicated that 59 percent of a random sample of 1,500 Americans supported a border fence to control immigration (Rasmussen Reports 2010). Only a minority of voters were in opposition: 26 percent. After the March 2010 shooting deaths of American Consulate employees in Ciudad Juarez, Mexico, 49 percent believed that preventing drug trafficking was more important than stopping unauthorized entry.

The data from Operation Gatekeeper in the almost completely fenced San Diego sector, where border fencing originated, has been used to argue that it is effective because apprehension of unauthorized border crossers is greatly reduced (Haddal et al. 2009). The USBP views fencing as a "force multiplier" because it allows them to concentrate on targeted enforcement. USBP considers the displacement of migrant crossing attempts to remote rural areas, as opposed to congested urban regions, as presenting a tactical advantage.

Public figures such as Patrick Buchanan, former Congressman Duncan Hunter, and FOX television journalist Glenn Beck have advocated building a fence along the entire 2,000-mile U.S.-Mexico border. Buchanan (2006), for instance, believes that it would show the exact border location, separate the two nations, and permanently enhance security. Although the limited border fences already in place have been likened to the Berlin Wall, he does not agree. After World War II, the Berlin Wall was constructed between the zone occupied by the North American Treaty Alliance and that occupied by the Soviet Union in Berlin, Germany, to prevent Eastern Europeans and Soviet citizens from crossing into a non-Communist zone and permanently immigrating. Supporters of a U.S.-Mexico border wall feel that the Berlin Wall locked a population in and made them captive. In contrast, the proposed wall would keep unauthorized entrants out. Is the glass half empty or half full?

Complete fencing of the border would leave 200 openings or ports of entry for vehicles, trucks, and railroads, allowing trade, travel, and border tourism. The mere sight of the border fence is considered a major deterrent to individuals and small groups trying to cross. It has been suggested that a $2 crossing fee would help finance construction of the fence, paying back the cost over time.

One positive impact of the Tijuana–San Diego fence was that land values rose on the U.S. side of the border within 14 miles of the fence. Supporters of fence construction indicate that it would make national parks like the Organ Pipe Monument, Indian reservations such as that of the Tohono-O'odham in southern Arizona, and ranches safer places.

Patrick Buchanan (2006) suggests that the fence might be perceived positively by Mexican border residents because of the increased risk of crime in border-crossing zones such as the Tijuana–San Diego corridor. Prior to the construction of a 14-mile fence in this area, there were border bandits and gangs that committed rape, robbery, and even homicide. This gang activity was separate from drug smuggling, an additional concern. Border homicides occurred at a rate of 10 per year and decreased to zero after the fence was installed. Drug busts of SUVs and trucks dropped from 300 a month to zero along the fence.

The deterrence of crossing reduces opportunity to further exploit unauthorized border crossers. Mexico experiences a high level of corruption because of the low salaries of government employees (Velasco 2005). The Mexican police and military stationed on the U.S.-Mexico border and at ports of entry have been accused of rape, robbery, and physical assault on unauthorized individuals crossing through Mexico from Central and South America. Both the Mexican police and military seek them out throughout Mexico, particularly at Mexico's southern border, to take their money and/or deport them. Women have been sexually assaulted, and unauthorized migrants are alleged to have been beaten to death. Recent corruption concerns involve bribery and intimidation of Mexican and even U.S. law enforcement and government officials by drug trafficking organizations (Cook 2007).

An unrecognized human rights issue is that fencing in remote desert or mountainous border regions would prevent the deaths—due to dehydration, heat exhaustion, cold exposure, starvation, and/or injury—of hundreds of unauthorized crossers. It would also stop the accumulation of areas of trash left by unauthorized crossers in fragile desert and mountain ecological zones. Ranchers and other property owners would no longer be subject to trespassing on their lands. The more the border is fenced, the more unauthorized entrants are funneled into specific areas, making land enforcement more efficient. However, this approach will work only if the land border is almost completely fenced.

The U.S. public has been chiefly concerned about unauthorized immigration and terrorism. The U.S.-Mexico border is a major drug and human smuggling platform, and transnational organized criminal groups employ high technology to counter each step in the escalation of border control. There is concern that the profit motive would cause such groups to accept payment from terrorists attempting to cross and/or to assist them in transporting weapons of mass destruction, such as dirty bombs or hazardous, active biological organisms such as anthrax. Repeatedly, the issues of the war on terror have been linked to U.S.-Mexico border security, although the 9/11 incident did not involve U.S.-Mexico border crossers.

The chief motivation, however, may not originate from the war on terror. Border security has been a part of the war on drugs since the tight control of the Florida coastal drug smuggling corridor resulted in displacement of drug trafficking to the U.S.-Mexico border. Ultimately, the government may view fence placement as a national security issue primarily connected to drugs, although it is represented as an effort to control immigration and terrorism. There are areas along the U.S.-Mexico border in which even the USBP is threatened by heavily armed drug smugglers.

Opponents of Border Fencing

Felipe Calderón, the president of Mexico (2007–present), ministers of several Latin American countries, and Mexican intellectuals consider the construction of a border wall to be unnecessary and even counterproductive. The Mexican press has condemned the wall project as a xenophobic and racist act. Many Mexican papers have run political cartoons showing Uncle Sam putting up a fence covered with insults to Mexicans. The construction of a border fence is viewed as a major slap in the face by the nation of Mexico. It implies that the United States is superior to Mexico and that social problems originate on the Mexican side, not the American side. The United States is protected from Mexico, not vice versa.

Fence opponents in Mexico, Central America, and Latin America argue that an approach that respects labor rights and human dignity is needed. Mexicans regard the fence as a negative response to individuals who work hard and contribute to the North American economy; they are concerned that it will affect ties between Mexicans and family members living in the United States. Mexicans liken fence extension to the Berlin Wall and view it as a hostile act.

Tony Payan (2006) contends that the border-wall mindset has weakened the ties between the United States and Mexico. There is a sense of separation that undermines cross-border social ties and makes it difficult to negotiate binational solutions to problems like unauthorized immigration. Today, border residents are less likely to visit one another, and twin cities on the U.S. and Mexico sides are more socially if not geographically distant. Texas governor Rick Perry (2000–present) opposes the fence because it undermines trade; he suggests that technology should be used to promote safe and legal migration and cross-border contact.

Liberal opponents view a fence as a way of keeping Mexican citizens out and believe that preventing freedom of human movement is a human rights issue. The fencing of San Diego, California; El Paso, Texas; and Nogales, Arizona, was undertaken as an effort to deter individuals from crossing. Wayne Cornelius (2006) found that, from 1994 to 2004, a total of 2,978 border migrants died while attempting to enter the United States from Mexico. Cornelius (2006, 784) points out that "To put this death toll in perspective, the fortified U.S. border with Mexico has been more than ten times deadlier to migrants from Mexico during the last nine years than the Berlin Wall was to East Germans throughout its twenty-eight year existence."

Controversy has ensued because border crossers have been diverted to the Sonora Desert and Baboquivari Mountains in Arizona. The fencing of limited areas of the border channeled migrants to different areas that pose a threat to life for those who cross. Primary causes of death are exposure/heat, drowning, and motor vehicle accidents (Guerrette 2007). When the movement of people across the border is squeezed, they will try other areas or methods. In the southwestern desert, migrants are not able to carry much water; they become exposed to intense heat and cold and sometimes get lost. Drowning deaths occur along Texas's Rio Grande River and the Colorado River in California when irrigation water is released and sudden flooding occurs. Tension between the United States and Mexico has increased because of these deaths, which could have been prevented by more open borders.

Academicians have conducted research showing that, although fencing funnels migrants from attempted entry in certain zones, it does not stop unauthorized immigration (Garcia-Goldsmith et al. 2007; Massey 2009). A major unintended consequence of border fencing and other types of escalation of control has been that human smuggling networks have become more organized and profitable (Massey 2009). Unauthorized entrants pay large sums in advance to be smuggled in, or they may pay off huge debts afterwards. Unwittingly, escalation in law enforcement on the border has increased the profitability of human smuggling and created a new transnational organizational structure that people must rely on. In the past, individuals tried to cross on their own or employed small-scale smugglers. Each time border control is escalated, criminal organizations realize greater opportunity. If a debt is owed after crossing, migrants may be coerced or enslaved to pay it off. Ultimately, U.S. border security must to consider the reasons that migrants are so desperate and to deal with the demand for drug consumption in the United States more effectively.

Environmentalists are also opposed to border fencing, which disrupts the ecology of desert regions and riverine systems. The San Diego border fence constructed as a part of Operation Gatekeeper is in a 3.5-mile area of marsh. In 2005, a federal judge ruled against a lawsuit brought by the Sierra Club and other environmental groups to protect the sensitive ecological balance of the Tijuana River marshes. It is one of the few intact estuaries and coastal lagoon systems in southern California. A more general objection to fencing at most rural points of the border is that it hampers the migration of wild animals.

In south Texas, many lawsuits were brought against the border fence. The fence disrupts the use of private property, placing a barrier between animals and water or ranchers and their own land. It has had social consequences such as dividing the campus of the University of Texas at Brownsville into U.S. and Mexican areas. A coalition of Texas mayors and other public officials sought to stop the fence, but their effort to bring the issue before the U.S. Supreme Court was unsuccessful. To facilitate fencing, the secretary of the Department of Homeland Security issued 30 waivers of laws protecting endangered species, migratory birds, deserts or forests, antiquities, Native American graves, and rancher's property rights.

Opponents of extended border fencing argue that the tactic is insufficient and that better intelligence and innovative solutions are needed. They point out that the cost estimate is $70 billion. Some conservative opponents of fencing, including the Border Fence Project, are against federal attempts to fence the border and found the present legislation, the Secure Border Fence Act of 2006, very flawed. Their reasoning is that only 700 miles will be fenced and a great deal of coverage will be electronic; they also worry that personnel to respond will be underfunded. They argue that a delay in fence building will result in surges of crossers in unfenced areas. Finally, they point out that, in their opinion, the federal government does not do a good job of repairing, maintaining, or guarding current fencing. Existing areas of 15-foot-high steel-and-concrete fencing have been successfully overcome for temporary periods with hacksaws and acetylene or plasma torches, huge ladders, and even bungee jumping cords.

Methods used by smugglers to circumvent the border fence include tunnels and cave-like passages used to smuggle people, drugs, and contraband. A total of 101 tunnels have been discovered between 1990 and 2008 (Haddal et al. 2009). Circumventing the fence is a response to increased CBP enforcement. In 2006, Congress passed the Border Tunnel Prevention Act to increase criminal penalties. A tunnel builder can get up to 20 years. Improvements in intelligence gathering and tunnel detection are occurring but attempts continue to be made.

Fencing the border to stop unauthorized entry was immediately linked to 9/11 and preventing terrorist incursion despite the fact that none of the 9/11 terrorists entered through the U.S.-Mexico border. Instead, they came by air and overstayed visas that were, in some cases, fraudulent. Opponents think it is an error to connect 9/11 with southern border security. The real issues at the U.S.-Mexico border are much more varied. Drug smuggling of cocaine, heroin, marijuana, and methamphetamine is a multibillion-dollar business connected to illegal money laundering.

The construction of a border fence completely overlooks the relationship of the United States, a high-income country, to Mexico and other Central and South American middle- or low-income countries. Issues in economic development are associated with unauthorized immigration for economic motives. Border fencing is a unilateral, not a bilateral or multilateral, effort that addresses the economic development of the sending countries (Payan 2006). Recently, the need to address socioeconomic issues in Mexico was recognized in the context of combating drug trafficking and related violence by increasing economic opportunity (Thompson and Lacey 2010).

Peter Skerry (2006) maintains that the primary reason for building a border fence was never about undocumented immigration. He contends that politicians want to stop drug traffickers. It is easy for public figures to merge and blur the issues of unauthorized immigration, counterterrorism, and—with renewed emphasis—drug trafficking. The secretary of Homeland Security has the authority to waive all laws that prevent national security measures, which makes the process of opposing the wall and developing binational and global solutions to major issues problematic. Globalization has made us one world, and the use of national sovereignty to build a wall can easily be perceived as national arrogance and disregard for the concerns of other nations.

Conclusion

Prior border fences did not stop unauthorized immigration. The Secure Border Fence Act of 2006 does not seal off the entire border. As a result, it has the potential to channel unauthorized entrants to rural regions of Arizona, New Mexico, and Texas or to direct human smugglers to turn toward air and coastal routes. Many observers think that only a guest-worker program in combination with a fence would deal with the issue of unauthorized immigration from Mexico. This solution, however, does not take into account people from Central and South America who travel north to make unauthorized crossings or people who are legally admitted and overstay their visas. There are unauthorized immigrants from many areas of the world in the United States who did not cross a land border to enter. Meanwhile, the government's central concerns for building a wall include transnational drug smuggling and counterterrorism. Controversy will continue as the government and the public consider whether it is possible for a nation to seal itself off in a rapidly globalizing world.

See also **Drug Trafficking and Narco-Terrorism; Human Smuggling and Trafficking; Immigration Reform (vol. 3)**

Further Reading

Archibold, Randal C., "Budget Cut for Fence on U.S.-Mexico Border." *New York Times* (March 16, 2010). http://www.nytimes.com/2010/03/17/us/17fence.html

Billeaud, Jacques, "Fence Alone Cannot Plug Border." MSNBC.com. May 28, 2010. http://www.msnbc.msn.com/id/37387658/ns/us_news-immigration_a_nation_divided

Buchanan, Patrick, *State of Emergency: The Third World Invasion and Conquest of America.* New York: Thomas Dunn Books/St. Martin's Press, 2006.

Cook, Coleen W., *Congressional Research Service Report: Mexico's Drug Cartels.* 2007. http://ftp.fas.org/sgp/crs/row/RL34215.pdf

Cornelius, Wayne A., "Controlling 'Unwanted Immigration': Lessons From the United States. 1993–2004." *Journal of Ethnic and Migration Studies* 31, no. 4 (2006): 775–794.

Downes, Lawrence, "The Not-So-Great-Wall of Mexico." *New York Times* (April 20, 2008). http://www.nytimes.com/2008/04/20/opinion/20sun4.html

Dunn, Timothy, *Blockading the Border and Human Rights: The El Paso Operation That Remade Immigration Enforcement.* Austin: University of Texas Press, 2009.

Garcia-Goldsmith, Raquel M., Melissa McCormick, Daniel Martinez, and Inez Magdelena Duarte, *The "Funnel Effect" and Recovered Bodies of Unauthorized Immigrants Processed by the Pima County Office of the Medical Examiner, 1990–2005.* Report Submitted to the Pima County Board of Supervisors. Tucson, AZ: Binational Immigration Institute. Mexican American Research and Studies Center, University of Arizona, 2006.

Guerette, Rob T., "Immigration Policy, Border Security, and Migrant Deaths: An Impact Evaluation of Life-Saving Efforts under the Border Safety Initiative." *Criminology and Public Policy* 6, no. 2 (2007): 245–266.

Haddal, Chad C., Yule Kim, and Michael John Garcia, "Congressional Research Service: Border Security: Barriers Along the U.S. International Border." March 16, 2009. http://www.fas.org/sgp/crs/homesec/RL33659.pdf

Hayworth, J. D., Testimony before the United States Senate Committee on the Judiciary, Subcommittee on Immigration, Border Security and Citizenship, Hearing on Securing the Borders and America's Ports of Entry, What Remains to be Done. May 20, 2009. http://judiciary.senate.gov/pdf/5-20-09HayworthTestimony.pdf

Liptak, Adam, "Power to Build U.S. Border Fence Is Above U.S. Law." *New York Times* (April 8, 2008). http://www.nytimes.com/2008/04/08/us/08bar.html

Massey, Douglas, Testimony before the United States Senate Committee on the Judiciary, Subcommittee on Immigration, Border Security and Citizenship, Hearing on Securing the Borders and America's Ports of Entry, What Remains to be Done. May 20, 2009. http://judiciary.senate.gov/hearings/testimony.cfm?id = 3859&wit_id = 7939

Nevins, Joseph, *Operation Gatekeeper: The Rise of the "Illegal Alien" and the Making of the U.S.-Mexico Boundary.* New York: Routledge, 2002.

Nunez-Nieto, Blas, and Yule Kim, *CRS Report for Congress: Border Security: Barriers Along the U.S.-Mexico Border.* Washington, DC: Congressional Research Service, 2008.

Payan, Tony, *The Three U.S.-Mexico Border Wars: Drugs, Immigration and Homeland Security.* Westport, CT: Praeger Security International/Greenwood Publishing Group, 2006.

Rasmussen Reports, "59% Say U.S. Should Continue to Build Fence on the U.S.-Mexico Border." March 18, 2010. http://www.rasmussenreports.com/public_content/politics/current_events/mexico/59_say_u_s_should_continue_to_build_fence_on_u_s_mexico_border

Reese, April, "U.S.-Mexico Fence Building Continues Despite Obama's Promise to Review Effects." *New York Times* (April 16, 2009).

Romero, Fernando, *Hyperborder: The Contemporary U.S.-Mexico Border and Its Future.* New York: Princeton Architectural Press, 2008.

Skerry, Peter, "How Not to Build a Fence." *Foreign Policy* (September/October 2006): 64–67.

Thompson, Ginger, and Marc Lacey, "U.S. and Mexico Revise Joint Anti-Drug Strategy." *New York Times* (March 24, 2010). http://www.nytimes.com/2010/03/24/world/americas/24mexico.html

Velasco, Jose Luis, *Insurgency, Authoritarianism and Drug Trafficking in Mexico's "Democratization."* New York: Routledge, 2005.

C

CLASS JUSTICE

Gregg Barak and Paul Leighton

Karl Marx maintained that the root of most crime and injustice could be found in class conflict. Within and without the academies of crime and justice, this contention is highly controversial. In fact, it is so controversial that here in the United States the whole idea of class itself is often in a state of political and social denial. Unlike gendered justice and sexism or racial (ethnic) justice and racism, class justice and classism has not been recognized in either the substantive or procedural sides of the law. Opponents of class justice argue that we are not only a so-called classless society but also a democracy in which all individuals are subject to due process, equal protection, and the rule of law. Although proponents of class justice do not take issue with the fact that no person is above the law, they do contend that many actions are beyond incrimination and adjudication, whereas other actions are selectively enforced and differentially punished according to class interests.

Background

Throughout most of the 19th century and well into the 20th, a blatant kind of class justice prevailed in the selective enforcement and differential application of the criminal and civil law to the haves and the have-nots. The laws themselves were heavily influenced by a reverence for private property and laissez-faire social relations. In terms of commercial transactions, the philosophy of the day was caveat emptor, "let the buyer beware." In the area of business, farmers and new merchants alike were allowed the freedom to expand their particular domains and to compete and acquire both property and capital with little legal interference. By contrast, labor was highly regulated. Unions were considered an illegal interference with freedom of contract and an unlawful conspiracy infringing upon the employer's property rights.

The administration of criminal (and civil) justice was chaotic, often corrupt, and subject to the buying of law enforcement and juries. An independent and decentralized criminal justice system designed for a more homogenized, pioneer, and primarily agricultural society was ill adapted for the needs of an increasingly complex, urban, and industrialized society. A social and cultural environment that was experiencing increasing numbers of immigrants from southern and eastern Europe, a changing means of rapid communication and transportation, and an expanding presence of wage-earning working classes called for a coordinated system of criminal justice.

By the end of the 19th century, the buying of justice that had prevailed earlier (available to those who could afford representation in the legislatures, in the courts, and in the streets) was threatening the very legitimacy of criminal justice in the United States. The initial laissez-faire emphasis on the right to acquire private property had blossomed into a full-fledged national preoccupation with wealth and power. Political corruption became widespread, and political machines dominated urban areas: "The machines controlled city governments, including the police and the courts. Payrolls were padded and payoffs were collected from contractors" (Edelstein and Wicks 1977, 7). Graft and other forms of bribery contributed not only to the buying of justice by those who could afford it but also to a changing national morality. Rackets, "pull," and protection were common antidotes to stubborn legal nuisances. Prevailing values of wealth and success predominated as guiding principles of right and wrong. "The ability to 'make good' and 'get away with it' offsets the questionable means employed in the business as well as professional worlds. Disrespect for the law and order is the accompanying product of this scheme of success" (Cantor 1932, 145).

Those who were marginalized—especially the poor, unemployed, women, and people of color—were rarely if ever in a position to buy justice. As the marginalized groups of immigrants and others grew in urban centers across the United States and as the miscarriages of justice flourished, the need to reform the institutions of criminal justice grew because the country was beginning to experience bitter class wars. The working classes aggressively resisted exploitation through on-the-job actions and wide social movements. To combat challenges to the emerging monopoly or corporate order of industrial capitalism, the wealthy ruling classes initially employed illegal violence, such as the hiring of thugs and private armies. Later, they retained the services of private security companies, such as Pinkerton's, to infiltrate and break up worker organizations.

Key Events

Double Standards of Justice

In 1964, William Rummel received three years in prison after being convicted of a felony for fraudulently using a credit card to obtain $80 worth of goods.

Five years later, he passed a forged check in the amount of $28.36 and received four years. In 1973, Rummel was convicted of a third felony: obtaining $102.75 by false pretenses for accepting payment to fix an air conditioner that he never returned to repair. Rummel received a mandatory life sentence under Texas's recidivist statue. He challenged this sentence on the grounds that it violated the Eighth Amendment's prohibition of cruel and unusual punishment by being grossly disproportionate to the crime.

In *Rummel v. Estelle* (1980), the U.S. Supreme Court affirmed Rummel's life sentence for the theft of less than $230 that never involved force or the threat of force. Justice Louis Powell's dissent noted "it is difficult to imagine felonies that pose less danger to the peace and good order of a civilized society than the three crimes committed by the petitioner" (*Rummel v. Estelle 1980*, 295). However, Justice William Rehnquist's majority opinion stated there was an "interest, expressed in all recidivist statues, in dealing in a harsher manner with those who by repeated criminal acts have shown that they are simply incapable of conforming to the norms of society as established by its criminal law" (*Rummel v. Estelle* 1980). After "having twice imprisoned him for felonies, Texas was entitled to place upon Rummel the onus of one who is simply unable to bring his conduct within the norms prescribed by the criminal law" (*Rummel v. Estelle* 1980).

Now consider the case of General Electric (GE), which is not considered a habitual criminal offender. Nevertheless it has been prosecuted for diverse crimes over many decades. In the 1950s, GE and several companies agreed in advance on the sealed bids they submitted for heavy electrical equipment. This price-fixing defeated the purpose of competitive bidding, costing taxpayers and consumers as much as a billion dollars. GE was fined $437,000—a tax-deductible business expense—the equivalent of a person earning $175,000 a year getting a $3 ticket. Two executives spent only 30 days in jail, even though one defendant had commented that price-fixing "had become so common and gone for so many years that we lost sight of the fact that it was illegal" (Hills 1987, 191).

In the 1970s, GE made illegal campaign contributions to Richard Nixon's presidential campaign. Widespread illegal discrimination against minorities and women at GE resulted in a $32 million settlement. Also during this time, three former GE nuclear engineers—including one who had worked for the company for 23 years and managed the nuclear complaint department—resigned to draw attention to serious design defects in the plans for the Mark III nuclear reactor because the standard practice was "sell first, test later" (Hills 1987, 191).

In 1981, GE was convicted of paying a $1.25 million bribe to a Puerto Rican official to obtain a power plant contract. GE has pleaded guilty to felonies involving illegal procurement of highly classified defense documents, and in 1985 it pleaded guilty to 108 counts of felony fraud involving defense contracts related to the Minuteman missile. In spite of a new code of ethics, GE was convicted in three more criminal cases over the next few years, in addition to paying $3.5 million to settle cases involving retaliation against four whistle-blowers who helped reveal the defense fraud. (GE subsequently lobbied Congress to weaken the False Claims Act.) In 1988, the government returned another 317 indictments against GE for fraud in a $21 million computer contract.

In 1989, GE's stock brokerage firm paid a $275, 000 civil fine for discriminating against low-income consumers, the largest fine ever under the Equal Credit Opportunity Act. A 1990 jury convicted GE of fraud for cheating on a $254 million contract for battlefield computers, and journalist William Greider reported that the $27.2 million fine included money to "settle government complaints that it had padded bids on two hundred other military and space contracts" (Greider 1996, 4).

Because of tax changes that GE had lobbied for and the tax cuts passed under President Ronald Reagan generally, GE paid no taxes between 1981 and 1983, when net profits were $6.5 billion. In fact, in a classic example of corporate welfare, GE received a tax rebate of $283 million during a time of high national deficits even though the company eliminated 50,000 jobs in the United States by closing 73 plants and offices. Further, "Citizen GE," whose advertising slogan has been "Brings good things to life," is one of the prime environmental polluters and is identified as responsible for contributing to the damage of 47 sites in need of environmental cleanup in the United States alone.

Even though felons usually lose political rights, GE's political action committee contributes hundreds of thousands of dollars to Congress each year, and it now owns NBC television, with all of its influence. In spite of having been convicted of defrauding every branch of the military, representatives from GE are frequently invited to testify before Congress. If the corporation's revenues were compared with the gross domestic product of countries, it would be among the top 50 largest economies in the world. With this kind of political, economic, and social power, it is easy to understand why "three strikes and you're out" does not apply to the big hitters like GE.

The pattern outlined in these examples was reinforced in 2003, when the Supreme Court upheld a 50-year sentence for two acts of shoplifting videos from Kmart. Under California's three-strikes law, Leandro Andrade's burglary convictions from the 1980s counted as the first two, and the prosecutor decided to charge the shoplifting incidents as strikes, which carry a mandatory sentence of 25 years each. The Supreme Court, citing *Rummel v. Estelle,* held that the sentences were neither disproportionate nor unreasonable (*Lockyer v. Andrade* 2003).

At the same time, Andrew Fastow, Enron's chief financial officer, negotiated a plea bargain for 10 years in prison. Fastow had been instrumental in fraud, which resulted in the largest bankruptcy in U.S. history at that time. He had worked the deals to launder loans through allegedly independent entities to make them appear as revenue for Enron, and he helped push the accountants to approve the deals and used the massive banking fees Enron paid to silence Wall Street analysts who asked questions about Enron's finances. Fastow was originally charged with 109 felony counts, including conspiracy, wire fraud, securities fraud, falsifying books, as well as obstruction of justice, money laundering, insider trading, and filing false income tax returns. The sentence was negotiated in an environment in which getting tough on corporate crime was seen as a high priority (Leighton and Reiman 2004).

Class, Crime, and the Law

The rich and powerful use their influence to keep acts from becoming crimes, even though these acts may be more socially injurious than those labeled criminal. Further, they are also able to use mass-mediated communication to shape the public discourse and moral outrage about crime. In short, the corporate elite's relative monopoly over the airways allows them to act as so-called transmission belts for creating consensus over what is and is not a crime. For example, Jeffrey Reiman, in the eighth edition of *The Rich Get Richer and the Poor Get Prison* (2007), notes that multiple deaths that result from unsafe workplaces tend to get reported as accidents and disasters, whereas the term *mass murder* is reserved exclusively for street crime. Although there are differences between the two, especially in the level of intentionality, it is not clear that one should be a regulatory violation and the other a crime.

If the point of the criminal law is to protect people's well-being, then why was no crime committed in the 2005 deaths of 12 miners in West Virginia? "Time and again over the past four years, federal mining inspectors documented the same litany of problems at central West Virginia's Sago Mine: mine roofs that tended to collapse without warning. Faulty or inadequate tunnel supports. A dangerous buildup of flammable coal dust" (Warrick 2006, A4). In the two years before this explosion, the mine was cited 273 times for safety violations, one-third of which were classified as "significant and substantial," and "16 violations logged in the past eight months were listed as 'unwarrantable failures,' a designation reserved for serious safety infractions for which the operator had either already been warned, or which showed 'indifference or extreme lack of care'" (Warrick 2006, A4). This state of affairs seems to fit within the criminal law categories of knowing, reckless, or negligent, but most matters like this stay within the realm of administrative sanctions and the civil law.

Outside of mining, the situation is the same. From 1982 to 2002, the Occupational Safety and Health Administration (OSHA), which has primary responsibility for the nation's workplace safety, identified 1,242 deaths it concluded were related to "willful" safety violations. Only 7 percent of cases were referred for prosecution, however, and "having avoided prosecution once, at least 70 employers willfully violated safety laws again, resulting in scores of additional deaths. Even these repeat violators were rarely prosecuted" (Barstow 2003). One of the many barriers is that causing the death of a worker by willfully violating safety laws is a misdemeanor with a maximum sentence of six months in jail; therefore, such cases are of little interest to prosecutors. This level of punishment was established in 1970 by Congress, which has repeatedly rejected attempts to make it tougher; consequently, harassing a wild burro on federal lands carries twice the maximum sentence of causing a worker's death through willful safety violations. Compare the lack of change in the punishment for a worker's death with the escalating toughness for all types of street crime, in which Congress's "tough on crime" attitude led to three-strikes laws, expansion of the number of strikable offenses, mandatory minimums, increasingly severe sentencing guidelines, and increased offenses eligible for the death penalty. Since the early 1990s, however, Congress has voted down all laws to increase penalties for workplace deaths, even recent modest proposals to increase the maximum penalty to 10 years (Barstow 2003).

In terms of class justice generally, much of the harmful and illegitimate behavior of the elite members of society has not traditionally been defined as criminal, but nearly all the harmful and deviant behavior perpetrated by the poor and the powerless, the working and middle classes, is defined as violating the criminal law. Thus, basing crime-control theory and practice on a neutral criminal law ignores the fact that the legal order and the administration of justice reflect a structural class bias that concentrates the coercive power of the state on the behaviors of the relatively poor and powerless members of society. These omitted relations of class justice reveal the importance of two systemic operations in the administration of criminal justice: selective enforcement and differential application of the law. Selective enforcement of harms by the law refers to the fact that most harm perpetrated by the affluent is "beyond incrimination" (Kennedy 1970). As for the harms committed by the politically and economically powerful that do come within the purview of criminal law, these are typically downplayed, ignored, or marginalized through differential application of leniency and/or compassion.

Similarly, criminologist Stephen Box suggests that one of the most important advantages of corporate criminals lies "in their ability to prevent their actions from becoming subject to criminal sanctions in the first place" (Braithwaite 1992, 89).

Although certain behaviors may cause widespread harm, criminal law does not forbid abuses of power in the realm of economic domination, governmental control, and denial of human rights. As we saw in the opening narrative of this entry, being a habitual offender is against the law in most areas, where "three strikes and you're out" applies to street criminals. But habitual offender laws do not apply to corporate persons (like GE) that can repeatedly commit serious crimes without being subjected to these statutes or to the legal possibility of a state revoking a corporation's charter to exist.

In some cases, harmful actions will be civil offenses rather than criminal ones, but the difference is significant because civil actions are not punishable by prison and do not carry the same harsh stigma. A plea to civil or administrative charges does not amount to an admission of guilt and thus cannot be used against a business in other related litigation. Other destructive behavior may not be prohibited by civil law or regulations created by administrative agencies. In this respect, the tobacco industry produces a product that kills 400,000 people each year, but its actions are not illegal, not a substantial part of the media campaign of the Office for National Drug Control Policy or Partnership for a Drug Free America, or even subject to federal oversight as a drug.

When corporations are charged, they can use their resources to evade responsibility. Criminologist James Coleman (1985) did an extensive study of the enforcement of the Sherman Antitrust Act in the petroleum industry and identified four major strategies that corporations employ to prevent full application of the law. First is endurance and delay, which includes using expensive legal resources to prolong the litigation and obstruct the discovery of information by raising as many motions and legal technicalities as possible. Second is the use of corporate wealth and political connections to undermine the will of legislators and regulators to enforce the law's provisions. Third is secrecy and deception about ownership and control to prevent detection of violations and make them more difficult to prove. Fourth are threats of economic consequences to communities and the economy if regulations are passed and/or fully enforced.

One of the classic statements on this topic, first referred to by former General and President Dwight D. Eisenhower as the "military–industrial complex," is a book by C. Wright Mills called *The Power Elite* (1956). He contended that an elite composed of the largest corporations, the military, and the federal government dominates life in the United States. Mills argued that these three spheres of power are highly interrelated, with members of each group coming from similar upper-class social backgrounds, attending the same private and Ivy League universities, even belonging to the same social or political organizations. In addition to their mutual "ruling class interests," corporate elites also make large political donations to both the Republicans and Democrats to ensure their access to the law-making process.

Reiman suggests that the result of these relations is that law is like a carnival mirror. It distorts our understanding of the harms that may befall us by magnifying the threat from street crime because it criminalizes more of the conduct of poor people. At the same time, it distorts our perception about the danger from crime in the office suites by downplaying and not protecting people from the harms perpetrated by those above them in the class system. As a consequence, both the criminal law and the administration of justice do "not simply *reflect* the reality of crime; [they have] a hand in *creating* the reality we see" (Reiman 1998, 57). Thus, to say that the criminal law appropriately focuses on the most dangerous acts is a problematic statement because the criminal law shapes our perceptions about what is a dangerous act.

Reiman also argues that the processing of offenders serves to "weed out the wealthy." Selective enforcement means that many harmful acts will not come within the realm of criminal law, and if they do, it is unlikely that they will be prosecuted, "or if prosecuted, not punished, or if punished, only mildly" (Reiman 1998, 57). This observation is consistent with the analysis in Black's highly referenced and acclaimed book *The Behavior of Law* (1976). Black sought to discover a series of rules to describe the amount of law and its behavior in response to social variables such as stratification, impersonality, culture, social organization, and other forms of social control. When it comes to issues of class, the variables of stratification and social organization are the two most relevant.

Black proposed that the law varies directly with hierarchy and privilege, so that the more inequality in a country, the more law. He also applied his proposition to disputes between two parties of unequal status and wealth. Based on a wide variety of cases, Black concluded there is likely to be more law in a downward direction, such as when a rich person is victimized by a poorer one. This means the use of criminal rather than civil law, for example, and a greater likelihood of a report, investigation, arrest, prosecution, and prison sentence. In contrast, when the wealthier harms the poorer, Black predicted there would be less law, meaning civil law, monetary fines rather than jail, and therapeutic sanctions rather than punitive ones. Further, Black argued that there is likely to be more law in the downward direction when an individual victimizes a group high in social organization, such as a corporation or the state. Conversely, less law and a pattern of differential application are likely to be the result of a corporate body or the state victimizing individuals or groups of individuals that have lower levels of social organization, such as poor communities.

Conclusion

Although attention has been paid to examples from occupational safety, the analysis provided here also applies to financial crimes, including several episodes of massive and widespread fraud. For example, Representative Frank Annunzio, who was chairman of the House Subcommittee on Financial Institutions that investigated the prosecution of criminals involved in the savings and loan (S&L) wrongdoings of the late 1980s, made the same points that Reiman and Black do in his opening remarks to one congressional hearing:

> Frankly, I don't think the administration has the interest in pursuing Gucci-clad white-collar criminals. These are hard and complicated cases, and the defendants often were rich, successful, prominent members of their upper-class communities. It is far easier putting away a sneaker-clad high school dropout who tried to rob a bank of a thousand dollars with a stick-up note, than a smooth talking S&L executive who steals a million dollars with a fraudulent note. (Hearings 1990, 23)

These comments highlight the difficulty and reluctance in prosecuting upper-class criminals even though the harm done is much greater than that due to street crime. Some S&L executives personally stole tens of millions of dollars and others were responsible for the collapse of financial institutions that needed government bailouts to the tune of $1 billion. The total cost of the S&L bailout ultimately climbed to about $500 billion, yet few S&L crooks went to prison, and the ones who received prison sentences got an average of two years, compared with an average of nine years for a bank robber (Hearings 1990).

After such expensive and widespread fraud, Congress briefly decided to get tough, but it soon removed all the regulations put in place to safeguard against similar fraud.

According to the authors of *Big Money Crime*, soon after the S&L crisis, Congress went on a wave of "cavalier" financial deregulation, creating the "paradox of increasing financial deregulation coming on the heels of the most catastrophic experiment with deregulation in history" (Calavita, Pontell, and Tillman 1997, 10). These actions set the stage for the 2002 financial crimes involving Enron, WorldCom, Global Crossing, Tyco, and several other billion-dollar corporations. Although a few of the responsible chief executives found themselves doing time behind bars, most of those involved in these frauds and crimes found themselves escaping, courtesy of class justice. At the same time, the victims of these crimes—workers, consumers, investors, retirees, and more—received little or no compensation, despite the fact that many lost their life savings.

Historically then, based on the past—long-term and short-term—and on the present, and given the prevailing political and economic arrangements, and barring a major revolution in the organization of multinational or global capitalism, class justice is looking very secure into the foreseeable future. It received a painful prick from the American populace after the collapse—and government bailout—of various Wall Street investment firms and major banks and insurers in 2008–2009; but very few if any of the custodians of what suddenly had become "toxic assets" ended up being prosecuted. To borrow the rhetoric of the time, Main Street was angry at Wall Street for the latter's misuse of investors' funds (in the form of "collateralized debt obligations" and other financial inventions), but expressions of anger and calls for additional financial regulation was as far as the matter went.

See also **African American Criminal Injustice; Corporate Crime; Social Justice; Environmental Justice (vol. 4)**

Further Reading

Auerbach, Jerold S., *Unequal Justice: Lawyers and Social Change in Modern America*. New York: Oxford University Press, 1977.

Barak, Gregg, Paul Leighton, and Jeanne Flavin, *Class, Race, Gender, and Crime: The Social Realties of Justice in America*, 3d ed. Lanham, MD: Rowman & Littlefield, 2010.

Barstow, David, "When Workers Die: U.S. Rarely Seeks Charges for Deaths in Workplace." *New York Times* (December 22, 2003). http://reclaimdemocracy.org/weekly_2003/when_workers_die.html

Braithwaite, John, "Poverty, Power and White Collar Crime." In *White Collar Crime Reconsidered*, ed. Kip Schlegel and David Weisbord. Boston: Northeastern University Press, 1992.

Calavita, Kitty, Henry Pontell, and Robert Tillman, *Big Money Crime*. Berkeley and Los Angeles: University of California Press, 1997.

Cantor, Nathaniel E., *Crime: Criminals and Criminal Justice*. New York: Henry Holt, 1932.

Coleman, James, "Law and Power: The Sherman Antitrust Act and Its Enforcement in the Petroleum Industry." *Social Problems* 32, no. 3 (1985): 264–274.

Edelstein, Charles D., and Robert J. Wicks, *An Introduction to Criminal Justice*. New York: McGraw-Hill, 1977.

Greider, William, *Who Will Tell the People? The Betrayal of American Democracy.* New York: Simon and Schuster, 1996.

Hartmann, Thom, *Unequal Protection: The Rise of Corporate Dominance and the Theft of Human Rights.* San Francisco: Berrett-Koehler, 2009.

Hearings before the Subcommittee on Financial Institutions Supervision, Regulation, and Insurance of the Committee on Banking, Finance, and Urban Affairs, U.S. House of Representatives, 101st Congress, 2nd Session, "When Are the Savings and Loan Crooks Going to Jail?" Washington, DC: U.S. Government Printing Office, 1990, 23.

Hills, Stuart, ed., *Corporate Violence: Injury and Death for Profit.* Savage, MD: Rowman & Littlefield, 1987.

Kennedy, Mark, "Beyond Incrimination: Some Neglected Facets of the Theory of Punishment." *Catalyst* 5 (Summer 1970): 1–30.

Leighton, Paul, and Jeffrey Reiman, "A Tale of Two Criminals: We're Tougher on Corporate Criminals, but They Still Don't Get What They Deserve." Supplement to Jeffrey Reiman, *The Rich Get Richer and the Poor Get Prison,* 7th ed. Boston: Allyn and Bacon, 2004. http://paulsjusticepage.com/RichGetRicher/fraud2004.htm

Lockyer v. Andrade, 538 U.S. 63 (2003).

Mills, C. Wright, *The Power Elite.* New York: Oxford University Press, 1956.

Reiman, Jeffrey, *The Rich Get Richer and the Poor Get Prison,* 8th ed. Boston: Allyn and Bacon, 2007.

Rummel v. Estelle, 445 U.S. 263 (1980).

Sheldon, Randall G., *Controlling the Dangerous Classes: A History of Criminal Justice in America,* 2d ed. Boston: Allyn and Bacon, 2007.

Simon, David, *Elite Deviance,* 9th ed. Boston: Allyn and Bacon, 2007.

Walker, Samuel, Cassia Spohn, and Miriam DeLone, *The Color of Justice: Race, Ethnicity, and Crime in America.* Boston: Wadsworth, 2006.

Warrick, Joby, "Safety Violations Have Piled Up at Coal Mine." *Washington Post* (January 6, 2006): A4.

CORPORATE CRIME

Richard D. Hartley and Michael Shally-Jensen

The focus on, study of, and prosecution for corporate crime is a relatively new phenomenon—one that has recently gained wide public attention. For criminologists, "corporate crime" refers to acts in violation of the law that are committed by businesses, corporations, or individuals within those entities. Corporate crime is also closely associated with white-collar crime, organized crime, and state–corporate crime. Although most of us do not think of businesses, corporations, or presidents and CEOs of companies when we think of criminals, corporate and white-collar offenses actually cause more deaths, physical injury, and property loss than the Uniform Crime Report's eight serious index offenses together (Kappeler, Blumberg, and Potter 2000).

Since the beginning of the 21st century, we have observed unparalleled levels of corporate malfeasance and financial wrongdoing. The economic crisis of 2008–2009 highlighted the extraordinary risks Wall Street investment banks had been taking with other people's money. Federal and state officials investigating possible illicit activities by these banks (Goldman Sachs, among them) focused on counterinvestments made by the banks' own top executives against faulty investment products (derivatives) they were selling to their clients, as well as on the likelihood that the banks hid risks from the rating agencies that evaluate financial products for consumers. Several years earlier, the bankruptcies of WorldCom and Enron raised public ire about the legitimacy of reported corporate profits. Xerox, for example, doctored its books to show $1.4 billion more in profits than was actually there, and WorldCom itself overstated its profits to the tune of $3.8 billion. The top-level officers in these companies have also been accused and convicted of wrongdoing. Some top executives have enjoyed the rewards of the sales of their companies' stocks prior to filing for bankruptcy and have been charged with fraud in the process. Scott Sullivan of WorldCom made $35 million this way; Kenny Harrison and Kenneth Lay of Enron made $75 million and $220 million, respectively, from the sales of company shares; and Gary Winnik of Global Crossing made $500 million in the two years before his company went bankrupt ("Corporate America's Woes, Continued" 2002). The accounting firms in charge of these companies' books were also implicated in many of the scandals. Three accounting firms—Arthur Andersen LLP, KPMG, and Ernst and Young—were all charged with violations, and Andersen was forced out of business because of it.

Companies and their employees have traditionally been able to safeguard themselves from government inquiries, the media, and shareholders because of the authority and influence they have over the information they release about company transactions. These companies are complex organizations to the extent that they can engage in shady business dealings while at the same time keeping some employees inside the corporation, and many shareholders outside of the corporation, blind to this devious corporate conduct (Simon 2006). Criminal actions of this nature continue because of the benefits the corporations enjoy and the minimal risks of being caught and punished for wrongdoing (Gray, Frieder, and Clark 2005). Others, however, have suffered some punishment; former Tyco CEO Dennis Kozlowski was sentenced to 8 to 25 years for misappropriating $400 million of the company's money. John and Tim Rigas are currently serving 15 and 20 years respectively for fraud and conspiracy related to their company, Adelphia. Ex-Enron CFO Andrew Fastow received a 6-year prison term for his role in the company's wrongdoing. Even Martha Stewart served 5 months in prison for obstructing justice in the investigation of her sale of ImClone stock.

The costs of corporate crime are beyond compare, totaling more than the combined price of all other crime *plus* the cost of operating the criminal justice system (Simon 2006). Actual costs are hard to gauge; however, research undertaken by Congress estimates the price of corporate crime at roughly $200 billion annually (Coleman 1985). Couple this with the fact that penalties are rarely imposed (or, if they are imposed, are not severe enough to guarantee compliance in the future), and it becomes obvious why corporate malfeasance continues.

Corporate Crime Typologies

It is necessary to distinguish between corporate and white-collar crime. The latter offenses are those "socially injurious and blameworthy acts committed by individuals or groups of individuals who occupy decision-making positions in corporations and businesses, and which are committed for their own personal gain against the business, and corporations that employ them" (Frank and Lynch 1992, 17). In other words, white-collar crimes are largely individual crimes benefitting the perpetrator or perpetrators. The case of Bernard Madoff, who ran the largest Ponzi scheme in U.S. history without the knowledge of others in his firm, is a recent example of white-collar crime. Corporate crimes, on the other hand, are those "socially injurious and blameworthy acts, legal or illegal, that cause financial, physical, or environmental harm, committed by corporations and businesses against their workers, the general public, the environment, other corporations and businesses, the government, or other countries" (Frank and Lynch 1992, 17).

This entry focuses on corporate crime. Such crime, at least for present purposes, encompasses those acts that are beneficial not for the individuals inside the corporation but instead for the corporation itself. Some overlap with white-collar offenses does exist, however, considering that the individuals who engage in these behaviors and represent the corporations are usually in a position to benefit from the illegal actions they undertake. Likewise, the line between organizational crime and corporate crime is indistinct, since criminals can often start corporations with the intention of committing crime or laundering their earnings from crime. This entry focuses mainly on the corporations themselves and provides more limited coverage of the individuals in the corporations.

Historical Background

Corporations have been in existence since the time of the Romans (Geis 1988). During this time, corporations existed in order to set up and control such legal entities as universities, churches, and associations. The king, in other words, gave corporate status to these entities, essentially granting them the ability to have legislative and judicial powers over themselves (Clinard and Yeager 1980). The East India Company is probably the first entity with such recognized corporate powers. Established in 1602, it is said to have been the first multinational corporation that issued stocks (Mason 1968). In the four centuries following the genesis of the East India Company, the corporation developed and its characteristics took shape. Legally speaking, a corporation had the following characteristics: "it was a body chartered or recognized by the state; it had the right to hold property for a common purpose; it had the right to sue and be sued in a common name; and its existence extended beyond the life of its members" (Clinard and Yeager 1980, 22). Corporations of the 17th and 18th centuries engaged in many egregious acts. Using and trading African Americans as slaves and destroying Native American culture are two glaring examples (Sale 1990).

The Industrial Revolution and expanding enterprise in the 18th and early 19th centuries produced very wealthy and influential capitalist corporations. These effectively avoided regulation and control even though they engaged in such activities as fraud, price gouging, labor exploitation, manipulation of stocks, and maintaining unsafe work environments (Myers 1907; Clinard and Yeager 1980). The genesis of corporations in America was similar; such entities as towns, churches, associations, and universities became trusts with certain legal powers and authority. Colonial Americans disliked many of the British corporations that were ruling the American colonies. The Revolutionary War was fought in part to rid the colonies of British monopolistic rule. After the signing of the Declaration of Independence, Adam Smith ([1776] 1998) stated that the idea that corporations were needed for the betterment of government was unfounded. For the next 100 years, corporate charters, and therefore control over corporations and trusts, was rigid. Public opposition was fierce, and very few charters were approved; even when they were approved, legislatures limited the number of years they could last. At the expiration date, the corporation would be terminated and its shareholders would enjoy the division of assets. The colonists wanted to be free from the exploitation they suffered under British rule. After the Revolutionary War, the Founding Fathers were nervous about the power of corporations. Through various legal means, they limited the role of corporations in society solely for business purposes. Corporations could not interfere in other aspects of society. Several conditions were set forth regarding the establishment and activities of corporations: Corporate charters (licenses to exist) were granted for a limited time and could be revoked promptly for violating laws. Corporations could engage only in activities necessary to fulfill their chartered purpose. Corporations could not own stock in other corporations or own any property that was not essential to fulfilling their chartered purpose. Corporations were often terminated if they exceeded their authority or caused public harm. Owners and managers were responsible for criminal acts committed on the job. Corporations could not make any political or charitable contributions or spend money to influence lawmaking (Reclaim Democracy 2004).

The nature of corporations changed in Britain in 1844, with the passage of the UK Joint Stock Companies Act, which essentially allowed a corporation to define itself and its purpose. Investors in a corporation could now collect funds for a specified purpose. Control over corporations at this point moved from being a responsibility of the government to one of the courts. Limited liability was awarded to shareholders in 1855, meaning that the assets of individuals in the corporation would be protected from any bad behavior in which the corporation might engage. A landmark U.S. court decision in 1866 in the case of *Santa Clara County v. Southern Pac. R. Co.* (1886) granted corporate personhood, which meant that corporations could now enjoy many of the rights and responsibilities of individuals. These rights included ownership of property, signing of binding contracts, and payment of taxes.

Several court cases would come to shape the idea of the corporation in the early formation of the republic. In the case of *The Rev. John Bracken v. the Visitors of William and Mary College,* the central issue was whether or not the charter grant of William and Mary College could be altered. The court decided that the corporation (the college) could indeed make changes—in other words, reorganize the curriculum and faculty— and that this would not violate the original charter.

The U.S. Supreme Court heard arguments on a similar matter in 1818. In the case of *Dartmouth College v. Woodward* (1819), Chief Justice John Marshall, the very same man who had argued in favor of the changes to the charter of William and Mary College, had to decide whether the state of New Hampshire could rewrite the charter of Dartmouth College, thereby intervening in its academic operations. Justice Marshall, writing for the majority, declared that it most certainly could not.

Less than 10 years later, the Supreme Court decision in the case of *Society for the Propagation of the Gospel in Foreign Parts v. Town of Pawlet* (1830) expanded the rights of corporations to be similar to those of natural persons.

During the Industrial Revolution, the United States was rapidly expanding both economically and geographically. Production and manufacturing swelled, as did international trade. In order to protect themselves from competition, large manufacturing businesses became corporations. These corporations began to take over not only the business world but also U.S. courts, politicians, and society (Brown 2003). Corporations soon tried to unchain the fetters that controlled their business dealings. It should not come as a surprise that corporations were granted personhood through the rulings of many of these court cases: the justices of the Supreme Court had loyalty to the propertied class.

The Nature of a Corporation

A corporation is a legal entity comprising persons but one that in some ways exists apart from those persons. It is this separation that gives corporations distinctive authority and control over its practices. The most important aspects of incorporation include the ideas of limited liability and perpetual lifetime. Limited liability gives members of a corporation limited personal liability for the debts and actions of the corporation. The key benefits of limited liability include the following:

1. A corporation has separate legal entity and distinction from its shareholders and directors, which means that both the directors and the company have completely separate rights and existences.
2. The liability of shareholders is limited to the amount unpaid on any shares issued to them.

3. Shareholders cannot be personally liable for the debts of the company.

4. Creditors can look to the company for payment, which can only be settled out of the company's assets; thus generally, the personal assets of the shareholders and directors are protected.

5. The company's name is protected by law; no one else is allowed to use it in that jurisdiction.

6. Suppliers and customers can have a sense of confidence in a business (Benefits of a Limited Company 2006).

Perpetual lifetime is also important to a corporation because it means that its structure and assets are permitted to exist past the lifetime of its members. These features give corporations tremendous power and ability in the business world. Individuals who own shares of stock in a corporation are called shareholders; nonprofit organizations do not have shareholders. Usually, a corporation will have a board of directors overseeing operations for the shareholders and administering the interests of the corporation. If a corporation were to dissolve, the members would share in its assets, but only those assets that remained after creditors were paid. Again though, through limited liability, members can be held responsible only for the amount of shares they had in the corporation.

The Corporation Today

Corporations today are looked at in both a positive and negative light. They are seen as the heart of capitalist and free-market economies and an outgrowth of the entrepreneurial nature of U.S. society. However, they are also seen as the mechanism by which exploitation of the people in the labor market exists. David O. Friedrichs (1996) best describes what corporations mean for society today:

> Many people hold corporations in high esteem. Millions of people are employed by corporations and regard them as their providers. Many young people aspire to become corporate employees. Corporations produce the seemingly endless range of products we purchase and consume, and they sponsor many of the forms of entertainment (especially television) we enjoy. They are also principal sponsors of pioneering research in many fields and a crucial element in national defense. Corporations are important benefactors of a large number of charities, public events, institutions of higher learning, and scientific enterprises. And of course the major corporations in particular, with their large resources, are quite adept at reminding us of their positive contributions to our way of life. (67)

Indeed, the corporation of the 21st century has its interests in profits and growth. The large corporations of today are vast and have enormous wealth. Yearly profits from U.S. corporations were estimated some years ago to be about $500 billion annually (Korten 1999), a figure that has only increased since. The cost of industry to U.S. taxpayers, however, is easily more than $2.5 trillion per year (Estes 1996). Corporate exploitation of the citizenry and the workforce in society is not a shock, given the fact that profits are the main objective of the corporation. Stockholders and managers alike have a general interest in maximizing profits at the expense of others. Since corporate management usually holds a hefty share of the company's stock, managers tend to proceed with their own interests in mind, thereby augmenting their own wealth while common stockholders and workers consume the costs.

Corporate America is also well positioned to advance its interests through political corruption. Because of their abundant resources, corporations can have enormous influence on the polity and the outlining of public policy. The people at the top of corporations, the government, and the military all have connections to one another that allow them to advance common interests. If it is hard to believe that the American political system could be bought, consider that corporate donations to both political parties account for over 70 percent of their fund-raising contributions (Greidner 1991). Corporations have also been able to hide most of the political influence they enjoy and remain free from liability because the government has deregulated control over many of the industries that these corporations control.

The corporations of today have also been able to gain increasing control over key economic and political institutions because of mergers. The large corporations are conglomerates, meaning that they have gobbled up smaller companies and multiple industries, becoming producers of a wide array of products. These mergers and takeovers have led to corporations being able to cross-subsidize, meaning that they can sustain one business with the profits from another. Conglomerates have increased in size, number, and market share owing to multibillion-dollar mergers occurring in the 1980s. An outcome of these mergers has been the ability of these companies to expand their businesses geographically to the point where they now compete in the global marketplace and have widespread foreign and domestic assets. The increasing globalization of the world marketplace has allowed corporations to further violate laws in the name of profit without taking responsibility for their actions. By becoming multinational, corporations can, for example, violate the antitrust laws of a country in which they do business while obeying the antitrust laws of their own country.

Although Third World countries and the citizens who inhabit them do enjoy some advantages from globalized economic business, they too pay a penalty in terms of workforce abuses. As the global marketplace expands, the wrongdoings of these multinational corporations are likely to become more pronounced (Friedrichs 1996).

Laws and Legal Origins of Corporate Crimes

Although images of crime and criminals today have increasingly included the actions of business executives and members of the upper class, this has not always been the case. Corporations historically have been able to avoid prosecution because of the limited liability they have written into their charters. It has also been difficult to bring charges against an entity because of a lack of a body to punish and because the populace finds it difficult to grasp the idea that corporations, which are not persons, could offend. Nevertheless, there has been a rapid rise in the criminal liability that corporations can be accountable for under various laws concerning securities, antitrust violations, and the environment. Charges against corporate offending are normally levied against individuals in the corporation; however, the corporation itself can be held responsible and sanctioned for certain offenses. At both the federal and state levels, legislation has been promulgated against corporate criminal offenses. The U.S. Constitution, under its commerce clause, allows the control of corporate offenses by the federal government. Numerous federal agencies also play a part in enforcing this legislation. Such agencies as the Internal Revenue Service, the Environmental Protection Agency, the Federal Bureau of Investigation, the Secret Service, the Securities and Exchange Commission, and others attempt to control and regulate corporate activity.

Early notions of liability held that a corporation could not have criminal charges applied to it. Holding a corporation liable was difficult for a number of reasons (Khanna 1996). First, corporations are fictional entities, not individuals. Second, there are moral problems in proving that a corporation is capable of formulating criminal intent. Third, courts had trouble making corporations criminally responsible for acts not listed in their charters. Finally, difficulty stemmed from criminal procedural rules that the accused be brought into court. In the United States, two doctrines have been of primary use in holding corporations criminally responsible: the Model Penal Code, section 2.07, which makes the corporation responsible for the behaviors of leaders in the organization, and *respondiat superior*, which holds the employer responsible for the criminal acts of its employees. Even though these two doctrines are in place, many prosecutors fail to act against corporations because the shareholders, not the corporate elite, will suffer most from any punishment a corporation receives. The Supreme Court applied the *respondiat superior* doctrine initially in the case of *New York Central & Hudson River Railroad v. United States,* where the company was not applying mandated shipping rates to all customers equally. The Supreme Court decided that this action violated the Elkins Act, and the corporation was subject to penalties under that act.

Other courts have also made similar rulings under the *respondiat superior* doctrine; however, critics have pointed out that the doctrine is better suited for civil torts than criminal liability. Section 2.01 of the Model Penal Code ameliorates this criticism because it enforces liability for the actions of corporate employees. Today, there are only two instances when corporations cannot be held liable for criminal actions: if the corporation is incapable of committing the crime (these would involve such acts as arson) or where there is no fine attached as punishment for the action. The Model Penal Code outlines three categories of corporate offenses. The first requires *mens rea*, or a guilty mind, and traditionally comprises individual offenses, including embezzlement and fraud. Corporations may be charged in these cases if "the offense was authorized, requested, commanded, performed or recklessly tolerated by the board of directors or by a high managerial agent acting in behalf of the corporation within the scope of his office or employment" (Model Penal Code § 2.07 [1] [c]). The second category of offenses includes such acts as collusion calling for *mens rea* that can be committed by corporations. Corporations can be punished for these offenses if, during the scope of employment, an agent acted to benefit the corporation. Under § 2.07 (5) of the Model Penal Code, however, the corporation may not be punished if "the defendant proves by a preponderance of evidence that the high managerial agent having supervisory responsibility over the subject matter of the offense employed due diligence to prevent its commission." The third category covers the strict liability crimes. Under the Model Penal Code, and on the basis of the *respondeat superior* rule, corporations can be held liable consistent with strict liability principles; in other words, there is no need to show intent to benefit a corporation.

The case of *New York Central & Hudson River Railroad v. United States* provides the framework for the idea that a corporation can be held liable for the deeds of agents acting in the capacity of their jobs. The notion of agents acting within their employment capacity is important in charging liability to the corporation. Other components of imputing liability are that employees have the authority to carry out the behavior in question. This authority "attaches when a corporation knowingly and intentionally authorizes an employee to act on its behalf" (Viano and Arnold 2006, 314). The government also has to show that the individual whose actions are in question does indeed have a relationship to the agency (*United States v. Bainbridge Management* 2002). The concept of acting within the scope of an agent's authority has generally been determined in different ways with regard to federal and state control. Federally, corporate criminal liability can be imputed based on the responsibilities of the agent, not his or her rank (*In re Hellenic* 2001). The goal of the government is to impute liability on the corporation through an action of an employee.

At the state level, some states have limited assigning criminal liability only to those in a high managerial position. For instance, 18 Pa. C.S.A. § 307 states that liability may be imputed if "the commission of the offense was authorized, requested, commanded, performed or recklessly tolerated by the board of directors or by a high managerial agent acting in behalf of the corporation within the scope of his office or employment." Other states have applied liability through judicial precedent *(North Dakota v. Smokey's Steak-house, Inc.* 1991). Further, others have been able to impute liability in cases even where high-level management disapproved of the employee's actions (*New Hampshire v. Zeta Chi Fraternity* 1997; *Ohio v. Black on Black Crime, Inc.* 1999). However, corporate criminal liability will not be imposed unless the actor behaved in a manner deliberately intended to benefiti the corporation. This can be the case even if, for instance, the corporation did not actually benefit. The corporation would not be criminally liable where the employee's behaviors were counter to the benefit of the corporation (*Standard Oil Company of Texas v. United States* 1962).

Recent Legislation

Sarbanes-Oxley Act

The Sarbanes-Oxley Act of 2002, also called the Public Company Accounting Reform and Investor Protection Act of 2002, was enacted in response to a number of questionable business practices by major corporations (Sarbanes-Oxley Act of 2002, Pub. L. No. 107–204, 116 Stat. 804 [2002])—specifically, the Enron, WorldCom, and Tyco debacles, which caused a deterioration in the trust of the accounting and reporting practices of these companies. Included in this legislation were increases in punishments under the White Collar Crime Penalty Enhancement Act. The penalty increases included longer prison sentences for those found guilty of certain Employee Retirement Income Security Act (ERISA) infractions. In addition, falsely certifying Securities and Exchange Commission (SEC) reports became criminal under the Sarbanes-Oxley Act. In all, nearly a dozen sections are included in the act, obligating certain accountabilities of corporate officials and mandating penalties for their violation. The act also set up the Public Company Accounting Oversight Board, whose charge it is to regulate, inspect, and discipline accounting firms. Major provisions of the Sarbanes-Oxley Act include

1. Obligation for public companies to assess and give details of the efficiency of their fiscal reporting
2. Requirement that CEOs and CFOs certify their fiscal reports
3. Increased penalties, both civil and criminal, for security law infringement
4. Stipulation that no personal loans can be given to any executive officer
5. Requirement of independent auditing committees for companies registered on stock exchanges
6. Guarantee of back pay and compensatory damages, and protection of employees who act as whistleblowers

Criminal Antitrust Penalty Enhancement and Reform Act

Legislation against antitrust violations is not new. The Sherman Antitrust Act was promulgated in 1890 to place a limit on monopolistic practices. Although this act was, for the most part, unenforced for the last 100 years, President George W. Bush signed the Criminal Antitrust Penalty Enhancement and Reform Act in 2004. This act essentially raised the upper limit penalties in cases of corporate crime to $1 million and 10 years imprisonment for convicted individuals and $100 million fines for corporations found guilty of antitrust violations. Corporations and their agents may now face severe penalties if convicted.

Types of Corporate Crime

As stated earlier in this chapter, corporate crime involves injurious acts that result in physical, environmental, and financial harms, committed by entities for their own benefit (Frank and Lynch 1992). Although there is overlap with white-collar crime, occupational crime, and other types of crime, corporate crime encompasses those behaviors that are engaged in by a corporation for its benefit. Corporate crime can result in political and economic consequences as well as physical harm, injury, and death to persons. Friedrichs (1996) sets forth a comprehensive list of corporate offenses that includes fraud, tax evasion, price fixing, price gouging, false advertising, unfair labor practices, theft, monopolistic practices, toxic waste dumping, pollution, unsafe working conditions, and death.

Fraud, Tax Evasion, and Economic Exploitation

Fraud, tax evasion, and economic exploitation have serious consequences for society and the citizenry because they allow corporations to raise their profits, lessen their tax burdens, and at the same time underpay their employees. Fraud covers violations of the Internal Revenue Code and involves corporations defrauding the government and taxpayers, usually through contractual agreements they hold with the government.

The war in Iraq that began in 2003 provided numerous instances, in an attempt to make a larger profit, of companies overcharging the U.S. government—and ultimately taxpayers—for services rendered. A report by Congress shows that the Department of Defense had 149 contracts in Iraq with 77 different companies that were worth approximately $42 billion; this report also shows that, according to government auditors, Halliburton, the largest contractor in Iraq, and its subsidiaries, namely Kellogg, Brown, and Root, submitted questionable bills in the amount of $1.4 billion (U.S. Senate Democratic Policy Committee 2005). Testimony from former Halliburton employees revealed that the company charged the U.S. government $45 for cases of soda, $100 to clean 15-pound bags of laundry, and $1,000 for video players; it also torched and abandoned numerous $85,000 trucks instead of making the minor repairs the trucks needed.

Other examples of fraud include (1) the effort to clean up the damage to the Gulf Coast caused by Hurricane Katrina, where a report to Congress identifies 19 government contracts worth about $8.75 billion that overcharged, wasted, or otherwise mismanaged the money received from the government), and (2) the health care industry, where, for example, in July 2006, Tenet Healthcare agreed to pay back $900 million to the federal government for violations of Medicare billing (although the company is alleged to have stolen $1.9 billion).

Recently, Congress and the Securities and Exchange Commission (SEC) investigated the actions of the Wall Street investment firm Goldman Sachs in the lead-up to the 2008–2009 financial crises. Goldman was alleged to have sold high-risk or faulty investment products (specifically, a kind of mortgage-backed security) while at the same time hedging its bets that the products would fail in the market, thus allowing the firm to profit at investors' expense. There were also allegations that Goldman (and others) deceived the rating agencies that assist consumers in evaluating investment products. By July 2010, Goldman had decided to settle the case with the SEC—for the sum of $500 million. A week later, Congress passed, and President Barack Obama signed, the Dodd-Frank Wall Street Reform and Consumer Protection Act, a law aimed at restricting the kinds of practices that caused Goldman to be investigated.

Price Fixing, Price Gouging, and False Advertising

With price fixing, companies that are supposed to be competitors collude to manipulate the cost of items, keeping them artificially high and thereby maximizing profits. Archer Daniels Midland (ADM), among other companies, was convicted of price fixing commodities used in common processed foods. The company paid a $100 million antitrust fine. Similarly, Hoffman-La Roche, a vitamin company, was fined $500 million for attempting to fix the price of some vitamins worldwide, and several music industry firms have been accused of fleecing consumers to the tune of $480 million in CD overpricing (Simon 2006).

Price gouging involves taking advantage of consumers who are at risk, raising prices during times of scarcity of products, or charging the highest price possible because of monopolies, manipulation of the market, or biases in the law. U.S. corporations have long been accused of taking advantage of the poor. "Many food chains find that it costs 2 or 3 percent more to operate in poor neighborhoods, yet low-income consumers pay between 5 and 10 percent more for their groceries than those living in middle-income areas" (Simon 2006, 12). During times of scarcity of products, price gouging is frequent. In 2004, the southeastern coast of the United States was hit by a number of hurricanes. In the aftermath of the storms, the Florida Department of Agriculture and Consumer Services received more than 3,000 complaints of price gouging by hotels, gas stations, and other retail service providers (Simon 2006).

False advertising is nothing new, either. Consumers in the United States have been deceived into purchasing billions of dollars of products or services that never lived up to their claims. Food products giving false nutritional values and products claiming certain utility through false demonstrations are examples of false or deceptive advertising. Before reforms were enacted in 2009, credit card companies routinely promoted cards with no fees in bold print and, in small type, hid additional costs and contradictory information, including calculations of interest for new purchases.

Corporate Theft, Exploitation, and Unfair Labor Practices

A typical scenario of white-collar offending involves employees stealing from their employers, but the opposite is sometimes also true. Examples are companies that bilk employees out of proper overtime pay, violate minimum wage laws, fail to make Social

Security payments, or use employee pension funds improperly. Not allowing labor to unionize, strike, or collectively bargain are three examples of unfair labor practices. The result is a loss of millions of dollars by employees who cannot negotiate or who are passed over for promotion on the basis of race, ethnicity, gender, or age. One of the largest alleged exploiters of labor in the United States is Wal-Mart. The allegations of wrongdoing against Wal-Mart are numerous and varied (Buckley and Daniel 2003). Charges of unfair labor practices make up most of the charges filed against the company, although there have also been reports of violations of health coverage among Wal-Mart employees (Bernhardt, Chaddha, and McGrath 2005).

Unsafe Environmental Practices

The most prevalent form of corporate crime may be pollution. Corporations account for a large share of environmental violations. As of 2010, corporations were manufacturing more toxic waste than ever, in excess of 600 pounds per person annually, and improper disposal of this deadly waste occurs in about 90 percent of cases (Friedrichs 1996). The detrimental consequences of this are obvious: about 25 percent of U.S. residents will get cancer in their lifetimes, and a study by Cornell University finds that roughly 40 percent of deaths worldwide can be attributed to environmental pollutants (Segelken 2006). Pollution has also been linked to health problems other than cancer—things like birth defects, heart and lung disease, and sterility (Brownstein 1981). The Exxon Valdez oil spill in 1989 and the BP–Deepwater Horizon spill in 2010 are two of the worst cases of environmental pollution in world history. In 1991, Exxon pleaded guilty to criminal charges and paid a $100 million fine, followed three years later by payment of $5 billion in punitive damages. In the case of BP–Deepwater Horizon, investigations were ongoing as of mid-2010; but even in the early stages questions were raised about the readiness and safety status of key pieces of equipment used by the company in extracting oil from the Gulf of Mexico.

Unsafe Consumer Products

Again, corporations may not intend to harm consumers, but their desires to maximize profits often lead them to cut corners when it comes to product safety. Everything from the food we eat, to the medicines we take, to the vehicles we drive, to any of the products we use on a daily basis can be dangerous to our health and well-being. According to the Consumer Product Safety Commission (2003), whose charge it is to protect the public from unreasonable risks of serious injury or death, injuries, deaths, and property damage from consumer product incidents cost us more than $700 billion annually. Deaths occurring from unsafe products or product-related accidents are alleged to number 70,000 annually (Consumer Product Safety Commission 2003). Although the FDA promulgates the regulation and proper labeling of food products, corporations seem to lure us into eating unhealthy and mislabeled foods that may, because of processing, lead to many preventable diseases.

Consumer products imported into the United States from foreign companies have fueled a number of recent safety warnings. According to Schmidt (2007), roughly 25,000 shipments of food arrive in the United States each day from over 100 countries; the FDA inspects about 1 percent of these imported foods, down from 8 percent in 1992. The U.S. Department of Agriculture, on the other hand, inspects about 16 percent of imported meats and poultry, but about 80 percent of the U.S. food supply is the responsibility of the FDA (Schmidt 2007). The Centers for Disease Control and Prevention (CDC) estimates that there are 5,000 deaths and 76 million illnesses caused by unsafe food in the United States annually (Schmidt 2007). Funding for FDA food safety has increased in recent years, but it is still not adequate.

Recently, the pharmaceutical industry has been one of the main culprits in much of the unsafe manufacturing and distribution of products that have a variety of adverse consequences for users, one of which is death. The pharmaceutical industry had profits of $35.9 billion in 2002, which accounted for half of the profits of all the Fortune 500 companies in that same year (Public Citizen's Congress Watch 2003). Despite these profits and the exorbitant salaries received by the CEOs of these companies, the nation is not necessarily healthier because of the behaviors of some corporations in this industry. When pregnant women used the drug thalidomide in the 1960s, many of their babies were born with severe defects; this was an early example of the harmful effects that unregulated and untested drugs can have. Dow Corning provides another example of a corporation that did not conduct adequate testing or divulge the potential harmful effects of the silicone breast implant, one of its products, before putting it on the market. More recently, Vioxx and Bextra, two drugs used for treating arthritis and pain, were found to increase the risk of heart attack or stroke, and the drug Prozac and similar antidepressants were found to be linked to higher rates of suicide among youth. Women who took hormone replacement drugs (to relieve symptoms of menopause) were discovered to be at risk of developing breast cancer (Mintzes 2006).

The Consumer Product Safety Commission is responsible for overseeing over 15,000 products for the public's protection. More than 800 persons die annually from materials that are not protected against flammability, and another 800 perish and 18,000 are injured from unsafe equipment (Consumer Product Safety Commission 2003). The bottom line is that these corporations are more worried about their profits than the health and safety of the consumers who purchase them. Even with tougher laws, increased prosecution, heftier fines, and negative publicity, these companies have been unaffected and continue to be the most profitable corporations in the nation.

Unsafe Working Conditions

In 2003, the Bureau of Labor Statistics, a division of the U.S. Department of Labor, reported 4.4 million work-related illnesses and injuries (Reiman 2007). According to Reiman (2007), "Much or most of this carnage is the consequence of the refusal of management to pay for safety measures, of government to enforce safety, and sometimes of management's willful defiance of existing law" (82). Although accurate statistics are hard to come by, deaths caused by inhalation of asbestos—and the fatalities from unsafe conditions in the chemical, mining, and textile industries throughout our history—speak volumes about the numbers of persons who have died prematurely due to unsafe work environments.

Conclusion: The Study of Corporate Crime

Why is it important to study corporate crime? The primary reasons for doing so, and doing more of it, are as follows:

1. There is still debate about whether current research and theorizing about crime can extend to white-collar and corporate criminals.
2. There has been a lack of focus on enforcement of these crimes.
3. With an increase in globalization of companies, there will be more opportunities to offend unless laws against corporate criminal liability are further formalized.
4. Despite increased pressure to punish corporate criminals, little funding has been allocated to the control and prevention of white-collar and corporate offending by comparison with that dedicated to street crime.
5. Because many large corporations have made headlines owing to their engagement in egregious behavior, the public has shown a renewed interest in the subject of corporate crime.
6. The impact of corporate offending regarding death and monetary loss amounts to a far greater detriment to society than all eight Uniform Crime Reports index offenses (i.e., homicide/manslaughter, robbery, rape, assault, burglary, larceny/theft, motor vehicle theft, and arson) added together.
7. If we can increase the public's appreciation of the seriousness of corporate offending, the result may be increased pressure on the legislature and criminal justice system to give higher priority to the enforcement of laws against these offenses.

See also **Class Justice; Bank Bailouts (vol. 1); Executive Pay (vol. 1); Corporate Governance (vol. 1); Corporate Tax Shelters (vol. 1)**

Legal Citations

Dartmouth College v. Woodward, 17 U.S. 518 (1819).

In re Hellenic, 252 F.3d 391 (2001).

New Hampshire v. Zeta Chi Fraternity 696 A.2d 530 (1997).

North Dakota v. Smokey's Steakhouse, Inc. 478 N.W. 2d 361(1991).

Ohio v. Black on Black Crime, Inc. 736 N.E. 2d 962 (1999).

Santa Clara County v. Southern Pac. R. Co. 118 U.S. 394 (1886).

Society for the Propagation of the Gospel in Foreign Parts v. Town of Pawlet, 29 U.S. 480 (1830).

Standard Oil Company of Texas v. United States 307 F. 2d 120 (1962).

United States v. Bainbridge Management, No. 01 CR 469–1, 6 (2002).

Further Reading

Benefits of a Limited Company Web site. 2006. fletcherkennedy.com/benefits_of_a_limited_company.html

Bernhardt, Annette, Anmol Chaddha, and Siobhán McGrath, "What Do We Know About Wal-Mart? An Overview of Facts and Studies for New Yorkers." *Brennan Center for Justice.* August 2005.

Brown, Bruce, *The History of the Corporation.* Sumas, WA: BF Communications, 2003.

Brownstein, R., "The Toxic Tragedy." In *Who's Poisoning America—Corporate Polluters and Their Victims in the Chemical Age,* ed. R. Nader, R. Brownstein, and J. Richard. San Francisco: Sierra Club Books, 1981.

Buckley, Neil, and Caroline Daniel, "Wal-Mart vs. the Workers: Labour Grievances Are Stacking Up Against the World's Biggest Company." *Financial Times* (November 20, 2003).

Clinard, Marshall B., and Peter Yeager, *Corporate Crime.* New York: Free Press, 1980.

Coleman, James, *The Criminal Elite.* New York: St. Martin's Press, 1985.

"Corporate America's Woes, Continued." *Economist* (November 28, 2002).

Consumer Product Safety Commission, *2003 Annual Report.* www.cpsc.gov/cpscpub/pubs/reports/2003rpt.pdf

Estes, Ralph, *Tyranny of the Bottom Line.* San Francisco: Berrett-Koehler, 1996.

Frank, Nancy K., and Michael J. Lynch, *Corporate Crime, Corporate Violence: A Primer.* Albany, NY: Harrow and Heston, 1992.

Friedrichs, David O., *Trusted Criminals: White Collar Crime in Contemporary Society.* Belmont, CA: Wadsworth, 1996.

Geis, Gilbert, "From Deuteronomy to Deniability: A Historical Perlustration on White-Collar Crime." *Justice Quarterly* 5 (1988): 7–32.

Gitlow, Abraham L., *Corruption in Corporate America: Who Is Responsible? Who Will Protect the Public Interest?* Lanham, MD: University Press of America, 2007.

Gray, Kenneth R., Larry A. Frieder, and George W. Clark, *Corporate Scandals: The Many Faces of Greed.* St. Paul, MN: Paragon House, 2005.

Greidner, William, "Who Will Tell the People: Betrayal of American Democracy." *Washington Post* (September 30, 1991).

Hartmann, Thom, *Unequal Protection: The Rise of Corporate Dominance and the Theft of Human Rights.* New York: Rodale Press, 2002.

Kappeler, V., M. Blumberg, and G. Potter, *The Mythology of Crime and Criminal Justice.* Prospect Heights, IL: Waveland Press, 2000.

Khanna, V. S., "Corporate Criminal Liability: What Purpose Does It Serve?" *Harvard Law Review* 109 (1996): 1479.

Korten, David, *The Post-Corporate World.* San Francisco: Berrett-Koehler, 1999.

Mason, Edward S., "Corporation." In *International Encyclopedia of the Social Sciences,* Vol. 3, ed. David L. Sills and Robert K. Merton. New York: Macmillan and Free Press, 1968.

Michalowski, Raymond J., and Ronald C. Kramer, eds., *State-Corporate Crime: Wrongdoing at the Intersection of Business and Government.* New Brunswick, NJ: Rutgers University Press, 2006.

Mintzes, Barbara, "Disease Mongering in Drug Promotion: Do Governments Have a Regulatory Role?" *PLOS Medicine* 3 (April 2006): e198.

Myers, Gustavus, *History of the Great American Fortunes.* New York: Modern Library, 1907.

Public Citizen's Congress Watch, "2002 Drug Industry Profits" (2003). www.citizen.org/documents/Pharma_Report.pdf

Reclaim Democracy, *Our Hidden History of Corporations in the United States* (2004). www.reclaimdemocracy.org

Reiman, Jeffrey, *The Rich Get Richer and the Poor Get Prison: Ideology, Class, and Criminal Justice,* 8th ed. Boston: Allyn and Bacon, 2007.

Rosoff, Stephen M., Henry N. Pontell, and Robert H. Tillman, *Profit without Honor: White-Collar Crime and the Looting of America.* Upper Saddle River, NJ: Prentice Hall, 2007.

Sale, Kirkpatrick, *The Conquest of Paradise.* New York: Knopf, 1990.

Schmidt, Julie, "U.S. Food Imports Outrun FDA Resources." *USA Today* (March 18, 2007).

Schwartz-Noble, Loretta, *Poisoned Nation: Pollution, Greed, and the Rise of Deadly Epidemics.* New York: St. Martin's Press, 2007.

Segelken, Roger, "Environmental Pollution and Degradation Causes 40 Percent of Deaths Worldwide, Cornell Study Finds." *Cornell News.* September 30, 1998. www.news.cornell.edu/releases/Sept98/ecodisease.hrs.html

Simon, David R., *Elite Deviance.* Boston: Pearson/Allyn and Bacon, 2006.

Smith, Adam, *An Inquiry into the Nature and Causes of the Wealth of Nations.* New York: Oxford University Press, 1998 [1776].

U.S. Senate Democratic Policy Committee, *Halliburton's Questioned and Unsupported Costs in Iraq Exceed $1.4 Billion.* U.S. House of Representatives Committee on Government Reform, 2005.

Viano, Michael, and Jenny Arnold, "Corporate Criminal Liability." *American Criminal Law Review* (March 22, 2006).

CRUEL AND UNUSUAL PUNISHMENT

William L. Shulman

The Eighth Amendment to the U.S. Constitution, in one of its major pronouncements, prohibits the imposition of cruel and unusual punishment. Although most of the issues addressed by the U.S. Supreme Court regarding the interpretation of this clause center on applications of capital punishment, the true battleground has concerned something different. The question of whether the Eighth Amendment requires the Court to strike down sentences of any type as being "disproportionate"—that is, sentences that seem to be greater than the crime warrants—has been a contentious and confusing one with regard to which the Court has struggled to define its role generally and to articulate a test or standard when it has chosen to rule on the proportionality of sentences.

Background

In the Court's own words, such law as it has established in the proportionality area is a "thicket of Eighth Amendment jurisprudence" and has not been "a model of clarity" (*Lockyer v. Andrade* 2003). Although the Court has found death sentences to be disproportionate in crimes other than murder (*Coker v. Georgia* 1977) and disproportionate where the defendant is either mentally retarded (*Atkins v. Virginia* 2002) or a juvenile (*Roper v. Simmons* 2005), it has struggled to define its involvement in noncapital sentences.

For a long period extending through the 20th century, it appeared that the Court was prepared to intervene only in a non–death sentence if that sentence involved something harsh and unusual in addition to incarceration. In *Weems v. U.S.* (1910), for example, the defendant received a 12-year sentence to be served in hard and painful labor, with the defendant chained at the wrists and ankles, for the crime of falsifying a public document. In addition, the punishment included the loss of civil rights such as parental authority and permanent surveillance by the government. The Court, in striking down the sentence as a violation of the Eighth Amendment, noted that other more serious crimes in the jurisdiction were punished less severely; it suggested that the punishment was not just but was of "tormenting" severity (*Weems v. U.S.* 1910, at 381).

Weems notwithstanding, the cases of *Rummel v. Estelle* (1980) and *Hutto v. Davis* (1982) appeared to represent the norm of the Court's approach to this issue. William James Rummel was charged under Texas law with obtaining $125 under false pretenses, a felony in Texas. Moreover, because Rummel had previously been convicted of fraudulent use of a credit card to obtain $80 worth of goods and with passing a forged check in the amount of $28.36, he qualified under Texas law as a habitual criminal. Rummel was prosecuted and convicted under that recidivist statute and given the mandatory life sentence the statute provided. The life sentence under Texas law involved the possibility that the defendant could be paroled in as early as 12 years, a factor the Court thought important in assessing the true nature of the punishment.

The Court, in reviewing and denying Rummel's Eighth Amendment challenge, stated that to the extent that proportionality claims had been successful, they had been raised in the context of capital cases and had been a function of the Court's long-standing view of the unique nature of death as a punishment. The Court further stated that non–death sentence challenges had been successful only exceedingly rarely and involved an unusual corporal type of punishment like that found in *Weems*. The *Rummel* Court could not have been clearer when it stated, "Given the unique nature of the punishments considered in *Weems* and in the death penalty cases, one could argue without fear of contradiction by any decision of this Court that for crimes concededly classified and classifiable as felonies, that is, as punishable by significant terms of imprisonment in a state penitentiary, the length of the sentence actually imposed is purely a matter of legislative prerogative" (*Rummel v. Estelle* 1980, at 274).

Two years after *Rummel*, the Court decided in *Hutto* that a prison term of 40 years and a fine of $20,000 for possession and distribution of approximately nine ounces of marijuana was not disproportionately in violation of the Eighth Amendment and was a matter of legislative prerogative. The fact that the opinion was per curiam (signed by the Court as a whole and not authored by any one justice) seemed to underscore the strength of the Court's hands-off approach.

Key Events

The key event occurring just a year after *Hutto* was the Supreme Court case of *Solem v. Helm* (1983), in which the Court seemingly broke with, if not clear precedent, at least with the strong tenor of its prior proportionality cases. *Solem*, which dealt with a similar situation to *Rummel*, announced what is clearly a proportionality test to assess the constitutionality of noncapital sentences under the Eighth Amendment.

The *Solem* test contained three objective factors a court should consider in determining if the sentence imposed is consistent with the Eighth Amendment. First, a court should look to the gravity of the offense and the harshness of the penalty. Second, a court should compare the sentences imposed on other criminals in the same jurisdiction. Finally, courts should compare the sentences imposed for commission of the same crime in other jurisdictions.

When the Court applied this three-pronged test to the facts of *Solem*, it held the sentence of life without parole to be disproportionate to the crime involved and cruel and unusual in violation of the Eighth Amendment. First, Helm, the defendant, was convicted of the offense of writing a "no account" check for $100. This, in turn, triggered the application of South Dakota's recidivist statute owing to his prior record of six nonviolent felonies. Under the statute, a defendant would receive a mandatory life sentence without the possibility of parole (unlike *Rummel*, in which parole was a possibility). In assessing the gravity of the offense in relation to the harshness of the penalty, the Court clearly came down on the defendant's side.

In terms of the application of the second part, the Court noted that in South Dakota, Helms was sentenced to the same punishment reserved for much more serious crimes such as murder, kidnapping, first-degree rape, and other violent crimes. Finally, in assessing how the defendant would have been treated in other jurisdictions, the Court noted that in 48 of the 50 states, he would have received a less severe sentence.

The significance of this case was its remarkable departure from the Court's long years of hands off on this issue. After what had clearly been a position of deferring to state legislatures and their assessments of the proper punishments for crimes, *Solem* seemed to open up the possibility that the courts had entered the fray. The question the case presented was whether the Supreme Court was truly committed to this new activist approach or viewed the case as an aberration dealing with a particularly unusual set of facts and circumstances.

Further Legal Developments

Of course, the cases discussed in the background section make up a significant portion of the Court's legal decisions in this area. It has been the Court's work since *Solem*, however, that has either, depending upon your perspective, fixed the aberration of *Solem* or further muddied the waters with another unworkable standard.

The case of *Harmelin v. Michigan* (1991) was the first important proportionality case after *Solem*. It involved the application of a Michigan mandatory life sentence law for certain drug offenses. Harmelin, the defendant, was convicted of possessing 672 grams of cocaine and sentenced to a mandatory life sentence without the possibility of parole. Early in the opinion, it was clear how the Court was going to deal with *Solem*'s insistence on performing the three-part proportionality test when it characterized the *Solem* decision as "scarcely the expression of clear and well established constitutional law." (*Harmelin v. Michigan* 1991, at 965). Justice Antonin Scalia's lengthy and scholarly discussion of the history of the Eighth Amendment and its historical precedent in the English Declaration of Rights of 1689 supported his interpretation that the amendment prohibited only cruel and unusual punishment (in other words, the manner, not the length, of the punishment) and did not support a proportionality requirement. Important to his interpretation was the notion that proportionality as a legal concept goes back to the Magna Carta and that numerous states at the time of the Constitution had specific provisions requiring proportionality in their sentencing laws, meaning that had the framers intended to graft that notion to the Eighth Amendment, they were well acquainted with the idea and could easily have done so. Scalia concluded his analysis by stating that the "cruel and unusual" language of the Eighth Amendment relates to the method of punishment only and not to the length of the punishment.

The final pronouncement of the Court on this matter came in *Ewing v. California* (2003), a case that dealt with the application of California's three-strikes law to a defendant with a lengthy history of criminal convictions but whose only triggering crime was the theft of three golf clubs. Ewing was sentenced under the statute to 25 years to life in prison.

Although the opinion did not garner a majority of the Court, the reasoning of Justice Sandra Day O'Connor's lead opinion relied on the framework set out by Justice Anthony Kennedy in his earlier concurrence in *Harmelin*. Kennedy found that the Eighth Amendment recognizes a limited proportionality principle in noncapital cases, which forbids the imposition of extreme sentences that are "grossly disproportionate" to the crime (*Ewing v. California* 2003).

Justice Kennedy identified four principles to consult before making the final determination under the Eighth Amendment. The Court was to look at the primacy of the legislature, the variety of legitimate penological schemes, the nature of the federal system, and the requirement that proportionality review be guided by objective factors. In applying these factors to the specifics of *Ewing*, the Court focused primarily on California's legitimate interests of deterring and incapacitating offenders with long and serious records. These legitimate penological interests, when combined with the primacy of (deference to) the legislature, shaped the Court's affirmation of the sentence.

Conclusion

Although the concept of proportionality of punishment has a long and rich history in England going back to the Magna Carta, and although it has been recognized and applied in capital and noncapital cases in the United States for almost a century, it appears to have gone the way of the Edsel and the dial phone (Donham 2005; see sec. IV for an excellent summary of historical evidence). The future of the Supreme Court's Eighth Amendment jurisprudence, in other words, does not appear to include general proportionality as a working doctrine.

Instead, there appear to be three vastly different approaches on the table, none of which appears to garner a majority of the Court's votes. There is the more liberal

MAYBE WE WERE WRONG: THE REFORM MOVEMENT IN SENTENCING

It is no coincidence that *Rummel*, *Solem*, and *Harmelin* occurred during the decade of the 1980s, a decade ushered in by the so-called War on Drugs and the movement to mandatory long-term sentences. States followed the call from the federal government that what was needed to stem the drug and violence epidemic in this country was a tougher "lock-'em-up" correctional policy. What followed was the increase of arrests and longer sentences, often triggered by recidivist or "three strikes" laws, and the construction of new prisons.

Lawmakers and policy makers have begun to look at the wisdom of that movement, which has several disturbing results. The policies of locking up offenders for longer times and denying them parole opportunities have resulted in an increasingly elderly and infirm prison population (at great cost to the public) and caused many inmates—denied any incentive for early release—to become unmanageable.

Reform efforts have come on both state and federal levels. On the federal level, the Second Chance Act addresses the issue of prisoner reentry and would authorize funding for model community programs to assist inmates who are reentering society. On the state level, a growing number of states have either eliminated some mandatory sentencing laws, eliminated recidivist or three-strikes laws, or reinstituted discretionary parole for certain offenses.* At the same time, in 2009 the state of Texas found it fit to execute (for rape and murder) Bobby Wayne Woods, a man whose IQ was between 68 and 86 and could therefore, in the eyes of his defense attorneys and others, claim mental incompetence (McKinley 2009).

*"The Right Has a Jailhouse Conversion." *New York Times Magazine* (December 24, 2006): 47; Families Against Mandatory Minimums. "State Responses to Mandatory Minimum Laws." 2010. http://www.famm.org

position of Justices Ruth Bader Ginsburg and Stephen Breyer, and presumably of Sonya Sotomayor and Elena Kagan (both new appointees), which suggests that a return to the *Solem* three-part test is appropriate. At the other end of the spectrum, Justices Antonin Scalia and Clarence Thomas adhere to the position that the Eight Amendment contains no proportionality requirement. Finally, and perhaps the most likely ground to be taken, is Justice Kennedy's concurring opinion in *Harmelin*, which recognizes a "narrow proportionality principle" in the Eighth Amendment. Of the two Bush appointees, Chief Justice John Roberts and Associate Justice Samuel Alito, we know only that they have upheld the right to use lethal injection in capital cases and were in the minority in a ruling deciding whether life sentences for juvenile offenders constitutes cruel and unusual punishment—five justices, including Kennedy, stated that such sentences are improper (except in certain homicide cases) (Barnes 2008; Bravin 2010).

It is also possible to envision a case in which all nine justices would agree on reversing a particular sentence under the Eighth Amendment if it were so extreme as to be unacceptable to any rational person at any time at any place. The idea that legislatures could make overtime parking a felony punishable by life is theoretically possible without a proportionality principle. This notion particularly irked Justice Byron White in his *Harmelin* dissent (*Harmelin v. Michigan* 1991, at 1018), but it may take more than chiding from fellow justices about frightening scenarios to gain unanimity in an area in which most justices have seemed content to go their own way.

See also **Death Penalty; Prisons—Supermax; Three-Strikes Laws**

Legal Citations

Atkins v. Virginia, 536 U.S. 304 (2002).

Coker v. Georgia, 433 U.S. 584 (1977).

Ewing v. California, 538 U.S. 11 (2003).

Harmelin v. Michigan, 501 U.S. 957 (1991).

Hutto v. Davis, 454 U.S. 370 (1982).

Lockyer v. Andrade, 538 U.S. 63, 66 (2003).

Roper v. Simmons, 125 S.Ct. 1183 (2005).

Rummel v. Estelle, 445 U.S. 263 (1980).

Solem v. Helm, 463 U.S. 277 (1983).

Weems v. U.S., 217 U.S. 349 (1910).

Further Reading

Barnes, Robert, "Justices Uphold Lethal Injection Procedure." *Washington Post* (April 17, 2008).

Bravin, Jess, "Justices Restrict Life Terms for Youth." *Wall Street Journal* (May 18, 2010).

Cusac, Anne-Marie, *Cruel and Unusual: The Culture of Punishment in America.* New Haven, CT: Yale University Press, 2009.

Donham, Joy M., "Note: Third Strike or Merely a Foul Tip? The Gross Disproportionality of *Lockyer v. Andrade.*" *Akron Law Review* 38 (2005): 369.

Evans, Kimberly Masters, *Capital Punishment: Cruel and Unusual?* Detroit: Gale, 2008.

Frost, Natasha, *The Punitive State: Crime, Punishment, and Imprisonment across the United States.* New York: LFB Scholarly Publishing, 2006.

Jarvis, Brian, *Cruel and Unusual: Punishment and U.S. Culture.* London and Sterling, VA: Pluto Press, 2005.

McKinley, James C., Jr. "Killer with Low IQ Executed in Texas." *New York Times* (December 3, 2009).

Melusky, Joseph Anthony, *Cruel and Unusual Punishment: Rights and Liberties under the Law.* Santa Barbara, CA: ABC-CLIO, 2003.

Whitman, James Q., *Harsh Justice: Criminal Punishment and the Widening Divide between America and Europe.* New York: Oxford University Press, 2003.

CYBERCRIME

Bernadette H. Schell

According to a 2009 study conducted by the McAfee antivirus company and entitled "Unsecured Economies: Protecting Vital Information," data theft and breaches from cybercrime likely cost businesses whose networks were hacked as much as $1 trillion globally. This huge cost included both losses in intellectual property rights as well as expenditures for losses in productivity and network damage repair. These cost projections were based on the survey responses of more than 800 chief information officers in the United States, Germany, the U.K., Japan, China, India, Dubai, and Brazil. Respondents said that the breaches amounted to about $4.6 billion in losses, and the repairs were estimated to be as high as $600 million (Mills 2009).

The respondents conjectured that the recent global economic recession had increased the security risks for business and government networks, given that over 40 percent of displaced or laid-off employees were the main threat to sensitive and proprietary information found on networks. When asked which countries posed the biggest threats as state cybercriminals, there were marked differences. Over 25 percent of the overall survey respondents said that they avoided storing data on networks in China because of their likelihood of being attacked, while about 47 percent of the Chinese respondents suggested that the United States poses the biggest threat to the security of their online data (Mills 2009).

Cybercrime and Hackers Defined

The growth and spread of the Internet globally within the past 20 years has fostered the growth of a variety of online crimes as well as national cybersecurity strategies and laws aimed at curbing these unwanted behaviors. In fact, an interesting debate has developed concerning the definition of online crimes, one using the terms "cybercrime" (or "cyber crime") and "computer crimes." Typically, cybercrimes occur because an individual who uses his or her special knowledge of cyberspace for personal or financial gain, and computer crimes typically involve a special knowledge of computer technology. Moreover, the interrelated nature of these behaviors further complicates the definition process; thus, many experts and the media seem to utilize these two terms interchangeably (Furnell 2002). The term "cybercrime" is used here to refer to any crime completed on or with a computer.

Broadly speaking, cybercrime includes such activities as electronic commerce, intellectual property rights (IPR) or copyright infringement, privacy rights infringement, and identity theft—a type of fraud. The domain of cybercrime also includes online child exploitation, credit card fraud, cyberstalking and cyberbullying, defaming or threatening other online users, gaining unauthorized access to computer networks (commonly known as "hacking"), and overriding encryption to make illegal copies of software or movies. Accepting that variations on the parameters constituting such unlawful acts, as well as the penalties associated with these criminal acts, vary from one jurisdiction to another globally, this continually evolving list of common cybercrimes is relevant and globally applicable (Schell and Martin 2006).

Some experts further suggest that cybercrimes are not all that different from traditional crimes. Whereas cybercrimes occur in an online environment, traditional crimes occur terrestrially. One of the best known cybercrime typologies classifies behavior along lines similar to those found in traditional crime typologies (Wall 2001).

Cybercrimes tend to include two common criminal acts: *trespassing* (defined as entering unlawfully into an area to commit an offence) and *theft* (defined as taking or exercising illegal control over the property of another to deprive the owner of that asset (Furnell 2002).

Individuals who break into networks to cause damage or to receive personal or financial gain are commonly referred to in the media as "hackers," but many in the computer underground insist that the more appropriate term for the mal-inclined techies wreaking havoc on networks is "cracker" or "Black Hat." Talented tech savvies paid by industry and governments to find vulnerabilities in software or networks are known in the computer underground as "White Hats" (Schell, Dodge, and Moutsatsos 2002).

As technologies evolve, so do the cybercriminal activities and labels. For example, the threat posed by a new form of cybercrime called "carding"—the illegal acquisition, sale, and exchange of sensitive online information—has increased in recent years (Holt and Lampke 2010). Those who engage in such activities are known simply as "carders."

Today, the major types of cybertrespassing and cybertheft include but are not limited by these categories (Schell and Martin 2004):

- Flooding: a form of cyberspace vandalism resulting in denial of service (DoS) to authorized users of a Web site or computer system
- Infringing intellectual property rights (IPR) and copyright: a form of cyberspace theft involving the copying of a target's copyright-protected software, movie, or other creative work without getting the owner's consent to do so

- Phreaking: a form of cyberspace theft or fraud conducted by using technology to make free telephone calls
- Spoofing: the cyberspace appropriation of an authentic user's identity by nonauthentic users, causing fraud or attempted fraud and commonly called "identify theft"
- Virus and worm production and release: a form of cyberspace vandalism causing corruption and maybe even the erasing of data

The Four Critical Elements of Traditional Crimes and Cybercrimes

According to legal expert Susan Brenner (2001), both traditional land-based crimes and cybercrimes cause *harm*—to property, to persons, or to both. Furthermore, as in the real world, in the virtual world there are politically motivated crimes, controversial crimes, and technical nonoffenses. In U.S. jurisdictions and elsewhere, traditional and cybercrimes involve four key elements:

- *Actus reus* (the prohibited act or failing to act when one is supposed to be under duty to do so)
- *Mens rea* (a culpable mental state)
- *Attendant circumstances* (the presence of certain necessary conditions)
- *Harm* (to persons, property, or both)

Perhaps an example or two will illustrate more clearly these critical elements. One of the best-known cyberstalking-in-the-making cases reported in the popular media of late involved a young man named Eric Burns (also known by his online moniker Zyklon). Burns's claim to criminal fame was that he attacked the Web pages of about 80 businesses and government offices whose pages were hosted by Laser.Net in Fairfax, Virginia.

An obviously creative individual, Burns designed a program called "Web bandit" to identify computers on the Internet that were vulnerable to attack. He then used the vulnerable systems to advertise his love for a high school classmate named Crystal. Through his computer exploits, Burns was able to advertise worldwide his unrelenting love for Crystal in the hope that if he could get her attention, he could have her longer-term. Unfortunately, the case did not end on a happy note for Burns. After he was caught and convicted by U.S. authorities, the 19-year-old pleaded guilty to defacing Web pages for NATO and Vice President Al Gore. In November 1999, the judge hearing the case ruled that Burns should serve 15 months in U.S. federal prison for his illegal exploits, pay more than $36,000 in restitution, and not be allowed to touch a computer for 3 years after his supervised prison release. Ironically, Crystal attended the same high school as Burns but hardly knew him. In the end, she helped the authorities capture him (U.S. Department of Justice 1999).

Citing the four elements of cybercrimes, cyberperpetrator Burns gained entry into computers and unlawfully took control of the property—the Web pages owned by

NATO and Vice President Al Gore. Burns entered with the intent of depriving the lawful owner of error-free Web pages (*mens rea*). By society's norms, Burns had no legal right to alter the Web pages by advertising his love for Crystal; he was not authorized to do so by the rightful owners (*attendant circumstances*). Consequently, Burns was liable for his unlawful acts, for he illegally entered the computer networks (i.e., criminal trespass) to commit an offense once access was gained (i.e., data alteration). As the targeted users realized that *harm* was caused to their property, the judge hearing the evidence ruled that Burns should be sent to prison for his criminal actions as well as pay restitution.

In recent times, there have also been some alleged cybercrimes involving harm or death to Internet-connected persons. For example, in late May 2010, a U.S. judge ordered a former Minnesota nurse facing charges in the suicides of two individuals to keep off the Internet until the cybercriminal case is heard and resolved. William Melchert-Dinkel, aged 47, appeared in a Minnesota court on "assisted suicide" charges. The father of two children is accused of coaxing Nadia Kajouji, an 18-year-old Canadian student, and Mark Dryborough, a 32-year-old British man, to commit suicide. Police allege that Melchert-Dinkel met both in online suicide chat rooms. According to court documents, this alleged cybercriminal had made online suicide pacts with about 10 or 11 individuals all over the world—indicating that, unlike most land crimes, the Internet has no geographical boundaries. Apparently Melchert-Dinkel would go into chat rooms using the monikers "carni," "Li Dao," or "falcon.girl," introducing himself as a female nurse. He seemed to use his medical knowledge to offer advice on suicide methods to online users seeking such. The charges are believed to represent the first time that assisted suicide laws—commonly used in mercy killing cases—have been applied to the virtual world. The teenaged victim in this bizarre case was studying at a university when she drowned herself two years ago, apparently on the advice of Melchert-Dinkel (Doolittle 2010).

The Changing Virtual Landscape and Presenting Challenges

There is little question that the virtual landscape has changed considerably just in the last 10 years, for in North America and globally, more people have become connected to the Internet, largely because of increasing affordability. Using Canada as one case in point, according to Statistics Canada, in 2009, some 80 percent of Canadians aged 16 and over used the Internet for personal reasons—a figure that shows an increase in usage by 7 percent since 2007 (the last time the survey was conducted). In short, almost 22 million Canadians aged 16 or over are active in the virtual world. Affordability, however, remains a key factor. Although there is a 94 percent Internet usage in Canadian households when income levels exceed $85,000 a year, there is only a 56 percent Internet usage in households where the income is less than $30,000 a year. Developing economies as well as developed economies see the economic sustainability importance of having citizens Internet-connected. According to a 2009 Internet World Stats study, China is, in fact, the number 1 most online-connected location worldwide (El Akkad 2010).

In fact, the virtual world is becoming so crowded on a nationwide basis that the Internet as we know it today seems to be reaching its limits. Some experts have estimated that quite soon—and likely before 2012—the number of new devices able to connect to the World Wide Web will plummet as the world exhausts its IP addresses—unique codes providing access to the Internet. Part of the problem is that the Internet was built around the Internet Protocol Addressing Scheme version 4 (IPv4), having about 4 billion addresses and now running low. Back in the 1970s, when the Internet was just becoming popular, 4 billion addresses probably seemed like plenty. Internet Protocol Addressing Scheme version 6 (IPv6) is on its way in, having trillions more addresses available and ready for the taking. The problem, say the experts, is that businesses and governments are slow in adapting their technology to IPv6. Thus there is the fear that there could be a major online crunch before 2012 (Kesterton 2010).

As more and more citizens become Internet-connected, new opportunities for communicating and exchanging information with others online come into existence, such as the development and growth of popular social networks like Facebook. However, accompanying the positive evolution of Internet usages is the dark side, whereby tech-savvy criminals continually search for new ways to cause harm to property and to persons in the virtual world.

Faced with stricter Internet security measures worldwide, some mal-inclined spammers, for example—marketers conning online users to buy their products or services after deriving mailing lists from many online sources, including scanning Usenet discussion groups—have now begun to borrow pages from corporate America's economic sustainability rule books: They, too, are outsourcing. Sophisticated spammers are now paying tech-savvy folks in India, Bangladesh, China, and other developing nations to overcome tests know as "captchas," which ask Internet users to type in a string of somewhat obscured characters to prove that they are human beings and not spam-generating robots. ("Captchas," pioneered by Luis von Ahn, a computer science professor at Carnegie Mellon, is an acronym for "completely automated public Turing test to tell computers and humans apart.")

The current charge-out rate for the borrowed talent ranges from about 80 cents to $1.20 for each 1,000 deciphered boxes, based on estimates provided by online exchanges like Freelancer.com, where many such projects are bid on weekly. Where jobs are scarce, becoming involved in such a money-making proposition provides a way for some hungry online citizens to avoid starving to death. Professor von Ahn says that the cost of hiring people, even as cheaply as it may appear, should limit the extent of such operations, since only profitable spammers who have already determined various ways to make money through devious online techniques can afford such operations. Some of these outsourced operations appear to be fairly sophisticated, involving brokers and middlemen. Large enterprises, such as Google, that utilize captchas technogy argue that paying people to solve captchas proves that the tool is working, at least in part, as an effective anticybercrime measure (Bajaj 2010).

There is little question that, globally, cybercrime in recent years has become more "organized," often involving underground gangs and Mafia-like hierarchies hiring needed talent to get the cybercrime job done and keep the coffers flush with cash. Since 2002, botnets, in particular, are recognized as a growing problem. A "bot," short form for "robot," is a remote-controlled software program acting as an agent for a user (Schell and Martin 2006). The reason that botnets are anxiety-producing to organizations and governments, alike is that mal-inclined bots can download malicious binary codes intended to compromise the host machine by turning it into a "zombie." A collection of zombies is called a "botnet." Although botnets have been used for spamming and other nefarious online activities, the present-day threat is that if several botnets form a gang, they could threaten—if not cripple—the networked critical infrastructures of most countries with a series of coordinated distributed denial of service (DDoS) attacks, bringing nations' economies to a standstill (Sockel and Falk 2009).

Botnets have been crafted by individuals not intentionally out to cause harm to property or persons but who are later co-opted into gangs with alternative motives. Sometimes the creators of the botnets are later blamed for the damages caused.

For example, in a New Zealand hearing held on July 15, 2008, Justice Judith Potter discharged without conviction Owen Walker, a teenage hacker involved in an international hacking group known as "the A-Team" (Farrell 2007). Walker was alleged to have been engaged in some of the most sophisticated botnet cybercrime ever seen in New Zealand. Even though Walker pleaded guilty to six charges during his trial—including accessing a computer for dishonest purposes and damaging or interfering with a computer system—he walked away from the courthouse without going to jail. Walker was part of an international ring of 21 hackers, and his exploits apparently cost the local New Zealand economy about $20.4 million in U.S. dollars. Had he been convicted, the teen could have spent up to seven years in prison.

In his defense, Walker said that he was motivated to create bots not by maliciousness but by his intense interest in computers and his need to stretch their capabilities—the line often cited by White Hat hackers as justification for their exploits (Gleeson 2008). The judge ordered Walker to pay $11,000 in costs and damages, although the botnet creator said that he did not receive any of the approximately $32,000 "stolen" resulting the course of the cybercrime in question (Humphries 2008).

Measures Governments Worldwide Have Enacted to Curb Cybercrime

Clearly, the continually evolving nature of cybercrime has caused considerable consternation for governments globally. It is tough for governments and their authorities to stay ahead of the cybercriminal curve because the curve keeps changing. Moreover, there is a widespread belief that if cybercriminals are to be stopped in their tracks and dealt with by the global justice system, countries must work together to stop this online "problem," which knows no boundaries. Simply stated, as the nature of cybercrime has evolved from single-person exploits to international cybergangs and Mafia-like structures, the need for more effective legal structures to effectively prosecute and punish those engaged in such costly behaviors has also increased exponentially.

In the United States in particular, most newsworthy cybercrime cases have been prosecuted under the computer crime statute 18 U.S.C. subsection 1030. This primary U.S. federal statute criminalizing cracking was originally called the Computer Fraud and Abuse Act (CFAA), modified in 1996 by the National Information Infrastructure Protection Act and codified at 18 U.S.C. subsection 1030, Fraud and Related Activity in Connection with Computers. If caught in the United States, crackers are often charged with intentionally causing damage without authorization to a protected computer. A first offender typically faces up to five years in prison and fines up to $250,000 per count, or twice the loss suffered by the targets. The U.S. federal sentencing guidelines for cracking have been expanded in recent years to provide longer sentences if exploits lead to the injury or death of online citizens—such as the recent case involving allegations against American William Melchert-Dinkel. In the United States, targets of cyber-crimes can also seek civil penalties (Evans and McKenna 2000).

After the September 11, 2001, terrorist attacks on the World Trade Center and the Pentagon, the U.S. government became increasingly concerned about terrorist attacks of various natures and increased homeland security protections. To this end, the U.S. Congress passed a series of laws aimed at halting computer criminals, including the 2002 Homeland Security Act, with section 225 known as the Cyber Security Enhancement Act of 2002. In 2003, the Prosecutorial Remedies and Tools against the Exploitation of Children Today Act (PROTECT Act) was passed to assist law enforcement in their efforts to track and identify cybercriminals using the Internet for child exploitation purposes. Also in 2003, the Can Spam Act was passed, aimed at decreasing the harm issues raised by online spammers.

President Barack Obama has identified cybersecurity as one of the most serious economic and national security challenges facing the United States today—a challenge that he affirmed the United States was not adequately prepared to counter effectively. Shortly after taking office, Obama ordered a complete review of federal efforts to defend the U.S. information and communication online infrastructure and the development of a more comprehensive approach for securing the information highway.

In May 2009, Obama accepted the recommendations of the Cyberspace Policy Review to select an executive branch cybersecurity coordinator who would have regular access to the president and to invest hugely into cutting-edge research-and-development efforts to meet the present-day digital challenges. The president also wanted to build on the Comprehensive National Cyber Security Initiative (CNCI) launched by President George W. Bush in the National Security Presidential Directive of January, 2008. President Obama has also called on other nations to develop similar comprehensive national cybersecurity policies and action plans as a means of securing cyberspace for online citizens worldwide (U.S. National Security Council 2010).

Other countries have followed the U.S. lead and cries for virtual world interventions. For example, on May 28, 2010, the Canadian government announced its National Strategy and Action Plan to Strengthen the Protection of Critical Infrastructure (Public Safety Canada 2010). Other countries have also enacted anti-intrusion legislation similar to the crime statute 18 U.S.C. subsection 1030 enacted in the United States. For example, section 342.1 of the Canadian Criminal Code is aimed at a number of potential harms, including theft of computer services, invasion of online users' privacy, trading in computer passwords, and cracking encryption systems. Moreover, breaking the digital encryption on a movie DVD—even if copying it for personal use—would in the near future make individual Canadians liable for legal damages up to $5,000 if a tougher copyright law proposed by the present Canadian federal government is enacted in 2010 (Chase 2010).

Finally, it must be emphasized that although the battle to keep cybercriminals at bay is a problem that will continue into the future, countries worldwide are committed to putting sizable resources into meeting the challenge. The Global Cyber Law Survey of 50 countries recently found that 70 percent of these had legislation against unauthorized computer access as well as against data tampering, sabotage, malware or malicious software usage, and fraud.

See also **Identity Theft; Advertising and the Invasion of Privacy (vol. 1); Internet (vol. 4); Surveillance—Technological (vol. 4)**

Further Reading

Bajaj, Vikas, "Spammers Pay Others to Answer Security Tests." *New York Times* (April 25, 2010).

Brenner, Susan W., *Cybercrime: Criminal Threats from Cyberspace.* Santa Barbara, CA: Praeger, 2010.

Chase, S., "New Bill Cracks Down On Copyright Pirates." *Globe and Mail* (June 3, 2010): A4.

Doolittle, R., "Internet Ban for Man Accused in Teen Suicide." *Toronto Star* (May 26, 2010): GT2.

El Akkad, O., "Communications: Canadian Internet Usage Grows." *Globe and Mail* (May 11, 2010): B9.

Evans, M., and B. McKenna,"Dragnet Targets Internet Vandals." *Globe and Mail* (February 10, 2000): A1, A10.

Farrell, N., "Hacker Mastermind Has Asperger Syndrome." *New Zealand Herald* (December 3, 2007). http://www.theinquirer.net/inquirer/news/1038901/hacker-mastermind-asperger-syndrome

Furnell, S., *Cybercrime: Vandalizing the Information Society.* Boston, MA: Addison Wesley, 2002.

Gleeson, Sheenagh, "Freed Hacker Could Work for Police." *New Zealand Herald* (July 16, 2008). http://www.nzherald.co.nz/nz/news/article.cfm?c_id = 1&objectid = 10521796/

Holt, T. J., and E. Lampke,"Exploring Stolen Data Markets On-Line: Products and Market Forces." *Criminal Justice Studies* 33, no. 2 (2010).

Humphries, M., "Teen Hacker Owen Walker Won't Be Convicted." July 17, 2008. http://www.geek.com/articles/news/teen-hacker-owen-walker-wont-be-convicted-20080717

Kesterton, M., "Social Studies: A Daily Miscellany of Information." *Globe and Mail* (May 31, 2010): L6.

McQuade, Samuel C., III, ed., *Encyclopedia of Cybercrime.* Westport, CT: Greenwood Press, 2009.

Mills, Elinor, "Study: Cybercrime Cost Firms $1 Trillion Globally." January 28, 2009. http://news.cnet.com/8301–1009_3–10152246–83.html

Public Safety Canada, "Ministers Announce National Strategy and Action Plan to Strengthen the Protection of Critical Infrastructure." May 28, 2010. http://www.publicsafety.gc.ca/media/nr/2010/nr20100528-eng.aspx?rss = true

Schell, B. H., J. L. Dodge, and S. S. Moutsatsos, *The Hacking of America: Who's Doing It, Why, and How.* Westport, CT: Quorum Books, 2002.

Schell, B. H., and C. Martin, *Webster's New World Hacker Dictionary.* Indianapolis, IN: Wiley, 2006.

Schell, B. H., and C. Martin, *Cybercrime.* Santa Barbara, CA: ABC-CLIO, 2004.

Sockel, H., and L. K. Falk, "Online Privacy, Vulnerabilities, and Threats: A Manager's Perspective." In *Online Consumer Protection: Theories of Human Relativism,* ed. K. Chen and A. Fadlalla. Hershey, PA: Information Science Reference, 2009.

U.S. Department of Justice, "'Web Bandit' Hacker Sentenced to 15 Months Imprisonment, 3 Years of Supervised Release, for Hacking USIA, NATO, Web Sites." November 19, 1999. http://www.justice.gov/criminal/cybercrime/burns.htm

U.S. National Security Council, The Comprehensive National Cyber Security Initiative. 2010. http://www.whitehouse.gov/cybersecurity/comprehensive-national-cybersecurity-initiative

D

DEATH PENALTY

Robert M. Bohm

Few issues in criminal justice are as controversial as the death penalty. For most people who support the death penalty, the execution of killers (and people who commit other horrible acts) makes sense. Death penalty supporters frequently state that executions do prevent those executed from committing heinous crimes again and that the example of executions probably prevents most people who might contemplate committing appalling crimes from doing so. In addition, many death penalty supporters simply believe that people who commit such crimes deserve to die—that they have earned their ignominious fate.

For opponents, the death penalty issue is about something else entirely. For many opponents, the level of death penalty support in the United States is a rough estimate of the level of maturity of the American people. The not-so-subtle implication is that a mature, civilized society would not employ the death penalty. Opponents maintain that perpetrators of horrible crimes can be dealt with effectively by other means and that it makes little sense to kill some people, however blameworthy they may be, to teach other people not to kill. These opponents argue that although the perpetrators of terrible crimes may deserve severe punishment, that punishment need not be execution. This entry provides a brief history of the penalty's development in the United States.

Background

The first person executed in what is now the United States was Capt. George Kendall, a councilor for the Virginia colony. He was executed in 1608 for being a spy for Spain. The fact that he was executed was not particularly unusual, because the death penalty was just another one of the punishments brought to the New World by the early European settlers.

Since Kendall's execution in 1608, more than 19,000 executions have been performed in what is now the United States under civil (as opposed to military) authority. This estimate does not include the approximately 10,000 people lynched in the 19th century. Nearly all of the people executed during the past four centuries in what is now the United States have been adult men; only about 3 percent have been women. Ninety percent of the women were executed under local as opposed to state authority, and the majority (87 percent) were executed prior to 1866. About 2 percent of the people executed have been juveniles—that is, individuals who committed their capital crimes prior to their 18th birthdays. Most of them (69 percent) were black and nearly 90 percent of their victims were white.

Key Events

It is important to understand that all of the significant changes in the practice of capital punishment in the United States—culminating in its complete abolition in some jurisdictions—are the result of abolitionist efforts. Those efforts created (1) degrees of murder, which distinguish between murders heinous enough to warrant death and those murders that do not; (2) a reduction in the number of offenses warranting the death penalty (except for the federal government and some states since 1994); (3) the hiding of executions from public view; and (4) a decreased number of annual executions. Although abolition of the death penalty has been their unremitting goal, abolitionists have been far more successful in reforming its practice.

Degrees of Murder

Because of the efforts of Pennsylvania Attorney General and later U.S. Attorney General William Bradford and Philadelphia physician and signer of the Declaration of Independence Benjamin Rush, both early death penalty abolitionists, Pennsylvania became the first state in legal proceedings to consider degrees of murder based on culpability. Before this change, the death penalty was mandated for anyone convicted of murder (and many other crimes) regardless of circumstance. Neither Bradford nor Rush believed that capital punishment deterred crime, citing the example of horse stealing, which at the time was a capital offense in Virginia and the most frequently committed crime in the state. Because of the severity of the penalty, convictions for the crime were hard to obtain.

Limiting Death-Eligible Crimes

Pressure from abolitionists also caused Pennsylvania in 1794 to repeal the death penalty for all crimes except first-degree murder. Between 1794 and 1798, Virginia and Kentucky joined Pennsylvania in abolishing the death penalty for all crimes except first-degree murder; New York and New Jersey abolished the penalty for all crimes except murder and treason. Virginia and Kentucky, both slave states, confined the reforms to free people; slaves in those states were still subject to a long list of capital crimes. When New Jersey, Virginia, and Kentucky severely restricted the scope of capital punishment, they also appropriated funds for the construction of their first prisons; Pennsylvania and New York had established prisons earlier. Still, a half-century would pass before the first state abandoned capital punishment entirely.

Hiding Executions from the Public

Between 1800 and 1850, U.S. death penalty abolitionists helped change public sentiment about public executions, especially among many northern social elites. In 1800, public hangings were mostly solemn events regularly attended by members of all social classes and touted as having important educational value. But by midcentury, members of the upper classes were staying away from them because in their minds they had become tasteless, shocking, rowdy, sometimes dangerous, carnival-like spectacles. This view, however, may have been more a matter of perception than reality, as eyewitness accounts suggest that decorum at public executions had not changed that much. In any event, the elite began to view those who attended executions as contemptible rabble out for a good time and concluded that any educational value public hangings once had was being lost on the less respectable crowd.

Another problem with public hangings during this period was that attendees were increasingly sympathizing with the condemned prisoners, weakening the position of the state. Indeed, some of those who met their fate on the gallows became folk heroes. Increasing acceptance of the belief that public executions were counterproductive because of the violence they caused was yet another change. Stories were circulated about the violent crimes being committed just before or after a pubic hanging by attendees of the event.

For these reasons, Connecticut, in 1830, became the first state to ban public executions. Pennsylvania became the second state to do so in 1834. In both states, only a few authorized officials and the relatives of the condemned were allowed to attend. By 1836, New York, New Jersey, Massachusetts, Rhode Island, and New Hampshire had enacted similar policies. By 1860, all northern states and Delaware and Georgia in the South had shifted the site of executions from the public square to an enclosed jail yard controlled by the sheriff and deputies. By 1890, some states had moved executions to inside the jail or a prison building. The last public execution was held in Galena, Missouri, in 1937.

From Mandatory to Discretionary Capital Punishment Statutes

In 1837, Tennessee became the first state to enact a discretionary death penalty statute for murder; Alabama did the same four years later, followed by Louisiana five years after that. All states before then employed mandatory death penalty statutes that required anyone convicted of a designated capital crime to be sentenced to death. The reason for the change, at least at first and in the South, undoubtedly was to allow all-white juries to take race into account in deciding whether death was the appropriate penalty in a particular case. Between the Civil War and the end of the 19th century, at least 20 additional jurisdictions changed their death penalty laws from mandatory to discretionary ones. Illinois was the first northern state to do so in 1867; New York was the last state to make the change in 1963. The reason most northern states switched from mandatory to discretionary death penalty statutes, and another reason for southern states to do so, was to prevent jury nullification, which was becoming an increasing problem. "Jury nullification" refers to a jury's knowing and deliberate refusal to apply the law because, in the given case, a mandatory death sentence was considered contrary to the jury's sense of justice, morality, or fairness.

From Local to State-Authorized Executions

A major change took place in the legal jurisdiction of executions during the time of the Civil War. Before the war, all executions were conducted locally—generally in the jurisdiction in which the crime was committed. But on January 20, 1864, Sandy Kavanagh was executed at the Vermont State Prison. He was the first person executed under state as opposed to local authority. This shift in jurisdiction was not immediately adopted by other states. After Kavanagh, there were only about two state- or federally authorized executions per year well into the 1890s; the rest were locally authorized. That pattern would shift dramatically during the next 30 years. In the 1890s, about 90 percent of executions were imposed under local authority, but by the 1920s, about 90 percent were imposed under state authority. Today, all executions except those conducted in Delaware and Montana and by the federal government and the military are imposed under state authority.

States Abolish the Death Penalty

In 1846, the state of Michigan abolished the death penalty for all crimes except treason and replaced it with life imprisonment. The law took effect the next year, making Michigan, for all intents and purposes, the first English-speaking jurisdiction in the world to abolish capital punishment. The first state to outlaw the death penalty for all crimes, including treason, was Rhode Island in 1852; Wisconsin was the second state to do so a year later. Not until well after the Civil War did Iowa (in 1872) and Maine (in 1876) become the next states to abolish the death penalty. Legislatures in both states reversed themselves, however, and reinstated the death penalty in 1878 in Iowa and in 1883 in Maine. Maine reversed itself again in 1887 and abolished capital punishment and, to date, has not reinstated it. Colorado abandoned capital punishment in 1897 but restored it in 1901.

During the first two decades of the 20th century, six states outlawed capital punishment entirely (Kansas, 1907; Minnesota, 1911; Washington, 1913; Oregon, 1914; South

Dakota, 1915; Missouri, 1917) and three states (Tennessee, 1915; North Dakota, 1915; Arizona, 1916) limited the death penalty to only a few rarely committed crimes, such as treason or the first-degree murder of a law enforcement official or prison employee. Tennessee also retained capital punishment for rape. In addition, 17 other states nearly

CHALLENGING THE LEGALITY OF CAPITAL PUNISHMENT

Although specific methods of execution had been legally challenged as early as 1890 and procedural issues earlier than that, the fundamental legality of capital punishment itself was not subject to challenge until the 1960s. It had long been argued that the U.S. Constitution—or, more specifically, the Fifth Amendment—authorized capital punishment and that a majority of the Framers did not object to it. Given such evidence, it made little sense to argue that capital punishment violated the Constitution. That conventional wisdom was challenged in 1961. In an article published in the *University of Southern California Law Review*, Los Angeles lawyer Gerald Gottlieb, an affiliate of the local American Civil Liberties Union (ACLU) branch, suggested that "the death penalty was unconstitutional under the Eighth Amendment because it violated contemporary moral standards, what the U.S. Supreme Court in *Trop v. Dulles* (1958) referred to as 'the evolving standards of decency that mark the progress of a maturing society.'" The key question raised by Gottlieb's interpretation, of course, was whether the United States, in fact, had evolved or progressed to the point at which standards of decency no longer permitted capital punishment. For a small group of abolitionist lawyers with the National Association for the Advancement of Colored People (NAACP) Legal Defense and Educational Fund (LDF), the answer was yes.

LDF lawyers turned their attention to the death penalty in the 1960s primarily because of the racially discriminatory way it was being administered. Later, however, when they began accepting clients actually facing execution, they realized that they had to raise issues having nothing to do with race. With this change in focus, there was no longer any reason not to take on the cases of white death row inmates too, so they did. In attempting to achieve judicial abolition of the penalty, LDF lawyers plotted a general strategy to convince the Supreme Court that the death penalty was employed in a discriminatory way against minorities and to otherwise block all executions by challenging the legal procedures employed in capital cases (the so-called moratorium strategy). If successful, their plan would accomplish three goals: First, it would make those who were still executed appear to be unlucky losers in a death penalty lottery. Second, if the death penalty were used only rarely, it would show that the penalty was not really needed for society's protection. Third, if all executions were blocked, the resulting logjam of death row inmates would lead to an inevitable bloodbath if states ever began emptying their death rows by executing prisoners en masse. The LDF lawyers did not believe the country could stomach the gore and would demand abolition of the penalty.

The LDF's moratorium strategy worked. In 1968, executions in the United States were unofficially suspended until some of the more problematic issues with the death penalty could be resolved. The moratorium on executions would last 10 years, until 1977, when Gary Gilmore asked to be executed by the state of Utah.

abolished the death penalty or at least seriously considered abolition, some of them several times. The momentum, however, failed to last. By 1920, five of the states that had abolished the death penalty earlier had reinstated it (Arizona, 1918; Missouri, 1919; Tennessee, 1919; Washington, 1919; Oregon, 1920). No state abolished the death penalty between 1918 and 1957. In contrast, after World War II, most of the advanced western European countries abolished the death penalty or severely restricted its use.

Legal Decisions by the U.S. Supreme Court

Furman v. Georgia

On January 17, 1972, Furman's lawyers argued to the Supreme Court that unfettered jury discretion in imposing death for murder resulted in arbitrary or capricious sentencing in violation of their client's Fourteenth Amendment right to due process and his Eighth Amendment right not to be subjected to cruel and unusual punishment. Furman's challenge proved successful and, on June 29, 1972, the U.S. Supreme Court set aside death sentences for the first time in its history. In its decision in *Furman v. Georgia, Jackson v. Georgia,* and *Branch v. Texas* (all three cases were consolidated and are referred to here as the *Furman* decision), the Court held that the capital punishment statutes in the three cases were unconstitutional because they gave the jury complete discretion to decide whether to impose the death penalty or a lesser punishment in capital cases. The majority of five justices pointed out that the death penalty had been imposed arbitrarily, infrequently, and often selectively against minorities. A practical effect of *Furman* was the Supreme Court's voiding of 40 death penalty statutes and the sentences of more than 600 death row inmates in 32 states. Depending on the state, the death row inmates received new sentences of life imprisonment, a term of years, or, in a few cases, new trials.

It is important to note that the Court did not declare the death penalty itself unconstitutional. It held as unconstitutional only the statutes under which the death penalty was then being administered. The Court implied that if the process of applying the death penalty could be changed to eliminate the problems cited in *Furman,* then it would pass constitutional muster.

The backlash against *Furman* was immediate and widespread. Many people, including those who had never given the death penalty issue much thought, were incensed at what they perceived as the Supreme Court's arrogance in ignoring the will of the majority and its elected representatives. They clamored to have the penalty restored. Obliging their constituents, the elected representatives of 36 states proceeded to adopt new death penalty statutes designed to meet the Court's objections. The new death penalty laws took two forms. Twenty-two states removed all discretion from the process by mandating capital punishment upon conviction for certain crimes (mandatory death penalty statutes). Other states provided specific guidelines that judges and juries were to use in deciding if death were the appropriate sentence in a particular case (guided discretion death penalty statutes).

Woodson v. North Carolina and Gregg v. Georgia

The constitutionality of the new death penalty statutes was quickly challenged, and on July 2, 1976, the Supreme Court announced its rulings in five test cases. In *Woodson v. North Carolina* and *Roberts v. Louisiana,* the Court voted 4–5 to reject mandatory statutes that automatically imposed death sentences for defined capital crimes. Justice Potter Stewart provided the Court's rationale. First, Stewart admitted that "it is capricious to treat similar things differently" and that mandatory death penalty statutes eliminated that problem. He added, however, that it also "is capricious to treat two different things the same way." Therefore, to impose the same penalty on all convicted murderers, even though all defendants are different, is just as capricious as imposing a penalty randomly. To alleviate the problem, then, some sentencing guidelines were necessary. Thus, in *Gregg v. Georgia, Jurek v. Texas,* and *Proffitt v. Florida* (hereafter referred to as the *Gregg* decision), the Court voted 7–2 to approve guided discretion statutes that set standards for juries and judges to use in deciding whether to impose the death penalty. The Court's majority concluded that the guided discretion statutes struck a reasonable balance between giving the jury some direction and allowing it to consider the defendant's background and character and the circumstances of the crime.

It is noteworthy that the Court approved the guided discretion statutes on faith, assuming that the new statutes and their procedural reforms would rid the death penalty's administration of the problems cited in *Furman.* Because guided discretion statutes, automatic appellate review, and proportionality review had never been required or employed before in death penalty cases, the Court could not have known whether they would make a difference. Now, more than 30 years later, it is possible to evaluate the results. A large body of evidence indicates that the reforms have had negligible effects.

Coker v. Georgia and Eberheart v. Georgia

The Supreme Court has repeatedly emphasized that the death penalty should be reserved for the most heinous crimes. In two cases decided in 1977, the Court, for all intents and purposes, limited the death penalty to aggravated or capital murders only. Aggravated or capital murders are murders committed with an aggravating circumstance or circumstances. Aggravating circumstances (or factors) or special circumstances, as they are called in some jurisdictions, refer "to the particularly serious features of a case, for example, evidence of extensive premeditation and planning by the defendant, or torture of the victim by the defendant." At least one aggravating circumstance must be proven beyond a reasonable doubt before a death sentence can be imposed. (To date, all post-*Furman* executions have been for aggravated murder.) The Court ruled in *Coker v. Georgia* that the death penalty is not warranted for the crime of rape of an adult woman in cases in which the victim is not killed. Likewise, in *Eberheart v. Georgia,* the Court held that the death penalty is not warranted for the crime of kidnapping in cases in which the victim is not killed. Traditionally, both rape and kidnapping have been capital crimes regardless of whether the victim died.

Lockett v. Ohio and Bell v. Ohio

One of the changes to death penalty statutes approved by the Court in *Gregg* was the requirement that sentencing authorities (either juries or judges) consider mitigating circumstances before determining the sentence. Mitigating circumstances (or factors), or extenuating circumstances, refer "to features of a case that explain or particularly justify the defendant's behavior, even though they do not provide a defense to the crime of murder" (e.g., youth, immaturity, or being under the influence of another person). The requirement that mitigating circumstances must be considered has been the subject of several challenges. The first test was in 1978 in the cases of *Lockett v. Ohio* and *Bell v. Ohio*. In those cases, one of the issues was whether defense attorneys could present only mitigating circumstances that were listed in the death penalty statute. The Court held that trial courts must consider any mitigating circumstances that a defense attorney presents, not just those listed in the statute. The only qualification to this requirement is that the mitigating circumstance must be supported by evidence.

Pulley v. Harris

In *Pulley v. Harris* (1984), the Court decided that there was no constitutional obligation for state appellate courts to provide, upon request, proportionality review of death sentences. Since *Pulley,* many states have eliminated the proportionality review requirement from their statutes, whereas other states simply no longer conduct the reviews.

Lockhart v. McCree

In *Lockhart v. McCree* (1986), the Court ruled that prospective jurors whose opposition to the death penalty is so strong that it would prevent or substantially impair the performance of their duties as jurors at the sentencing phase of the trial may be removed for cause. Stated differently, as long as jurors can perform their duties as required by law, they may not be removed for cause because they are generally opposed to the death penalty. To date, *Lockhart v. McCree* is the latest modification to the Court's earlier *Witherspoon* decision. In *Witherspoon v. Illinois* (1968), the Court rejected the common practice of excusing prospective jurors simply because they were opposed to capital punishment. The Court held that prospective jurors could be excused only for cause. That is, jurors could be excused only if they would automatically vote against imposition of the death penalty, regardless of the evidence presented at trial, or if their attitudes toward capital punishment prevented them from making an impartial decision on the defendant's guilt.

McCleskey v. Kemp

The most sweeping challenge to the constitutionality of the new death penalty statutes was *McCleskey v. Kemp* (1987), wherein the Court considered evidence of racial discrimination in the application of Georgia's death penalty statute. Recall that in the *Furman* decision, racial discrimination was cited as one of the problems with the pre-*Furman* statutes. The most compelling evidence was the results of an elaborate statistical analysis of post-*Furman* death penalty cases in Georgia. That analysis showed that Georgia's new statute produced a pattern of racial discrimination based on both the race of the offender and the race of the victim. In *McCleskey*, the Court opined that evidence such as the statistical analysis—which showed a pattern of racial discrimination—is not enough to render the death penalty unconstitutional. By a vote of five to four, it held that state death penalty statutes are constitutional even when statistics indicate they have been applied in racially biased ways. The Court ruled that racial discrimination must be shown in individual cases—something McCleskey did not show in his case. For death penalty opponents, the *McCleskey* case represented the best, and perhaps last, chance of having the Supreme Court again declare the death penalty unconstitutional.

Atkins v. Virginia

In *Atkins v. Virginia* (2002), the Court ruled that it is cruel and unusual punishment to execute the mentally retarded. A problem with the *Atkins* decision is that the Court did not set a standard for what constitutes mental retardation. That issue was left to the states to decide. Texas became the first to test the law when it pursued, successfully, the execution (in 2009) of Bobby Wayne Woods, a convicted murderer, who had an IQ of between 68 and 86.

Roper v. Simmons

In *Roper v. Simmons* (2005), the Court held that the Eighth and Fourteenth Amendments forbid the imposition of the death penalty on offenders who were under the age of 18 at the time their crimes were committed.

Baze v. Rees

In this case (2008) the Court ruled that execution by lethal injection did not constitute "cruel and unusual punishment" and therefore was acceptable under the U.S. Constitution.

Conclusion

Globally, the death penalty is trending toward abolition. As of this writing, more than half of the countries in the world—104 of them—have abolished the death penalty in law or practice. All of the major U.S. allies except Japan have abolished the death penalty. On the other hand, only 58 countries and territories have retained the death penalty and continue to apply it; 35 other countries retain it on paper but have not applied it in a decade or more.

In the United States, 14 jurisdictions do not have a death penalty, and among the 39 jurisdictions that do have one, only a handful use it more than occasionally and almost all of them are located geographically in the South. More than 70 percent of all post-*Furman* executions have occurred in the South. Still, executions are more concentrated than the 70 percent figure suggests. Five states—Texas, Virginia, Oklahoma, Missouri, and Florida—account for 65 percent of all post-*Furman* executions; three states—Texas, Virginia, and Oklahoma—account for 53 percent of them; Texas and Virginia account for 45 percent of them; and Texas alone accounts for 36 percent of them. Thus the death penalty today is a criminal sanction that is used more than occasionally in only a few nonwestern countries, a few states in the U.S. South, and two U.S. border states. This is an important point because it raises the question of why those death penalty—or more precisely, executing—jurisdictions in the world need the death penalty, whereas all other jurisdictions in the world—the vast majority—do not.

In the states noted previously, the death penalty has proved stubbornly resilient and will probably remain a legal sanction for the foreseeable future. One reason is that death penalty support among the U.S. public, at least according to the major opinion polls, remains relatively strong. According to a 2009 Gallup poll, for example, 65 percent of adult Americans favored the death penalty for persons convicted of murder, 31 percent opposed it, and 5 percent did not know or refused to respond (Gallup 2010). It is unlikely that the practice of capital punishment could be sustained if a majority of U.S. citizens were to oppose it. However, in no year for which polls are available has a majority of Americans opposed the death penalty (the first national death penalty opinion poll was conducted in December 1936).

The abiding faith of death penalty proponents in the ability of legislatures and courts to fix any problems with the administration of capital punishment is another reason for its continued use in some places. However, the three-decade record of fine-tuning the death penalty process remains ongoing. Legislatures and courts are having a difficult time "getting it right," despite spending inordinate amounts of their resources trying.

Many people support capital punishment even though they are ignorant of the subject. It is assumed by abolitionists that if people were educated about capital punishment, most would oppose it. Unfortunately, research suggests that educating the public about the death penalty may not have the effect the abolitionists desire. Although information about the death penalty can reduce support for the sanction—sometimes significantly—rarely is the support reduced to less than a majority, and the reduction in support may be only temporary.

Two major factors seem to sustain death penalty support in the United States: (1) the desire for vindictive revenge and (2) the symbolic value it has for politicians and law enforcement officials. According to Gallup, 50 percent of all respondents who favored the death penalty provided retributive reasons for their support: 37 percent replied "An eye for an eye/They took a life/Fits the crime," and another 13 percent volunteered "They deserve it." The reasons offered by the next largest group of death penalty proponents (by only 11 percent each) were "Save taxpayers money/

Cost associated with prison" and "Deterrent for potential crimes/Set an example." No other reasons were given by more than 10 percent of the death penalty proponents (Gallup 2010).

The choice of "An eye for an eye" has been called *vindictive revenge* because of its strong emotional component. Research shows that the public supports the death penalty primarily for vindictive revenge. Those who responded "An eye for any eye" want to repay the offender in kind for what he or she has done. Research also shows that people who support the death penalty for vindictive revenge are generally resistant to reasoned persuasion. That is, they are less likely to change their position on the death penalty when confronted with compelling evidence that contradicts their beliefs.

Politicians continue to use support for the death penalty as a symbol of their toughness on crime. Politicians who oppose capital punishment are invariably considered soft on crime. Criminal justice officials and much of the public often equate support for capital punishment with support for law enforcement in general. It is ironic that although capital punishment has virtually no effect on crime, the death penalty continues to be a favored political silver bullet—a simplistic solution to the crime problem used by aspiring politicians and law enforcement officials. In sum, although the global trend is toward abolishing the death penalty, pockets of resistance in the United States remain and will be difficult to change.

See also **Class Justice; Cruel and Unusual Punishment; DNA Usage in Criminal Justice; Eyewitness Identification; Miscarriages of Justice**

Note

Sources for virtually all material in this entry may be found in Robert M. Bohm, *Deathquest III: An Introduction to the Theory and Practice of Capital Punishment in the United States,* 3d ed. (Cincinnati, OH: Anderson, 2007).

Further Reading

Acker, James R., Robert M. Bohm, and Charles S. Lanier, eds., *America's Experiment with Capital Punishment: Reflections on the Past, Present and Future of the Ultimate Penal Sanction,* 2d ed. Durham, NC: Carolina Academic Press, 2003.

Bakken, Gordon Morris, *Invitation to an Execution: A History of the Death Penalty in the United States.* Albuquerque: University of New Mexico Press, 2010.

Banner, Stuart, *The Death Penalty: An American History.* Cambridge, MA: Harvard University Press, 2002.

Bedau, Hugo, and Paul Cassell, eds., *Debating the Death Penalty: Should America Have Capital Punishment?* New York: Oxford University Press, 2004.

Bohm, Robert M., *Deathquest III: An Introduction to the Theory and Practice of Capital Punishment in the United States,* 3d ed. Cincinnati, OH: Anderson, 2007.

Gallup, "Death Penalty." 2010. http://www.gallup.com/poll/1606/death-penalty.aspx

Haney, Craig, *Death by Design: Capital Punishment as a Social Psychological System*. New York: Oxford University Press, 2005.

Sundby, Scott E., *A Life and Death Decision: A Jury Weighs the Death Penalty*. New York: Palgrave Macmillan, 2007.

DNA USAGE IN CRIMINAL JUSTICE

Julia Selman-Ayetey

Deoxyribonucleic acid (DNA) is one of the most valuable discoveries of the 20th century. Imported from the medical and scientific fields, the application of DNA technology in the criminal justice system has revolutionized the way crimes are investigated and prosecuted. Once considered an irrelevant and "stupid molecule" (Watson 1997, 2), DNA is now frequently considered a reliable and powerful silent witness able to identify or eliminate suspects as well as clinch convictions. However, its use in the criminal justice system is not without controversy. Indeed, its use raises quite a number of ethical concerns, and its ability to incriminate the innocent, while less known, is well documented. This has occurred through administrative and technical errors and disturbingly through deliberate distortion of forensic analysis and findings as well as evidence planting. This entry is by no means a comprehensive treatise on DNA; it is meant simply to introduce the reader to some of the contentious issues surrounding the use of DNA in the criminal justice system.

Background

DNA is a molecule located in the nuclei of all cells other than red blood cells and, with the exception of monozygotic (identical) twins, is unique to individuals. "Surprisingly, unlike the unwavering excitement that now surrounds DNA, the discovery of its structure was accompanied by much less fanfare" (Selman 2003, 10). The molecule's rise to prominence only followed the realization that it carried vital genetic information, including disease, from parent to offspring—essentially a "blueprint of life." Since its discovery, DNA technology has been used in a variety of settings, from gene therapy in clinical medicine to genetic engineering in plants and animals for improved agricultural productivity. It has also been applied in a number of other disciplines, such as anthropology, theology, philosophy, law, and, of more relevance to this entry, criminal justice systems the world over.

The use of DNA in police investigations was the result of significant scientific advances made primarily by Sir Alec Jeffreys, professor of genetics at the University of Leicester in England. Jeffreys coined the term "DNA fingerprinting" after discovering that certain regions (loci) of DNA have a high degree of variability that makes them virtually unique to individuals (Jeffreys 1985).

This simple scientific fact was first used in a criminal context in a rather complicated double rape and murder case known as the Pitchfork case. In 1987, it emerged that a man had given his blood sample to the police, but had identified it as that of his colleague, Colin Pitchfork. When he was overheard talking about the switch and this was reported to the police, Pitchfork was arrested. DNA analysis confirmed that he had raped both girls. Pitchfork confessed to the murders and was sentenced to life in prison.

The original method created by Jeffreys was initially used by British police forces; however, owing to the expense and great length of time it took to generate a DNA fingerprint, both the British and U.S. criminal justice systems now use what is accurately referred to as "DNA profiling." The difference between the two DNA identification methods is an important one, as Jeffreys states:

Unfortunately—and particularly in the United States—the term "DNA fingerprinting," which we specifically apply to the original multi-locus system in which we look at scores of markers, has been corrupted to be used in almost any DNA typing system. That has created a problem in court, because DNA profiling does not produce DNA fingerprints....So this is a semantic problem, but a serious one. (Jeffreys 1995)

DNA profiling involves extracting DNA from biological samples taken from hair, body tissue, or fluids such as saliva, semen, or blood. Forensic analysis of loci on the DNA then produces a DNA profile. DNA profiling is less conclusive than DNA fingerprinting, as it examines considerably fewer loci or markers of a person's DNA. At

THE PITCHFORK CASE

In November 1983, in the small town of Narborough, England, Lynda Mann was raped and strangled to death. The search for her killer proved futile. In 1986, Dawn Ashworth, another teenage girl, was also found dead in Narborough after having been raped. Semen samples revealed that the killer of both girls had the same blood type. Police later arrested a local teenage boy, who falsely confessed to killing Ashworth but denied involvement in the death of Mann.

Aware of Professor Jeffreys' work with DNA fingerprinting, police submitted semen samples from both murder cases along with a sample of the suspect to Jeffreys for DNA testing. Forensic analysis concluded that the rapist in these cases was not the local boy. It did, however, indicate that the killer in both instances was the same person. Then, in 1987, Leicester police conducted the world's first mass screening by asking almost 5,000 men in the area to provide blood or saliva samples to absolve themselves of the offense. After six months of processing all the samples, there was still no match. Later that year, someone overheard that a man had substituted his sample for that of Colin Pitchfork, his colleague, who was tested and subsequently arrested.

present, DNA profiling cannot examine all the differences between people's DNA; thus, although they will not have the same entire DNA sequence or genome, there is a remote chance that two unrelated people could have the same DNA profile. Hence the discriminatory power of any DNA profile increases with the number of loci tested. When DNA typing first started being used to facilitate police investigations in England and Wales, the standard analysis involved the examination of 6 loci. Now they examine 10 (plus 1 that indicates gender). The United States currently examines 13 sites. Given the number of loci that are now examined, unrelated people are extremely unlikely to have the same DNA profile, and if they are collected and analyzed correctly, DNA profiles are accepted by scientists as well as the courts as being conclusive enough to establish identification irrefutably.

It is this consensus that has greatly contributed to the establishment and expansion of DNA databases. The use of DNA databases enables new profiles to be compared against those already stored on the system. Matches may be found on examining evidence from two (or more) crime scenes, which may mean that a particular suspect was involved in both crimes, and, as is often the case, a match can be made between an individual and a crime scene. Although a match alone does not prove involvement in a crime, it can provide unquestionable proof that a person was present at the scene of a crime. This, together with other evidence, may illustrate beyond a reasonable doubt that an individual is the offender.

Key Events

The first official forensic database, the National DNA Database (NDNAD), was established in the United Kingdom in 1995. Having previously operated local and state databases, the United States followed suit in 1998 when its national DNA database, the National DNA Index System (NDIS), was launched under the authority of the DNA Identification Act of 1994 (Federal Bureau of Investigation 2009). The NDIS together with local and state databases make up the Combined DNA Index System (CODIS). CODIS stores profiles on two indexes. The Forensic Index contains profiles recovered from crime scenes, whereas profiles of convicted offenders or certain categories of arrestees are held under the Offender Index (Federal Bureau of Investigation 2009). The U.S. national DNA database currently contains profiles of approximately 0.5 percent of the population. In comparison, the British national database is estimated to have profiles of over 10 percent of the population (of England and Wales), or 5.53 million profiles (National Policing Improvement Agency [NPIA] 2009).

The potential of DNA technology was pushed further with the introduction of DNA dragnets or sweeps (or mass screenings, as they are called in the United Kingdom). Dragnets involve requesting a group of individuals who fit a general description of the suspect to voluntarily provide a DNA sample for profile analysis in order to exclude themselves as suspects. The first dragnet was used in the United Kingdom in the Colin Pitchfork case. Since then, this method has become increasingly common in Europe, including a dragnet in Germany in 1998 that sampled DNA from 16,000 men in an attempt to find the perpetrator of the murder of a young girl (Dundes 2001). Although there have been about a dozen DNA dragnets in the United States (Duster 2008), this method of "elimination by numbers" has been used less frequently here than in Britain owing to potential conflicts with the Fourth Amendment, which provides, among other things, protection against unreasonable searches and seizures.

Familial searching is another milestone in DNA applications in the criminal justice system. It is predominantly used in cases in which a crime-scene profile has failed to match a suspect profile on the national DNA database. Familial searching involves probing the database to find profiles similar to the one taken from the crime scene in the hope of being led to the suspect. The profiles that are found to be similar to the one from the crime scene would be from individuals who have a high probability of being relatives of the perpetrator. This is viable because people inherit 50 percent of their DNA from each parent. Thus, close family members such as parents, children, siblings, and even aunts and uncles are likely to share some genetic markers. This approach was first used in the United Kingdom in 2002. (In 2002, a DNA familial search led to the identification of an offender who was deceased. In 2003, familial searches led to the identification of two other offenders in the United Kingdom, one of whom was Craig Harman, who was convicted of manslaughter in 2004.) It was initiated in the United States in 2003, so that familial searching is still relatively new. At present, familial searches are not likely to become a regular occurrence in criminal investigations primarily because of the cost of running such a search (estimated at $9,000 per search in 2004) ("Sins of the Fathers" 2004). As forensic DNA technology continues to develop and costs decrease, however, law enforcement may want to make familial searches common practice.

Both these applications of DNA forensic technology raise important issues regarding ethics, confidentiality, civil liberties, and human rights (Williams and Johnson 2006; Haimes 2006). Clearly, it is important that all issues of concern be brought to the public forefront for debate and that the government and relevant bodies implement appropriate legislation, policies, and procedures to ensure that innocent individuals and families are not adversely affected. This may require the amendment of laws that have recently been passed without adequate public discussion.

Legal Decisions

During early uses of DNA as evidence, the main assistance with admissibility the courts had was the standard as laid out in *Frye v. United States*. Under the *Frye* test, scientific evidence could be admitted only if it had "gained general acceptance in the particular field in which it belongs" (*Frye v. United States*). In 1993, however, with the use of DNA profiles becoming more prevalent, the Supreme Court set a new standard

DNA AND THE CRIMINAL JUSTICE SYSTEM SINCE 1987

- 1987: The first DNA exoneration and mass screening took place in the double murder investigation of Lynda Mann and Dawn Ashworth in England. In Florida, rapist Tommy Lee Andrews became the first ever to be convicted on the basis of DNA evidence.
- 1988: Colin Pitchfork, the first man apprehended on the basis of DNA profiling, was sentenced to life in prison for the murders of Mann and Ashworth.
- 1989: Gary Dotson became the first person in the United States to be exonerated and released from prison thanks to DNA results.
- 1993: Kirk Bloodsworth was released from prison on June 28, 1993, making him the first person on death row to be exonerated by DNA evidence in the United States. Also, Dr. Kary B. Mullis won the Nobel Prize in Chemistry for the invention of the polymerase chain reaction (PCR) method. Prior to the PCR method, DNA analysis was slow, required large quantities of sample, and involved difficulty in analyzing mixed or contaminated samples. PCR enabled profiles to be produced from minute and degraded samples of DNA. In addition to its applications in other fields, PCR enabled DNA profiling to be used in a larger number of cases.
- 1994: For the very first time, analysis of nonhuman DNA led to the identification and apprehension of a criminal. Royal Canadian Mounted Police officers had hairs from a man's pet cat analyzed, which pointed to him as the murderer of his wife.
- 2001: In May, the Criminal Justice and Police Act (CJPA) of 2001 came into force in England and Wales. This law authorizes the retention of DNA samples and profiles of anyone charged with any offense that carried a penalty of imprisonment or anyone charged with a few specified noncustodial offences.
- 2002: The number of exonerated death row inmates in the United States based on DNA testing reached 100.
- 2004: In England, Craig Harman became the first person in the world to be prosecuted and convicted as a result of DNA database familial searching. In the United States, President George W. Bush signed the Innocence Protection Act, which amended the federal code to permit postconviction DNA testing and established a grant program to help states defray the costs of testing.
- 2006: The DNA Fingerprinting Act of 2005 became law in the United States. This legislation permits the DNA sampling of foreign citizens detained on federal grounds and reduced the stage at which a DNA profile can be uploaded onto the federal database from charge to arrest. It also authorized government funds to support the analysis and retention of all DNA samples and profiles on the national database. Furthermore, this act requires individuals who would like their profiles removed from the database to file certified documents stating that they have been acquitted or have had charges dismissed before their requests can be processed.

- 2009: The longest-serving prisoner ever to be exonerated by DNA evidence, James Bain of Florida, was released after spending 35 years in prison. Also, the U.S. Supreme Court ruled (in *Melendez-Diaz v. Massachusetts*) that crime lab analysts are required to submit to cross-examinations in trials where data from their labs is used as evidence.

in *Daubert v. Merrell Dow Pharmaceuticals, Inc.* This standard expanded the *Frye* test by recognizing the need to highlight issues that might bias or mislead the jury. In particular, it permitted for the first time the admission of new factors, such as publications and probabilities of error, to assist with evaluating the degree of reliability (*Daubert v. Merrell Dow Pharmaceuticals, Inc.*). One of the most significant cases regarding the use of DNA typing in criminal trials was *People v. Castro* (1989). This case fervently contested the admissibility of DNA evidence in court. In its opinion, the Court issued recommendations that would encourage fair and just use of DNA evidence. The Court held that it should be provided with chain of custody of documents and details of any defects or errors. It also held that laboratory results should be provided both to the defense counsel and the court.

Although a number of state and federal cases have created a gateway into the courtroom for forensic DNA evidence, courts have also declined to admit DNA evidence. Some of these cases involved laboratories that had unreliable or dubious practices (*Schwartz v. State* 1989).

In addition to being used as evidence to convict suspects, DNA technology is increasingly being used to exonerate previously convicted individuals. On June 12, 2006, for the very first time, the U.S. Supreme Court considered the standards necessary to reopen a postconviction death penalty case involving DNA evidence. After Paul House had served more than 19 years on death row, the Supreme Court held that he was entitled to a new trial (*House v. Bell* 2006). House was originally convicted of murder, but recent DNA analysis showed that the body fluids found on the victim's clothes were not his. This new evidence was sufficient to meet the precedent for postconviction claims of innocence as set out in *Schlup v. Delo* (1995).

In addition to case law, DNA has also affected legislation. The Innocence Protection Act was tabled to the U.S. Senate in February 2000. On October 30, 2004, the Justice for All Act of 2004, which includes the Innocence Protection Act of 2004, became law. This act seeks to do a number of things, the most significant of which are to (1) enhance and protect the rights of crime victims; (2) reduce the backlog of untested DNA samples; (3) expand forensic laboratories; (4) intensify research into new DNA testing technologies; (5) develop training programs on the proper collection, preservation, and analysis of DNA evidence; and (6) facilitate the exoneration of innocent individuals through postconviction testing of DNA evidence.

In December 2003, a private citizen submitted to the attorney general's office in California a proposed initiative titled DNA Fingerprint, Unsolved Crime and Innocence Protection Act. (Bruce Harrington submitted the proposal after his brother and sister-in-law had been murdered some years earlier.) This proposal sought to widen the category of instances in which DNA samples could be taken and profiles stored on the state's database. Proposition 69, as the proposal became known, was approved by voters in California on November 2, 2004. The effect of this enactment was that as of November 3, 2004, the following categories of people will have a DNA sample taken and uploaded onto the state and national DNA database: (1) any person, adult or juvenile, convicted of any felony (including any person in prison, on probation, or on parole for any felony committed prior to November 3, 2004, or any person on probation or any other supervised release for any offense and who has a prior felony); (2) any person convicted of any sex or arson offense or attempt; and (3) adults arrested for murder, voluntary manslaughter, or felony sex offenses (which includes rape) or attempt to commit one of these crimes (Office of the Attorney General 2007).

Furthermore, as of January 2, 2009, all adults arrested for any felony are subject to DNA collection and retention. Prior to the passing of Proposition 69, only those convicted of a serious felony such as rape and murder had to submit DNA samples (California Legislative Analyst's Office 2004). Thus Proposition 69 has effectively resulted in the massive expansion of California's DNA database. It is worth noting that Louisiana, Minnesota, Texas, and Virginia already have legislation that authorizes taking DNA samples from adults arrested for a felony. There is therefore a clear trend toward a so-called DNA-based criminal justice system.

Conclusion

As a result of ongoing advances by scientists, extensive legislation, support from police and prosecutors, and substantial funding from the government, the drive to expand the application of DNA technology in the criminal justice system continues. Currently, scientists at the University of Southampton in the United Kingdom are in the process of developing a method of forensic analysis that could enable DNA samples to be transformed into profiles at the scene of the crime ("Forensic Science Hots Up" 2008). Furthermore, DNA profiling involving testing for race and other physical characteristics has slowly begun. Scientists now have the ability to decipher from DNA analysis the gender and age of an individual, and research is currently being conducted toward identifying eye, hair, and skin color. This can obviously assist the police with composing more accurate descriptions of a suspect. Although this could significantly facilitate criminal investigations, it also raises a number of sociological and ethical issues: What defines race? Is it what the public see, or is it what the individual knows or believes he or she is? How do we deal with a situation in which racial genetic testing reveals information the individual did not know and may not have wanted to know about himself or herself?

Could racial DNA profiling lead to eugenics? These are just some of the issues (Duster 2008; Ossorio 2006). Perhaps appropriately, testing for racial characteristics has not yet become common practice. Before further steps are taken to increase its utilization, serious consultation with sociologists, criminologists, ethicists, psychologists, geneticists, and lawyers must be conducted.

Given the benefits of the use of DNA technology in the criminal justice system and the perceived breaches of rights it begets, particularly for those who are acquitted or never charged, there have been calls by some to collect DNA samples and store DNA profiles of all citizens on forensic databases. Proponents of a forensic database holding DNA profiles of the entire citizenry argue that it will reduce racial discrimination in the disproportionate storage of profiles of ethnic minorities and simultaneously increase fairness, as everyone would be incurring the same degree of threat to privacy. Furthermore, because everyone would know that their DNA was on the database, proponents also hold that such a database would act as a deterrent (Williamson and Duncan 2002; Kaye and Smith 2004; Smith, Kaye, and Imwinkelried 2001; Tracy and Morgan 2000).

Arguments against this proposal include issues relating to the presumption of innocence and the right to avoid self-incrimination (embodied in the Fifth Amendment in the United States), not to mention the potential misuses of genetic information by government agencies as well as others, such as insurance companies and employers who might benefit from such information. Given the immense financial cost and practical difficulties alone, the prospect of implementing such an idea is fraught with numerous obstacles. Given the speed at which DNA legislation has expanded, however, many believe implementation of these ideas is a real possibility and perhaps inevitable. The key question is whether this will happen explicitly with public debate or by stealth.

DNA, DNA profiles, databases, and related applications have irreversibly changed the way humans think about life, disease, and the resolution of crime. However, it is its use in the criminal justice system that continues to attract the most controversy (Harmon 1993; Neufeld 1993; McCartney 2006). The use of DNA in the criminal justice system provides numerous benefits resulting in more convictions of the guilty and more exonerations of the innocent. It also raises serious questions, including but not limited to privacy, probable cause, coercion, consent, confidentiality, civil liberties, subjective identity, and other ethical considerations. Many of these concerns are legitimate, particularly because the introduction of legislation often occurs devoid of public scrutiny. The recent vote on Proposition 69 illustrates that public consultation has been initiated. It is necessary that future consultations be complemented with a discussion of the relevant concerns so that the public can form an educated opinion. Much more public debate is essential to avoid the introduction of unfair legislation and practices and to prevent miscarriages of justice that would ultimately affect us all.

See also **Expert Witness Testimony; Miscarriages of Justice; Biotechnology (vol. 4)**

Further Reading

Aronson, Jay D., *Genetic Witness: Science, Law, and Controversy in the Making of DNA Profiling.* New Brunswick, NJ: Rutgers University Press, 2007.

California Legislative Analyst's Office, "Proposition 69: DNA Samples, Collection, Database, Funding, Initiative Statute." 2004. http://www.lao.ca.gov/ballot/2004/69_11_2004.htm

Clark, George Woody, *Justice and Science: Trials and Triumphs of DNA Evidence.* New Brunswick, NJ: Rutgers University Press, 2008.

Daubert v. Merrell Dow Pharmaceuticals, Inc., 113 S.Ct. 2786 (1993).

Dundes, Lauren, "Is the American Public Ready to Embrace DNA as a Crime- Fighting Tool? A Survey Assessing Support for DNA Databases." *Bulletin of Science, Technology and Society* 21, no. 5 (2001): 369–375.

Duster, Tory, "DNA Dragnets and Race: Larger Social Context, History, and Future." *GeneWatch* 21 (2008): 3–5. http://www.councilforresponsiblegenetics.org/pageDocuments/4Z1DPHLC1I.pdf

Federal Bureau of Investigation, *CODIS* (2009). http://www.fbi.gov/hq/lab/html/codisbrochure_text.htm

"Forensic Science Hots Up." *Highlights in Chemical Biology.* October 31, 2008. http://www.rsc.org/Publishing/Journals/cb/Volume/2009/1/Forensic_science.asp

Frye v. United States, 293 F. 1013. D.C. Cir. (1923).

Haimes, Erica, "Social and Ethical Issues in the Use of Familial Searching in Forensic Investigations: Insights from Family and Kinship Studies." *Journal of Law, Medicine and Ethics* 34, no. 2 (2006): 263–276.

Harmon, Rockne P., "Legal Criticisms of DNA Typing: Where's the Beef?" *Journal of Criminal Law and Criminology* 84, no. 1 (1993): 175–188.

House v. Bell, 547 U.S. 518 (2006).

Jeffreys, Alec, "DNA Profiling and Minisatellites." *Science Watch.* 1995. http://archive.sciencewatch.com/interviews/sir_alec_jeffreys.htm

Jeffreys, Alec J., Victoria Wilson, and Swee Lay Thien, "Hyper Variable 'Minisatellite' Regions in Human DNA." *Nature* 314 (1985): 67–73.

Kaye, D. H., and Michael E. Smith, "DNA Databases for Law Enforcement: The Coverage Question and the Case for a Population-Wide Database." In *DNA and the Criminal Justice System: The Technology of Justice,* ed. David Lazer. Cambridge, MA: MIT Press, 2004.

Lazer, David, ed., *DNA and the Criminal Justice System: The Technology of Justice.* Cambridge, MA: MIT Press, 2004.

Lee, Henry C., and Frank Tirnady, *Blood Evidence: How DNA is Revolutionizing the Way We Solve Crimes.* Cambridge, MA: Perseus, 2003.

Lynch, Michael, et al., *Truth Machine: The Contentious History of DNA Fingerprinting.* Chicago: University of Chicago Press, 2009.

McCartney, Carole, "The DNA Expansion Programme and Criminal Investigation." *British Journal of Criminology* 46 (2006): 175–192.

National Policing Improvement Agency (NPIA), The National DNA Database: Statistics (2009). http://www.npia.police.uk/en/13338.htm

Neufeld, Peter, "Have You No Sense of Decency?" *Journal of Criminal Law and Criminology* 84, no. 1 (1993).

Office of the Attorney General, State of California, Department of Justice, Bureau of Forensic Services, "Proposition 69: FAQs." 2007. http://ag.ca.gov/bfs/content/faq.htm

Ossorio, Pilar N., "About Face: Forensic Genetic Testing for Race and Visible Traits." *Journal of Law, Medicine and Ethics* 34, no. 2 (2006): 277–292.

People v. Castro, 545 N.Y.S. 2d. 985. NY Sup. Ct. (1989).

Rudin, Norah, and Keith Inman, *An Introduction to Forensic DNA Analysis*, 2d ed. Boca Raton, FL: CRC Press, 2001.

Schlup v. Delo, 513 U.S. 298 (1995).

Schwartz v. State, 447 N.W. 2d 422 (1989).

Selman, Julia, "From Human Cell to Prison Cell: A Critique of the Use of DNA Profiling in the British Criminal Justice System." Master's thesis, University of Cambridge, 2003.

"The Sins of the Fathers." *Economist* (April 24, 2004): 60.

Smith, Michael E., David H. Kaye, and Edward J. Imwinkelried, "DNA Data from Everyone Would Combat Crime, Racism." *USA Today* (July 26, 2001). http://www.usatoday.com/news/opinion/2001-07-26-ncguest2.htm

Tracy, Paul E., and Vincent Morgan, "Big Brother and His Science Kit: DNA Databases for 21st Century Crime Control?" *Journal of Criminal Law and Criminology* 90, no. 2 (2000): 635–690.

Watson, James D., *The Double Helix: A Personal Account of the Discovery of the Structure of DNA* London: Weidenfeld and Nicolson, 1997.

Williams, Robin, and Paul Johnson, *Genetic Policing: The Uses of DNA in Police Investigations.* Cullompton, U.K.: Willan, 2008.

Williams, Robin, and Paul Johnson, "Inclusiveness, Effectiveness and Intrusiveness: Issues in the Developing Uses of DNA Profiling in Support of Criminal Investigations." *Journal of Law, Medicine and Ethics* 34, no. 2 (2006): 234–247.

Williamson, Robert, and Rony Duncan, "DNA Testing For All." *Nature* 418 (2002): 585–586.

DOMESTIC VIOLENCE INTERVENTIONS

Venessa Garcia

Domestic violence and the question of whether to intervene into the family dwelling affected by physical or psychological abuse has, until recently, been controversial because of the different viewpoints regarding the issue as one of privacy versus one of public accountability. Once domestic violence was viewed as a social problem, the controversies shifted to what was the appropriate form of intervention or who should be responsible for carrying out domestic violence practices—law enforcement and criminal justice agencies or social and human service agencies. Another set of controversies surrounding domestic violence practices stems from the often competing or contradictory goals of punishment versus rehabilitation.

Background

Historically, domestic violence was seen as a private trouble. It occurred within the privacy of a man's own home. He was in charge of all affairs and persons residing in his home, and he had the right to chastise his wife. According to the Old Testament, women were the source of all evil. Under English common law, the husband was allowed to chastise his wife with restraint. Based on religious beliefs, the law limited the husband's violence. With the secularization of society, however, this violence became problematic. Nevertheless, in the colonies, a new liberal Lockean philosophy focusing on public order became the foundation for the establishment of domestic violence laws that remained under the umbrella of private order for centuries (Buzawa 2002).

It was not until the 1970s that feminists adopted the concern for violence against women. Domestic violence came to be understood as the domination of men over women in all spheres of a patriarchal society. In opposition to past liberal philosophy, feminists argued that the power and domination at the root of domestic violence required that society redefine this violence as a social problem instead of a private family affair. This argument followed C. Wright Mills's sociological tenet that personal troubles are in fact public issues (Mills 1976) and that society would eventually come to change domestic violence practices.

Although the 1970s Battered Women's Movement worked to change domestic violence laws, practices of the 1980s still reflected the definition of domestic violence as a private issue. According to the Uniform Crime Report, in 1989 women were six times more likely than men to be victimized by a spouse, ex-spouse, boyfriend, or girlfriend. Within a nine-year period, intimates committed 5.6 million violent acts against women, an annual average of almost 626,000. One-quarter of these assaults were reported to the police. It was reported that half of the complaints were an effort to prevent the abuse from recurring, whereas one-quarter were attempts to punish the abuser. Half of the victims who reported domestic violence to the National Crime Victimization Survey claimed to have had no response from the police because, as they were informed, this was a private matter (Harlow 1991).

Today in the United States, an incident of domestic violence against women occurs every 15 seconds. Research has found that battering is the single largest cause of injury to women. Annually, roughly 1 million women seek medical attention as a result of domestic violence, and their husbands or boyfriends commit 30 percent of all homicides against women (Belknap 2006). These statistics hardly suggest that such incidents are private matters. Yet research has found that 75 percent of all stranger assaults result in arrest and court adjudication, whereas only 16 percent of all family assaults, usually charged as misdemeanors and not felonies, result in arrest and court adjudication (Dobash 1978).

Key Legal and Social Moments

In terms of legal responses to domestic violence, it is believed that under English common law, Judge Sir Francis Buller in the 1780s stated that a husband can physically chastise his wife as long as he did not use a stick thicker than his thumb (Table 1). This became known as the *rule of thumb*. Others claim, however, that there is no reference to this statement in English common law. It is known that as early as 1655, the Massachusetts Bay Colony prohibited domestic violence. In 1824, however, a husband's right to assault his wife became codified under state law. The Mississippi State Supreme Court ruled that the husband had a right to chastise his wife physically, though in moderation (*Bradley v. State* 1824). Although the rule of thumb was referenced in this case, it was not used to justify the decision. In 1871, however, Alabama became the first state to recognize a wife's right to legal protection against her husband's physical abuse (*Fulgham v. State* 1871). Unfortunately, this ruling soon became a paper promise, since victims found that the criminal justice system still held strongly to the belief that domestic violence was a private trouble. In 1879, the court ruled that a man cannot be criminally prosecuted for assaulting his wife unless the violence was cruel or created permanent injury (*State v. Oliver* 1879). Even as recently as 1962, a husband's right to chastise his wife physically was legalized in *Joyner v. Joyner.*

It was not until the 1970s, with the Battered Women's Movement, that domestic violence began to be recognized as a social problem. Specifically, in 1977, Oregon became the first state to legislate mandatory arrest, and in 1979 President Jimmy Carter established the Office of Domestic Violence; however, the landmark case that truly took hold of domestic violence practices was *Thurman v. City of Torrington* (1984). *Thurman* was a civil case in which it was recognized that police had a legal responsibility to respond to and protect victims of domestic violence. The $2.3 million awarded to Tracy Thurman was the key moment that changed police practice in their responses. Although, by 1983,

TABLE 1. Legal Changes in Domestic Violence Practices

Rule of thumb. It is commonly believed that under English common law, Judge Sir Francis Buller in the 1780s stated that a husband can physically chastise his wife as long as he does not use a stick thicker than his thumb (rule of thumb). Others, however, claim no reference to this statement in English common law.

Bradley v. State (1824). A husband had a right to physically chastise his wife, though in moderation.

State v. Oliver (1879). The criminal law did not apply to a husband's assault unless the violence was cruel or led to permanent injury to his wife.

Joyner v. Joyner (1962). A husband had a right to use force to compel his wife to "behave" and "know her place."

Thurman v. City of Torrington (1984). In this civil case, police were found to be negligent in responding to and protecting victims of domestic violence.

State v. Ciskie (1988)* and ***State v. Baker*** (1980).** These were the first cases to uphold the use of "battered woman syndrome" evidence via expert testimony.

---

*State v. Ciskie, 110 Wash. 2d 263 (1988).

**State v. Baker, 424 A.2d 171. (NH S.Ct. 1980).

every state had made legal remedies in response to the demands of the Battered Women's Movement, many were still reluctant to intervene in so-called family matters. The *Thurman* case changed this practice.

Another key moment in domestic violence practices was the Minneapolis Experiment (Sherman and Berk 1984). The Minneapolis Experiment, conducted in 1984, found that as compared with previous practices, arrest was a greater deterrent to domestic violence. As a result of this experiment as well as the *Thurman* decision, many states implemented mandatory arrest laws. Since 1984, however, replication of the Minneapolis Experiment has found that arrest works as a deterrent only for the six months immediately following the arrest and not more. Thus the debate still continues: what is the most effective way to address domestic violence? Nonetheless, by 1986, some 46 percent of police departments in cities with populations greater than 100,000 had a proarrest policy based on probable cause. In 1984, it was only 10 percent (Steinman 1990, 2).

Domestic Violence Theories

Three major theories have influenced domestic violence practices. Individually oriented theories examine the character of both the batterer and the battered. These theories have brought about many negative myths and stereotypes about domestic violence and especially about the abused woman. Most people saw battered women as pathological. Recidivists were seen as masochistic, weak, or sick or women who sought out batterers. For this reason, women were referred to psychologists and various social service agencies. In responding to domestic violence calls, many police officers believed that the man's violence was justified because the woman constantly nagged him; for a man to use physical force, the woman must be at fault. In these cases, the police almost always sided with the man.

The big question with domestic violence was why did the woman remain in an abusive relationship? Many people believed that she was getting a meal ticket, and after so long, why did she complain now? Many concluded that she wanted to get revenge after a recent fight with her abuser. The assumption here was that she purposely provoked him until he was angry enough to strike her, and when he did, she called the police. Another myth that the criminal justice and judicial systems utilized was that these women never pressed charges; they were weak-willed women who could not follow through. Therefore the police did not waste valuable police time, as well as taxpayers' money, arresting the man, especially if he and the abused woman were married. Unfortunately, there is still evidence of these victim-blaming practices within the criminal justice system in the making of arrests and the choosing of prosecutorial actions.

Family-oriented and subcultural theories focus on characteristics within the family and on socialization patterns. According to these theories, the characteristics of the family predict future violence; that is, violence begets violence. In other words, adults who experience or witness violence during childhood are more prone to becoming violent adults or battered adults. Children are often socialized that women are the property of men or that violence against one's spouse is acceptable. Unfortunately, some of these children grow up to be police officers. Within these theories, however, people believe that violence occurs in minority families, low-income families, and families containing alcohol or substance abusers. In responding to domestic violence calls, police who follow these myths generally do not consider such situations serious because they believe that the cultures of these families condone violence.

Feminist theories erased many of these myths from the minds of many people, although not all. These theories utilize a macrolevel analysis. They point to the structural violence in Western society. The privatized family structure makes domestic violence an individual problem, not a societal one. Accordingly, our male-dominated society keeps women economically and emotionally dependent on their men, giving them few or no options for a violence-free life. Feminists argue that the male-dominated criminal justice and judicial systems allow and even encourage this to happen. It was the fight of feminists that forced the police to change their policies toward domestic violence. This change was not the result of the acceptance of the feminist theories, however; instead, it was a result of feminist grassroots movements to sue police departments for failing to protect female victims.

Domestic Violence Practices

Police Responses

In the early 1980s and prior to that time, police as well as the courts felt that domestic violence was a private matter in which they should not interfere. According to police, it was not real police work; therefore, the police should not be dragged into it. Domestic violence was given very low priority and avoided if possible. In fact, during the mid-1960s, police departments in urban areas with high crime rates, such as Detroit, were actually screening out domestic violence calls.

Police domestic violence policies are evident in their training manuals. According to the Police Training Academy in Michigan, until recent changes in domestic violence policies, police officers were instructed to avoid arrest whenever possible and to appeal to the vanity of the individuals involved (Martin 1983). In responding to a call, the police were to tell the woman to consider time lost and court costs. The officer was to inform the couple that his only interest was to prevent a breach of the peace. He would recommend a postponement owing to the unavailability of a judge or court session, even if untrue. This statement was premised on the belief in the myth that battered women often changed their minds about pressing charges before the case came to court. He explained that she would probably reconcile with her abuser before the hearing. Police even went as far as scaring the woman, making her realize that pressing charges would infuriate her abuser, possibly making him retaliate worse than ever. In addition, she had to realize that the police could not babysit her.

In California, the Training Bulletin on Techniques of Dispute Interventions also advised officers to avoid arrest except to protect life and property and preserve the peace. In addition, it instructed the officer to encourage the victim to reason with her attacker. In Detroit as in many other cities, police precincts received more calls involving domestic violence than complaints of any other serious crime. Detroit's training consisted of 240 hours, yet only 3 to 5 hours were dedicated to this most frequent and recurrent crime. Officers were trained to avoid action as well as injury to themselves. Domestic violence was not a crime unless there was severe injury, and many times no action was taken even then. The International Association of Police Chiefs stated that it was unnecessary to create a police matter when only a family matter existed.

In domestic violence cases, the police saw their role as that of preservers of the family. This meant that no police action was taken even if it meant persuading the woman not to press charges or denying that she could be helped in any way. The police played mediator roles in attempting to reunite the couple. Arrests were made only when there was a disruption of the peace or the possibility that the police would have to be called back to the scene.

All studies have shown that police were reluctant to intervene in domestic violence. They were even more reluctant if the couple was married, moving the incident farther into the private realm. A husband had more right over his wife than a boyfriend did because an unmarried couple did not constitute a family. Police were also reluctant to intervene in the domestic affairs of recidivists. Over time, officers became detached from a woman who constantly cried for help but did not leave her abuser. In response to these calls, police often arrived with the intention of keeping the peace but no intention of intervening.

As mentioned previously, police officials practiced a no-arrest policy. Yet when police did arrest, there were strict guidelines. To begin, there had to be a witness present other than the abused woman and her children. This was something that rarely occurred because domestic violence usually occurs within the privacy of a home. If an arrest was made, no matter how serious the abuse, it had to be witnessed by an officer and was charged as a misdemeanor. This also almost never happened. To assault another person in front of a police officer is to challenge and show disrespect for the authority of the police. Nonaction protected the officer from personal danger and liability of false arrest. When a woman had a man arrested for domestic violence, many times she would drop the charges. This allowed the man to sue the police department for false arrest. In order to release themselves from this liability, either no arrest was made or the woman was forced to make a citizen's arrest.

A study conducted by the FBI found that domestic disturbances caused the greatest number of officer deaths and injuries. This study created a panic as well as a reluctance to respond to domestic violence calls. In responding to these crimes, oftentimes officers responded in an aggressive manner in order to protect themselves from any unforeseeable dangers. Their response often made the woman feel that she was a criminal as well. When the FBI released its statistics to the police departments, it created a panic among officers, and police precincts started screening domestic violence calls. However, it was later found and reported that the FBI report overstated the number of officer deaths by three times the actual number. What the FBI did was combine bar fights, gang activities, and restraining deranged people into one disturbance category. In actuality, between 1973 and 1982, only 62 out of 1,085 deaths occurred because of domestic violence. This is a very small number, considering that police spend much more time at a domestic violence call than at any other type of call.

Court Procedures

In a 1975 New York conference on abused wives, Justice Yorka Linakis stated, "There is nothing more pathetic than to see a husband going to his home—usually in the company of a policeman—to collect his meager belongings" (Martin 1983). A Michigan circuit court judge argued that violence is provoked; therefore, the wife should be cited for contempt on this basis and both should be sentenced to jail. Prior to changes caused by the Battered Women's Movement, these were the kinds of attitudes a battered woman would encounter in court. Courts were highly insensitive to a woman's distress. This insensitivity was caused by the ignorance of the problem, inadequate laws, and a heavy backlog of other, more important cases.

When a woman decided to bring charges against her assailant, she had the choice of using a criminal court or a family court. The purpose of criminal court is to punish the criminal and deter the crime. If taken to criminal court, domestic violence is considered a crime. Within this broad category is physical injury, sexual abuse, rape, attempted rape, harassment, threat of physical abuse, death, destruction of another's property, kidnapping or involuntary confinement, or violation of a protection order. The state filed a criminal charge when an arrest was made or when a victim filed a private criminal complaint. A private criminal complaint was filed when the victim did not call the police or did call but the police failed to show up or did not make an arrest when they arrived. Penalties in a criminal court consist of a jail sentence, a fine, or a term of probation. Although normally there is not enough evidence in a domestic violence case for a conviction, a case must be proved beyond a reasonable doubt. The result is usually a warning to the abuser stating that further violence will be prosecuted. If there is enough evidence for a conviction, the prosecutor will usually arrange a plea bargain, bringing the charges down to a misdemeanor or, more often, a violation resulting in probation or, less seriously, a warning.

Although by 1983, in response to the demands of the women's movement, every state had made new legal remedies available to women, many were still reluctant to intervene in family matters. For this reason, most domestic violence cases have been thrown out of criminal court and sent to family court. In family court, a woman could file for a divorce, custody of children, and alimony from her husband. Major problems with family court, though, are that only spouses and couples with children are allowed to file for remedies. This bars cohabitants and other intimates, who would not receive help and support otherwise, from seeking remedies. Although family court would be of greater help to an economically dependent woman with no occupational training, it is designed to protect the family assailant rather than the family victim. It has been recognized that family court is inappropriate for handling felony cases, since it provides the assailant with counsel and leaves the woman to fend for herself.

There were various civil remedies for which a battered woman could file. An order of protection or restraining order requires the abuser to refrain from violence and stay away from the victim. It can last up to one year. Violation of this order is contempt of court and is punishable by a jail sentence of up to six months, a fine, both, or a term of probation. A major problem with obtaining an order of protection is that it takes several days to receive, and often police do not enforce it, claiming that they have no record of the order or that it is a civil not a criminal matter and therefore out of their hands. In order to be protected while she waits for the order of protection, a woman can file for a temporary order of protection. This order can be obtained at night and on weekends. A victim of domestic violence can also file for damages or a peace bond. The problem with these remedies is that they require the abuser to give money to the court that could otherwise be used to support the victim and her children.

Conclusion

Although much of the domestic violence research as well as legislative changes and court decisions have focused on police practices, much has also been done to change prosecutorial and judicial practices. Specifically, prosecutors tend to oversee victim/witness units that tend to deal predominantly with victims of domestic violence. These units inform the victims of the processing of their cases and aid them in understanding the justice process as well as obtaining victim compensation. Within the courts, domestic violence courts have been implemented. These courts are organized so as to give a substantial focus to these sensitive and complex cases; however, research is still needed to assess the effectiveness of these practices. For example, although most police agencies have implemented proarrest policies, researchers have found that the discretion has been taken from the police and given to the prosecutor. Specifically, prosecutors tend to screen out many of these domestic violence cases before they can reach the courts. Furthermore, domestic violence courts are not usually fully structured. Instead, they operate much as early U.S. circuit courts did, in which the domestic violence court convenes one or two days a week and is overseen by one judge or sometimes a commissioner.

Questions of domestic violence practices have been present since the codification of the law; however, these practices did not truly become controversial until the 1970s, and although these interventions or lack thereof may have peaked in their controversial nature, their legacies die hard. For example, although most police departments have mandatory arrest policies, many police officers still hesitate to make arrests. Then, when an arrest is made, the offender is usually charged with a misdemeanor, even when serious injuries have occurred. Furthermore, officer attitudes during arrest often reveal the prevalence of the private-trouble ideology within society. Finally, the fact that many domestic violence crimes go unreported reveals further problems in improving domestic violence practices. Victims do not report these crimes for many reasons. Sometimes victims do not believe that the police can or will do anything to help them, and sometimes victims themselves define the problem as a private trouble. As with many other controversies in criminal justice, the cultural roots at the heart of the problem suggest that domestic violence practices will remain controversial for some time to come.

See also **Domestic Violence—Behaviors and Causes (vol. 3)**

Further Reading

Belknap, Joanne, *The Invisible Woman: Gender, Crime, and Justice,* 3d ed. Belmont, CA: Wadsworth, 2006.

Bradley v. State, 1 Miss. 156 (1824).

Buzawa, Eve S., and Carl G. Buzawa, *Domestic Violence: The Criminal Justice Response,* 3d ed. Newbury Park, CA: Sage, 2002.

Davis, Richard L., *Domestic Violence: Intervention, Prevention, Policies, and Solutions.* Boca Raton, FL: CRC Press, 2008.

Dobash, R. Emerson, and Russell P. Dobash, "With Friends Like These Who Needs Enemies: Institutional Supports for the Patriarchy and Violence against Women." Paper presented at the 9th World Congress of Sociology, Uppsala, Sweden, July 1978.

Fulgham v. State, 46 Ala. 146–147 (1871).

Gosselin, Denise Kindshi, *Heavy Hands: An Introduction to the Crimes of Family Violence,* 3d ed. Upper Saddle River, NJ: Prentice Hall, 2004.

Harlow, Caroline W., *Female Victims of Violent Crime.* Washington, DC: U.S. Department of Justice, 1991.

Martin, Del, *Battered Wives.* New York: Pocket Books, 1983.

Mills, C. Wright, *The Sociological Imagination.* New York: Oxford University Press, 1976 [1959].

Roberts, Albert R. ed., *Handbook of Domestic Violence Intervention Strategies: Policies, Programs, and Legal Remedies.* New York: Oxford University Press, 2002.

Sherman, Lawrence W., and R. A. Berk, "The Specific Deterrent Effects of Arrest for Domestic Assault." *American Sociological Review* 49 (1984): 261–272.

State v. Oliver, 70 N.C. 60, 61–62 (1879).

Steinman, Michael, "Lowering Recidivism among Men Who Batter Women." *Journal of Police Science and Administration* 17 (1990): 2.

Thurman v. City of Torrington, 595 F. Supp 1521. D. Conn. (1984).

DRUG TRAFFICKING AND NARCO-TERRORISM

JUDITH ANN WARNER

When politicians and journalists speak about the U.S. -Mexico border, drug trafficking is viewed as only part of the problem of border security. Preventing terrorist entry and unauthorized immigration are the chief issues. Drug trafficking occurs at all U.S. ports of entry, including the U.S. -Mexico border, the U.S.-Canada border, airports, and sea lanes. Despite the War on Drugs, cocaine, marijuana, methamphetamines and heroin are regularly crossed and bring billions into the hands of criminals. Conceivably, heightened border enforcement could have an impact on Mexican drug trafficking organizations (DTOs). Yet despite all of the efforts made by the White House and Congress to strengthen the border, drug smugglers can respond with ever more sophisticated and brutal acts. Indeed, drug trafficking represents a national security threat, because widespread corruption and drug-related violence could destabilize the government of Mexico (Grayson 2010).

Mexican drug trafficking organizations grow and transport marijuana and heroin and are active in manufacturing "meth" (methamphetamines). Estimates are that 90 percent of cocaine sold in the United States enters through the Mexico border. Alternately, the billions in profit realized from drug sales have created money laundering ventures and enabled the DTOs to purchase smuggled arms, including automatic weapons. The subsequent corruption and drug-related violence causes further concern owing to the possibility of "spillover violence," including kidnappings, torture and homicide in the United States.

The Dimensions of the Problem

The U.S. government has resisted the legalization of marijuana, heroin, and cocaine because of their psychotropic effects. In the 1960s, the United States began to take international action to enforce drug prohibition (Andreas and Nadelman 2006). The major focus was on the Colombia Cali and Medellín cartels and stopping the smuggling of Colombian cocaine to Florida from the Caribbean. Another concern was cross-border smuggling of marijuana and heroin from Mexico. The Drug Enforcement Administration (DEA) was successful in stopping Colombian cocaine smuggling through the Caribbean in the late 1980s and 1990s thanks to an increased naval presence. Colombian cocaine cartels then turned to Mexican smugglers and began using their services, making the U.S.-Mexico border the major route of entry (Payan 2006). Patrick Buchanan, a media commentator, has referred to the change in drug smuggling routes from sea to land as the "Colombianization of Mexico."

Mexican government officials have an informal tradition of overlooking or actively colluding with drug smugglers (Beittel 2009, 7–8). Through the 1990s, the acceptance of bribes was part of a process of accommodation in which the ruling party, the PRI

(Partido Revolucionario Institutional, or Institutional Revolutionary Party) operated in tandem with Mexican DTOs (Velasco 2006; Grayson 2010). From the mid-1980s through 1992, the U.S. government certified the degree to which foreign governments cooperated in stopping drug trafficking (Beittel 2009, 2–3). Under pressure from the United States, Mexican officials participated in crop eradication programs and made some arrests. The working relationship between Mexican and U.S. officials was characterized by mistrust. After 2002, the United States classified countries considered to be ineffective against drug traffickers and associated this effort with sanctions affecting assistance. When Vincente Fox became president of Mexico (2000–2006), his PAN (Partido Acion Nacional, or National Action Party) ended the PRI's 71-year hold on the presidency and political appointments; it also inadvertently disrupted long-term relations of collusion and corruption with drug traffickers (Velasco 2005).

The destabilization of Mexican drug trafficking interorganizational relations and territorial control was an unexpected consequence of the development of a viable two-party system in Mexico, its "democratic transition" (Velasco 2005). Immediately, as Mexico's democratic practice became stronger, President Fox began binational cooperation to suppress drug smuggling. By 2006, some 79,000 Mexicans had been arrested on charges related to drug smuggling (Cook 2007, 3–4). Statistics indicate that low-level drug smugglers and dealers made up 78,831 of the arrests, hit men made up 428, lieutenants 74, financial officers 53, and cartel leaders—the apex of decision making—15. Tijuana DTO leader Francisco Arellano Felix and Gulf DTO leader Osiel Cárdenas Guillén were arrested. Although Guillén was apparently able to continue operations from inside a Mexican prison for a time, attempts by rival drug organizations to control lucrative trafficking routes (such as Interstate Highway 35 in Texas) led to turf wars characterized by spiraling violence and brutality in Mexican border cities and, later, throughout Mexico (Cook 2007, 11–12).

In 2005, conflict over control of the "plaza" (territory) between rival Gulf and Sinaloa DTOs in Nuevo Laredo and Laredo, among the principle ports of entry for cocaine and marijuana, led to the deaths of 135 people. Most of these dead were cartel members, but a journalist, city council member, 13 Mexican police, and the Nuevo Laredo police chief were also killed. In response, President Fox sent federal Mexican troops to Nuevo Laredo to control the situation. Texas Governor Rick Perry sent additional police and equipment to aid the border cities. Both U.S. and Mexican officials have become concerned that the major drug DTOs pose a threat to border security. In September 2008, a total of 175 arrests were made in Mexico, the United States, and Italy to control the violent Gulf drug cartel.

Felipe Calderón, the current Mexican president (2007–present), has increased law enforcement activity against DTOs and narco-terrorism. He considers drug trafficking–related violence a threat to Mexico's national stability (Beittel 2009, 3). The drug-related lawlessness has spread geographically, escalated, and incorporated terrorist elements.

Narco-terrorism is defined as using terror as a tactic to increase drug trafficking profits (Casteel 2003). In reference to other international drug trafficking, the concept of narco-terrorism also refers to using profits from drug trafficking, such as heroin sales, to fund terrorism. At present, Mexican DTOs have not formed ties to international terrorists.

Mexican drug trafficking organizations have used hit men and gang-precipitated torture and violence to intimidate the public and government officials (Cook 2007, 6–9; Beittel 2009, 5–6). The Mexicans who have been killed include elected government representatives, journalists, police chiefs and other law enforcement officers, prosecutors, and civilians of all ages. Pamela L. Bunker, Lisa J. Campbell, and Robert J. Bunker (2010, 145–146) of the Counter-OPFOR Corporation state: "Because many of the police forces and judicial systems in Mexico have been corrupted and compromised and therefore arrest and prosecution rates are extremely low, the probability of ever being brought to justice is almost non-existent for most individuals and groups engaging in killings, torture and beheadings."

Narco-terrorism involves the use of brutality and murder to intimidate the civilian population and authorities. Individuals may be kidnapped for failure to pay drug debts or in order to demand ransom payments. Forms of torture include beatings, knife cuts, breaking bones, sexual abuse, and starvation. Extreme torture includes the use of acid, water, fire, electricity, water boarding, and suffocation (Bunker, Campbell, and Bunker 2010). Prior to homicide or afterward, bodies may be subject to decapitation (*decapitado*), quartering (*descuartizado*), placement in a car trunk (*encajuelado*), wrapping/binding in a blanket (*encobijado*), sealing in a metal storage drum (*entambado*), or depositing in an acid bath (*pozoleado, guisado*) (Bunker, Campbell, and Bunker 2010, 146). Drug-related killings in Mexico increasingly involve short-term torture such as inflicting nonfatal wounds prior to death. These tactics involve the intended effect of intimidation for political or economic gain, but they can also be ritualized, as when narco-cults (*narco-cultos*) carry them out in a ritualized manner connected to a plea for divine intercession, as when a sacrifice is made to Saint Death (*La Santa Muerte*). In Mexico, headless or tortured bodies are being left in public places connected to marijuana growing regions or cartel-controlled areas. Law enforcement officers who turn down bribes may find their names on lists attached to corpses.

The Mexican population perseveres and has taken action against the escalating violence, which can result in death and injury for civilians. In August 2008, a massive public protest against the violence involving hundreds of thousands of marchers occurred in Mexico City and throughout Mexico. In 2010, Mexican government estimates were that, since 2007, some 22,700 people had been killed (Castillo 2010). In 2007, a total of 2,837 were murdered. By 2009, the total killed reached 9,635, tripling the death toll. The border city of Ciudad Juarez has reported 4,324 deaths since 2006, the highest rate in Mexico. From January to March 2010, the death toll was 3,365—violence of epidemic proportions. Deaths in Ciudad Juarez included a pregnant employee of the

U.S. Consulate, her husband, and another husband of a consulate employee (Lacey and Thompson 2010).

Drug trafficking and unauthorized immigration are discussed as issues of lawlessness along the U.S.-Mexico border, but most people in the region are law-abiding. The chief problem has been that, as U.S. border enforcement has escalated, the smuggling of both drugs and people has become more sophisticated. In Mexico, destabilization of relations between drug trafficking organizations (owing to the arrest of leaders and competition for territory) is given as the chief reason for the increased violence. Nevertheless, DTOs are sufficiently powerful and well armed to engage in violent conflict with law enforcement and the Mexican military. It is questionable whether the death toll should be seen as evidence of success from the pitting of drug traffickers against one another because of the degree of harm to the civilian population as well as economic consequences, such as loss of tourism and trade for Mexico.

This situation would not occur if there were not a demand for drugs in the United States and a lack of economic opportunity in Mexico. President Barack Obama (2009–present) and Hillary Clinton, his secretary of state, have acknowledged that the United States shares responsibility for the problem because of the high demand for drugs in the country and the relative ineffectiveness of current programs in quelling that demand.

DRUG TRAFFICKING AND GLOBAL INEQUALITY AT THE U.S.-MEXICO BORDER

Democrats and Republicans are united in using law enforcement as a means to combat drug trafficking, but they do not emphasize the role of global inequality between the United States and Mexico as a factor in this trade. Drug trafficking is estimated to be the most profitable form of organized crime worldwide. It is thought that some $80 billion per year is spent on drugs crossed through the U.S.-Mexico border region. Although the exact figure spent is unknown, U.S.-Mexico inequalities fuel this multibillion-dollar trade. Mexico has a high unemployment rate and a low minimum wage. The demand for drugs in the United States is high; there are an estimated 20 million users who are willing to pay high prices for drugs. The wage disparity between the United States and Mexico makes working for drug cartels attractive for many young Mexican men in border communities. Many of the recruits are low-skilled laborers who have a hard time finding jobs. Drug trafficking skills—physical aggression, playing the role of a bodyguard, using a gun, and driving a vehicle across the border—can be learned quickly. The easy money earned from smuggling is much greater than what is available from legitimate employment in Mexico. It is actually surprising that the vast majority of Mexicans resist involvement in this criminal enterprise.

Drug Trafficking Organizations and Distribution Networks

In the 1980s, Mexico had one drug trafficking organization, headed by Felix Gallardo. When drug trafficking in the Caribbean was brought under control, Colombian cocaine traffickers joined forces with Mexicans. As the war on drugs heated up along the border, interorganizational disputes marred the operation of the border-wide cartel, and Gallardo (in prison) ordered it split into four separate organizations: the Gulf Cartel (Southeast Texas), the Juarez Cartel (Southwest Texas), the Sinaloa Cartel Federation (Texas, New Mexico, and Arizona), and the Tijuana Cartel Federation (California) (Cook 2007, 1–2). Originally, the arrests of Tijuana Federation leader Javier Arellano Felix and Guild Cartel leader Osiel Cárdenas Guillén led to an intercartel alliance. Later, the U.S. Project Reckoning heavily disrupted the U.S. and European transport networks (U.S. Attorney, Southern District of New York 2008). Abroad, 600 arrests were made and $72 million in currency was taken. Inside the United States, 12,000 kilograms of cocaine, $60 million in currency, and 750 arrests connected to 750 distribution networks were major outcomes. Today, the territory of the Gulf Cartel is chiefly controlled by Los Zetas, a paramilitary group of former Mexican military who served as enforcers for a period of time. Mexican drug organizations are known to operate in 195 cities and to send drugs to 230 cities.

Specialized professionals and high technology are stepping up the response of trafficking organizations—and the potential for violent conflict. According to the FBI, the Zetas, highly trained former Mexican soldiers, have become involved in smuggling both drugs and people into the United States, probably displacing the Gulf Cartel. The Zetas have surveillance operatives, checkpoints, and high technology. They have been linked to the possibility of smuggling special-interest entrants into the United States—that is, individuals who may or may not be connected to terrorism who originate from sending countries identified as having terrorist organizations.

The Calderón government has confiscated 70 tons of cocaine, 4,000 tons of marijuana, and 43,000 tons of methamphetamine precursor ingredients (Berrong 2009). The Mexican cartels have been able to thwart every effort to stop trafficking because they are flexible and adaptive organizations. Tony Payan (2006), an international relations and foreign policy specialist, characterizes the war on drugs at the border as a cat-and-mouse game in which the United States has tactical victories such as drug seizures and arrests but is losing in the conflict. U.S. escalation in personnel and technology has always resulted in DTO adaptation and a continued supply of drugs.

Drug Transport Methods at Border Crossings and Border Checkpoints

Heroin and cocaine have been too valuable to risk crossing in between ports of entry, as U.S. Border Patrol (USBP) agents could become aware and seize the load. As a result, most drugs are crossed through ports of entry. Social networks built on corruption on both sides of the border facilitate drug transport. Attempts are made to bribe U.S.

Customs officers, sheriffs, and law enforcement personnel, and some give in to the offer of large sums of money.

DTOs often use vehicles rather than human carriers ("mules") because it is impossible for customs to inspect every vehicle and item that crosses the border. The Bureau of Transportation Statistics indicates that the following numbers of vehicles, cargo containers, and individuals crossed in 2009: 2,432,495 trucks, 1,555,466 loaded truck containers, 146,058 loaded rail containers, 6,348 rail passengers, 135,775 buses, 1,445,200 bus passengers, 40,576,475 personal vehicles, 91,139,705 vehicle passengers, and 23,538,289 pedestrians. Checking is done at random or on the basis of customs officers' intuition, depending on signs of anomalies or driver nervousness. All roads located past the border leading into the U.S. interior also have checkpoints that are frequently manned by officers with drug-sniffing dogs. Payan indicates that many of the vehicles that cross drugs go through points of entry (POEs) rather than between them. It is estimated that 70 percent of drugs are crossed through the southwestern border in this way. Mexico has become the major supplier of marijuana, brown heroin, and Colombian cocaine.

In the past, cars, vans, and pickup trucks have been the favorite vehicle for crossing drugs. Today, this method is used by small operators. Hidden compartments in ordinary places in the vehicle are created. The drugs are then basted with masking scents tested by the cartels' own drug-sniffing dogs. Vehicles are crossed in two ways. The first involves going to the checkpoint and hoping that drug-sniffing dogs, the reaction of the driver to stress, and the thoroughness of the inspection will not expose the drugs. The second method is to cross cars in groups and let one be caught, distracting officials from the others. Often workers are placed in locations where they can see if an inspector is distracted. But the best way to smuggle drugs is to bribe a U.S. officer working at a port of entry to let drugs pass through. Several cases in which law enforcement has been bribed turn up every year. A single corrupt official can allow massive quantities to be crossed, preventing other drug enforcement activities from stopping the flow.

Since the passage of the North American Free Trade Agreement, tractor trailer trucks have been extensively used to transport drugs. This is the preferred method of the largest cartels. The escalation of technologies used in the war on drugs has made it harder to bribe officials because of the risk of being caught. Now the drug cartels must spend millions on bribes in order to find Americans working at ports of entry who will take the risk.

Diversified Organized Crime Tactics

Controlling two types of smuggling, of people and drugs, has allowed the DTOs to use unauthorized migrants as a border-patrol diversion in order to cross drugs in a different area. Undocumented immigrants pay protection money to the cartels; then the cartels divert the immigrants to certain routes designed to attract USBP activity and remove attention from the route through which drugs will be smuggled.

Fencing, National Guard troops, and additional USBP personnel have made it more risky to use traditional drug smuggling routes. There has been a significant increase in the amount of cocaine and marijuana seized. National Guard groups placed along the Arizona border have resulted in a significant increase in detained unauthorized migrants as well. It is plausible that this has cut into the DTOs' profit margins, prompting them to use of alternative methods.

U.S. Border Patrol Confrontations with Cartel Smugglers

The greatest risk that USBP officers take lies in dealing with drug smugglers and trafficking organizations. The USBP makes more drug smuggling arrests than any law enforcement agency, including the Drug Enforcement Administration (DEA). Drug smugglers use violence to avoid arrest and will risk killing USBP officers. In effect, a major activity of the USBP has become drug interdiction rather than immigrant apprehension.

USBP officers' jobs involve working individually in remote regions away from witnesses. In cases of human smuggling, they may face resistance, but drug smugglers may try to kill them. In June 1998, Alexander Kirpnick was shot and killed while attempting to apprehend five marijuana smugglers in the desert hills near Nogales, Arizona. Similar killings occurred in 2008 and 2009.

One issue in confronting drug smuggling is that the USBP is literally outgunned. The drug cartels have access to automatic assault rifles, while each USBP officer has only a revolver. Former Laredo, Texas, Sheriff Rick Flores (2005–2008) points out that smugglers have automatic assault weapons, rocket-propelled grenades, and Kevlar helmets with level-four body armor similar to that of the military.

The violence of drug smugglers' reactions to attempts to stop and arrest them has increased. In the past, the sight of law enforcement would result in smugglers dropping the drugs or abandoning vehicles. Human smugglers would be arrested with the rest of the group. Currently, drug cartels are firing on the USBP, engaging in reckless high-speed chases, and initiating standoffs at the U.S.-Mexico border. The United States has no jurisdiction to pursue any smugglers into Mexico.

DTOs control increasingly sophisticated technology. Spotters using high-power binoculars, and encrypted radios are placed in the mountains. Despite the placement of interior checkpoints, smugglers slip through by crossing private property. The income realized from drugs allows them to invest in high technology, and they have even been able to decipher the USBP's encrypted communication.

Spillover Violence and Unintended Effects of U.S. Border Policy

Both Mexican and U.S. national security is threatened by narco-terrorism. Director of Homeland Security Janet Napolitano believes that drug-related violence in Mexico has the potential to spill over to the United States. Spillover violence incidents include trafficker-to-trafficker homicide and planned attacks on U.S. citizens, officials, or physical infrastructure (Peters 2009). Since Mexican DTOs have drug distribution networks reaching numerous U.S. cities, such attacks could become widespread. Those attacks that have already occurred in the United States involved mainly border cities. Such incidents have included inter-DTO homicide, kidnapping of smugglers or family members, and attacks on USBP officers. The *National Drug Assessment, 2010* (Department of Justice National Drug Intelligence Center 2009, 16), states that "Direct violence similar to the conflicts occurring among major DTOs in Mexico is rare in the United States." Indirect violence such as kidnappings and DTO conflicts may be more frequent. DTO "discipline" can include kidnapping, beating, torture and murder of organization members who fail to deliver drugs or money. Drug users may be kidnapped if they do not pay. Phoenix, Arizona, reported 267 kidnappings related to drug or human smuggling in 2009 (Department of Justice National Drug Intelligence Center 2009, 16). At present, U.S.-Mexico border cities are not experiencing heightened violence. For example, only 17 murders were reported in El Paso in 2008, and there were 13 through December 25, 2009 (Johnson 2009).

In Mexico, kidnapping is a major problem. Through 2005, hundreds of Mexicans and sixty American citizens were kidnapped (Blumenthal 2005). Drug-related violence includes murder of government officials, journalists, and innocent bystanders. Threats have been made against Americans news media and journalists. DTOs seek to intimidate government, law enforcement, and the media as a way of reducing press coverage and public reaction. The U.S. State Department advises Americans to be alert and take precautions when they are traveling in Mexico.

Peter Andreas (2009), a political scientist, suggests that that there is an unintentional and reinforcing impact of the U.S. attempt to control its southern border with Mexico and the expansion of drug and human smuggling. He refers to this effect as unintentionally symbiotic and points out that the criminal justice complex at the border has been greatly expanded as a result. Throughout most of the 20th century, the southern border has been ineffectively policed and the Immigration and Naturalization Service, as it was then known, now renamed Immigration and Customs Enforcement (ICE) and a part of the Department of Homeland Security, did a largely symbolic job. Today, the worsening of the problem necessitates new strategies that may result in overturning past policy.

Strategies to Address the Problem

The War on Drugs and Expansion of Drug Trafficking

There are two views on whether border security initiatives are curbing drug trafficking. Payan (2006) feels that despite the expansion of USBP and Drug Enforcement administration personnel on the border, the quantity of drugs seized each year continues to increase, along with the total volume of drugs being trafficked. Drug trafficking organizations are so successful at moving product that the price of drugs on the street in urban cities has declined. The federal government's border-control policy has not succeeded in controlling the cartels. The alternative view, put forth by the House Committee on Homeland Security, is that federal and state efforts to secure the border have resulted in the cartel's current efforts to control human smuggling and enter into extortion, because drug seizures are making inroads on their profits. The controversy over whether the U.S.-Mexico border can be controlled cannot be resolved by examining rates of seizure of drugs, as supply can be increased if seizures are increased. Only information on street prices and availability can resolve this issue, and such data have not been a major concern in the debate over the impact of escalation in border security personnel and technology.

The Mérida Initiative

The United States' primary international program for control of drug trafficking is called the Mérida Initiative (Seelke and Ribando 2009). Mexico, Central America, the Dominican Republic, and Haiti are participants. Issues addressed include drug trafficking, arms smuggling, money laundering, and transnational organized crime. For three years, $1.4 billion in technological assistance and training will be provided. In particular, helicopters, speedboats, and computerized intelligence systems for data sharing were to lead the investment. After an expenditure of $700 million, Congress voted to withhold funds pending review of the program's efficacy (Landler 2009).

Can yet another United States program for control of international trafficking succeed? Drug trafficking through the U.S.-Mexico border has ties with transnational organized crime in Mexico, Central America, the Caribbean, and South America. Developing nations lack the funds, training, and technology to confront drug transit and associated crime. Furthermore, organized crime thrives in ungoverned social space (Velasco 2005; Grayson 2010). Weak national governments need to be strengthened and to gain credibility (Olson and Donnelly 2009). Democratic governments, as opposed to dictatorships, are not considered absolutely essential, but they are seen as being more effective at controlling crime. The widespread bribery and collusion of government and law enforcement officials allows drug trafficking organizations to gain political control. The lower standard of living and salaries increase the attractiveness of criminal offers, especially where law enforcement and judiciaries are weak.

Mexican citizens have protested and reform of law enforcement is occurring in Mexico. When local police proved ineffective owing to bribery and intimidation, the federal police were reorganized as a national police force. As drug-related violence escalated, the Mexican military was brought in. Twenty-four thousand military personnel have been involved in countertrafficking; they are thought to have had some effect in reducing violence, but primarily by displacing it or creating a condition of stalemate (Cook 2007). Local, state, and federal police and increasingly the military have been bribed and even recruited for work with drug trafficking organizations (Velasco 2005, 106–108).

Both police and the military have low salaries and poor working conditions. Less educated applicants are attracted to the low-prestige occupation of law enforcement.

Police are easily corrupted because of their low pay and the Mexican history of corruption, particularly at the municipal and state levels. There is an established social climate that will be difficult to challenge or change without improving salaries and living conditions (Velasco 2005). The Mérida initiative and other U.S. binational programs support the professionalization of Mexican law enforcement.

Efforts are being directed toward reform of Mexico's judicial system. Mexico has an inquisitorial justice system but is enacting reforms that would move it toward adversarial justice, as in the United States (Olson 2008). Prosecution in inquisitorial systems involves evidence collection by prosecutors, who issue recommendations that lead to closed-door verdicts. The individual is *not* presumed innocent until proven guilty. Oral prosecution and defense, cross-examination of witnesses, and defendant access to evidence is limited. People are held until they can establish their innocence. It is thought that Mexico will have switched to an adversarial system of justice by 2015.

President Calderón has strengthened control over the Mexican military, but it is incomplete (Cook 2007; Grayson 2010). Reports of human rights violations point to disappearance, torture, murder, and arbitrary detention (Amnesty International 2009). Amnesty International (2009) documented five cases involving 35 individuals in a period of 12 months during 2008–2009 and has released information on other incidents. It is difficult to prosecute military personnel. Amnesty International (2009, 5) released the following quotation: "If you report us, something worse will happen to you, and no one will do anything to us because we are soldiers." Crimes committed by the military are tried in a separate military judicial system, which may violate the Mexican Constitution. Amnesty International (2009, 22) indicates that

> when abuses are committed by members of the military the response of the state at
> all levels is ineffective. The failure of both civilian and military authorities to take

ECONOMIC GLOBALIZATION, DRUGS, AND THE BORDER

Drug demand creates pressure at the border, where the United States is trying to exercise sovereignty, prevent the entry of drugs, and conduct trade. Controlling drugs potentially compromises the North American Free Trade Agreement transborder economic connection, which promotes opening the border instead of closing it. In the confusion of apprehending migrants and letting trade goods flow across the border, both drugs and humans have often gotten through.

The logic of securing the border to open it for trade is contradictory. The reason for considering globalization as a factor in the expansion of this problem is that many nations have opened their borders to increased trade and tourism, generating new criminal opportunities. The U.S.-Mexico border smuggling issue is a part of a larger global crime nexus in which powerful international organized crime syndicates operate. The linkage between Colombian cocaine cartels and Mexican drug traffickers reflects globalization.

468 DRUG TRAFFICKING AND NARCO-TERRORISM

timely effective action to prevent and punish these grave human rights violations is tantamount to complicity. In some instances, the lack of cooperation by some military and civilian authorities with relatives or other relevant authorities, such as court officials or members of the [National Human Rights Commission] trying to establish truth and justice may even amount to concealment.

Steps taken within the military justice system to investigate these abuses and hold those responsible to account do not constitute a real intent to bring the perpetrators to justice. The lack of independence and transparency of the military justice system ensures victims and relatives are frequently denied access to justice. Consequently Mexico appears to be unwilling or unable genuinely to carry out investigations and prosecutions against its military.

The United States will withhold 15 percent of Mérida funding if human rights violations by the military are not efficaciously handled (Seelke and Ribando 2009). In general, equity and transparency are needed to increase the credibility of the Mexican justice system and reduce corruption within it (Olson 2008). The Mérida initiative seeks to provide resources for investigating and prosecuting crime related to drug trafficking. Unfortunately, Mexican law enforcement lacks scientific and legal skills. Organized criminals are present within all sectors of the criminal justice system, from patrol to prison, and without oversight.

Controversy ensued when the U.S. Joint Forces Command (2008, 36) labeled Mexico a potential "failing state." Mexican President Calderón and other officials reacted extremely negatively to this assertion and maintained that there is no area in Mexico that is not under state control. Secretary of State Hillary Clinton (Clinton 2009) stated that she does not believe that Mexico has any "ungovernable territories." Mexican authorities maintain that DTOs are weakening and that they are turning on each other owing to diminishing market share (Associated Press 2009). Jane's Information Group (2009) has taken the position that drug traffickers only need to subvert the state through corruption rather than defeat it.

Mexico, a developing country with a limited budget, has a power asymmetry with the United States. This asymmetry contributes to the drug interdiction issue, because Mexico sees U.S. intervention as a challenge to its national sovereignty. Mexico resists any U.S. troop involvement on its soil. In Latin America, the United States is perceived as having a unilateral drug strategy rather than taking part in cooperative multinational efforts. The Obama administration inherited the Mérida initiative and is changing direction. A new emphasis will be placed on developing law enforcement and communities (Thompson and Lacey 2010). Law enforcement training and technology and improved screening of drugs and vehicles at crossing points will be renewed and expanded. The latest concern is building economic opportunity in communities affected by poverty and crime. The biggest shift has been away from military assistance.

Reducing U.S. Drug Demand

In the 1960s, the United States instituted an international drug prohibition policy. President Richard Nixon began the War on Drugs, which critics have considered a damaging policy that undermines U.S. interests in Mexico and other drug exporting nations. In Mexico, efforts have included crop eradication and drug interdiction. A policy debate is being waged over the efficacy of these efforts. Advocates believe that the supply of drugs has been reduced. Critics consider that drug prices are lower than ever, but the U.S. government does not report this fact. The Obama administration is making a departure from the rhetoric of the War on Drugs. On March 25, 2009, Secretary of State Hillary Clinton said: "Clearly what we are doing has not worked....Our insatiable demand for illegal drugs fuels the drug trade" (2009).

Critics of U.S.-Mexico drug policy believe that demand reduction among U.S. citizens would limit the earnings of drug trafficking organizations. The Obama administration has begun new initiatives for drug treatment and prevention (Hananel 2010) and seeks to abandon the phrase "War on Drugs." Drug Czar Gil Kerlikowski has stated: "Calling it a war really limits your options....Looking at this both as a public safety problem and a public health problem makes a lot more sense." The Obama plan calls for reducing the number of first-time users by 15 percent over five years and sets other goals for reducing driving under the influence of drugs, chronic drug usage, and drug-related deaths. Community antidrug programs will screen for drug use and mainstream medical facilities will be involved. Health personnel are encouraged to ask about drug use.

The debate on how to control drug use includes the idea of harm reduction through legalization. Norm Stamper, a former Seattle police chief, favors the legalization of drugs through state-run stores or distribution by registered pharmacists (Kristof 2009). Nicholas D. Kristof, *New York Times* op-ed columnist, points out that the drug war had three major impacts: (1) it greatly increased drug users in prison populations from 41,000 in 1980 to 500,000 in 2009; (2) it empowered organized crime and terrorists who make billions in profit; and (3) the money spent on law enforcement, $44.1 billion, could be spent in other ways, including treatment and prevention. It has been argued that drug treatment is more cost-effective than interdiction.

Mexico has preceded the United States in adopting harm reduction by passing a law to decriminalize possession of small amounts of drugs. Individuals will not be prosecuted but instead referred to drug treatment programs. Individuals will be required to enter a treatment center if they are found in possession of drugs a third time. This measure is in response the development of an internal drug addiction problem and designed to free up prison space for dangerous criminals. Critics of decriminalization argue that it will increase addiction.

In 2010, President Obama authorized 1,200 National Guard troops for the border and sought increased funds for border law enforcement (Archibold 2010). The *New York*

Times responded in an editorial that "adding a thousand or so border troops won't stop the cartels or repeal the law of supply and demand" ("Editorial" 2010).

Conclusion

Drug trafficking and the associated violence is the major problem at the U.S.-Mexico border. Every escalation in border security by U.S. Customs and Border Patrol, the DEA, and other federal agencies has been met with adaptation by the drug cartels. Although many officials in Mexico and some law enforcement officers in the United States have been bribed, both Mexico and the United States are increasingly choosing to confront the cartels. Mexico estimates that the trade is based on 20 million users in the United States. The law enforcement approach to the war on drugs has not reduced the demand. This suggests that reducing the motivation of American citizens for using drugs and rehabilitating drug users would be an alternative way of reducing demand.

The United States has engaged in many wars: a war on drugs, a war on terrorism, and conflict in Afghanistan and Iraq. Has it won any of these wars? What are the criteria for deciding? The United States is pursuing its strategy of constantly escalating a quasi-military struggle for control of the Mexican border. This strategy has never worked, and Mexican drug trafficking organizations adapt to change more rapidly than the Department of Homeland Security bureaucracy is able to do. It is unlikely that this problem will soon be resolved in the future any more than stopping cocaine smuggling in the Caribbean to Florida ended Colombian drug smuggling.

The United States may have waited too long to deal with the demand for illicit drugs in the United States. The billions of profit from drugs paid into Mexico, a country with a great deal of poverty, provide the motivation to engage in illegal trafficking. Drug lords are highly adaptable in finding ways to provide drugs, start habits, and maintain fixes. Imprisonment has not slowed demand. It remains to be seen if the prevention and treatment strategy of the Obama administration can be more effective.

See also **Border Fence; Human Smuggling and Trafficking; War on Drugs** (vol. 3)

Further Reading

Amnesty International, *Mexico, New Reports of Human Rights Violations by the Military.* Washington DC: Amnesty International, 2009. http://www.amnesty.org/en/library/asset/AMR41/058/2009/en/e1a94ad6-3df1-4724-a545-f0b93f39af69/amr410582009en.pdf

Andreas, Peter, *Border Games: Policing the U.S.-Mexico Divide,* 2d ed. Ithaca, NY: Cornell University Press, 2009.

Andreas, Peter, and Ethan Nadelmann, *Policing the Globe: Criminalization and Crime Control in International Relations.* New York: Oxford University Press, 2006.

Archibold, Randall C., "Obama to send up to 1,200 Troops to Border." *New York Times* (May 25, 2010). http://www.nytimes.com/2010/05/26/us/26border.html

Associated Press, "Mexican Cartels Use Migrants as DEA Decoys: Drug Smuggling Rings Take Over Human Trafficking Routes." May 1, 2007. http://www.cbsnews.com/stories/2007/05/01/national/main2746396.shtml

Beittel, June S., "Congressional Research Report for Congress: Mexico's Drug Related Violence." May 27, 2009. http://www.fas.org/sgp/crs/row/R40582.pdf

Berrong, Stephanie, "Cooperation on the Border." *Security Management* (April 2009). http://www.securitymanagement.com/article/cooperation-border-005427

Blumenthal, Ralph, "Texas Town Is Unnerved by Violence in Mexico." *New York Times* (August 11, 2005).

Buchanan, Patrick, *State of Emergency: The Third World Invasion and Conquest of America.* New York: St. Martin's Press, 2006.

Bunker, Pamela L., Lisa J. Campbell, and Robert J. Bunker, "Torture, Beheadings and Narcocultos." *Small Wars and Insurgencies* 21 (2010): 145–178.

Campbell, Howard, *Drug War Zone: Frontline Dispatches from the Streets of El Paso and Juárez.* Austin: University of Texas Press, 2009.

Casteel, Steven W., "Narco-Terrorism, International Drug Trafficking and Terrorism—A Dangerous Mix." Statement before the U.S. Senate Judiciary Committee. May 20, 2003. http://www.usdoj.gov/dea/pubs/cngrtest/ct052003.html

Castillo, Eduardo, "22,700 Killed in Drug Related Violence in Mexico Since '06." *Houston Chronicle* (April 13, 2010).

Chaddock, Gail Russell, "Congress Takes Aim at Modern-Day Slavery: Traffickers in Human Cargo for Sex Trade or Sweatshops Will Face Tougher Penalties." *Christian Science Monitor* 2 (2000).

Clinton, Hillary Rodham, U.S. Department of State. "Remarks with Mexican Foreign Secretary Patricia Espinosa after Their Meeting." Mexico City, Mexico, March 25, 2009.

Cook, Coleen W., *Congressional Research Service Report: Mexico's Drug Cartels.* October 16, 2007. http://ftp.fas.org/sgp/crs/row/RL34215.pdf

"Editorial: Troops and the Border." *New York Times* (May 27, 2010). http://www.nytimes.com/2010/05/28/opinion/28fri2.html

Grayson, George W., *Mexico: Narco-Violence and a Failed State.* New Brunswick, NJ: Transaction Publishers, 2010.

Hananel, Sam, "Obama Shifts Strategy Away from War on Drugs: Will Now Focus on Prevention and Treatment." *Boston Globe* (May 12, 2010). http://www.boston.com/news/nation/washington/articles/2010/05/12/obama_shifts_strategy_away_from_war_on_drugs

House Committee on Homeland Security, *Interim Report: A Line in the Sand: Confronting the Threat at the Southwest Border.* Washington DC: House Committee on Homeland Security. http://www.house.gov/sites/members/tx10_mccaul/pdf/Investigaions-Border-Report.pdf

Jane's Information Group, "Security Mexico." February 2009. http://www.janes.com/

Johnson, Kevin, "Violence Drops in U.S. Cities Neighboring Mexico." *USA Today* (December 28, 2009). http://www.usatoday.com/news/nation/2009-12-27-Mexico-border-violence_N.htm?csp = 34&utm_source=feedburner&utm_medium=feed&utm_campaign=Feed%3A+usatoday-NewsTopStories+%28News+-+Top+Stories%29

Kristof, Nicholas, "Time to Legalize Drugs?" *New York Times* (June 13, 2009). http://kristof.blogs.nytimes.com/2009/06/13/time-to-legalize-drugs

Lacey, Marc, "In Mexico, Ambivalence on a Drug Law." *New York Times* (August 23, 2009). http://www.nytimes.com/2009/08/24/world/americas/24mexico.html?scp=16&sq=Mexican%20drug%20cartels&st = cse

Lacey, Marc, "In Mexican Drug War, Investigators are Fearful." *New York Times* (October 16, 2009). http://www.nytimes.com/2009/10/17/world/americas/17juarez.html?partner=rss&emc=rss

Lacey, Marc, and Ginger Thompson, "Two Drug Slayings in Mexico Rock U.S. Consulate." *New York Times* (March 14, 2010). http://www.nytimes.com/2010/03/15/world/americas/15juarez.html

Landler, Mark, "Clinton Says U.S. Feeds Mexican Drug Trade." *New York Times* (March 25, 2009). http://www.nytimes.com/2009/03/26/world/americas/26mexico.html

Napolitano, Janet, "Napolitano's Testimony before Senate Homeland Security and Governmental Affairs Committee, Southern Border Violence: Homeland Security Threats, Vulnerabilities, and Responsibilities." Council on Foreign Relations. March 25, 2009. http://www.cfr.org/publication/18945/napolitanos_testimony_before_senate_homeland_security_and_governmental_affairs_committee_southern_border_violence.html

National Drug Intelligence Center, National Drug Threat Assessment 2009. December 2008. http://www.usdoj.gov/ndic/pubs31/31379/index.htm

Olson, Eric, "Six Key Issues in U.S.-Mexico Security Cooperation." Woodrow Wilson Center Mexico Institute. 2008. http://www.wilsoncenter.org/news/docs/Olson%20Brief.pdf

Olson, Eric L., and Robert Donnelly, "Report from the U.S.-Mexico Security Cooperation Working Group and A Conference on International Experiences in Combating Organized Crime: Confronting the Challenges of Organized Crime in Mexico and Latin America." 2009. http://www.wilsoncenter.org/news/docs/Confronting%20Challenges%20of%20Organized%20Crime-%20Eric%20Olson%20Robert%20Donnelly.pdf

Payan, Tony, *The Three U.S.-Mexico Border Wars: Drugs, Immigration and Homeland Security*. Westport, CT: Praeger Security International, 2006.

Peters, Katherine McIntire, "DEA: Mexican Drug Violence is a Sign of Progress, Not Failure." *Government Executive* (April 15, 2009). http://www.govexec.com/dailyfed/0409/041509kp1.htm

Richardson, Chad, *On the Edge of the Law: Culture, Labor and Deviance on the South Texas Border*. Austin: University of Texas Press, 2006.

Seelke, Claire Ribando, Congressional Research Service Report for Congress: Merida Initiative for Mexico and Central America: Funding and Policy Issues, August 21, 2009. http://www.wilsoncenter.org/news/docs/CRS%20Mérida%20Initiative%20for%20Mexico%20and%20Central%20America%20Funding%20Policy%20Issues.pdf

Sele, Andrew, "Money, Guns and Drugs: Are U.S. Inputs Fueling Violence on the U.S.-Mexico Border?" Testimony by Andrew Sele to the House Subcommittee on National Security and Foreign Affairs. March 9, 2009. http://nationalsecurity.oversight.house.gov/documents/20090313115456.pdf

Sheridan, Mary Beth, "Clinton: U.S. Drug Policies Failed: Fueled Mexico's Drug War." *Washington Post* (March 26, 2009). http://www.washingtonpost.com/wp-dyn/content/article/2009/03/25/AR2009032501034.html

Thompson, Ginger, and Marc Lacey, "U.S. and Mexico Revise Joint Anti-Drug Strategy." *New York Times* (March 23, 2010). http://www.nytimes.com/2010/03/24/world/americas/24mexico.html

U.S. Attorney, Southern District of New York, "175 Alleged Gulf Cartel Members and Associates Arrested in Massive International Law Enforcement Operation." September 17, 2008. http://www.usdoj.gov/usao/nys/pressreleases/September08/projectreckoningpr.pdf

U.S. Joint Forces Command, "The Joint Operating Environment 2008: Challenges and Implications for the Future Joint Force." December 2008. http://www.jfcom.mil/newslink/storyarchive/2008/JOE2008.pdf

Velasco, Jose Luis, *Insurgency, Authoritarianism and Drug Trafficking in Mexico's "Democratization."* New York: Routledge, 2005.

DWI AND DRUG TESTING

Angela Taylor

Policies that target driving while intoxicated (DWI) or that permit so-called suspicionless drug testing of specified groups (employees, students) demonstrate the conflict between promoting public health and safety and constricting individual liberty and privacy *(Skinner v. Railway Labor Executives' Association* 1989). Anti-DWI laws are programs designed to reduce the damage caused by the mix of alcohol and driving, which kills and injures thousands of Americans each year. Mass drug testing policies, whether by employers or in schools, are viewed by advocates as means of ensuring well-being and integrity in workplace and academic settings, with the added bonus of discouraging drug use generally.

Opponents of these mass testing policies are concerned, for example, about the effects on certain constitutional rights. One scholar has noted that changes in judicial conceptions of the proper scope of government power have occurred in the wake of attempts to regulate traffic (Laurence 1988, 136–166). This is nowhere more evident than in the case of anti-DWI policies and is echoed in the case of drug testing policies. In a series of court decisions addressing these policies, constitutional safeguards, particularly those related to due process and protection against unwarranted search and seizure, have been narrowed. Widespread public outcry about these practices has largely been muted; citizens appear to be willing to trade freedom for safety, or perceived safety, because it is unclear that these policies are the most effective means of mitigating the damages of drug and alcohol use. The full implications of these losses for situations beyond the narrow issues of DWI and drug use have yet to be seen.

Background

DWI policies were enacted against the backdrop of certain facts about use of alcohol and drugs in the United States. It is undeniable that alcohol increases the chances of driving mishaps. In fact, a 0.04 percent blood alcohol concentration (BAC), an amount much less than the current limit of 0.08 percent, can lead to driving errors (Ross 1992, 19). Data from 2008 show that close to one third (32 percent) of U.S. traffic fatalities, or some 11,773 deaths, are linked to alcohol use (Centers for Disease Control and Prevention 2009). Nevertheless, substantial numbers of individuals report driving after having used alcohol: there are approximately 159 million such incidents each year (Voas et al. 1998, 267–275). Further, only a fraction of those who report DWI are ever arrested for it; recent figures demonstrate an arrest prevalence of approximately 1 percent (Voas et al). Drunk driving is more common among males and those between 21 and 34 years of age. It is more likely to occur at night and on weekends, generally the times when leisure activities take place (Voas et al). Whites, persons of mixed race, and Native Americans most often report driving under the influence, whereas blacks, Hispanics, and mixed-race individuals most often report being arrested (Caetano and McGrath 2005).

Drug-testing polices are part of the arm of drug policy that focuses on prevention, specifically by lowering the prevalence of use in order to decrease its consequences, including addiction, and other negative aspects of use, like accidents, illness, lowered productivity, and so forth. Employer-based drug testing is a common procedure. Most recent data show that 46 percent of workers report that their employers test for drugs (Carpenter 2006). This figure is down from 49 percent in 1997 (U.S. Department of Health and Human Services 2007). Drug tests, generally using urine as the biological matrix, are done for a number of reasons, most often for pre-employment screening, during postaccident investigations or in cases of suspected on-the-job use. Random drug testing is done largely in settings where safety-related testing occurs.

Drug testing expanded from the workplace into schools following concerns over drug use by youth. According to one study, 18 percent of schools engaged in testing, mostly of students in high school (Yamaguchi, Johnston, and O'Malley 2003). This number, valid in 2001, has likely changed in the wake of the 2002 *Board of Education v. Earls* decision, which expanded categories of students who could be tested. Mass drug testing also takes place in the criminal justice system, from pretrial to probation or parole supervision. Such testing has not generated the controversy that other forms have created. This is likely due to the reduction in rights of those subject to criminal penalties.

DID YOU KNOW?

The mandatory guidelines for federal workplace drug testing (which apply to workplaces of both the federal government and government contractors) require an employer to conduct two tests before a urine test can be reported positive for a drug or be considered an adulterated or substituted sample. The first test is referred to as the initial test and second as the confirmatory test.

Source: Substance Abuse and Mental Health Services Administration (SAMHSA). "Analytical Testing Methods" (2005).

Key Events

A major review of alcohol and driving, published in 1968, was the first government document to officially link drunk driving and accidents (Ross 1992, 175). Even so, DWI was seen as basically a traffic problem or a by-product problem of alcohol use (Gusfield 1988, 109–135). This changed in 1980 with the rise of an organization called Mothers against Drunk Driving (MADD), started by Candy Lightner, who lost her 13-year-old to a drunk driver. MADD and similar organizations pushed to make penalties and criminal justice enforcement against drunk drivers more stringent. Drunk driving came to be viewed as a moral problem, with campaigns portraying drunk drivers as villains of the road, thus increasing the public ire directed toward those offenders (Gusfield 1988, 109–135).

The movement was very successful in obtaining changes in DWI and alcohol policies, among them (1) lowering the limit of acceptable blood alcohol for drivers; (2) sobriety checkpoints, which are defined areas where police will check vehicles to see if passengers are intoxicated or have some other alcohol-related violation; (3) administrative suspensions; (4) getting the drinking age raised from 18 to 21; and (5) increased penalties for offenders, mostly for recidivists but also for first-timers (Gusfield 1988, 109–135).

These efforts were facilitated by the ability of the federal government to use its power over state funding of transportation projects to push states into drafting various laws designed to reduce driving under the influence. States were threatened with loss of highway construction funds unless they altered their laws according to federal dictates. Recent efforts in this regard include pushing for a reduction of the acceptable blood alcohol limit to 0.08 percent from 0.10 percent and mandating certain penalties for repeat offenders, including compelling the use of ignition interlocks. These last are devices designed to prevent a car from being turned on unless the driver registers a blood alcohol level below a given amount.

These changes met with some opposition, some of which centered on use of the Breathalyzer, and to the training of officers in discerning driver impairment. This likely reflects the overwhelming influence of "per se" laws (using a zero-tolerance measure), which penalize having a breath alcohol level above a given amount. A casual Internet survey reveals a cottage industry of defense attorneys advertising methods of fighting the test and DWI charges in general. Other challenges came from concern over the penalties, in particular administrative license suspensions and sobriety checkpoints. These wound up in the courts.

How have these policies worked in reducing DWI? The percentage of drunk-driving deaths has gone down in recent years. Some research has linked this to various drunk-driving penalties, most specifically those directed at youth, such as raising the drinking age (Laurence 1988, 136–166). However, it is likely that other factors—for instance, a decline in the use of alcohol—are important as well.

Drug use exploded as a societal concern during the 1980s. This altered focus was linked to a variety of factors, including general concern over crime combined with the heightened use of crime as an issue in elections; the rising cocaine and, later, crack epidemic; and highly publicized incidents (such as the Len Bias cocaine overdose). These factors all contributed to an environment of increased public worry about drug use. Meanwhile, advances in the science and the technology of drug-testing devices made the process quicker and more efficient and thus more feasible to carry out on a mass scale. Arguably, workplace drug testing had its inaugural in 1986, when President Ronald Reagan ordered that government agencies drug-test employees who worked in jobs featuring a high risk of injury. This proclamation ushered in the age of employee drug testing, with drug testing in other arenas to follow (Crowley 1990, 123–139).

As with DWI policies, the use of such tests was questioned, largely by civil libertarians and some drug policy experts. They portrayed the tests as inaccurate and decried their intrusion into personal privacy, noting that the bodily fluids used could provide additional information about the person, from disease status to pregnancy. They also disputed the stated reasons for testing—ensuring safety—arguing that policies that addressed impairment of all kinds (from illicit to licit drugs to fatigue) would be more fruitful (Crowley 1990, 123–139).

How has workplace testing affected drug use? Data from one drug-testing laboratory show a decline in the number of workers testing positive for drugs, from 13.8 percent in 1988 to 4.5 percent in 2004 (Carpenter 2006, 795–810). A recent study argues that workplace tests do affect drug use generally, although less than is often presumed (Yamaguchi 2003).

Key Legal Decisions

Court challenges to DWI and drug-testing policies have resulted in a gradual redrawing of the line between individual freedom and government intrusion. Take, for instance, administrative suspensions, seen by some as a violation of due process, because one's license is taken away at the point of the DUI arrest. The Supreme Court in *Mackey v. Montrym* upheld these with the caveat that the person obtains a hearing shortly after the suspension (1979).

This opened the door to a more severe application of these laws; today, almost all states have laws using administrative suspension to punish the mere refusal to take a breath test (Insurance Institute for Highway Safety 2007). The Supreme Court in *Michigan Department of State Police v. Sitz* upheld sobriety checkpoints, which are effectively suspicionless searches (1990). They reasoned that rather than being a police action, checkpoints feature the state acting in its capacity to regulate public safety and thus are more akin to housing or restaurant inspections than crime fighting.

Regarding drug testing, the Supreme Court in *Skinner v. Railway Labor Executives' Association* ruled in 1989 that monitoring employees involved in "safety sensitive" positions was a state interest overriding the right of individuals not to have their persons (bodily fluids) seized (via drug test) without probable cause. The Court broadened its interpretation of the government's interest in the case of *National Treasury Employees Union v. Von Raab* to include concerns about customs workers facing promotion into positions that placed them at great risk, not for safety violations but for personal corruption owing to increased contact with drugs in large quantities (1989). These two cases were cited as precedent in upholding drug testing of students, first in *Vernonia School District v. Acton* (1995), in which random drug testing of student athletes was approved, and then in *Board of Education v. Earls* (2002), which gave the nod to a program in Oklahoma that randomly tested all students involved in extracurricular activities.

What is notable about these court decisions is the basis on which they were decided. Specifically, these policies were upheld as promoters of health and safety and on the basis of administrative rather than criminal justice considerations (Crowley 1990, 123–139). This is important, as it demonstrates a potential limit to the Court's reach regarding such policies. Evidence for this can be seen by the types of testing plans overturned by the Court, among them a hospital-based program that tested pregnant women, with positive results immediately provided to law enforcement for purposes of prosecution (*Ferguson v. City of Charleston* 2000), and a Georgia law that used drug testing as a condition for candidacy for local office (*Chandler v. Miller* 1997).

Drugged Driving

One topic that could loom large in future discussions of both DWI and drug-testing policy concerns the issue of drugged driving, or driving under the influence of drugs (DUID). Although it has a low prevalence rate (approximately 5 percent of those from a 2003 Substance Abuse and Mental Health Services Administration survey admitted to drugged driving, versus roughly 16 percent who admitted to DWI) (Substance Abuse and Mental Health Services Administration 2003), it has emerged as the next step in the evolution of concern over the negative effects of substance use. Recent attention speaks to a push to make drugged driving the next arena in the fight over automobile safety (Leinwand 2004; Armentano 2005).

Compared with the case for alcohol use, there is little science linking specific levels of drug use to impairment or to car accidents, making solutions to the drugged driving problem more difficult to enact. Most states have laws prohibiting DUID. Most define the offense based on actual impairment; however, several states define the offense based on per se grounds. There is potential for fresh court challenges based on the enforcement of those laws, particularly if authorities criminalize the presence of substances (marijuana metabolites, for instance) with no psychoactive impact whatsoever, as has been done in some cases.

Drugged driving is also important because it provides a friendly setting for the use of alternative—that is, non–urine based—drug-testing technologies, in particular those using saliva. Saliva tests have the potential to capture current intoxication and thus to indicate current impairment (Cone 1997). Some European countries have conducted

---

DID YOU KNOW?

According to the Institute of Behavior and Health, supported by data from the 2007 National Roadside Survey:

- Up to 20 percent of automobile crashes in the United States are caused by drugged driving. This translates into about 8,600 deaths, 580,000 injuries, and $33 billion in damages each year.
- Drugs are present more than seven times as often as alcohol among weekend nighttime drivers in the United States, with 16 percent of drivers testing positive for drugs compared with 2 percent testing at or above the legal limit for alcohol.

Source: "Drugged Driving: A National Priority." http://druggeddriving.org

---

evaluation studies of saliva tests for roadside testing of drugged drivers, with mixed success (Roadside Testing and Assessment). Because they are less intrusive than urine testing, such tests are very attractive for most drug-testing goals. Additionally, the technology can easily be converted for use in testing surfaces for the presence of drugs. Such devices are being evaluated for use in schools (McFarland 2006).

The increasing prominence of alternative testing comes in the context of a reduction in employer drug testing, possibly owing to concerns over cost. Some view the push for roadside testing as a cynical attempt to improve the flagging fortunes of the drug testing industry. Others have seen it as a possible boon to public safety. One thing does remain evident: conflicts over testing policies and the challenges they pose to individual freedom are far from over.

See also **Search Warrants; Addiction and Family (vol. 3); Drugs (vol. 3)**

Further Reading

Armentano, Paul, "Drug Test Nation." *Reason* (February 12, 2005). http://www.reason.com/news/show/32881.html

Board of Education v. Earls, 122 S.Ct. 2559 (2002).

Caetano, Raul, and Christine McGrath, "Driving while Intoxicated (DUI) among U.S. Ethnic Groups." *Accident Analysis and Prevention* 37 (2005): 217–224.

Carpenter, Christopher S., "Workplace Drug Testing and Worker Drug Use." *Health Services Research* 42, no. 2 (2006): 795–810.

Carruth, Bruce et al., *Assessment and Treatment of the DWI Offender.* New York: Routledge, 2002.

Centers for Disease Control and Prevention, "Impaired Driving Fact Sheet." 2009. http://www.cdc.gov/MotorVehicleSafety/Impaired_Driving/impaired-drv_factsheet.html

Chandler v. Miller, 520 U.S. 305 (1997).

Cone, E. J., "New Developments in Biological Measures of Drug Prevalence." In *The Validity of Self-Reported Drug Use: Improving the Accuracy of Survey Estimates,* NIDA Research Monograph 167, ed.

Lana Harrison and Arthur Hughes. Washington, DC: U.S. Department of Health and Human Services, 1997. http://www.nida.nih.gov/pdf/monographs/monograph167/108–129_Cone.pdf

Crowley, Donald W., "Drug Testing in the Rehnquist Era." In *Images of Issues: Typifying of Contemporary Social Problems,* ed. Joel Best. New York: Walter de Gruyter, 1990.

Ferguson v. City of Charleston, 532 U.S. 67 (2000).

Gusfield, Joseph, R., "The Control of Drinking and Driving in the United States: A Period in Transition." In *Social Control of the Drinking Driver,* ed. Michael D. Laurence, John R. Snortum, and Franklin E. Zimring. Chicago: University of Chicago Press, 1988.

Insurance Institute for Highway Safety, "DUI/DWI Laws." Insurance Institute for Highway Safety, Highway Loss Data Institute, 2007. http://www.iihs.org/laws/state_laws/dui.html

Jacobs, James, *Drunk Driving: An American Dilemma.* Chicago: University of Chicago Press, 1992.

Karch, Steven B., *Workplace Drug Testing.* Boca Raton, FL: CRC Press, 2007.

Laurence, Michael D., "The Legal Context in the United States." In *Social Control of the Drinking Driver,* ed. Michael D. Laurence, John R. Snortum, and Franklin E. Zimring. Chicago: University of Chicago Press, 1988.

Leinwand, Donna, "Growing Danger: Drugged Driving." *USA Today* (October 21, 2004). http://www.usatoday.com/news/nation/2004–10–21-cover-drugged-driving_x.htm

Mackey v. Montrym, 443 U.S. 1 (1979).

McFarland, Art, "A New Weapon to Detect Drugs in Schools." 7Online.com, *WABC-TV News.* November 13, 2006. http://abclocal.go.com/wabc/story?section=our_schools&id=4757591

Michigan Department of State Police v. Sitz, 496 U.S. 444 (1990).

National Highway Traffic Safety Administration (NHTSA), *Countermeasures That Work: A Highway Countermeasure Guide for State Highway Safety Offices.* Washington, DC: NHTSA, 2007.

National Treasury Employees Union v. Von Raab, 489 U.S. 656 (1989).

Roadside Testing and Assessment, http://www.rosita.org

Ross, H. Laurence, *Confronting Drunk Driving: Social Policy for Saving Lives.* New Haven, CT: Yale University Press, 1994.

Sawvel, Patty Jo, *Student Drug Testing.* Boston: Cengage Gale, 2006.

Skinner v. Railway Labor Executives' Association, 489 U.S. 602 (1989).

Substance Abuse and Mental Health Services Administration, *Driving under the Influence among Adult Drivers.* Rockville, MD: Center for Mental Health Services, Substance Abuse and Mental Health Services Administration, 2003. http://www.oas.samhsa.gov/2k5/DUI/DUI.pdf

U.S. Department of Health and Human Services, Office of Applied Studies, "Worker Drug Use and Workplace Policies and Programs: Results from the 1994 and 1997 National Household Survey on Drug Abuse" (2007). http://www.oas.samhsa.gov/NHSDA/A-11/WrkplcPlcy2–06.htm#P136_7936

Vernonia School District v. Acton, 515 U.S. 646 (1995).

Voas, Robert B., et al., "Drinking and Driving in the United States: The 1996 National Roadside Survey." *Accident Analysis and Prevention* 30 (1998): 267–275.

Woody, Robert Henley, *Search and Seizure: The Fourth Amendment for Law Enforcement Officers.* Springfield, IL: Charles C. Thomas, 2006.

Yamaguchi, Ryoko, Lloyd D. Johnston, and Patrick M. O'Malley, "Relationship between Student Illicit Drug Use and School Drug-Testing Policies." *Journal of School Health* 73 (2003): 159–164.

E

EXPERT WITNESS TESTIMONY

Allison M. Cotton

The purpose of expert witness testimony is to provide findings of fact for the decision-making process of semijudicial or judicial bodies or to provide the various courts of law with factual information on which to base a resolution, ruling, or verdict (Dorram 1982). The controversies surrounding the use of expert witnesses and expert testimony may revolve around issues such as whether experts may be abusing their power to influence the outcomes of adjudication, be providing better evidence than lay persons, or be speaking on matters relevant to cases that are outside of their expertise, but the controversies are not limited to these issues. Before an individual may be allowed to offer opinion testimony as an expert, however, it must be established not only that the subject of the opinion is proper for expert testimony but also that the individual offering the opinion is "a person skilled at touching the matter of inquiry" (Gothard 1989).

Expert testimony today is very much like a corrida, the traditional bullfight. It has precisely prescribed rituals. The beginning, which is the bailiff's opening statement to the public to rise upon the entrance of the judge, is like the music of the bullfight. The ending, like the dragging out of the bull by the mules, is the moment when the gavel is slammed down. In between, the expert witness is the bull in the arena. The various attorneys entitled to cross-examine will treat him or her exactly as a bull is treated—although in this case the pics, lances, and swords are metaphorical. Just as the traditional bullfight has established stages, so does the proper expert testimony. Stage 1 is the swearing in and identification of the witness, which is followed by stage 2, the statement and presentation of the witness's professional qualifications. If they are not accepted, that is the end of the testimony. The bull is dead; bring in the next bull (Dorram 1982, 4).

Background

The first documented forensic expert was Antistius, who was asked to examine Julius Caesar's corpse to determine the cause of his death (Meyer 1999). In his opinion, Antistius declared that only one of the 24 sword wounds he suffered actually caused Caesar's death and that it was the sword wound that perforated his thorax (Meyer 1999, 2). In the beginning, then, only medical experts were allowed to provide expert testimony, and then only related to their specific field of practice, such as chemistry, biology, or psychiatry. In fact, experts, specifically medical experts, have been used in English courts since the 14th century and in the common law courts of North America for more than 200 years (Meyer 1999). Since the mid-1980s, social workers have been recognized by courts as having sufficient expertise in several fields of practice and, subsequently, have been qualified as experts in courts of law (Gothard 1989).

Legal Developments

The Federal Rules of Evidence (FRE), the Frye test, and the *Daubert* guidelines form the basis for determining the admissibility of expert medical or scientific testimony (McHenry et al. 2005). Although the FRE are meant to be applied to federal court proceedings, many state courts have adopted them as a guide for dealing with expert witness testimony. Various sections of the FRE outline the "knowledge, skill, experience, training or education" levels required of experts and allow for judicial discretion in determining who constitutes an expert witness and whether the testimony is relevant to jury deliberations (McHenry et al. 2005). Besides, expert testimony must be based on information that is generally accepted in the scientific community, according to *Frye v. United States* (1923), in which the court decided that a technique used for performing a lie detector test must be "generally accepted within the scientific community before expert opinion about data gained from use of the technique is admissible into evidence" (see *Frye v. United States* 1923). The Frye test, then, is used as the legal basis for judges to exclude expert testimony based on information, principles, or opinion not falling within those parameters.

In 1993, the U.S. Supreme Court provided guidelines for expert witnesses in the federal court case of *Daubert v. Merrell Dow Pharmaceuticals, Inc.* when it ruled that expert testimony should be based on information that has been subjected to the scientific method rather than on unsupported speculation (see *Daubert v. Merrell Dow Pharmaceuticals Inc.* 1993). The court also directed trial judges to determine whether expert testimony is relevant and based on valid scientific evidence (*Daubert v. Merrell Dow Pharmaceuticals Inc.* 1993). Further, the Court gave its support to the FRE guidelines, which permit judges to appoint their own independent expert witnesses. In so doing,

FEDERAL RULES OF EVIDENCE

- FRE 702: Authorizes judges to allow the admission of expert testimony when it "will assist the trier of fact to understand the evidence or determine a fact in issue." Under this rule, a witness may be classified as an expert on the basis of knowledge, skill, experience, training, or education.
- FRE 703: Permits an expert to base his or her opinion on information "perceived or made known to him or her at or before the hearing" and establishes that a qualified expert's testimony should be based upon information or data reasonably relied upon by experts in the particular field forming opinions or references on the subject.
- FRE 704: Provides the basis for allowing an expert to offer an opinion on ultimate factual issues, namely, causality.
- FRE 705: Permits an expert witness to offer an opinion "without prior disclosure of the underlying facts or data (on which the opinion is based) unless the court requires otherwise." This rule establishes that the expert witness "may in any event be required to disclose underlying facts or data on cross examination."
- FRE 706: Gives judges the authority to appoint their own independent expert witness to ensure that the expert testimony is relevant and scientifically valid.

Source: Christopher R. McHenry, Walter L. Biffl, William C. Chapman, and David A. Spain, "Expert Witness Testimony: The Problem and Recommendations for Oversight and Reform." *Surgery* 137, no. 3 (2005): 275.

the Court proclaimed that an expert witness must be able to determine the relevant facts of a case, define the standard of care for management of a specific problem, determine whether a physician's action conformed or deviated from the standard of care, and assess the relationship between the alleged substandard care and the patient's outcome (McHenry et al. 2005, 275). The problem with this standard of application, according to Christopher McHenry, is that "very little constraint is applied to the testimony of an expert, often giving him or her inordinate latitude to comment on things that are outside his or her area of expertise" (McHenry et al. 2005, 276). Once the expert has been qualified as such, then the person on the stand, under oath, is allowed to expound upon various topics and issues relevant to the trial, oftentimes without having any brakes applied to his or her utterances, in part because the expert testimony becomes a performance that is not unlike a regular stage performance. What the expert must convey in the course of the performance is that he or she is indeed an expert and that his or her opinion should be taken seriously (Dorram 1982, 51).

Controversies in Expert Witness Testimony

Problems with expert witnesses and expert witness testimony have included the fact that some experts have been allowed not only to testify about medical facts but also to offer opinions about material issues of the criminal trial. Their opinions may influence decisions involving criminal sentencing or involuntary commitment, for example (Faust and Ziskin 1988). The issue here becomes whether some experts have abused the power to be able to influence the outcome of trials and have turned the criminal trial into a kind of "legalized gamble" (Meyer 1999, 3), particularly because, when judgments have rested on common sense or stereotypes rather than empirical knowledge, professionals have not been shown to outperform lay persons in terms of accuracy; that is, studies show that professional clinicians do not in fact make more accurate clinical judgments than laypersons (Faust and Ziskin 1988, 34).

Another issue that complicates the use of expert testimony is the interrelated specialties that have arisen in the medical field such that experts can defer endlessly to colleagues who possess more specialized knowledge of the issue at bar.

Whereas 50 years ago medicine was still primarily an art rather than a science, medicine is now interlinked with a plethora of technical and scientific occupations. The proliferation of information and specialties has become such that large health care providers now employ specialists in primary care and farm out patients for further specialized treatment. In fact, some specialties have become so compartmentalized that surgeons, chemotherapists, and radiation specialists no longer feel comfortable weighing the advantages of competing treatment modalities for certain types of diseases, such as cancer of the uterus or prostate gland (Meyer 1999, 3).

Additionally, there is some concern over the rather subjective nature of expert testimony, not only because testimony by a so-called expert is often allowed by judges even though other physicians or scientists do not regard the individual's credentials as those of an expert in a particular field (McHenry et al. 2005, 276) but also because the perception exists that an expert can be found to support any point of view as long as the financial compensation is right (McHenry et al. 2005, 276). Moreover, there is no peer review of expert witness testimony to ensure its merit or validity (McHenry et al. 2005, 276). These and other problems not mentioned here contribute to increasing skepticism about the veracity and reliability of expert witness testimony.

Moreover, judges and juries are not bound by expert witness testimony; the jury members (and the trial judge) are free to accept or reject the expert's testimony in whole or in part (Gutheil 1998). Attorneys, therefore, must base the decision of whether to offer expert testimony on the likelihood of that expert being able to connect with the jury—that is, to leave an impression that is favorable to winning the verdict. Jury instructions do not require members to heed the advice of experts; in fact, some jury instructions encourage jurors to exercise their own judgment as to whether to believe or include the opinions of experts in their deliberations.

There is also some evidence to suggest that jurors use intuition, credentials, and mannerisms to determine the veracity of expert witness testimony. Put another way, there is nothing to prevent jurors from using their gut feelings about an expert, the prestige of the institutions from which the expert graduated, or the appearance of the expert on the stand

CRIME LAB ANALYSTS AS EXPERT WITNESSES

Until a U.S. Supreme Court ruling in 2009, *Melendez-Diaz v. Massachusetts*, it was common practice for prosecutors in criminal cases to submit data from crime labs in support of their cases without calling as witnesses the scientists who prepared those data. Under the *Melendez-Diaz* ruling, however, crime lab analysts are required to appear in court and submit to cross-examination.

The decision states that forensic analysts must testify under the Sixth Amendment Confrontation Clause granting defendants the right to confront witnesses against them. Previously analysts could be subpoenaed to court to explain their reports or methodology, but in practice that rarely happened.

In his majority opinion, Justice Antonin Scalia refuted the argument that forensic reports consist of neutral facts. As Scalia observed, "Forensic evidence is not uniquely immune from the risk of manipulation. . . . Confrontation is designed to weed out not only the fraudulent analyst, but the incompetent one as well. Serious deficiencies have been found in the forensic evidence used in criminal trials." Thus, as with expert witnesses generally, an analyst's bona fides or professional judgment may be questioned in cross-examination.

In his dissenting opinion, Justice Anthony M. Kennedy strongly opposed the majority's interpretation of the Confrontation Clause, claiming that the Court had carelessly brushed aside a century of precedent for dealing with scientific evidence. "The Confrontation Clause is not designed, and does not serve, to detect errors in scientific tests." Justice Kennedy asserts. "That should instead be done by conducting a new test. Or, if a new test is impossible, the defendant may call his own expert to explain to the jury the test's flaws and the dangers of relying on it. And if, in an extraordinary case, the particular analyst's testimony is necessary to the defense, then, of course, the defendant may subpoena the analyst."

It was expected that the ruling would create a significant backlog in cases handled by crime labs, as analysts undertake to prepare formal testimony to justify their research results in court.

Sources: Rebecca Waters. "Supreme Court Ruling Requires Crime Lab Analysts to Testify." *Forensic Magazine* (July 1, 2009), http://www.forensicmag.com/News_Articles.asp?pid= 595; Jennifer E. Laurin. "*Melendez-Diaz v. Massachusetts, Rodriguez v. Houston,* and Remedial Rationing." *Columbia Law Review Sidebar* 109/82 (August 18, 2009), http://www. columbialawreview.org/articles/i-melendez-diaz-v-massachusetts-i-i-rodriguez-v-city-of-houston-i-and-remedial-rationing

to determine the veracity of the expert's testimony even though these supposed markers of accuracy are potentially prejudicial (Faust and Ziskin 1988). In fact, some evidence suggests that jurors tend to ignore the expert testimony presented on the stand during the trial and, instead, choose to use their own life experiences or common sense to determine guilt or innocence. In such cases, the expert's efforts to persuade may well succeed if it aligns more closely with common belief (Faust and Ziskin 1988).

When asked about the defense's case, one juror said: "I think they tried to prove that he was mentally incapable of understanding what he was doing and brain damaged…which didn't have any effect on me because I know that you can get psychiatrists to argue anything because it's not an exact science." And another juror concluded that "the defense had to show much and they did a good job. We just didn't buy it" (Cotton 2002, 234).

Several efforts to reform the expert witness process have been undertaken in recent decades (between 1987 and 1998) by respected medical organizations; specifically, the American Academy of Pediatrics, the American Academy of Neurologic Surgeons, the American Academy of Orthopedic Surgeons, and the American Medical Association have published guidelines and/or passed resolutions that subject expert witnessing to peer review and disciplinary sanctions (McHenry et al. 2005, 276). In 2004, the American College of Surgeons issued a statement that includes recommended qualifications and guidelines for behavior of the physician who acts as an expert witness (American College of Surgeons 2004, 22–23). In support of the effort to maintain the integrity of expert witnessing, the Collaborative Defense Network for Expert Witness Research, founded in 1984, collects information on and researches the background of expert witnesses (http://www.idex.com). The company offers a wide range of expert witness services, such as testimonial history searches, trial depositions and transcripts, state license discipline searches, and articles by the expert, among others.

Conclusion

In the final analysis, there is much to be said about the need for expert witness testimony in this age of complicated medicine and science. If the jury cannot tell sanity from insanity based on their own experience, for example, then persons must guide them with special expertise in the recognition of this hidden condition (Freemon 2001). Only trained experts can separate the individual who is insane in a partial way, or only with regard to certain subjects, from the normal person (Freemon 2001, 361). Nevertheless, it is expected that the same types of controversial issues surrounding the use of expert witness testimony will persist into the future.

See also **DNA Usage in Criminal Justice; Eyewitness Identification; Insanity Defense**

Further Reading

American College of Surgeons, "Statement on the Physician Activity as an Expert Witness." *Bulletin of the American College of Surgeons* 89, no. 3 (2004): 22–23. http://www.facs.org/fellows_info/statements/st-8.html

Bronstein, Daniel A., *Law and the Expert Witness*, 3d ed. Boca Raton, FL: CRC Press, 2007.

Candilis, Philip J., Robert Weinstock, and Richard Martinez, *Forensic Ethics and the Expert Witness.* New York: Springer 2007.

Cotton, Allison, "Who Is This Defendant? A Study of Capital Punishment and the Effort to Attribute Personality." Ph.D. dissertation, University of Colorado at Boulder, 2002.

Daubert v. Merrell Dow Pharmaceuticals Inc., 509 U.S. 579, 593–7 (1993).

Dorram, Peter B., *The Expert Witness*. Chicago: American Planning Association, 1982.

Faust, David, and Jay Ziskin, "The Expert Witness in Psychology and Psychiatry." *Science* 241, no. 4861 (1988): 31–35.

Fisher, Jim, *Forensics under Fire: Are Bad Science and Dueling Experts Corrupting Criminal Justice?* New Brunswick, NJ: Rutgers University Press, 2008.

Freemon, Frank R., "The Origin of the Medical Expert Witness." *Journal of Legal Medicine* 22 (2001): 349–373.

Frye v. United States, 293 F. 1013. (D.C. Cir. 1923).

Gothard, Sol, "Power in the Court: The Social Worker as an Expert Witness." *Social Work* 34, no. 1 (1989): 65–67.

Gutheil, Thomas G., *The Psychiatrist as Expert Witness*. Washington, DC: American Psychiatric Press, 1998.

Harris, Rebecca C., *Black Robes, White Coats: The Puzzle of Judicial Policymaking and Scientific Evidence*. New Brunswick, NJ: Rutgers University Press, 2008.

McHenry, Christopher R., et al., "Expert Witness Testimony: The Problem and Recommendations for Oversight and Reform." *Surgery* 137, no. 3 (2005): 274–278.

Meyer, Carl, ed., *Expert Witnessing: Explaining and Understanding Science*. Boca Raton, FL: CRC Press, 1999.

Sales, Bruce Dennis, *Experts in Court: Reconciling Law, Science, and Professional Knowledge*. Washington, DC: American Psychological Association, 2005.

EYEWITNESS IDENTIFICATION

Allison M. Cotton

Eyewitness identifications are an important component of U.S. criminal investigation, particularly in those phases of the trial process involving evidence, prosecution, and plea negotiation (Sporer, Malpass, and Koehnken 1996). In fact, evidence provided by eyewitnesses is sometimes the only evidence linking a suspect to a crime (Sporer, Malpass, and Koehnken 1996). For that reason, eyewitness identifications are controversial because, although some witnesses may be confident about their description of a suspect, there are inherent witness-based problems in face-recall techniques, which may limit the ultimate effectiveness of most systems in current use (Sporer, Malpass, and Koehnken 1996). Moreover, from the point of view of criminal investigation, accurate face recall is of considerable importance, not only because the penalties for crime in the United States range from probation to death but also because show ups, lineups, and photo arrays rely solely on the accuracy of face recall to build a case.

Eyewitness *mis*identification is the single most significant factor behind wrongful convictions in the United States. According to the Innocence Project, it has played a role in over 75 percent of convictions that subsequently were overturned on the basis of DNA evidence (Innocence Project).

Issues involving eyewitness testimony, specifically the reliability of eyewitness testimony, can be divided into two categories: (1) errors in describing the actual event and (2) errors in describing the persons involved. Problems in the latter category focus primarily on eyewitness identification of suspects that necessitates a reliance on face-recall data to connect the specific characteristics of suspects' faces with the events of a crime.

Face Recall

Generally speaking, people tend to process faces holistically. This means that the faces we encounter form an impression in our minds that incorporates the major details of the faces as well as where the specific features on a face are configured to make a person look the way that he or she appears to us in our recollection. The width of a person's face, the length of the nose, as well as the distance between a person's eyes, for example, are processed together as a combination of features that is then recorded as an image taking into account the relationship of the features to one another. In a recognition task, witnesses are presented with a target and search their store of faces until a response of familiarity is evoked. Such familiarity can easily be confused with recall from the actual features of the person who was viewed at the crime scene.

The task of face recall is generally much more difficult than that of recognizing faces, and this difficulty may well be exacerbated by techniques that require the witness to select items from a set of pictorial illustrations and assemble them into a picture of a whole face. The two aspects of the task—decomposition of a holistic image into elements and visual scrutiny of pictorial elements—may each interfere with the witness's ability to maintain a visual image of the face she or he is trying to recall (Innocence Project).

Therefore eyewitness identifications must be viewed cautiously (Terry 1994).

A Case Study

Jennifer Thompson (Doyle 2005), the first victim in the court's narrative, is blonde and tiny, five feet tall, weighing 100 pounds. She speaks quietly and ends her sentences with the rising, interrogative lilt characteristic of girls raised in the South. It is easy to see the traces of her upbringing as the adored daughter of suburban North Carolina business executives.

But it is easy to see something else in Jennifer's interview, too: the iron resolve with which she survived her attack and pursued her attacker and the unflinching honesty with which she is determined to tell the story of the assault and its aftermath. During the rape, her mind was racing:

At that point, I realized that I was going to be raped and I didn't know if this was going to be the end, if he was going to kill me, if he was going to hurt me and I decided that what I needed to do was outsmart him. Throughout the evening, I would turn on lights, even if it was just for a second, and he would tell me, "Turn the lights off." And at one point, he bent down and turned on my stereo and a blue light came off of the stereo and it shone right up to his face and... and I was able to look at that. When I went into the bathroom, I turned the light on and he immediately told me to shut it off, but it was just long enough for me to think, "Okay, his nose looks this way" or "His shirt is navy blue, not black," little, brief pieces of light that I could piece together as much as I could piece together.

Jennifer escaped to a neighbor's house and was taken to a local hospital emergency room, where a rape kit was prepared. There, she was interviewed for the first time by Burlington police captain Mike Gauldin. The qualities that strike a viewer watching Jennifer's interview struck Detective Gauldin during their initial encounter: "She was so determined during the course of the sexual assault to look at her assailant well, to study him well enough so that, if given an opportunity later, she would be able to identify her assailant," Gauldin remembered. "A lot of victims are so traumatized, so overcome with fear during the course of the sexual assault itself, that it's unusual to find somebody that's capable of having that presence of mind."

Gauldin asked Jennifer to help a police artist prepare a composite drawing of the rapist. That drawing was widely circulated, and it generated an anonymous tip. An informant

INTERVIEWING EYEWITNESSES AT THE SCENE

The U.S. Department of Justice provides guidelines on working with eyewitnesses from the point of the first phone call regarding an incident to the conduct of the suspect lineup and other procedures. For example, law enforcement officers performing a preliminary investigation following the report of an incident are advised to:

1. Establish rapport with the eyewitness.
2. Inquire about the witness's condition.
3. Use open-ended questions (e.g., "What can you tell me about the car?"); augment with closed-ended questions (e.g., "What color was the car?").
4. Clarify the information received with the witness.
5. Document the information received from the witness, including the witness's identity, in a written report.
6. Encourage the witness to contact investigators with any further information.
7. Encourage the witness to avoid contact with the media or exposure to media accounts concerning the incident.
8. Instruct the witness to avoid discussing details of the incident with other potential witnesses.

Source: U.S. Department of Justice, *Eyewitness Evidence: A Guide to Law Enforcement.* http://www.ncjrs.gov/pdffiles1/nij/178240.pdf

provided Gauldin with the name of a man with a criminal record, a man who worked at Somer's Seafood Restaurant in the neighborhood of Jennifer's apartment, a black man with a habit of touching white waitresses and teasing them about sex. The caller said the man owned a blue shirt similar to the shirt Jennifer had seen on the night of the rape. Gauldin placed that man's photograph in an array of six individual mug shots of black men and asked Jennifer whether she recognized anyone. The composition of the array was fair, and no one stood out unduly. Gauldin played it straight: He made no effort to prompt Jennifer or tip her off to his suspect. Jennifer remembers her photo identification this way: "It didn't take me very long. It took me minutes to come to my conclusion. And then I chose the photo of Ronald Cotton. After I picked it out, they looked at me and they said, 'We thought this might be the one,' because he had a prior conviction of the same… same type of circumstances sort of."

Armed with Jennifer's identification, Gauldin obtained a search warrant and set out to arrest Ronald Cotton. Cotton was not at home, but Gauldin did find two pieces of evidence in Cotton's room: a red flashlight like one described by the second rape victim and a shoe with a foam insert consistent with foam found on the floor at Jennifer's apartment. When Cotton heard about Gauldin's search, he turned himself in at the police station "to clear things up." Cotton gave Gauldin an alibi, but his alibi did not check out. Gauldin arranged to have Cotton stand in a live lineup.

Jennifer methodically examined the line of six black men arrayed across the front of a room at police headquarters. "They had to do the steps to the right, to the left, and then turn around," she recalled. "And then they were instructed to do a voice presentation to me. They had to say some of the lines that the rapist had said to me that night so I could hear the voice, because the voice was a very distinct voice."

Jennifer narrowed her choices to the man wearing number 4 and Ronald Cotton, who was wearing number 5. She had the police put the lineup members through their routine again. Then she was sure: "It's number 5," she said. Later, Gauldin explained what had happened: "That's the same guy. I mean, that's the one you picked out in the photo."

"For me," Jennifer remembered "that was a huge amount of relief, not that I had picked the photo, but that I was sure when I looked at the photo that [it] was him and when I looked at the physical lineup I was sure it was him." She was still sure when she testified in court and identified Ronald Cotton.

She was just as sure when she faced Cotton again, in a second trial ordered by the North Carolina Supreme Court. There was a new challenge this time. Cotton's lawyers had pursued inmate rumors that the Burlington rapes actually had been committed by a convict named Bobby Poole. At Cotton's second trial, Poole was brought into court and shown to Jennifer. Jennifer did not flinch then either. "I thought," she told *Frontline*, "Oh, this is just a game. This is a game they're playing." It was not Poole, Jennifer told the jurors, "I have never seen him in my life." She told them it was Cotton. At the second trial, the other Burlington victim testified for the first time, and she also positively identified

Cotton. Cotton was convicted again, and Jennifer was elated. "It was one of the happiest days of my life," she recalled. Now she knew for certain that Cotton was never going to get out. She had forced herself to go through two trials; she had picked the right man; she had her justice. "I was sure as I can be," she remembers.

But Jennifer Thompson was wrong. The second Burlington victim was wrong. Mike Gauldin and the Burlington police, despite their conscientious, by-the-book investigation, were wrong. The 24 jurors who in two separate trials had convicted Ronald Cotton were wrong.

Procedural Issues between Cops and Prosecutors

Mistaken identifications are not uncommon in our system of justice. The police actually see lots of misidentification during criminal investigations. In fact, witnesses—20 to 25 percent in one survey—routinely identify fillers in photo arrays or lineups. These confident but mistaken witnesses never make it to the prosecutors because their cases are screened out, but they are a regular feature of an investigator's life. The prosecutors, by contrast, seldom see a case unless the police have a solid identification and something to corroborate it (Doyle 2005). For that reason, it can be said that the police are primarily responsible for the outcome of eyewitness identifications and consequently take great care to make sure that the procedures for conducting show ups, photo arrays, and lineups are closely followed. Contrarily, anything resembling standardized procedures represents a potential danger for prosecutors because defense lawyers are viewed as being eager to pounce on any deviation from the new standard procedures (Doyle 2005). Although following routine procedures may be a fundamental part of police culture, it may sometimes place an extra burden on prosecutors, who want to be able to exercise their judgment in preparing a case for trial. It has therefore been argued that the science of memory must count in police stations and courtrooms (Doyle 2005), not only to alleviate the perils of mistaken identifications based on poor processes, but also to ensure the accuracy of prosecution.

The Science of Memory

In 1975, Lavrakas and Bickman found that in a study of 54 prosecuting attorneys in a large metropolitan community, "an eyewitness identification and the victim's memory of the incident (which is also an eyewitness account) are far more important than any other characteristics a witness possesses, such as age, race, or level of income" (Loftus 1996, 12). Lavrakas and Bickman interpreted the prosecutors' responses to mean that having a witness who could recall events accurately was absolutely crucial to the just resolution of criminal cases. The likeableness of the witness as well as his or her appearance and presentation on the stand during the trial were also shown to influence the perception of credibility. Most important, however, was the ability of the witness to portray confidence on the stand as well as to give an accurate description of events that could not be easily influenced when the added pressure of cross-examination was applied by the defense. Indeed, this is a difficult task, because defense lawyers are sometimes very well trained in cross-examination techniques that can lead to inconsistent results, particularly when small details of events are challenged over long periods of time.

When we experience an important event, we do not simply record that event in memory as a videotape recorder would. The situation is much more complex. Nearly all of the theoretical analyses of the process divide it into three stages. First, there is the *acquisition* stage—the perception of the original event—in which information is encoded, laid down, or entered into a person's memory system. Second, there is the *retention* stage, the period of time that passes between the event and the eventual recollection of a particular piece of information. Third, there is the *retrieval* stage, during which a person recalls stored information. This three-stage analysis is so central to the concept of the human memory that it is virtually universally accepted among psychologists (Loftus 1996).

In sum, once the information associated with an event has been encoded or stored in memory, some of it may remain there unchanged whereas some may not.

Background

The three most common types of eyewitness identifications, all of which offer their own relative advantages and disadvantages to criminal investigations occurring in the United States, are among several techniques for identifying suspects that law enforcement officials use to buttress their case for arrest. First, lineups of the sort that appear in popular movies and television shows depicting a suspect who is escorted into a room with three to five supposedly similar-looking people to stand before a witness to a crime have routinely been scrutinized owing to the questionable similarity of the participants' physical characteristics. In *Martin v. Indiana* (1977), for example, in which the description of the suspect was that of a tall 32-year-old African American, only 2 out of 12 people in the lineup were African American and one of them was only five feet three inches tall.

Second, photo lineups in which eyewitnesses attempt to identify suspects from an array of photographs are not generally considered as reliable as live lineups owing to the variable quality of the photos. Photo arrays continue to be used because of the diversity of treatments available to the administrators of the photo lineups, such as adding additional photos to the lineup so that the witness must choose from an array of numerous photos as opposed to the numeric limitations of a live lineup. Also, additional photos of the actual suspect can be added to the photo array in varying poses and with various ornamentation, such as with or without a beard or glasses. Still, issues arise with the fairness of such techniques where justice is concerned because, for example, when a suspect appeared in 14 of 38 photos, a New Jersey court ruled, in *State v. Madison* (1988), that the photo array was impermissibly suggestive (*State v. Henderson* 1988).

Finally, police usually arrange show ups when they present a single suspect to a witness and ask, "Is he the one who raped you?" Show ups have been criticized for inherent prejudice owing to the nature of the show up, because they usually happen immediately after the crime, and some witnesses may view the fact that the police have apprehended the person as a sign that the person is guilty of the crime. The U.S. Supreme Court, however, has not ruled that this procedure constitutes a constitutional due process violation if there is additional reason to believe that the suspect is in fact the guilty party. Some state courts, however, as in the case of *People v. Guerea* (1974), have routinely ruled that show ups violate due process. In short, mistaken identification was observed to be the major source of error contributing to wrongful convictions in recent years (Sporer, Malpass, and Koehnken 1996).

A Key Moment

Hugo Muensterberg is credited with having performed one of the earliest experimental demonstrations of eyewitness misidentification in Berlin in 1902 when, as a college professor, he staged a fight between students during a lecture. It was so arranged that one of the actors appeared to have shot another with a pistol. Students attending the lecture were asked to write down their account of the fight immediately following the event, but only 26 percent of the students were able to give somewhat accurate details, and even those presented some erroneous facts, such as nonattributed and misattributed language and actions (Muensterberg 1908).

Important Persons and Legal Decisions

Three landmark cases that first established constitutional parameters regarding eyewitness identification in criminal trials established procedural standards: (1) In *United States v. Wade* (1967), the Supreme Court held that because a postindictment lineup is a "critical stage" of prosecution, the defendant had a right to have an attorney present (*United States v. Wade* 1967). (2) *Gilbert v. California* (1967) augmented the ruling set forth in *Wade* by holding that "a per se exclusionary rule as to such testimony can be an effective sanction to assure that law enforcement authorities will respect the accused person's constitutional right to the presence of his counsel at the critical lineup" (*Gilbert v. California* 1967). And (3) *Stovall v. Denno* (1967) created a standard whereby the identification procedure may not be "so unnecessarily suggestive and conducive to irreparable mistaken identification that [the suspect is] denied due process of law."

Additional challenges to the procedures set forth by the Supreme Court standards have questioned the constitutionality of eyewitness identifications based primarily on the Sixth Amendment right to counsel. Arguments for Sixth Amendment protection, for example, suggest that suspects are entitled to an attorney if identification occurs at a preliminary hearing, even before the indictment, but not if the identification is conducted as a part of an on-the-scene show up. Besides, it is well known that although states may increase rights provided by the Constitution (including the Sixth Amendment), states cannot decrease its protections. Pennsylvania, for example, requires an attorney at all postarrest lineups, and Tennessee provides the right to counsel as soon as an arrest warrant is issued. New York even requires the presence of an attorney if a suspect wants to waive his or her right to counsel as an added protection for the validity of the waiver (Sporer, Malpass, and Koehnken 1996). To that end, "The vast majority of eyewitness identification cases have been decided on due process grounds" (Sobel 1988, 110).

It should also be noted that *Neil v. Biggers* (1972) outlined the following five witness factors to be used in considering whether the defendant's due process rights have been violated: (1) opportunity of the witness to view the criminal at the time of the crime, (2) the witness's degree of attention, (3) the accuracy of the witness's prior descriptions, (4) the witness's level of certainty, and (5) the time lapse from the crime to the identification (*Neil v. Biggers* 1972). Opportunity to view can involve factors such as whether the crime and the identification occurred in daylight, as well as the distance and time duration within which the crime occurred. The case of *Gilliard v. LaVallee* (1974) provided the foundation for considering time duration in eyewitness identifications because, in that case, the kidnap victims were able to view their captors for up to six hours (*Gilliard v. LaVallee* 1974). Similarly, the degree of attention paid by eyewitnesses to the crime at the time that it occurred can be said to influence the credibility of eyewitness identifications. Attention is high when undercover officers are making a drug deal (*State v. Denny* 1984), for example, but low when an assailant awakens a victim during an incident (*People v. Leonard* 1978). Prior descriptions may cause inconsistency and may not be allowed in trial proceedings in cases where a witness provides a physical description of a suspect at the scene of a crime by height and weight, for example, but it is later determined that the height and weight of the suspect are significantly different from what the witness first reported.

Although it is commonly agreed that certainty is ascertained with the traditional standard set forth in *Neil v. Biggers,* "that a confident witness is an accurate witness" (Sporer, Malpass, and Koehnken 1996), there is some evidence to suggest that the relative certainty with which a witness identifies a suspect cannot, in fact, be correlated with the degree of accuracy. For example, time lapse can greatly influence the degree of accuracy regardless of the degree of confidence displayed by witnesses. Generally, there is no due process violation based on the length of time lapse between the event and the identification, but the accuracy of identifications has not been shown to increase with time; for example, two years did not present a problem to the New Hampshire court in *State v. Cross* (1986).

Still, other factors may also influence eyewitness identification, such as unconscious transference, which usually occurs when a person actually seen in an unrelated place or context is mistakenly identified as the offender in an eyewitness identification procedure. Also, identifications made by people in some occupations, such as college professors

(*Plummer v. State* 1980), lawyers (*Robinson v. State* 1985), and security guards (*Royce v. Moore* 1972) are sometimes viewed by trial participants as being more credible.

Conclusion

In 2001, New Jersey became the first state with guidelines strongly recommending that police use a sequential method of photo identification rather than displaying an array of photos of suspects (Harry 2001). Studies have shown that the new method, which does not allow witnesses to compare mug shots side by side, drastically cuts the number of mistaken identifications. Based primarily on a U.S. Justice Department study commissioned in 1999, the results of which showed that many cases overturned with DNA evidence relied heavily on witness identifications of suspects, the push for the sequential method came from law enforcement officials rather than persons who had been wrongly convicted or their advocates (Harry 2001). Further, there has been opposition to the variability with which many police departments around the country process eyewitness identifications; for that reason, it has been argued that the problem of misidentification can be avoided by scripting data collection with police departments (Wells and Olson 2003). In addition, conditions are being found in which eyewitness certainty might be more closely related to eyewitness identification accuracy than was once thought, especially when external influences on eyewitness certainty are minimized; but the difficulty of exploring that relationship remains because of a perceived disconnect between social science and policing. Police records, for example, do not distinguish between eyewitnesses who make identifications of a filler and those who make no identifications, which can result in a serious underestimation of the rate of filler identifications (Wells and Olson 2003).

Finally, in a law review article published in 2002, Dori Lynn Yob suggested that the problems with a state-by-state approach point to a broader solution: the adoption of mandatory, uniform, nationwide standards (Yob 2002). She goes on to argue that such a broad set of standards would be most effectively implemented through a U.S. Supreme Court decision and proposes that the following changes be made: (1) The witness should be instructed prior to the lineup that the perpetrator may or may not be present and that he or she should not feel pressured to make an identification. (2) The composition of the lineup should not cause a suspect to stand out unduly. (3) Fillers in the lineup should be chosen to fit the eyewitness's initial description of the culprit rather than to resemble the suspect. (4) When there is more than one witness, a different lineup should be created for each witness, with only the suspect remaining the same. (5) Lineups should always be conducted by someone unconnected to the case who does not know the identity of the suspect. (6) Mock witnesses should be used to test the neutrality of each lineup, and blank lineups should always be used. (7) Sequential lineups should always be used. And (8) lineups should always be videotaped.

In Yob's view, "uniform nationwide guidelines would likely have an impact on the amount of erroneous eyewitness evidence because the guidelines would help attorneys identify and object to faulty identification procedures," and "a critical look at the problems with eyewitness identification evidence should be included in the curriculum of certain high school and college classes"(Yob 2002), not only because students at the high school level are more likely to incorporate the education into civic duties they learn to fulfill as they develop but also because most people do not attend college. For that reason, we are more likely to capture the hearts and minds of the young people in high school today before they become the jurors, judges, and police of tomorrow.

See also **DNA Usage in Criminal Justice; Expert Witness Testimony; Miscarriages of Justice**

Legal Citations

Gilbert v. California, 388 U.S. 263; 87. S. Ct. (1967).

Gilliard v. LaVallee, 376 F. Supp. 205. (S.D. N.Y., 1974).

Martin v. Indiana, 438 F. Supp. 234. (N.D. Ind., 1977).

Neil v. Biggers, 409 U.S. 188. (1972).

People v. Guerea, 78 Misc. 2d 907, 358 N.Y.S. 2d 925.

People v. Leonard, 66 A.D.2d 805, 410 N.Y.S. 2d 885. (1978).

Plummer v. State, 270 Ark. 11, 603 S.W.2d 402. (1980).

Robinson v. State, 473 So.2d 957 Miss. (1985).

Royce v. Moore, 469 F.2d 808. (1st Cir., 1972).

State v. Cross, 128 N.H. 732, 519A.2d 272. (1986).

State v. Denny, 350 N.W.2d 25. (N.D., 1984).

State v. Henderson, 109 N.J. 223, 536 A.2d 254. (1988).

Stovall v. Denno, 388 U.S. 293; 87 S. Ct. (1967).

United States v. Wade, 388 U.S. 218; 87 S. Ct. (1967).

Further Reading

Cutler, Brian, and Margaret Bull Kovera, *Evaluating Eyewitness Identification.* New York: Oxford University Press, 2010.

Doyle, James M., *True Witness: Cops, Courts, Science, and the Battle against Misidentification.* New York: Palgrave Macmillan, 2005.

Harry, Jennifer L., "DNA Evidence Changes Identification Methods." *Corrections Today* 63, no. 6 (2001): 3–5.

Innocence Project, "Eyewitness Misidentification." http://innocenceproject.org/understand/Eye witness-Misidentification.php

Loftus, Elizabeth F., *Eyewitness Testimony.* Cambridge, MA: Harvard University Press, 1996.

Muensterberg, H., *On the Witness Stand: Essays on Psychology and Crime.* New York: Doubleday, 1908.

Rossmo, D. Kim, *Criminal Investigative Failures*. Boca Raton, FL: CRC Press, 2008.

Sobel, N. R., *Eyewitness Identification: Legal and Practical Problems*. New York: Clark Boardman, 1988.

Sporer, Siegfried Ludwig, Roy S. Malpass, and Guenter Koehnken, eds., *Psychological Issues in Eyewitness Identification*. Mahwah, NJ: Erlbaum, 1996.

Terry, Roger L., "Effects of Facial Transformations on Accuracy of Recognition." *Journal of Social Psychology* 134, no. 4 (1994): 483–489.

Wells, Gary L., and Elizabeth A. Olson, "Eyewitness Testimony." *Annual Review of Psychology* 19 (2003): 277–296.

Yob, Dori Lynn, "Mistaken Identifications Cause Wrongful Convictions: New Jersey's Lineup Guidelines Restore Hope, but Are They Enough?" *Santa Clara Law Review* 43 (2002): 213.

G

GANG INJUNCTION LAWS

Rebecca Romo and Xuan Santos

Throughout the United States, in both urban and rural regions, people perceive juvenile crime and gang violence as a menace to society. Although recent statistics show a relative decline in crime rates, gang crime remains the center of attention. Although youth increasingly join street organizations for social status and respect among their peers, the media allege that these gangs disrupt the quality of life of their communities. Tracey L. Meares and Dan M. Kahan (1998) argue that the high rates of crime that continue to plague inner-city communities rob residents of their security, undermine legitimate economic life, and spawn pathological cultures of violence that ruin the lives of victims and victimizers alike. Community residents, gang experts, and prosecutors have alleged that these so-called superpredators (Krisberg 2005) intimidate citizens and force them to submit to their authority so that they can sell drugs, party in public, stash weapons, and commit crimes with impunity.

Chris Swecker, assistant director of the Criminal Investigative Division of the FBI, said before the subcommittee on the Western Hemisphere of the U.S. House of Representatives Committee on Foreign Affairs that "Gangs are more violent, more organized, and more widespread than ever before. They pose one of the greatest threats to the safety and security of all Americans. The Department of Justice estimates that 30,000 gangs with 800,000 members impact 2,500 communities across the U.S." (Swecker 2005). Swecker highlights the mainstream discourse and ideology on gang violence, which suggests a threat to communities across the United States by describing gangs as disrupting the moral fabric of U.S. society. Accordingly, advocates of gang injunction laws maintain that these civil codes provide law enforcement with more tools to fight gangs and reduce crime. On the other hand, critics and opponents of gang injunction laws maintain that they are ineffective and a waste of taxpayers' dollars, which could be better spent on community development and crime prevention.

Background

To date, there are no accurate figures on the number of gangs or gang members or the extent of gang crime in the United States. Sociologist Malcolm Klein, one of the leading experts in this field, estimated in the 1990s that there were between 800 and 1,000 cities with gang crime problems, with more than 9,000 gangs and 400,000 gang members (Klein 1995). In 2002, the National Youth Gang Survey found that cities with gang problems more than doubled Klein's figures, with a total of 2,300. Figures from the 2006 survey showed the total dropping only slightly (to 2,199). It found a total of 26,500 gangs with an estimated 785,000 members in the United States; these were approximately 46 percent Latino or Latina and 34 percent African American (FBI Law Enforcement Bulletin 2009). Most data on gang members collected by law enforcement derive from self-identification, monikers, tattoo insignia, community input (gang members, community workers, neighbors, teachers, and family members), and gang members'

GANG INJUNCTION LAWS IN CALIFORNIA

California Civil Code § 3479: Nuisance Defined

A nuisance is anything which is injurious to health, including, but not limited to, the illegal sale of a controlled substances, or is indecent or offensive to the senses, or an obstruction to the free use of property, or unlawfully obstructs the free passage or use, in the customary manner of any navigable lake, or river, bay, stream, canal, or basin, or any public park, square, street, or highway, is a nuisance.*

California Civil Code § 3480 Public Nuisance Defined

A public nuisance is defined as one which affects at the same time an entire community or neighborhood, or any considerable number of persons, although the extent of the annoyance or damage inflicted upon individuals may be unequal.**

---

* California Law Search. "California Civil Code Section 3479." 2006. http://california-law-search.com/civ/3479–3484.html
** California Law Search. "California Civil Code Section 3480." 2006. http://california-law-search.com/civ/3479–3484.html

DID YOU KNOW?

In order to determine if you have a case and an effective gang injunction, you must accomplish the following:

- Survey crime in the area to identify problem areas, individuals, and activities
- Gather quality-of-life information to prove neighborhood damaged by gang nuisance
- Identify community stakeholders and determine what the community believes are so-called fear factors
- Examine law enforcement local expertise; identify necessary declarants for court documents
- Search for nexus of:

  1. Criminal activity
  2. Nuisance activity
  3. Individual gang members

Source: Julie Bishop, *Gang Injunctions: A Primer.* Los Angeles: City Attorney's Office, 1998.

style of dress and demeanor—among the many characteristics that law enforcement officials use to determine gang membership.

Nevertheless, law enforcement agencies claim they lack the funding and resources to combat gang activity and to protect communities. In addition, law enforcement and politicians pump fear into the public in order to acquire resources and the permission to mount an all-out attack on gangs. The climate of fear nurtured by law enforcement officials has paved the way for the rise of gang injunctions and restraining orders on street organizations. California became the first state to develop a hard-hitting gang injunction procedure by applying public nuisance laws to enforce civil injunctions that prohibit suspected gang members from engaging in either legal or criminal activities in public spaces known as *free zones* or *safety zones* (Burdi 2007). Free zones and safety zones map out the areas in a community, usually consisting of a few square blocks, where gang members may not associate with one another.

Gang injunction laws allow prosecutors to use public nuisance doctrines prohibiting lawful and unlawful behavior at their discretion. Civil procedures do not require jury trials, defense counsel, or the burden of proving guilt beyond a reasonable doubt.

Operationalizing These Laws

For a gang injunction petition to be honored in civil court, the prosecutors must establish two sources who identify defendants. Prosecutors often rely upon the community residents, law enforcement intelligence, and informants to establish a person's gang activity.

Once this is accomplished, the prosecution must serve gang members with paperwork adjudicating them to the lawsuit, and once served, the injunction becomes effective. During the injunction hearings, the defendant's preexisting gang activity is exposed, even if he or she has not been arrested or convicted of a crime. This represents a disturbing trend in criminal justice in which crimes are punished before they actually happen. Most requests for gang injunctions are granted; however, the judge has discretionary power to change the terms of the injunction. In addition, the judge may exclude named individuals from the complaint owing to poor evidence implicating an individual to gang affiliation or for failure to serve an individual with a copy of the complaint.

In an effort to expel gang members from a target area, on October 26, 1987, the Los Angeles city attorney and former mayor James Hahn became the first to use a public nuisance abatement lawsuit in *People v. Playboy Gangster Crips*. This injunction barred 23 individually identified gang members from breaking 6 of 23 injunction terms, which, under California law, were already illegal. Although this injunction was not completely successful, it established a legal precedent in the use of the public nuisance doctrine to combat an entire urban street organization instead of individuals (L.A. City Attorney Gang Prosecution Section 1995, 325–331).

Jeffrey Grogger, professor of urban policy at Harvard University, dispels the myth that all gang injunctions operate in the same way. He argues that prohibited activities vary somewhat, but they typically include a mix of activities already forbidden by law, such as selling drugs or committing vandalism, and otherwise legal activities, such as carrying a cell phone or associating in public view with other gang members named in the suit. Once the injunction is imposed, prosecutors can pursue violations of the injunction in either civil or criminal court. The maximum penalty for civil contempt is a $1,000 fine and five days in jail. The maximum penalty under criminal prosecution is a $1,000 fine and six months in jail. Although civil procedures result in less stringent penalties, they have the advantage that their penalties can be imposed without criminal due process (Grogger 2002).

In 1993, the most complete gang injunction issued thus far took place in the community of Rocksprings in San Jose, California, an area that gang members from Varrio Sureño Trece, Varrio Sureño Town, or Varrio Sureño Locos (VSL) claimed as their turf (Castorena 1998). Silicon Valley residents felt unsafe and threatened because gang members congregated on sidewalks and lawns, where it was alleged that VST and VSL gang members engaged in a plethora of drug sales, violent activities, loitering, and lewd conduct. The residential condition made people afraid of having their children play outside and deterred residents from having visitors because they were afraid of gang reprisal in the four-square-block neighborhood.

As a result, the city of San Jose issued a gang injunction against 38 members of the three named gangs. It enjoined and restrained these individuals from engaging in the following activities: intimidating witnesses, which meant confronting, annoying, harassing, challenging, provoking, assaulting, or battering any person known to be a witness to or victim of a crime; grouping together (driving, gathering, sitting, and standing) with other known Trece/VSL associates in public or any place accessible to the public; carrying any firearms (imitation or real) and dangerous weapons on their persons or in the public view or any space accessible to the public; fighting anywhere in public view (streets, alleys, private and public property); using gang gestures (hand signs, physical gestures, and discourses) describing or referring to any of the three gangs; wearing clothing bearing the name or letters spelling out the name of a gang; selling, possessing, or using illegal drugs or controlled substances without a prescription (prohibiting anyone from knowingly remaining in the presence of such substances as well); the public consumption of alcohol anywhere in public view or in any place accessible to the public; spray painting or applying graffiti on any public (alleys, block walls, streets) or private property (residences or cars); possessing any graffiti paraphernalia (spray cans, paint markers, etching tools, white-out pens, acrylic paint tubes, various paint cap tips, razor blades, or other known graffiti tools) unless going to or from art class; or trespassing on private property. Gang members were also required to honor a daily curfew from 10:00 P.M. to sunrise unless they were going to a legitimate meeting or entertainment activity, engaging in a business trade, profession, or occupation, or involved in an emergency situation. They were enjoined from looking out for another person to give warning that a law enforcement officer was approaching by whistling, yelling, or signaling and also violating the law in any other way (thus prohibiting violence and threats of violence, including assault and battery, murder, rape, and robbery by force or fear).

Defendants from the three gangs challenged the unconstitutional vagueness of this court order in *People ex rel. Gallo v. Acuña,* and an appeals court threw out 15 of the 25 original provisions. As a result, the San Jose city attorney appealed two provisions to the California Supreme Court: the terms that prohibited gang members from congregating in safe zones and one barring them from harassing or threatening inhabitants who complained about gang activities. The California Supreme Court approved the use of civil antigang injunctions by rejecting the constitutional challenge to the use of a public nuisance abatement injunction against street gangs. This decision took into consideration the interest of the community while restricting the First Amendment rights of free speech and association of gang members.

According to Justice Janice Brown, "To hold [that] the liberty of the peaceful, industrious residents of Rocksprings must be forfeited to preserve the illusion of freedom for those whose ill conduct is deleterious to the community as a whole is to ignore half the political promise of the Constitution and whole of its sense....Preserving peace is the first duty of government, and it is for the protection of the community from the predations of the idle, the contentious, and the brutal that government was invented" (*People ex rel. Gallo v. Acuña* 1997). The *People ex rel. Gallo v. Acuña,* a landmark California

Supreme Court decision, paved the way for municipal government across the state to use similar gang suppression tactics to curtail gang activities.

For example, in 2006, Dennis Herrera, the San Francisco city attorney, sought an injunction against the Oakdale Mob Gang because of their reputation for distributing drugs and contributing to an increasing rate of violent crime, including harming and killing rival gang members and witnesses. To protect residents, Herrera pushed for punishing any gang member who violated a curfew order of 10:00 P.M. or who congregated with other gang members within a four-block safety zone. There were also many other

INEFFECTIVENESS OF GANG INJUNCTION LAWS

In 1995, the city of Pasadena, California, instituted two separate gang injunction laws. The city later discarded the gang injunction after the Pasadena Police Department and other governing bodies found it difficult to control gang activity as crime spilled over to other regions, making their efforts a complete failure. The failure of gang injunction laws stems from their inadequate ability to address the complex structure of gangs and the emerging crime issues in neighboring areas.*

In 1997, the Southern California division of the American Civil Liberties Union (ACLU) conducted a 10-year longitudinal study on the effectiveness of gang injunction laws. The ACLU focused on the efficacy of the 1993 injunction law against the predominantly Latino Blythe Street Gang. The ACLU found that gang injunction laws do not meet their objectives in reducing the long-term crime incidences in Blythe Street's safety zone.**

Opponents of gang injunction laws argue that they are expensive and deplete city resources. The constitutional cost of embarking on a gang injunction campaign ranges from $400,000 to $500,000. Several civil libertarians, social justice organizations (e.g., Books not Bars), and law enforcement practitioners argue in favor of investing funds in educational programs geared at preventing crime. Take, for example, Father Gregory Boyle, a Jesuit priest who founded Homeboy Industries in the community of Boyle Heights in East Los Angeles. Although many organizations quickly condemn gang members, Homeboy Industries offers an alternative to punitive approaches by offering gang members their first chance by helping them to become gainfully employed. Boyle believes that the best way to deal with gangs requires a major shift in moving away from the symptoms of gangs to addressing the social disease leading to gang formation. Boyle believes that gang injunctions fail to address the structure of poverty and law enforcement's misdiagnosis of the problem.***

*Matthew Mickle Werdegar. "Enjoining the Constitution: The Use of Public Nuisance Abatement Injunctions against Urban Street Gangs." *Stanford Law Journal* 51 (1999): 404–445.
**American Civil Liberties Union. "False Premise, False Promise: The Blythe Street Gang Injunction and Its Aftermath," 1997. http://www.streetgangs.com/injunctions/topics/blythe report.pdf/
***Gregory Boyle, guest lecturer, University of California–Santa Barbara, Sociology 144, Chicana/o Communities, February 26, 2004.

restrictions (Martin 2006). Similarly, in 2005, San Diego County District Attorney Terri Perez filed a court order prohibiting known gang members from grouping together with other associates, displaying gang signs, wearing gang attire, carrying weapons, selling illegal narcotics in public, or fighting in areas of downtown Vista (Klawonn 2005). The widespread use of injunction laws to combat neighborhood gang problems has now appeared in Austin, Los Angeles, Phoenix, Sacramento, San Antonio, San Diego, San Francisco, San Jose, and Stockton.

Many law practitioners believe that the relative reduction of crime in communities derives from law agencies holding an entire group of gang members accountable for the actions of individuals. From a law enforcement standpoint, gang injunction laws address status offences and nuisance activities before they become felonious. Julie Bishop, the leading project attorney on gang injunctions for the Los Angeles city attorney's office, argues that communities benefit from gang injunction laws:

> [T]hey have an amazing, immediate deterrent effect on the entire [gang] group's activity, not just the few who are "sued" by the City Attorney. They complement Neighborhood Recovery Efforts and address the gang problem from a group perspective. They save traditional law enforcement response for the chronic serious offenders. They have a preventive aspect in that they repeatedly warn defendants of the consequences of continuing their behavior. (Bishop 1998, 2)

Conclusion

As local and federal agencies attempt to ameliorate the gang problem, recent trends reveal a drop in the overall crime rate. At the core, these Draconian gang injunction laws attempt to deter individuals from committing future crimes at the expense of their constitutional rights while exacerbating police repression and extending the prison system in communities of color. As noted in the 1998 National Youth Gang Survey, approximately 80 percent of gang members are African American and Latino or Latina. Gang injunction laws disproportionately affect youth and adult gang members of color.

Victor M. Rios, sociology professor at the University of California–Santa Barbara, argues that the ever-expanding power and punitiveness of criminal justice policies and practices affect every member of poor racialized communities in multiple ways, especially urban youth of color. For example, law enforcement often applies gang injunctions to minorities because of their race, not because they have demonstrated substantial evidence of gang activity or crime. This process has increased the probability of harassment of many law-abiding people of color. Rios notes that this so-called hypercriminalization of communities of color is derived from surveillance, security, and punitive penal practices centered on controlling black and brown populations preemptively—before they have even committed a criminal act (Rios 2006).

Lawrence Rosenthal argues that the enforcement of conventional laws, accordingly, allows the police enormous freedom to undertake a variety of quite heavy-handed measures against the residents of inner-city minority communities—authority that officers who may harbor racial biases are frequently accused of misusing (Rosenthal 2002). The taking away of constitutional rights of expression and assembly, like forbidding gang members from interacting with lifelong friends, brothers, and sisters in the same family or banning street attire, does not address the systemic conditions that create gangs. Gang injunction laws exacerbate institutional racism when youths of color—blacks, Latinas, Latinos, and Southeast Asians, for example—are deemed to be suspicious and criminal even if they do not belong to a gang. This means that anyone who fits a gang member profile within the confines of a safe zone may be detained, searched, and arrested without probable cause.

See also Juvenile Justice; Gangs (vol. 3)

Further Reading

Allan, Edward L., *Civil Gang Abatement: The Effectiveness and Implications of Policing by Injunction.* New York: LFB Scholarly Publishing, 2004.

Bishop, Julie, *Gang Injunctions: A Primer.* Los Angeles, CA: City Attorney's Office, 1998.

Burdi, Jerome, "City Safe Zones Would Ban Gangs." *Topix.* January 27, 2007. http://www.topix.net/content/trb/2458370624183364534840215139892182419688

Castorena, Deanne, *The History of the Gang Injunctions in California.* Los Angeles, CA: Sage, 1998.

Delaney, Tim, *American Street Gangs.* Upper Saddle River, NJ: Pearson/Prentice Hall, 2006.

Denfeld, Rene, *All God's Children: Inside the Dark and Violent World of Street Families.* New York: Public Affairs, 2009.

FBI Law Enforcement Bulletin, Summary. http://www.fbi.gov/publications/leb/2009/june2009/bulletin_reports.htm

Fremon, Celeste, *G-dog and the Homeboys: Father Gregory Boyle and the Gangs of East Los Angeles.* Santa Fe: University of New Mexico Press, 2004.

Grogger, Jeffrey, "The Effects of Civil Gang Injunctions on Reported Violent Crime: Evidence from Los Angeles County." *Journal of Law and Economics* 45 (2002): 69–90.

Klawonn, Adam, "Injunction Sought for 89 in Vista Gang." *San Diego Tribune* (June 8, 2005).

Klein, Malcolm W., *The American Street Gang.* New York: Oxford University Press, 1995.

Klein, Malcolm W., *Street Gang Patterns and Policies.* New York: Oxford University Press, 2006.

Krisberg, Barry, *Juvenile Justice: Redeeming Our Children.* Thousand Oaks, CA: Sage, 2005.

L.A. City Attorney Gang Prosecution Section, "Civil Gang Abatement: A Community Based Policing Tool of the Office of the Los Angeles City Attorney," In *The Modern Gang Reader,* ed. Malcolm W. Klein, Cheryl L. Maxon, and Jody Miller. Los Angeles, CA: Roxbury, 1995.

Martin, Adam, "City Attorney Seeks Injunction against S.F. Gang." *Examiner* (October 23, 2006).

Meares, Tracy L., and Dan M. Kahan, "Law and (Norms of) Order in the Inner City." *Law and Society Review* 32, no. 4 (1998): 183–209.

People ex rel. Gallo v. Acuña, 929 P.2d 596, 623 (Cal., 1997) (J. Mosk, dissenting) cert. denied, 117 S. Ct. 2513.

Rios, Victor M., "The Hyper-criminalization of Black and Latino Male Youth in the Era of Mass Incarceration." *Souls* 8, no. 2 (2006): 40–54.

Rodríguez, Luis, *Hearts and Hands: Creating Community in Violent Times.* New York: Seven Stories Press, 2001.

Rosenthal, Lawrence, "Gang Loitering and Race." *Journal of Criminal Law and Criminology* 91, no. 1 (2002): 99–160.

Swecker, Chris, "Statement of Chris Swecker, Assistant Director, Criminal Investigative Division, Federal Bureau of Investigation, Before the Subcommittee on the Western Hemisphere, House International Relations Committee, April 20, 2005." http://www.fbi.gov/congress/congress05/swecker042005.htm/

GUN CONTROL

Matt Nobles

Few topics in the realm of U.S. justice and politics elicit a more polarizing response than that of gun control. Issues in gun policy range from the moral to the practical, with implications for law, economics, public health, and a host of other disciplines. At the center of the debate is the fundamental question of whether firearms, specifically those owned and wielded by private citizens, do more harm than good in deterring violent crime. Despite intense scrutiny from so many fields, however, scholars have reached few solid conclusions to date. The answers to even basic questions (who is victimized, how many are victimized, and at what cost are they victimized) are fiercely disputed, resulting in a nebulous yet hotly contested understanding of the interplay between guns and crime.

U.S. gun policy is a complex and difficult issue characterized roughly by its two diametrical sides: the pro-gun (or gun rights) camp, which argues that guns are a constitutionally protected social necessity, and the anti-gun (or gun control) camp, which asserts that guns are a fundamentally unsafe and extremely costly means to facilitate a variety of social ills. Data exist to support both sides; the difficulty lies in separating partisanship and underlying attitudes from empirical observation and objective analysis. In truth, the isolation of such objectivity may be a logical impossibility.

Background

Outside the United States, guns are sometimes a contentious issue, but rarely at the level witnessed here. Many Westernized nations feature tighter controls on private firearm ownership, particularly for certain types of weapons that could, in the view of their governments, be more readily used to facilitate crime. Australia, for example, experienced a period with relatively little gun regulation prior to the 1980s and 1990s, when a series of high-profile shooting incidents incited progressively harsher reform. Now, guns in Australia are tightly controlled, with restrictions on ownership based on the category of firearm and the evaluation of so-called genuine need on the part of the possessor. Although some low-level debate remains over gun control policies in other countries, there is a veritable firestorm of political, academic, and litigious action on all sides of the gun control issue in the United States.

This issue begins with the interpretation of the U.S. Constitution's Second Amendment. Broadly, the amendment is concerned with security through self-defense; the key difference between the gun rights and gun control perspectives lies with precisely who is entitled to self- defense and how that defense is to be manifested.

Supporters of gun rights believe that the Second Amendment applies to individual-level possession of firearms, whereas supporters of gun control argue that the intent was to provide for the formation and readiness of peacekeeping forces such as the army or state militias. (Since the federal Militia Act of 1903, individual state militias have been organized into the National Guard and have been tasked with supplementing army units overseas and providing domestic support in relief of natural disasters.) In the former perspective, the right and responsibility of self-defense carries an individualistic connotation. In the latter, self-defense is provided for generally by the state, through publicly governed mechanisms such as police, who are entrusted with powers of arrest and tasked with maintaining order. Additional points concerning the amendment have also been debated and promoted, including the right to rebel against government tyranny.

At present, the prevailing attitude in the United States asserts the gun rights perspective—that the Second Amendment protects and guarantees individual possession. Gun rights supporters, particularly the National Rifle Association (NRA), endorse the interpretation that a "well regulated militia," as quoted in the amendment, refers to an armed populace and not only to governmental bodies such as the U.S. Army or National Guard. The NRA, founded in 1871, is the oldest continuously operating civil liberties organization in the United States. It is also, perhaps more significantly, one of the largest and best-funded lobbying organizations in the United States today. Beginning with a more conservative shift in the late 1970s, the NRA has championed laws that promote gun rights and emphasize gun safety for millions of shooting enthusiasts. The opinion about gun rights and the Second Amendment is consistently reflected in public opinion polls on gun ownership. For example, a Gallup poll conducted in 2008 demonstrated that 73 percent of respondents believed that the wording of the Second Amendment indicates a guarantee of private ownership as well as the formation of state militias (Gallup 2008).

THE CONSTITUTIONAL RIGHT TO BEAR ARMS

The Second Amendment, as passed by Congress and later ratified by the states:

A well regulated militia being necessary to the security of a free State, the right of the People to keep and bear arms shall not be infringed.

NATIONAL RIFLE ASSOCIATION

The National Rifle Association (NRA) was founded in 1871 to promote sport shooting and it remains involved in programs to promote firearms safety in the context of hunting and marksmanship. However, it has now become the most influential lobbying group in favor of the individual right theory of the Second Amendment. The NRA (http://www.nra.org/) claims just under 3 million members. In 2004, the NRA Political Victory Fund supported 265 candidates for U.S. House or Senate seats, prevailing in 254 races.* Because the NRA considers personal firearm ownership a fundamental civil right, it opposes all firearms regulations not specifically targeted at persons already shown to be unfit to handle weapons by criminal or mental health history. It also usually opposes bans on particular weapons or firearms paraphernalia and regards firearms registration as a precursor to confiscation. The NRA's response to gun violence is to advocate vigorous enforcement of existing limitations on who may own firearms and severe penalties for unlawful use of firearms.

Legal opinion on the gun control issue seems divided, with both sides claiming victory. In some instances, both pro- and anti-gun advocates claim victory in the very same case. The case of *United States v. Miller* (1930), for example, is cited by the Brady Campaign (2007) as evidence of the courts' interpretation in favor of gun possession by militia members only, whereas the same case is cited by the NRA (Tahmassebi 2000) as evidence of support for the constitutional guarantee of individual ownership. Dozens of other contradictory instances may be found in federal and circuit court opinions dating back more than a century.

Legal Developments

The use and control of firearms in the United States has traditionally been approached from a fundamentally permissive position, with individual ownership largely unregulated. Notable exceptions to this position exist for the nature and type of firearm, the characteristics of its owner, and the provisions of its transfer—all factors that are monitored by the government. A series of federal laws have provided the framework for this means of gun control in the United States since the Prohibition era. The first and perhaps most influential of these laws was the National Firearms Act of 1934, which placed severe limitations on individuals who wished to own small arms and accessories that were generally assumed to facilitate violent crime. Among the regulated items covered in the act were sound suppressors (or silencers), destructive devices such as hand grenades, short-barreled rifles and shotguns, and fully automatic machine guns. The act makes the unlicensed possession or transfer of such items a criminal offense punishable by up to 10 years in federal prison and/or a substantial monetary fine plus forfeiture of all items that violate the act. The National Firearms Act has remained in effect, largely unaltered, and has enjoyed bipartisan support for more than 70 years—a remarkable feat, given the frequency of legal challenges to legislative gun control.

Specific forms of gun control in the United States have also been enacted through laws intended to supplement the National Firearms Act of 1934. One such provision, the Gun Control Act of 1968 (Chapter 44 of Title 18, U.S. Code), was established following the high-profile assassinations of Martin Luther King Jr. and Robert Kennedy. This act provided tighter regulation of interstate commerce dealing with firearms, established the Federal Firearms License program to prevent individuals from purchasing guns through direct mail order or from out-of-state dealers, and mandated that all firearms produced in or imported into the United States bear a serial number for identification purposes.

Certain provisions of the Gun Control Act of 1968 were later clarified and amended in the Gun Owners Protection Act of 1986 (18 U.S.C. § 921 et seq.). This legislation featured several key decisions favoring gun rights supporters. First, it included a formal prohibition of governmental registries linking private guns to individuals. Second, it offered protection for federal firearms licensees from "abusive" inspections on the part of the Bureau of Alcohol, Tobacco, and Firearms. Third, it established a "safe passage" clause for gun owners traveling to and from legal shooting-related sporting events, effectively immunizing them from prosecution for possession or transportation of firearms outside their home jurisdictions. Finally and most critically, the act also clarified the list of persons denied private firearm ownership on public safety grounds, such as individuals who are fugitives from justice or those who have been adjudicated to be mentally ill. An amendment was added in 1996 (the Lautenberg Amendment) to prevent ownership for those who have been convicted of domestic violence and those subject to court-issued restraining orders.

Additional restrictions on gun ownership have been imposed since the Gun Owners Protection Act of 1986. In 1993, President Bill Clinton signed the Brady Handgun Violence Protection Act (18 U.S.C. § 921 et seq.) into law. The act was named for former Ronald Reagan Press Secretary James Brady, who was wounded in an assassination attempt by John Hinckley Jr. in 1981. It established a five-day waiting period for handgun purchases involving a federal firearms licensee (dealer) and a private individual (customer). The waiting period was intended to provide an opportunity for criminal background checks on the purchaser, but this system was replaced in 1998 with the establishment of the computerized National Instant Check System (NICS). NICS provides the same functionality but takes only minutes instead of days, thus preserving the original intent of the Brady Act while streamlining its implementation.

Nevertheless, gaps were found in the system in the wake of a deadly mass shooting carried out by Seung-Hui Cho, a Korean American student, on the campus of Virginia Tech in Blacksburg, Virginia, in April 2007. Cho was known to have a history of serious mental illness and, as such, should have been prevented from purchasing firearms. After the shooting (in which 32 people died), Congress acted to strengthen NICS by ensuring that any prohibiting information regarding the status of a person with a psychiatric condition be made available during the background check process. The NICS Improvement Act was signed into law in January 2008.

For its part, the U.S. Supreme Court, until its 2010 *McDonald v. Chicago* decision, had never ruled on whether the Second Amendment addresses a fundamental individual right to possess firearms at the state level. The closest the Court had come to judgment on this issue was in a 2008 case, *District of Columbia v. Heller* (2008), which centered on the right of an individual to bear arms inside the U.S. federal district (Washington, DC). In that case, a District of Columbia law that banned persons from owning handguns (pistols) and automatic and semiautomatic weapons, and that required any firearms (rifles) held inside the home to have trigger locks was declared unconstitutional. Gun rights proponents proclaimed the ruling a major victory, while gun control advocates lamented it even while observing that it was narrowly worded.

Hence the importance of *Mcdonald* (2010) in clarifying matters. In that case, Chicago firearms restrictions similar to those previously put in place in Washington, DC, were

THE GUN-FREE SCHOOL ZONES ACT OF 1990 AND THE ASSAULT WEAPONS BAN OF 1994

The only major state or federal gun control law that has been struck down by the Supreme Court is the Gun-Free School Zones Act of 1990. The law was designed to curtail gun-related violence in schools, having been enacted after a number of high-profile school shootings. The act established a ban on the possession of firearms within 1,000 feet of a school and set a penalty of $5,000 or five years' imprisonment, or both, for violators. Soon enough, however, the law was challenged by gun rights advocates, and in *U.S. v. Lopez* (1995) the U.S. Supreme Court ruled that in drafting the law Congress had exceeded its authority to regulate commerce (in this case, commerce in guns). The Second Amendment played no part in that decision. The Court left open the possibility, however, that school districts could set out their own restrictions on the presence of guns within their jurisdictions.

The wide-ranging Assault Weapons Ban of 1994, affecting semiautomatic handguns, rifles, and shotguns, was part of the larger Violent Crime Control and Law Enforcement Act of that same year. The ban made the production of so-called assault weapons that included two or more functional or cosmetic features such as threaded barrels, bayonet mounts, and telescopic stocks illegal in the United States from 1994 to 2004. This law was rendered immaterial, however, owing to poorly conceived definitions and a variety of adaptations on the part of domestic gun manufacturers; the industry was able to work its way around it. As the law's expiration date of September 2004 approached, it became clear that there was insufficient support in Congress to renew it. It passed out of law and, to date, has not been taken up anew.

put to the test by gun rights advocates. A Court of Appeals had upheld the restrictions, and when the case came to the Supreme Court it was initially expected that the justices might limit the scope of their ruling to the Chicago ban and its constitutionality. However, the conservative majority on the Court used the *McDonald* case to address the deeper issue of Second Amendment rights and their applicability to the states. In its 5–4 decision, the Court stated that the Second Amendment is to be regarded (under the Fourteenth Amendment's due process clause guaranteeing individual freedoms and protections) as ensuring the individual's right to bear arms. The opinion noted that certain firearms restrictions mentioned in the *Heller* case, such as those "prohibit[ing]…the possession of firearms by felons or mentally ill" as well as "laws forbidding the carrying of firearms in sensitive places such as schools and government buildings, or laws imposing conditions and qualifications on the commercial sale of arms," remain valid and are not affected by the *McDonald* ruling (*McDonald v. Chicago* 2010). But wholesale bans on guns in cities or other localities and burdensome restrictions on their access and use by individuals are prohibited under *McDonald*.

Important Perspectives

Groups and individuals who espouse a gun rights outlook are quick to highlight the apparent positive value of gun possession through the use of statistics on defensive gun use. In 1991, criminologist Gary Kleck argued that defensive use is widely successful: individuals with guns are more likely to prevent the completion of the attempted crime and are less likely to become injured during the event. However, the nature and extent of defensive use is hotly contested. Kleck and colleague Marc Gertz claim that defensive use is underreported, estimating as many as 2.5 million overall defensive gun uses per year (1995), whereas critics claim that the actual number is much smaller (owing to sampling and methodological biases), perhaps around 100,000 overall defensive gun uses per year (Cook, Ludwig, and Hemenway 1997). This disagreement is typical of competing research on gun policy.

Proponents of a strict gun control model point to evidence of the various gun-related costs borne by society. One of those costs may include an increased risk of victimization that accompanies gun possession. The use of firearms accounts for the second highest total of nonnatural deaths in the United States (behind motor vehicle accidents), and the overall homicide rate in the United States is significantly greater than that in other industrialized nations (McClurg, Kopel, and Denning 2002). The exact magnitude of the inequity is a matter of which set of statistics one chooses to use. Given the high prevalence of firearm-related homicide, one might presume that gun possession could pose a direct victimization risk if legal guns were used against their owners during the commission of a crime. The number and availability of stolen guns, which are frequently instrumental in the commission of violent crime, may also indirectly influence victimization risk for the rest of the population.

GUN MANUFACTURERS AND LIABILITY

In 2005 President George W. Bush signed the Protection of Lawful Commerce in Arms Act (PLCAA) (119 Stat. 2095 [2205]), a law aimed at prohibiting suits against gun manufacturers for injuries suffered by the unlawful misuse of their products. The perceived need addressed by the PLCAA was protection of the firearms industry from a wave of litigation against gun manufacturers and distributors that was often driven by local government officials claiming reimbursement for expenses caused by gun violence. The targeting of manufacturers as parties who were at least partly liable in some cases (as when guns were made to be easily converted to automatic weapons) was at the time hailed by gun control advocates and local law enforcement officials as an innovative and necessary legal solution. However, the Republican-controlled legislative and executive branches of the federal government saw matters in a different light and moved instead to protect manufacturers.

Costs may also be economic in nature. For groups concerned primarily about the costs rather than the benefits of guns, the debate over gun control has spilled over into disciplines such as public health, which has a unique perspective and responsibility as typical first responders to gun violence. The financial burden for emergency response, hospital care, and opportunity costs from lost wages due to gunshot injuries is enormous—around $2 billion by some estimates (Cook and Ludwig 2000, 65). Some researchers have begun to regard gun violence as analogous to a public health epidemic, best visualized with epidemiological models showing patterns of spatial distribution (Fagan, Zimring, and Kim 1998), similar to the spread of diseases such as influenza and requiring a similar mobilization of public resources to combat. Self-inflicted injuries carry a cost as well; gun-control advocates note that the prevalence of self-inflicted gunshots in the United States drives the overall trend in gun deaths, with more than 50 percent of gun-related deaths attributable to suicide (Cook and Ludwig 2000, 16–18).

In the 1990s, a well-organized movement, backed financially and philosophically by the NRA, began to generate grassroots support for "concealed carry" legislation. These laws require government officials to issue licenses to people who wish to carry concealed weapons, absent compelling reasons for denial (e.g., a history of mental illness, substance abuse problems, outstanding warrants, etc.); that is, such a license would be issued to anyone who applied and met minimum state-imposed criteria. Notably missing from the application process is an evaluation of the individual's need to carry a weapon, a controversial part of the concealed-carry debate. Proponents of these laws believe that the mechanism for private citizens to obtain licenses to carry concealed firearms would translate into a general deterrence of violent crime. In other words, more guns on the street would equal more opportunity for self-defense.

An interesting resource for the concealed-carry movement was John Lott Jr.'s book *More Guns, Less Crime: Understanding Crime and Gun-Control Laws* (Lott 1998). The book provides complex statistical analyses of the impact of shall-issue permitting laws on violent crime using 15 years of crime rate data for all counties in the United States. Lott reaches the conclusion that the adoption of shall-issue permitting laws results in a decrease for key violent crime rates such as homicide and rape, whereas the laws apparently cause small increases in less serious crime such as larceny and auto theft. He surmises that criminals behave in a manner consistent with rational motives, and increases in general deterrence (leading to the more widespread use of legally concealed weapons) trigger a change in specialization for career criminals. Lott also concludes that suicide and accident rates related to firearms are unaffected by shall-issue laws.

Despite the complex methodology and expansive data used in the analysis, Lott's conclusions in *More Guns, Less Crime* failed to convince some academics. A series of critical reviews of Lott's book appeared almost immediately in scholarly journals and the popular press. For example, researchers at Carnegie Mellon University reanalyzed Lott's original data in an effort to identify trends that could skew his results (Black and Nagin 1998). This reanalysis omitted a single state, Florida, which was hypothesized to bias Lott's original conclusions owing to a period of high violence from the international drug trade and instability regarding intensive legislative actions to control guns. The effect of removing Florida from the analysis was dramatic: nearly all effects of shall-issue laws on violent crime rates became nonsignificant.

Conclusion

The issue of gun ownership is unlikely to become less controversial in the near term. Indeed, the debates about the true benefits and costs of guns may continue for generations. The future of private gun possession in the United States is, to this point, a matter of constitutional entitlement. On a positive note, many key issues dealing with gun control that work on a nonpartisan basis (e.g., possession bans for the mentally ill) seem to enjoy a popular consensus in the United States and elsewhere. This may prove to be a philosophical common ground if comprehensive and balanced gun control reform is ever attempted.

On a more practical level, the issue of whether gun control has an effect on crime is largely unsettled. Evidence suggests that there may be a positive benefit of gun ownership in terms of lawful self-defense and deterrent value under certain circumstances and when the analyses are conducted using certain types of data. Contradictory evidece suggests that violent victimization rates increase with gun ownership and that guns carry a heavy societal price tag. Accelerated population growth, the rising cost of health care, and the expansion of certain political agendas suggest that the societal cost of guns may rise in the near future. Although violent crime may be generally in decline, gun crime may rise in certain segments of the population that are most at risk, including minorities and young males. The precise nature of the increase and the appropriate policy response will be fiercely contentious issues.

See also **Right-Wing Extremism; School Violence; Interest Groups and Lobbying (vol. 1)**

Further Reading

Black D., and D. Nagin, "Do Right-to-Carry Laws Deter Violent Crime?" *Journal of Legal Studies* 27, no. 1 (1998): 209–219.

Brady Campaign to Prevent Gun Violence, http://www.bradycampaign.org

Burbick, Joan, *Gun Show Nation: Gun Culture and American Democracy.* New York: New Press, 2006.

Cook, Philip J., and Jens Ludwig, *Gun Violence: The Real Costs.* New York: Oxford University Press, 2000.

Cook, Philip J., Jens Ludwig, Jens and David Hemenway, "The Gun Debate's New Mythical Number: How Many Defensive Uses per Year?" *Journal of Policy Analysis and Management* 16, no. 3 (1997): 463–469.

Crooker, Constance E., *Gun Control and Gun Rights.* Westport, CT: Greenwood Press, 2003.

District of Columbia v. Heller, 554 U.S. (2008).

Doherty, Brian, *Gun Control on Trial: Inside the Supreme Court Battle over the Second Amendment.* Washington, DC: Cato Institute, 2009

Fagan, J., F. Zimring, and J. Kim, "Declining Homicide in New York City: A Tale of Two Trends." *Journal of Criminal Law and Criminology* 88, no. 4 (1998): 1277–1307.

Gallup, "Public Believes Americans Have Right to Own Guns." March 27, 2008. http://www.gallup.com/poll/105721/public-believes-americans-right-own-guns.aspx.

Hemenway, David, *Private Guns, Public Health.* Ann Arbor: University of Michigan Press, 2006.

Kleck, Gary, and M. Gertz, "Armed Resistance to Crime: The Prevalence and Nature of Self-Defense with a Gun." *Journal of Criminal Law and Criminology* 86, no. 1 (1995): 150–182.

Kleck, Gary, *Point Blank: Guns and Violence in America.* New York: Aldine De Gruyter, 1991.

Lautenberg Amendment, 18 U.S.C. § 922(g)(8).

Lott, John R., Jr., *More Guns, Less Crime: Understanding Crime and Gun-Control Laws,* 2d ed. Chicago: University of Chicago Press, 1998.

Ludwig, Jens, and Philip J. Cook, *Evaluating Gun Policy: Effects on Crime and Violence.* Washington, DC: Brookings Institution Press, 2003.

McClurg, Andrew, David B. Kopel, and Brannon Denning, eds., *Gun Control and Gun Rights: A Reader and Guide.* New York: New York University Press, 2002.

McDonald v. Chicago, 561 U.S. ___ (2010).

Melzer, Scott, *Gun Crusaders: The NRA's Culture War.* New York: New York University Press, 2009.

National Rifle Association Institute for Legislative Action, "The Constitution, Bill of Rights, and Firearms Ownership in America" (2006). http://www.nraila.org/Issues/Articles/Read.aspx?ID=192/.

Spitzer, Robert J., *Gun Control: A Documentary and Reference Guide.* Westport, CT: Greenwood Press, 2009.

Tahmassebi, Stefan B., "The Second Amendment and the U.S. Supreme Court.," National Rifle Association Institute for Legislative Action (2000), http://www.nraila.org/Issues/Articles/Read.aspx?ID=7/.

United States v. Miller, 307 U.S. 174 (1939).

U.S. v. Lopez, 514 U.S. 549 (1995).

Wellford, Charles, John V. Pepper, and Carol V. Petrie, eds., *Firearms and Violence: A Critical Reader.* Washington, DC: National Academies Press, 2005.

H

HUMAN SMUGGLING AND TRAFFICKING

Claudia San Miguel and Annie Fukushima

The concerns about illegal immigration expressed in the popular media, such as television news shows and talk radio programs, can be misleading. These shows often overlook the factors underlying migration and disregard the jeopardy that migrants face in dealing with the smugglers who bring them across the border or the traffickers who enslave them. Despite the dangers involved, many undocumented migrants come to the United States to look for work or to join their families, hoping to settle permanently. Others, entering the country under even less favorable circumstances, come at the hands of human traffickers. Human smugglers and traffickers are international criminals. Nevertheless, it is not surprising that as border-enforcement efforts continue to raise the stakes for both migrants and smugglers/traffickers, incidents of coercion and predation will increase in number and intensify in degree.

Although persons smuggled into the country most often are looking for work, women and children are trafficked both into the United States and internationally for the purpose of forced prostitution and enslavement. Of necessity, this is a process involving trickery and coercion. The United States has responded by passing legislation and directing efforts toward international cooperation. This legislation may represent a good faith effort on the part of lawmakers, but efforts on the ground to stop the massive problem of human smuggling and trafficking have produced mixed results.

Background

The process of globalization has minimized the impact of the distance between communities across the world. Although global migration is not new, the speed with which it is occurring and the shifting dynamics are. Why do people migrate? Their reasons may include finding a job, reunifying family, getting married, or fulfilling the demand for labor by migrants. Nevertheless, in some cases migrants lose control and are maneuvered into criminal activities or enslavement under conditions of coercion by smugglers or traffickers. Those who are categorized as undocumented immigrants are welcomed as cheap and dispensable labor but refused permanent legal resident status. This makes modern migrants from countries that are considered the global south (developing nations), particularly women and children from these countries, vulnerable to criminals.

In the 20th and 21st centuries, the gender dynamics of global migration have shifted. Since 1970, the migration of women has increased on a global scale in a phenomenon referred to as the feminization of migration. Although women have yet to earn equal hourly wages in most countries, including the United States, they now constitute 50 percent of the world's migrants. Women migrants are impacted by the creation of binary categories that have developed to label migration as either coerced (trafficked) or voluntary (smuggled). Such simple polarizations of migration are insufficient to describe the nature of the migration process and the vulnerability of women to human traffickers.

The U.S. West Coast has a deeply embedded migratory relationship with Latin America—one that generates racialized (race-based) perceptions of human trafficking and smuggling. Americans stereotype Mexico and Latin America as regions involved in smuggling; they assume that the United States has little or no criminal involvement. The experiences of those involved, however, reveal a complex picture of interlinkage between countries of the so-called global north (industrialized nations) and the global south.

Human Smuggling

Undocumented migrants cross U.S. national borders without a border-crossing identification card. These cards are issued by U.S. consulates to visitors for tourism or business, temporary workers, and refugees. These cards are denied to individuals who cannot establish sufficient financial means or pass the security check required of entrants from countries designated as places that harbor terrorists.

The United States has the largest and most diverse flow of undocumented workers among the developing nations. Undocumented Mexicans, Central Americans, and other Latin American workers are employed in agriculture, manufacturing, and the service sector, including jobs ranging from maids to waiters. This is a historical process that began as early as the 1940s, when the United States implemented the Bracero program to legally bring migrant workers into the United States. Today, although many foreign-born individuals are admitted as legal immigrants, a substantial number enter as undocumented migrants, often assisted by smugglers. They may stay for a period of time and then return to their country of origin, or they may remain permanently as unauthorized immigrants. Although people who are smuggled enter the United States illegally, they often face the additional risk of being "trafficked" for nefarious purposes. A migrant who seeks to enter voluntarily but is coerced into forced prostitution or enslaved to perform labor has been trafficked by organized crime.

Since 9/11, protection of the U.S. border has been a key focus of U.S. national security. One goal of the U.S. Border Patrol is to combat human smuggling and human trafficking. However, even as U.S. borders have been tightened, immigrants looking for employment opportunities continue to enter the United States from Latin America. A 2008 Pew Hispanic Center survey showed that the number of illegal immigrants entering the United States had declined from an average of 800,000 per year in 2000–2004 to 500,000 per year in 2005–2008. U.S immigrants are racially and ethnically diverse, but the mass media tend to focus on antismuggling initiatives aimed at Latin Americans coming through the southern U.S. border. In San Diego, California, and other major crossing points, large-scale crackdowns on human smuggling rings occasionally take place. Employers in the agricultural and service sectors, in particular, cautiously welcome unauthorized immigrants, but the tightening of U.S. borders and the arrest of migrant laborers and smugglers have made employers' access to such cheap labor more difficult.

Human Smuggling and Coercion

It is often assumed that those who are smuggled across national boundaries undertake the journey of their own free will; they are neither coerced into acting nor deceived in any significant way because they have entered into contracts or paid for the service. Those who are smuggled are grouped with other, voluntary migrants who come to pursue economic opportunities (economic migration) or to be reunited with their families.

Human smuggling is the facilitation, transportation, attempted transportation, or illegal entry of a person or persons across an international border through deception, as through the use of fraudulent documents or by other means involving no identification. Definitions of smuggling in U.S. policy suggest that the person being smuggled is cooperating with the smuggler. These definitions do not fully take account of actual or implied coercion and consider that the illegal entry of one person is being facilitated by another (or more than one). The use of this notion of cooperation, however, is debatable, as often some element of coercion or deception is involved.

Although the U.S. public focuses on the smuggling of Mexican and, to a lesser extent, Central American and Latin American undocumented immigrants, this is just part of a much larger picture. Smuggling cannot be understood in a vacuum because it is a complex transnational phenomenon. It is not only a U.S. reality but a global one. Human smuggling is not limited to the United States, although the United States has the largest number of unauthorized immigrants. Other countries that have been and remain major destinations include Germany, Canada, and Australia.

Human smuggling is the process of bringing in unauthorized entrants. According to the U.S. Immigration and Naturalization Act, it is a felony for a smuggler and a civil offense (at least for the first incident) for a migrant to engage in this activity. The methods of smuggling include self-smuggling, smuggling by professional organizations/networks, and smuggling by independent entrepreneurs known as coyotes in the case of Latin American emigration or snakeheads in the case of Asian emigration. This criminal activity is very profitable. In the first decade of the 21st century, a Chinese migrant might pay from $25,000 to $30,000 to attempt unauthorized entry to the United States. The smuggling fee itself places international migrants into a coercive situation because of the length of time it takes for a person and relatives from a developing country to pay off such a debt. If payment is delayed, relatives in the country of origin may be threatened.

Human smuggling involves high risks for both smugglers and migrants. A coyote—also known as a *pollero*—is a person paid to smuggle a migrant from Mexico, Central America (including El Salvador, Guatemala, and Honduras), or Latin America across the U.S.-Mexico border. Coyotes are despised by some on both sides of the border for profiting from migrants. As the borders have become increasingly militarized, dependency on smugglers has increased, and smugglers are able to coerce ever larger payments from undocumented immigrants. Coercion becomes intensified when smugglers connected to drug traffickers ask immigrants to carry in marijuana or other drugs as part of their fee. Coercion has also increased because urban border enforcement has increasingly pushed migrants to cross in more remote and often more dangerous areas, requiring that they push themselves beyond their normal limits. Environmental factors, such as summer heat exposure in the Arizona desert, can cause serious physical harm and even death. In some cases smugglers abandon incapacitated members of a group, who can only hope that a U.S. Border Patrol officer will find them before dehydration, heat stroke, and starvation end their lives. Others risk suffocation while hidden in the backs of trucks.

Undocumented smuggling of Asian emigrants has historically utilized maritime routes and received relatively less media attention. Maritime smuggling has been associated with the rape of women migrants, malnourishment, and unhealthy conditions of concealment. Snakeheads smuggling Chinese into the United States are reported to have stopped using maritime routes through Seattle, Washington. The new route is by air. One positive, indirect consequence of this change is a reduction of exposure to harm owing to the short duration of attempted entry. In 2004, the United Nations Convention signed the Smuggling of Migrants by Land, Air, and Sea Protocol at its Vienna meeting to control human smuggling, trafficking, and transnational organized crime.

Global smuggling networks include a wide variety of source countries and routes, including the often neglected Canadian border. Cases of human smuggling through

Canada from Asia and Eastern Europe were highlighted during a 2006 indictment in Detroit, Michigan, which revealed that undocumented migrants sometimes rode inside or held onto the sides of freight trains traveling through rail tunnels or were smuggled in ferries, car trunks, the cargo trailers of semi trucks, and, in some cases, small boats. Even in such instances coercion can be involved, the migrants sometimes being unaware of what is expected of them until the time of the crossing.

Regardless of how much is paid and where migrants are from, the end result is the same: migrants who are smuggled into a country reach their destination only if they survive the process. In 2000, more than 100 Chinese were found hiding in several ships in U.S. and Canadian ports, including three who arrived dead in a cargo ship called the *Cape May;* they died of malnutrition and dehydration. Migrants contracting with human smugglers must deal with fear as well as the risk of death.

Forced Migration

Forced migration—or the flight of refugees and displaced individuals fleeing ethnic cleansing, political conflict, famine, and other traumatic situations—often involves a degree of coercion. It is most often a situation of political coercion but is sometimes due to traumatic necessity. Displaced people around the globe are diverse but they have all been affected by economic and political turmoil in their home countries. A displaced person is often a refugee or asylum seeker.

Refugees

Refugees are, by definition, individuals who, because of a conflict involving the nation-state in which they live, are forced to flee. This type of forced migration is especially severe when entire groups face persecution on the basis of their ethnicity. The legal concept of a refugee was created in 1951, when a Refugee Convention formulated by a United Nations Conference on the Status of Refugees and Stateless Persons was adopted. Individuals protected under the category of refugee flee their countries because of persecution or conflict. Their primary international oversight organization is the United Nations' High Commission on Refugees (UNHCR), which was developed in conjunction with the UN protocol to protect, assist, and provide monetary support for refugees.

Central American Refugees

Mexican, Central American, and Latin American migration has been treated as something that is freely motivated, as compared with migrations from Asia or Africa. This has created controversy, because the United States was involved in covert warfare in Central America during the 1980s and chose to treat displaced individuals and families as economic migrants rather than refugees. Immigrant advocates in the United States took up these migrants' cause by documenting the existence of death squads and other political persecution during the Central American civil wars. As a result, there have been several periods of legalization of Central Americans in the United States resulting from judicial decisions. Currently, Latin America is not considered a major region producing forced migration.

Human Trafficking

Trafficking in persons has been defined as the modern-day form of slavery and is perhaps among the most profitable transnational crimes next to the sale of drugs and arms. This transnational crime has been subject to international and national attention. Publicity and human rights advocacy has helped pave the way for the creation of international and national laws to stop the sale and enslavement of persons. However, controversy exists over the extent of the protection these laws provide, especially the Victims of Trafficking and Violence Prevention Act of 2000 (VTVPA), a law drafted and implemented by the United States. Because a significant number of persons who are trafficked become vulnerable victims of this crime owing to grim economic circumstances in their native countries, controversy also exists over the extent to which victims contribute to their own victimization and whether the United States should provide any legal protection for them. Opposing views focus on the extent to which the law should protect victims (such as prostitutes, sex workers, and agricultural workers) who might initially have agreed to be transported across national or international borders in order to find employment and then became enslaved.

Defining the Problem

Trafficking in persons has a broad definition. The Protocol to Prevent, Suppress, and Punish Trafficking in Persons (the Palermo Protocol), which is the leading and most recent international legislation to stop the sale and enslavement of persons, defines human trafficking in persons as

> The action of: recruiting, transporting, transferring, harboring, or receiving persons
>
> By means of: the threat or use of force, coercion, abduction, fraud, deception, abuse of power or vulnerability, or giving payments or benefits to a person in control of the victim
>
> For the purpose of: exploitation, which includes exploiting the prostitution of others, sexual exploitation, forced labor, slavery or similar practices, and the removal of organs.

Using the international definition as a foundation, the U.S. Congress adopted the VTVPA, which is the leading U.S. law against trafficking. This law categorizes human trafficking into two primary components: sex trafficking and labor trafficking. Both types of trafficking are defined as involving the recruitment, harboring, transportation, provision, or obtaining of a person. Sex trafficking is for the purpose of initiating a commercial sex act by force, fraud, or coercion; the law particularly focuses on sex trafficked individuals who are below 18 years of age, specifying even greater penalties in such cases. Labor trafficking involves the use of force, fraud, or coercion to subject a person to labor under conditions of involuntary servitude, peonage (debt bondage, often to work off a smuggling fee), or slavery.

Human trafficking can also be understood within the context of the methods and/ or activities of the trafficker(s)—those who actively engage in the sale and enslavement of persons. The trafficker usually recruits persons, either adults or children, to be sold into slavery. Recruitment generally involves some form of deception or fraud, such as lying about finding and/or providing legitimate employment for the recruited. Recruitment can also involve the abduction of persons. The trafficker then needs to make the transaction or sale of the person in exchange for money or another service. This usually involves transporting a person to a specific destination. Finally, the receipt or transfer of the person to the paying customer or client must be made. The threat or use of force or any other means of coercion is present throughout all phases of the sale. Additionally, once the transfer to the paying customer has been made, the trafficked person is further exploited by being forced to work as a prostitute, agricultural worker, domestic servant, or anything else against her or his will. Although human trafficking may not necessarily involve the sale, transportation, or transfer of a person across international borders, victims of this crime are usually sold on an international scale, human trafficking must be classified as a transnational crime.

The Scope and Nature of Human Trafficking

Although since the fall of the Soviet Union in the early 1990s the sale of drugs and arms have become the most profitable transnational crimes, human trafficking remains well known in the 21st century. Today, it is estimated that 21 million people are victims of human trafficking. In the United States alone, government estimates indicate that between 600,000 and 800,000 individuals are victims of trafficking each year. One of the reasons for this is that the sale of human beings is highly profitable. In fact, it is estimated to be the third most profitable international crime next to the sale of weapons and drugs. The profits of the global human trafficking enterprise are estimated at $7 billion to $10 billion a year. Other reasons for its prevalence may be the belief (of the traffickers) that there is a relatively low risk of being apprehended and punished. Law enforcement's preoccupation with stopping the sale of weapons and drugs leaves criminals with the impression that human trafficking laws will not be enforced and that their chances of being arrested and incarcerated are minimal at best. This false sense of security also drives the willingness of traffickers to continue their work.

Human trafficking results in a form of slave labor or involuntary servitude. It is a venture that thrives on the exploitation of humans for financial or economic reasons. In fact, one could argue that human trafficking is a more profitable business than other transnational crimes, such as arms trafficking or drug smuggling, because humans can be sold over and over again. Thus, unlike drugs and arms, which are usually sold to only one customer for a one-time profit, humans can be resold to different customers and sold numerous times for an exponential amount of profit. Typically, victims of human trafficking are sold and enslaved to perform a variety of jobs, the most common of which involves working in some capacity in the sex industry as a prostitute or exotic entertainer. This is the case for most women and children.

Children are often trafficking victims of sex tourism operations. Sex tourism or child sex tourism occurs when people of one country, usually because of the strict enforcement of human trafficking laws, travel to a foreign location for sexual gratification. They travel with the knowledge the government of the country being visited is unwilling or unable to enforce laws against trafficking or prostitution. Such child sex tourism has been thriving in Mexico and Latin America. Children are also used as camel jockeys (camel riders in races) in some countries or forced to work as domestic servants or in sweatshops.

In most cases, victims of human trafficking are forced to do various kinds of jobs because the traffickers insist that they must pay an impending debt—money ostensibly used by the trafficker to purchase fraudulent travel documents or pay for travel expenses. Essentially, the traffickers create a situation of debt bondage where the victims must provide services to earn their freedom. However, freedom is rarely a possibility because the trafficker is constantly adding to the debt. Overinflated living expenses, medical expenses, and other expenses, including the trafficker's commission, keep the victim from earning her or his freedom.

There are some who wonder why victims do not attempt to escape their captors and why they choose to remain enslaved. The answer is actually quite simple. Victims do not choose to remain enslaved and they do not attempt to escape for fear of harm to themselves or their families. Victims are continuously warned that if they try to flee or call the authorities, they will be killed. Harm to family members is also threatened. The psychological abuse of constantly fearing for one's life or the lives of loved ones is enough to cripple any attempts to escape.

Psychological manipulation at the hands of the traffickers is not the only factor that keeps victims from escaping. Most victims fear that they will be arrested, since most are without legal documents or authorization. What makes matters worse is that travel visas, even if fraudulent, are taken from the victims as soon as they reach their place of destination. Fear of arrest for violating immigration laws keeps victims from contacting authorities. Physical abuse is also a factor that keeps victims from escaping. In addition, constant supervision by their captors makes it virtually impossible for these people to attempt an escape.

Current Efforts to End Trafficking

The international community has been tackling the problem of human trafficking since the early 1900s, when a 1904 international treaty banned trafficking in white women for prostitution—the so-called white slave trade. In the mid-20th century, further international treaties were created to address this problem. For instance, in 1949, the United Nations, of which the United States is a member, signed an international treaty to suppress the sale of humans. More recently, in 2000, a total of 148 countries were signatories to an international treaty to prevent, suppress, and punish those who traffic in persons. This international treaty, known as the Palermo Protocol because it was signed by the various nations in Palermo, Italy, makes it a crime to recruit, transfer, harbor, or purchase a person for the purpose of any type of exploitation. It also makes the sale of organs a crime. The Palermo Protocol considers a victim's consent irrelevant, meaning that any person who is abducted, deceived, forced, or suffers other forms of coercion or initially agrees to be transported across borders shall be treated as a victim if she or he suffers any form of exploitation. The victims shall receive help to return to their country or city of origin and shall receive any medical, legal, or psychological assistance needed.

Conclusion

Human smuggling and trafficking have come to be two of the most profitable transnational crimes. Their profitability is highly dependent on a steady flow of desperate, vulnerable, and exploitable persons and a steady supply of customers in the United States willing and able to benefit from such transactions. Like other economic ventures, human smuggling and trafficking thrive from the supply of seekers and victims and the demand for them. These phenomena are thus significantly affected by global factors, such as economic and political instability, both of which are effects of globalization. Although globalization has certainly helped make the transport and/or sale of humans the transnational enterprises that they are, human smuggling and trafficking have extensive histories. Both flourished despite early- and mid-20th-century agreements and laws to control their spread. Today, both have once again captured the attention of the world and become high law enforcement priorities for the United States. Perhaps they have become so in part because the United States is a prime destination country both for illegal migrants and victims of trafficking.

See also **Border Fence; Drug Trafficking and Narco-Terrorism; Immigration and Employment Law Enforcement; Globalization (vol. 1); Immigrant Workers (vol. 1); Immigration Reform (vol. 3)**

Further Reading

Bales, Kevin, *Disposable People: New Slavery in the Global Economy.* Berkeley: University of California Press, 2004.

Batstone, David, *Not for Sale: The Return of the Global Slave Trade, and How We Can Fight It*. New York: HarperOne, 2007.

DeStefano, Anthony M., *The War on Human Trafficking: U.S. Policy Assessed*. New Brunswick, NJ: Rutgers University Press, 2007.

Gaynor, Tim, *Midnight on the Line: The Secret Life of the U.S.-Mexico Border*. New York: Thomas Dunne Books, 2009.

Kyle, David, and Rey Koslowski, eds., *Global Human Smuggling: Comparative Perspectives*. Baltimore, MD: Johns Hopkins University Press, 2001.

Ngai, Mai, *Impossible Subjects: Illegal Aliens and the Making of Modern America*. Princeton, NJ: Princeton University Press, 2004.

Payan, Tim, *The Three U.S-Mexico Border Wars: Drugs, Immigration, and Homeland Security*. Westport, CT: Praeger, 2006.

Skinner, E. Benjamin, *A Crime So Monstrous: Face-to-Face with Modern-Day Slavery*. New York: Free Press, 2009.

Zhang, Sheldon X., *Smuggling and Trafficking in Human Beings: All Roads Lead to the United States*. Westport, CT: Praeger, 2007.

I

IDENTITY THEFT

Bernadette H. Schell

Identity theft, or masquerading, is a legal term used to define the malicious theft and consequent misuse of someone else's identity to commit a crime. Land-based identity theft can occur if a burglar, say, breaks into someone's home and steals the homeowner's credit cards, driver's license, and Social Security card and then uses these to buy things using a false identity. Identity theft, or masquerading, is fraudulent criminal behavior (Schell and Martin 2005).

In the modern age, identity theft can and does occur in the virtual world. In this venue, it often involves the cybercriminal's hacking into a computer network to obtain personal information on online users—such as their credit card numbers, birth dates, and Social Security numbers—and then using this information in an illegal manner, such as purchasing things with the stolen identity or pretending to be someone of higher professional status to gain special and undeserved privileges. Because of the huge financial and reputational harms it can cause for victims, identity theft is one of the fastest-growing and most devastating crimes in the United States and globally.

On February 21, 2005, ChoicePoint, Inc., a data warehouse having 17,000 business customers, had its massive database of client personal information hacked. Consequently, the company said that about 145,000 consumers across the United States may have been adversely affected by the breach of the company's credentialing process. The company said that the criminals not only obtained illegal access but used stolen identities to create what seemed to be legitimate businesses wanting ChoicePoint accounts. The cybercriminals then opened 50 accounts and received abundant personal data on consumers—including their names, addresses, credit histories, and Social Security numbers (Weber 2005).

As a result of the ChoicePoint breach and those occurring in 2005 at the LexisNexis Group (affecting 310,000 clients), the Bank of America (affecting about 1.2 million federal employees having Bank of America credit cards), and Discount ShoeWarehouse (affecting about 1.2 million clients), U.S. politicians called for hearings and ramped-up regulations to protect consumers against identity theft or masquerading. These breaches also prompted many U.S. states to propose more than 150 bills aimed at regulating online security standards, increasing identity theft and fraud protections, increasing data broker limitations, increasing limits on data sharing, and improving the process to clients regarding security breach notifications (Associated Press 2005; McAlearney 2005).

According to a recent article in *Forbes,* identity theft and related online fraud increased considerably in 2009. The article cited over 11 million victims—at an estimated cost of $54 billion. A year earlier, just under 10 million people were allegedly targeted—at an estimated cost of $48 billion. Interestingly, the cost to individual victims as a result of network data breaches has declined from $498 in 2008 to $373 in 2009. Who, then, is covering the costs for the personal harms inflicted on innocent victims as a result of identity theft? Increasingly, affirm the experts, it is the financial institutions to whom land-based and online citizens entrust their money and from whom they receive assurances of privacy protection regarding personal information. Even as the cost of fraud mitigation continues to spiral out of control, financial institutions are bringing the out-of-pocket expenses for identity theft victims as close to zero as possible so as to maintain their clients' confidence in the system. Losing customers over the longer term because of fractured consumer confidence translates into the institutions' investing in shorter-term remedies for assisting identity theft victims to become financially and psychologically "whole" again as quickly as possible (Merrill 2010).

The Four Critical Elements of Traditional and Identity Theft Crimes

According to legal expert Susan Brenner (2001), both traditional land-based crimes and cybercrimes like identity theft cause *harm*—to property, persons, or both. Some innocent victims of identity theft even incur prison records when false criminal charges are filed. As in the real world, there are politically motivated crimes, controversial crimes, and technical nonoffenses in the virtual world. In U.S. jurisdictions and elsewhere, traditional and cybercrimes like masquerading involve four key elements:

- *Actus reus* (wrongful act, or the physical component of a crime)
- *Mens rea* (a culpable mental state)
- *Attendant circumstances* (the presence of certain necessary conditions)
- *Harm* (to either persons or property, or both)

Perhaps an example can illustrate these critical elements more clearly. One such identity theft case that made world headlines occurred in 2001. It involved U.S. waiter Abraham Abdullah., a hacker who was arrested and imprisoned for defrauding financial institutions of about $20 million by using an identity theft scheme. Abdullah selected his targets' identities from the Forbes 400 list of America's wealthiest citizens; his targets included Steven Spielberg, Oprah Winfrey, Martha Stewart, and Warren Buffett. Then, with the help of his local library's computer, Abdullah used the Google search engine to glean financial information about these wealthy U.S. citizens. He also used the information obtained from forged Merrill Lynch and Goldman Sachs correspondence to persuade credit reporting services (like Equifax) to give him detailed financial reports on the targets. Such reports were then used by Abdullah to dupe banks and financial brokers into transferring money to accounts controlled by him (Credit Identity Theft.com 2008; Schell, Dodge, and Moutsatsos 2002).

This case illustrates that with mere access to the library's computer and the Internet, this cybercriminal was able to initiate a surprisingly simple process of masquerading by gaining unauthorized access to credit card and brokerage accounts. His scheme was revealed when he sent a fake e-mail message to a brokerage house requesting a transfer of $10 million to his bank account in Australia from an account owned by millionaire Thomas Siebel. Abdullah, an American, was tried according to U.S. jurisdictional law and sent to prison (Schell 2007).

In terms of the four elements of the crime, Abdullah gained entry into and unlawfully took control of the property—the sensitive information in credit card and brokerage accounts (*actus reus*). He entered with the intent of depriving the lawful owner of sensitive information (*mens rea*). By society's norms, Abdullah had no legal right to gain access to credit card and brokerage accounts of targeted wealthy individuals for his own financial gain. He clearly was not authorized to do so by the rightful owners (*attendant circumstances*). Consequently, Abdullah was liable for his unlawful acts, for he illegally entered the private accounts (i.e., criminal trespass) to commit an offense once access was gained (i.e., identity theft and fraud). As the targeted users eventually realized that *harm* was caused to their financial property, the judge hearing the evidence ruled that Abdullah should spend some time behind prison bars.

Phishing and Pharming: Relatively New Forms of Identity Theft

Within the past several years, a relatively new form of identity theft has emerged called "phishing." This refers to various online techniques used by identity thieves to lure unsuspecting Internet users to illegitimate Web sites so that the thieves can "fish for" sensitive personal information—to be later used for criminal acts like identity theft and fraud. These illegitimate or rogue Web sites are commonly designed to look as though they came from legitimate, branded, and trusted businesses, financial institutions, and government agencies. Often the cyberthieves deceive vulnerable Internet users into disclosing their financial account information or their online usernames or passwords (Public Safety Canada 2009).

The more aware Internet users receiving phishing emails from supposedly legitimate banks or financial institutions are likely to realize that the cyberthieves may have used spamming techniques (i.e., mass e-mailing) to send the same message to thousands of people. Many of those receiving the spam do not have an account or client relationship with the business or financial institution sending the said e-mail, so they may just ignore the message. The cybercriminals creating phishing e-mails, however, hope that some e-mail recipients will actually have an account with the legitimate business; thus the recipients may believe that the e-mail has come from a "trusted" source and will therefore release the requested personal information (Public Safety Canada 2009). According to a 2004 report released by Gartner, Inc., an IT marketing research firm, phishing exploits cost banks and credit card companies an estimated $1.2 billion in 2003—and since then the costs have continue to climb.

Like phishing, pharming is a technique used by cybercriminals to get personal or private (typically financially related) information by "domain spoofing." Instead of spamming targets with ill-intended e-mail encouraging them to visit spoof Web sites appearing to be legitimate, pharming poisons a domain name system server by putting false information into it. The outcome is that the online user's request is redirected elsewhere. Often, the online user is totally unaware that this process is occurring because the browser indicates that the online user is at the correct Web site. Consequently, Internet security experts view pharming as a more of a serious menace, primarily because it is more difficult to detect. In short, although phishers try to "scam" targets on a one-on-one basis, pharming allows ill-intentioned cybercriminals to scam large numbers of online targets all at once by effectively using the domain spoofing technique (Schell 2007).

What, therefore, should Internet users do about phishing and pharming? According to the U.S. Department of Justice and Canada's Department of Public Safety and Emergency Preparedness, Internet users should keep three points in mind when they see e-mails or Web sites that may be part of a phishing or pharming scheme (Public Safety Canada 2009):

1. Recognize it. If one receives an unexpected e-mail from a bank or credit card company saying that one's account will be blocked if one does not confirm the billing information, one should *not* reply or click on any links in the e-mail.

2. Report it. One should contact the bank or credit card company if one has unwittingly supplied personal or financial information. One should also contact the local police, who will often take police reports even if the crime may ultimately be investigated by another law enforcement agency. The identity theft case should also be immediately reported to the appropriate government agencies. In the United States, online users should contact the Internet Crime

Complaint Center, or IC3 (http://www.ic3.gov/). In Canada, online users should contact Phonebusters (the antifraud online group) at info@phone-busters.com. Canadian and American agencies such as these are compiling data about identity theft to determine trends in this domain.

3. Stop it. Online users should become familiar with the safe online practices of one's financial institutions and credit card companies; typically, for example, such businesses will not utilize e-mail to confirm an existing client's information. Moreover, a number of legitimate targeted financial institutions have distributed contact information to online users so that they can quickly report phishing or pharming incidents. Finally, online users having the Internet Explorer browser can go to the Microsoft security home page to download special fixes protecting them against certain phishing schemes.

Other Legal Means for Controlling Identity Theft and Fraud

Because of its often anonymous and decentralized composition, the Internet is fertile ground for identity theft and fraud. Fraud, defined by law, is viewed as an intentional misrepresentation of facts made by one person, knowing that such misrepresentation is false but will, in the end, induce the other person to act in some manipulated fashion resulting in injury, harm, or damage to the person manipulated. Thus, fraud may include an omission of facts or an intended failure to state all of the facts. Knowledge of the latter would be needed to prevent the other statements from being misleading. In cyberterms, spam is often sent in an effort to defraud another person into purchasing a product or service that he or she has no intention of purchasing. Fraud can also occur through other means, such as online gaming, online auctions, or false claims of inheritance or lottery wins (Schell 2007).

Recently in the United States, the Sarbanes-Oxley Act (SOA) was passed as a reaction to accounting misdeeds in companies like WorldCom and Enron, but its passage has fraud implications as well, particularly with regard to online personal information storage. With the vast amounts of personal information stored on company computers, fraud opportunities abound. A major problem prompting the passage of the SOA was that companies storing large amounts of information have tended to give little thought to what is being stored in company or institutional networks—or how securely it is being stored. Consequently, occasional occurrences of fraud or alterations of data by hackers have gone undetected. Some experts have argued that, rather than spending lots of money to store data in accordance with SOA compliance provisions, companies should allocate funds to determine exactly what kinds of information must be stored and for how long (Schell 2007).

In the spring of 2010, a number of Web site companies—including Google, Microsoft, and Yahoo—faced consumer and advocacy group backlash for keeping Internet search records for too long. These companies were told in writing by European Union (EU) officials probing possible breaches of EU data privacy law that "their methods of making users' search data anonymous" continue to breach EU data protection rules. The group also told Google—the world's largest search engine—to shorten its data storage period from nine months to six months or face harsh penalties for noncompliance. Shortening the data storage period would adversely affect the search engine companies' potential for generating advertising revenue, for they rely on users' search queries to target more specific advertising. It is important to note that search engine companies are competing for online market share, whereby consumer queries are expected to generate a whopping $32.2 billion in advertising revenue just for 2010. Technically speaking, a user's search history contains a footprint of the user's interests and personal relations. This very personal information can be misused in many ways, so consumer protections are required (Bloomberg News 2010).

Also in the spring of 2010, following numerous complaints from online users, the social networking Web site Facebook announced four reforms to more easily control access to their personal data. The complaints started when Facebook announced features like "instant personalization," which tailors other Web sites to users' Facebook profiles. In fact, so many online consumers became irate with Facebook that thousands of them planned to "de-friend" the $24 billion social media corporation as a sign of protest on Monday, May 31, 2010 (Zerbisias 2010).

In a news conference on May 26, 2010, Facebook CEO Mark Zuckerberg said that the company had offered a lot of controls to date, but if consumers found them too hard to use, then consumers won't feel that they have enough control—so the company needed to improve things. The following four reforms were announced to make it easier for online consumers to decline the instant personalization feature: (1) one simple control was created so users can see the content they post—everyone, friends of their friends, or just their friends; (2) the amount of basic information that must be visible to everyone has also been reduced, and the information fields will no longer have to be public; (3) the company has made it simpler for users to control whether applications and Web sites can access any of users' information; and (4) with these changes, the overhaul of Facebook's privacy model was said to be complete ("Facebook" 2010).

Despite these announced reforms, Canada's Office of the Privacy Commissioner warned Facebook that the company still was not complying with Canadian federal privacy laws. The Office noted that Facebook's new settings continue to require users to publicly reveal their names, profile information, pictures, gender, and networks to the broader Internet population. Under Canadian law, companies are bound to give consumers full control over how their personal data are used, thus enabling them to curb identity theft and affiliated cybercrimes. The office put Facebook on notice that it will continue to monitor the situation to ensure that the social networking site complies with the law (McNish and El Akkad 2010).

Identity Theft, Phishing, and Pharming: Defying the Online Tenets of Privacy, Security, and Trust

Identity theft, phishing, and pharming defy the basic online tenets of privacy, security, and trust (PST). Recent public surveys have shown that a number of consumers are still afraid to buy goods and services online because they fear that their personal information will be used by someone else. In recent times, trust seals and increased government regulation—such as the SOA—have become two main ways of promoting improved privacy disclosures on the Internet. Trust seals often appear on e-business Web sites—including green Trust images, the BBBOnLine (Better Business Bureau OnLine) padlocks, and a host of other privacy and security seals. In fact, some companies are paying up to $13,000 annually to display these logos on their Web sites in hopes of having consumers relate positively to their efforts to provide online privacy (Schell and Holt 2010).

Generally, businesses and government agencies take two kinds of approaches to prevent security breaches: (1) proactive approaches to prevent security breaches—such as preventing hackers from launching attacks in the first place (typically through various cryptographic techniques) and (2) reactive approaches—by detecting security threats "after the fact" and applying the appropriate fixes or "patches." These two approaches combined generally allow for comprehensive network solutions (Schell and Holt 2010).

Without question, a major barrier to the success of online commercial and social networking Web sites has been the fundamental lack of faith between business and consumer partners. This lack of trust by consumers is largely caused by their having to provide detailed personal and confidential information to companies on request. Also, when purchases have been made online, consumers fear that their credit card numbers may be used for purposes other than those for which permission was given. And from the business partner's trust vantage point, the company is not really sure if the credit card number the consumer gives is genuine or in good credit standing. In short, "communicating" with unknowns through the Internet elicits two sets of questions that call for reflection: First, what is the real identity of the other person(s) on the Internet, and can their identities somehow be authenticated? Second, how reliable are the other persons on the Internet, and is it safe to interact with them (Schell and Holt 2010)?

To respond to these queries, in recent years a number of products have been developed to assist in the authentication process, including the following (Schell 2007):

- Biometrics, which assesses the users' signatures, facial features, and other biological identifiers
- Smart cards, which contain microprocessor chips running cryptographic algorithms and store a private key
- Digital certificates, which contain public or private keys—the value needed to encrypt or decrypt a message

- SecureID, a commercial product using a key and the current time to generate a random number stream that is verifiable by a server, thus ensuring that a potential users puts a verifiable number on the card within a set amount of time (such as 5 or 10 seconds)

The Bottom Line

Despite the goodwill and multiple technical and legal means to protect privacy, security, and trust provisions online, should we affirm that online consumers can rest assured that cyberspace is a risk-free environment in which they can safely communicate with others, buy things, and socially network? To answer this question, on March 4, 2005, a team of researchers at Seattle University "surfed" the Internet with the intent of harvesting social insurance and credit card numbers. In less than 60 minutes, they found millions of names, birth dates, and Social Security and credit card numbers—using just one Internet search engine, Google. The researchers warned that by using the right kind of sophisticated search terms, a cybercriminal could even find data deleted from company or government Web sites but temporarily cached in Google's extraordinarily large data warehouse. The problem, the researchers concluded, was not with Google per se but with companies allowing Google to enter into the public segment of their networks (called the DMZ) and index all the data contained there. Although Google and other search engine companies do not need to be repaired, companies and government agencies must understand that they are exposing themselves and their clients by posting sensitive data in public places. The bottom line is that even today, with many provisions in place to keep online consumers safe, there remain identity theft and related crime risks (Schell and Martin 2006).

See also **Cybercrime; Advertising and the Invasion of Privacy (vol. 1); Internet (vol. 4); Surveillance—Technological (vol. 4)**

Further Reading

Associated Press, "Data Brokerages: LexisNexis Database Hit by ID Thieves." *Globe and Mail* (March 10, 2005): B13.

Biegelman, Martin T., *Identity Theft Handbook: Detection, Prevention, and Security.* Hoboken, NJ: Wiley, 2009.

Bloomberg News, "Web Firms Breach Data Privacy, EU Group Says." *Toronto Star* (May 27, 2010): B3.

Brenner, Susan W., "Is There Such a Thing as Virtual Crime?" *California Criminal Law Review* 4, no. 1 (2001): 105–111.

Credit Identity Theft.com, "Identity Theft of Celebrities and Wealthy." September 29, 2008. http://creditidentitysafe.com/articles/identity-theft-of-celebrities-and-wealthy.htm

"Facebook Seeks End to Privacy War." *Toronto Star* (May 27, 2010): B3.

Hoffman, Sandra K., *Identity Theft: A Reference Handbook.* Santa Barbara, CA: ABC-CLIO, 2010.

McAlearney, Shawna, "Privacy: How Much Regulation Is Too Much?" April 28, 2005. http://security.networksasia.net/content/privacy-how-much-regulation-too-much

McNish, J., and O. El Akkad, "Facebook Piracy Changes under Fire." *Globe and Mail* (May 27, 2010): B11.

Merrill, Scott, "Identity Theft Costs Rise Overall, While Costs per Victim Decline." February 10, 2010. http://www.crunchgear.com/2010/02/10/identity-theft-costs-rise-overall-while-costs-per-victim-decline

Public Safety Canada, "Phishing: A New Form of Identity Theft." 2009. http://www.publicsafety.gc.ca/prg/le/bs/phish-eng.aspx

Schell, B. H., *The Internet and Society*. Santa Barbara, CA: ABC-CLIO, 2007.

Schell, B. H., J. L. Dodge, and S. S. Moutsatsos, *The Hacking of America: Who's Doing It, Why, and How*. Westport, CT: Quorum Books, 2002.

Schell, B. H., and T. J. Holt, "A Profile of the Demographics, Psychological Predispositions, and Social/Behavioral Patterns of Computer Hacker Insiders and Outsiders." In *Online Consumer Protection: Theories of Human Relativism*, ed. K. Chen and A. Fadlalla. Hershey, PA: Information Science Reference, 2010.

Schell, B. H., and C. Martin, *Webster's New World Hacker Dictionary*. Indianapolis, IN: Wiley, 2006.

Weber, H. R., "Criminals Access ChoicePoint's Information Data." *Globe and Mail* (February 22, 2005): B15.

Zerbisias, A., "Facebook under Fire: Is Social Site Getting a Little Too Friendly?" *Toronto Star* (May 20, 2010): A4.

IMMIGRATION AND EMPLOYMENT LAW ENFORCEMENT

E. Andreas Tomaszewski

Although most people understand the contributions immigrants make to the U.S. culture and economy, a much-contended issue is that of illegal immigration and what to do about it. Associated with legal and illegal immigration are the issues of employment, as this is the preferred way for most people to make a living. The controversies come from the lack of consensus on what immigration policies should look like, and these revolve around questions such as: Who should be allowed to immigrate to the United States? How many people should be allowed to immigrate? How can people be prevented from entering the United States illegally, meaning without having obtained legal permission to enter? What should be done when illegal immigrants are found by law enforcement? Are immigrants not responsible for a large number of crimes? Do immigrants not take work away from Americans? Does immigration not increase the likelihood of terrorist attacks on U.S. soil by foreign extremists?

In the past few years, anywhere from close to three quarters of a million to around 1 million people enter the United States as legal immigrants annually (MPI Staff and

WHERE DO IMMIGRANTS LAND AND SETTLE?

Traditional so-called gateway states for past immigrants to the United States were California, New York, Texas, Florida, New Jersey, and Illinois.

More recently, newer immigrants have started to settle in states that had customarily seen relatively few of them: Georgia, North Carolina, Massachusetts, Washington, Ohio, South Dakota, Delaware, Missouri, Colorado, New Hampshire, Michigan, Montana, Connecticut, and Nevada.

Jernegan 2005). The numbers went down after the September 11, 2001, attacks, as the responsible terrorists had entered the United States legally, which led to significant changes to the immigration system. According to the U.S. Census Bureau's 2005 American Community Survey (which counts only households, not residents in institutions such as universities or prisons), 35.7 million of the close to 289 million people currently living in the United States are immigrants, which represents 12.4 percent of the population, up from 11.2 percent in 2000. Further, from 1990 to 2000, the total population showed a 57 percent increase in the foreign-born population, to 31.1 million from 19.8 million (Lyman 2006).

Background

Immigration has always played a very important part in the history of the United States, a country of immigrants. It owes its existence to people who came to the new world of their own free will (early European settlers and more recent immigration) and against their will (enslaved Africans), all of whom contributed greatly to making the United States what it is today (Zinn 2003). Europeans began settling the area north of the Rio Grande in North America in the 1500s, and the first black people landed in English America in 1619. The first U.S. census in 1790 showed close to 4 million people living in the colonies. The largest number of voluntary travelers by far came from England (2 million), followed by Scotland (163,000), Germany (140,000), and Holland (56,000). Almost 700,000 of the total population of the day were slaves from Africa.

Today, estimates of the numerical size of the group of illegal immigrants vary greatly, depending on who generates them. They range from 7 million to 20 million and almost any figure in between (Knickerbocker 2006). A consensus, of sorts, has formed around estimates between 11 and 12 million (Pew Hispanic Center 2010; Yen 2010). U.S. immigration officials have said that since 2003, the number of illegal immigrants has grown by as much as 500,000 a year, although in recent years the total has flattened out (Pew Hispanic Center 2010).

A growing problem has arisen from the large number of children born in the United States to parents with no legal status. This automatically makes the children U.S. citizens, whereas their parents remain illegal, which makes it very difficult to develop policies for this group of immigrants (Knickerbocker 2006). Having understood a long time ago the importance of immigration and a system that controls it, the various U.S. administrations have developed and changed policies with the goals of reducing the number of illegal immigrants and regulating their impact on the domestic labor market. Assessments regarding the success of these policies vary greatly, and mid-2010 saw numerous attempts to significantly revamp immigration law.

Legal Developments

The persistent desire of foreigners to start a new life in the United States and the state's need to control exactly who is able to do so made the creation of immigration policy imperative. After a significant period of time without immigration policies, the Immigration Act of 1819, which set standards for vessels bringing immigrants (Martz, Croddy, and Hayes 2006), was the first piece of legislation dealing with this issue. Subsequently, immigration laws have been revamped virtually once a decade.

Following the American Civil War, several states passed immigration laws. The Supreme Court decided in 1875 that the regulation of immigration was a federal responsibility. After immigration increased drastically in 1880, a more general Immigration Act was introduced in 1882, which levied a head tax on immigrants and prevented certain people (e.g., convicts and the mentally ill) from entering the United States. State boards or commissions enforced immigration law with direction from U.S. Treasury Department officials (Smith 1998) before the Immigration Service was established in 1891 (Center for Immigration Studies n.d.). Finally, following a renewed surge in immigration after World War II, a quota system based on the national origin of immigrants was introduced in 1921 (Martz, Croddy, and Hayes 2006). This system was revised in 1924, and Congress created the U.S. Border Patrol as an agency within the Immigration Service in the same year. Under the modified system, immigration was limited by assigning each nationality a quota based on its representation in the previous U.S. census.

In 1951, a program that had allowed Mexican seasonal labor to work in U.S. agricultural businesses (the Bracero Program, started by California) was turned into a formal agreement between the United States and Mexico. Congress recodified and combined all previous immigration and naturalization law in 1952 into the Immigration and Nationality Act (INA). Along with other immigration laws, treaties, and conventions of the United States, the INA relates to the immigration, temporary admission, naturalization, and removal (deportation) of foreign nationals. The national origins system remained in place until 1965, when Congress replaced it with a preference system designed to unite immigrant families and attract skilled immigrants to the United States. This was in response to changes in the origins of immigrants that had taken place since the 1920s: the majority of immigrants were no longer from Europe but from Asia and Latin America.

It was also the first time that immigration and employment were linked, as efforts were made to offset the domestic shortage of people with certain skills by bringing in immigrants who met certain criteria. Although several acts at various times allowed refugees to enter the United States and remain—for example, after World War II, people from communist countries were allowed in, as were other refugees from Europe—a general policy regulating the admission of refugees was put in place only with the Refugee Act of 1980. This act defines a refugee as a person leaving his or her own country because of a "well-founded fear of persecution on account of race, religion, nationality, membership in a particular group, or political opinion" (Martz, Croddy, and Hayes 2006).

A significant change to immigration policies was made in 1986, when the Immigration Reform and Control Act was passed; one of the provisions included in the act made it illegal for employers to knowingly hire illegal immigrants. Following this, many modifications to existing laws and introductions of new laws continued to focus on illegal immigration and the employment of undocumented immigrants, as did the reform debates of 2006–2007 and 2010. The Illegal Immigration Reform and Immigrant Responsibility Act of 1996 authorized more border patrol agents along the 2,000-mile United States–Mexico border, created tougher penalties for smuggling people and creating forged documents, and initiated an expedited removal process for immigrants caught with improper documents.

Throughout history, considerations regarding race have always influenced immigration policies; legislation ranges from having some racist undertones to being blatantly racist (Zinn 2003; Vellos 1997). Examples that stand out include the following: the Chinese Exclusion Act of 1882; the Immigration Act of 1907, which limited the number of

TRENDS IN IMMIGRATION

Whereas people from European countries dominated early stages of immigration, this is no longer the case; for some time now, the majority of immigrants have come from Latin America, South America, and Asia.

The phrase "Mexicanization of U.S. immigration" refers to a more than decade-long trend of Mexicans coming to the United States legally and illegally.

Historically, the peak immigration decade was 1901 to 1910, when 8.8 million legal immigrants were admitted to the United States. The 1990s surpassed this, even without taking into account illegal immigrants.

Because immigrants who came to the United States in the mid-20th century (after World War II) are now dying off, the percentage of European-born immigrants has dropped by almost 30 percent since 2001.

Recent data show that foreign-born people and their children make up 60 percent of the population in the most populous city in the United States: New York. A similar trend can be seen in many of the suburban counties around the city: in 24 of them, 20 percent of the residents are now foreign-born.

The three countries of origin from which the majority of immigrants have come and continue to come are Mexico (totaling approximately 11.6 million in 2007), China (just over 2 million), and India (1.7 million).

Japanese immigrants; the National Origins (First Quota) Act of 1921, which favored immigration from northern European countries at the expense of southern and eastern European nations; and the National Origins (Second Quota) Act of 1924, which continued the discrimination against southern and eastern Europeans and imposed new restrictions on Asian immigration. Arguably, provisions in the 2001 Patriot Act discriminate against certain ethnic and religious groups (Middle Easterners and Muslims) because of their alleged connections with terrorist organizations.

Key Events and Issues

Within the last 100 years, three events that affected immigration and corresponding legislation in the United States stand out: World War I (1912–1918), World War II (1939–1945), and the terrorist attacks of September 11, 2001. This last event led the government under President George W. Bush to introduce the USA Patriot Act in the same year, which established the U.S. Department of Homeland Security and made the U.S. Department of Citizenship and Immigration Services (CIS) a bureau within it (CIS has an Office of Immigration Statistics, which collects data to discern immigration trends and inform policy formulation).

Further, Title 8 of the Code of Federal Regulations (CFR) was amended in 2002 and 2003. (The U.S. Code and the Code of Federal Regulations codify federal laws, including those that deal with immigration [Title 8 in both documents].) The Immigration and Naturalization Service (INS), which was in charge of immigration and enforcement of immigration law for so long as part of the U.S. Department of Justice, no longer exists. Aside from the creation of the CIS within the large bureaucratic structure of the Department of Homeland Security, some functions have been streamlined. For example, whereas the U.S. Department of Customs and Immigration and the INS used to be in charge of related tasks, U.S. Immigration and Customs Enforcement (ICE, also a part of Homeland Security) was carved out of the old Customs Department and now focuses exclusively on these issues, such as the arrest and removal of a foreign national who, in governmental language, is called an alien. The formal removal of an alien from the United States was called deportation before the Illegal Immigration Reform and Immigrant Responsibility Act of 1996, and such a measure must be ordered by an immigration judge after it has been determined that immigration laws have been violated. The Department of Immigration and Customs Enforcement can execute a removal without any punishment being imposed or contemplated (U.S. Department of Citizenship and Immigrations Services).

Foreign nationals entering the United States generally fall into one of three categories: lawful permanent residents (LPRs), nonimmigrants, and undocumented migrants (illegal immigrants). Documents have to be issued by U.S. immigration authorities for individuals in the first category, also referred to as permanent resident aliens, resident alien permit holders, and green card holders. A noncitizen of the United States can fall into this category upon arrival by either having obtained the document through the more common and often lengthy application process or by having won it in the "green card lottery," which makes a certain number of green cards available every year. These documents are also referred to as immigrant visas because the holder is allowed to reside and work in the United States without restrictions under legally recognized and lawfully recorded permanent residence as an immigrant. The Immigration Act of 1990 set the flexible numerical limit of individuals falling into this category at 675,000 annually. Exempt from these limits are several categories of people, including immediate relatives of U.S. citizens, refugees, and asylum seekers.

Nonimmigrants may or may not require permission (a visa) to enter, depending on their purpose for entering the country (work, business, study, travel) and nationality. In general, tourists and business travelers from most Western countries do not have to apply for a visa at a U.S. embassy or consulate general in their country of citizenship, although this is always subject to change (as was done after 9/11). Those who plan to stay in the United States temporarily to study or work must apply for authorization to do so prior to their arrival. It is not guaranteed that such an application, which often takes six months or more, will be approved or processed in time. For example, improved security measures, increased background checks of applicants, and prolonged processing times after 9/11 have significantly lengthened the process.

U.S. employers wanting to employ a foreign national on the basis of his or her job skills in a position for which qualified authorized workers are unavailable in the United States must obtain labor certification. This is one of many instances in which the U.S. Department of Labor is involved with matters pertaining to foreign nationals. Labor certification is issued by the secretary of labor and contains attestations by U.S. employers as to the number of U.S. workers available to undertake the employment sought by an applicant and the effect of the alien's employment on the wages and working conditions of U.S. workers similarly employed. Determination of labor availability in the United States is made at the time of a visa application and at the location where the applicant wishes to work.

There are literally dozens of nonimmigrant visa classifications, including the following, which are among the most common. Students who want to study at U.S. colleges and universities are issued F-1 visas; those participating in cultural exchange programs (including academics and researchers from abroad) get J visas, which generally cannot be renewed; temporary workers with specialized knowledge and skills (including academics and researchers from abroad) get H and other visas. For professionals from Canada or Mexico, there is the TN category under North American Free Trade Agreement (NAFTA) regulations.

Each year, Congress decides how many visas are to be issued in each category. Although holders of different types of H and other visas play an increasing role in the U.S. economy, significantly fewer have been authorized in recent years despite high demand by U.S. employers. The annual cap is typically reached within the first few months of the fiscal year. For example, for fiscal year 2009, the cap of 65,000 (in fiscal years 2001 to 2003, it was 195,000) was reached in just 8 days. (In fiscal year 2005, the same cap was reached on the first day of the fiscal year.)

Further, it is standard practice that J visas are associated with a particular educational institution, just as TN and H visas are tied to a particular employer. If the student wants to change universities or the worker his or her employer, a new document must be issued. The length of time that these visas are valid varies, and an application for renewal must be filed with immigration authorities before they expire. Otherwise, the visa holder loses eligibility to do what the document had authorized could be done. Upon expiration of a visa, a new document must be applied for at a U.S. embassy or consulate general in the visa holder's country of citizenship. Upon expiration of the visa, the immigrant student or worker can no longer legally study or work in the United States and generally can remain in the United States no longer than six months.

People falling in the last category, that of undocumented migrants, are commonly referred to as illegal immigrants, which means that they entered the country without proper documents and without authorization and knowledge of U.S. immigration authorities. Enforcement of immigration and employment law focuses on this group. They cross the border at unsecured locations, such as forests and rivers, or between inspection points (official border crossings), or they pass inspection with forged documents or cross the border hidden in vehicles. The majority of illegal immigrants come from Mexico and other Latin, Central, and South American countries in hopes of finding work and a better economic future.

Although not discussed very often, a large number of undocumented migrants, especially from Mexico, are leaving the United States each year (counterflow). For example, INS data show that, in the 1990s, around half as many people who entered the United States unauthorized every year left it again (Martz, Croddy, and Hayes 2006). In fact, many unauthorized Mexicans do not want to immigrate permanently; they want to get a job, make some money (unemployment and poverty rates are very high in Mexico), and return home to their families. Smaller numbers of illegal immigrants cross the United States–Canada border or come by sea.

Many people who try to enter the United States without authorization (e.g., their applications were rejected because they did not meet certain criteria, they thought they would be rejected, or they never applied for whatever reason) risk their lives. For example, from 1998 through 2002, more than 1,500 illegal immigrants died trying to cross into the United States, mostly of exhaustion and exposure. Another risk in trying to cross the border alone is that of getting caught by the U.S. Border Patrol, whose job it is to stop illegal immigration. If that happens, they are generally not detained or charged but sent back across the border. To lower these risks, many pay a lot of money for the services of guides, called coyotes, organized in bands, which make millions of dollars each year. The guides may accompany them to a location where the border is not secured properly or smuggle them across the border. Being smuggled in the back of a truck or in a container, however, is risky, too, as such immigrants have suffocated or died of heat exhaustion or lack of water.

Once on U.S. soil, undocumented migrants try to find work and accommodation and become the responsibility of Department of Immigration and Customs Enforcement, which tries to find them and, if successful, take them back across the border; undocumented migrants are generally not charged. With access to the right networks, finding a job can be relatively easy. Further, many employers prefer to hire illegals because it increases their profit margin. Although the employers can charge the same for their products or services, they can pay the migrants less. Industries that hire a large number of undocumented workers include service industries, natural resources, and construction (National Employment Law Project). The Immigration Reform and Control Act of 1986 included a provision for employer sanctions if employers hired, recruited, or referred for a fee aliens known to be unauthorized to work in the United States. Violators of the law are subject to a series of civil fines for violations or criminal penalties when there is a pattern or practice of violations (historically, the latter was inconsistently enforced).

Although the Department of Labor is in charge of enforcing labor-related laws and regulations, such as the Fair Labor Standards Act, which, among other things, provides minimum wage and overtime protections and thus also protects illegal workers, the enforcement of immigration laws is out of its jurisdiction. For better or worse, historically, cooperation between the agencies that enforce immigration laws, on the one hand, and employment laws, on the other, has been less than stellar. Despite the provisions of the 1986 law, employers of illegal immigrants were not at the center of enforcement activities for a long time, although increasing attention was paid to the issue in the 1990s.

For example, in 1999, a total of 417 civil fine notices were issued to employers. During the first years of the George W. Bush administration, less attention was paid to employers and only three civil fine notices were issued in 2003. In 2002, one year before Immigration and Customs Enforcement (ICE) was created within the Department of Homeland Security (DHS), 25 criminal charges were brought against employers. Following bipartisan pressure on the administration in spring 2006, DHS Secretary Michael Chertoff announced a campaign that promised to focus on employers suspected of hiring illegal workers and included more serious sanctions than previously, such as felony charges, huge financial penalties, and the seizure of assets. The more aggressive enforcement of immigration and employment laws by ICE led to 445 criminal arrests of employers within the first seven months of 2006 and to the deportation of the majority of 2,700 illegal immigrants who worked in these operations (Preston 2006).

Conclusion

With anti-immigrant sentiments on the rise between 2001 and 2010, the percentage of people polled who felt that immigrants are a burden because they take jobs and housing away from citizens grew from 38 percent to 52 percent. Similarly, the percentage of those who felt that immigrants strengthened the United States with their hard work and talents dropped from 50 percent to 41 percent. Into the foreseeable future, at last three controversial debates will continue.

First, several commentators and officials—for example, in Texas, California, and Arizona—have suggested that there is an immigration crisis. Although responsible analyses show that this is not the case, the fact remains that a significant number of immigrants come to and live in the United States illegally. This creates several problems, including an increased likelihood for members in this group to be economically exploited (working for less than the minimum wage, not getting paid overtime or not getting paid at all, working in dangerous and labor law–violating environments, etc.), and being at higher risk for criminal victimization (particularly violence against women), as perpetrators of such crimes know that their victims are not likely to report their victimization to representatives of the state (National Employment Law Project).

The number of undocumented immigrants in the United States alone should be reason enough to undertake a comprehensive reform of U.S. immigration policies, regardless of whether the argument is the policies' lack of effectiveness or a humanitarian one that emphasizes the human, civil, and constitutional rights of unauthorized workers and immigrants in general. Two proposals for reform, one from the Senate and one from the House of Representatives, were discussed in 2006 but failed to pass. After the state of Arizona enacted, in 2010, a law giving police the authority to stop and question anyone suspected of being an illegal immigrant, leaders at the federal level, including President Barack Obama, are speaking of the need to renew the debate for comprehensive immigration reform.

In general, visa screening, border inspections, and the tracking of foreigners have been tightened as compared to the pre-9/11 years (MPI Staff and Jernegan 2005). For example, it requires non–U.S. citizens, including those residing in the United States temporarily (and legally), to provide border inspectors with digital fingerprints and a digital photo, which are taken by the inspector upon entry into the United States. Further, temporary legal residents have to obtain a bar-coded printout when leaving the United States, which they have to turn in when they return. Prior to this change, immigration authorities had no record of an alien who left the country.

Finally, another controversy ensues over the implementation of the National Security Entry-Exit Registration System (NSEERS), which requires all foreigners from countries with alleged ties to terrorist organizations to register with the government. In December 2002, this led to the detention without bond of thousands of immigrants from Iraq, Iran, and several other countries, although there was no evidence that these individuals had been involved in any terrorist or other criminal activity (Flowers 2003). Although the situation has improved somewhat in recent years, it is clear that many of the legislative changes are here to stay, and critics wonder if immigration restrictions associated with the so-called War on Terror are yet another and more subtle way to discriminate against potential immigrants from particular backgrounds. Still, after a car bomb attempt in Times Square in May 2010 by a naturalized U.S. citizen from Pakistan, sentiments in favor of strict law enforcement were again on the rise.

Little disagreement exists that immigration policies should play an important part in efforts to keep the United States and its residents safe, as is the case with the associated need to know where foreigners are and what they do and to ensure that they engage in legal employment. The problem is, however, to find a way to achieve that which is agreeable to the majority, if not all.

See also **Border Fence; Human Smuggling and Trafficking; Patriot Act; Racial, National Origin, and Religion Profiling; Immigrant Workers (vol. 1); Immigration Reform (vol. 3)**

Further Reading

Brotherton, David C., and Philip Kretsedemas, eds., *Keeping Out the Other: A Critical Introduction to Immigration Enforcement Today.* New York: Columbia University Press, 2008.

Center for Immigration Studies, "History." n.d. http://cis.org/topics/history.html

Chomsky, Aviva, *They Take Our Jobs! and 20 Other Myths about Immigration.* Boston: Beacon Press, 2007.

Cieslik, Thomas, David Felsen, and Akis Kalaitizidis, eds., *Immigration: A Documentary and Reference Guide.* Westport, CT: Greenwood Press, 2009.

Daniels, Roger, *Coming to America: A History of Immigration and Ethnicity in American Life,* 2d ed. New York: Harper Perennial, 2002.

Flowers, Christine, "The Difficulties Immigrants Face in the Post-9/11 World: How the War on Terrorism Has Changed Their Legal Status." *FindLaw's Writ: Legal News and Commentary* (May 1, 2003). http://writ.news.findlaw.com/commentary/20030501_flowers.html

Johnson, Kevin R., *Opening the Floodgates: Why America Needs to Rethink Its Borders and Immigration Laws.* New York: New York University Press, 2007.

Knickerbocker, Brad, "Illegal Immigrants in the U.S.: How Many Are There?" *Christian Science Monitor* (May 16, 2006). http://www.csmonitor.com/2006/0516/p01s02-ussc.html/

Lyman, Rick, "Census Shows Growth of Immigrants." *New York Times* (August 15, 2006). http://www.nytimes.com/2006/08/15/us/15census.html?ex=1313294400 and en=faeaaa9792c67f0c and ei=5088 and partner=rssnyt and emc=rss

Martin, Philip L., *Importing Poverty? Immigration and the Changing Face of Rural America.* New Haven, CT: Yale University Press, 2009.

Martz, Carlton, Marshall Croddy, and Bill Hayes, *Current Issues of Immigration, 2006.* Washington, DC: Constitutional Rights Foundation, 2006.

Mills, Nicolaus, *Arguing Immigration: The Debate over the Changing Face of America.* New York: Touchstone, 2007.

MPI Staff and Kevin Jernegan, "A New Century: Immigration and the U.S." *Migration Policy Institute* (Migration Information Source). 2005. http://www.migrationinformation.org/Profiles/display.cfm?ID=283

National Employment Law Project, "Immigrant Worker Project." n.d. http://www.nelp.org

Newton, Lina, *Illegal, Alien, or Immigrant: The Politics of Immigration Reform.* New York: New York University Press, 2008.

Pew Hispanic Center, "U.S. Unauthorized Immigration Flows Are Down Sharply since Mid-Decade." September 1, 2010. http://pewhispanic.org/files/reports/126.pdf

Preston, Julia, "U.S. Puts Onus on Employers of Immigrants." *New York Times* (July 31, 2006): sec A1.

Smith, Marian, "Overview of INS History." *U.S. Citizenship and Immigration Services Online.* 1998. http://www.uscis.gov/portal/site/uscis/menuitem.5af9bb95919f35e66f614176543f6d1a/?vgnextoid=b7294b0738f70110VgnVCM1000000ecd190aRCRD and vgnextchannel=bc9cc9b1b49ea110VgnVCM1000004718190aRCRD

Swain, Carol M., ed., *Debating Immigration.* New York: Cambridge University Press, 2007.

Takaki, Ronald, *A Different Mirror: A History of Multicultural America,* rev. ed. Boston: Back Bay Books, 2008.

U.S. Department of Citizenship and Immigration Services, Home Page. http://www.uscis.gov

Vellos, Diana, "Immigrant Latina Domestic Workers and Sexual Harassment." *American University Journal of Gender and the Law* 407 (1997): 407–432.

Yen, Hope, "Number of Illegal Immigrants in U.S. Declining." MSNBC. September 1, 2010. http://www.msnbc.msn.com/id/38961638/ns/us_news-immigration_a_nation_divided

Zinn, Howard, *A People's History of the United States: 1492–Present.* New York: HarperCollins, 2003.

INSANITY DEFENSE

CATHERINE D. MARCUM

The issue of mental health and insanity has been a controversial one in the court system since the early 13th century. At the time, defendants claiming mental health issues during the commission of a crime were able to pursue different types of judicial outcomes rather than being classified as simply guilty or not guilty. However, the progression of the insanity defense has changed, especially over the past 100 years, which has changed the understanding of its tenets for both the defendant and the general public.

Background

One of the earliest recorded tests for insanity was the "wild beast" test. Created in the 13th century by an English judge in King Edward's court, the defendant was deemed insane by demonstrating that his or her mental capacity was not greater than that of a wild beast (Lunde 1975). In the early 18th century, the defendant was deemed insane if he or she could no more control his or her actions than a wild beast (*Washington v. United States* 1967); in other words, the defendant claiming insanity was unable to maintain any sort of self-control and therefore was unable to refrain from committing the crime with which he or she was charged.

The first insanity case involving "not guilty by reason of insanity" as a separate verdict of acquittal was the *Hadfield* decision. In 1800, James Hadfield attempted to murder King George III with a firearm. He claimed that God had called upon him to undergo self-sacrifice in order to carry out the act. His defense counsel argued that he was delusional and murder of the king was not an intention of Hadfield in his right mind. The jury's verdict of not guilty by reason of insanity was groundbreaking in initiating a new era of criminal defense (Caesar 1982; Gall 1982; Robin 1997).

Legal Developments

Although the *Hadfield* decision was an important pioneering step, it was not until almost 50 years later that the landmark McNaghten case drastically changed the insanity defense. In 1843, Daniel McNaghten planned to assassinate England's Prime Minister Robert Peel but accidentally murdered his secretary instead. During the trial, McNaghten's attorneys presented psychiatric testimony stating he was under the form of mental delusions that caused him to attempt the murder of Peel. The jury determined that McNaghten had no soundness of mind at the time of the offense and was found not guilty by reason of insanity. He was committed to Bedlam, where he remained until his death (Biggs 1955). The *McNaghten* decision was not taken well by the residents of England, especially Queen Victoria, who demanded a legislative review of the case. The House of Lords called a judges' review of the law's standards of the insanity defense. From this meeting, the *McNaghten rule* (*Rex v. McNaghten* 1843), or "right-wrong" test of insanity, was formed, which based a decision of insanity on the perception of the defendant's knowledge of right and wrong. The test was instituted in not only England but also the United States.

The main criticism of the *McNaghten* rule was that it considered only impairments of personality and not mentally ill offenders' inability to emotionally restrain themselves but still have the recognition that an act is wrong. This "irresistible impulse test," whose origins date back to 1840, was recognized as a separate basis of a determination of insanity. In 1929, the court of appeals in the District of Columbia held in *Smith v. United*

JUSTICE TINDEL'S ARTICULATION OF THE *MCNAGHTEN* RULE

"To establish a defense on the ground of insanity, it must be proved that, at the time of the committing of the act, the party accused was laboring under such a defect of reason, from disease of the mind, as not to know the nature and quality of the act he was doing; or if he did know it, that he did not know that he was doing what was wrong. The mode of putting the latter part of the question to the jury on these occasions has generally been whether the accused at the time of doing the act knew the difference between right and wrong."

States that an accused must be able not only to prove the inability to determine right and wrong but also to demonstrate the failure to control impulse (Robin 1997).

In 1954, the Court of Appeals for the District of Columbia found that the *McNaghten* rule, used by all federal courts and many states as a test of insanity for approximately 100 years, was outdated. A modernized version of the rule was implemented with the *Durham* rule, as the *McNaghten* rule was found to disregard advances in medical science (*Durham v. United States* 1945). Monte Durham was convicted of housebreaking in a bench trial; his only defense was that he was of unsound mind. Judge David Bazelon created the *Durham* rule, which stated that a defendant was not responsible for a crime if the act was a result of a mental disease. The purpose of the new rule was to enable communication between psychiatric experts and the court to ensure proper evaluation of potential insanity (Robin 1997).

The *Durham* rule was used as the court standard of insanity for approximately two decades. However, an updated definition of insanity was adopted from the American Law Institute (ALI) as a result of *United States v. Brawner* (1972): "A person is not responsible if at the time of such conduct as a result of mental disease or defect he lacks substantial capacity to appreciate the wrongfulness of his conduct or to confirm his conduct to the requirements of law" (pp. 66–67). The purpose of the ALI-*Brawner* test, or substantial capacity test, was to cease the reliance on psychiatric testimony and allow the jury to determine insanity. It is also noted in the substantial capacity test that mental disease does not include irregularities caused by recidivist behavior and antisocial behavior.

Shortly after implementation of the ALI-*Brawner* test, John Hinckley attempted to assassinate President Ronald Reagan on March 30, 1981. At trial, his psychiatrist testified that Hinckley suffered from schizophrenia and was unable to comprehend the magnitude of his act, even though he knew it was illegal. Based on the instruction of the law, the jury found Hinckley not guilty by reason of insanity and a national fury arose ("Insane on All Counts" 1982). The congressional response was the Insanity Defense Reform Act of 1984.

Prior to the passage of the Insanity Defense Reform Act, the majority of federal jurisdictions did not differentiate between the verdict of "not guilty by reason of insanity" and "not guilty"; in other words, a person judged not guilty by reason of insanity was treated the same by law as a person acquitted of a crime (Liu 1993). These jurisdictions did not require courts to inform the jury of the legal consequences of a not guilty by reason of insanity verdict because they felt as if the jury had no role in sentencing. The general rationale was that instruction of the repercussions of such a verdict would divert the jury from their roles as fact finders and compromise verdicts (*Pope v. United States* 1962). Defendants who were given the verdict not guilty by reason of insanity actually benefited in their defense because their burden of proof was different than that other cases. Generally, in federal and state courts, the burden of proof only had to meet a reasonable doubt regarding sanity.

After the Hinckley decision and the argued discrepancies of the insanity defense, Congress passed the Insanity Defense Reform Act of 1984, which made several changes to the federal law. First, the act allowed defendants to offer evidence that, at the time they committed a crime, demonstrated they were unable to appreciate the wrongfulness of their crime. Second, the responsibility of the burden of proof was switched from the prosecutor to the defense, which had to prove insanity with clear and convincing evidence. Next, the verdict not guilty by reason of insanity became a separate verdict along with guilty and not guilty. Finally and most important, the act addressed a serious loophole in federal law that allowed a defendant to escape commitment after being judged not guilty by reason of insanity (Ellias 1995).

Controversies of the Insanity Defense

The utilization of the insanity defense is not as cut and dried as is stated in the Insanity Defense Reform Act and has caused much controversy with the public. For instance, one might assume that the commitment of a person to a mental institution based on a verdict of not guilty by reason of insanity equates to commitment for life. However, this is not necessarily the case. In *Foucha v. Louisiana* (1992), the U.S. Supreme Court ruled that a person could not be held indefinitely through commitment with the verdict of not guilty by reason of insanity; therefore, once deemed not a threat to society and "cured," a person could be released back into society. This may be seen as unfair compared with the probable life sentence received by many other persons convicted of the same type of crime.

A second controversy is the fact that not all states afford the right to the insanity defense. States such as Montana, Idaho, and Utah have banned the use of the insanity defense. In 2006, the U.S. Supreme Court upheld in *Clark v. Arizona* (2006) that states have the right to deviate from or even totally abolish the use of the defense tactic.

Conclusion

After implementation of the Insanity Defense Reform Act, empirical studies found that the majority of jurors were aware that the verdict not guilty by reason of insanity

---

ANDREA YATES

One of the best-known cases of the insanity plea was that of Andrea Yates. In March 2002, Yates was convicted of drowning three of her five children and sentenced to life in prison. However, in July 2006, her conviction was reversed and she was found not guilty by reason of insanity and committed to a state mental hospital in Texas. Because of the Insanity Defense Reform Act of 1984, Yates did not avoid commitment despite her verdict of not guilty by reason of insanity.

equated to the involuntary commitment to a mental hospital for the defendant (Ellias 1995). Although early use of the claim of insanity caused media buzz of the assumed overuse of the defense, public perception has settled into the realization of the small frequency of its actual use as well as the necessity of the defense. Although the potential for abuse of the insanity defense is there, as well as the constant controversy over its use, many would argue that there is benefit there for the often mistreated mentally ill offender. Rather than treating such a person like a "wild beast," there are other options that will offer them the best treatment possible.

See also **Death Penalty; Expert Witness Testimony; Mental Health (vol. 3)**

Legal Citations

Clark v. Arizona, Docket No. 05–5966 (2006).

Durham v. United States, 214 F.2d 862 (1954).

Foucha v. Louisiana, 504 U.S. 71 (1992).

Pope v. United States, 298 F.2d 507 (5th Cir. 1962).

Rex v. McNaghten, Clark and Finnelly, 200, 8 *Eng.* Rep 718, House of Lords (1843).

Washington v. United States, 390 F.2d 444 (1967).

Further Reading

American Law Institute (ALI), *Model Penal Code*. Philadelphia: Author, 1962.

Biggs, John, *The Guilty Mind*. New York: Harcourt, Brace, 1955.

Caesar, B., "The Insanity Defense: The New Loophole." *Prosecutor* 16 (1982): 19–26.

Ellias, R., "Should Courts Instruct Juries As to the Consequences to a Defendant of a 'Not Guilty by Reason of Insanity' Verdict?" *Journal of Criminal Law and Criminology* 85, no. 4 (1995): 1062.

Erickson, Patricia E., *Crime, Punishment, and Mental Illness: Law and the Behavioral Sciences in Conflict*. New Brunswick, NJ: Rutgers University Press, 2008.

Ewing, Charles Patrick, *Insanity: Murder, Madness, and the Law*. New York: Oxford University Press, 2008.

Flew, Anthony, *Crime, Punishment, and Disease*. New Brunswick, NJ: Transaction Publishers, 2002.

Gall, C. A., "The Insanity of the Insanity Defense." *Prosecutor* 16 (1982): 6–13.

"Insane on All Counts: Is the System Guilty?" *Time* (July 5, 1982): 26–27.

Liu, Joseph P., "Note, Federal Jury Instructions and the Consequences of a Successful Insanity Defense" *Columbia Law Review* 93 (1993): 1223, 1229.

Lunde, D. T., *Murder and Madness*. New York: Norton, 1975.

Robin, G., "The Evolution of the Insanity Defense: Welcome to the Twilight Zone of Mental Illness, Psychiatry, and the Law." *Journal of Contemporary Criminal Justice* 13, no. 3 (1997): 224–235.

Shaw, Matthew F., *After the Insanity Defense: When the Acquitted Return to the Community*. New York: LFB Scholarly Publishing, 2007.

Simon, Rita J., and Heather Ahn-Redding, *The Insanity Defense, the World Over.* Lanham, MD: Lexington Books, 2006.

Szasz, Thomas, *Law, Liberty, and Psychiatry: An Inquiry into the Social Uses of Mental Health Practices.* Syracuse, NY: Syracuse University Press, 1989.

Torrey, E. Fuller, *The Insanity Defense: How America's Failure to Treat the Seriously Mental Ill Endangers Its Citizens.* New York: Norton, 2008.

Worth, Richard, *The Insanity Defense.* New York: Chelsea House, 2001.

J

JUVENILE JUSTICE

Christopher Bickel

The history of juvenile justice in the United States contains contradictory and competing ideas about juvenile delinquency and its solutions. Hence, juvenile justice policies have shifted along a continuum of incarceration at the one end and rehabilitation at the other. During times of moral panic over youth delinquency—which are often laced with racial fear and anxiety—the United States has shifted to an incarceration model that relies heavily on punitive policies of discipline. At other times, juvenile justice polices have embodied a model of rehabilitation that stresses support services and counseling for juveniles. Recently, one of the more controversial issues revolving around juvenile is whether juveniles who commit so-called adult crimes should be regarded as adults and subject to the same kinds of punishment or should be cared for as youths in need of treatment and understanding.

Background

The first institution in the United States to address juvenile delinquency was the House of Refuge in New York City. Established in 1825, this institution held not only children convicted of crimes but also those whose only crime was living in poverty. Soon after the opening of the first House of Refuge, reformers opened similar houses in Boston and Philadelphia. The public justification for the Houses of Refuge was explicitly religious. Wealthy reformers believed that impoverished children lacked the proper Christian values and morals, including a strong work ethic and respect for authority. As a result, reformers designed the Houses of Refuge to reform youth through disciplined activity, prayer, work, and a heavily regimented day. On the one hand, the Houses of Refuge provided an alternative to the harsh conditions of adult jails and prisons, where children were frequently held. On the other hand, house residents were subjected to harsh training where corporal punishment and punitive working conditions were common.

Underneath the religious rhetoric of the conservative reformers was an intense fear of the poor, who, if organized, posed a threat to their class privilege. This gave rise to a widespread moral panic about rising juvenile delinquency among poor and working-class youth. At the time, massive economic disparity between the rich and poor profoundly shaped the social landscape. The industrial elite heavily exploited the labor of working-class and immigrant populations in the factories. Riots over working conditions were commonplace. The wealthy elite grew ever more weary and saw the Houses of Refuge as providing necessary reforms to control working-class youth (Krisberg 2005).

Since the construction of first House of Refuge, there has been contentious debate about how best to confront juvenile delinquency. Although the early reformers argued for institutionalization, others questioned the utility of institutions for children. In the 1850s, organizations like the Children's Aid Society argued that the Houses of Refuge were likely to expose children to criminal behavior and lead to more crime. The Children's Aid Society was part of a broader movement called the Child Savers, which argued that the Christian family was the ideal place to combat juvenile delinquency and socialize children. Child Saver organizations established programs to relocate children from the city to families in the west. These families, in theory, would raise the children with so-called proper Christian morals and values and offer better living conditions for the impoverished. In practice, however, the children's new families often treated them as delinquent stepchildren and exploited their labor for profit (Krisberg 2005).

Although the Child Savers argued against institutionalization for white immigrants, they raised few questions about the institutionalization of Native American children in boarding schools and African American children on plantations. In fact, many Child Savers urged the government to provide more funding for the construction of boarding schools for Native American children. Given prevailing stereotypes, Child Savers argued that the Native American family was immoral, backward, and unfit to raise children. Boarding schools, they believed, were the proper place to socialize Native American children. The boarding schools forbade children to use their first language, severed family ties, and attempted to replace Native American culture with Protestant values and morals. Boarding school staff forced children to cut their hair upon arrival and adopt European American ways of dress and demeanor. In their attempts to reform Native American children, boarding schools often relied on violent forms of discipline, not unlike those found in the early Houses of Refuge (Finkelstein 2000).

Despite resistance to institutionalization, juvenile reform schools continued to grow in the cities, especially in the Northeast. Throughout the late 1800s, the state increasingly participated in the construction and management of reform schools. In 1899, Illinois established the first juvenile court charged with hearing all cases involving juveniles. The court was founded on the idea of *parens patriae,* which asserts that children are developmentally unlike adults. Given this, the state has a vested interest in protecting the welfare of children, who cannot protect themselves. Before 1899, the legal system made no formal distinction between adults and children (Austin and Irwin 2001). After the formation of the Illinois juvenile courts, other states soon followed. Juvenile courts sought to control juvenile delinquency through rehabilitation rather than punishment. The courts had the power to remove children from their homes and sentence them to training schools. Although rehabilitation was the goal, the training schools continued to feel like places of punishment to those confined.

Throughout the early 1900s, reformers continued to experiment with different strategies to control juvenile delinquency. With the rise of the social sciences, researchers explored the causes of delinquency and began to offer social policies based on systematic research. Early criminologists, like Cesare Lombroso, argued that criminality was genetic and traceable by studying the structure and shape of the human body. Biological explanations posited that if people were born criminal, attempts to rehabilitate them would inevitably fail. Other researchers, like William Healy, questioned the more biological explanations and instead argued that juvenile delinquency was a symptom of a child's surroundings—their peers, family, and so on—which all affected their mental health.

The more environmental explanations for juvenile delinquency gathered strength with the creation of the Chicago School of Sociology. Sociologist Clifford Shaw systematically studied juvenile delinquency in Chicago during the 1930s. He argued that delinquency was the product of social disorganization in neighborhoods, which experienced a breakdown of more conventional institutions like the family and church. Informed by theories of social disorganization, the Chicago School helped to develop more preventative strategies to combat juvenile delinquency. Social workers were sent out into the community to organize residents and create community institutions that would prevent juvenile delinquency. For Shaw, reform schools were of limited value because they did not address the social causes of delinquency, specifically the structural breakdown of communities. The key to solving problems of juvenile delinquency was to strengthen community ties and institutions. Despite Shaw's call for more preventative measures, juvenile institutions continued to grow throughout the 1940s and 1950s.

The Modern Period: From Deinstitutionalization to Getting Tough

The 1960s gave birth to a new wave of thinking about juvenile delinquency, which challenged the continued institutionalization of juveniles. With the rise of the Black Power movement, Chicano Movement, and American Indian Movement, community residents began to argue for more control over the institutions that confined their children.

Many questioned the need for more juvenile institutions, which activists argued were not about rehabilitation or reform but rather about controlling and patrolling communities of color. The social uprisings of the 1960s provided the backdrop to the formation of more community-based solutions. Instead of removing children from the community to large-scale institutions, activists argued for more preventative programs, group homes, and transition homes.

Activist calls for deinstitutionalization came to fruition in 1972 when Jerome Miller, director of the Massachusetts Department of Youth Services, closed down all juvenile reform schools and transferred the children to smaller residential programs, where they received personalized counseling from trained professionals rather than punishment from prison guards. These new community-based programs were far more successful in reducing recidivism rates that the youth prisons that existed prior to 1972. Following in Miller's footsteps, President Richard Nixon established the 1973 National Advisory Commission on Criminal Justice Standards and Goals. The commission recommended that all large-scale juvenile justice institutions be closed and replaced by more community-based programs (Mauer 1999). Juvenile prisons, the commission argued, were more likely to increase crime than to prevent it, because children rarely received the necessary rehabilitation in prison-like facilities. In institutions, children learned more about crime and developed a distaste for people in positions of authority, all of which increased the chances that they would reoffend. Nixon, however, disregarded the report, paving the way for increased use of juvenile prisons. Although various states continued to experiment with deinstitutionalization for juveniles, these efforts all but disappeared during the 1980s and 1990s, with the rise of the "get tough on crime" movement.

Although juvenile crime rates during the 1970s and early 1980s remained fairly constant, there was a substantial increase in juvenile crime from 1987 to 1994, especially crimes involving firearms. For example, teenage homicide rates doubled between 1985 and 1994 (National Criminal Justice Commision 1996). Conservative criminologists, academics, commentators, and politicians seized the opportunity to push a "get tough on crime" agenda that argued for less rehabilitation and more punishment. John DiIulio, a political scientist at Princeton, became an academic poster child for this movement when he coined the racially charged word *superpredator*. DiIulio, and a cohort of other conservative academics, used that word to describe a new kind of juvenile offender who was sociopathic, remorseless, and very dangerous. DiIulio's argument, fraught with racial stereotypes, maintained that the new youthful offender lacked a moral conscience and values.

This framing of youth crime is reminiscent of how the early reformers framed white immigrant youth during the creation of the Houses of Refuge. DiIulio warned that, by the year 2010, nearly 270,000 superpredators would be roaming the streets, resulting in an unprecedented crime wave. This stoked the already burning flames of racial and class anxiety and thus served to justify new laws and penalties for juvenile offenders.

Rehabilitation, conservatives argued, would not work with this new type of juvenile offender. The media ran with the story. Every school shooting, juvenile homicide, and violent crime became a testament to the rise of the superpredator, which became a racially imbued code word for children of color in the inner city. By 1994, nearly 40 percent of all print news that covered children was about crime and violence, mostly involving children of color (Hancock 2000).

Time, however, did not lend much support to DiIulio's thesis of the superpredator. Crime rates began to drop after 1994, and the crime wave he had predicted never hit. In fact, juvenile crime rates have continued to drop. Moreover, DiIulio's description of a new kind of juvenile delinquent failed to match the data on incarcerated children. Of the 106,000 children in secure facilities in 1997, the overwhelming majority were incarcerated for nonviolent offenses. Thirty-six percent of juveniles were incarcerated for crimes against persons. Only 2 percent of incarcerated children had committed homicide, and 6 percent committed sexual assault. The majority of incarcerated children, or 73 percent, had committed nonviolent offenses. Property offenses, like auto theft and shoplifting, accounted for 32 percent. Drug offenses accounted for 9 percent, mostly for drug possession. Public order violations, like being drunk in public, accounted for 10 percent. Technical violations of patrol accounted for 13 percent (Office of Juvenile Justice and Delinquency Prevention 1999).

This portrait of incarcerated children is a far cry from the myth of the violent superpredator. Nonetheless, politicians continued to sound the alarm. By capitalizing on the public's racial anxiety and fear of crime, politicians seized their newly found political capital to win elections. This paved the way to making the juvenile justice system of the United States one of the most punitive in the world and one of the largest incarcerators of children.

Moreover, the 1980s and 1990s saw the passing of several punitive laws designed to target youth crime at the federal, state, and local levels. At the federal level, the Violent and Repeat Juvenile Offender Act of 1997 encouraged more prosecution of juvenile offenders, increased penalties for gang-related offenses, and increased the use of mandatory minimums for juvenile offenders. At the state level, an increasing number of states passed laws to lower the age at which juveniles could be tried as adults. Some states allowed children as young as 14 years of age to be tried in adult criminal courts. In 2000, California, for example, passed Proposition 21, the Juvenile Crime Initiative, which increased the penalties for gang-related felonies; mandated indeterminate life sentences for carjacking, drive-by shootings, and home invasion robbery; made gang recruitment a felony; and required adult trials for children as young as 14 charged with serious sex offenses and murder. Proposition 21 passed with 62 percent of the vote, even though crime rates among juveniles had decreased during the previous six years.

At the local level, city prosecutors sought restraining orders against specific gangs in the community. These orders are known as gang injunctions and prohibit actions like walking down the street in groups of four or more, wearing certain kinds of clothes, and associating with other gang members. These activities are not crimes in any other neighborhoods except those where injunctions apply. Those who violate these rules can be held for violating a court order, resulting in up to six months in jail for participating in illegal activities. Moreover, those convicted of gang-related felonies face additional penalties aside from the actual crime for being in contempt of court for violating the restraining orders.

Los Angeles, for example, has nearly 30 gang injunctions that target more than 35 different gangs, nearly all of them comprising people of color. Although police departments praise gang injunctions as a vital tool in their war on gangs, the use of gang injunctions has raised questions among civil rights advocates because they overwhelmingly target people of color. The use of gang injunctions is quite similar to the way in which white southerners used the Black Codes to criminalize and incarcerate large numbers of recently freed African Americans after the abolition of slavery. Black Codes included laws against loitering, socializing in large groups, and vagrancy that applied only to African Americans, much as restraining orders apply only to specific communities (Bennett 1993).

A massive increase in the number of children of color in the juvenile justice system has accompanied these new federal, state, and local "get tough" policies. Although African Americans represent roughly 13 percent of the population, they make up nearly 40 percent of all incarcerated children. Latinos represent 13 percent of the general population but 21 percent of incarcerated children in public institutions. Native Americans also have a high rate of incarceration, but because of their relatively low numbers in the general population, they represent only 1 percent of the incarcerated population. Asians and Pacific Islanders account for 2 percent of the incarcerated population. These low numbers, however, mask the high incarceration rates of Cambodian, Laotian, Hmong, and Samoan children (Office of Juvenile Justice and Delinquency Prevision 1999).

These statistics reflect widespread institutional racism within the juvenile justice system. According to the 2007 report *And Justice for Some,* by the National Council on Crime and Delinquency, Latino and African American youth are far more likely to be incarcerated in state institutions, even when controlling for the type of offense and prior records. Latino youth are three times more likely to be incarcerated than their white counterparts and spend 112 days longer in secure settings than their white counterparts. African American children are six times more likely to be incarcerated and spend, on average, 61 more days confined than their white counterparts (National Council on Crime and Delinquency 2007). Moreover, although white children are more likely to use drugs, children of color are three times more likely to be incarcerated for drug crimes (Krisberg 2005).

WHITE AND BLACK JUSTICE

Sara Steen, a professor at Vanderbilt University, and George Bridges, a professor at the University of Washington, provide insight into how race structures the process of juvenile justice. Bridges and Steen systematically studied the written reports submitted by probation officers to the juvenile court system. These reports, based on interviews with accused children, contain the children's life histories and the probation officers' sentencing recommendations. After looking at hundreds of reports, Bridges and Steen found that, when they were explaining the crimes of black children, probation officers pointed to negative attitudes and personality traits, such as a lack of respect for the law and authority. For white children, however, probation officers highlighted more environmental factors, like family and drug abuse. As a result, Steen and Bridges found that probation officers recommended longer sentences for black children because they were perceived to be dangerous and a threat to society.* Racial stereotypes, they argued, heavily shape the processing of children of color throughout the juvenile justice system.

*George Bridges and Sara Steen, "Racial Disparities in Official Assessments of Juvenile Offenders: Attributional Stereotypes as Mediating Mechanisms of Juvenile Offenders." *American Sociological Review* 63 (August 1998): 554–570.

Conditions of Confinement: Incarceration versus Rehabilitation

Children awaiting trial are often confined to juvenile detention centers located in their communities. Once children are sentenced, they are usually transferred to state institutions located in rural communities far away from their homes. Secure institutions for juveniles, whether detention centers or youth prisons, vary greatly depending on the state. Most states base their juvenile justice policies on the incarceration model and confine youth to large, prison-like institutions equipped with cells, steel doors, and heavy locks. Services and rehabilitation programs are scarce, because the goal of rehabilitation has been replaced with that of punishment. Other states, however, organize juvenile justice around policies of rehabilitation and run smaller, community-based institutions that offer substantial counseling and rehabilitation programming.

Under the incarceration model, juvenile detention centers and youth prisons treat their captives as human objects to be worked upon, shaped, and molded to meet institutional demands. Much like the early Houses of Refuge, juvenile detention centers and prisons strictly enforce obedience, passivity, and deference to people in positions of authority. In juvenile detention centers and youth prisons, children are subjected to a series of rules and punishments that, in theory, are supposed to help reform their behavior.

Behavior management programs are often used to achieve these ends. Such programs outline all institutionally acceptable and unacceptable behaviors and impose an artificial hierarchy on the youth, marking those with and those without certain privileges. If a child follows all the rules and obeys the instructions of the guards, they are rewarded with extra time out of their cells, later bedtimes, and more access to the phone.

If children break these institutional rules or defy the orders of the guards, they may be punished with cell confinement, which in theory should last anywhere from eight hours to three days but in reality may last for several months.

If a child, for example, has a pencil in his or her cell, or if he or she possesses more than five books, the child may be locked in the cell for 16 hours. If a child tucks his or her pants into socks or is found with sagging counting blues (baggy blue jeans), he or she may be locked in the cells for two days. If a child floods the cell, he or she may be locked in the cell for a minimum of three days, with additional punishment depending on behavior while confined (Bickel 2004).

Grounded in simple operant conditioning, the underlying assumption of this system, known as the level system, is that if compliance is rewarded and noncompliance punished, the youth, like mice in a Skinner box, will eventually learn to adhere to the rules of the institution and, by extension, those of society. Although the level system is the primary tool of social control inside the secured walls, it is justified on the grounds that if children can be trained to follow rules inside the detention facility, these newly instilled values will follow them once they leave it.

Depending on the institution, children may spend their time housed in large barracks-style housing units or in cells similar to those used to house adults in prisons: seven- by eight-foot cinderblock rooms each containing a bed, a stainless steel sink and toilet, and a steel door with a narrow window. On average, children spend nearly 14 hours a day inside their cells. When they are confined to cells for long periods of time, children often feel angry, frustrated, and bored, leading many to conclude that they are merely being warehoused (Bickel 2004). The stringent rules and punishments exacerbate these feelings among detained and incarcerated youth and set the stage for intense conflict between the confined and the confiners, or guards, who must enforce the rules and impose punishments.

Guards and the Incarceration Model

Guards work in juvenile facilities for a variety of reasons. Some want to work with children and counsel them. Others, however, work in juvenile institutions because such jobs provide a stable and secure source of income. Guards come from all walks of life. Some are college graduates, others are retired from the military, and others are high school graduates. Increasingly, states require that guards have at least a college education or military experience. Few guards, however, have significant training dealing with incarcerated children, especially those in large, prison-like institutions that operate under the incarceration model.

The training that guards receive varies from state to state but usually consists of a stint in a training academy and a probationary period of on-the-job training. In

Washington, for example, new recruits must attend a two-week training academy course at some time during their six-month probationary period of employment. At the academy, guards learn how to observe the children, use disciplinary techniques, and use physical force. During this training, guards learn to always be on the alert in dealing with detained and incarcerated children. Implicit and sometime explicit in their training is the assumption that the children are, at best, troubled and, at worst, downright dangerous. The *Washington State Juvenile Workers Handbook,* for example, warns new recruits that "the first step in preparing to deal with offenders is to understand the sociopathic personality" (Criminal Justice Training Commission n.d.) The handbook, then, lists characteristics of the so-called sociopathic personality, reminiscent of DiIulio's myth of the superpredator: irresponsible, self-centered, feels little or no guilt, sees staff as objects for exploitation, compulsive liar, strong drive for immediate gratification, and adept at manipulation. "You must recognize that a majority of the offender population will be sociopathic to some degree," the handbook warns (Criminal Justice Training Commission n.d.).

Although guards are taught to be deeply suspicious of the children, they are offered little education on how larger social forces shape the children's response to the justice system. Guards, for example, are not taught about the effects of poverty or racism on the lives of detained children, nor is there any discussion of how racial and class biases affect how guards interact with and perceive their charges. In short, guards leave the academy ill prepared to deal with incarcerated children in any way except as potential threats. They are taught little that might help them bridge the gap between the two warring worlds found in most juvenile detention centers and youth prisons.

Rather than teaching understanding and building bridges between the guards and children, the academy trains guards to distrust incarcerated youth at every turn, thus exacerbating the conflict between the two sides (Bickel 2004).

The Incarceration Model and Abuse

On April 1, 2003, cameras caught two juvenile prison guards physically assaulting two children in a Stockton, California, youth facility. One guard punched a child in his head and face more than 28 times while the child was in a fetal position, arms protecting his head. Aside from the repeated closed-fist punches, guards dropped their knees with heavy force several times on the back of the child's head and neck. Although the incident was caught on tape, the county district attorney dropped all charges against the guards.

This incident, coupled with increasing public scrutiny of the California Youth Authority (CYA), led to an intensive review of juvenile prisons in the state. The CYA is one of the largest justice systems in the United States, housing more than 4,300 youth, 84 percent of whom are children of color. The CYA relies heavily on the incarceration model to structure institutional policies and practices. Barry Krisberg, director of the

National Council on Crime and Delinquency, released his report of the CYA in December 2003. Krisberg found extensive abuse in the six CYA institutions he investigated.

During the first four months of 2003, one state institution documented more than 535 incidents of the use of chemical restraints, such as mace and pepper spray. Mace and pepper spray are used throughout juvenile facilities in the United States and are usually used to break up large disturbances. The 2003 review of the CYA, however, found that chemical restraints were frequently used to remove children from their cells, even when there was no clear reason to do so. Guards refused to allow many children to wash off the chemicals, leaving severe chemical burns on their skin. During the same four-month period, there were 109 incidents involving physical restraints and 236 incidents involving mechanical restraints. Mechanical restrains involve forcing children to rest on their knees for long periods of time with their hands bound behind their backs (Krisberg 2003).

Aside from the use of chemical, physical, and mechanical restraints, Krisberg also found that 10 percent to 12 percent of the youths were housed in restrictive facilities where they spent 23 hours a day in their cells, with one hour out for recreation. Often, during that one hour of recreation, children were chained in five-point restraints, with ankles locked together and wrists locked to the waist, making it difficult to exercise. Other children were released to small cages called Special Program Areas.

In addition to abuse at the hands of guards, Krisberg also found significant ward-on-ward violence in the CYA. In the six institutions he studied, there were more than 4,000 ward-on-ward physical assaults and 1,000 cases of sexual harassment. This averages to about 10 assaults per day in six institutions having a combined total population of 3,800 youths. The 2003 CYA review highlights the rampant violence that youths experience from both guards and other inmates. Although the CYA is one of the larger and more violent youth prison systems in the United States, there is no doubt that violence looms large in the minds of all children who are incarcerated (Krisberg 2003).

The push toward incarcerating more juveniles in secure facilities has produced some troubling results. If the success of incarceration strategies is measured by how many children are rearrested after their release, then most states that operate under the incarceration model are failing miserably. In California, for example, nearly 91 percent of those released from the CYA are arrested within three years (Center for Juvenile and Criminal Justice 2007). In Pennsylvania, nearly 55 percent are rearrested within 18 months, and in Utah, 79 percent are rearrested within a year (Krisberg 2005). These failure rates, coupled with media stories of abuse, have led some organizations to call for a shift from the incarceration model to a rehabilitation model. Organizations like Books Not Bars of Oakland, California, organize formerly incarcerated youth and their parents to protest the continued operation and expansion of large-scale youth prisons. Through protests and political lobbying, Books Not Bars pressures local and state officials to close the large institutions and replace them with smaller facilities that focus on rehabilitation.

Their efforts, along with the efforts of other youth justice organizations, have led to a significant drop in the number of youths confined in the CYA.

Alternatives to Incarceration: The Shift to Rehabilitation

Activist demands to close large-scale youth prisons and jails echo the child advocates of the 1930s and 1960s, who challenged the increasing reliance on juvenile institutionalization. Some states, like Missouri, have cast aside the incarceration model in favor of a rehabilitation model that relies heavily on preventative programs, alternatives to incarceration, and community-based solutions. In 1983, Missouri closed its large institutions for juveniles and opened several small community-based rehabilitation centers throughout the state, where residents could be located closer to home. Although most states have facilities that house 100 or more youths, Missouri's institutions house no more than 36 children per facility (Missouri Division of Youth Services 2000). Missouri also has a number of different types of facilities, ranging from small, secure institutions to group homes to day treatment centers.

Unlike the large youth prison of other states, Missouri's secure facilities have no cells or barracks-style housing units. Instead, the children are housed in dormitory settings and are allowed to wear their own clothing rather than institutional uniforms. Guards are replaced with college graduates who receive specialized training on how best to interact with the children they supervise. As a result, Missouri experiences far less conflict between staff and the youths, paving the way for supportive relationships to develop. Moreover, rather than being closed institutions, community organizations are a vital part of the programming, as children are allowed to leave the facilities to work in the community on supervised projects. Missouri also has several group homes where children charged with less serious offenses are held. In these homes, youths are allowed to attend school and work outside of the facility.

Missouri's rehabilitation model has been far more successful than those in other states. The recidivism rate in Missouri is far lower than those of California, Utah, and Pennsylvania. Only 9 percent of the youths are reincarcerated in juvenile or adult facilities after their release (Missouri Division of Youth Services 2000). Moreover, because the facilities in Missouri do not rely heavily on guards, the security costs to run them are far lower than those of other states. Whereas California spends nearly $80,000 to house a child in the CYA, Missouri spends $40,000, with far better results. Missouri continues to be a model for other states and may signal a future shift in national juvenile justice policies.

Conclusion

The history of juvenile justice in the United States has revolved around several competing approaches to dealing with juvenile delinquency. From the early calls for confinement within Houses of Refuge to the more recent demands for deinstitutionalization in Massachusetts and Missouri, juvenile justice has always shifted and changed with the times. During periods of moral panic laced with racial anxiety and fear, the United States has moved toward punitive strategies that expose children, especially children of color, to systemic violence and abuse. As youth advocates and activists highlight the failure of more punitive polices, however, states are beginning to search for more effective strategies that move from incarceration to rehabilitation.

See also **Alternative Treatments for Criminal Offenders; Gang Injunction Laws; Juveniles Treated as Adults; School Violence; Gangs (vol. 3)**

Further Reading

Austin, James, and John Irwin, *It's about Time: America's Imprisonment Binge.* Stamford, CT: Wadsworth, 2001.

Bennett, Lerone, *Before the Mayflower: A History of Black America.* Chicago: Johnson, 1993.

Bickel, Christopher, "Jaded by the System: Authoritarianism and Resistance in a Juvenile Detention Center." Unpublished manuscript, University of California, Santa Barbara, 2004.

Books Not Bars, http://www.booksnotbars.org

Center for Juvenile and Criminal Justice, *Reforming the Juvenile Justice System.* Boston: Beacon Press, 2007.

Criminal Justice Training Commission, *Juvenile Workers Academy,* Part 2, "Supervision." Olympia, WA: n.d.

Finkelstein, Barbara, "A Crucible of Contradictions: Historical Roots of Violence Against Children in the United States." In *The Public Assault on America's Children: Poverty Violence and Juvenile Injustice,* ed. V. Polakow. New York: Teachers College Press, 2000.

Hancock, LynNell, "Framing Children in the News: The Face and Color of Youth Crime in America." In *The Public Assault on America's Children: Poverty Violence and Juvenile Injustice,* ed. V. Polakow. New York: Teachers College Press, 2000.

Krisberg, Barry, *General Corrections Review of the California Youth Authority.* San Francisco: National Council on Crime and Delinquency, December 2003.

Krisberg, Barry, *Juvenile Justice: Redeeming Our Children.* Thousand Oaks, CA: Sage, 2005.

Mauer, Marc, *Race to Incarcerate.* New York: New Press, 1999.

McShane, Marilyn D., and Frank P. Williams III, eds., *Youth Violence and Delinquency: Monsters and Myths.* Westport, CT: Praeger, 2007.

Missouri Division of Youth Services, "System Change through State Challenge Activities." *Juvenile Justice Bulletin.* Washington, DC: Office of Juvenile Justice and Delinquency Prevention, March, 2000.

National Council on Crime and Delinquency, *And Justice for Some: Differential Treatment of Youth of Color in the Justice System.* San Francisco: Author, 2007.

National Council on Crime and Delinquency, http://www.nccd-crc.org; Center on Juvenile and Criminal Justice, http://www.cjcj.org

National Criminal Justice Commission, *The Real War on Crime,* ed. Steven Donziger. New York: Harper Perennial, 1996.

Office of Juvenile Justice and Delinquency Prevention, *Juveniles in Correctional Facilities.* Washington, DC: U.S. Department of Justice, 1999.

Polakow, Valarie, *The Public Assault on America's Children: Poverty Violence and Juvenile Injustice.* New York: Teachers College Press, 2000.

Scott, Elizabeth S., *Rethinking Juvenile Justice.* Cambridge, MA: Harvard University Press, 2008.

JUVENILES TREATED AS ADULTS

Cary Stacy Smith and Li-Ching Hung

Since the mid-1990s, fear of juvenile crime and criminals has undermined what was considered the norm for many years; that is, the idea that most crimes committed by juveniles should be tried in a juvenile court. Using a punitive adult model for adolescents and preteens required the courts to assume that the youthful transgressor was equal to an adult in terms of culpability; naturally, there was and is widespread disagreement on this issue. Some argue that it is the height of folly to think that an average teenager is incapable of understanding criminal proceedings, whereas others state that it is highly unethical for judges and district attorneys to prosecute adolescents in an adult venue (Steinberg 2005). Other controversies question the wisdom, for example, of placing youths in institutional situations where they are likely to experience physical and/or sexual abuse.

Background

In 1899, the first juvenile court system within the United States was established in Cook County, Illinois; shortly thereafter, juvenile courts spread to all states of the union.

Within juvenile courts, adolescent offenders are treated differently than their adult counterparts. For instance, what is considered legal for adults may not be legal for juveniles. Violations known as status offenses—such as being truant, running away from home, and using alcohol—are behaviors that are not against the law for adults but are

COMPARATIVE VIOLENCE IN ADULT AND JUVENILE INSTITUTIONS

Fifty percent of children incarcerated in adult prisons reported being attacked with a weapon, and 10 percent reported having been sexually attacked. Only 1 percent reported the same in a juvenile institution.

Source: Vincent Shiraldi and Jason Zeidenberg, "The Risks Juveniles Face When They Are Incarcerated with Adults." Justice Policy Institute (1997). www.justicepolicy.org/images/upload/97-02_REP_RiskJuvenilesFace_JJ.pdf

considered infractions if performed by juveniles. The primary aim of juvenile courts is to guide, not punish, adolescents who have violated the law. In addition, although adult law focuses on the offense, juvenile law focuses on the offender, and attempts are made to rehabilitate any transgressors. Other differences include the following: (1) juveniles are adjudicated rather than pronounced guilty, (2) juvenile records may be sealed at the judge's discretion, and (3) juveniles do not have the right to a jury trial. Moreover, juveniles are usually placed in special facilities, away from hardened, adult criminals. With serious crimes, however, exceptions are made (Jonson-Reid 2004).

Law enforcement has the option of preventative detention, meaning that a youth may be detained for his or her protection or the community's protection. Because the juvenile court system is highly individualized, sentences vary from court to court and state to state and may cover a wide range of community-based and residential options. The disposition is based on an adolescent's history and the severity of his or her offenses and includes a significant rehabilitation component. Moreover, the disposition can be for an unspecified period; the court has the authority to send a youth to a specific facility or program until he or she is deemed rehabilitated or until he or she reaches the age of majority. The disposition may also include a restitution component and can be directed at people other than the offender, such his or her parents. Parole combines surveillance with activities to reintegrate the juvenile into the community.

One reason juveniles are transferred to criminal court is the general belief that if adolescents (both violent and nonviolent) are exposed to the adult criminal justice system, any criminal urges would be extinguished. Unfortunately, the literature does not back this supposition. A 1996 study looked at 2,738 juvenile offenders transferred to criminal court in Florida with a matched sample of nontransferred juveniles. Juveniles tried as adults were more likely to be incarcerated, incarcerated for longer periods than those who remained in the juvenile system, and had a higher recidivism rate. Within two years, they were more likely to reoffend, to reoffend earlier, to commit more subsequent offenses, and to commit more serious subsequent offenses than juveniles retained in the juvenile system (Bishop, Frazier, Lanza-Kaduce, and Winner 1996).

Studies on Juveniles and Justice

During 2003, a study titled Adolescent Development and Juvenile Justice, conducted by the John D. and Catherine T. MacArthur Foundation Research Network, examined more than 1,400 people between the ages of 11 and 24 in Philadelphia, Los Angeles, northern and eastern Virginia, and northern Florida. Each participant was given an intelligence test and later asked to respond to several hypothetical legal situations, such as whether confessing to a police officer if he or she committed a crime was a smart move. Interestingly, the researchers found that one-third of those aged 11 to 13 and one-fifth of those aged 14 to 15 could not understand the proceedings regarding their alleged crimes, nor could they supply help to their defense lawyers. The study recommended that states reconsider the minimum age at which juveniles may be tried as adults or that a system for evaluating defendants' competency be created.

The report was released on the heels of a 10-year effort by states trying to make it easier to try children as adults (Steinberg 2005).

The question is this: Is it OK to place children with adults in prison, where the older convicts will likely teach them how to be successful criminals and where they will probably experience both physical and sexual abuse? For example, one 17-year-old adolescent held with adult convicts in an Idaho jail was sexually tortured and murdered by the adult inmates. In Ohio, a 15-year-old girl was sexually assaulted by a deputy jailer after being placed in an adult jail for a minor infraction, and in Kentucky, approximately 30 minutes after a 15-year-old was put in a jail cell following an argument with his mother, he hanged himself. In one year, four children held in Kentucky jails committed suicide (Zeidenberg and Schiraldi 1997).

In 1989, a study compared how youths were treated at a number of juvenile training schools with those serving time in adult prisons. Unsurprisingly, five times as many adolescents held in adult prisons answered yes to the question "Has anyone attempted to sexually attack or rape you?" In addition, the statistics regarding youth rape in prisons were coupled with the fact that children placed with adults were twice as likely to report being physically abused by staff. The juveniles in adult prison were also 50 percent more likely to report being attacked with a weapon. Close to 10 percent of the youth interviewed reported a sexual violation.

Little research exists regarding any quantitative data on rape, suicide, and assault rates among the thousands of juveniles sentenced to adult prisons each year or the 65,000 children who pass through the jail system. Several states classify suicide under deaths due to "unspecified" causes in their yearly reports, thus making the problem invisible. Rape in prison is listed under inmate assault; hence, the problem is opaque. Approximately 25,000 children each year have their cases transferred to criminal court instead of being tried in juvenile courts, where the majority of convicted defendants are usually set free by the time they turn 21 (Senate Committee on the Judiciary 2000).

Many judges will not prosecute youths as adults, as in the case of Nathaniel Abraham. At age 11, he was charged with first-degree murder and was to be prosecuted under a 1997 Michigan law that allowed adult prosecutions of children of any age in serious felony cases. Abraham was eventually convicted of second-degree murder, but the presiding judge felt that the new law was flawed and sentenced him to youth detention rather than life imprisonment (Steinberg 2005). In Texas, Lacresha Murray, an 11-year-old girl, was convicted twice for the death of a 2-year-old who spent the day in her home. After extensive questioning, without guardians or an attorney present, she admitted that she might have dropped and then kicked the toddler. The presiding judge dismissed all criminal charges leveled against her (Fritsch, Caeti, and Hemmens 1996).

Key Events

According to the National Center for Juvenile Justice, a private, nonprofit research group, between 1992 and 1999, every state except Nebraska passed laws making it easier for juveniles to be tried as adults. Even though Nebraska passed no new laws on the subject during that seven-year period, it is among the 14 states and the District of Columbia that allow prosecutors to file charges against juveniles in criminal court (Fritsch, Caeti, and Hemmens 1996). Each of the 50 states has specific provisions that determine whether certain juveniles may be tried as adults in criminal court (for example, those charged with capital crimes or other serious felonies). This procedure is commonly called a *transfer to criminal court* and has three primary mechanisms: judicial waiver, statutory exclusion, and concurrent jurisdiction.

- Forty-five states have judicial waiver provisions, in which the juvenile court judge has the vested authority to waive juvenile court jurisdiction and transfer the case to criminal court if he or she feels that the crime committed warrants more punishment than is commonly meted out within the juvenile justice system.
  - Threshold criteria that must be met before the court may consider waiver: generally a minimum age, a specified type or level of offense, a sufficiently serious record of previous delinquency, or some combination of the three.
  - In all states in which discretionary waiver is authorized, the juvenile court must conduct a hearing at which the parties are entitled to present evidence bearing on the waiver issue. Generally, state law specifies factors a court must weigh and findings it must make in order to arrive at the determination that a juvenile is no longer amenable to treatment as a juvenile.
  - The prosecution usually bears the burden of proof in a discretionary waiver hearing; however, some states designate special circumstances under which this burden may be shifted to the child. Generally, a prosecutor seeking a waiver to criminal court must make the case for waiver by a preponderance of the evidence.

- Twenty-nine states have statutory exclusion laws excluding youths who commit certain serious offenses and/or repeat offenses from the jurisdiction of the juvenile court. These laws are different from mandatory waiver laws in that, with statutory exclusion, the adult court has jurisdiction over a case from the beginning, without a juvenile court waiver hearing.
- Seventeen states allow for concurrent jurisdiction of offending youth in both the juvenile and adult court systems. Adolescents aged 14 or older who commit certain felonies are subject to transfer to adult criminal court for prosecution at the discretion of the judge. Transfer proceedings are mandatory in instances

of murder or aggravated malicious wounding. Prosecutors in instances of lesser felonies may also directly file for jurisdictional transfers. Once initiated, any transfer to adult court may be petitioned for reverse waiver back to juvenile court (Fritsch, Caeti, and Hemmens 1996).

In addition to state governments, the federal government also has the option of treating children as adults. There are many federal rules regarding juveniles, too many to detail here, including Federal Rule 106, which states the Federal Bureau of Investigation and other federal law enforcement agencies should aid local and state authorities in the apprehension of gang members. The rule's language is condescending, stating that local law enforcement has become frustrated with the state criminal systems and that federal assistance is sorely needed. Most defendants serve a bare minimum of time, however, and although the adult criminal system is ineffective in curtailing gang violence, the juvenile system is much worse. Most juvenile delinquents are handled by the state and are usually released immediately or lightly punished; thus, the states need guidance from the federal government (U.S. Department of Justice 1997b).

On the other hand, violent criminals (both adult and adolescent) are gaining a keen respect for the federal criminal system. They are aware of the abolition of parole as well as the severe guidelines and enhanced sentencing for drug- and firearms-related federal crimes. It is imperative for the safety of the citizens of the United States that U.S. attorneys' offices become more involved in seeking out the most serious juvenile offenders for prosecution as delinquents or transferring them for criminal prosecution as adults (U.S. Department of Justice 1997a); all may be found in the *Criminal Resource Manual* (U.S. Department of Justice 1997c).

Federal Rule 126 states that juveniles charged with serious offenses and who have prior criminal history and have proved unreceptive to treatment in the juvenile justice system may be considered for transfer to adult status. Any decision to transfer should be based upon discussion with the investigating agents, a prosecution policy that targets the most serious juvenile offenders, and a comparison of effective alternatives that may be available in the given state jurisdiction (U.S. Department of Justice 1997a).

Federal Rule 140 discusses the mandatory transfer of juveniles to adult status. Adult status for juveniles is mandatory if the acts were committed after his or her 16th birthday and would be tried as felonies involving the use, attempted use, or threatened use of physical force against another. In addition, if a substantial risk of physical force was used against another in committing the offense or if a juvenile has previously been found guilty of an act for which an adult would face prison time, such an offender may be transferred to adult status. Finally, the act must be one of the offenses set forth in this rule or an offense in violation of a state felony statute (U.S. Department of Justice 1997d).

Conclusion

Several states have laws saying that it is legal to sentence an adolescent to death if he or she was convicted of a capital offense. On March 1, 2005, the U.S. Supreme Court in *Roper v. Simmons* struck down the use of capital punishment for offenders committing crimes before the age of 18. In 1993, Christopher Simmons (who was 17 at the time) formulated a plan with two younger friends to murder Shirley Crook. In essence, the plan was to commit burglary and murder by breaking and entering, tying up Ms. Crook, and then tossing her from a bridge. At the trial's conclusion, Simmons was sentenced to death. He first moved for the trial court to set aside the conviction and sentence, citing, in part, ineffective assistance of counsel. His young age and impulsivity, along with a troubled background, were brought up as issues that Simmons claimed should have been raised at the sentencing phase. The trial court rejected the motion, and Simmons appealed. Finally, the case was argued in the U.S. Supreme Court. Justice Anthony Kennedy, writing for the majority, cited sociological and scientific articles stating that juveniles are immature and lacking a sense of responsibility as compared with adults (*Roper v. Simmons* 2005).

The Court noted that in recognition of the comparative immaturity and irresponsibility of juveniles, almost every state prohibited those younger than age 18 from voting, serving on juries, or marrying without parental consent. The studies also found that juveniles are more vulnerable to negative influences and outside pressures, including peer pressure. They have less control, or experience with control, over their own environment. Thus, the Court held that executing someone who was younger than age 18 at the time of the murder was committed was cruel and unusual punishment (*Roper v. Simmons* 2005). In a subsequent case from 2010, *Graham v. Florida,* the Court determined that life imprisonment for a juvenile offender convicted of any crime other than homicide likewise constitutes cruel and unusual punishment and must not be applied (Liptak 2010).

Little disagreement exists regarding the minute number of teens who should be tried in the adult criminal justice system (with the prominent exception of the death penalty) if they pose a sincere threat to those around them. Likewise, there is little bickering about severely delinquent adolescents (rapists, murderers, arsonists, etc.) receiving commensurate punishment for the scope of their crimes. However, thousands of young people are being prosecuted daily within the adult system, although many are charged with nonviolent crimes. This should give cause for quiet reflection, because the primary reason for youth courts was and is to adjudicate young people who had broken the law in a nonviolent fashion. If society punishes adolescents as it does adults, even if their transgressions do not warrant it, does the get-tough policy benefit the public?

Sadly, the prevailing mindset of many lawmakers is "If you do the crime, do the time—regardless of age." Thus, many adolescents and preteens whose crime was of a nonviolent nature will remain incarcerated with adult criminals, who will continue their physical and sexual abuse of children—all at taxpayer expense.

See also Gang Injunction Laws; Juvenile Justice; Prison Sexual Assault; Gangs (vol. 3)

Further Reading

Bishop, D. M., C. E. Frazier, L. Lanza-Kaduce, and L. Winner, "The Transfer of Juveniles to Criminal Court: Does It Make a Difference?" C*rime and Delinquency* 42 (1996): 171–191.

Butts, J., and G. Halemba, *Waiting for Justice: Moving Young Offenders through the Juvenile Court Process.* Pittsburgh, PA: National Center for Juvenile Justice, 1996.

Dawson, R. O., "The Future of Juvenile Justice: Is It Time to Abolish the System?" *Journal of Criminal Law and Criminology* 81 (1990): 136–155.

Fritsch, E. J., T. J. Caeti, and C. Hemmens, "Spare the Needle but not the Punishment: The Incarceration of Waived Youth in Texas Prisons." *Crime and Delinquency* 42, no. 4 (1996): 593–609.

Jonson-Reid, M., "Child Welfare Services and Delinquency: The Need To Know More." *Child Welfare* 83, no. 2 (2004): 157–174.

Kupchik, A., *Judging Juveniles: Prosecuting Adolescents in Adult and Juvenile Courts.* New York: New York University Press, 2006.

Liptak, Adam, "Justices Limit Life Sentences for Juveniles." *New York Times* (May 17, 2010). www.nytimes.com/2010/05/18/us/politics/18court.html

Puzzanchera, C. M., "Delinquency Cases Waived to Criminal Court, 1988–1997." *OJJDP Fact Sheet.* Washington, DC: U.S. Government Printing Office, 2000.

Roper v. Simmons, 543, U.S. 551 (2005).

Scott, Elizabeth S., *Rethinking Juvenile Justice.* Cambridge, MA: Harvard University Press. 2008.

Senate Committee on the Judiciary, "Putting Consequences Back into Juvenile Justice at the Federal, State, and Local Levels." Washington, DC: Government Printing Office, 2000.

Steinberg, L., *A Prospective Study of Serious Adolescent Offenders in Philadelphia.* Philadelphia: Pennsylvania Council on Crime and Delinquency, 2005.

U.S. Department of Justice, "Rule 106, Federal Involvement in Prosecuting Gang Activity." *Title 9: Criminal Resource Manual.* Washington, DC: U.S. Government Printing Office, 1997a.

U.S. Department of Justice, "Rule 126, Treating Juveniles as Adults for Criminal Prosecution—Generally." *Title 9: Criminal Resource Manual.* Washington, DC: U.S. Government Printing Office, 1997b.

U.S. Department of Justice, *Title 9: Criminal Resource Manual.* Washington, DC: U.S. Government Printing Office, 1997c.

U.S. Department of Justice, "Rule 140, Mandatory Transfer of Juveniles to Adult Status." *Title 9: Criminal Resource Manual.* Washington, DC: U.S. Government Printing Office, 1997d.

Zeidenberg, J., and V. Schiraldi, *The Risks Juveniles Face When They Are Incarcerated with Adults.* Washington, DC: Justice Policy Institute, 1997. http://www.cjcj.org/pubs/risks/riskspr.html.

M

MIRANDA WARNINGS

Jo-Ann Della Giustina

"You have the right to remain silent." We hear it on television, in the movies, and in music lyrics. The Miranda warnings have become so embedded in routine police practices that they have become a part of our national culture. Yet, they remain controversial. The Miranda rule was intended to protect against coerced confessions but has been criticized for tying the hands of law enforcement and favoring criminals. Moreover, some argue that it provides a method by which a guilty person can go free.

Shortly after ruling that the Fifth Amendment privilege against self-incrimination was applicable to the states (*Miranda v. Arizona* 1966), the U.S. Supreme Court ruled in the 1966 landmark case of *Miranda v. Arizona* that a person in police custody must be informed of his or her constitutional right against self-incrimination before being questioned. Without the Miranda warnings, any statement given during a custodial interrogation is not admissible in court proceedings. The Court stated that "[t]he prosecution may not use statements…stemming from questioning initiated by law enforcement officers after a person has been taken into custody or otherwise deprived of his freedom of action in any significant way, unless it demonstrates the use of procedural safeguards effective to secure the Fifth Amendment's privilege against self-incrimination" (*Brown v. Mississippi* 1936). The Court explained that the Miranda rule goes to the root of the "concepts of American criminal jurisprudence: the restraints society must observe consistent with the Federal Constitution in prosecuting individuals for crime" (*Brown v. Mississippi* 1936).

Background

During the early 20th century, the Supreme Court applied a due process voluntariness test, rooted in common law (*Leyra v. Denno* 1954), to determine the admissibility of a suspect's confession. The due process test weighs all the surrounding circumstances, including the details of the interrogation and the characteristics of the detainee. Early cases explained that the use of physical brutality and psychological pressure violate due process rights by overcoming a detainee's will.

While voluntariness has remained a requirement for confessions, the Court changed its focus in the 1960s. In 1964, the Court decided two landmark cases. In *Malloy v. Hogan,* the Court applied the Fifth Amendment's self-incrimination clause to the states, and in *Escobedo v. Illinois,* the Court ruled that the police violated the detainee's right to counsel because they did not advise him of his constitutional privilege to remain silent or his right to consult with his attorney. As a result, his statements were inadmissible.

Two years later, the Supreme Court decided *Miranda v. Arizona,* in which the Court remarked that reliance on the traditional totality of the circumstances test was inadequate to insure that a custodial confession would be voluntary. The Court noted that custodial police interrogation, by its very nature, isolates and pressures the individual. Because of this inherent compulsion in custodial surroundings, the Court presumed that all statements given during custodial police interrogation are compelled unless the detainee is informed of his or her right to remain silent and to have an attorney present during the interrogation and then knowingly and voluntarily waives those rights. The coercion inherent in custodial interrogations blurs the line between involuntary and voluntary statements, thereby increasing the risk that an individual will not be guaranteed his or her constitutional privilege against self-incrimination.

To ensure that police interrogation conforms to the Fifth Amendment requirements, the Court established concrete constitutional guidelines for law enforcement agencies and the courts. Under those guidelines, the admissibility of a statement given during custodial interrogation depends on whether the police provided the detainee with procedural safeguards sufficient to secure the Constitution's privilege against self-incrimination. The police must inform the detainee that he or she has the right to remain silent, that any statement he or she makes can be used against him or her in a court of law, that he or she

---

THE MIRANDA WARNINGS

A detainee has the right to remain silent.

Any statement a detainee makes can be used against him or her in a court of law.

A detainee has the right to the presence of an attorney during any interrogation.

If the detainee cannot afford an attorney, one will be appointed prior to any questioning.

has the right to the presence of an attorney, and that if he or she cannot afford an attorney, one will be appointed prior to any questioning.

Key Legal Cases

Since the Miranda decision, the Court has clarified, narrowed, and reinforced the Miranda rule. One significant issue clarified is when custody occurs. Custody does not necessarily mean a formal arrest. Instead, it is based on how a reasonable person in the detainee's situation would perceive his or her freedom to leave (*Michigan v. Mosley,* 1975). A person is in custody when the police have exerted physical or psychological authority so that a reasonable person would not believe that she or he was free to leave. In *Thompson v. Keohane* ((1981), the Court described the Miranda custody test as follows: "Two discrete inquiries are essential to the determination: first, what were the circumstances surrounding the interrogation; and second, given those circumstances, would a reasonable person have felt he or she was not at liberty to terminate the interrogation and leave."

Custody, however, is not the only issue clarified by the Court. Miranda warnings are required only before a detainee is interrogated. If the police do not question the detainee, no Miranda warnings are needed. Moreover, standard booking questions, such as name, date of birth, and address, are allowed without Miranda warnings.

The Court has given direction to law enforcement on what actions must be taken if the detainee invokes the right to silence or to an attorney. Pursuant to *Michigan v. Mosley* (1984), if the detainee indicates that he or she does not want to be interrogated, the police must immediately stop the questioning. However, the police may resume the interrogation after a significant period of time has passed and a new set of Miranda warnings is given.

In contrast, *Edwards v. Arizona* ((1971), established a bright-line rule that once a person in custody asserts her or his right to an attorney, the interrogation must end until an attorney is present. If the police subsequently initiate a discussion in the absence of an attorney, the detainee's statements are presumed involuntary even if he or she signs a waiver. An exception to this rule exists if either the detainee or the police ask a question relating to routine incidents of the custodial relationship (e.g., food, water, etc.) because it does not represent a desire to open up a more generalized discussion related directly or indirectly to the investigation.

Moreover, a detainee may subsequently waive the right to have an attorney present after he or she has invoked his or her right by reopening the dialogue with the authorities. It must be shown that the accused initiated the conversation in a manner indicating a desire and willingness to open a generalized discussion about the investigation. There must then be a knowing and intelligent waiver of his or her right to counsel's presence during questioning. Any waiver must be unbadgered, which depends on the particular facts and circumstances of each case.

There has been some confusion over whether the police must provide an attorney if the detainee requests one but cannot afford to pay for that attorney. The Miranda rule does not require that a lawyer be present at all times to advise detainees in the police station. Instead, it prescribes only that the police may not question the detainee without an attorney present if the detainee has invoked his or her right to counsel. In other words, if the detainee cannot afford to pay for an attorney but requests counsel, the police cannot question him or her unless they provide an attorney before any questioning occurs. There is no requirement that the police provide an attorney if no interrogation is conducted.

Public criticism of the Miranda warnings has led to a weakening of its requirements. Since the early 1970s, the Supreme Court has created numerous exceptions to the Miranda warnings, resulting in many un-Mirandized statements being legally admitted into evidence.

A narrow public safety exception was created in *New York v. Quarles* (2004). If public safety merits, the police officer may ask reasonable questions to secure his or her own safety or the safety of the public prior to the Miranda warnings without jeopardizing the admissibility of the statement. An example of a proper public safety question is to ask the detainee about the location of an abandoned weapon. Similarly, under the so-called stop-and-identify exception, an officer may ask a suspect his or her name and address without providing Miranda warnings.

Another exception was established in *Harris v. New York* ((1976), which allowed a detainee's un-Mirandized custodial statements to be used to impeach his credibility during his trial testimony. Because the detainee did not claim that his prior inconsistent statements were coerced or involuntary, the Court explained, they were admissible because the Miranda rule was not a license for the defendant to use perjury.

In addition to carving out exceptions to the Miranda rule, the Supreme Court has also reinforced the rule. In *Missouri v. Seibert* (2004), the Court struck down the police technique of giving the Miranda warnings only after a detainee had made an incriminating statement. Police officers were interrogating a detainee without Miranda warnings until he or she gave an incriminating statement. At that point, the officer would inform the detainee of his or her constitutional rights, obtain a waiver of those rights, and have the detainee repeat the statement. The Court declared that this type of coordinated and continuing interrogation is improper because it is likely to mislead the detainee.

Further, in *Doyle v. Ohio* (1976), the Court ruled that the prosecution could not comment at trial on a detainee's silence after Miranda warnings are given. The Court explained that using a detainee's silence to impeach him or her at trial would be fundamentally unfair and a deprivation of due process rights.

In 2000, the Court reaffirmed the Miranda opinion in *Dickerson v. United States.* Relying on the rule of *stare decisis,* or the principle of precedent, the Court reaffirmed *Miranda v. Arizona* despite its recognition that the Miranda rule may allow a guilty defendant to go free if incriminating statements are excluded at trial. The Court held that Miranda is a constitutional rule that has become so embedded in routine police practices that it has become a part of our national culture. The Court rejected the argument that the Miranda rule ties the hands of law enforcement and the courts. It declared that the police have adjusted their practices to the rule's requirements as its meaning has become clear by Supreme Court cases subsequent to *Miranda v. Arizona.* The Court concluded that those cases "have reduced the impact of the *Miranda* rule on legitimate law enforcement while reaffirming the decision's core ruling that un-warned statements may not be used as evidence in the prosecution's case" (*Dickerson v. United States* 2000 [italics in original]).

Miranda and Terrorism

Miranda holds as the law of the land insofar as civilian courts are concerned. In the case of suspected terrorists, however, where the assumption is that military tribunals will be employed, Miranda warnings do not apply. Under the administration of George W. Bush, terrorist suspects, such as those detained at the U.S. facility in Guantanamo, were not Mirandized. The intention was to subject the detainees to military trials. By 2009, with Guantanamo scheduled to close (albeit later than planned), some commentators noted that the absence of Miranda warnings in these cases limited U.S. prosecutors' abilities to try them—at least under any civilian jurisdictions. At a minimum, such cases raised legal questions, thus opening the door for possible challenges down the road. Initially, therefore, the incoming Obama administration sought to cover its bases by Mirandizing all new terrorist suspects (including the "Christmas Day bomber," Umar Farouk Abdulmutallab). Following the attempted car-bombing of Times Square in May 2010 (by Faisal Shahzad), however, the administration announced that it would no lon-ger Mirandize terrorist suspects and would most likely pursue military justice in these cases (Perez 2009; Savage 2010).

Conclusion

There was an intense political reaction following the Miranda decision. Law enforce-ment and prosecutors argued that it was a major blow to their ability to solve crimes; po-litical officials argued that criminals would go free. Eventually, its acceptance grew. Since *Miranda v. Arizona* has been upheld as a constitutional decision, the debate seems to be closed—at least in the case of civilian courts. The Court has reinforced the principle that detainees will be protected by the Fifth Amendment but has not foreclosed the possibil-ity that further exceptions to the Miranda rule will be established in the future.

See also **Miscarriages of Justice; Patriot Act; Search Warrants**

Legal Citations

Brown v. Mississippi, 297 U.S. 278 (1936).
Dickerson v. United States, 530 U.S. 428 (2000).

Doyle v. Ohio, 426 U.S. 610 (1976).

Edwards v. Arizona, 401 U.S. 222 (1971),

Escobido v. Illinois, 378 U.S. 478 (1964).

Harris v. New York, 426 U.S. 610 (1976).

Leyra v. Denno, 347 U.S. 556 (1954).

Malloy v. Hogan, 378 U.S. 1 (1964).

Michigan v. Mosley, 423 U.S. 96 (1975).

Miranda v. Arizona, 384 U.S. 436 (1996).

Missouri v. Seibert, 543 U.S. 600 (2004).

New York v. Quarles, 542 U.S. 600 (2004) and 542 U.S. 177 (2004).

Thompson v. Keohane, 451 U.S. 477 (1981).

Yarborough v. Alvarado, 541 U.S. 652 (2004).

Further Reading

Dershowitz, Alan M., *Shouting Fire: Civil Liberties in a Turbulent Age.* Boston: Little, Brown, 2002.

Perez, Evan, "Miranda Issues Cloud Gitmo Cases." *Wall Street Journal* (June 12, 2009). http://online.wsj.com/article/SB124476465967008335.html

Rotunda, Kyndra Miller, *Honor Bound: Inside the Guantanamo Trials.* Durham, NC: Carolina Academic Press, 2008.

Savage, Charlie, "Administration Supports Limits on Miranda Rule." *New York Times* (May 10, 2010): A1.

Stuart, Gary L., *Miranda: The Story of America's Right to Remain Silent.* Tucson: University of Arizona Press, 2004.

White, Welsh S., *Miranda's Waning Protections.* Ann Arbor: University of Michigan Press, 2001.

Wrightsman, Lawrence S., and Mary L. Pittman, *The Miranda Ruling: Its Past, Present, and Future.* New York: Oxford University Press, 2010.

MISCARRIAGES OF JUSTICE

ROBERT M. BOHM

Miscarriages of justice are not like other criminal justice controversies. Typically, people oppose miscarriages of justice; however, sometimes folks will promote miscarriages of justice for other purposes. When people agree that miscarriages of justice have occurred, they are almost universally condemned. However, controversies may arise over whether or not a miscarriage of justice has occurred. Making matters more complicated are issues of intent. Some of the miscarriages are unintentional or accidental. They are committed by fallible human beings who are simply attempting to do their jobs as best they can. Other miscarriages are intentional and venal. People commit them to further personal or professional agendas. This entry examines miscarriages of justice in the United States, what they are, what causes them, and possible remedies.

A miscarriage of justice has been defined as "a grossly unfair outcome in a judicial proceeding, as when a defendant is convicted despite a lack of evidence on an essential element of the crime" *(Black's Law Dictionary* 2000, 811). This definition focuses narrowly on wrongful convictions, which have received the most interest of scholars writing in this area but are only one type of miscarriage of justice. Miscarriages of justice also include wrongful arrests, wrongful charges or indictments, and wrongful sentences. They may include harassment by a law enforcement officer, an attorney failing to file a timely appeal, or correctional officials failing to release an inmate in a timely fashion once his or her sentence has expired. As such, the police and other law enforcement officials, defense attorneys, prosecutors, judges, and jurors as well as correctional officials commit miscarriages of justice.

Two general types of miscarriages of justice are "errors of due process" and "errors of impunity" (Forst 2004). Errors of due process involve "unwarranted harassment, detention or conviction, or excessive sanctioning of people suspected of crime" (Forst 2004, 10). "Errors of impunity" involve "a lapse of justice that allows a culpable offender to remain at large" (Forst 2004, 23) or, in some other way, to escape justice. Errors of due process can cause errors of impunity. In other words, if a person is arrested, convicted, and imprisoned for a crime that he or she did not commit, there is a good chance that the real offender will remain free to prey on other people. On the other hand, there is also a chance that the real offender will be arrested, convicted, and imprisoned for another crime. Although either type of error can undermine the integrity and legitimacy of the criminal justice process, (Forst 2004, 212–219) the bulk of the scholarship to date has focused on errors of due process.

Background

Until recently, the subject of miscarriages of justice—whether errors of due process or errors of impunity—had not received much scholarly attention from social scientists and especially criminologists. In fact, prior to Yale Law Professor Edwin Borchard's pioneering book *Convicting the Innocent* (1932), conventional wisdom suggested that innocent people were almost never wrongfully convicted. That such injustices probably occurred more frequently than most people thought was criminal justice's little secret.

Much of the newer miscarriages of justice research has focused on capital punishment. A principal reason is that capital cases generally receive more scrutiny than other felony cases because of the punishment's finality and the requirement that an appellate court review capital convictions and/or sentences. It is likely, however, that the miscarriages in capital cases that have been revealed represent only the tip of the proverbial iceberg of all miscarriages of justice, either in capital cases or in all criminal cases. The problem is that there is no official record of miscarriages of justice, so it is impossible to determine precisely how many there are and how often they occur.

The public is no longer so sanguine about the infallibility of the justice system. For example, in a 2009 Gallup poll of adults nationwide, 59 percent of respondents thought,

A STUDY OF EXONERATIONS IN THE UNITED STATES

Law Professor Samuel R. Gross and his colleagues identified 328 exonerations from 1989 through 2003.* They claim that it is "the most comprehensive listing of exonerations to date." They defined "exoneration" as "an official act declaring a defendant not guilty of a crime for which he or she had previously been convicted." According to the researchers, the 328 exonerations in their list represent only the "tip of an iceberg" and do not include, for example, the mass exonerations of the approximately 135 innocent defendants who were victims of the rogue officers of the Los Angeles Police Department's Rampart division in 1999–2000 or the 39 innocent drug defendants framed by a Tulia, Texas, undercover police officer in 2003. The researchers found that the rate of exonerations increased dramatically over the 15-year period—that is, there were many more "discovered" exonerations toward the end of the period than at the beginning.

Ninety-seven percent of the exonerations discovered by Gross and his colleagues involved defendants convicted of murder and/or rape. Forty-four percent of the wrongfully convicted defendants were cleared by DNA evidence, including 88 percent of those convicted of rape. The cause of the wrongful convictions in nearly 90 percent of the rape cases was eyewitness misidentification, especially cross-racial misidentification involving a black defendant and a white victim. The main cause of the wrongful convictions in murder cases was perjury on the part of the real killers, supposed participants, or eyewitnesses to the crime; jailhouse snitches and other untrustworthy police informants; police officers; and state forensic scientists. Another major factor in wrongful murder convictions was false confessions. Juveniles (almost all of them were either black or Hispanic) and the mentally disabled were particularly vulnerable to false confessions. On average, exonerated defendants served more than 10 years in prison for crimes they did not commit.

The exonerations occurred in four ways: (1) In 77 percent of the cases, the courts dismissed criminal charges after new evidence of innocence was presented. (2) In about 13 percent of the cases, governors or other authorized executive officers issued pardons based on evidence of innocence. (3) In approximately 9 percent of the cases, defendants were acquitted at retrial after evidence was presented that they had no role in the crimes for which they were convicted. (4) Finally, in 1 percent of the cases, states posthumously admitted that defendants who had died in prison were innocent.

*Samuel R. Gross et al., "Exonerations in the United States, 1989 through 2003." 2004. http://www.internationaljusticeproject.org/pdfs/ExonerationReport4.19.04.pdf

"in the past five years, a person was executed who was, in fact, innocent of the crime with which he or she was charged" (Gallup 2009). That was down somewhat from 73 percent who so believed in 2003, according to Gallup. A Harris poll conducted in 2008 similarly found that up to 95 percent of adults nationwide thought that innocent people sometimes were wrongly convicted of murder—a statistic that has held remarkably steady since at least 1999 (Polling Report 2009).

Key Events

This remarkable turnaround in the public's belief about miscarriages of justice was the result of a combination of events. The most important arguably was the advent of DNA profiling. DNA evidence is now used to link or eliminate identified suspects to a crime, identify "cold hits" where a sample from a crime scene is matched against numerous cases in a DNA database and a positive match is made and to clear convicted rapists and murderers years after they began serving their sentences. A second important and related development was the establishment in 1992 of the Innocence Project by Law Professors Barry Scheck and Peter Neufeld at the Benjamin N. Cardozo School of Law in New York City. The project uses law students in a clinical law program to provide *pro bono* legal services to inmates who are challenging their convictions based on DNA evidence. The student lawyers are supervised by practicing attorneys. The project has represented or assisted more than 100 cases in the United States, including several death penalty cases, where convictions have been reversed or overturned. Today, there is a national network of more than 40 Innocence Projects throughout the United States. Scheck and his colleagues, underscoring the importance of DNA evidence, found that "of the first eighteen thousand results [of DNA tests] at the FBI and other crime laboratories, at least five thousand prime suspects were excluded *before* their cases were tried" (Scheck 2001, xx). That is, more than 25 percent of the prime suspects were wrongly accused.

Another development was additional revelations that people convicted of capital crimes and sentenced to die were actually innocent. In Illinois, investigations by Northwestern University journalism professor David Protess and his students provided proof of innocence. In 1998, Northwestern University hosted the first National Conference on Wrongful Convictions and the Death Penalty. Attending were 35 former death row inmates. Some of them told their stories about almost being executed and how they had been wrongly convicted. In 1999, the *Chicago Tribune* published two major series. The first series documented prosecutor misconduct throughout the United States; the second series examined problems with Illinois's capital punishment system that contributed to such a large percentage of its death row inmates being exonerated because of their innocence. Based largely on the series by the *Chicago Tribune* and the fact that Illinois had released 13 condemned inmates from death row since 1977 while executing 12, Republican Governor George Ryan, himself a proponent of the death penalty, imposed a moratorium on capital punishment in Illinois in January 2000. In May 2000, Governor Ryan charged a special commission he created with producing a comprehensive report on the administration of capital punishment in Illinois. In April 2002, Governor Ryan received the completed report, which contained 85 recommendations for changes in the Illinois capital punishment system. Declaring the Illinois capital punishment system to be broken, in January 2003, just days before he was to leave office, Governor Ryan pardoned four death-row inmates and commuted the sentences, mostly to life in prison without possibility of parole, of the remaining 167 inmates on Illinois's death row. Between 1973 and November 2006, a total of 123 people in 25 states have been released from death row with evidence of their innocence (Death Penalty Information Center 2006). Some probably innocent death row inmates were not as lucky and have been executed (Bohm 2003).

Reasons and Remedies

The proximate reasons for these miscarriages of justice are now well documented. They include shoddy investigation and misconduct by the police; eyewitness misidentification, perjury by prosecution witnesses, false confessions, guilty pleas by innocent defendants, prosecutor misconduct, judicial misconduct or error, bad defense lawyers, and jury problems.

Remedies to miscarriages of justice are also well known. Among the recommendations are the following: provide good attorneys, punish the misconduct of defense attorneys, improve police investigations, interrogations, and the handling of evidence, improve eyewitness identification techniques and procedures, improve the work and credibility of crime lab technicians, require DNA testing, set rigorous standards for jailhouse snitches/informants, improve police training, punish police misconduct, guide prosecutors' charging decisions, improve disclosure requirements, punish prosecutor misconduct, provide better training and certification of trial judges in capital cases, give trial judges veto power in capital cases (when juries impose death sentences), eliminate time limits and other constraints on claims of actual innocence, increase the resources and scope of innocence projects, collect relevant data, establish innocence commissions, and provide assistance and indemnity.

Conclusion

The integrity and legitimacy of the criminal justice process depends largely on efforts to eliminate injustice. Miscarriages of justice threaten the very foundation of society. When criminal suspects and defendants are not treated fairly and accorded the rights guaranteed to them by the U.S. Constitution, the legitimacy and authority of the state are called into question. Citizens who lose faith in the state's ability to dispense justice are likely to employ vigilante justice, resulting in social chaos.

To move analysis of this subject forward, the federal and state governments should be required by statute to compile an annual miscarriage of justice registry, listing all known cases of miscarriages of justice and their causes. Such a registry would not only provide an indication of the problem's magnitude but it would also be an excellent resource to use in evaluating criminal justice administration. It could reveal what works well and what is in need of change. Also needed is theorizing and investigation of the more fundamental causes of miscarriages of justice as well as the political will, organizational commitment, and resources to implement and monitor the remedies.

See also **Death Penalty; DNA Usage in Criminal Justice; Eyewitness Identification; Police Corruption; Public Defender System; Three-Strikes Laws**

Further Reading

Black's Law Dictionary, 7th ed. St. Paul, MN: West Group, 2000.

Bohm, R. M., *Deathquest II: An Introduction to the Theory and Practice of Capital Punishment in the United States*. Cincinnati, OH: Anderson, 2003.

Cohen, Stanley, *The Wrong Men: America's Epidemic of Wrongful Death Row Convictions*. New York: Carroll & Graf, 2003.

Death Penalty Information Center, "Innocence." 2006. http://www.deathpenaltyinfo.org

Forst, Brian, *Errors of Justice: Nature, Sources, and Remedies*. New York: Cambridge University Press, 2004.

Gallup, "In U.S., Two-Thirds Continue to Support Death Penalty." October 13, 2009. http://www.gallup.com/poll/123638/in-u.s.-two-thirds-continue-support-death-penalty.aspx

Lytle, Leslie, *Execution's Doorstep: True Stories of the Innocent and Near Damned*. Boston: Northeastern University Press, 2008.

Polling Report, "Are you in favor of the death penalty for a person convicted of murder?" Gallup poll, Oct. 1–4, 2009. http://www.pollingreport.com/crime.htm

Robinson, Paul H., and Michael T. Cahill, *Law Without Justice: Why Criminal Law Doesn't Give People What They Deserve*. New York: Oxford University Press, 2006.

Scheck, Barry, P. Neufeld, and J. Dwyer, *Actual Innocence: When Justice Goes Wrong and How to Make It Right*. New York: Signet, 2001.

Westervelt, Saundra D., and John A. Humphrey, eds., *Wrongly Convicted: Perspectives on Failed Justice*. Newark, NJ: Rutgers University Press, 2001.

P

PATRIOT ACT

Cary Stacy Smith and Li-Ching Hung

On September 11, 2001, al Qaeda terrorists, wielding box cutters, skyjacked and then crashed jets into the World Trade Center and Pentagon. Exactly 45 days later, on October 26, 2001, President George W. Bush signed Public Law 107–56. The act's formal title is "Uniting and Strengthening America by Providing Appropriate Tools Required to Intercept and Obstruct Terrorism Act"; however, it is better known as the USA Patriot Act, or simply "Patriot Act" (PA). Fifteen federal statutes were affected by the PA, some in major ways; that is, law-enforcement and intelligence personnel were provided with legal tools for fighting international and domestic terrorism. Once the PA was passed, the Bush administration and many others heralded it as a much-needed tool for combating terrorism and preventing future attacks on the United States. With the passing of time, however, critics of the PA have voiced concerns that the act violates basic constitutional guarantees of civil rights.

One major boon for authorities was how the PA streamlined the legal processes for obtaining authorization for surveillance on suspicious individuals as well as seizing money that may be used to support terrorism. The act also required financial institutions to report any suspicious activity, to effectively identify new customers, to sever all ties to fraudulent banks located in foreign countries, and to maintain anti–money laundering programs at all times. In addition, banks were encouraged to share information with federal, state, and local law enforcement agencies, while the federal government was empowered to confiscate the property of any individual or organization either performing terrorist acts or who had plans to do so. The PA expanded the definitions of money laundering and fraudulent activities—such as those, involving American credit cards that fall under the definition of supporting terrorism (see also Smith and Messina 2004).

The PA also changed the various requirements needed for the issuance of search warrants. Prior to September 11, 2001 (9/11), local judges, or the Foreign Intelligence Surveillance Court (used only when foreign spying was suspected), issued warrants authorizing electronic surveillance, such as wiretaps. Before the PA was passed, foreign intelligence gathering had to be the sole reason (Smith and Messina 2004). After 9/11, any federal judge could issue a nationwide warrant to tap phones and e-mail or any instrument a suspect could conceivably use. Examples include (1) "sneak and peek" search warrants; (2) permitted delays in serving some warrants until seven days after the surveillance authorized by the warrants; and (3) the requirement that libraries, bookstores, and Internet service providers are required to supply information about how their clients use their various services. Regarding foreign suspects, federal agents could (until 2007, when the policy was revised) request authorization for "warrantless" searches when the gathering of foreign intelligence was thought significant reason for the searches.

Background

The PA was a compromise of the Anti-Terrorism Act of 2001 (ATA), a legislative package intended to strengthen the nation's defense against terrorism. The ATA contained provisions vastly expanding the authority of law enforcement and intelligence agencies to monitor private communications and access personal information. The final legislation

THE 10 TITLES OF THE PATRIOT ACT

The Patriot Act has 10 titles, each containing numerous sections. They are:

Title I: Enhancing domestic security against terrorism—deals with measures that counter terrorism.

Title II: Enhanced surveillance procedures—gives increased powers of surveillance to various government agencies and bodies. There are 25 sections in this title, with one of the sections (section 224) containing a sunset clause.

Title III: International money-laundering abatement and antiterrorist financing act of 2001.

Title IV: Protecting the border.

Title V: Removing obstacles to investigating terrorism.

Title VI: Providing for victims of terrorism, public safety officers, and their families.

Title VII: Increased information sharing for critical infrastructure protection.

Title VIII: Strengthening the criminal laws against terrorism.

Title IX: Improved intelligence.

Title X: Miscellaneous.

included a few beneficial additions from the administration's initial proposal. Examples are a sunset provision, which provided that several sections of the PA would automatically expire after a specified period of time unless Congress renewed them, concerns about aspects of the electronic surveillance provisions, and an amendment providing judicial oversight of law enforcement's use of the FBI's Carnivore system (a method of electronic surveillance). On the other hand, the PA still retained provisions expanding the government's investigative authority, especially with respect to the Internet. Those provisions address issues that are complex and implicate fundamental constitutional protections of individual liberty, including the appropriate procedures for interception of information transmitted over the Internet and other rapidly evolving technologies.

One primary purpose for the PA was stopping terrorists from staying within the United States. When reasonable grounds exist to believe that foreign visitors pose a threat to national security, they can be arrested and held for seven days without being charged, pending investigation or their deportation. Judicial review is nonexistent, except for habeas corpus, while the U.S. attorney general has the right to order aliens held indefinitely if no countries agree to accept them upon deportation (Brasch 2005).

The PA makes one liable for deportation, even if a person associates unknowingly with terrorists or terrorist organizations. In order to identify and track suspects, the act substantially increases rewards for information regarding terrorism, expands the exemptions to the Posse Comitatus Act of 1878, and gives the U.S. attorney general permission to collect samples of DNA from convicted federal prisoners. Domestic terrorism, a new category, is added; that is, an act intended to negatively influence governmental policy or to coerce civilians by intimidation committed by any citizen of the United States. Such acts, whether by citizens or foreigners, include attacking mass transportation, releasing biological agents, using weapons or explosives, spreading false information about terrorist attacks, or conspiring with terrorists (Etzioni 2004).

Legal Decisions

Congressman James F. Sensenbrenner introduced the Patriot Act into the House of Representatives as H.R. 3162. The act swept through Congress quickly with little dissent. House Resolution 3162 was introduced in the House of Representatives on October 23, 2001. Assistant Attorney General Viet D. Dinh and Michael Chertoff (future secretary of the Department of Homeland Security) were the primary drafters of the PA. The bill passed in the House of Representatives on October 24, 2001, as it did in the Senate (with one dissenter and one senator not voting) on October 25, 2001. President George W. Bush signed the bill into law on October 26, 2001 (Smith and Messina).

Quite possibly the single most controversial aspect of the act was Section 215, which dealt with a very narrow implied right of federal investigators to access library and bookstore records. The section allowed FBI agents to obtain a warrant *in camera* from the

THE PATRIOT ACT AND FOREIGN INTELLIGENCE

The act follows and amends a series of acts that are related to the investigations of foreign intelligence. These include:

1. The Foreign Intelligence Surveillance Act (FISA), which was passed in 1978 and defined who could be investigated; targets were usually engaged in espionage or international terrorism. In 2004, FISA was permitted to target "lone wolf" terrorists without showing that they were members of a terrorist group or agents of such a group or of any other foreign power.
2. The USA Act was passed on October 12, 2001, and subsequently folded into the USA Patriot Act. Under the USA Act, a terrorist who was not an agent of a foreign power could be the target of a federal investigation of foreign intelligence.
3. The Financial Anti-Terrorism Act was passed on October 17, 2001, and also folded into the USA Patriot Act. It increased the federal government's powers to investigate and prosecute the financial supporters of terrorism.

See also W. M. Brasch, *America's Unpatriotic Acts: The Federal Government's Violation of Constitutional and Civil Rights* (New York: Peter Lang, 2005).

United States Foreign Intelligence Surveillance Court for library or bookstore records of anyone connected to an investigation of international terrorism or spying. The section never specifically mentions and civil libertarians argued that the provision violated patrons' human rights; it has become known as the "library provision."

It is unknown how many individuals or organizations have been charged or convicted under the act. Throughout 2002 and 2003, the Justice Department adamantly refused to release numbers. John Ashcroft in his 2004 statement *The Department of Justice: Working to Keep America Safer* claimed that 368 individuals were criminally charged in terrorism investigations, although the numbers 372 and 375 were later used. Of these, he stated that 194 (later 195) resulted in convictions or guilty pleas. In June 2005, President Bush reported that investigations yielded over 400 charges against terrorists, with more than half resulting in convictions or guilty pleas. In some cases, federal prosecutors chose to charge suspects with nonterror-related crimes for immigration, fraud, and conspiracy (Smith and Messina 2004).

Members of the U.S. Congress from both sides of the aisle have tried to curb some of the act's policies. In 2003, Senators Lisa Murkowski (R-AK) and Ron Wyden (D-OR), introduced the Protecting the Rights of Individuals Act, which revised several provisions of the Patriot Act to increase judicial review. For example, instead of PEN/Trap warrants—a device used to collect all numbers dialed on a phone keypad after a call has been connected—based on the claims of law enforcement, rather, they would be based on "specific and articulable facts that reasonably indicate that a crime has been, is being, or will be committed, and that information likely to be obtained by such installation and use is relevant to the investigation of that crime" (see also Cole and Dempsey 2002).

Congressman Bernie Sanders (I-VT) with Reps. Jerrold Nadler (D-NY), John Conyers Jr. (D-Mich.), C. L. Otter (R-Idaho), and Ron Paul (R-Texas) proposed an amendment to the Commerce, Justice, State Appropriations Bill of 2005 that would cut off funding to the Department of Justice for searches conducted under Section 215. The amendment initially failed to pass the House with a tie vote, 210–210. Although the original vote came down in favor of the amendment, the vote was held open and several house members were persuaded to change their votes (Cole and Dempsey 2002).

The courts have also spoken out against the act. U.S. District Judge Audrey Collins ruled that Section 805 (which classifies "expert advice or assistance" as material support to terrorism) was vague and in violation of the First and Fifth Amendments, marking the first legal decision to set a part of the act aside. The lawsuit against the act was brought by the Humanitarian Law Project, representing five organizations and two U.S. citizens who wanted to provide expert advice to Kurdish refugees in Turkey. Groups providing aid to these organizations had suspended their activities for fear of violating the act, and they filed a lawsuit against the Departments of Justice and State to challenge the law, claiming the phrase "expert advice or assistance" was too vague. Collins granted the plaintiff's motion that "expert advice or assistance" is impermissibly vague but denied a nationwide injunction against the provision. The plaintiffs were granted "enjoinment" from enforcement of the provision (Chesney 2005).

Conclusion

In terms of the act remaining as it was in 2001, when it was signed into law, the future looks dim. To date, eight states (Alaska, California, Colorado, Hawaii, Idaho, Maine, Montana, and Vermont) and hundreds of cities and counties (including New York City; Los Angeles; Dallas; Chicago; Eugene, Oregon; Philadelphia; and Cambridge, Massachusetts) have passed resolutions against the PA in its present form. In Arcata, California, an ordinance was passed that bars city employees (including police and librarians) from assisting or cooperating with any federal investigations under the act that would violate civil liberties. In addition, a group called The Bill of Rights Defense Committee helped coordinate local efforts to pass resolutions. The validity of these ordinances is in question, however, since under the Constitution's supremacy clause, federal law supersedes state and local laws. However, others have opined that the federal employees, in using such procedures for investigations, violate the Constitution's clauses in the fourth amendment, and in these cases, the Constitution overrides the act's provisions (Chesney 2005; Bill of Rights Defense Committee).

See also **Immigration and Employment Law Enforcement; Miranda Warnings; Racial, National Origin, and Religion Profiling; Search Warrants; Surveillance—Technological (vol. 4)**

AMERICAN FEELINGS ABOUT THE PATRIOT ACT

According to a USA Today/CNN poll, the percentage of Americans having negative feelings about the act has grown (see Table 1). Originally, the Patriot Act had a sunset clause to ensure that Congress would have to take active steps to reauthorize it. The United States had never enacted into law anything like this act; thus people needed time in which to gauge whether or not it needed modification. From the beginning, the primary criticisms leveled at the Patriot Act centered upon civil liberties. In 2006, the reauthorization resolution was passed and contained 27 safeguards designed for maintaining civil liberties.

The 27 safeguards are as follows:

Safeguard 1: requiring high-level approval and additional reporting to Congress for Section 215 requests for sensitive information such as library or medical records

Safeguard 2: statement of facts showing relevance to a terrorism or foreign spy investigation required for Section 215 requests

Safeguard 3: explicitly allowing a FISA court judge to deny or modify a Section 215 request

Safeguard 4: requiring minimization procedures to limit retention and dissemination of information obtained about U.S. persons from Section 215 requests

Safeguard 5: explicitly providing for a judicial challenge to a Section 215 order

Safeguard 6: explicitly clarifying that a recipient of a Section 215 order may disclose receipt to an attorney or others necessary to comply with or challenge the order

Safeguard 7: requiring public reporting of the number of Section 215 orders

Safeguard 8: requiring the Justice Department's independent inspector general to conduct an audit of each Justice Department use of Section 215 orders

Safeguard 9: explicitly providing for a judicial challenge to a National Security Letter (NSL)

Safeguard 10: explicitly clarifying that a recipient of a National Security Letter may disclose receipt to an attorney or others necessary to comply with or challenge the order

Safeguard 11: providing that a nondisclosure order does not automatically attach to a National Security Letter.

Safeguard 12: providing explicit judicial review of a nondisclosure requirement to a National Security Letter

Safeguard 13: requiring public reporting of the number of National Security Letters

Safeguard 14: requiring the Justice Department's independent inspector general to conduct two audits of the use of National Security Letters

Safeguard 15: requiring additional reporting to Congress by the Justice Department on use of National Security Letters

Safeguard 16: requiring the Justice Department to recertify that nondisclosure of a National Security Letter is necessary

Safeguard 17: narrowing the deference given to the Justice Department on a National Security Letter nondisclosure certification

Safeguard 18: requiring a report to Congress on any use of data-mining programs by the Justice Department

Safeguard 19: requiring notice be given on delayed-notice search warrants within 30 days of the search

Safeguard 20: limiting delayed-notice search warrants extensions to 90 days or less

Safeguard 21: requiring an updated showing of necessity in order to extend the delay of notice of a search warrant

Safeguard 22: requiring annual public reporting on the use of delayed-notice search warrants

Safeguard 23: requiring additional specificity from an applicant before roving surveillance may be authorized

Safeguard 24: requiring court notification within 10 days of conducting surveillance on a new facility using a "roving" wiretap

Safeguard 25: requiring ongoing FISA court notification of the total number of places or facilities under surveillance using a "roving" wiretap

Safeguard 26: requiring additional specificity in a FISA court judge's order authorizing a "roving" wiretap

Safeguard 27: providing a four-year sunset on FISA "roving" wiretaps

TABLE 1. Does the U.S. Patriot Act Go Too Far?

Date	Too Far	Not Too Far
August 25–August 26, 2003	22%	69%
November 10–November 12, 2003	22%	65%
February 16–February 17, 2004	26%	64%
April 13–April 16, 2005	45%	49%

Table Source: USA Today, USA Today/CNN/Gallup Poll Results (May 20, 2005), http://www.usatoday.com/news/polls/tables/live/2004–02–25-patriot-act-poll.htm

Further Reading

Abele, Robert P., *A User's Guide to the USA Patriot Act and Beyond.* Lanham, MD: University Press of America, 2005.

Bill of Rights Defense Committee, "Resolutions Passed and Efforts Underway by State." http://www.bordc.org/list.php?sortAlpha = 1

Brasch, Walter M., *America's Unpatriotic Acts: The Federal Government's Violation of Constitutional and Civil Rights.* New York: Peter Lang, 2005.

Chang, Nancy, *Silencing Political Dissent.* New York: Seven Stories Press, 2002.

Chesney, R. M., "The Sleeper Scenario: Terrorism Support Laws and the Demands of Prevention." *Harvard Journal on Legislation* 42, no. 1 (2005): 1–91.

Cole, D., and J. X. Dempsey, *Terrorism and the Constitution: Sacrificing Civil Liberties in the Name of National Security,* 2d ed. New York: Norton, 2002.

Etzioni, Amitai, *How Patriotic Is the Patriot Act?* New York: Routledge, 2004.

Foerstel, Herbert N., *The Patriot Act: A Documentary and Reference Guide.* Westport, CT: Greenwood Press, 2008.

Goldberg, Danny, et al., *It's a Free Country: Personal Freedom in America after September 11.* New York: Nation Books, 2003.

Pious, Richard M., *The War on Terror and the Rule of Law.* Los Angeles: Roxbury, 2006.

Schulhofer, Stephen J., *Rethinking the Patriot Act: Keeping America Safe and Free.* New York: Century Foundation, 2005.

Smith, Norris, and Lynn M. Messina, *Homeland Security.* New York: H. W. Wilson, 2004.

POLICE BRUTALITY

Jessica S. Henry

Police brutality refers to the use of excessive force against a civilian. The controversies that surround the topic of police brutality relate to different definitions and expectations over what is meant by excessive force. Indeed, police officers are expressly authorized to use necessary, reasonable force to perform their duties. As Jerome Skolnick, an influential police scholar in the United States, underscores: "as long as members of society do not comply with the law and resist the police, force will remain an inevitable part of policing." (Skolnick and Fyfe 1993). Others would quickly point out that there is also a difference between legitimate or legal force and illegitimate or excessive force by the police. They would argue, too, that the use of force is not only a question of reacting to citizen violations of the law and resistance but may also involve an array of actions that do not lawfully conform to the spirit of the law. Police brutality might include, for example, the unlawful beating of a citizen by an officer under the cover of the law or the brutality of other citizens or fellow officers who unjustly harm others that is overlooked or even condoned. Thus, the issue of police brutality turns not simply on the presence of force but on its degree, kind, reasonableness, and even on omission.

Although police brutality may also be said to occur whenever the police use violent force that is excessive, some scholars have limited that definition to include excessive force that is conscious and deliberate, as compared with the good-faith mistake of an officer who uses unnecessary force in the face of an unexpected situation. In contrast, the Communications Assistance for Law Enforcement Act (CALEA) accreditation standard does not contemplate the intent of the officer. Rather, it permits officers to use "only the force necessary to accomplish lawful objectives" and describes excessive force as any level of force that is more than necessary.

Background

Modern police forces were established in the 1830s and 1840s and were marked primarily by corruption and inefficiency. Indeed, police agencies throughout the 1800s and early 1900s were as often involved in violence and crime as the alleged perpetrators of crime.

At the turn of the 19th century, police use of excessive force had a widespread and accepted place in law enforcement. In interrogating suspects, the police would routinely beat suspects with fists, blackjacks, and rubber hoses to extract information. These police "interrogations," otherwise known as the "third degree," were conducted in hot, tiny, overlit rooms.

USE OF FORCE

Every day, law enforcement officers face danger while carrying out their responsibilities. When dealing with a dangerous—or unpredictable—situation, police officers usually have very little time to assess and determine the proper response. In such situations, good training can enable the officer to react properly to the threat or possible threat and respond with the appropriate tactics to address the situation, possibly including some level of force, if necessary, given the circumstances.

The U.S. Commission on Civil Rights has stated that "in diffusing situations, apprehending alleged criminals, and protecting themselves and others, officers are legally entitled to use appropriate means, including force." In dozens of studies of police use of force there is no single, accepted definition among researchers, analysts, or the police. The International Association of Chiefs of Police (IACP), in its study *Police Use of Force in America 2001*, defined use of force as "the amount of effort required by police to compel compliance by an unwilling subject." The IACP also identified five components of force: physical, chemical, electronic, impact, and firearm. To some people, though, the mere presence of a police officer can be intimidating and seen as use of force.

The Bureau of Justice Statistics, in *Data Collection on Police Use of Force*, states that "the legal test of excessive force . . . is whether the police officer reasonably believed that such force was necessary to accomplish a legitimate police purpose." However, there are no universally accepted definitions of *reasonable* and *necessary* because the terms are subjective. A court in one jurisdiction may define *reasonable* or *necessary* differently than a court in a second jurisdiction. More to the point is an understanding of the improper use of force, which can be divided into two categories: "unnecessary" and "excessive." The unnecessary use of force would be the application of force where there is no justification for its use, while an excessive use of force would be the application of more force than required where use of force is necessary.

Source: "Use of Force." Cops: Community Oriented Policing Services (U.S. Department of Justice). 2010. www.cops.usdoj.gov/default.asp?Item=1374

In 1928, President Herbert Hoover established the Wickersham Commission, which was charged in part with examining law enforcement police practices. Finding widespread brutality and corruption, in 1931 the Wickersham Commission reported that torture was routinely employed by police officers against suspects to elicit confessions. In one infamous example of police excesses, the commission described a suspect who was held by the ankles out of a third-story window. It also identified rampant corruption within police departments nationwide and linked brutality to routine police practices. The Wickersham Report drew unprecedented attention to the issue of police brutality and coerced confessions.

As a result of the Wickersham Report, the use of the third degree became less common. It did not, unfortunately, eliminate the practice entirely. For instance, a 2006 report issued after a four-year, $6 million investigation revealed that, during the 1970s and 1980s, Chicago police officers, under the leadership of Commander Jon Burge, routinely used torture to elicit confessions from hundreds of suspects. The torture techniques employed by the police included the use of cattle prods placed against a suspect's genitals, the shoving of a loaded gun into a suspect's mouth, or the placement of a plastic typewriter cover over a suspect's head until he lost consciousness. Other suspects were beaten with fists, kicks, and telephone books. Nearly all the victims were people of color. Notwithstanding the public furor over the report, no state prosecutions were planned as of the time of this writing.

The use of the third degree was not the only technique highlighted by the Wickersham Report. Rather, that report brought to light the endemic and institutional nature of police brutality among police departments across the country. Many of the then-identified issues relating to police brutality continue today. In 1991, for instance, 60 years after the Wickersham Report, the Christopher Commission issued its report on the use of force by the Los Angeles police department. That report, which called for new standards of accountability, described a police department and culture where the use of excessive force, primarily against people of color, was not uncommon. Its conclusions and recommendations were eerily reminiscent of its predecessor report.

The Christopher Commission's conclusions again were echoed several years later. In 1998, Human Rights Watch issued a nearly 400-page report analyzing police brutality and accountability throughout the United States. It concluded that police brutality is endemic to police departments nationwide and that there are inadequate measures in place to address and correct the pervasiveness of the issue. Human Rights Watch also made a series of nonbinding recommendations to increase police accountability and transparency in police practices. Whether any of these recommendations will be implemented in a systemic manner remains to be seen.

Key Moments/Events

In the 20th and 21st centuries, the phrase "police brutality" became inextricably linked with the names of individuals such as Rodney King, Abner Louima, or Amadou Diallo.

So too, police brutality has been linked with some of this nation's worst public riots. The following discussion focuses on several high-profile instances of police brutality. It is not meant to be exhaustive but rather to highlight significant events that altered the nation's consciousness about police brutality.

Many of the worst riots or rebellions in the 20th century stemmed from allegations of police brutality. The damage from the riots in terms of loss of life and property destruction was massive, while the damage between the community and the police department in some cases has yet to be repaired.

For instance, on March 3, 1991, there were riots in Los Angeles in response to an infamous beating caught on videotape. Rodney King, an African American, was speeding on a Los Angeles freeway. After King refused to pull over for fear that his probation would be revoked, 11 police cars and a police helicopter gave chase. King subsequently refused to exit his car. Police officers forcibly dragged him from the car and shot him twice with a taser gun. Four officers beat him with a nightstick at least 56 times, while dozens of other officers stood by and watched. King suffered brain damage and 16 broken bones. An amateur photographer captured the entire incident on videotape, which was subsequently and repeatedly shown on television throughout the world. After a jury that did not include a single African American person acquitted the officers, five days of rioting erupted in the streets of Los Angeles.

A little more than a decade earlier, on December 17, 1979, Miami erupted in violence. According to police reports, Arthur McDuffie, an African American, made an obscene gesture to a police officer and sped away on his motorcycle. After a police chase through Miami's streets, which involved at least 12 police cars, McDuffie was captured and severely beaten by six white police officers. He died four days later. Although it was revealed at trial that the officers initially had lied about the source of McDuffie's injuries, an all-white jury acquitted the officers. After the verdict, Miami erupted in three days of racially charged rioting.

Of course, not all instances of police brutality result in rioting. Indeed, there was no rioting in response to one of the worst cases of brutality in recent years. On August 9, 1997, Haitian immigrant Abner Louima was arrested outside a Brooklyn nightclub after a fight in which he had not participated. At the 70th precinct in Brooklyn, several officers, including Justin Volpe, brutalized Louima. Volpe sodomized Louima by plunging a broomstick into his rectum and mouth while his hands were cuffed behind his back. Louima suffered extensive internal injuries and required several surgeries.

In another high-profile example of brutality, Johnny Gammage, an African American, was driving a luxury car when he was pulled over by the Pittsburgh police on October 12, 1995. Gammage exited his car carrying a cell phone, which officers claimed appeared to be a gun. Officers on the side of the road detained him, and he died there. The coroner identified the cause of death as suffocation caused by pressure on the back and neck. Although all three officers charged with involuntary manslaughter were acquitted, Gammage's death led to an extensive Justice Department investigation into police practices in Pittsburgh.

Under strikingly similar circumstances, Amadou Diallo, a 22-year-old unarmed street vendor from Guinea, was mistakenly shot and killed by the police. As he stood in the doorway to his apartment on February 4, 1999, four police officers in plain clothes fired 41 shots, hitting him 19 times. The officers later claimed that he was drawing a gun when they opened fire. What the officers took for a gun was, in fact, his wallet. Although the four officers were acquitted after trial, which was moved from the Bronx to Albany, New York, the City of New York agreed to pay $3 million dollars to resolve the Diallo family's civil rights lawsuit.

Lawsuits and Other Remedies to Reduce Police Brutality

Lawsuits have proven to be one effective way of controlling police practices. The U.S. Department of Justice is empowered to bring suit against police departments under the 1994 Violent Crime Control Act. This act authorizes the Justice Department to sue police departments where there has been an alleged "pattern or practice" of abuse. The impact of these "pattern" suits has been dramatic. The Justice Department has sued and entered into consent decrees with numerous police departments: the New Jersey Police Department to limit its reliance on racial profiling in traffic stops; an Ohio police force to reduce its use of excessive force; the Pittsburgh police department to institute increased oversight and accountability; and the Los Angeles police department (LAPD) over the Rampart scandal, where, in August 2000, a federal judge ruled that the government's antiracketeering statute—known as the RICO Law, created to fight organized crime—could be used against the police. A court-appointed monitor works to ensure that the departments are in compliance with consent decrees. These pattern lawsuits have the potential to bring broad, sweeping change to police practices and reduce the use of excessive force.

Individual citizens who have been abused by the police can also sue police departments for monetary damages. The cost of these lawsuits can be significant. For instance, in the 1990s, the Detroit police department paid an average of $10 million dollars per year to resolve lawsuits arising from police misconduct. In response to these and other lawsuits, some police departments have taken steps to address and reduce police misconduct. For instance, the Los Angeles County Board of Supervisors arranged for a special counsel to investigate problems within the LAPD, recommend reforms, and ultimately reduce the cost of litigation.

Criminal prosecution is an additional legal avenue that can be used to deter police brutality. Prosecutors, however, traditionally have been reluctant to pursue criminal charges against individual police officers. This, in part, reflects the dependent relationship of prosecutors, who rely on the police to secure convictions and do not wish to damage these institutionalized relationships. Moreover, convictions against police officers are difficult to obtain both because it is hard to prove beyond a reasonable doubt that an officer used excessive force with criminal intent and jurors tend to empathize with the police and therefore are reluctant to convict them of crime.

Criminal convictions against police officers are relatively rare, but they do occur. In the case of Abner Louima, for instance, Justin Volpe pled guilty to anally penetrating Louima with a broomstick and was sentenced to 30 years in federal prison. Charles Schwarz also went to trial in the Louima case. Although was initially convicted of obstruction of justice and was sentenced to 15 years federal imprisonment, his conviction was overturned by an appellate court. Schwarz finally pled guilty to perjury and was sentenced to five years' imprisonment. And the convictions of the remaining three police officers were overturned by a federal appeals court. Whether these types of convictions and their mixed results will deter other officers from brutality is not clear. In contrast, an acquittal often, albeit unintentionally, sends a public message that the police can "get away" with murder.

Another potential mechanism for controlling police brutality is through the use of civilian complaint boards. These boards may serve as independent reviewers of citizen complaints, aid in monitoring police departments, or help with policy review. Although many of these boards have been criticized for a wide range of reasons, they may aid in increasing the transparency of police departments, which in turn may improve public confidence in the complaint process. However, complaint review boards are only as effective as the mandate given to them by the community and the degree of cooperation demonstrated between the police, prosecutor, politicians, and review board.

Conclusion

Police brutality remains a challenge within law enforcement today. The frequency with which police brutality occurs may decline in the future, with effective mechanisms to ensure police accountability and a continued emphasis on police professionalism. Although isolated instances of police brutality may be unavoidable, a number of accountability measures can be implemented in an effort to reduce overall patterns of police brutality.

Police departments traditionally have turned inward in an effort to regulate the conduct of their officers. An internal affairs unit (IAU) is responsible for investigating allegations of misconduct and brutality. The "blue curtain" or the "blue wall of silence" refers to the informal code among police officers that constrains them from reporting the misdeeds of other officers. The refusal to "rat out" a fellow officer remains a cultural norm within police departments. Therefore there are significant cultural limitations to an IAU investigation. Moreover, the investigations conducted by IAUs are typically cloaked in secrecy. Thus it is extremely difficult to assess whether and to what extent police departments in fact are monitoring their operations.

There are, however, external methods of monitoring and curbing police brutality, as discussed in the previous section. These accountability measures together may begin to affect the national police culture in which brutality is accepted, overlooked, or ignored. Until measures such as these are implemented, however, the excessive use of force by individual police officers is unlikely to come to an end.

See also **Miscarriages of Justice; Police Corruption**

Further Reading

Alpert, Geoffrey P., and Roger G. Dunham, *Understanding Police Use of Force: Officers, Suspects, and Reciprocity.* Cambridge, UK: Cambridge University Press, 2004.

Chevigny, Paul, *Edge of the Knife: Police Violence in the Americas.* New York: New Press, 1995.

Holmes, Malcolm D., *Race and Police Brutality: Roots of an Urban Dilemma.* Albany: State University of New York Press, 2008.

Human Rights Watch, *Shielded from Justice: Police Brutality and Accountability in the United States.* New York: Human Rights Watch, 1998.

Nelson, Jill, *Police Brutality: An Anthology.* New York: Norton, 2001.

Skolnick, Jerome, and James J. Fyfe, *Above the Law: Police Practices and Procedures.* New York: Free Press/Macmillan, 1993.

Williams, Kristian, *Our Enemies in Blue: Police and Power in America,* rev. ed. Boston: South End Press, 2007.

POLICE CORRUPTION

Marilyn Corsianos

Although there is still some debate over the meaning of the term *police corruption*, the primary controversy has to do with how police corruption stemming from the abuse of police power or authority can be reduced. Since the beginning of formal policing in the 1800s, various groups have demanded more measures to identify and control police corruption and increase police accountability to members of the public. But, what exactly does *police corruption* refer to?

Some acts of police behavior are universally condemned. Others generate disagreement and debate and some police actions clearly violate laws, while yet others violate internal departmental policies. Herman Goldstein defines police corruption as "the misuse of authority by a police officer in a manner designed to produce personal gain for the officer or others" (1997). Similarly, Lawrence Sherman defines police corruption as "an illegal use of organizational power for personal gain" (Sherman 1974, 30).

By contrast, Robert H. Langworthy and Lawrence H. Travis III define police corruption as "the intentional misuse of police power. In practice, this definition means that before something can be called police corruption, two things must be established. First, it must be shown that police powers were misused. Second, it must also be shown that the officer(s) misusing police power intended to misuse it. Whether the motive is money, personal gain, or gain for self or others is not important except insofar as it helps to show intentional misuse of power" (Langworthy and Travis 2003, 414).

It is difficult if not impossible to know the extent of police corruption beyond the reported cases. The victims of police corruption typically report these cases to police authorities. Police officers who participate in acts of corruption have no incentives to report their own corrupt activities and risk losing their jobs and/or facing prosecution in criminal courts. Also, officers who witness acts of police corruption usually have no incentive to come forward and report the misconduct by their fellow officers. As accepted members of the police culture, they are expected to respect the police occupational culture and code of silence.

Moreover, citizens who willingly engaged in acts of corruption with the police have no motive to report their own involvement or that of the officer. In addition, citizens who were less willing participants in the corruption (e.g., citizens who accept an officer's proposal to pay him or her a fee in exchange for not receiving a citation), or citizens who observe a corrupt transaction may decide not to report these incidents because they are either fearful of retribution or believe that the police will not bother with an investigation. Furthermore, only a handful of sociological or criminological studies have been done on police corruption, and they are typically case studies that look at one or a few police agencies.

Findings from case studies often present difficulties in making generalizations from one police department to the next. For obvious reasons, many academics encounter difficulties in gaining access to police agencies and finding a sample of officers willing to participate in a study of police corruption. Researchers who have been successful in conducting such studies have often spent significant time with particular officers, establishing themselves as trustworthy researchers.

Background

Evidence of police corruption in the United States can be traced back to the beginnings of formal police organizations in the 1800s. From the mid-1800s to the early 1900s, the police were appointed by elected political officials who expected police to respond to a variety of neighborhood demands in order to ensure votes during the next election. In addition, officers were selected from the neighborhoods they would serve in order to reflect the interests of the neighborhood residents (Walker 1977). Police officers had to answer to political leaders and to the individual neighborhoods they served (Kelling and Moore 1988). This meant that they operated differently throughout the different neighborhoods, which led to a great deal of controversy regarding police accountability and police roles (Conley 1995).

Police discretion was not monitored. The police had the power to arrest on suspicion and could apply physical force to members of the public (Miller 1977). Evidence suggests that during elections, some officers prevented supporters of opposing parties from casting their ballots using intimidation, arrest, and/or physical force. Police officers also protected the illegal operations of political leaders and/or accepted bribes by owners of illegal operations (Fogelson 1977). Police corruption was commonplace, given the lack of controls on police and their close relationship to politicians and neighborhoods.

By the early 1900s, citizens began to demand reform and accountability. People demanded that the police become a legitimate profession by separating the police from politics, create rules to guide police behavior, distance the police from the communities they were expected to serve, hire police based on qualifications and not political connections, and require special training and skills to fulfill police roles. But despite these accomplishments, along with more recent changes in community policing/community problem solving initiatives, police corruption has not been eliminated.

Different levels of police corruption may be found within police organizations today. They include police agencies where only a few officers participate in corrupt practices as well as agencies with departments where the majority of officers engage in corruption but do so independently, and agencies where corruption is organized and shared among most of the members of the department (Sherman 1974).

Moreover, scholars have identified different types of police corruption (Inciardi 1987). Examples of police corruption vary depending on the definition of police corruption used (Stoddard 1979). For instance, some scholars identify the acceptance of free or discount merchandise or services by officers as a form of police corruption. However, if merchants offer the discounts without any police influence or abuse of power, this particular act is not necessarily a corrupt practice.

Key Events

Recent highly publicized cases show the public that police corruption continues to exist, and they provide citizens with information on how they occur (Corsianos 2003). The cases that often receive a lot of publicity are those that involve excessive use of force, which includes deadly force, by police officers. Deadly force by the police results in an average of 373 civilian deaths each year. The majority of those killed by the police are young and male and a disproportionate number are African American (Brown and Langan 2001). The following is a list of some key incidents of excessive use of force applied by the police as well as incidents involving other types of police corruption.

> 2005–2010: In New Orleans, six unarmed people were shot by police on the Danziger Bridge while riding out the floodwaters of Hurricane Katrina (2005); two of them died. Another officer, Lt. Michael Lohman, arrived later at the scene and colluded with the officers present in creating a story about having been

COMMISSIONS' FINDINGS

The Knapp Commission

It was the Knapp Commission in 1972 that first brought attention to the New York Police Department (NYPD) when the commission released the results of more than two years of investigations into allegations of corruption. In 1970, NYPD officer Frank Serpico went public on the widespread corruption within the police agency. New York City Mayor John Lindsay established the Knapp Commission to investigate the allegations. The commission found widespread corruption such as bribery, especially amongst narcotics officers. As a result, many officers were prosecuted and many more lost their jobs. The commission's findings led to the following recommendations: (1) commanders should be held accountable for their subordinates' actions; (2) commanders should file periodic reports on areas that would breed corruption; (3) field offices of the Internal Affairs Division should be created at all precincts; and (4) undercover informants should be placed in all precincts. A massive restructuring took place and strict rules and regulations were implemented to ensure that this level of police corruption would never happen again.

The Mollen Commission

Many of the Knapp Commission's issues of concern resurfaced again in the early 1990s, as a new corruption scandal emerged. Several officers were accused of selling drugs and assaulting suspects. Mayor David Dinkins appointed a commission in 1992, headed by Judge Milton Mollen, to investigate the allegations. The Mollen Commission report, published in July 1994, described an internal accountability system that was flawed in most respects and discussed the relationship between corruption and brutality. The report read, "Today's corruption is not the corruption of Knapp Commission days. Corruption then was largely a corruption of accommodation, of criminals and police officers giving and taking bribes, buying and selling protection. Corruption was, in its essence, consensual. Today's corruption is characterized by brutality, theft, abuse of authority and active police criminality."

The commission evaluated the department's procedures for preventing and detecting that corruption and recommended changes and improvements to those procedures. Some of the recommendations included improving recruitment and applicant screening, officer performance evaluations, police management, enforcement of command accountability and internal affairs operations, and creating and/or improving integrity training, drug testing, and corruption screening. Also, the Commission to Combat Police Corruption (CCPC) was created in 1995 based upon the recommendations of the Mollen Commission. The Mollen Commission believed that the creation of an independent commission to monitor the anti-corruption activities of the police department would help stop the recurring cycles of corruption.

The Christopher Commission

In 1991, Rodney King, an African American, was struck 56 times with batons by Los Angeles police officers after being stopped by police following a car chase. After the King incident, a commission headed by former Secretary of State Warren Christopher was created

(*continued*)

(*continued*)

to conduct an examination of the structure and operation of the Los Angeles Police Department (LAPD). The commission looked at the recruitment and training practices, internal disciplinary system, and citizen complaint system. In addition, they reviewed a five-year period of internal use of force reports, Mobile Digital Terminal (MDT) transmissions between police cars and police stations, and 83 civil damages cases involving excessive force settled by the city attorney for more than $15,000. The commission also held hearings and interviewed numerous officials and residents.

The commission's report was released in July 1991, and it concluded that racism and sexism were widespread and that a significant number of LAPD officers repetitively used excessive force against the public. The commission also criticized management for their lack of leadership and for failing to control these officers. They also noted that the department often rewarded the problem group of officers with positive evaluations and promotions.

The Christopher Commission made several recommendations to identify, control, and reduce police corruption.

fired on by the victims. They planted a gun on the bridge to bolster their story, and Lohman altered the police reports. A state investigation was launched in 2006 but went nowhere. Federal investigators launched their own inquiry in 2009, bringing charges of a cover up in April 2010.

1999: Amadou Diallo, an African immigrant with no criminal record, was shot and killed by the police. Four New York City police officers fired 41 shots, claiming that Diallo looked suspicious, ignored their commands, and reached for a gun. Diallo, however, was unarmed and was reaching for his wallet when he was shot and killed.

1997: Abner Louima was sodomized with a plunger by a New York City police officer and then the plunger was shoved into his mouth, breaking his front teeth. This act was committed at a police precinct in the presence of several officers, but no one came forward to report the assault. Given the extent of Louima's injuries, he was taken to a hospital where details of the assault were made public.

1997: Six former law officers from Texas were indicted on drug trafficking and corruption charges for smuggling more than 1,700 pounds of marijuana into the country.

1995: The FBI began investigating police corruption charges involving Philadelphia's 39th District. The case concerned a cadre of officers who raided crack houses, shook down drug dealers, and generally trampled on individual rights in order to obtain convictions. By the end of the investigation in 1997, about 100 cases had been overturned.

1994: Hidalgo County Sheriff Brig Marmolejo Jr. was sentenced to seven years in federal prison for taking $151,000 in bribes to allow a drug trafficker to have special privileges in jail.

TYPES OF CORRUPT ACTIVITIES

1. The demand by officers that citizens buy police merchandise in which officers use threats of citation or arrest to make the sale
2. The acceptance of cash or gifts by officers, in exchange for ignoring some violation on the part of the citizen
3. Lying as a witness to cover up the actions of oneself or another officer
4. The taking of cash or expensive items for personal use from a crime scene/call
5. The use of race as a key factor in police decisions to stop and interrogate citizens (referred to as racial profiling, race-based policing, or race-biased policing)
6. A planned burglary or theft by officers while on duty
7. The use of excessive force (e.g., assault, deadly force) by officers on members of the public

1992: Malice Green was pulled from his car by Detroit police officers and beaten to death.

1992–1999: LAPD officers working for the prestigious antigang unit CRASH, in the Rampart Division, were found to be responsible for numerous corrupt activities involving physical beatings, shootings, planting of evidence, falsifying police reports, and falsifying evidence and testimony about their actions in court.

Conclusion

The debate continues on how to limit police abuse of powers and more specifically police corruption. Various groups have demanded stricter measures to identify police corruption, control police behavior, and increase accountability (Walker 2005). Some suggestions include the following:

1. Create open and accessible citizen complaint procedures

Citizens should be given detailed information on how to file a complaint against a police officer. The process should be explained to the public and a time frame should be provided. Police Web sites should post information on the complaint process and citizens should be informed via community newsletters and the police working at various precincts.

2. Create external citizen oversight/complaints agencies

These agencies consist of official panels of citizens who investigate complaints of police misconduct and police corruption. Police departments should be expected to cooperate with these agencies by law and turn over all documents relating to the alleged act or acts of police corruption and should have access to locating and interviewing witnesses and the police officers.

3. Create official corruption units

Official corruption units (similar to the one created in New York City in the early 1990s) should consist of a combination of prosecutors, investigators, and paralegals. Such a unit should work in conjunction with the district attorney's office and should be authorized to investigate the corruption of any public official including police officers and maintain a relationship with police departments' internal affairs bureaus. Upon discovering evidence of police corruption, they should attempt to discover the extent of the corruption within particular units and/or the entire organization by turning corrupt police into undercover "spies" in order to collect evidence as to the extent of corruption and use them in courtroom prosecutions.

4. Create early intervention computerized databases

These databases should be used to collect detailed information on police behavior and practices (e.g., the number of vehicles they stop, the race and sex of the citizens they stop to question, the number of complaints made against them, the nature of the complaints, etc.). This information should be monitored and evaluated internally for any possible patterns of misconduct by police.

5. Demand more accountability on the part of elected officials who can influence police actions through their control over police budgets and the tenure of police administrators

In recent years, citizen complaints about the police practice of racial profiling has led to the passage of legislation mandating that police agencies keep statistics on the race of citizens stopped and questioned by police for traffic violations.

6. Create professionalism within the police and eliminate the "blue code of silence"

Police departments should become more selective in the hiring process and have a preference for applicants with college degrees. In addition, better training should be offered to new recruits. Focus should be given to classes on professionalism, conflict resolution, race relations, gender relations, police accountability, and integrity. Officers with better education and better training will be less likely to participate in police corruption and will be more likely to come forward and report such cases.

See also **Miscarriages of Justice; Police Brutality; Racial, National Origin, and Religion Profiling**

Further Reading

Brown, J. and P. Langan, *Policing and Homicide, 1976–1998: Justifiable Homicide by Police, Police Officers Murdered by Felons.* Washington, DC: Bureau of Justice Statistics, 2001.

Burris, John L., and Catherine Whitney, *Blue vs. Black: Let's End the Conflict between Cops and Minorities.* New York: St. Martin's Griffin, 1999.

Conley, J. A., "The Police in Urban America, 1860–1920." In *The Encyclopedia of Police Science*, 2d ed., ed. W. G. Bailey. New York: Garland, 1995.

Corsianos, Marilyn, "Discretion in Detectives' Decision Making and 'High Profile' Cases." *Police Practice and Research: An International Journal* 4, no. 3 (2003): 301–314.

Fogelson, R. M., *Big-City Police*. Cambridge, MA: Harvard University Press, 1977.

Goldstein, H., *Policing a Free Society*. Cambridge, MA: Ballinger, 1977.

Inciardi, J., *Criminal Justice*, 2d ed. New York: Harcourt Brace Jovanovich, 1987.

Ivkovic, Sanja Kutnjak, *Fallen Blue Knights: Controlling Police Corruption*. New York: Oxford University Press, 2005.

Kelling, G. L., and M. H. Moore, *The Evolving Strategy of Policing*. Washington, DC: U.S. Department of Justice, 1988.

Langworthy, Robert H., and Lawrence F. Travis III, *Policing in America: A Balance of Forces*, 3d ed. Upper Saddle River, NJ: Prentice Hall, 2003.

Levitt, Leonard, *NYPD Confidential: Power and Corruption in the Country's Greatest Police Force*. New York: Thomas Dunne Books, 2009.

Miller, W. R., *Cops and Bobbies: Police Authority in New York and London, 1830–1870*. Chicago: University of Chicago Press, 1977.

Prenzler, Tim, *Police Corruption: Preventing Misconduct and Maintaining Integrity*. Boca Raton, FL: CRC Press, 2009.

Roberg, Roy, Kenneth Novack, and Gary Cordner, *Police and Society*. New York: Oxford University Press, 2008.

Sherman, L., ed., *Police Corruption: A Sociological Perspective*. Garden City, NY: Anchor, 1974.

Stoddard, E., "Organizational Norms and Police Discretion: An Observational Study of Police Work with Traffic Violators." *Criminology* 17, no. 2 (1979): 159–171.

Walker, Samuel, *A Critical History of Police Reform: The Emergence of Police Professionalism*. Lexington, MA: Lexington Books, 1977.

Walker, Samuel, *The New World of Police Accountability*. Thousand Oaks, CA: Sage, 2005.

Weitzer, Ronald John, and Steven A. Tuch, *Race and Policing in America: Conflict and Reform*. New York: Cambridge University Press, 2006.

Williams, Kristian, *Our Enemies in Blue: Police and Power in America*. Cambridge, MA: South End Press, 2007.

Withrow, Brian L., *Racial Profiling: From Rhetoric to Reason*. Upper Saddle River, NJ: Pearson/Prentice Hall, 2006.

PRISON CONSTRUCTION

Byron E. Price

Because the United States has the largest prison population and the highest rate of incarceration in the world, the expansion of its capacity to hold more prisoners is a very contentious one. Perhaps the most controversial question revolves around whether or not U.S. correctional policy should be in the business of building new prisons or whether it should be finding alternatives to imprisonment. These debates or questions, of course, raise related issues that include but are not limited to: punishment versus rehabilitation, privatization versus antiprivatization, and the abolition of parole and probation versus a moratorium on new prison construction.

Background

In the 1990s, in an effort to keep pace with a marked increase in the prison population, prison construction likewise rose to unprecedented levels (Martin and Myers 2005). The additional prison boom coupled with the public's disgust with rehabilitation efforts fueled the imprisonment boom, which lèd to more prison construction, especially between 1990 and 1995. During this time period, 213 new prisons were constructed nationwide (Martin and Myers 2005). During the 1990s, corporations saw the growth of prisons as an economic opportunity and several of them entered the prison construction business. The main two corporations were Corrections Corporation of American (CCA) and the Geo Group—formerly known as Wackenhut (see CCA's and the Geo Group's Web sites, respectively http://www.correctionscorp.com/ and http://www.thegeogroupinc.com/). These corporations changed the way prisons were built. They built speculative prisons (Collins 1998); that is, they built prisons without the state's involvement. They were able to seek financing from Wall Street investment firms such as E. F. Hutton to finance this speculative construction and sidestep the need to float taxpayer-supported bonds, the traditional method of financing new prison construction (Price 2006a). With the advent of prisons for profit, prison construction has become a lucrative industry, and this has led to more punitive laws and more lobbying for laws that increase the prison population.

Legal Decisions

Since 1965, lawsuits charging that overcrowding in prisons constitutes a form of cruel and unusual punishment, and is therefore a violation of prisoners' civil rights, have been brought in virtually every state (Levit 1996). As overcrowding of prisons has continued to swell, most federal, state, and local offici
als have recognized the need to delegate correctional responsibilities to nongovernmental organizations (Segal 2002).

Federal regulations govern this policy and can be found in 18 U.S.C. Sec. 4082(b), which "remands all federal offenders to confinement in any available, suitable, and appropriate institution or facility, whether maintained by the Federal Government or otherwise" (Segal 2002). Prison conditions and prison overcrowding resulted in other class action suits, such as those brought in *Mattison v. South Carolina Department of Corrections*—filed in 1976, consent decree signed in 1978; and in *Nelson v. Leeke*—filed in 1982, decree signed in 1985. Based on the successful argument made by these parties, the South Carolina Department of Corrections agreed to work to eliminate overcrowding by raising staffing levels, upgrading facilities, and making other administrative changes. Following the agreement, five new prisons were built and a number of other units were refurbished (South Carolina Department of Corrections 2007).

Lawsuits have been brought against states across the United States by various plaintiffs charging cruel and unusual punishment as the basis for grievances concerning prison overcrowding. (AELE Law Enforcement Legal Center 2010). Because of the lawsuits brought by various prisoners, courts passed laws mandating that states address their prison crowding problems. Courts also passed enabling legislation that made way for states to privatize prisons and authorize more prison construction. The legal challenges to prison overcrowding enhance the arguments of those critics who oppose the punitive model, which calls for mass incarceration as opposed to rehabilitation. The challenges and lawsuits reinforce their position; they argue that too much emphasis is being placed on incarceration and building more prisons. Instead they assert that states should reform laws that increase the prison population and direct that money away from prison construction into educational programs. Prisons have become such a profitable industry that corporations owning prisons make billions of dollars off prisoners' labor and the per diem the states pay them to house prisoners. Detractors of prison building assert that the laws are driving the legal challenges and more thought should be given to policy that diverts money from education to correction. Proponents of for-profit prisons ask: What is wrong with inmates working and picking up a trade they can use upon release from prison? Critics respond that prisoners are paid slave wages while corporations make millions of dollars in profits.

Controversies in Prison Construction

The major challenge for policy makers responsible for setting correctional policy center around four competing and contentious issues that will affect the future of prison construction in the United States. The first challenge for policy makers is to determine which option is more feasible, building new prisons or seeking alternative methods to incarceration. Because of the "the get tough on crime" and "war on drugs" campaigns, coupled with an increasing trend of politicians running on get-tough platforms, the current climate appears to be in support of building more prisons (although recent economic conditions have produced something of a dampening effect). Have these campaigns been successful in deterring crime? The jury is still out, but both campaigns (the war on drugs and getting tough on crime) have been successful in adding to the growth of the U.S. prison population. The question is at what cost? If these campaigns are deemed successful, then the policy of punishment first may become the status quo, critics fear.

The debate about punishment versus rehabilitation is the second major challenge that will affect future prison construction. Advocates of punishment applaud the current policy to incarcerate and incapacitate for longer periods of time. They assert that these people are criminals and should be locked up, and why should society care about citizens who disobey the law? Since rehabilitation does not work, and if private prisons will help us keep them locked up, then private prisons should be welcomed. On the other hand, proponents of rehabilitation and alternative methods to incarceration contend that resources should be directed into diversion programs and not prison development. The United States incarcerates 500,000 more people than China, although China has five times our population, and private prisons would only expand this number.

Whether to privatize prisons or not is the third major controversy and challenge for policy makers concerned with the growth of prisons. The debate rages on but has taken on added impetus with the introduction of private probation and private prisons. Private prisons present a challenge to policy makers because supporters of private prisons and probation are perceived as having a vested interest in the business of incarceration. Other scholars contend that this is not the case; governments cannot continue to spend exorbitant amounts on prison construction. As long as private prisons are monitored, there should not be a problem. Furthermore, because of various mandatory sentencing laws (e.g., truth-in-sentencing and three-strikes laws) and the imprisonment boom they have generated, privatization is a reasonable alternative, particularly considering the dire straits that many state budgets are in. Yet opponents of prison privatization contend that the new prison construction is being fueled by for-profit prison corporations lobbying and writing laws via the Criminal Justice Task Force committee of the American Legislative Exchange Council—a nonprofit private conservative organization based in Washington, D.C., that writes model privatization and criminal justice legislation. They point to the chart in Table 1 as proof of why for-profit prisons are driving the prison construction boom.

The table shows the number of states passing laws that drive up the prison population and create the need for new prison construction as a result of lobbying. Lobbying for laws favorable to its industry is unethical, and creating a need for new prison construction is unconscionable, commentators contend, and that is why private corporations should not be in the business of incarceration. Also, the opponents of prison privatization maintain that a decreasing crime rate is bad for business for prison corporations and that is why they lobby for laws favorable to their industry.

One of the major issues of prison construction is location, or siting. As the rate of prison construction has risen, so too has the importance of debates concerning siting (Martin 2000; Abrams 1992; Shichor 1992). Although there are concerns in respect to siting a prison, especially as it involves the impact on those communities, in some circles the perceived economic development benefits trump the concerns concomitant with siting prisons. An adverse aspect of prison siting for economic development purposes is that prison construction leads to a modest population loss in many urban communities as urban prisoners are exported outside their communities to rural communities (where prisons are often the largest employers). Because of a quirk in the census, which often counts prisoners in the communities where they are housed

TABLE 1. Impact of For-Profit Prison Lobbying

Legislation	Number of Enactments	States
Truth in Sentencing Act (inmates serve at least 85 percent of their sentences)	25	Arkansas, California, Connecticut, Florida, Georgia, Illinois, Indiana, Louisiana, Massachusetts, Michigan, Mississippi, Missouri, Montana, Nevada, New Hampshire, North Carolina, North Dakota, Oklahoma, South Carolina, South Dakota, Tennessee, Texas, Virginia, West Virginia, Wyoming
Habitual offender/three strikes (life imprisonment for a third violent felony)	11	Arkansas, Florida, Indiana, Montana, New Jersey, North Carolina, South Carolina, Tennessee, Vermont, Wyoming
Private correctional facilities	4	Arkansas, Connecticut, Mississippi, Virginia
Prison industries (requires prisoners to work for private companies)	1	Mississippi

(a policy that changed in many districts for the 2010 census), urban communities historically have lost political and economic clout to the communities where prisoners are shipped. This is one of the main objections to siting prisons for economic development purposes. If the practice does continue in selected districts, then the way the census counts prisoners should be adjusted.

The impetus for the prison construction boom is fueled by the ever-expanding prison population (Lawrence and Travis 2004) and the economic development needs of many rural white communities, critics argue. As prison populations continue to spiral out of control and the willingness of states to build more correctional facilities has not abated, many states and federal agencies are having a difficult time housing prisoners because they are running out of space and prisons are usually overcrowded.

For-profit prison corporations have stepped in to attempt to relieve the overcrowding problems, but they create a need for more prisons with their lobbying efforts and vested interest in the business of incarceration, critics argue. On the other hand, proponents of privatization contend that they are only responding to states' calls for relief as a result of court orders imposed on states to address their overcrowding problems. A benefit of private prison construction is that they can finance construction through lease contracts and lease purchasing agreements versus the traditional way states pay for prison construction, such as "financing construction by cash appropriations (the pay-as-you-go approach) or by issuing general obligation bonds. The former puts the whole financial burden of construction on the state's annual budget. Bonds create problems by requiring voter approval and are restricted by debt limitations (Joel 1998). Critics of for-profit prison construction contend that the taxpayers should determine if they want more prisons versus having private entities determine policy, especially those with a vested interest in new construction. They also want to know whether, once the prisons are financed by for-profit prison corporations, the corporations are accountable to the citizens or to their stockholders. Corporations consider this argument nonsense. They cite competition as the reason why it behooves them to deliver quality service. If they fail to deliver quality service, they assert, they lose money and their competitors can step in and take control of their business.

The final challenge for policy makers is the debate surrounding the abolition of parole and probation versus a moratorium on new prison construction. It is argued that parole and probation must be abolished because they do not work and are too costly. If there were enough prisons, there would be no need to worry about probation and parole because there would be enough space to house prisoners eligible for parole and probation. Moreover, because rehabilitation appears to be a dismal failure, more prisons and laws are needed to incapacitate criminals, according to lobbyists and other advocates of prison construction.

On the other hand, critics of the punishment-first mentality also take issue with the idea of abolishing parole and probation—which is favored by today's correctional culture. They contend that the emphasis should be on rehabilitation and providing a second chance to those who have made mistakes, not on expanding the prison population and new prison construction. Additionally, citizens for criminal justice reform insist that the get-tough-on-crime tactics and punitive philosophy that permeate American society diverts the United States from rehabilitation and creates problems for the future. They ask why we have become a society that does not provide a second chance to those who may have had a momentary had a lapse in judgment. This group factors in structural impediments to human development such as racism, and how racism has handicapped certain minority groups who are disproportionately affected by incarceration and the pursuit of prisons as an economic development apparatus. As a result of their advocacy, states like Illinois are emphasizing rehabilitation as a solution to the high number of repeat offenders and costly jails (Paulson 2006). These groups point out the fact that if federal parole is reinstated it will reduce the costs of the federal prison system by reducing the need to undertake new prison construction. They maintain that "the entire, current budget…earmarked for new prison construction can be eliminated" (Armsbury 2005). Additionally, the argument is made that not enough money is spent on education, treatment, and job training in prison; as a result, prisoners are not equipped to return to society, which heightens the likelihood of recidivism.

PRIVATE PRISON COMPANIES

Private prison companies increase profits in several ways. Known as an economy of scale, the company is paid based on the number of inmates housed. In this case, much like a hotel, there is pressure to fill every available bed every night. To fill the prisons, companies contract with other states and transport inmates to facilities that are not full. In addition, the lower the level of security provided, the lower the cost to the company. The results can sometimes be disastrous for inmates, staff, and communities alike.

For example, in 1997, under pressure to fill empty beds at the medium-level security Northeast Ohio Correctional Center, the Corrections Corporation of America (CCA), under contract with the state, imported maximum-security-level inmates from Washington, D.C. Within one year, 20 stabbings and 6 escapes occurred. Empty prison beds in private facilities, depending on the contract, can also increase private prison profits. In this situation the state guarantees the company that it will pay as if 95 percent of the beds were full—even if they are empty. For instance, in 2001, Mississippi legislators diverted $6 million to pay for nonexistent "ghost inmates" after the CCA threatened to close down its Tallahatchie facility. In a publicly run facility, empty prison beds result in cost savings to taxpayers.

Another way prison companies increase profit is to cut costs, which often results in decreased quality of services and increased costs to taxpayers. The potential areas for cost cutting include but are not limited to inmate transportation, guard training/pay, and medical care, all of which can adversely affect the safety and security of inmates, guards, and citizens. For example, over a three-year time period, 21 violent prisoners escaped during transport by private companies. Training for corrections officers in state-operated facilities averages 12 to 16 weeks, while private companies offer an average of 3 weeks of training. Following the escapes and murders at the Northeast Ohio Correctional Center, an investigation reported that staff and officers, including supervisors, were inexperienced and undertrained. In the privately run Santa Fe Detention Center (New Mexico) alone, an investigative team found more than 20 cases in which inmates died as a result of negligence, indifference, inadequate training, or overzealous cost cutting.

—*Donna Selman-Killingbeck*

On the other hand, detractors of rehabilitation policy point out that those inmates should not receive a free college education, because citizens who have never been incarcerated cannot get a college degree for free. The rejoinder to this comment by advocates of rehabilitation as opposed to incarceration is: What person in his or her right mind would go to prison for a free college education? The reason prisons continue to expand is because of the move away from restorative justice policy, which advocates that everyone needs a second chance. The Second Chance Act, geared toward helping ex-offenders reintegrate into society, focuses on jobs, housing, mental health, substance abuse, and strengthening families; it is the kind of effort that should be undertaken, proponents of restorative justice assert. FedCURE is also a policy the government should pursue because it would reinstitute the old parole and good time laws, which would allow inmates to be paroled at the federal level. (Congress abolished parole in the Comprehensive Crime Control Act of 1984.) However, federal prisoners may earn a maximum of 54 days of good-time credit per year against their sentences.

Critics of alternative methods to incarceration reply that people who commit crimes should not be rewarded for good behavior while incarcerated for crimes they have committed against society. Proponents of rehabilitation ask: Where is the compassion? They pose this question to policy makers with a predilection for punishment, because research shows that the majority of prisoners are nonviolent drug offenders. Furthermore, they note that at least one past president, George W. Bush, was in his youth a nonviolent drug offender who received a second chance. What if he had not benefited from an alternative method of incarceration? They cite many other individual cases as examples of why alternative methods to incarceration should be considered for nonviolent offenders.

Another controversy surrounding the abolition of parole and probation is the idea of privatized probation. Because parole and probation are considered to be too costly, proponents of privatized probation contend that if states are unwilling to abolish probation and parole, they should privatize them. This would help manage the crimes that are being committed by probationers and parolees who should have never been released or pardoned in the first place. Because people who have been paroled and placed on probation keep committing crimes, they drive the need for more prison construction and more police officers. However, advocates of "lock them up and throw away the key" happily report that the tactic of being tough on crime has reduced violent crime—thus a justification for more prisons.

Enough is enough, opponents of incarceration argue. They aver that the United States has locked up more people than any other country and that it leads the world in incarceration. They are initiating a campaign for a moratorium on prisons. Advocates of this movement maintain that states can save money by using funds to actively pursue alternatives to imprisonment for as many people as possible. They also point out that according to the Bureau of Justice Statistics, it costs about $25,000 per year to incarcerate each of the 2.2 million people in the U.S. prisons. This costs as much as annual tuition at a good college, they contend. Proponents of increased use of imprisonment purport that prisons are a necessary evil in our society. Policy leaders in the opposing camp believe that the incarceration of prisoners places their children "at increased risks for many of the social ills that trip up our younger members of society, for instance, truancy, teen pregnancy, drug use, gang involvement and sexually transmitted diseases and infections" (Price 2006a, 40). If laws will not be reformed because policy makers cannot risk being labeled soft on crime, they should at least be designed to help the children who are being "consigned to the juvenile justice system and social bureaucracies" (Price 2006a, 40) in the United States because a parent is being removed from the household (usually the breadwinner) and incarcerated.

Conclusion

Research on prison construction reveals a trend toward fewer prisons being built in the near future, but individual facilities will become larger (Dallao 1997). Another trend taking place is that facilities being built today are different from the ones built in the past (Dallao 1997). These trends appear to be national in scope. Other trends worth examining are the use of more technology, the use of more prefabricated materials, and higher costs of prison construction.

In the wake of the severe economic recession of 2008–2009, prison construction has slowed in many areas even while there has been a shift toward increased acceptance of prison-building projects in the eastern region of the United States (Reutter 2010). This trend is a complete reversal of the previous prison construction trend. Although prison construction has shifted eastward to a degree and fewer prisons are being built, the overall trend is still toward long periods of incarceration. In recent years, federal prisons and the numerous jails throughout the country have experienced a climb in prison population as a result of a crackdown on immigration. This, too, seems a trend that likely will continue—unless new laws are enacted that overhaul the current immigration system.

See also **African American Criminal Injustice; Alternative Treatments for Criminal Offenders; Immigration and Employment Law Enforcement; Prison Sexual Assault; Prisons—Supermax; Three-Strikes Laws; War on Drugs**

Further Reading

Abrams, K., S. Abrams et al., "Issues in Siting Correctional Facilities: An Informational Brief." http://www.nicic.org/pubs/1992/010591.pdf

AELE Law Enforcement Legal Center, "Private Prisons and Their Employees: Civil Liabilities and Defenses." September 2010. http://www.aele.org/law/2010all09/2010-09MLJ301.pdf

American Legislative Exchange Council (ALEC), http://www.alec.org

Armsbury, C., "Reinstating Federal Parole is Smart Economics." *Razor Wire* 8, no. 2 (November 2005).

Collins, William C., *Privately Operated Speculative Prisons and Public Safety: A Discussion of Issues.* Washington, DC: Corrections Program Office, Office of Justice Programs, United States Department of Justice, 1998.

Corrections Corporation of America (CCA), http://www.correctionscorp.com

Dallao, Mary, "Prison Construction Trends: States Build Fewer but Larger Facilities." *Corrections Today* 59, no. 2 (1997): 70.

"Drug Policy Analysis: Education versus Incarceration." http://www.drugpolicy.org/communities/race/educationvsi

Gangi, Robert, Vincent Schiraldi, and Jason Zeidenberg, *New York State of Mind? Higher Education vs. Prison Funding in the Empire State, 1988–1998.* Washington, DC: Justice Policy Institute, 1998.

Geo Group Inc., http://www.thegeogroupinc.com

Gottschalk, Marie, *The Prison and the Gallows: The Politics of Mass Incarceration in America*. New York: Cambridge University Press, 2006.

Hallet, Michael A., *Private Prisons in America: A Critical Race Perspective*. Urbana: University of Illinois Press, 2006.

Hughes, Kristen A., *Justice Expenditure and Employment in the United States, 2003*. Washington, DC: U.S. Department of Justice, Office of Justice Programs, 2006.

Joel, Dana, "A Guide to Prison Privatization." Heritage Foundation. 1998. http://www.heritage.org/Research/Crime/BG650.cfm

Lawrence, Sarah, and Jeremy Travis, "The New Landscape of Imprisonment: Mapping America's Prison Expansion." Urban Institute. 2004. http://www.urban.org/url.cfm?ID=410994

Levit, S. D., "The Effect of Prison Population Size on Crime Rates: Evidence from Prison Overcrowding Litigation." *Quarterly Journal of Economics* 111, no. 2 (1996): 319–351.

Lynch, Mona, *Sunbelt Justice: Arizona and the Transformation of American Punishment*. Stanford, CA: Stanford Law Books, 2010.

Martin, R., and D. L. Myers, "Public Response to Prison Sitting." *Criminal Justice and Behavior* 32, no. 2 (2005): 143–171.

Martin, Randy, "Community Perceptions about Prison Construction: Why Not in My Backyard." *Prison Journal* 80, no. 3 (2000): 266.

May, John P., and Khilid R. Pitts, eds., *Building Violence: How America's Rush to Incarcerate Creates More Violence*. Thousand Oaks, CA: Sage, 2000.

McShane, Marilyn D., *Prisons in America*. New York: LFB Scholarly Publishing, 2008.

Paulson, A., "New Tack on Teen Justice: A Push away from Prisons." *Christian Science Monitor* (December 8, 2006): 2.

Pratt, Travis C., *Addicted to Incarceration: Corrections Policy and the Politics of Misinformation in the United States*. Los Angeles: Sage, 2009.

Price, Byron Eugene, "Incarceration Nation: For Profit Prison Companies' Success Comes at a Huge Social Cost." *Worth* (August 2006a): 40.

Price, Byron Eugene, *Merchandizing Prisoners: Who Really Pays for Prison Privatization?* Westport, CT: Praeger, 2006b.

Reutter, David M., "Economic Crisis Prompts Prison Closures Nationwide, but Savings (and Reforms) Are Elusive." *Prison Legal News* (September 13, 2010).

Segal, Geoffrey, "Corporate Corrections? Frequently Asked Questions about Prison Privatization." Reason Foundation. November 1, 2002. http://www.reason.org/corrections/faq_private_prisons.shtml

Selman, Donna, and Paul Leighton, *Punishment for Sale: Private Prisons, Big Business, and the Incarceration Binge*. Lanham, MD: Rowman & Littlefield, 2010.

Shichor, D., "Myths and Realities in Prison Siting." *Crime and Delinquency* 38, no. 1 (1992): 70–87.

South Carolina Department of Corrections, "A Chronology of Major Events/Developments." 2007. www.doc.sc.gov/about_scdc/about.jsp

Useem, Bert, and Anne Morrison Piehl, *Prison State: The Challenge of Mass Incarceration*. New York: Cambridge University Press, 2008.

PRISON SEXUAL ASSAULT

Tawandra L. Rowell

With the increase in the number of persons incarcerated over the past few decades, the problem of prison sexual assault has become a matter of concern and controversy. Although there is limited empirical evidence on sexual behavior in correctional environments and much debate over the occurrence and frequency of sexual assaults in total institutions, criminologists acknowledge that sexual assault occurs on a regular basis (Bosworth and Carrabine 2003; Struckman-Johnson and Struckman-Johnson 2000; Wooden and Parker 1982). Many concerns apply to those involved in prison sexual assaults, which are traumatic experiences that have consequences for both inmates and correctional officials, including an increase in the escalation of violence within the institution (Fleisher 1989), suicide (Hanser 2002; Lockwood1980), and related health issues, such as HIV (Gido 2002; McGuire 2005).

Background

According to Beck and Hughes (2005), over the past 20 years the total number of inmates who have been sexually assaulted has probably exceeded 1 million. Sexual assaults in correctional environments are difficult for inmates to escape owing to the highly controlled environment of correctional institutions. Because of this restrictive environment of the prison setting (inmates are prevented from roaming the facility freely), sexual assaults are often heard, witnessed by other inmates, and most often rumored to have taken place (Tewksbury1989a), making these public events. This creates fear and anxiety among other inmates housed within the facility, which can also lead to other forms of violence (Dumond 1992).

Perhaps one of the most frustrating aspects of examining nonconsensual sexual behavior in prison environments is the lack of a clear definition from which to operate. The majority of studies fail to define the sexual terminology for the readers who must interpret their findings (Saum et al. 1995). It is also not uncommon for prison sex researchers to create confusion for inmates participating in such studies when they fail to define whether the behavior being studied is in fact considered sexual assault (Kunselman et al. 2002).

Various definitions have been used to study prison sexual assault, which could be partly responsible for the wide range of rates of male prison sexual assault (Davis 1968). However, even though various questions and definitions have been utilized, over the past few decades a limited number of prison sexual assault studies have given rough estimates regarding the prevalence of sexual assaults in correctional institutions. The findings indicated that between zero and 21 percent of inmates are involved in sexual assaults (Struckman-Johnson and Struckman-Johnson 2000; Davis 1968; Hensley, Tewksbury and Castle 2003; Struckman-Johnson et al. 1996; Tewksbury 1989b).

Both male and female inmates are affected by prison sexual assaults. Although female sexual assault in prison had been documented as early as 1968 (Fishman 1968), the vast majority of research on sexual assault in prison environments involves male inmates (Gaes and Goldberg 2004). Sexual assaults involving female prisoners are rare, largely because most researchers have assumed that sexual behavior between female inmates occurs on a consensual basis (Owen 1998).

In male prison environments especially, the exhibition of aggressive behavior, especially aggressive sexual behavior, promotes individuals to a higher status in the prison sexual hierarchy, one that ensures that they will be relatively free of the threat of violence from others (although there are exceptions), which aggressively furthers an individual's goal of exhibiting his masculinity (Kupers 2001). Prison sex researchers would agree that inmates engaging in sexual assaults can be placed into certain nearly universal categories, particularly as punks, jockers ("studs"), or wolves (Donaldson 1993).

Inmates involved in prison sexual assaults are labeled based on the sexual roles they portray (Struckman-Johnson et al. 1996). This determines the treatment that inmates receive from their fellow inmates as well as from correctional officers (Saum et al. 1995). Then, should they ever be transferred or incarcerated elsewhere, their labels follow them from institution to institution (Struckman-Johnson 1996).

Prison Sexual Assault Research

Studies of Female Sexual Assault

Over the past decade, only a few studies on sexual assault involving female inmates have emerged. Struckman-Johnson and colleagues (1996) examined sexual coercion among female and male inmates in Nebraska correctional facilities. Approximately 7 percent of their female respondents reported that they had been sexually coerced. Next, Struckman-Johnson and Struckman-Johnson (2000) examined sexual assault within seven correctional institutions in the Midwest. The authors reported that between 6 and 9 percent of their sample had been sexually assaulted.

Utilizing letters sent by one female offender over a five-year period, Alarid (2000) qualitatively examined sexual coercion among female inmates. She discovered that such behavior between female inmates is predominantly consensual and that the sexual coercion that does occur in this environment is generally not reported to correctional authorities. According to Alarid, 75 to 80 percent of female inmates tend to experiment with or be involved in some type of consensual sexual relationship while incarcerated, which is in direct contrast with what has been reported in male correctional institutions, where sexual assaults are believed to be more violent and to involve more inmates.

Studies of Male Sexual Assault

Even though prison sex researchers have largely ignored female inmates, studies of male prison sexual assault are also relatively scarce. Such studies tend to report higher prevalence rates than those conducted in female correctional institutions (Struckman-Johnson and Struckman-Johnson 2000; Tewksbury 1989b). In 1968, Davis conducted one of the first empirical studies designed to examine prison sexual behavior by examining sexual assaults within the Philadelphia Prison System (PPS). He interviewed 3,304 out of 60,000, or approximately 5 percent, of all inmates who passed through the PPS over a two-year period. According to Davis, the sexual assaults in PPS were indicative of an environment that encouraged aggressive sexual behavior.

Since Davis's study was conducted in 1968, results from numerous empirical studies on sexual behavior, particularly sexual assault, among male inmates have been published (Struckman-Johnson and Struckman-Johnson 2000; Tewksbury 1989b). Although 3 percent of Davis's respondents admitted to being victims of prison sexual assaults, estimates from more recent studies indicate that the proportion of male inmates involved in sexual activities while incarcerated, both consensual and nonconsensual, could exceed 15 to 20 percent (Struckman-Johnson and Struckman-Johnson 2000; Wooden and Parker 1982). Nonconsensual sexual behaviors are reportedly the most frequent type of sexual behavior occurring in correctional institutions (Hensley, Koscheski, and Tewksbury 2005). Table 1 summarizes the limited number of previous studies on male prison sexual assault.

In the 1980s a renewed interest sparked a series of prison sexual assault studies. These produced low prevalence estimates (Owen 1998), ranging from 1 to 28 inmates. Over the past 10 years, prison sex researchers continued their inquiries, leading to additional studies attempting to document the frequency and dynamics of prison sexual assaults. This next series of studies captured estimates ranging from 2 to 375 inmates, perhaps the highest prevalence rate yet reported (Owen 1998). Even though the rates vary, the fact that sexual assaults are occurring in correctional environments should compel correctional authorities and criminal justice professionals to devote more attention to this important issue (Struckman-Johnson et al. 1996).

Until recently, prison sexual assault was largely neglected by researchers and legislators. However, the few studies that have been conducted provide important information regarding the extent to which incarcerated individuals are involved in coercive sexual activities. More recently, the federal government has recognized the serious situation involving sexual assaults in correctional settings, passing the first piece of legislation designed to address the issue of sexual assault in correctional environments.

Challenges in Prison Sexual Assault Research

Disclosure

Prior literature has insisted that the underreporting of sexual assault is consistent and universal (Watkins and Bentovin 2000). Many inmates, particularly male inmates, are reluctant to admit any behavior that may result in their being considered less masculine (Wooden and Parker 1982). For instance, only 29 percent of the victims in

TABLE 1. Prevalence Rates from Previous Sexual Assault Studies

Authors	Sample Size	Prevalence	Question Asked
Davis 1968	3,304	2.9 percent (97 inmates)	Not reported.
Carroll 1977	21	40 sexual assaults/year	Based on the reports of informants; questions not reported.
Lockwood 1980	76	1.3 percent (1 inmate)	Informants and staff reported one or two sexual assaults a year.
Nacci and Kane 1982	330 in 17 federal prisons	1 percent assaulted (3 inmates)	Asked if anyone had forced or attempted to force the inmate to perform sex against his will.
Wooden and Parker 1982	200	14 percent (28 inmates)	I have been pressured to have sex against my will __ times.
Tewksbury 1989b	150	0 percent	How many times have you been raped in this prison? While in this prison, how many times has another male tried to have sex with you using threat or force?
Saum, Surrat, Inciardi, and Bennett 1995	101	5.9 percent (1 inmate)	Not reported.
Struckman-Johnson, Struckman-Johnson, Rucker, et al. 1996	474	21 percent (99 inmates)	Since the time you have been in this prison, has anyone ever pressured or forced you to have sexual contact (touching of genitals, oral, or anal sex) against your will?
Hensley, Tewksbury, and Castle 2003	174	1.2 percent (2 inmates)	Not reported.
Hensley, Koscheski, and Tewksbury 2005	142	8.5 percent (12 inmates)	Since you have been incarcerated, has another inmate sexually assaulted you?
Beck and Harrison 2007	23,398 (incl. females)	4.5 percent	Varied (part of National Inmate Survey, involving 146 state and federal prisons).

THE CORRECTIONS OFFICERS HEALTH AND SAFETY ACT

In 1998, the U.S. House of Representatives approved the Corrections Officers Health and Safety Act of 1998, which requires mandatory HIV testing of federal prisoners sentenced to a period of incarceration of six or more months.* Even with the approval of the Corrections Officers Health and Safety Act legislation in 1998, mandatory HIV testing programs have been slow to develop. To date, only 19 state prison systems require HIV testing upon entry into correctional institutions; a few others routinely offer voluntary testing or provide it upon request or clinical indication.**

Since many inmates and correctional officers may be exposed to HIV/AIDS while housed or employed in a correctional environment, the need to diligently focus on the impact of sexual assault cannot be overemphasized. However, research regarding sexual assault is difficult to conduct in prison environments. Prison sex researchers have admitted that there are significant challenges related to conducting research in this area, including gaining access to prison populations and convincing inmates to disclose such sensitive information.**

---

*K. K. Rapposelli et al., "HIV/AIDS in Correctional Settings: A Salient Priority for the CDC and HRSA." *AIDS Education and Prevention* 14 (2002): 103–113.

**H. M. Eigenberg, "Male Rape: An Empirical Examination of Correctional Officers' Attitudes toward Male Rape in Prison." *Prison Journal* 68 (1989): 39–56.

Struckman-Johnson and colleagues' (Tewksbury 1989b) study of 1,700 male inmates reported their sexual assault experience to correctional authorities. When inmates do agree to participate, convincing them to report their participation in sexual behavior honestly can be challenging. Even when researchers and research teams emphasize that participants' responses will be completely confidential and anonymous, it may be difficult to convince inmates to disclose such sensitive personal information.

Prisoners may underestimate their participation in this behavior because they are concerned with possible repercussions from fellow inmates and correctional officers (Kunselman et al. 2002). Some researchers would argue that there is a widespread inmate code or culture that discourages inmates from reporting sexual assaults regardless of their roles in such behavior (Stastny and Tyrnauer 1982).

The Inmate Code

The inmate or prison code, as it is commonly known, includes a set of unwritten rules designed to help new inmates survive in the prison community. As in the case of other subcultures of deviance, inmates are expected to conform to unorthodox norms, in this case the inmate code. Clemmer (1958) claimed that inmates show solidarity and heighten their status by adhering to the inmate code. Those who refuse to conform to the prison subculture distance themselves from their fellow inmates, which can lead to serious consequences. For those who conform to the prison subculture, the social distance between them and their fellow inmates is reduced, which can contribute to developing positive relationships. These, in turn, can later serve to protect inmates from abuses such as sexual assault (Fong and Buentello 1991).

Embarrassment at having been sexually victimized or fear of being prosecuted for the perpetration of a sexual assault may discourage participants from disclosing such behavior. Since engagement in sexual assault stigmatizes inmates, they are reluctant to admit that these events occur (Kunselman et al. 2002). Although previous studies demonstrate that male inmates are willing to disclose some information (Struckman-Johnson and Struckman-Johnson 2000; Wooden and Parker 1982), the choice to reveal information regarding one's involvement in sexual assault in the prison environment can have consequences, making inmates reluctant to truly admit their involvement in sexual assaults for fear of being considered "snitches" (Clemmer 1958).

Snitching

Snitching, or providing information to correctional officials about events that have transpired or will transpire in the institution, is strictly forbidden by the prison inmate code. This is perhaps its most important violation and a taboo that has stubbornly persisted (Clemmer 1958). Anyone who dares to report such an occasion to prison authorities will surely endure severe consequences, including physical injury, constant taunting and verbal threatening, and even death on some occasions. "If an inmate reports a sexual assault, even without naming the assailant, he will be labeled a 'snitch,' and a contract will automatically be placed on him, and his life expectancy will be measured in minutes" (Cahill 1990).

The severe consequences associated with snitching protect even rapists from being reported to correctional authorities (Struckman-Johnson et al. 1996). Snitches often find themselves in protective custody, or PC, for their own protection. Convincing prisoners to admit involvement in sexual activities while incarcerated has proven difficult for many researchers. Therefore it is especially important that the research team emphasize the confidential and anonymous nature of inmates' their responses.

Generalizability

Most studies on inmate sexual assault have involved one correctional institution, making generalizations regarding other correctional institutions statistically impossible. However, the information gained from these studies can help to elucidate the nature of prison sexual assaults and the extent to which inmates are exposed to sexually transmitted infections in this environment. Many criminal justice researchers have been able to capture the nature of sexual behavior in male correctional environments. As reported earlier,

THE PRISON RAPE ELIMINATION ACT OF 2003

In 2003, President George W. Bush signed the Prison Rape Elimination Act of 2003 (PREA), which requires correctional institutions to provide data on sexual assaults within their respective facilities. The PREA was initially proposed owing to dissatisfaction with the lack of research being conducted on rape in America's prisons. Additionally, it seeks to address the insufficient training of correctional officers and deficiencies in correctional officials' response to sexual assault in their respective facilities (Prison Rape Elimination Act of 2003, Public Law No. 108–79).

A National Prison Rape Elimination Commission was established to examine federal, state, and local policies regarding prevention of prison sexual assault.

The PREA requires a firm commitment from the nation's correctional institutions. Since the PREA has been implemented, increased attention has been focused on sexual assaults in correctional environments. This is particularly important given the public health consequences for those engaged in these types of activities.

researchers have reported that a fair number of inmates admit to engaging in these types of behaviors. Future research efforts in this area can be worthwhile and could provide much needed insight into inmates' involvement in prison sexual assaults.

Consequences of Sexual Assaults

Numerous consequences may afflict those involved in sexual assaults. Although prison sexual assault studies examine the prevalence of such behavior, they rarely focus on the consequences affecting the individuals that are involved (Dumond and Dumond 2002). All of those involved may experience some physical consequences, particularly the risk of contracting an infectious disease. However, these inmates may experience other physical injuries as well.

Sexual assaults are very devastating experiences for victim, who reportedly experience many emotional, physical, and psychological sequelae (Krebs 2006; Robertson 2003). Victims admit experiencing frequent suicidal thoughts, and some have attempted to commit suicide. Lockwood claimed that 38 percent of the sexual assault victims in his study admitted to having contemplated suicide. Thirty-six percent of Struckman-Johnson's (1996) Nebraska prisons sample indicated that they had experienced suicidal thoughts.

Although most victims do not physically harm themselves following involvement in sexual assaults, there are other physical consequences for those involved in such events. Sexual assaults are usually quite violent and involve the infliction of injuries onto victims and sometimes perpetrators as well (when victims choose to fight back). Physical injuries sustained in sexual assaults include lacerations, bruising, tissue damage, abrasions, and internal injuries (Dumond 2001). In the case of male inmates, sexual assaults usually involve more than one aggressor, thus increasing the likelihood that this pursuit will be successful (O'Donnell 2004), which also inflicts more pain and injury on the victim. Sexual assaults have occasionally caused the death of victims (Saum et al. 1995). All inmates who are involved in some capacity in sexual activity while incarcerated run the risk of contracting an infectious disease (Dumond 2001).

Spread of Infectious Diseases

Correctional institutions tend to concentrate individuals with infectious diseases (Hammett, Harmon, and Rhodes 2002). In the United States, the prevalence of infectious diseases is approximately four times greater among prisoners than among the general population (Golembeski and Fullilove 2005). Especially where male inmates are concerned, the risk of contracting sexually transmitted diseases from other inmates is greatly increased. This is an especially serious concern because those who are incarcerated generally engage in more risk-taking behavior, which may place them at risk for contracting HIV/AIDS (Grinstead et al. 1999; Krebs and Simmons 2002).

Generally condoms are not readily available in prison. Ninety-six percent of prisons consider condoms contraband (Hammett, Harmon, and Maruschak 1999). This is especially problematic given the fact that many inmates habitually engage in risky sexual behavior, and these behaviors continue in prison (Krebs and Simmons 2002).

Since the majority of correctional systems do not provide testing for infectious diseases unless an inmate has a valid reason for requesting it (reasons can range from being exposed to blood in the workplace to being involved in a fight with another inmate) (Krebs and Simmons 2002), it is difficult to report the rates of infectious diseases accurately. The spread of infectious diseases such as tuberculosis (TB), hepatitis B (HBV) and C (HCV), human immunodeficiency virus (HIV), and acquired immunodeficiency syndrome (AIDS) in correctional communities has been documented (Beck and Hughes 2005; Braithwaite and Arriola 2003). However, HIV/AIDS in this environment is becoming the most pressing concern for correctional authorities.

According to Swartz, Lurigio, and Weiner (2004), the first AIDS case was discovered among prison inmates in 1983. Since this discovery, the spread of HIV/AIDS in correctional settings has been documented (Andrus et al. 1989; Dean, Lansky, and Fleming 2002). The prevalence of AIDS infection is over twice as high in state and federal prisons than among the general U.S. population, and in previous years it has been as much as five times higher (Braithwaite and Arriola 2003; Bureau of Justice Statistics 2009). Every state in the nation has reported at least one male HIV-positive inmate (Krebs and Simmons 2002). In 2008, national data from the Bureau of Justice Statistics indicated that an estimated 19,924 state inmates and 1,538 federal inmates were HIV-positive.

Conclusion

With the passage of the PREA, interest in the sexual behavior of inmates is expected to increase, hopefully producing research surpassing that which has been conducted in the past. Continued research in this area could have tremendous implications for individuals who are negatively affected by prison sexual assaults. It is hoped that the increase in inquiries will lead to more innovative approaches to examining such a taboo and timely topic, which will eventually lead to more effective and thorough approaches that will fulfill the directive of the Prison Rape Elimination Act (PREA) eliminating sexual assaults in correctional environments.

It is especially important to gather information on HIV risk-related behavior while individuals are still incarcerated. Previous studies on male prison sexual assaults pose many problems, from ineffective sampling techniques that limit generalizability to failing to include important information in the wording of questionnaires. Further research in this area is desperately needed. It could help correctional officials to develop interventions designed to inform and protect those who are believed to be vulnerable to such attacks. Further studies should aim to evoke serious discussion about sexual assault in U.S. correctional institutions.

Correctional institutions are responsible for providing safe and secure living and working environments that will help incarcerated individuals to become productive members of society upon their release. If inmates are persuaded to provide correctional authorities with essential information regarding such behavior, it may encourage the latter to develop programs and allow interventions designed to address these issues. Since the passage of the PREA in 2003, correctional authorities have been required to provide information regarding the number of sexual assaults occurring in their facilities. Further research on prison sexual assault involving inmates and correctional staff could bring awareness of the situation to correctional authorities, possibly prompting them to address this issue more effectively.

The majority of incarcerated individuals return to their communities after a stay of three to five years (Blumstein and Beck 1999, 17–61). Since individuals at risk of contracting HIV frequently move between their home communities and prisons, those who engage in sexual assault will have the potential to transmit it to those residing in their home communities once they are released, which is increasingly becoming a topic of discussion (Braithwaite et al. 2005). An inmate's involvement in sexual assaults while incarcerated can have a tremendous impact on the communities to which they will return. Given the fact that most prisoners will resume sexual activity soon after release (Dolan, Lowe, and Shearer 2004), continuing to ignore such a serious issue can have severe consequences for society overall.

See also **Juveniles Treated as Adults; Prison Construction**

Further Reading

Alarid, L. F., "Sexual Assault and Coercion Among Incarcerated Women Prisoners: Excerpts from Prison Letters." *Prison Journal* 80 (2000): 391–406.

Andrus, J. K., D. W. Fleming, C. Knox, et al., "HIV Testing in Prisoners: Is Mandatory Testing Mandatory?" *American Journal of Public Health* 79 (1989): 840–42.

Beck, Allen J., and Paige M. Harrison, *Sexual Victimization in State and Federal Prisons Reported by Inmates, 2007.* Washington, DC: Bureau of Justice Statistics, 2007. http://bjs.ojp.usdoj.gov/index.cfm?ty = pbdetail&iid = 1149

Beck, Allen J., and T. A. Hughes, *Sexual Violence Reported by Correctional Authorities, 2004.* Washington, DC: U.S. Department of Justice, July 2005.

Blumstein, A., and A. Beck, "Factors Contributing to the Growth in U.S. Prison Populations." In *Prisons,* ed. M. Tonry and J. Petersilia. Chicago: University of Chicago Press, 1999.

Bosworth, M., and E. Carrabine, "Reassessing Resistance: Race, Gender and Sexuality in Prison." Punishment and Society 3 (2003): 501–15.

Braithwaite, R. L., and K.R.J. Arriola, "Male Prisoners and HIV Prevention: A Call for Action Ignored." *American Journal of Public Health* 93 (2003): 759–763.

Braithwaite, R. L., et al., "Short-Term Impact of an HIV Risk Reduction Intervention for Soon-to-Be-Released Inmates in Georgia." *Journal of Health Care for the Poor and Underserved* 16 (2005): 130–39.

Bureau of Justice Statistics, *HIV in Prisons 2007–2008.* Washington DC: National Institute of Justice, 2009.

Cahill, T., "Prison Rape: Torture in the American Gulag." In *Men and Intimacy: Personal Accounts Exploring the Dilemmas of Modern Male Sexuality,* ed. F. Abbott. Freedom, CA: Crossing, 1990.

Chonco, N. R., "Sexual Assaults among Male Inmates: A Descriptive Study." *Prison Journal* 69 (1989): 72–82.

Clemmer, D., *The Prison Community.* Boston: Christopher Publishing House, 1958.

Davis, A. J., "Sexual Assaults in the Philadelphia Prison System and Sheriffs' Vans." *Trans-Action* (1968): 8–16.

Dean, H. D., A. Lansky, and P. L. Fleming, "HIV Surveillance Methods for the Incarcerated Population." *AIDS Education and Prevention* 14 (2002): 65–74.

Dolan, K., D. Lowe, and J. Shearer, "Evaluation of the Condom Distribution Program in New South Wales Prisons, Australia." *Journal of Law, Medicine and Ethics* 32 (Spring 2004): 124–131.

Donaldson, S., "A Million Jockers, Punks, and Queens: Sex among Male Prisoners and Its Implications for Concepts of Sexual Orientation." 1993. http://spr.igc.org/en/stephendonaldson/doc_01_lecture.html

Dumond, R. W., "The Impact and Recovery of Prison Rape." 2001. http://www.spr.org/pdf/Dumond.pdf

Dumond, R. W., "The Sexual Assault of Male Inmates in Incarcerated Settings." *International Journal of the Sociology of Law* 20 (1992): 135–157.

Dumond, R. W. and D. A. Dumond, "The Treatment of Sexual Assault Victims." In *Prison Sex: Practice and Policy,* ed. Christopher Hensley. Boulder, CO: Lynne Rienner, 2002.

Fishman, J. F., *Crucibles of Crime: The Shocking Story of the American Jail.* Montclair, NJ: Patterson Smith, 1968.

Fleisher, Mark S., and Jessica L. Krienert, *The Myth of Prison Rape: Sexual Culture in American Prisons.* Lanham, MD: Rowman & Littlefield, 2009.

Fleisher, Mark E., *Warehousing Violence.* Newbury Park, CA: Sage, 1989.

Fong, R. S., and S. Buentello, "The Detection of Prison Gang Delinquency: An Empirical Assessment." *Federal Probation* 55 (1991): 66–69.

Gaes, G. G., and A. L. Goldberg, *Prison Rape: A Critical Review of the Literature.* Washington, DC: National Institute of Justice, 2004.

Gido, Rosemary L., "Inmates with HIV/AIDS: A Growing Concern." In *Prison Sex: Practice and Policy,* ed. Christopher Hensley. Boulder, CO: Lynne Rienner, 2002.

Golembeski, C., and R. Fullilove, "Criminal (In)justice in the City and Its Associated Health Consequences." *American Journal of Public Health* 95 (2005): 1701–1706.

Grinstead, O. A., B. Zack, B. Faigeles, et al., "Reducing Postrelease HIV Risk among Male Prison Inmates." *Criminal Justice and Behavior* 26 (1999): 453–465.

Hammett, T. H., P. Harmon, and W. Rhodes, "The Burden of Infectious Diseases among Inmates of and Releases from U.S. Correctional Facilities, 1997." *American Journal of Public Health* 92 (2002): 1789–1794.

Hammett, T. H., P. Harmon, and L. M. Maruschak, *HIV/AIDS in Correctional Facilities, Inmate Education Programs, Inmate Health Care, Jails and Jail Inmates, and HIV/AIDS.* Washington, DC: National Institute of Justice, July 1999.

Hanser, R., "Inmate Suicide in Prison." *Prison Journal* 82 (2002): 459–477.

Hensley, Christopher, ed., *Prison Sex: Practice and Policy.* Boulder, CO: Lynne Rienner, 2002.

Hensley, Christopher, M. Koscheski, and R. Tewksbury, "Examining the Characteristics of Male Sexual Assault Targets in a Southern Maximum-Security Prison." *Journal of Interpersonal Violence,* 20 (2005): 667–679.

Hensley, Christopher, R. Tewksbury, and T. Castle, "Characteristics of Prison Sexual Assault Targets in Male Oklahoma Correctional Facilities." *Journal of Interpersonal Violence* 18 (2003): 595–606.

Krebs, C., and M. Simmons, "Intraprison HIV Transmission: An Assessment of Whether It Occurs, How It Occurs, and Who Is at Risk," *AIDS Education and Prevention* 14 (Suppl. B, 2002): 53–64.

Krebs, C. P., "Inmate Factors Associated with HIV Transmission in Prison." *Criminology and Public Policy* 5 (2006): 113–136.

Kunselman, J., R. Tewksbury, R. W. Dumond, and D. A. Dumond, "Nonconsensual Sexual Behavior." In *Prison Sex: Practice and Policy,* ed. Christopher Hensley. Boulder, CO: Lynne Rienner, 2002.

Kupers, T. A., "Rape and the Prison Code." In *Prison Masculinities,* ed. D. Sabo, T. A. Kupers, and W. London. Philadelphia: Temple University Press, 2001.

Kuznel, Regina G., *Criminal Intimacy: Prison and the Uneven History of Modern American Sexuality.* Chicago: University of Chicago Press, 2008.

Lockwood, D., *Prison Sexual Violence.* New York: Elsevier, 1980.

McGuire, D. M., "The Impact of Prison Rape on Public Health." *California Journal of Health Promotion* 3 (2005): 72–83.

O'Donnell, I., "Prison Rape in Context." *British Journal of Criminology* 44 (2004): 241–255.

Owen, B., *In the Mix.* Albany: State University of New York Press, 1998.

Robertson, J. E., "Rape among Incarcerated Men: Sex, Coercion, and STDS." *AIDS Patient Care and STDS* 14 (2003): 423–430.

Sabo, Don, Terry A. Kupers, and Willie London, eds., *Prison Masculinities.* Philadelphia: Temple University Press, 2001.

Saum, C. A., H. L. Surrat, J. A. Inciardi, et al., "Sex in Prison: Exploring the Myths and Realities." *Prison Journal* 75 (1995): 413–430.

Stastny C., and G. Tyrnauer, *Who Rules the Joint? The Changing Political Culture of Maximum-Security Prisons in America.* Lexington, MA: Lexington Books, 1982.

Struckman-Johnson C., and D. Struckman-Johnson, "Sexual Coercion Rates in Seven Midwestern Prison Facilities for Men." *Prison Journal* 80 (2000): 379–390.

Struckman-Johnson, C., D. Struckman-Johnson, L. Rucker, et al., "Sexual Coercion Reported by Men and Women in Prison." *Journal of Sex Research* 33 (1996): 67–76.

Swartz, J. A., A. L. Lurigio, and D. A. Weiner, "Correlates of HIV-Risk Behaviors: Implications for Tailored AIDS Prevention Programming." *Prison Journal* 84 (2004): 486–504.

Tewksbury, R. A., "Fear of Sexual Assault in Prison Inmates." *Prison Journal* 69 (1989a): 62–71.

Tewksbury, R. A., "Measures of Sexual Behavior in an Ohio Prison." *Sociology and Social Research* 74 (1989b): 34–39.

Watkins B., and A. Bentovin, "Male Children and Adolescents as Victims: A Review of the Current Knowledge." In *Male Victims of Sexual Assault,* ed. G. C. Mezey and M. B. King. Oxford, UK: Oxford University Press, 2000.

Wooden, Wayne S., and Jay Parker, *Men behind Bars: Sexual Exploitation in Prison.* New York: Plenum, 1982.

PRISONS—SUPERMAX

Jeffrey Ian Ross

Supermax prisons are controversial for several reasons, not limited to their lockdown policies, lack of amenities, prisoner isolation techniques, strategies of dehumanization, and overall conditions of confinement. Over the past two decades in the United States, correctional systems at the state and federal levels have introduced or expanded the use of supermax prisons (King 1999). These facilities—also known as special (or security) handling units (SHUs) or control handling units (CHUs)—are either stand-alone correctional institutions or wings or annexes inside an already existing prison.

Background

Supermax prisons are a result of the recent growth in incarceration that has occurred throughout many of the world's advanced industrialized countries (Toch 2001). In October 1983, after the brutal stabbing to death of two correctional officers by inmates at the federal maximum-security prison in Marion, Illinois, the facility implemented a 23-hour-a-day lockdown of all convicts. The institution slowly changed its policies and practices and was retrofitted to become what is now considered a supermax prison. In 1994, the federal government opened its first supermax prison in Florence, Colorado, specifically designed to house supermax prisoners. The facility was dubbed the "Alcatraz of the Rockies."

In the years that followed, many state departments of corrections built their own supermax prisons. Part of the reason for the proliferation of supermax prisons is the conservative political ideology that started in the Reagan administration (1981–1989). During the 1980s, as a response to an increase in the public's fear of crime and to the demise of the "rehabilitative ideal," a punitive agenda took hold of criminal justice and led to an increased number of people incarcerated. This approach was carried forward by George H. W. Bush (1989–1993), Reagan's Republican successor.

Originally designed to house the most violent, hardened, and escape-prone criminals, supermaxes are increasingly used for persistent rule breakers, convicted leaders of criminal organizations (e.g., the Mafia) and gangs, serial killers, and political criminals (e.g., spies and terrorists) (Lovell et al. 2001; Bruton 2004). In some states, the criteria for admission into a supermax facility and the review of prisoners' time inside are very loose or even nonexistent.

The number of convicts being sent to supermax prisons is growing. The supermax maintained by the Federal Bureau of Prisons (FBOP) in Florence, Colorado, for example, incarcerates about 430 people, including such notable criminals as "Unabomber" Ted Kaczynski, Oklahoma City bombing coconspirator Terry Nichols, and former FBI agent and Soviet/Russian spy Robert Hanssen. Nevertheless, only a fraction of those incarcerated in state and federal prisons are sent to a supermax facility. In 2004, approximately

LIST OF SUPERMAX PRISONS IN THE UNITED STATES

Federal Supermax Prisons

United States Penitentiary Administrative Maximum Facility (ADX) in Florence, Colorado, opened 1994. (*Note:* the United States Penitentiary Facility in Marion, IL, which was converted to a supermax in 1983, was downgraded to a medium-security prison in 2006.)

Selected Well-Known State Supermaxes

Maryland Correctional Adjustment Center (MCAC), Baltimore, Maryland, opened 1988

Minnesota Correctional Facility—Oak Park Heights (MCF-OPH), Stillwater, Minnesota, opened 1983

Tamms Correctional Center, Tamms, Illinois, opened March 1998

Varner Supermax, Grady, Arkansas, opened 2000

Wallens Ridge State Prison, Big Stone Gap, Virginia, opened April 1999

25,000 inmates were locked up in this type of prison, representing well under 1 percent of all the men and women who are currently incarcerated across the country (Harrison and Beck 2005; Mears 2005).

The U.S. detention facility located at the Guantanamo Bay military installation is effectively a supermax prison. It houses approximately 190 persons suspected of participating in terrorist activities directed against the Unites States. Numerous controversies, however, surround the Guantanamo detainees and their legal status. Indeed, the prison itself is considered by many to lie outside the jurisdiction of the U.S. legal system, although the U.S. Supreme Court has ruled that the prisoners must, at least be allowed to challenge their detentions in U.S. courts. Because of the controversies involved, the Guantanamo prison is slated to close in 2011 or 2012 and an existing facility in Thomson, Illinois, is to be outfitted as a supermax unit to house most of the remaining detainees.

Conditions of Confinement

One of the more notable features of all supermax prisons is the fact that prisoners are typically locked down 23 hours a day. Other than supervision by correctional officers (COs), prisoners have virtually no contact with other people (fellow convicts or visitors). Access to phones and mail is strictly and closely supervised or restricted. Supermax prisoners have very limited access to privileges such as watching television or listening to the radio.

Supermax prisons also generally do not allow inmates to either work or congregate during the day. (There are notable exceptions. The Maryland Department of Corrections, for example, allows some supermax inmates to congregate during yard time.) In addition, there is absolutely no personal privacy; everything the convicts do is monitored, usually through a video camera that is on all day and all night. Communication with the correctional officers typically takes place through a narrow window on the steel door of the cell and/or via an intercom or microphone system.

Although cells vary in size and construction, in general, they are 12 by 7 feet in dimension. A cell light usually remains on all night long, and furnishings consist of a bed,

OTHER COUNTRIES THAT HAVE SUPERMAX OR SIMILAR FACILITIES

Al Hayer Prison, Riyadh, Saudi Arabia

Goulburn Correctional Centre, Goulburn, New South Wales, Australia

Special Handling Unit, Ste-Anne-des-Plaines, Quebec Canada

Centro de Readaptação Provisória de Presidente Bernardes, Presidente Bernardes, São Paulo, Brazil

Penitenciaría de Combita, Colombia

C Max, Pretoria, South Africa

a desk, a stool made of poured concrete, and a stainless steel sink and toilet. In spite of these simple facilities and the fact that prisoners' rehabilitation is not encouraged (and is next to impossible), supermax prisons are more expensive than others to build and run.

In supermaxes, inmates rarely have access to educational or religious materials or services. Almost all toiletries (e.g., toothpaste, shaving cream, and razors) are strictly controlled (Hallinan 2003). When an inmate is removed from his cell, he typically has to kneel down with his back to the door. Then he is required to place his hands through the door to be handcuffed.

Effects of Incarceration

When it comes to supermax prisons, the mass media and academia have been relatively silent because it is difficult for reporters and researchers to gain access to these or most other penal facilities. In addition, correctional professionals are reluctant to talk with outsiders for fear that they may be unnecessarily subjected to public scrutiny. And even though comprehensive psychological data on individuals kept in these facilities are lacking, numerous reports have nonetheless documented the effects.

All told, the isolation, lack of meaningful activity, and shortage of human contact takes its toll. Supermax prisoners often develop severe psychological disorders, including delusions and hallucinations, which may have long-term negative effects (Rhodes 2004). Furthermore, the conditions inside supermax prisons have led several corrections and human rights experts and organizations (like Amnesty International and the American Civil Liberties Union) to question whether these prisons are a violation of (1) the Eighth Amendment to the U.S. Constitution, which prohibits the state from engaging in cruel and unusual punishment and/or (2) the European Convention on Human Rights and the United Nations' Universal Declaration of Human Rights, which were established to protect not only the rights of people living in the free world but also of those behind bars.

Supermax prisons have plenty of down sides, and not just for the inmates (Lippke 2004). Some people have suggested that all supermax prisons are part of the correctional–industrial complex (see, for example, Christie 2003). Most of the supermaxes in the United States are brand new or nearly so. Others are simply freestanding prisons that were retrofitted. According to a study by the Urban Institute, the annual per-cell cost of a supermax is about $75,000, compared with $25,000 for each cell in an ordinary state prison.

We have plenty of superexpensive supermax facilities—two-thirds of the states now have them. But they were designed when crime was considered a growing problem, and now we have a lower rate of violent crime, which shows no real sign of a turn for the worse. However, as good as these prisons are at keeping our worst offenders out of the way, the purpose of the supermax is in flux.

Conclusion

No self-respecting state director of corrections or correctional planner will admit that the supermax concept was a mistake. And one would be wrong to think that these prisons can be replaced by something drastically less costly. But prison experts are beginning to realize that, just like a shrinking city that finds itself with too many schools or fire departments, the supermax model must be made more flexible in order to justify its size and budget.

One solution is for these facilities to house different types of prisoners. In May 2006, Wisconsin Department of Corrections officials announced that, over the past 16 years, the state's supermax facility in Boscobel—which cost $47.5 million (in 1990) and has a capacity of 500 inmates—has always stood at 100 cells below capacity. It will house maximum-security prisoners, or serious offenders, but individuals who represent a step down from the worst of the worst.

The Maryland Correctional Adjustment Center, also known as the Baltimore Supermax prison, opened in 1989 at a cost of $21 million with room for 288 inmates. Like its cousin in Wisconsin, it has never functioned at capacity. It holds not only the state's most dangerous prisoners but also 100 or so inmates who are working their way through the federal courts. It also serves as the home for Maryland's 10 death row convicts.

Converting cells is one approach, but not the only one. Other ideas include building more regional supermaxes and filling them by shifting populations from other states. This would allow complete emptying out of a given supermax and then closing it down or converting it to another use.

There is also the possibility that some elements of the supermax model could be combined with the approaches of traditional prisons, creating a hybrid that serves a wider population. But different types of prisoners would have to be kept well away from each other—a logistical problem of no small concern.

See also **Cruel and Unusual Punishment; Prison Construction; Prison Sexual Assault**

Note

The last section of this article draws from Jeffrey Ian Ross, "Is the End in Sight for Supermax," *Forbes* (April 18, 2006). http://www.forbes.com/blankslate/2006/04/15/prison-supermax-ross_cx_jr_06slate_0418super.html/

Further Reading

Begg, Moazzam, and Victoria Brittain, *Enemy Combatant: A British Muslim's Journey to Guantanamo and Back.* London: Free Press, 2006.

Bruton, James H., *The Big House: Life inside a Supermax Security Prison.* St. Paul, MN: Voyageur Press, 2004.

Christie, Nils, *The Prison Industrial Complex.* London: Routledge, 2003.

Hafetz, Jonathan, and Mark Denbeaux, eds., *The Guantanamo Lawyers: Inside a Prison Outside the Law*. New York: New York University Press, 2009.

Hallinan, Joseph T., *Going up the River*. New York: Random House, 2003.

Harrison, Paige M., and Allen J. Beck, "Prisoners in 2004." *BJS Bulletin*. Washington DC: U.S. Department of Justice, 2005. http://www.ojp.usdoj.gov/bjs/pub/pdf/p04.pdf

King, Roy D., "The Rise and Rise of Supermax: An American Solution in Search of a Problem." *Punishment and Society* 1 (1999): 163–185.

Lippke, Richard L., "Against Supermax." *Journal of Applied Philosophy* 21, no. 2 (August 2004): 109–124.

Lovell, David, et al., "Who Lives in Supermax Custody?" *Federal Probation* 64 (2000): 33–38.

Mears, Daniel P., *Supermax Prisons: Examining the Impacts and Developing a Cost-Benefit Model*. Washington, DC: National Institute of Justice, 2005.

National Commission on Safety and Abuse in Prison, "Commission on Safety and Abuse in America's Prisons." 2006. http://www.prisoncommission.org

Neal, Donice, ed., *Supermax Prisons: Beyond the Rock*. Lanham, MD: American Correctional Association, 2002.

Rhodes, Lorna A., *Total Confinement: Madness and Reason in the Maximum Security Prison*. Berkeley: University of California Press, 2004.

Riveland, Chase, *Supermax Prison: Overview and General Considerations*. Longmont, CO: National Institute of Corrections, 1998.

Shalev, Sharon, *Supermax: Controlling Risk through Solitary Confinment*. Uffculme, UK: Willan Publishing, 2009.

Toch, Hans, "The Future of Supermax Confinement." *Prison Journal* 81 (2001): 376–388.

PUBLIC DEFENDER SYSTEM

Roslyn Muraskin and Matthew Muraskin

For over 50 years now, indigent defendants—that is, those accused of crimes but unable to afford an attorney—have had the right to obtain legal counsel at no cost to themselves by making use of state public defender systems. With that central point settled, the controversies in this area revolve around a number of other issues. For instance, when does the right to use a state-appointed attorney come into play in the state's intervention into a person's life as law enforcement attempts to find culpability for a criminal offense? Is there an appropriate time when the right to counsel may be waived by an accused indigent? Answers to these questions affect the lives of most persons accused of a criminal offense in the United States. For example, in 1998, two-thirds of federal felony defendants could not afford to retain their own counsel, and in 75 of the most populous counties in the United States the figure was 82 percent (U.S. Department of Justice 2001). Other issues have to do with such questions as what is the best way to provide legal services for the indigent and what level of poverty qualifies one for assigned counsel.

Are we reaching indigents who reside outside of the most populous areas in the country? Finally, and overarching most or all of these issues, is the public defender system capable of handling the task we have assigned it using the resources we have provided?

Background

The Sixth Amendment to the U.S. Constitution provides that "[I]n all criminal prosecutions, the accused shall enjoy the right to...have the Assistance of Counsel for his defense." Even earlier than that, Benjamin Austin argued at the Constitutional Conventions, "As we have an Attorney General who acts in behalf of the State, it is proposed that the Legislature appoint another person (with a fixed salary) as Advocate General for all persons arraigned in criminal prosecutions; whose business should be to appear in behalf of all persons indicted by the State's Attorney." (Smith and Bradway 1936, 53). But the idea remained dormant for the next 100 years.

In 1896, however, bills were introduced in 12 state legislatures to establish public defender officers. By 1917, public defender bills had been introduced in 20 states. By 1926, there were 12 working public defender offices, and by 1933 at least 21 offices were up and running in the United States (Barak 1980). However, the right to have such a defense was pretty much a hollow one until the middle of the 20th century, as the vast majority of defendants who were too poor to hire a lawyer on their own came from other jurisdictions. Indeed, the National Legal Aid and Defender Association reports on their Web site that, until the middle of the 20th century, most criminal defense lawyers worked on a *pro bono* basis even in capital cases after being appointed by the individual trial judges; and although there were a few programs to provide representation (i.e., the New York

---

PUBLIC DEFENDER

The idea of a public defender is actually quite old. Such a system existed in ancient Rome. Later, the ecclesiastical courts of the Middle Ages provided an office of advocate for the poor and an office of the procurator of charity. Both offices were honorable positions, as these courts recognized the needs of accused persons in matters of legal representation. As early as the 15th century, Spain has had an officer corresponding to a public defender. And in 1889, Belgium began a policy of public defense. By the turn of the 20th century, the laws of the following countries provided an office of defenders: Argentina, Belgium, Denmark, England, France, Germany, Hungary, and Mexico. In the United States, the following states had adopted public defender systems by 1993: California, Connecticut, Illinois, Indiana, Minnesota, Nebraska, Ohio, Tennessee, and Virginia.

Source: Gregg Barak, *In Defense of Whom? A Critique of Criminal Justice Reform* (Cincinnati, OH: Anderson, 1980).

City Legal Aid Society starting in 1896 and the Los Angeles Public Defender in 1914), such services were limited to the largest cities in the country.

Legal Developments

In 1932, the U.S. Supreme Court began a many-year process to change the law to require the appointment of counsel to indigents, first in state capital cases (*Powell v. Alabama*) and then, six years later, to all federal prosecutions *(Johnson v. Zerbst)*. When faced with the question of requiring counsel for indigents in state noncapital cases in 1943, however, it refused to do so *(Betts v. Brady)*. It was not until 1963, in *Gideon v. Wainwright*, that the right was extended to state felony cases, and in 1972 *(Argesinger v. Hamlin)*, the Supreme Court held that there was a right to assigned counsel for an indigent in any type of criminal proceeding in which there was a possibility of incarceration. In 1961, the right was extended to pretrial situations at the very beginning of the judicial process (*Hamilton v. Alabama*) and even before, in postarrest interrogations (*Miranda v. Arizona* 1966) and lineups (*United States v. Wade* 1967), as well as after conviction on appeals (*Douglas v. California* 1963).

With the issue of an indigent's right to assigned counsel settled, there now is a vast and continually developing body of law, both federal and state, setting forth the parameters of exactly when the right to counsel attaches and whether and when it can be waived.

Counsel can be waived at any stage of the proceedings; however, the right to counsel attaches at the time of arraignment and even before if the police intend to conduct an interrogation or a lineup. The developing body of law primarily focuses on the factual circumstances surrounding whether there was a valid waiver or not. The controversy revolves around the facts. Did what happen amount to a waiver or not? Did the questioning start before the Miranda warnings; did they precede the questioning, or did they come afterward? Was the person in custody so as to require warnings?

A prime example would be as follows: A detective asks a defendant in custody if he wants to tell his side of the story. The defendant says yes, and before any Miranda warnings are given, the defendant starts to incriminate himself, at which point the officer finally gives Miranda warnings. The question is whether what took place before the warnings were given was substantive in nature or even whether it was a question to ask at all. There is no such thing as a little bit of questioning; you either are questioned or are not, and this is where controversy lies.

Indigent Defense Services

To implement the now required delivery of indigent criminal defense services, several different programs have developed within most localities. They presumably handle conflicts (i.e., multiple defendants or conflicting loyalties such as prior representation of the victim now accusing the defendant), keep costs down, or provide work for private lawyers.

One method of delivery is by means of a public defender who is a government official, either appointed (i.e., New York) or elected (i.e., Florida) in a particular locality, who—along with his or her staff of lawyers, investigators, and so forth—provides representation to the indigent with a government budget line usually much lower than that of the district attorney. In some localities, such as New York City and its neighboring counties of Nassau and Suffolk, private and separate legal aid societies contract with the local government to provide the major representation in the same manner and structure as a public defender.

Service delivery may also be made with an assigned counsel panel of private lawyers who have agreed to provide representation, as selected, for a previously agreed and usually hourly fee set by a governmental body. The fee usually paid to the assigned counsel is much lower than the normal fee for the service. Indeed, in New York State, the hourly fee was raised to $75 in 2003, having been at $40 per hour since 1985. Another option to provide the required legal services is through a contract with one or more lawyers to handle a specific number of cases for a set fee.

Determination of indigence varies by locality and is usually done by the court making the assignment, the agency or lawyer to be assigned, or by some screening agency set up for that purpose or is a part of some other branch of the executive department of the locality.

According to the Bureau of Justice Statistics, 964 public defender offices across the nation handled 5.8 million indigent defense cases in 2007, at a total expenditure of $2.4 billion (U.S. Department of Justice 2009). This cost, however, is mostly a local one, with county governments in the 100 most populous counties picking up about 60 percent of the tab, although in some states such as New York it is a completely local cost. Maine is the only state having no public defender offices; it provides indigent defense services through private attorneys.

Misdemeanors accounted for about 40 percent of all cases handled by state-based public defender offices and about 50 percent of the cases handled by county-based offices. Misdemeanors were followed by non–capital felony cases (25 percent of state cases and 32 percent of county cases) and by appeals cases (1 percent and a negligible fraction, respectively) (U.S. Department of Justice 2009).

As for staffing and caseloads, the same statistics indicate that more than 17,000 attorneys were employed by public defender offices in 2007, some 4,000 at the state level and nearly 13,000 at the county level. Each state public defense attorney handled, on average, 147 misdemeanor cases, 88 felony cases, and 3 appeals cases in 2007. County-based public defenders handled, on average, 164 misdemeanors and 2 appeals. Half of all state-based public defender offices had formal caseload limits in place in 2007, whereas less than one fifth of county-based programs had the same limits. (In nearly 40 percent of the county-based programs, however, attorneys had the authority to refuse appointments because of caseload.) (U.S. Department of Justice 2001).

Stresses to the System[1]

Over the past several years there have been an increasing number of cases in which public defenders' offices, underfinanced and overburdened with cases, have failed to meet expectations. Indigent defense programs in Louisiana, Florida, Georgia, Missouri, Kentucky, New York, and Michigan, among others, have been identified as needing overhaul. Indeed, in some cases it is the public defenders themselves who have sued for changes, as they recognize that they no longer can manage high caseloads and at the same time provide adequate representation to each of their clients. Often, there is pressure on defendants to plead guilty to lesser charges in exchange for lighter sentences—one way to avoid the time and expense of a trial. This and other forms of "rushed justice," along with instances of faulty lawyering (stemming from unmanageable caseloads and/or inadequate training and experience), have produced a rise in the number of wrongful convictions. State budget cuts across the nation in the wake of the 2008–2009 financial crisis have only made matters worse (Eckholm 2008; "Hard Times" 2008; Glaberson 2010).

Whether the trend will turn around anytime soon is an open question at this point. Louisiana, for one, has implemented large-scale changes intended to ensure that both the letter and spirit of *Gideon v. Wainwright* are addressed. New York only recently (2010) was ordered by the state supreme court to fix its broken public defender system, and what that state does may serve as a model for other states. Meanwhile, several states and districts faced with challenges to their public defender systems have already begun the process of self-examination and public discussion.

See also **Alternative Treatments for Criminal Offenders; Class Justice; Miranda Warnings; Poverty and Race (vol. 1)**

Note

1. This section and parts of the previous one were contributed by Michael Shally-Jensen.

Further Reading

Barak, Gregg, *In Defense of Whom? A Critique of Criminal Justice Reform.* Cincinnati, OH: Anderson, 1980.

Braswell, Michael C., Belinda R. McCarthy, and Bernard J. McCarthy, *Justice, Crime and Ethics,* 6th ed. Cincinnati, OH: Anderson, 2006.

Eckholm, Erik, "Citing Workload, Public Lawyers Reject New Cases." *New York Times* (November 8, 2008).

Glaberson, William, "Court Rules that Suit on Public Defender System Can Proceed." *New York Times* (May 6, 2010).

Grisham, John, *The Innocent Man: Murder and Injustice in a Small Town.* New York: Doubleday, 2006.

"Hard Times and the Right to Counsel." *New York Times* (November 21, 2008).

Muraskin, Roslyn, and Matthew Muraskin, *Morality and the Law.* Upper Saddle River, NJ: Prentice Hall, 2001.

Muraskin, Roslyn, and Albert R. Roberts, *Visions for Change: Crime and Justice in the 21st Century,* 5th ed. Upper Saddle River, NJ: Prentice Hall, 2008.

Rhode, Deborah L., *Access to Justice.* New York: Oxford University Press, 2004.

Robinson, Matthew B., *Justice Blind? Ideals and Realities of American Criminal Justice,* 3d ed. Upper Saddle River, NJ: Prentice Hall, 2008.

Smith, Reginald H., and John S. Bradway, *Growth of Legal-Aid Work in the United States.* Bulletin No. 607. Washington, DC: U.S. Government Printing Office, Department of Labor, 1936.

U.S. Department of Justice, Bureau of Justice Statistics. "Indigent Defense Statistics." Washington, DC: U.S. Government Printing Office, October 1, 2001.

U.S. Department of Justice, Bureau of Justice Statistics, "Public Defender Offices, 2007." November 2009. http://bjs.ojp.usdoj.gov/content/pub/pdf/pdo07st.pdf

Weiss, Michael Scott, *Public Defenders: Pragmatic and Political Motivations to Represent the Indigent.* New York: LFB Scholarly Publishing, 2004.

Wice, Paul B., *Public Defenders and the American Justice System.* Westport, CT: Praeger, 2005.

R

RACIAL, NATIONAL ORIGIN, AND RELIGION PROFILING

Judith Ann Warner and Karen S. Glover

Racial profiling has eclipsed most other criticisms of the police–minority and immigrant relationship and has emerged as perhaps the most controversial social issue in that area. Singling out an individual on the basis of race or national origin for law enforcement scrutiny is generally called racial profiling. *Profiling* refers to criteria police use for traffic stops, but some definitions expand it to any police contact on the basis of suspicion in public spaces, and it is applied in the examination of immigration enforcement. A classic scenario involves a traffic stop of a minority motorist who is under suspicion for the possession of contrabands, specifically illegal drugs. An emergent scenario is the stopping of a Latino and questioning about documentation authorizing him or her to be in the country legally. The import of examining the traffic stop in particular is that it is potentially the first step into the criminal justice system and thus its effects are far-reaching.

Although the association of physical attributes with criminality has a long history, going back at least to Cesare Lombroso's "criminal man" theory from the late 19th century (Fattah 1997), the concept of racial profiling has been articulated as a particularly pressing social problem for our times and thus may be viewed as a somewhat distinct and more narrow issue than the more general concept of ethnic stereotyping. Should a person who appears to be racially different or of different national origin be stopped by law enforcement or questioned in public or in his or her home? Many unauthorized entrants and permanent resident aliens, on the surface, appear to be racially different or stand out because of ethnic or cultural differences. As a result, law enforcement has practiced racial and national-origin profiling in seeking out unauthorized immigrants for stops on the basis of suspicion of lacking documents or suspicion of committing a crime.

Key Events

Racial profiling processes in the police–minority relationship in the 21st century are embedded within a long history of minority stereotyping. The minority community, long vocal about a tense relationship with law enforcement that constrained citizenship protections, finally received confirmation of their suspicions following the publication of information on *Operation Pipeline,* the Florida drug interdiction program that linked minority status with drug trafficking.

More generally, racial profiling dominates the public discourse, particularly in minority communities, following high-profile events such as the killing of Amadou Diallo or the beating of Rodney King. Community members express outrage at these events and understand them as a consequence of race-based policing. After September 11, 2001, and the linking of terrorism with Middle Eastern identity that followed, the public discourse surrounding racial profiling assumed a different tone, even among many who were once adamantly opposed to the practice. "National security" concerns appeared to trump certain civil liberties immediately following the attack, although with the passage of time, this apparent dichotomy has subsided.

Since 9/11, immigrants have been singled out because they have come from terrorist-harboring nations or because they follow the traditional customs—in dress and so on—of Islam. This too is gives rise to profiling, on the basis of national origin, ethnicity, or religion as well as race. All are forms of profiling are controversial law-enforcement practices because they discriminate against the targeted groups. Profiling can be seen as a form of harassment of targeted immigrant communities. It is viewed as a discriminatory cause of differential crime rates between groups because people from profiled groups are more likely to be stopped by law enforcement or the U.S. Border Patrol and Immigration and Customs Enforcement. Nevertheless, officers need to identify unauthorized entrants and criminal suspects. How this is done is a subject of great controversy. Although racial profiling of citizens by police has been questioned, profiling of noncitizens on the basis of race, national origin, and religion has been a tool used in the war on terror and legitimated by the Supreme Court. At the same time, few citizens are aware of the extent to which their own rights are curtailed within 100 miles of a national border or by legislation passed to fight the war on terror.

Background

After passage of the 1965 Immigration and Nationality Act, the number of racially and ethnically diverse entrants into the United States increased. However, race is now understood to be more of a cultural idea than a biological reality (Omi and Winant 1994). Although race is a social concept constructed to justify hierarchical rankings between groups as "natural," many Americans still differentiate between racial groups based on skin color and other misleading observations. As a result, many white Americans have reacted very negatively to the perceived racial and cultural differences of the new immigrant population. These negative perceptions have led to a tolerance of racial profiling in policing and immigration enforcement.

The emergence of racial profiling as a unique concept in policing discourse occurred in the 1990s amid a confluence of issues. On the heels of relatively high crime rates associated with drug trafficking in the 1980s, several major cities in the United States implemented crime-control strategies intended to crack down on minor infractions of the law. Drug interdiction policies assumed a priority position in the nation's public discourse and became more and more defined (both formally and informally) by racial and ethnic status issues as well as high-profile incidents of the abuse of force by the police—such as the Rodney King beating. The discovery of a cooperative effort in the 1980s and 1990s between the U.S. Drug Enforcement Agency and the Florida Department of Motor Vehicles, titled *Operation Pipeline*, has been identified as a critical point in the emergence of the racial profiling controversy. This drug interdiction program linked drug courier profiles to the racial and ethnic status of motorists traveling on state highways between Florida and the north (Withrow 2006). Opponents of racial profiling dubbed the regular traffic stops of minorities as due to the "crime" of *driving while black*.

As described by Covington, long-term claims by minorities of being targeted by the police were often viewed as anecdotal accounts from overly sensitive, angry, and disgruntled minorities (Withrow 2006). In part because official documentation of the phenomenon was nonexistent, much of the law enforcement community initially rejected the idea that race-based policing occurred. Indeed, the body of criminological research now available on racial profiling has been established only since the mid-1990s. This predominantly quantitative research focuses on issues of disproportionality in law enforcement–initiated traffic stops.

The main inquiry is whether minorities are subject to traffic stops (considered seizures under Fourth Amendment protections against "unreasonable search and seizures" by the state) disproportionate to their representation in the general driving population. Two early standards of proof guided police discretionary powers in stopping citizens: Fourth Amendment protections against unreasonable seizures without probable cause and later the 1968 U.S. Supreme Court decision in *Terry v. Ohio*, which introduced the legal standard of "reasonable suspicion" into the realm of police powers. Studies generally point to racial disparity in traffic stops, with more minority motorists relative to white motorists being stopped by law enforcement (Covington 2001). Additional inquiries of the racial profiling research agenda include whether minorities are searched more often, are subject to longer stops, receive more punitive measures if penalized during a stop, and have higher "hit rates" for contraband once a traffic stop is made (Buerger and Farrell 2002). The bulk of the data on these additional inquiries suggests that the answer to all of the questions except the last, is yes. Other attempts to address racial profiling are found in popular press accounts and in legal journals. The legal journals in particular provide a great deal of information on racial profiling and emphasize important distinctions between legal and moral arguments surrounding this issue.

Once racial profiling of minorities became established in the nation's consciousness in the 1990s, Representative John Conyers (D-Michigan) introduced the Traffic Stops Statistics Act in 1997, which passed unanimously in the House of Representatives. Formidable opposition from national police organizations, concerned about the demands the bill would make on law enforcement, effectively neutralized the bill in the Senate (Withrow 2006). Recurring efforts to introduce a federal law to address the issue have followed, with varying degrees of success, including an executive measure by President Bill Clinton in 1999 mandating a nationwide collection of traffic stop data. Currently, most states have enacted or are considering legislation requiring the collection of data on traffic stops by local and state law enforcement. The combined federal and state efforts to collect data on racial profiling along with the lawsuit-generated studies (Withrow 2006), which provided the first empirical glimpse into the issue, have produced a body of data that generally point to racial disparity in the treatment of individuals subjected to examination in traffic stops by law enforcement (Johnson 2001).

The U.S. Department of Justice issued voluntary guidelines for collecting racial profiling data in 2000. These data are collected by the Racial Profiling Data Resource Center at Northeastern University. At present, at least 27 states are participating. The U.S. Department of Justice (2006), has demonstrated that young male African Americans (22 percent) and Latinos (17 percent) are more likely to be searched than non-Latino whites (8 percent). African Americans and Latinos are three times as likely as non-Latino whites to be threatened with force during a police stop. In Rhode Island, research indicated that minority members were twice as likely as whites to be searched during a traffic stop but less likely to be in possession of prohibited drugs (U.S. Department of Justice 2005). This reaffirms New Jersey research showing that African Americans and Latinos were the profiled targets of 75 percent of traffic stops resulting in a search in New Jersey.

The bulk of research on racial profiling concerns the causal dynamics of racial profiling and typically emerges from the conflict framework. For example, in a recent study, researchers used conflict theory to discuss the police–minority relationship and how the law is differentially enforced against minorities in order to protect white interests (Buerger and Farrell 2002). Other research looks at a conflict theory variant, group-position theory, to describe how dominant groups view the police as allies (Harris 2002). Some researchers have discussed how cognitive bias and its associated concept of in-group bias explain the disproportionate numbers of minority motorists stopped by the police (U.S. Department of Justice 2006). Racial prejudice, although rarely directly discussed (and not necessarily subsumed under the previously mentioned concepts), is another factor in examinations of racial profiling motivations (U.S. Department of Justice 2005). Spatial context is also looked to in explaining racial disparities in policing behavior (Petrocelli, Piquero, and Smith 2004). For example, low-socioeconomic-status communities comprising minorities predominantly may be subject to more patrolling and stops.

The empirical focus on racial disparity in traffic stops was followed by quantitative studies addressing factors leading to an individual's "perception" of being racially profiled (Wilson, Dunham, and Alpert 2004). Theory about the factors that shape citizens' "perceptions" of racial profiling focus on citizens' personal and vicarious experiences (Parker et al. 2004). Racial status is a determining factor in attitudes toward the police. Some theorize that the overall experience of racial oppression and other social institutions operates as a "priming" mechanism for minorities in shaping perceptions of police behavior (Bennett et al. 2004; Tyler and Wakslak 2004; Weitzer and Tuch 1999; Weitzer and Tuch 2004). Studies examining the effects of socioeconomic and racial status on perceptions of discrimination by the police have shown that class is not protective of negative perceptions of the police (Brown and Benedict 2002; Weitzer and Tuch 2005). Research examining the concept of procedural fairness to predict perceptions of racial profiling indicates that the quality of decision making, quality of treatment, and inferences about trustworthiness are the key criteria for minorities in assessing police behaviors (Weitzer and Tuch 2005). "Perception"-orientated research, however, has the potential to be critiqued for its emphasis on the psychological and the individual. There is the concern

---

RACIAL PROFILING AND DRUG INTERDICTION

Racial profiling is very much an issue of drug interdiction. Research on the common characteristics of suspected drug traffickers shows the wide range of traits that have been used to justify the targeting of individuals suspected of criminal activity.

Minorities driving expensive or old vehicles or rental cars
Nervousness when becoming aware of the police patrol car or excessive friendliness when approached by officer
Large quantities of food wrappers, and so on, indicating a long road trip
Too much or too little baggage
Use of air fresheners
Strict adherence to traffic codes upon noticing police patrol car
Visible religious paraphernalia (to deflect suspicion)

Source: Brian L. Withrow, *Racial Profiling: From Rhetoric to Reason* (Upper Saddle River, NJ: Pearson Prentice Hall, 2006).

RACIAL PROFILING OF A HISPANIC JUDGE: FILEMON VELA

David Harris, in his book *Profiles in Injustice* (2006), attests to how the Latino U.S. District Judge for South Texas Filemon Vela, was stopped by the U.S. Border Patrol in 1999 while on his way to hold court in Laredo, Texas. When he asked why his Ford Explorer was stopped, he was told there were too many people in the vehicle—although it could have held more. Judge Vela questioned whether the U.S. Border Patrol had the legal authority to stop him. Afterwards, his secretary made a complaint about the policies that resulted in this unjustified stop. The U.S. Border Patrol indicated that it would provide more information for officers so that only legal stops would occur.

In 2000, when Judge Vela was a passenger in another vehicle, he was stopped again. This time the reason given was that the car had tinted windows. These incidents convinced Judge Vela that all Hispanics are profiled to be stopped. Observation has been made that in any area designated as a border, whether an international airport or a highway close to the U.S.–Mexico border, government agents can stop and search people without a warrant, probable cause, or even a reasonable suspicion. The Supreme Court permits this on the basis of national sovereignty. The Court maintains that border stops and searches are legal because they are at the border. Farther inland, at checkpoints located away from a geographical border, the U.S. Border Patrol has wide discretion to act, including on the basis of Mexican physical appearance as one of multiple factors.

that research that treats racial matters in the context of "perceptions" or "ideas" has the effect of distancing structural elements of racial oppression. Examining racial matters as merely ideas "limits the possibility of understanding how it shapes… life chances" (Weitzer and Tuch 1999, 494–507).

The *Whren* Decision

The U.S. Supreme Court's 1996 decision in *Whren v. United States* is perhaps the most important legal ruling concerning racial profiling in the modern era. *Whren* examined whether the police could make a legal traffic stop under pretext. The Court determined that regardless of the initial subjective intentions of the police officer, an objective reason for a stop would make the stop legal (Johnson 2001). A classic example occurs when an officer suspects a motorist of possessing contraband but makes a traffic stop on the motorist under the "pretext" of failing to properly signal or some other minor traffic code violation. The officer then asks for the motorist's consent to search the vehicle, knowing that most citizens do not know that they have a right not to consent to a search. Although an argument may be made that the minor traffic code violation justifies the stop, the decisions about which motorists get stopped for the objective violation is the fundamental concern of racial profiling opponents. In a racially ordered society such as the United States, it is argued, minorities will bear the brunt of this form of policing. The 1996 *Whren* decision is viewed as a lesser standard of proof that an officer has to meet in order to make a legal stop and therefore represents a broadening of police discretionary powers. Other legal rulings in recent years demonstrate the debate that surrounds the racial profiling controversy.

This has happened so often in traffic that, as mentioned above, it is referred to as driving while black. Skin color is a very dubious basis for making a traffic stop. Many African American professionals driving more expensive cars get stopped because a police officer suspects that the car is stolen. This is experienced as both harassment and a form of discrimination against African Americans. Law enforcement policies have been adopted to reduce these incidents, but African Americans are citizens, whereas many new immigrants are not. Permanent resident aliens and undocumented immigrants have no protection from profiling. Thus, there is a spate of associated terms: driving while brown, driving while immigrant and, most recently, driving while Arab. On the other hand, non-Hispanic white Americans are privileged to receive less police attention and are less likely to be caught for drug possession at a traffic stop.

Unauthorized Immigrant Racial Profiling

The U.S. Border Patrol and the Immigration and Naturalization Service (INS), now the Bureau of Immigration and Customs Enforcement (ICE), originated the racial and national-origin profiling of immigrants. In the U.S.-Mexico border region, there are many Mexican American citizens and Mexican permanent-resident aliens. Because many attempting unauthorized entry over the border are Latino, Mexican citizens and legal Latino residents are more likely to be stopped than individuals of other nationalities. This is a historical practice. In the 1950s, Operation Wetback targeted Mexicans, and in 1986, when undocumented farm workers were eligible for legalization, there was a series of U.S. Border Patrol sweeps to confiscate their documents and deport them until this practice was contested by protestors and the media. The INS/ICE has pursued a very anti-immigrant enforcement strategy that is only partially controlled by immigrant advocates and media publicity.

In 1975, the Supreme Court decided in *United States v. Brignoni-Ponce* (422 U.S. 873) that since Mexicans were estimated to make up 85 percent of undocumented entrants, an officer could use "Mexican appearance" as a "relevant factor" for investigation provided that it was not the only ground for suspicion (Johnson 2001). One result has been that Mexicans—and now Central Americans—have been more likely to be deported than their statistical frequency in the undocumented population would merit. Immigration profiling has an adverse impact on citizens. If Mexican profiling occurs, then Hispanic citizens, permanent resident aliens, and individuals with visas may be stopped, interrogated, and detained as well as individuals of other ethnicity who are mistaken as Hispanic.

Kevin Johnson (2001) alleges that this policy places an unfair burden on the legal Hispanic population, which has greatly grown in size since 1973. He points out that the estimate that 85 percent of undocumented entrants were Mexican was always overinclusive and that current estimates place Mexicans at 50 percent of the undocumented population. The harms resulting from this policy include that it is embarrassing and humiliating to be stopped, causing emotional stress and the possibility that verbal and physical abuse will occur. Even more importantly, Mexican profiling undermines the status of Hispanics in American society and encourages a stereotype that characterizes Hispanics as "foreigners." This practice has even led to the unlawful arrest and deportation of legal permanent residents and citizens. Hispanics have become doubly suspect; they may be racially profiled as potential criminals or as potential undocumented entrants.

David Cole (2003), a lawyer and immigrant advocate, coined the phrase "driving while immigrant" to refer to police traffic stops based on immigrant racial profiling. Mexicans have been a major focus of the debate on profiling undocumented immigrants. The stereotype that Latinos are illegal can result in unrefined decisions to stop a person because he or she looks Mexican, which is presumably to be justified after the fact. The very low "reasonable suspicion" standard augments this. The U.S. Border Patrol often refers to this as "canned probable cause." David A. Harris, a legal scholar, believes immigrants are judged guilty on sight and disproportionately stopped; their crime or deportation rate will be elevated because non-Latino whites are less likely to be stopped.

Driving while brown, even though Latinos are racially classified as white, is no longer a Supreme Court criterion for stop and search in immigration enforcement. In 2000, the U.S. Court of Appeals for the Ninth Circuit disregarded the *United States v. Brignoni-Ponce* ruling and stated, in *United States v. Montero-Camargo* (177 F.3d 1113, 1118 9th Cir. 1999), that "Hispanic appearance is not a lawful basis for making a stop because it is a 'weak proxy' for undocumented status." The court opinion stated,

> We conclude at this point in our nation's history, and given the continuing changes in our racial and ethnic composition, Latino appearance is, in general, of such little probative value that it may not be considered as a relevant factor where particularized or individualized suspicion is required. Moreover, we conclude, for the reasons that we have indicated that it is also not an appropriate factor.

Some decisions, like that in *U.S. v. Montero-Camaro* (2000), have ruled that race was not a basis by which border patrol agents could detain individuals, while the *Brown v. City of Oneonta* (2000) decision ruled that the many black males who were questioned as potential rape suspects in a particular case did not have their Fourteenth Amendment protections violated (Cole 2003).

National Origin Profiling in Interior Immigrant Raids

There has been a long history of U.S. Border Patrol sweeps using physical appearance. In 1997, the Chandler police cooperated in stopping, detaining, and questioning residents using skin color as one cue. In 2001 the *New York Times* reported that INS/ICE officers in New York relied on racial and ethnic physical and social characteristics and accents to profile undocumented entrants (Sachs 2001). Relying on group probability as the basis for immigration enforcement, rather than individual suspicion, violates the provision for equal protection under the law provided by the Fourteenth Amendment. There was pressure to end this profiling, but then terrorist catastrophe resulted in a retraction of civil rights, especially for noncitizens.

Pressure on the U.S. Border Patrol is intense because conservatives demand more action while targeted groups, including Latinos, claim civil rights violations (Bennett 2004). In 2004, the Temecula Border Patrol conducted inland sweeps in Norco, Corona, and Escondido, California. Complaints resulted in the Department of Homeland Security denying that it gave authorization for the sweeps. Hispanic protests of immigrant sweeps occurred all over California. The *Los Angeles Times* indicated that more than 150 undocumented immigrants were arrested in San Bernardino and Riverside County, California (Wilson and Murillo 2004). Illustrating a connection between political expediency and reducing national origin profiling, in 2004, a presidential election year, the Latino vote was considered crucial and these sweeps were curtailed. The sweeps frighten both legal immigrants and foreign-born citizens.

Post-9/11 sweeps of undocumented immigrants are less open to public scrutiny because of the secrecy provisions allowed by the Patriot Act of 2001. To understand the level of public fear that can be generated, it must be understood that in the 2004 California sweeps, the U.S. Border Patrol questioned 9, 972 people on trolleys, at bus stops, in train stations, at other public transportation sites, and on the streets (Spagat 2004). They arrested 291 people, a very low strike rate for the degree of public scrutiny involved (Wilson and Murillo 2004).

After 9/11, U.S. Border Patrol efforts were expanded to include sweeps near the Canadian Border (Abramsky 2008). The community of Havre, Montana, considers the train inspections that occur now to be a sign of patriotic defense. Northern U.S. Border Patrol installation has been expensive; its captures include visa-overstaying tourists, undocumented Latinos looking for work, and potential asylum seekers and refugees—no individuals connected to terrorism. Abramsky, writing in *The Nation,* thinks these activities give a false picture of counterterrorism security. Nevertheless, a series of Supreme Court rulings has given the right to demand ID to law enforcement officers and limited the probable cause requirements for search and interrogation of individuals within 100 miles of the two international borders with Canada and Mexico.

In 2005, the Ninth Circuit Court of Appeals ruled in *U.S. v. Cervantes-Flores* that U.S. Border Patrol questions can be asked about citizenship, immigration status, and suspicious activities. Any additional search or detention must be justified by either consent or probable cause. Under provisions of post-9/11 legislation, however, the U.S. Border Patrol has been given additional powers.

National Origin Terrorist Profiling

The history of terrorist suspicion and profiling began with airline bombings such as that of Pan Am Flight 103 over Lockerbie, Scotland. Terrorist hijackings and bombings have been associated with Arabs and Muslims. In the mid-1990s, airports began profiling darker-skinned individuals who spoke Arabic or English with an Arabic accent (Harris 2002). In the mid-1990s, airport stops and searches of Arab and Muslim Americans became routine. Arab and Muslim Americans began to be stigmatized. After the 1996 crash of TWA Flight 800 over Long Island in which terrorism was initially suspected, Arab Americans began to be very harshly treated at airports. President Clinton appointed a commission to study airport security. The result was Computer Assisted Passenger Screening (CAPS), which selects passengers to screen based on their current reservation and not on their race, nationality, ethnicity or religion. Passengers are selected at random.

After 9/11 both President George W. Bush and Attorney General John Ashcroft adopted terrorist profiling on the basis of national origin and religion. Subsequently, Congress approved the Patriot Act. This act gave the INS unlimited power to detain noncitizens who were thought to have a connection to terrorism. A ruling by Ashcroft allowed ICE to suspend a judge's release order in immigrant cases. Proof of a link to terrorism or crime was not needed to detain noncitizens (Human Rights First 2004).

In 2006, a federal judge ruled that immigration law could be used to detain noncitizens on the basis of race, religion, or national origin. This measure supported racial, national origin, and religious profiling of noncitizens. It was made in reaction to a legal case involving the post-9/11 sweeps of Muslim immigrants, the vast majority of whom were not linked to terrorism. In particular, a sweep had been conducted in New York City, the site of the former World Trade Center. The INS and FBI, with assistance of New York City Police, profiled and arrested Muslim Middle Eastern and Southeast Asian immigrants. Many were detained and then deported if immigration violations were discovered.

Many noncitizens were arrested without knowing their rights and were denied due process of the law under the Illegal Immigration Reform and Individual Responsibility Act of 1996 (IIRIRA). The grounds for deportation established by IIRIRA provide for mandatory detention and deportation of permanent resident aliens who commit crimes classified as aggravated felonies. In other words, immigration law was used in a mostly fruitless search for terrorists, which resulted in many national origin or religiously profiled arrests and deportation. Deepa Fernandes (2007) states that INS and FBI agents did not identify themselves or show credentials before asking to see a profiled person's ID, often in their own homes. Immigrants were arrested if they could not provide documentation. These mass arrests were conducted secretly under the terrorist-investigation secrecy provision of the Patriot Act. Attorney General Ashcroft authorized mass arrest of Arab, Southeast Asian, and Muslim men. The noncitizens profiled in the antiterrorism sweep were interviewed by the INS and FBI. If no link to terrorism was established, they were turned over to the INS for prosecution based on immigration status. Immigrants, immigration advocates, and certain government officials protested the sweeps.

After 9/11 all noncitizen immigrant men from specified Arab and Muslim countries were asked to register with the government. Those profiled included persons from Bangladesh, Indonesia, Egypt, Bahrain, Iran, Iraq, Syria, Algeria, Morocco, North Korea, Oman, Jordan, Kuwait, Pakistan, Libya, Sudan, Saudi Arabia, Afghanistan, Algeria, Eritrea, Lebanon, Qatar, Somalia, Tunisia, the United Arab Emirates, and Yemen. The FBI wanted to interview 5,000 men between 18 and 33 years of age who had entered the United States after the year 2000 from countries identified as having al Qaeda activity. These interviews were designated as voluntary, but if the noncitizen did not appear, he or she was deemed to be guilty of an immigration violation (Fernandes 2007). At the interviews, visa overstayers were identified and ordered deported regardless of any connection to terrorism. Many men who had some form of legal status were detained until the INS cleared them. The detained and deported men often had wives and children who suffered emotionally and economically after the deportations. The immigrant community was horrified.

Federal requests led many states and communities to allow their police to make immigration-related inquiries. In both 2004 and 2005, some 35 police agencies were converted into ICE immigration enforcers. In Florida and other states, immigrant advocates have fought against using police to request immigration status. A negative consequence of using police to enforce immigration law is that immigrant communities fear reporting crime. Many police departments are resisting being used to enforce immigration law for this reason. Nevertheless, in 2005, the House of Representatives passed legislation allowing the police to enforce immigration laws, but the legislation has not passed the Senate.

During the antiterrorism national origin and religion sweep, the government encouraged individuals and communities to be on the lookout for suspicious behavior. The persons identifying people were often coworkers, neighbors, or ex-girlfriends. The reports were connected to possible terrorism, but the result was that many people who were simply out of compliance with visa documentation or residency registration or undocumented were detained and deported. Sometimes these deportations were engineered by people seeking revenge (Fernandes 2007). These individuals and their families were not allowed access to secret evidence. Many had no prior criminal record prior to deportation. Judges were given no authority to review cases in which deportation was mandatory. In addition, the inspector general of the Justice Department (2003) criticized the fact that bail was being denied in all of these cases with no judicial overrides. This meant that deportees would lack assistance of family and legal counsel owing to problems of access.

Amnesty International (2004), a human rights advocacy group, has found that between 9/11 and 2003, Arab American citizens, permanent resident aliens, undocumented

THE GENERAL ACCOUNTING OFFICE STUDY OF U.S. CUSTOMS RACIAL PROFILING

For many years, U.S. Customs used a complicated profile of 43 factors to decide when to search persons or transport. Their first priority was drug smuggling, although terrorist identification is equally important today. This profile was implemented at primary inspection and individuals were directed to secondary inspection or into a further series of ever more intensive and intrusive inspections. In 1999, this profile was disputed as racially biased and an investigation was undertaken by the General Accounting Office (GAO; now called the Government Accountability Office). The GAO found that customs inspectors disproportionately profiled African American women and that black, Hispanic, and Asian women were three times more likely to be strip searched than men of the same race and ethnic background. Latino women were significantly more likely to be x-rayed than non-Latino whites. The customs searches were biased both as to race and gender, and the rates at which contraband was found were highly disproportionate to the profile. In other words, there was a significantly greater probability of finding drugs when men or non-Latino whites were searched. The results of the GAO report suggested that behavioral cues and related information were much more reliable than racial profiling. Thereafter the number of searches declined and the number of hits—percentage of searches finding contraband—greatly increased.

Source: General Accounting Office, "U.S. Customs Service: Better Targeting of Airline Passengers for Personal Searches Could Produce Better Results." Report to the Honorable Richard J. Durbin, U.S. Senate. March 2000. http://www.gao.gov/new.items/gg0038.pdf

entrants, and visa overstayers have been three times more likely than whites to be profiled. Over 75 percent of Arab Americans report having been discriminated against since the destruction of the World Trade Center Towers. Arabs and South Asians have been asked to vacate airplanes because they made passengers anxious. In airports, Sikh Americans, who wear turbans as a part of their religion, have been asked to remove them.

Reasons for and against Racial and National Origin Profiling

In the United States, advocates for minority groups and immigrants argue that flawed ideas in law enforcement have associated race and national origin with crime. This has the impact of criminalizing minorities and immigrants. Such racial profiling in law enforcement is based on several reasons (Leadership Conference on Civil Rights 2004). The first is the stereotype that minorities/immigrants commit a majority of crimes and that profiling them is a good strategy for using police resources. A related idea is that most minority members/immigrants are criminals. Both assertions are baseless (Harris 2002; Leadership Conference on Civil Rights 2004). This linkage is based on prison statistics showing disproportionate rates of minority imprisonment. Unfortunately, few people connect racial profiling with higher imprisonment rates. Nor do they stop to think that non-Hispanic white privilege with regard to not being stopped or searched might contribute to their underrepresentation in the prison population (aided by their higher socioeconomic status and ability to hire good lawyers) (Harris 1999).

Proponents of racial profiling suggest that minorities are disproportionately subject to stops compared with whites because minorities are disproportionately involved in criminal activity, a variant of statistical discrimination theory. This framework suggests that it is rational, given the distribution of minorities in the criminal justice system, to target minorities for criminal behavior (Weitzer and Tuch 2005). More recent studies suggest that the rationale behind statistical discrimination explanations for racial profiling is discounted when considering the bulk of studies that show that the rates of contraband discovered in traffic stops, for example, are quite similar across racial and ethnic groups (Tomaskovic-Devey, Mason, and Zingraff 2004). Another common argument against the rational discrimination thesis is that racial profiling criminalizes minority groups as a whole, creating distrust or a disconnect between law enforcement and the community. A common refrain from proponents of the practice is that citizens who are innocent of wrongdoing should not be concerned about law enforcement contact or should look upon the practice as merely an inconvenience.

Research indicates that African Americans commit drug-related crimes at a rate that is proportional to their numbers in the population. Although they have been disproportionately profiled for traffic stops, there is a lower rate of finding evidence of drug possession than for when non-Hispanic whites are stopped. Indeed, a General Accounting Office Report (2000) has indicated the opposite. The reason is that race is not a reliable cue. Behavioral and informational cues are better. Switching away from disproportionate searching of minority women and increasing searches of men and non-Hispanic whites reduced the number of searches and greatly increased the success rate.

Another issue related to racial profiling is the stereotype that minorities and/or immigrants commit more violent crimes. This is not relevant to racial profiling. Profiling is practiced in relation to traffic stops, stop-and-frisk actions, and other nonviolent police actions. Many violent crimes have witnesses who can generate a description of whom to look for. Profiling is done in cases of hidden infractions, such as drug trafficking.

Racial profiling was treated as more of an issue prior to 9/11 and the resulting retraction of civil liberties. During the 2000 Bush-versus-Gore presidential election, candidate Al Gore introduced the topic of racial profiling and both George W. Bush and his running mate Dick Cheney came out against it. Conservative pundits continued to advocate it. John Derbyshire (2001) in the *National Review* defended racial profiling as an efficient police technique based on probability that best makes use of limited resources. George Will (2001), writing in the *Washington Post*, purported that using race as a basis for a traffic stop is reasonable as long as it is part of a *group* of risk factors used in assessing suspect behavior. He distinguished between hard profiling (race as the target characteristic) and soft profiling (race as part of a profile indicating suspicion). In addition, Will indicated that other factors might be the reason that minority drivers were more likely to be stopped, such as vehicle defects and so on.

In 2000, the Gallup public opinion poll showed that 81 percent of Americans were in favor of ending racial profiling. In February 2001, President George W. Bush stated that racial profiling "is wrong and we will end it in America" (U.S. Department of Justice 2003). Attorney General John Ashcroft took this as a charge from the president. Congress moved toward the generation of legislation to this effect. Next, the attacks of 9/11 created insecurity, and a rollback began on the push for the right of minorities not to be profiled. Nevertheless, immigrants and citizens have always been profiled in border regions and in the interior because of the unauthorized entrant issue.

Terrorist Profiling and Stereotypes

Terrorist profiling is based on unjustified stereotypes about the propensity of group members to engage in illegal activity. The majority of immigrants are law-abiding. Similarly, being Arab or Muslim does not make an individual a terrorist. Although all of the 9/11 hijackers were Arab nationals, many terrorists are of different backgrounds. Richard Reid, the "Shoe Bomber" of December 22, 2001, was of Jamaican ancestry with British citizenship. Theodore Kaczynski, the "Unabomber," and Timothy McVeigh were white American citizens who committed terrorist acts. John Walker Lindh (the "American Taliban") and other American citizens have been involved with the Taliban, al Qaeda, and other terrorist groups. Recently, Nigerian and Pakistani individuals have been taken into custody for attempted terrorist acts. "Jihad Jane" (Colleen LaRose), charged with recruiting terrorists to wage war on behalf of Muslims, is a native-born American.

Those who oppose national origin or terrorist profiling argue that the all-too-human way of thinking in terms of stereotypes rather than cues for terrorist behavior has hampered the search for terrorist operatives and hurt many innocent people. Terrorist profiling is a simplistic tactic that does not substitute for using behavior-based cues in enforcement (National Conference on Civil Rights Leadership 2004). Finally, terrorist profiling, like racial profiling, creates fear and alienates immigrant communities from law enforcement instead of encouraging them to help investigations.

Case Probability versus Class Probability as a Profiling Strategy

Gene Callahan and William Anderson (2001), both journalists, believe that the war on drugs has led to racial profiling. They state that when law enforcement uses class probability (i.e., stereotyping a group of socially differentiated individuals), it is profiling, and the claim can be made that individuals targeted on that basis have not received equal protection under the law. Instead, they suggest that law enforcement should use case probability when this is a factor but not all factors have been identified in targeting an offender. There are two ways of using information about race and ethnicity. Class probability stereotypes a group, but if the race or ethnicity of a suspect has been established by an officer or victim, it is reasonable to focus on finding a suspect with that social characteristic. In other words, it must be germane to a specific case, not part of a general surveillance strategy.

On the basis of case probability, the 9/11 terrorists exhibited several behavioral cues that could have excited suspicion: (1) they bought one-way tickets, (2) they made reservations just before the flights, and (3) they paid with large amounts of cash (in a plastic credit/debit card society). No one connected the dots. Everyone noticed after the fact that they were Arab nationals, which suggests that new recruits of different national origins would be used by always versatile terrorist groups in any new attack. One issue with advocating class (one-dimensional factor) probability is that post-9/11 terrorist profiling focused on national origin and religion with no strategy. Profiled permanent aliens and undocumented immigrants were denied the right to due process and legal counsel if they were "out of status," which means that their immigration paperwork was not current. Many individuals were mandatorily detained and deported, but there is still no connection between the U.S. immigrant communities and 9/11. Critics argue that this was a huge waste of law enforcement resources and taxpayer money in order that federal officials could state that immigrant communities did not contain terrorist organizations.

Profiling and Local Law Enforcement Controversy

287g Immigration Policing Agreements

The 1996 Illegal Immigration Reform and Immigrant Responsibility Act (IIRIRA) provided for local and state police to cooperate with federal agents in immigration enforcement through the 287g program (U.S. Immigration and Customs Enforcement 2010). In such cases a Memorandum of Agreement (MOA) is signed between the federal government and state or local policing agencies, and participants are supervised by Immigration and Customs Enforcement (ICE). The Obama administration has expanded 287g agreements. Currently, information on noncitizens with civil or criminal violations and/or under suspicion of terrorist connections is entered into a National Crime Information Center (NCIC) database and available to police.

In releasing official statements, officials argue that their deportation efforts especially target criminal aliens. This strategy has received criticism from immigrant advocates concerned about racial profiling and proenforcement conservatives who claim that prioritizing locating and deporting criminal aliens would lead to neglect of those who lack documents. The U.S. Government Accountability Office (2009, 4) found that ICE officials did not document, consistent with internal control standards, that they had enhanced community safety and security by targeting aliens committing violent or other serious crimes. Certain participating agencies arrested and deported aliens who had committed minor crimes like carrying an open container of alcohol. The Government Accountability Office (GAO) noted that if all 287g participants sought ICE detainment for deportable aliens, they would lack space for detention, including that designated for violent criminal aliens.

287g has primarily led to arrest of nonviolent unauthorized migrants and immigrants. The border metropolis of El Paso's Operation Linebacker resulted in 1,076 arrests of unauthorized entrants and drug charges against 4 noncitizens (Staudt 2008). Data on 287g alien arrests caused ICE to change the memoranda of agreement MOAs and stress that the purpose is to locate, imprison, and remove aliens who commit narcotics or human smuggling violations, gang or organized crimes, and sex-related offenses. Despite federal efforts to involve police, municipalities have not uniformly responded (Krestsedemas 2008, 341–342).

Arguments in favor of involving local and state police in federal immigration enforcement include that they are a "multiple force amplifier." If they are allowed to use immigration status as a factor in questioning and arrest, it increases the likelihood that unauthorized immigrants will be detected. Giving police the go-ahead to probe is considered to assist in detecting terrorist activity. The 9/11 Commission (Eldridge et al. 2004) found that 4 of the 9/11 hijackers were subject to routine traffic stops and could have been detained for speeding ticket or visa violations. An argument against expanding state and local police power is that it would alienate and reduce the cooperation of immigrant community residents. Communities with a concentration of unauthorized immigrants may be less cooperative and underreport crime and victimization to police if they fear that family or community members will be deported (Romero 2006; Martinez 2007). Community policing strategies necessitate frequent contact and good relations between police and neighborhood residents. Police and neighborhood relations are strained if there is fear (Martinez 2007). Furthermore, many immigrants' original homelands are characterized by police corruption and thus these people may be reluctant to trust American police. Racial and national origin screening is another cause for immigrant concern (Krestsedemas 2008, 346–351).

Arizona S.B. 1070: Support Our Law Enforcement and Safe Neighborhoods Act

Racial profiling controversy was renewed by the passage of Arizona Senate Bill 1070, the Support our Law Enforcement and Safe Neighborhoods Act. SB 1070 made it a state misdemeanor crime for a noncitizen to be in the United States without having federal visa or immigration documents, which are required to be carried, and authorizes police to enforce immigration law (Archibold 2010). State and local police are required to check immigration status if there is reasonable suspicion that an individual is an unauthorized entrant. Police can make a warrantless arrest on the basis of probable cause if they believe an individual without documents is an unauthorized alien. After arrest, individuals cannot be released until establishing legal status by criteria of § 1373(c) of Title 8 of the U.S. Code. A first-time offender can be fined $500 and given up to six months of jail time. In order to avoid arrest, permanent resident aliens and visitors with visas must carry identification documents such as an Arizona driver's license, a non-operator identification license, or any recognized federal, state, or local ID certifying immigration status.

Arizona's state and local police departments could have signed MOA's with the federal 287g program, but that would have required numerous legal contracts. Arizona's law is the first to require police to check immigration status. Both advocates and opponents of the bill gathered for praise or protest during the Arizona legislature's consideration of its passage (Harris, Rau, and Creno 2010). Arizona Governor Jan Brewer stated: "We must enforce the law evenly, and without regard to skin color, accent or social status" (Samuels 2010). The law inspired public protest, constitutional challenges, and calls for an economic boycott of Arizona. One result was the passage of Arizona 2162, which amends the law by stating: "prosecutors would not investigate complaints based on race, color or national origin."

Advocates of the law present ideas such as the "force multiplier" effect in the context of Arizona's upsurge in unauthorized immigration. Drug and human trafficking and spillover drug-related violence are major concerns. Being able to establish legal status aids law enforcement in preventing these activities. Nevertheless, immigration is the domain of federal law and the Arizona bill may be unconstitutional. Multiple lawsuits have been filed against it. An lawsuit filed by the American Civil Liberties Union argues that the bill violates the Supremacy Clause of the U.S. Constitution, which provides for federal authority over the states and, by legal precedent, immigration. Kurt Kobach, a law professor at the University of Missouri–Kansas City School of Law and codrafter of the AZ bill, argues that the bill is constitutional because of the principle of "concurrent enforcement." In other words, the state law parallels federal law, which makes first entry without authorization documentation a misdemeanor (Schwartz and Archibold 2010).

The leading criticism of the bill is that it justifies racial profiling (Schwartz and Archibold 2010). Thinking critically about behavioral or situational cues, it is difficult to come up with *any* that distinguish someone who is not lawfully in the country.

The criteria that might distinguish an unauthorized immigrant overlap with legal resident and native-born minority status are racialized physical features, language and/or accent, and signs of lower- or working-class social status. Ultimately, when police are asked to enforce immigration status, unless they ask everyone, any "suspicion" is likely to be based on racial or national origin profiling unless there is a cause for a traffic stop, such as speeding. Because there is no basis for visually distinguishing between unauthorized and legal residents, including citizens, the law has discriminatory implications.

Arizona S.B. 1070 is likely to result in a pattern similar to "driving while black," and individuals who have a "foreign" appearance are likely to experience traffic stops and

HENRY LOUIS GATES JR. AND THE BEER SUMMIT

An incident that garnered national attention briefly in 2009 was that involving the renowned African American scholar Henry Louis Gates Jr. After returning home to Cambridge, Massachusetts, from a trip abroad, Gates found that the front door to his house was jammed. His driver (who was also African American) tried to help him open it. A neighbor and a passer-by called the Cambridge police department to report suspicious activity, and when the police arrived Gates was arrested for disorderly conduct (he had objected loudly to the officers approaching him). Later the charges were dropped, and Gates and the arresting officer met with President Barack Obama at the White House to smooth over the matter. In February 2010 Gates donated the handcuffs that had been used in the arrest to the Smithsonian Institution. An independent review of the case later in the year reported that the situation could have been avoided and recommended changes in police procedures.

Source: Russell Contreras and Mark Pratt, "Henry Louis Gates Arrest 'Avoidable,' Report Says." *Huffington Post* (June 30, 2010). http://www.huffingtonpost.com/2010/06/30/henry-louis-gates-arrest-_n_630758.html

other public police encounters. The key to proving legal status is identification documentation, which can be legal or fraudulent. Citizens and legal permanent residents will have to carry valid IDs, an inconvenience Americans have strongly resisted when the idea of a national ID card has been proposed.

Conclusion

The broadening of state powers following the terrorist attacks on the United States in 2001 have limited the restrictions put on law enforcement, even at the local police level. Even prior to the attacks, the U.S. Supreme Court's *Whren* decision foreshadowed the direction of federal legislation toward a lessening of citizenry protections. Because the Fourth and Fourteenth Amendments to the U.S. Constitution are often posed as legal remedies to address racial profiling practices, there is limited movement toward criminalizing racial profiling under new law. Advocates of legislation to specifically address racialized issues in the legal realm contend that Fourth and Fourteenth Amendment protection claims are rarely successful legal strategies because of the high standards of proof that each require to prove discrimination.

Near the U.S.-Mexico border everyone is a suspect, citizen and noncitizen alike, with little recourse to Fourteenth Amendment rights regarding inspection of documents and vehicles. The problems of human and drug smuggling have made everyone a suspect to be questioned, and the Supreme Court has validated the right to see ID and to ask questions about suspicious behavior. In the interior, both citizens and noncitizens became suspects in the war on terror, but national origin and religious profiling focused on immigrant communities with, by and large, fruitless results. Citizens have not sufficiently considered the loss of civil liberties they suffered after 9/11 or when they should get them back, and most are unaware that they have diminished rights within 100 miles of a border.

Immigrant communities are composed of people who can help in the war on terror if they are not alienated by profiling. Will the government come to realize that all forms of profiling violate the Fourteenth Amendment right to equal protection under the law and waste resources that could be better expended in looking for behavioral and informational cues of unlawful activity? Why is it unlikely that driving as a citizen will become the basis of a profile? The debate will continue, and one has to judge whether simple stereotyping rather than good law enforcement practice is the basis of the law and make appropriate changes.

See also **Border Fence; Immigration and Employment Law Enforcement; Patriot Act; Police Brutality; Police Corruption; War on Drugs; Immigration Reform (vol. 3)**

Further Reading

Abramsky, Sasha, *American Furies: Crime, Punishment, and Vengeance in an Age of Mass Imprisonment.* Boston: Beacon Press, 2008.

Amnesty International, *Threat and Humiliation: Racial Profiling, Domestic Security, and Human Rights in the United States.* New York: Amnesty International, 2004. http://www.amnestyusa.org/racial_profiling/report/rp_report.pdf

Archibold, Randal C., "U.S.'s Toughest Immigration Law is Signed in Arizona." *New York Times* (April 23, 2010).

Bennett, Gary G., et al., "Perceived Racism and Affective Responses to Ambiguous Interpersonal Interactions among African American Men." *American Behavioral Scientist* 47 (2004): 963–976.

Bolton, Kenneth, and Joe R. Feagin, *Black in Blue: African-American Police Officers and Racism.* New York: Routledge, 2004.

Brown, Ben, and William Reed Benedict, "Perceptions of the Police: Past Findings, Methodological Issues, Conceptual Issues, and Policy Implications." *Policing: An International Journal of Police Strategies and Management* 25 (2002): 543–580.

Buerger, Michael E., and Amy Farrell, "The Evidence of Racial Profiling: Interpreting Documented and Unofficial Sources." *Police Quarterly* 5 (2002): 272–305.

Callahan, Gene, and William Anderson, "The Roots of Racial Profiling." *Reason* (August/September 2001). http://reason.com/archives/2001/08/01/the-roots-of-racial-profiling

Carmen, Alejandro del, *Racial Profiling in America.* Upper Saddle River, NJ: Pearson/Prentice Hall, 2008.

Cole, David, *Enemy Aliens: Double Standards and Constitutional Freedoms in the War on Terrorism.* New York: New Press, 2003.

Covington, Jeannette, "Round Up the Usual Suspects: Racial Profiling and the War on Drugs." In *Petit Apartheid in the U.S. Criminal Justice System,* ed. Dragan Milanovic and Katheryn K. Russell. Durham, NC: Carolina Academic Press, 2001.

Derbyshire, John, "Racial Profiling: Burning Hotter." *National Review* (October 5, 2001). http://old.nationalreview.com/derbyshire/derbyshire100501.shtml

Eldridge, Thomas R., et al., *9/11 and Terrorist Travel. Staff Report on the National Commission on Terrorist Attacks upon the United States.* 2004. http://govinfo.library.unt.edu/911/staff_state ments/911_TerrTrav_Monograph.pdf

Fattah, Ezazt A., *Criminology: Past, Present, and Future.* New York: St. Martin's Press, 1997.

Fernandes, Deepa, *Targeted: Homeland Security and the Business of Immigration.* New York: Seven Stories Press, 2007.

Georges-Abeyie, D., *The Criminal Justice System and Blacks.* New York: Clark Boardman, 1984.

Glover, Karen S., *Racial Profiling: Research, Racism, and Resistance.* Lanham, MD: Rowman & Littlefield, 2009.

Harcourt, Bernard E., *Against Prediction: Profiling, Policing, and Punishing in an Actuarial Age.* Chicago: University of Chicago Press, 2007.

Harris, Craig, Alia Beard Rau, and Glen Creno, "Arizona Governor Signs Immigration Law." *Arizona Republic.* April 24, 2010.

Harris, David A., *Profiles in Injustice: Why Racial Profiling Won't Work.* New York: Free Press, 2002.

Human Rights First, *In Liberty's Shadow: U.S. Detention of Asylum Seekers in the Era of Homeland Security.* New York: Human Rights First, 2004.

Johnson, Kevin R., "The Case Against Race Profiling in Immigration Enforcement." *Washington University Law Quarterly* 78 (2001): 675–736.

Kretsedemas, Philip, "What Does an Undocumented Alien Look Like? Local Enforcement and New Immigration Profiling." In *Keeping Out the Other: A Critical Introduction to Immigration Enforcement Today,* ed. David Brotherton and Philip Kretsedemas. New York: Columbia University Press, 2008.

Krivo, Lauren J., and Ruth D. Peterson, *Race, Crime, and Justice: Contexts and Complexities.* Thousand Oaks, CA: Sage, 2009.

Leadership Conference on Civil Rights, *Wrong Then, Wrong Now: Racial Profiling Before and After September 11.* Washington, DC: The Conference, 2004. http://www.civilrights.org/publica tions/wrong-then/racial_profiling_report.pdf

Martinez, Ramiro, "Incorporating Latinos and Immigrants into Policing Research." *Criminology and Public Policy* 6, no. 1 (2007): 57–64.

Muhammad, Khalil Gibran, *The Condemnation of Blackness: Race, Crime, and the Making of Urban America.* Cambridge, MA: Harvard University Press, 2010.

Omi, Michael, and Howard Winant, eds., *Racial Formation in the United States,* 2d ed. New York: Routledge, 1994.

Parker, Karen F., et al., "A Contextual Study of Racial Profiling." *American Behavioral Scientist* 47 (2004): 943-962.

Petrocelli, Matthew, Alex R. Piquero, and Michael R. Smith, "Conflict Theory and Racial Profiling: An Empirical Analysis of Police Traffic Stop Data." *Journal of Criminal Justice* 31 (2004): 1–11.

Romero, Mary, "Racial Profiling and Immigration Law Enforcement: Rounding Up of Usual Suspects in the Latino Community." *Critical Sociology* 32, no. 2–3 (March 2006): 447–473.

Sachs, Susan, "Files Suggest Profiling of Latinos Led to Immigration Raids." *New York Times* (May 1, 2001).

Samuels, Tanyanika, "New York Politicians Rip into Arizona Immigration Law." *New York Daily News* (April 24, 2010).

Schwartz, John, and Randal C. Archibold, "Law Faces a Tough Road through the Courts." *New York Times* (April 27, 2010).

Spagat, Elliot, "San Diego County Included in Recent Border Sweeps." *North County Times* (June 15, 2004).

Staudt, Kathleen, "Bordering the Other in the Texas Southwest: El Pasoans Confront the Local Sheriff." In *Keeping Out the Other: A Critical Introduction to Immigration Enforcement Today,* ed. David Brotherton and Philip Kretsedemas. New York: Columbia University Press, 2008.

Tomaskovic-Devey, Donald, Marcinda Mason, and Matthew Zingraff, "Looking for the Driving while Black Phenomena: Conceptualizing Racial Bias Processes and Their Associated Distributions." *Police Quarterly* 7 (2004): 3–29.

Tyler, Tom R. and Cheryl J. Wakslak, "Profiling and Police Legitimacy: Procedural Justice, Attributions of Motive, and Acceptance of Police Authority." *Criminology* 42 (2004): 253–281.

U.S. Department of Justice, Inspector General's Office, *The September 11 Detainees.* Washington, DC: Office of the Inspector General, 2003

U.S. Department of Justice, "Racial Profiling Fact Sheet." Washington, DC: Department of Justice, 2003.

U.S. General Accounting Office, *Racial Profiling: Limited Data Available on Motorist Stops.* Washington, DC: Government Printing Office, 2000.

U.S. Government Accountability Office, *Immigration Enforcement: Better Controls Needed over Program Authorizing State and Local Enforcement of Federal Immigration Laws.* Washington, DC: GAO, 2009.

U.S. Immigration and Customs Enforcement, "Delegation of Immigration Authority Section 287(g) Immigration and Nationality Act." January 2010. www.ice.gov/pi/news/factsheets/section287_g.htm

Weitzer, Ronald, and Steven A. Tuch, "Race and Perceptions of Police Misconduct." *Social Problems* 51 (2004): 305–325.

Weitzer, Ronald, and Steven A. Tuch, *Race and Policing in America: Conflict and Reform.* New York: Cambridge University Press, 2006.

Weitzer, Ronald and Steven A. Tuch, "Race, Class, and Perceptions of Discrimination by the Police." *Crime and Delinquency* 45 (1999): 494–507.

Weitzer Ronald and Steven A. Tuch, "Racially-Biased Policing: Determinants of Citizens' Perceptions." *Social Forces* 83 (2005): 1009–1030.

Will, George, "Exposing the 'Myth' of Racial Profiling." *Washington Post* (April 19, 2001).

Wilson, George, Roger Dunham, and Geoffrey Alpert, "Prejudice in Police Profiling." *American Behavioral Scientist* 47 (2004), 896–909.

Wilson, Janet, and Sandra Murillo, "Inland Latinos Alarmed by New Border Patrol Sweeps." *Los Angeles Times* (June 10, 2004).

Withrow, Brian L., *Racial Profiling: From Rhetoric to Reason.* Upper Saddle River, NJ: Pearson/Prentice Hall, 2006.

RIGHT-WING EXTREMISM

DANIEL L. SMITH-CHRISTOPHER AND JUDITH ANN WARNER

In both the United States and Europe, the late 20th century saw an upsurge in the formation of right-wing extremist groups and other groups often labeled *hate groups* (advocating the expulsion or destruction of an entire people because of race or religion). At the same time, there was an accompanying upsurge in the number of anti-Semitic and racist incidents of harassment and violence. Although most of these groups do not use explicitly religious arguments in defense of their ideologies and ideas, some of them most certainly do. In fact, in one recent study, it is stated that "if there were one thread that runs through the various far-right movements in American history it would be fundamentalist Christianity" (Michael 2003, 65). It is important to know about these groups, particularly because many of them have become quite sophisticated in their public presentation, often masking their true intentions behind quite normal sounding "research groups," "churches," or "cultural activities."

Variety of Groups

Extremist movements, hate groups, and militias have been a part of the American landscape for many decades. The Ku Klux Klan, one of the most notorious of the American-grown terrorist organizations, was originally formed in 1865, based originally in Pulaski, Tennessee. It has been responsible for literally hundreds of lynchings and killings, mostly (but not exclusively) in the southern United States, but it dwindled into virtual nonexistence before World War I. The Klan, however, was revived and refounded by William Simmons, a Christian pastor, in 1915, and advocated versions of the *Christian Identity* doctrine (see below), and recent Klan groups (there are now various splinter groups) have been implicated in violence and murders in the United States as recently as 1981.

Related extremist groups are the various *militias* that provide training in firearms and often advocate being prepared for an ideological battle or outright war between races or that comprise adherents of unacceptable beliefs.

Among the less violent groups but still advocating racism are organizing groups such as the Council of Conservative Citizens (CCC), founded in 1985 in Atlanta, Georgia, but now based in St. Louis, Missouri, with a membership of 15,000.

Finally, there are variations of the *Christian Identity* movements that take the form of a "churches," often using names such as Church of the Aryan Nation or Christian Identity.

Definitions and Membership

Scholars of right-wing groups define these movements in many different ways. How one defines them obviously has serious implications for how many movements fall within these definitions and therefore affect the statistics on how many such groups currently exist.

According to a 1996 study by the Center for Democratic Renewal (an important organization that is considered one of the main watchdog groups keeping tabs on right-wing extremism in the United States), "there are roughly 25,000 'hard core' members and another 150,000 to 175,000 active sympathizers who buy literature, make contributions, and attend periodic meetings" (Michael 2003, 1).

The breakdown of right-wing groups in the United States is presented in Table 1.

However, the Southern Poverty Law Center, one of the main sources of information for right-wing extremist groups, posts on its Web site a list by state of extremist groups active in the United States. Upon reviewing this list (and taking only the top 20 states for active hate groups), one discovers a somewhat surprising comparison with the previous list, suggesting that these groups have a wider geographical distribution than one might expect (see Table 2).

Studies of membership across the United States have reported that the execution of Timothy McVeigh, the main conspirator in the Oklahoma City bombing of the Alfred Murrah Federal Building on June 11, 2001, which killed 168 people, seems to have slowed membership growth in various American hate groups. However, only a few months later, the attack on the World Trade Center in New York City on September 11, 2001, stopped the downward trend in militia membership, and the movement began to pick up membership once again.

Characteristics of Extremist and Hate Groups

George Michael lists a number of characteristics that he suggests are generally common among extremist groups:

1. Small locus of identity. Groups tend to strongly identify themselves with very locally defined groups—at most a nation, but often a race within a nation or a race within a region. Members are not interested in recruiting beyond a select few because they view the rest of the world in highly negative terms.

TABLE 1. Right-Wing Groups in the United States

Region	KKK	Neo-Nazi	Skinhead	Christian Identity	Other	Patriot/ Militia	Total
East	16	23	6	1	30	16	92
South	69	28	6	20	54	51	228
Midwest	39	39	10	9	58	54	209
Southwest	9	9	12	2	23	36	91
West	5	31	6	14	51	60	167
Total	138	130	40	46	216	217	787

Source: Michael 2003, 2.

TABLE 2. Geographic Distribution
of Extremist Groups

1. Texas	66
2. California	60
3. Florida	51
4. New Jersey	44
5. Georgia	37
6. Tennessee	37
7. South Carolina	36
8. Alabama	32
9. Missouri	31
10. New York	31
11. North Carolina	29
12. Illinois	28
13. Louisiana	28
14. Pennsylvania	28
15. Ohio	27
16. Michigan	26
17. Mississippi	25
18. Arkansas	24
19. Virginia	22
20. Colorado	17

Source: Southern Poverty Law Center, "Hate Map,"
2009. http://www.splcenter.org/intel/map/hate.jsp

2. Low regard for democracy. Although most groups abide by federal rules, they often have a low regard for systems that give too much freedom to all people—including, of course, the excluded groups. This violates their sense of privilege and the feeling that their membership should be limited to a select few.
3. Antigovernment. Many groups view the federal government with great suspicion and see it as hopelessly under the control of particular groups.
4. Conspiracy view of history. Groups view historical as well as recent events according to complicated and dubious theories of conspiracy and control by some particular hated group.
5. Racism. Their views often exclude nonwhite races entirely, but in the case of those who also direct their hatred toward Roman Catholicism, even white Catholics liable to be targeted by hateful propaganda (Michael 2003, 5–6).

There can be differences, however, in certain categories of groups. Militia groups, for example, can be described somewhat differently, as suggested by Mulloy (2008), who cites some common denominators of members of militia groups:

1. Conservative outlook. These are worried about repressive government that imposes undesired limitations on them, usually including taxes and gun control.
2. Weekend adventurers. Some of the less ideological members are simply those who enjoy dressing in camouflage and "playing soldier" in the woods.
3. Libertarian conservatives. These argue against almost all forms of federal government, even if they accept some limited local government as valid.
4. Hardcore extremists. Such people harbor an obsessive conviction that the United States, indeed the world, is in the grip of an all-powerful conspiracy (Mulloy 2008, 3–4).

One can also add that militia and militia-like groups tend to be most active in states where there is a high percentage of gun owners, current and retired military personnel, and law enforcement personnel.

For Americans who fall into any of these categories, two events in the 1990s stand out as national tragedies that fueled a great deal of anger and resentment among some Americans who already tended to hold a conspiracy theory of suspicion toward government. The first was the attempted arrest of Randy Weaver in Ruby Ridge, Idaho, in August 1992. Weaver, a known white supremacist, was arrested for selling sawed-off shotguns to an undercover informant. When he did not appear for his trial, U.S. marshals went to his rural Idaho home to arrest him. The killing of the family dog led to a gun battle in which Weaver's son Sam was killed, as was a federal marshal. Weaver himself was wounded and his wife was killed. The 11-day siege ended when another known member of a so-called patriot group cooperated with the marshals and convinced Weaver to surrender.

The second event was the disastrous end of the police siege of the Branch Davidian religious movement near Waco, Texas, in February 1993. The decision to force an end to a long stand-off resulted in the death of many members of this religious cult. After a 51-day standoff, the FBI decided to invade the complex. In four hours, over 300 canisters of tear gas were injected into the complex and a fire broke out, which killed over 74 members of the movement, including children. Part of the ensuing controversy was stirred not only by the fact that the events were broadcast throughout the nation but also because many of the reasons cited by the government for its aggressive tactics turned out to be unsupported. For example, there was no evidence for the alleged child abuse, and there was no evidence of drug dealing, much less drug producing laboratories, and no massive stockpiling of weaponry. There is even some suggestion that the government enforcement agency known as the ATF (Bureau of Alcohol, Tobacco, and Firearms) wanted to show off a success in Waco in the light of upcoming congressional discussions about the future of the agency and its federal funding.

Most Americans saw these events as isolated incidents involving religious extremists or troubled individuals. But for those inclined to see conspiracies in the modern world, these events are frequently cited as "evidence" of deeper issues and are often used in virulent literature used to stir up hatred and support for extremist agendas.

Watching the Extremists

Even though there are many organizations that compile information on various extremist and hate groups (including, of course, the FBI), there are four main organizations that are widely noted for reliable information on right-wing extremism and are active in attempting to use legal means to limit such activities. These are:

1. The Anti-Defamation League (ADL), which was founded in 1913 in Chicago by attorney Sigmund Livingston as an organization intended to be a defense agency for Jews in the facing discrimination United States. However, the ADL had been active in organizing information and legal challenges against groups who advocate hatred and/or discrimination against many different minorities. Michael (2003, 15–16) even reports cases of grudging respect for the ADL among some of the groups it has targeted for its effective use of legal challenges (see http://www.adl.org).
2. The Southern Poverty Law Center (SPLC) was founded in 1971 by two lawyers, Morris Dees Jr. and Joseph Levin in Montgomery Alabama. Sometimes considered controversial because of the major fund-raising success of Morris Dees, the charismatic central figure of the SPLC, the organization has nonetheless emerged as one of the most effective in the United States in combating hate groups (Michael 2003, 21–22). SPLC investigations have resulted in "civil suits against many white supremacist groups for their roles in hate crimes. More than 40 individuals and nine major white supremacist organizations were toppled by SPLC suits in the Project's first 17 years" (see http://splcenter.org).
3. Political Research Associates, founded in Chicago in 1981, is "first and foremost a research organization" (Michael 2003, 27). It works to expose movements, institutions, and ideologies that undermine human rights. Two of its affiliates known for their efforts against hate groups are the Center for Democratic Renewal and the Policy Action Network (see http://www.publiceye.org/index.php).

The "Christian Identity" Movement

Among the most explicitly religious groups among the far-right and extremist organizations is the movement known as Christian Identity (variant but related groups appear with names like Church of the Aryan Nation and similar ones). A number of specific groups identify with variations on this train of thought, so it is important to briefly summarize some of the basic ideas encountered in these many versions.

Among the most common ideas that feed the Christian Identity movement ideas are those known as British Israelism or Anglo-Israelism. This is the belief that the white races of western Europe and especially the Celtic and Germanic peoples are direct descendents of the Lost Tribes of Israel. Thus, the "white" Americans and Commonwealth peoples (Australia, New Zealand, Canada, etc.) are descendants of Israelites and thus have a special status before God.

In the United States, more virulent forms of the Christian Identity movement became deeply anti-Semitic, believing that they had "replaced" the Jews as the true "chosen people of God" and that today's Jews are "descendants of Satan" (Eatwell 2009).

Among the most dangerous of the ideas circulated among Christian Identity followers is the notion of an impending great war between good and evil, largely to be fought between white people on the one side and all nonwhites aligned with the Jews on the other. Christian Identity adherents believe that there were many other people in the world before God made Adam and Eve, but that Adam and Eve were created white and that whites are therefore the ones that God especially cared for. Eve, however, had sex with one of the pre-Adam peoples (therefore nonwhite). Cain was born from this union and was the ancestor of all nonwhite peoples today. Abel, the true son of Adam, was the further ancestor of all white people.

This is then mixed with (very loose) interpretations of, for example, selected portions of the New Testament Book of Revelation, which speaks (symbolically) of a war between good and evil that will finally bind and destroy evil in the world. Some extremist

THE HUTAREE GROUP

In Michigan, in March 2010, nine members of an apocalyptic Christian militia group known as the Hutaree (pronounced Hu-TAR-ay) were arrested by FBI agents and charged with plotting to kill local law enforcement officers in the hope of bringing about a generalized antigovernment revolt. The group's plan was to attack police officers with weapons from its armament and then retreat to dug-in positions protected by land mines and other heavy weaponry. The Hutaree believed that such violence was religiously justified as a means of sparking the final battle between Christians and the Antichrist, here represented by the government. "Jesus wanted us to be ready to defend ourselves using the sword," stated the group's Web site. They had expected other Christian and antigovernment militias to join in. In this case, however, just the opposite occurred. With the FBI in pursuit, one of the Hutaree approached the commander of a neighboring militia to ask for assistance. Instead, the leader turned him down and moreover tipped law enforcement authorities as to the Hutarees' whereabouts. The rationale given by the informant was that it was the right thing to do. Observers who know the area in which the two groups operate speculate that the Hutaree is a fringe organization whose increasing religious zeal (and, to the extent it was known, willingness to kill cops) caused it to be disliked by the local populace.

Source: New York Times (March 30 and 31, 2010).

members within the Christian Identity movement advocate terrorist violence against minorities in the United States, even ahead of the "great war."

Members of Christian Identity movements have been implicated in violent acts in the United States, including the following:

- Eric Rudolph's bombing of the 1996 Atlanta Olympics, and his 1997 bombing of an abortion clinic in Birmingham, Alabama
- The burning of synagogues in Sacramento, California, in 1999
- The murder of a gay couple in Redding, California, the same year
- The attempted murder of five individuals at a Jewish Community Center in Los Angeles in 1999

There appear to be international connections as well, such as the Living Hope Church founded in South Africa by Rev. Willie Smith in the late 1990s in reaction to the fall of the Apartheid racist regime there.

Hate-Crime Laws

The FBI has defined hate crime, sometimes called bias crime, as "a criminal offense committed against a person, property, or society which is motivated, in whole or in part, by the offender's bias against a race, religion, disability, sexual orientation or ethnicity/national origin" (Shively 2005: 2). Almost all states have established criminal penalties for hate crimes. These penalties enhance the severity of punishment for a hate- or bias-motivated crime or establish hate crimes as a new category of crime (a process conceptualized by social scientists as criminalization).

Federal statutes require mandatory reporting of all crime, including hate crime, but there is inconsistency in reporting across all states. Civil rights and immigrant advocates believe that hate crime is unreported partly owing to differences in state and federal laws and their interpretation. Another cause of underreporting is the need for training on how to recognize and classify hate crime. This innovation in law enforcement is subject to further debate. There are lawmakers and lawyers who are not convinced that justice for all will be served by adding hate crime penalties.

Hate crime laws were federally enacted and then adopted by states for four reasons: (1) a bias-motivated crime is viewed as different from a traditional crime because it traumatizes an individual owing to his or her group affiliation; (2) hate crimes place stress on distinct social groups because they view themselves as targets and are subject to more stress than other groups; (3) hate crimes are regarded as particularly heinous because of their underlying motivation and their impact on society; and (4) law enforcement traditionally has not acted forcefully in cases of violence and property crime motivated by hate. Each of these arguments for hate crime laws is examined below.

The creation of hate crime legislation is based on the idea that hate- or bias-motivated crimes are a different type of crime than traditional criminal acts and that they are more serious. The consequences of hate crime include more negative psychological and emotional consequences for victims, increased violence, and greater physical injury. For example, an individual who is robbed and then beaten extensively because of his or her skin color, religion, or sexual preference has, arguably, had a more traumatic experience than an individual who is briefly assaulted, even if injured, and robbed.

Hate crimes have different consequences for communities because they threaten the safety of singled-out groups of people. No one wants to be a crime victim, and a hate crime indicates that members of a particular group are targets for more hate crime. The targeted group has an increased sense of risk of criminal victimization and views the situation as persecution.

Because of the perception that hate crime is more severe than conventional crime, laws have been created to increase penalties. Hate motivation is thought to make a crime more serious. A social message is sent that penalties will be increased in the hope that this type of crime will be deterred by concern about the increased consequences of conviction. For example, adolescents commit acts of vandalism, but the element of hate motivation and emotion is not usually evoked by this act. If the crime was not motivated by bias, such as breaking the windows of an abandoned house, it would carry a lesser punishment. Vandalism motivated by bias, such as painting swastikas and other hate symbols on a house or a church, would be punished more severely.

The last reason for the creation of hate crime laws and penalties is that victims of hate crimes have traditionally received less law enforcement protection. The hate crime aspect of such acts has not been investigated or is underprosecuted. In other words, hate crimes have been prosecuted in the same way as traditional crime or not prosecuted at all. The hate crime statutes in at least 12 states provide for more law enforcement training in the recognition of hate crime to increase the protection of targeted groups. Recently, federal efforts to train all state and local police departments in the documentation of hate crimes have been expanded. Hate crime laws contribute to an understanding of what hate crime is among both law enforcement and the general public. The general public has increasingly understood and accepted the idea that there is a separate category of crime characterized by hate.

See also **Border Fence; Gun Control; Racial, National Origin, and Religion Profiling; New Religious Movements (vol. 3)**

Further Reading

Barkun, Michael, *Religion and the Racist Right: The Origins of the Christian Identity Movement.* Chapel Hill, NC: University of North Carolina Press, 1996.

Eatwell, Roger, *Fascism and the Extreme Right.* London: Routledge, 2009.

Eatwell, Roger, and Cas Mudde, *Western Democracies and the New Extreme Right.* London: Routledge, 2004.

Hewitt, Christopher, *Political Violence and Terrorism in America: A Chronology*. Westport, CT: Praeger, 2005.

Hewitt, Christopher, *Understanding Terrorism in American: From the Klan to al Qaeda*. London: Routledge, 2002.

Juergensmeyer, Mark, *Terror in the Mind of God: The Global Rise of Religious Violence*, 3d ed. Berkeley, CA: University of California Press, 2003.

Michael, George, *Confronting Right-Wing Extremism and Terrorism in the USA*. London: Routledge, 2003.

Mulloy, D. J., *American Extremism: History, Politics and the Militia Movement*. London: Routledge, 2008.

Shively, M., *Study of Literature and Legislation on Hate Crime in America*. Washington, DC: National Institute of Justice, 2005.

S

SCHOOL VIOLENCE

LEANNE R. OWEN

In the final years of the 20th century, following a spate of widely publicized school shootings and other high-profile incidents of juvenile violence on school grounds, safety at American educational institutions became an issue. The primary controversy has revolved around whether school violence is a legitimate and realistic cause for worry or panic or whether the actual statistics are quite encouraging despite some political and/ or scholarly claims to the contrary. In other words, while some argue that our public schools are experiencing some kind of epidemic of violence, others maintain that citizens should rest assured that our public schools are relatively safe places.

Competing and often contradictory claims about the frequency or rarity of these types of happenings, as well as calls for legislative action aimed at their prevention, flooded the popular media and academic literature alike in the wake of more than a few high-profile shootings. As justification for the passage of the Violent and Repeat Juvenile Offender Accountability and Rehabilitation Act of 1999, it was stated that "Congress finds that juveniles between the ages of 10 years and 14 years are committing increasing numbers of murders and other serious crimes...the tragedy in Jonesboro, Arkansas, is, unfortunately, an all too common occurrence in the United States." In sharp contrast, the Final Report of the Bi-Partisan Working Group on Youth Violence asserted that "there are many misconceptions about the prevalence of youth violence in our society and it is important to peel back the veneer of hot-tempered discourse that often surrounds the issue...it is important to note that, statistically speaking, schools are among the safest places for children to be" (Center on Juvenile and Criminal Justice 2000).

Background

Public concern about school crime in general and violence in particular can be traced back to the origins of the public school system in the United States (Crews and Counts 1997). Additional attention was directed to the issue with the publication of the *Task Force Report: Juvenile Delinquency and Youth Crime* in 1967 and the Office of Education of the U.S. Department of Health, Education, and Welfare made suggestions as to the role schools could play in curtailing youth crime. Congressional hearings held at the time reflected the broad public concern about delinquency and violence in schools (U.S. Senate Committee on the Judiciary 1975); over the course of the years since, criminologists and laypersons alike have attempted to shed some light on the nature, extent, and root causes of school-based violence.

The three-year period between 1996 and 1999 in particular appeared to many Americans to be fraught with news stories about school violence, and the issue was frequently represented as signaling the beginning of a possible juvenile crime epidemic. On February 2, 1996, 14-year-old Barry Loukaitis opened fire on his algebra class in Moses Lake, Washington, killing two students and a teacher and wounding another individual. Later that month, in Bethel, Alaska, 16-year-old Evan Ramsey killed a fellow student as well as the principal, in addition to wounding two other persons. In October of the following year, in Pearl, Mississippi, 16-year-old Luke Woodham killed two classmates and injured seven. The month of December brought two high-profile cases; the first involved 14-year-old Michael Carneal, who opened fire on a prayer circle at Heath High School in West Paducah, Kentucky, killing three students and wounding five others. That same month, 14-year-old Colt Todd in Stamps, Arkansas, shot two of his classmates while they stood in the school parking lot.

In March 1998, in one of the most widely publicized school shootings, four students and a teacher were killed and 10 others wounded when Mitchell Johnson, age 13, and Andrew Golden, age 11, emptied Westside Middle School in Jonesboro, Arkansas, with a false fire alarm. The case received national coverage, and news magazines led with headlines such as "The Hunter and the Choirboy" (Labi 1998) and "The Boys behind the Ambush" (Gegax, Adler, and Pederson 1998). Throughout the country, politicians, academics, pediatricians, and parents alike were questioning how something like this could happen and what could be done to prevent similar tragedies in the future.

Four other incidents of school shootings were recorded in 1998, in Edinboro, Pennsylvania; Fayetteville, Tennessee; Springfield, Oregon; and Richmond, Virginia. The deadliest recorded school shooting until 2007 took place the following April in Littleton, Colorado, when 18-year-old Eric Harris and 17-year-old Dylan Klebold had plotted for a year to kill 500 people and blow up Columbine High School. At the end of their hour-long rampage, 12 students and a teacher were dead and an additional 23 people were seriously injured. Klebold and Harris then turned the guns on themselves, effectively ending any hopes of determining definitively what caused them to engage in such unthinkable behavior. Speculation was rife and law enforcement officials suggested that indications of what Klebold and Harris were plotting had existed prior to the attack. Klebold had written a graphic story about slaughtering preppy students as well as a detailed paper about Charles Manson. Harris, in addition to writing about Nazis and guns in schools, made notes about killing in a massacre "to-do" list, including such things as

THE AFTERMATH OF JONESBORO

In the aftermath of what was dubbed the Jonesboro Massacre, different groups of experts have attempted to respond to seemingly unanswerable questions in a variety of ways. Some wondered what stimuli in these children's lives could have possibly prompted them to kill; hunting, popular music, television programs, and violent films were all identified in varying degrees as questionable hobbies that may have exerted undue negative influences on these boys. Some questioned how Johnson and Golden gained access to firearms in the first place, and for these, the answers appeared to lie in restricting purchases and usage of guns. The Clinton administration sought to ban assault weapons as part of a larger, comprehensive effort to prevent crime, focusing on the idea of forbidding military-style weapons in the hopes that they would not fall into the wrong hands (specifically those of children).

For those individuals struggling with the incongruity of physiologically small, slight, immature beings demonstrating a capacity to act in the most violent and sadistic ways imaginable, emphasis appeared to be placed most intently upon the punitive versus the rehabilitative prospects of the criminal justice system. Debates ensued as to whether trying these young people as adults would act as a stronger general deterrent for others in the same age group contemplating similar actions or whether an area of greater concern was the distinct possibility that, if tried and sentenced as adults, these juveniles could conceivably spend the following two or three decades learning how to become better criminals and thereby cement their chances of becoming chronic and repeat offenders. The very ideological underpinnings of the juvenile court system were called into questions as arguments asserted that children were qualitatively different from adults and therefore deserved to be treated rather than punished. This view was countered by contentions that those who commit adult crimes should pay the adult price and do the adult time.

On a local level, the community of Jonesboro launched an $8.4 million federally funded three-year initiative to prevent school violence. Programs were developed to improve school safety as well as school-based and community mental health services, help with early childhood development, and promote education reform. A leadership academy for students was created in hopes of teaching students alternative methods of conflict resolution.

reminders to obtain gas cans, nails, and duffel bags. Further notes and diaries found after their deaths described instances of bullying victimization at school and repeated expressions of rage, hatred, and resentment.

Key Moments/Events

In light of the widespread coverage in the popular media of these high-profile incidents of school violence, the Justice Policy Institute examined data gathered from an earlier study conducted by the Centers for Disease Control and concluded that the likelihood of children becoming victims of school-based violence was as minute as "one in two million" (Olweus 1993). The following month, President Clinton addressed Americans and asserted that "the overwhelming majority of our schools are, in fact, safe" (CNN 1998), a comment reiterated by Attorney General Janet Reno and Education Secretary Richard W. Riley in the report titled *Early Warning, Timely Response: A Guide to Safe Schools* (Dwyer, Osher, and Warger 1998). Subsequent administrations have essentially reiterated such views.

BULLYING

One particular concern raised immediately following the Columbine tragedy was school bullying. A substantial amount of evidence appeared to exist that drew a direct correlation between persistent taunting and insults being leveled at Klebold and Harris and their subsequent outburst. Parents, teachers, counselors, and school administrators began expressing serious worries that bullying, if left unchecked, could result in the victims themselves becoming aggressors. Consequently, many schools began implementing strategies designed to prevent bullying, many modeled after the program developed by Daniel Olweus in Norway (Olweus 1993). A curriculum of conflict resolution was developed around the idea of minimizing antisocial and negative behavior, and programs began teaching children as young as kindergarten age about resolving disputes in a respectful and appropriate manner.

However, some criminologists suggest that bullying has not significantly decreased as a result of these efforts, positing instead that it has simply been transformed from the more overt, direct forms of action to a more invisible, indirect type. In other words, instead of children bullying their fellow classmates by hitting, kicking, punching, threatening, or tripping them—actions that would inevitably attract the attention of teachers and recess or hallway monitors and thus result in sanctions being imposed—they may instead resort to name-calling, instigating malicious gossip, spreading rumors, posting derogatory comments on social networking Web sites such as My Space or Facebook, or sending hateful text or e-mail messages to one another. Such actions may escape the notice of appropriate adult authorities and may therefore persist undeterred for an extended period of time, possibly resulting in physical, emotional, or psychological damage to the student being bullied. A case in South Hadley, MA, in 2010, in which a high school student hung herself in response to bullying, illustrates this point.

In *Indicators of School Crime and Safety 2009*, the 12th installment of a series of annual reports jointly compiled by the National Center for Education Statistics and the
Bureau of Justice Statistics, data are presented suggesting that students may actually be
better protected against the potentiality of violent crime victimization at school than
away from it. The report analyzes the incidence of violent deaths at school (defined
as a self- or other-inflicted death occurring on the school grounds) as well as nonfatal
student victimization. Violent deaths for children between the ages of 5 and 18 years
of age were determined to have declined from 30 to 21 between the 2006–2007 and
2007–2008 school years. During the 2006–2007 academic year (the latest year for which
complete data are available), 8 suicides were recorded among school-aged youth, which
statisticians have calculated translates into less than one suicide per million students.
During that same school year, 1,748 children within the same age range were victims of
homicide and 1,296 committed suicide away from school. The conclusion to be drawn
is that youth were nearly 60 times more likely to be murdered and 160 times more likely
to commit suicide away from school than at school (National Center for Education
Statistics 2009).

In addition to violent incidents in which students were killed, the *Indicators of School
Crime and Safety 2009* report also measured the incidence and frequency of nonfatal
violent victimizations of students, including such offenses as rape, sexual assaults, robbery, and aggravated assault. The authors determined that in each survey year between
1992 and 2007, students reported lower rates of serious violent victimization at school
than away from school. Approximately 118,000 students were victims of serious violent crimes at school in 2007 as compared with nearly 164,000 serious violent crime
victimizations away from school. Taken as a rate, this figure suggests that 4 students
between the ages of 12 and 18 years out of every 1,000 were victims of serious violent
crimes at school during this time period, compared with approximately 6 students out
of every 1,000 who were victimized away from school. In previous years the ratio was
even more dramatic (for example, 8 per 1,000 at school versus 24 per 1,000 away from
school in 1997). Less than 1 percent of school-aged children reported serious violent
crime victimization within the previous six months (National Center for Education
Statistics 2009).

Despite the publication and dissemination of this report and earlier editions of it, a
telephone poll by Hart and Teeter Research taken days after the shooting in Jonesboro,
Arkansas, revealed that 71 percent of 1,004 adult respondents thought it was very likely
or likely that a school shooting could happen in their community (Center on Juvenile
and Criminal Justice 2000, 5). A *USA Today* poll from April 21, 1999, conducted the
day after the Littleton, Colorado, shooting found that 68 percent of Americans thought
it was likely that a shooting could happen in their town or city and that respondents
were 49 percent more likely to be fearful of their schools than in the previous year. A
CBS News phone poll two days after the Littleton, Colorado, shooting (April 22, 1999)

found that 80 percent of Americans expected more school shootings, and the number of people listing crime as the most important problem increased fourfold (from 4 to 16 percent) in the week after the Littleton shooting. Two years later, a Gallup poll revealed that 63 percent of parents still thought it likely that a Columbine-type shooting could happen in their community (Gallup 2001). Matters were only made worse following a mass shooting on the campus of Virginia Tech in 2007 in which 32 people were killed. Although the incident took place on a college campus rather than within a local school district, students, teachers, parents, and administrators remained fearful regarding the prospect of further gun violence in U.S. schools (Fallahi et al. 2009).

Dewey G. Cornell of the Virginia Youth Violence Project has contended that despite the encouraging statistics demonstrating that school violence is not, as some would suggest, an epidemic, it is unsurprising that parents and politicians would be concerned that the opposite is true. He has stated "public perception is easily skewed by media attention to a handful of extreme cases" (Cornell 2003, 1). He alludes to the 2002 version of the *Indicators of School Crime and Safety* study and confirms that the rate of violent crime in public schools in the United States has declined steadily since 1994, with the rate of serious violent crime in 2001 holding steady at half of what it was in 1994 (Cornell 2003, 3).

Kenneth S. Trump, the president of the National School Safety and Security Service, has argued that the methodology of the *Indicators of School Crime and Safety* study is flawed and that school violence levels are not on the decline, as the research seems to claim. He posits that by utilizing reported crime incidents rather than random sampling, "the federal report grossly underestimates the extent of school crime" (Scarpa 2005, 19). Instead, Trump refers to statistics indicating that the number of school-associated violent deaths "jumped to 49 in 2003–2004, more than the two prior school years combined and greater than any school year since 1999" (Scarpa 2005, 19).

Part of the discrepancy may be attributed to the fact that the actual sources of data about school violence in particular and juvenile violence in general may offer contradictory evidence. The Surgeon General's Report on Youth Violence highlights this inconsistency, arguing that official reports and self-reports—the two primary means of obtaining information about violent acts committed by juveniles—are inherently at odds (Satcher 1999). Official reports rely on the number of recorded arrests of juveniles to measure the extent of their lawbreaking behavior, and the surge in arrests for violent crime between 1983 and 1993 is believed to be largely attributable to the proliferation of firearms use by teenagers and the subsequent increased likelihood that confrontations between individuals in that age cohort would turn not only violent but lethal. With an increasing number of schools in all jurisdictions today (rural, suburban, and urban) installing metal detectors and placing security officers on campus, the number of students carrying guns to school has dropped. It is therefore expected that altercations would be less likely to result in homicide and serious injury and thus less likely to draw the attention of police officers. By 1999, arrest rates for homicide, rape, and robbery had all dropped below the rates for 1983. Arrest rates for aggravated assault were higher in 1999 than they were in 1983 but had nonetheless declined significantly since 1994.

These official statistics are at odds with the data derived from self-reports of juveniles. Confidential surveys, according to the Surgeon General's Report, find that 13 to 15 percent of high school seniors report having committed an act of serious violence in recent years (1993 to 1998). These acts are unlikely to involve firearms and therefore generally do not draw the attention of law enforcement officials. It is estimated that between the early 1980s and late 1990s, the number of violent acts perpetrated by high school seniors increased by nearly 50 percent, a trend similar to that found in arrests for violent crimes in general for all age groups. The surgeon general concludes that youth violence remains an ongoing national problem, albeit one that is largely hidden from public view.

Important Persons/Legal Decisions

In the introduction to the third edition of his landmark book *Folk Devils and Moral Panics,* Stanley Cohen describes the phenomenon of school violence and argues that with the media coverage of each incident, the idea arose that bullying and school shootings were not only commonplace but becoming all too familiar. He alludes to the types of headlines generated by newspapers and magazines (not entirely dissimilar from those employed in the aftermath of the Jonesboro massacre)—such as "The Monsters Next Door: What Made Them Do It?" and "Murderous Revenge of the Trench Coat Misfits"—in identifying school violence as the subject of a modern-day moral panic. One characteristic of a moral panic, according to Cohen, is disproportionality; in other words, it is not that the events in question do not take place but rather that they do not take place with as alarming frequency as indicated by the media (Cohen 2005).

Cohen's arguments are substantiated by the work of Dewey Cornell, who demonstrates that the rate of violent crime in American public schools has declined since 1994 and that, since the late 1990s, the number of homicides committed at school has actually dropped from 35 in 1998, to 25 in 1999, to a low of 2 in 2002, and 4 in 2003 (Cornell 2003). Moreover, he calculates the actual risk of a student-perpetrated homicide taking place at a particular school by referring to the 53 million students who attend the nation's 119,000 public and private schools. He cites 2003 data from the National School Safety Center to demonstrate that between the 1992–1993 school year and the 2001–2002 school year, there were 93 incidents of student-perpetrator homicides on school grounds. Taken as an annual average, he contends that this translates to approximately 9.3 incidents each year over a 10-year period, which, when divided into the 119,000 schools in the United States, ultimately amounts to an annual probability of any school experiencing a student-perpetrated homicide of 0.0000781, or one in every 12,804. Put another way, a parent or teacher can expect a student to commit a homicide at a specific school once every 12,804 years. Cornell argues decisively that schools are not dangerous places but rather generally safe, constructive environments that may be, from time to time, plagued by random incidents of violence.

In 2008 Congress passed the School Safety Enhancements Act, which, among other features, made schools accountable for keeping students safe during their formative years. Schools now face legal action or potentially even closure if it is determined that the environment they provide is in any way unsafe or dangerous. To that end, schools have experimented with different strategies for the prevention of violence and crime. Some have, as mentioned previously, begun utilizing metal detectors and relying upon assistance from private security officers or police officials. Others have implemented dress codes to discourage the wearing of gang colors or gang insignia and to equalize fashion options regardless of the socioeconomic status of individual students (some of whom might be able to afford brand-name clothes while others could not, thereby causing a rift that might provide grounds for bullying or denigration). Many schools have begun incorporating peer mediation programs into their curricula, encouraging students to arbitrate disputes between their classmates and to ensure that each party is given a fair opportunity to voice concerns and express emotional responses. Some schools are finding these programs easier to implement than others, and research indicates that the selection of appropriate peer mentors and training of both the peer mentors and faculty or staff supervisors is key in bringing about a successful resolution.

Conclusion

It is uncertain whether these strategies will be effective in preventing school violence in the long run. Meta-analysis of the existing literature reflects mixed findings (Scheckner et al. 2004), suggesting that how a program is designed and developed as well as whether there is strong faculty and administrative support (specifically financial support) will have a strong impact on how successful it will be. What some criminologists find worrying is that as schools struggle to ensure safe environments for their students, lest they be court-ordered to close, they may find themselves attempting to conceal evidence of certain types of questionable behavior by arguing that it is not specifically indicative of an unsafe environment at school.

The *Washington Post* reported one such incident in Frederick County, Maryland, which involved a six-year-old girl being fondled by a middle schooler while being driven to her program for gifted students. The bus driver involved in the incident reported seeing middle-school boys describing sex acts to first-graders and attempting to shove a condom into another boy's mouth. When the bus driver told the six-year-old's mother about the fondling incident months later, he also mentioned that he had informed school officials; when pressed, the school denied having any record of the report. Beverly Glenn, the executive director of the Hamilton Fish Institute in Washington, explains that such actions are becoming increasingly common because schools do not want to be designated as unsafe for fear of losing students and consequently losing money. Instead, an increasing number of such incidents are being handled internally whenever possible, with the implicit justification that the acts themselves, if they take place as this one did on the way either to or from school, are not committed on school grounds and therefore do not render the school environment unsafe (Williams 2005).

It is unclear, then, precisely how useful and effective the various strategies—both school-based and legislative—have been in controlling school violence and whether the problem is actually escalating in severity or diminishing. What is certain is that whenever incidents involving children—either as victims or perpetrators—take place, the news media will report them and further promote the idea that the problem is "all too familiar" and is reaching "epidemic proportions." It is imperative, then, that readers and viewers analyze these reports critically in order to distinguish between fact and myth.

See also **Juvenile Justice; Juveniles Treated as Adults; Serial Murder and Mass Murder; Suicide and Suicide Prevention (vol. 3); Violence and Media (vol. 3)**

Further Reading

CBS News Poll, April 22, 1999.

Center on Juvenile and Criminal Justice, *School House Hype: Two Years Later.* San Francisco: Author, 2000.

CNN, "Clinton Unveils National Guide on School Violence: Program Designed to Help Identify Troubled Kids." August 27, 1998.

Cohen, S., *Folk Devils and Moral Panics,* 3d ed. New York: Routledge, 2005.

"Complete Listing of Worries." *Washington Post* (November 7, 1999).

Cornell, D., *Myths about Youth Violence and School Safety.* Richmond: University of Virginia, 2003.

Crews, G. A., and M. R. Counts, *The Evolution of School Disturbance in America: Colonial Times to Modern Day.* Westport, CT: Praeger, 1997.

Cullen, David, *Columbine.* New York: Twelve, 2009.

Donohue, E. D., V. Schiraldi, and J. Ziedenberg, *School House Hype: School Shootings and the Real Risks Kids Face in America.* Washington, DC: Justice Policy Institute, 1998.

Dwyer, K. P., D. Osher, and C. Warger, *Early Warning, Timely Response: A Guide to Safe Schools.* Washington, DC: Department of Education, 1998.

Fallahi, C. R., et al., "A Survey of Perceptions of the Virginia Tech Tragedy." *Journal of School Violence* 8, no. 2 (April 2009): 120–135.

Gegax, T., J. Adler, and D. Pederson, "The Boys behind the Ambush." *Newsweek* 131, no. 14 (1998): 20–25.

Gerler, E. R. Jr., ed., *Handbook of School Violence.* Binghamton, NY: Haworth, 2004.

Gillespie, M., *School Violence Still a Worry for American Parents.* Princeton, NJ: Gallup, 1999.

Labi, N., "The Hunter and the Choirboy." *Time* 151, no. 13 (1998): 28–37.

Lebrun, Marcel, *Books, Blackboards, and Bullets: School Shootings and Violence in America.* Lanham, MD: Rowman & Littlefield, 2009.

Murray, Thomas R., *Violence in America's Schools: Understanding, Prevention, and Responses.* Westport, CT: Praeger, 2006.

National Center for Education Statistics, *Indicators of School Crime and Safety 2009.* Washington, DC: National Center for Education Statistics, 2009. http://nces.ed.gov/programs/crimeindicators/crimeindicators2009/index.asp

Olweus, D., *Bullying at School: What We Know and What We Can Do.* London: Blackwell, 1993.

Satcher, D., *Youth Violence: A Report of the Surgeon General.* Washington, DC: U.S. Government Printing Office, 1999.

Scarpa, S., *District Administration* 41, no. 2 (February 2005): 19.

Schafer, W. E., and K. Polk, "Delinquency and the Schools." *Task Force Report: Juvenile Delinquency and Youth Crime.* Washington, DC: U.S. Government Printing Office, 1967.

Scheckner, S. S., et al., "School Violence in Children and Adolescents: A Meta-Analysis of the Effectiveness of Current Interventions." In *Handbook of School Violence,* ed. E. R. Gerler Jr. Binghamton, NY: Haworth, 2004.

USA Today/CNN/Gallup Poll Results, April 21, 1999.

U.S. Senate Committee on the Judiciary, *Our Nation's Schools—A Report Card: 'A' in School Violence in Vandalism. Preliminary Report of the Subcommittee to Investigate Juvenile Delinquency.* Washington, DC: U.S. Government Printing Office, 1975.

Williams, E., "As School Bus Sexual Assaults Rise, Danger Often Overlooked." *Washington Post* (June 14, 2005).

SEARCH WARRANTS

Keith G. Logan and Jonathan Kremser

In the 21st century, Americans are challenged with balancing the concern for individual rights with the need for public order through the administration of justice. We have seen license plates with the logo "Live Free or Die," a message intended not to encourage violence but rather to illustrate how Americans have traditionally sought to protect their personal liberties against unnecessary government intrusion. This conviction is perhaps best reflected in Benjamin Franklin's prophetic admonition that "they that can give up essential liberty to obtain a little temporary safety deserve neither liberty nor safety."

Beginning in the previous decade, however, in part through actions undertaken by President George W. Bush and his Attorney General Alberto Gonzales, questions have been raised about whose interpretation of the Bill of Rights is correct and whether the need for search warrants will prevail in all circumstances. Together, the president and attorney general chose to place a new test before the courts on the need for search warrants or similar lawfully issued orders. From 2002 until at least 2007, the National Security Agency (NSA) was directed to intercept international and domestic electronic communications without the authorization of a search warrant issued by a U.S. district court or other court order issued by the Foreign Intelligence Surveillance Act (FISA) Court.

Needless to say, these actions raised and continue to raise controversy among citizens, scholars, and the legal community as Americans have witnessed a loss of the historically strong standard needed to be met before agents of the government could enter a home, intercept mail, invade privacy, or collect electronic data from computers, cell phones, and bank records.

Background

In general, the United States has set a very high standard for government conduct in the hope that our privacy would be maintained and that our rights would not be violated. At the very beginning of this nation, the Framers sought to build popular support for the new government by amending the Constitution in 1887 with the Bill of Rights, which included protections against invasive government searches, securing "the Blessings of Liberty to ourselves and our Posterity" (as noted in the Preamble to the U.S. Constitution, 1787). Their belief in such principles as no taxation without representation illustrated their apparent desire to protect themselves against unreasonable government intrusion without legal justification.

It has not always been the law that agents of the government needed a lawfully issued search warrant based upon probable cause and signed by a neutral, detached judicial authority. In the past, without meeting this standard, evidence could be seized and later used in a criminal prosecution. Over the years, however, our legal system evolved to a point where law enforcement officers who violate the law of search and seizure usually find their evidence excluded and any conviction reversed.

The strength of Americans' belief in the sanctity of their homes and privacy is reflected in the words of the U.S. Constitution and its amendments. This document was designed to ensure that actions detested during British rule would not exist in the United States. And although it preserved the interests of the wealthy class of property owners (who else could afford to take six months off to travel to Philadelphia and write a Constitution?), the document also granted enough concessions to small property owners, middle-income merchants, and farmers, to build support for its ratification in the statehouses (see Zinn 2005).

During colonial times, representatives of the Crown routinely invaded citizens' homes; American colonists were subject to the abuses of general warrants, which permitted searches that did not specify the items to be seized or the person or place where they were to be found. An example of a general warrants was the writ of assistance that permitted a British tax collector and the collector's representatives to search colonial homes and other buildings to determine if there were goods present that did not bear the mark of a tax payment. These writs were not based upon probable cause and gave the bearer almost limitless authority. As was noted in *Boyd v. United States* (1886), the writs of assistance were "the most destructive of English liberty, and the fundamental principles of law, that ever was found in an English law book."

The Fourth Amendment to the Constitution is just one response to what the colonists found to be unjust treatment. It reads as follows: "The right of the people to be secure in their persons, papers, and effects against unreasonable searches and seizures, shall not be violated and no Warrants shall issue, but upon probable cause, supported by Oath or affirmation, and particularly describing the place to be searched and the persons or things to be seized."

Legal Decisions

Execution of a Search Warrant

The Fourth Amendment governs the proper execution of a search warrant. Police are generally required to knock and announce their identity and purpose before attempting

THE TYPICAL SEARCH WARRANT

A typical federal search warrant will be issued after a review of the application for the warrant, which will provide the probable cause that the government has for believing the person or item(s) to be seized are located in a particular place. The application is made under oath and lists the facts that the reviewer—a judicial authority—will evaluate in determining whether or not to issue the search warrant. If, upon review, the judge or magistrate finds that there is probable cause, the search warrant it will be authorized. If not, it will be denied.

The typical search warrant contains the following:

Caption or reference to the name of the court that is issuing the warrant name of the requesting individual (also known as the affiant).

Description of the place or person to be searched (location must be specific and located in an area where the judicial officer has jurisdiction). This standard of "particularity" requires that the description be sufficiently precise so that the officer executing the warrant can "with reasonable effort ascertain and identify the place intended" (see *Steele v. United States* 1925; *Coolidge v. New Hampshire* 1971; *United States v. Ross* 1982).

Detailed description of the property to be seized (scope of the search). This requires that the description leave nothing to the discretion of the officers (see *Marron v. United States* 1927).

When the warrant may be executed (the hours of the day or night), how the warrant may be executed (knock-and-announce or unannounced), and by whom (individual or agency/department).

Date and signature of the judicial officer who issued the warrant.

The reverse side or second page of the warrant will usually contain information regarding the return of the warrant. This information (the return) will reflect the date of service of the warrant and a list (inventory) of any items that were seized as a result of the search. The return will be certified by the executing individual and returned to the court in a timely manner. A copy of the warrant and a list of the seized items will be left at the location or with the person.

forcible entry (see *Wilson v. Arkansas* 1995). In response to law enforcement concerns about the need for flexibility, the U.S. Supreme Court held that this requirement is governed by a reasonableness standard. In *United States v. Banks* (2003), the Court concluded that a 15- to 20-second interval from the time the officers "knock and announce" until they enter by force was reasonable, given the possibility of destruction of evidence. Situations allowing for unannounced entries include the threat of physical violence or escape (see *United States v. Bates* 1996). Where there has been a violation of the knock-and-announce requirement, without more, the Court recently determined that the evidence should not be suppressed at trial (see *Hudson v. Michigan* 2006).

Exclusionary Rule

Most court decisions have upheld an individual's privacy right. When a search goes beyond the scope of the warrant or is conducted illegally or without a warrant, the defendant will move to have the evidence discovered during the search suppressed. After reviewing the facts surrounding the seizure of the evidence, the court, when appropriate, will support the suppression motion and the items will be excluded from being introduced during the trial. The key case for the exclusionary rule is *Weeks v. United States* (1914) in which the Court recognized that the use of illegally seized evidence against Weeks was a denial of his constitutional rights. In *Wolf v. Colorado* (1949), the Court recognized the importance of an individual's privacy against "arbitrary intrusion by the police"; it also recognized the significance of the *Weeks* decision, which held that "in a federal prosecution the Fourth Amendment barred the use of evidence secured through an illegal search and seizure." *Mapp v. Ohio* (1961) ensured that this right applied not only to federal law enforcement but also to state law enforcement through the due process authority of the Fourteenth Amendment.

The natural extension of the exclusionary rule came with cases involving derivative evidence, called the "fruit of the poisonous tree." In *Silverthorne Lumber Co. v. United States* (1920), the Court determined that evidence derived from an illegal search and subsequent seizure of accounting records (books, papers, and other documents) could not be used; it denied the government any use of the material gathered as a result of a "forbidden act" (see also *Silverman v. United States* 1961). The Court found that the wrong committed by the government tainted all the secondary evidence flowing from that illegality and was inadmissible as well. There are also cases where the Court has found that the wrong committed by the government is so attenuated or distanced from the illegally obtained evidence that such evidence has been accepted at trial (see *Nardone v. United States* 1937; *Wong Sun v. United States* 1963).

Exceptions

There are numerous exceptions to the criteria for the issuance of warrants and the admission of evidence as set forth in the Bill of Rights. Although several of the Supreme

Court's decisions have upheld the constitutional requirements, other case decisions have reduced the strength of a warrant requirement. Several exceptions to the strict requirements of search warrants are reflected in the following paragraphs:

Inevitable discovery and independent source: In *Nix v. Williams* (1984), the Court determined that the efforts of law enforcement personnel would likely have located the evidence (a body) and admitted it despite a constitutional violation (illegal questioning). In *Murray v. United States* (1988), the Court found that law enforcement personnel obtained evidence from an independent source in addition to the illegal source; it chose not to remove the evidence from admission. The independent source in this case was seen as a cure to the constitutional violation regarding the evidence.

Good faith exception: The courts have also decided not to penalize a law enforcement officer who acted in good faith to enforce a warrant that was no longer valid (see *United States v. Leon* 1984; *Massachusetts v. Sheppard* 1984; *Arizona v. Evans* 1995).

Incident to arrest: In *Chimel v. California* (1969), the Court rejected a search of the defendant's entire house without a search warrant; but incident to the defendant's arrest it did permit a search of the immediate area for weapons and other evidence. The Court found in *United States v. Robinson* (1973) that with a search warrant, a law enforcement officer could search the entire body of a defendant incident to the defendant's lawful custodial arrest. In *New York v. Belton* (1981), the Court permitted a search of the entire passenger compartment of an automobile incident to the lawful arrest of an occupant or recent occupant (see also *Von Cleef v. New Jersey* 1969; *Thornton v. United States* 2004). In *Maryland v. Buie* (1990), the Court found that as a "precautionary measure," law enforcement officers could conduct a search or protective sweep of the entire premises (adjoining the place of arrest) without a warrant to ensure a "reasonably prudent officer" that the area did not harbor danger that might place the officer's safety in jeopardy.

Stop and Frisk

In *Terry v. Ohio* (1968), the Court accepted a limited invasion of a person's privacy by allowing a pat-down of a subject's outer clothing. The Court determined that a law enforcement officer had the right to conduct a pat-down of an individual who was the subject of an investigative stop when the officer had a reasonable concern for his or her safety. The "outer clothing" was determined to include the passenger compartment of an automobile in *Michigan v. Long* (1983).

Plain touch or plain feel of an item incident to a "Terry stop" was noted in *Minnesota v. Dickerson* (1993). In this case the law enforcement officer, who had a reasonable concern for his safety, was legally permitted to conduct a pat-down of the defendant's outer clothing for weapons; the officer felt what he immediately recognized to be a lump of crack cocaine. The Court noted that when the "contour or mass makes its identity immediately apparent" to the law enforcement officer, there is no violation of the Fourth Amendment (*Minnesota v. Dickerson* 1993, at 376; see also *Coolidge v. New Hampshire* 1971, which supported the seizure of items of an incriminating nature that were not specifically named in the search warrant, but were in "plain view"). The key behind the plain touch/plain feel doctrine is that the law enforcement officer must be in a place he or she is legally authorized to be and conducting himself or herself in a lawful manner.

Warrantless Automobile Searches

Warrantless searches of automobiles, based on the Court's holding in *Carroll v. United States* (1925), were found constitutional. The Court determined that when law enforcement officers had probable cause to believe that the vehicle contained contraband, they could search the vehicle without a court-authorized search warrant. The key behind this search is the inherently mobile nature of the automobile and the potential for the destruction of evidence if not immediately seized; this has become known as the *Carroll doctrine.*

However, in *Scher v. United States* (1938), the Court also determined that a vehicle parked in an open garage by the defendant was still subject to a warrantless search by law enforcement officers applying the Carroll doctrine (see also *Chambers v. Maroney* 1970; *Michigan v. Thomas* 1982; *United States v. Ross* 1982; *California v. Carney* 1985; *Maryland v. Dyson* 1999). In *United States v. Tartaglia* (1989) the Court found the same exigent circumstances present in a train's roomette and accepted the application of the Carroll doctrine (see also *Cardwell v. Lewis* 1974 regarding exigent circumstances).

Close to the issue of searches is conducting an inventory. An inventory of a vehicle that has been impounded should not be confused with the issue of a search. Although there is less of an expectation of privacy, an inventory is conducted to safeguard the contents of a vehicle and protect the law enforcement officers from liability for any purported loss of its contents. Inventories are an accepted practice and generally must be part of the standard procedures for that agency or the action could be seen as an illegal search (see *South Dakota v. Opperman* 1976).

Emergencies and Hot Pursuit

In both emergency situations and the hot pursuit of a suspect, law enforcement officers may legally enter the private premises of an individual. In each situation, the law enforcement officer is legally permitted to be in that place without a search warrant. The officer may be responding to a 911 call for assistance or see what he or she believes to be an emergency, or the officer may be in hot pursuit of a suspected felon (murder, robbery, etc.) and has a reasonable basis to enter the premises. Upon entry for this lawful purpose, any evidence that the officer observes in plain view cannot be ignored. This would include weapons used in a robbery, drugs, and so on (see *Warden v. Hayden* 1967; *Mincy v. Arizona* 1978; *McDonald v. United States* 1948; *United States v. Gillenwaters* 1989).

Open Fields

In *Hester v. United States* (1924), the Court noted that the "special protection accorded by the Fourth Amendment to the people in their 'persons, houses, papers and effects' is not extended to the open fields." But the Court did not change the rule that a warrant was needed to search the house or its curtilage (see also *Oliver v. United States* 1984; *See v. City of Seattle* 1967; *California v. Ciraolo* 1986; *United States v. Dunn* 1987; *Florida v. Riley* 1989). Although not the same as an open field, the Court has determined that search warrants were not required in common or public areas, where individuals have less of an expectation of privacy (see *United States v. Nohara* 1993).

Consent

In any case where a search warrant is not present, an individual can always consent to a search. This would not violate the defendant's Fourth Amendment rights unless the consent was not "knowing" and "voluntary." *Schneckloth v. Bustamonte* (1973) noted that if there were police coercion, the consent would not be voluntary. Fraud or other forms of subtle coercion by a law enforcement officer would lead to the loss of the voluntariness of the consent (see also *Bumper v. North Carolina* 1968).

Electronic Eavesdropping

The subtle issue of an electronic invasion of privacy or searching without a warrant was once a simple issue. In *Olmstead v. United States* (1928), the Court determined that electronic eavesdropping (as in telephone communications) was not covered by the Fourth Amendment. The focus at that time was on the home/building and the concept of physical trespassing and not the individual's privacy. However, this changed with *Katz v. United States* (1967). The Court found that an individual could have a privacy expectation even when he or she was using a public telephone booth. It concluded that a search warrant would be required to intercept electronic communications. In other cases, the Court has looked closely at various means used to enhance what can be seen from outside a building—the use of which would result in an invasion of privacy without a warrant. In *Kyllo v. United States* (2001), the Court determined that the use of thermal imaging technology to determine activities inside a person's home was a clear invasion of his or her privacy and hence a warrantless search.

Other Investigations

Although this section on search warrants is directed at warrants related to criminal investigations, it should be noted that the Foreign Intelligence Surveillance (FISA) Court is also authorized to issue orders similar to search warrants that are applicable in intelligence investigations. Congress passed the Foreign Intelligence Surveillance Act (FISA) in 1978 in an effort to ensure that Fourth Amendment rights and civil liberties would not be abridged by the use of electronic surveillances, especially in conducting national security investigations (*United States v. United States District Court* 1972). However, there is a question of whether this has been successful (see *ACLU v. NSA* 2006).

Warrantless Wiretapping

Although President George W. Bush's position had been that it was not possible to conduct the surveillance program according to the FISA ("NSA Eavesdropping Was Illegal, Judge Says" 2010) and he argued that a warrant was not necessary because of the "war powers" provided to him in the Constitution and by the Congress, the American Civil Liberties Union (ACLU) challenged this position in U.S. District Court. In *ACLU v. NSA* (2006), the ACLU disputed the legality of the secret NSA program, commonly known as the Terrorist Surveillance Program (TSP). The district court held, in part, that the TSP violated the First and Fourth Amendments, the Constitution, and statutory law and then granted a permanent injunction regarding the continued operation of the TSP.

In a January 17, 2007, letter to Senators Patrick Leahy (chairman, Committee on the Judiciary) and Arlen Specter (ranking minority member, Committee on the Judiciary), Attorney General Gonzales stated: "any electronic surveillance that was occurring as part of the Terrorist Surveillance Program will now be conducted subject to the approval of the Foreign Intelligence Surveillance Court." He also wrote that on January 10, 2007, a FISA Court judge "issued orders authorizing the Government to target for collection international communications into or out of the United States where there is probable cause to believe that one of the communicants is a member or agent of al-Qaeda or an associated terrorist organization."

Further, in April 2010, on the basis of a case brought by an Oregon Islamic foundation that was being monitored by the government, a federal district judge ruled that the Bush administration had overstepped its authority in undertaking warrantless wiretapping. Among the comments in the judge's 45-page ruling was that the "theory of unfettered executive-branch discretion" created an "obvious potential for abuse" ("NSA Eavesdropping" 2010).

See also **Patriot Act; Surveillance—Technological (vol. 4)**

Legal Citations

ACLU v. NSA, 438 F. Supp. 2d 754 (D. Mich. 2006).

Arizona v. Evans, 514 U.S. 1 (1995).

Boyd v. United States, 116 U.S. 616, 625 (1886).

Bumper v. North Carolina, 391 U.S. 543 (1968).

California v. Carney, 471 U.S. 386 (1985).

California v. Ciraolo, 476 U.S. 207 (1986).

Cardwell v. Lewis, 417 U.S. 583 (1974).

Carroll v. United States, 267 U.S. 132 (1925).

Chambers v. Maroney, 399 U.S. 42 (1970).

Chimel v. California, 395 U.S. 754 (1969).

Coolidge v. New Hampshire, 403 U.S. 443 (1971).

Florida v. Riley, 488 U.S. 445 (1989).

Hester v. United States, 265 U.S. 57, 59 (1924).

Hudson v. Michigan, 547 U.S., 126 S. Ct. 2159 (2006).

Katz v. United States, 389 U.S. 347 (1967).

Kyllo v. United States, 533 U.S. 27, 34, 40 (2001).

Mapp v. Ohio, 367 U.S. 643 (1961).

Marron v. United States, 275 U.S. 192 (1927).

Maryland v. Buie, 494 U.S. 325 (1990).

Maryland v. Dyson, 527 U.S. 465 (1999).

Massachusetts v. Sheppard, 468 U.S. 981 (1984).

McDonald v. United States, 335 U.S. 451 (1948).

Michigan v. Long, 463 U.S. 1031 (1983).

Michigan v. Thomas, 458 U.S. 259 (1982).

Mincy v. Arizona, 437 U.S. 385 (1978).

Minnesota v. Dickerson, 508 U.S. 366 (1993).

Murray v. United States, 487 U.S. 533 (1988).

Nardone v. United States, 308 U.S. 338 (1937).

New York v. Belton, 453 U.S. 454 (1981).

Nix v. Williams, 467 U.S. 431 (1984).

Oliver v. United States, 466 U.S. 170 (1984).

Olmstead v. United States, 277 U.S. 438 (1928).

Scher v. United States, 305 U.S. 251 (1938).

Schneckloth v. Bustamonte, 412 U.S. 218 (1973).

See v. City of Seattle, 387 U.S. 541 (1967).

Silverman v. United States, 365 U.S. 505 (1961).

Silverthorne Lumber Co. v. United States, 251 U.S. 385 (1920).

South Dakota v. Opperman, 428 U.S. 364 (1976).

Steele v. United States, 267 U.S. 498, 503 (1925).

Terry v. Ohio, 392 U.S. 1 (1968).

Thornton v. United States, 124 U.S. 2127 (2004).

United States v. Banks, 124 S. Ct. 521 (2003).

United States v. Bates, 84 F. 3d 790 (6th Cir., 1996).

United States v. Dunn, 480 U.S. 294 (1987).

United States v. Gillenwaters, 890 F. 2d 679 (4th Cir., 1989).

United States v. Leon, 468 U.S. 897 (1984).

United States v. Nohara, 3 F. 3d 1239 (9th Cir., 1993).

United States v. Robinson, 414 U.S. 218 (1973).

United States v. Ross, 456 U.S. 798 (1982).

United States v. Tartaglia, 364 F. 2d 837 (D.C. Cir., 1989).

United States v. United States District Court, 407 U.S. 297 (1972)

Von Cleef v. New Jersey, 395 U.S. 814 (1969).

Warden v. Hayden, 387 U.S. 294 (1967)

Weeks v. United States, 232 U.S. 383, 398 (1914).

Wilson v. Arkansas, 514 U.S. 927 (1995).

Wolf v. Colorado, 338 U.S. 25, 28 (1949).

Wong Sun v. United States, 371 U.S. 471 (1963).

Further Reading

Bloom, Robert M., *Searches, Seizures, and Warrants: A Reference Guide to the United States Constitution.* Westport, CT: Praeger, 2003.

Bodenhamer, David J., *Our Rights.* New York: Oxford University Press, 2007.

Ferdico, John, *Criminal Procedure for the Criminal Justice Professional,* 10th ed. Belmont, CA: Thomson Wadsworth, 2008.

Ingram, Jefferson L., *Criminal Procedure, Theory and Practice,* 2d ed. Upper Saddle River, NJ: Pearson/Prentice Hall, 2008.

Ivers, Greg, and Kevin T. McGuire, *Creating Constitutional Change: Clashes over Power and Liberty in the Supreme Court.* Charlottesville: University of Virginia Press, 2004.

Moore, Robert, *Search and Seizure of Digital Evidence.* New York: LFB Scholarly Publishing, 2005.

Newman, Bruce A., *Against That "Powerful Engine of Despotism": The Fourth Amendment and General Warrants at the Founding and Today.* Lanham, MD: University Press of America, 2007.

"NSA Eavesdropping Was Illegal, Judge Says." *Washington Post* (April 1, 2010).

Zinn, Howard, *A People's History of the United States: 1492–Present.* New York: Harper Perennial, 2005.

SERIAL MURDER AND MASS MURDER

CHARLES I. BROOKS AND MICHAEL A. CHURCH

Serial killers murder again and again, sometimes over many years or even decades if they are not caught. Law enforcement officials, criminologists, psychologists, and sociologists all deal with some fundamental questions about serial killers:

- Do they leave "signatures," telltale signs unique to their style of killing?
- Do these killers have a common personality type that makes profiling them easier?
- Do serial killers differ from mass murderers?
- Can we prevent the development of a serial killer?

In considering these questions, we restrict our discussion to male perpetrators, because most serial killers are men. There are cases of female serial killers, but most theories and analyses are based on men. We focus here on representative research but also offer some clinical insights regarding prevention.

Do Serial Killers Leave "Signatures"?

Movies add to the suspense of a case by having the killer leave a characteristic clue with the body, something that tells investigators that the murderer has killed before. A perpetrator may, for instance, bury his victims face down and naked, with a stocking tied around the neck. These clues, called signatures, can include a variety of things unique to the killer. Initials might be carved in the body or a poem might be pinned to the body. A signature can also include evidence of a particular behavior involved in the killing. For instance, some perpetrators may have sex with the dead victim and others may require oral sex prior to the killing. Some may hide the body.

Douglas and Munn (1992a, 1992b) refer to a signature as a "calling card." These signatures can be specific behaviors or objects, but in either case they appear unique to the murderer. When such signatures are present, police are confident that the same killer is involved in the present and previous murders. Some investigators say that these signatures can change over time and become more developed or sophisticated throughout the murderous sequence. For example, the degree of postmortem mutilation may increase across victims.

Other law officials point out, however, that serial killers do not leave signatures in any consistent fashion, and signatures should not be considered a part of the puzzle. Serial killers show considerable variation in many aspects of their crimes, especially when the situation is different from victim to victim, as when a third party unexpectedly shows up during commission of the crime. Also, victims can vary greatly in how suspicious they may be of the perpetrator or how much control the attacker may need to use (e.g., gagging or binding the victim). Some serial murderers develop new strategies and techniques to decrease the probability of failing or being caught.

Bateman and Salfati (2007) analyzed murder cases in the files of the Homicide Investigation and Tracking System in Seattle, Washington. All the cases had been solved, and all involved the killing of at least five people. The investigators analyzed 450 murders. Victims included both children and adults, and the average age of the offender at the time of arrest was 30 years.

The investigators coded the cases according to whether crime scene behaviors did or did not occur, classified across six categories: body disposal, planning and control, mutilation, sexual offenses, theft, and weapon type. The researchers determined how frequently and consistently each of 35 crime scene behaviors occurred in the 450 serial homicides. The following behaviors occurred frequently (in at least 50 percent of the cases):

- Having a weapon at the scene (93 percent)
- Having sex after the killing (84 percent)
- Stealing something other than clothing (77 percent)
- Leaving body nude (77 percent)
- Vaginal sex (72 percent)
- Hiding the body (68 percent)
- Restraining the victim (66 percent)
- Leaving semen at the scene (63 percent)
- Using a knife to kill the victim (63 percent)
- Moving the body after the killing (61 percent)
- Torturing the victim (56 percent)
- Sexual assault (52 percent)

The following behaviors occurred consistently (at least 80 percent of the cases):

- Having a weapon at the scene (93 percent)
- Destroying evidence (93 percent)
- Bringing a crime kit to the scene (89 percent)
- Vaginal sex (88 percent)
- Theft (88 percent)
- Moving the body (87 percent)
- Torturing the victim (86 percent)
- Having sex after killing (84 percent)
- Hiding the body (84 percent)
- Oral sex by victim (85 percent)
- Using a ligature to kill the victim (84 percent)
- Restraining the victim (83 percent)
- Using a knife (82 percent)

The fact that so many of these behaviors occurred speaks against the notion that individual killers leave unique signatures. Individual offenders often showed consistency in general style, such as body disposal, mutilation, or weapons use, but the specific method of disposal, mutilation, and so on showed considerable variation. In other words, no individual profile emerged in most of the cases examined, and attempts to link a specific murder style to a specific serial killer were not fruitful.

The idea of unique signatures probably evolves because typically one serial killing case is occupying police in a given place at a given time. Thus, over a one-year period, there may be similar-age victims, all raped prior to killing, all left nude, and all stabbed with a knife. Such consistency points to signatures, but all these behaviors can be expected to occur with some consistency over several perpetrators. Thus, if both serial killers and other murderers are active in a given place simultaneously, the similarity of murders committed by the killers may suggest that one killer is involved.

Analysis of individual cases shows little evidence for a consistent profile. An individual offender might show general consistency in behaviors like body disposal, mutilation, or weapon use, but the specific method of disposal or mutilation, or the specific weapon, might show considerable variation. Serial killers adapt to different situations in killing their victims. Different killings may also reflect different moods of the killer, a need for novelty, or a slightly different motivation for killing one victim rather than another. Thus, analysis of individual behaviors to link homicide with a single murderer has not been supported by research published to date.

Do Serial Killers Have a Common Personality Type?

In our post–September 11 world, people worldwide have become more aware of terrorist threats and ways to prevent them. One prevention method used by law enforcement agencies in many countries is *profiling,* especially with respect to appearance and behavior. The question here is quite simple: In a particular place, such as an airport, can we observe the overt behavior of an individual who has specific physical features and decide that this person poses a risk? In the previous section, we noted limitations in trying to profile the serial killer's behavior by concentrating on unique crime signatures. Does the same difficulty occur if we use personality and background profiling to identifying serial killers?

Do serial killers show common *personality* dynamics? Are they all insecure introverts? Are they characteristically hostile or charming? Do they show similar *backgrounds?* Are there similar family, economic, and social-status factors common to serial killers? These questions involve performing critical analyses of these murderers from multiple points of view. Researchers look at childhood experiences, emerging behavior patterns during childhood and adolescence, and adult characteristics that can lead to these killers' destructive behavior.

It is important to remember that researchers look for links and relationships between things like childhood experiences and later adult behavior. The problem, of course, is that many adults who are not serial killers may also show some of those factors in their own backgrounds. By the same token, someone walking through an airport may show all the behavioral and physical signs of being a potential terrorist but may be a law-abiding citizen who has no intention of engaging such behavior. When we do profiling, we must always be aware of potential errors (false positives) in our analyses.

Schlesinger (2000) lists four types of serial killers based on who they kill and their motivation for doing so:

- The *visionary* is a psychotic who operates in a world of delusional thinking. The killer may believe, for instance, that he is called by God to rid the world of evil people.
- The *mission-oriented* killer is driven to kill only certain types of people, such as prostitutes or young single women.

- The *hedonistic* killer murders for the thrill of it or for sexual gratification.
- The *power control* killer needs to demonstrate his control over the victim. Killing is an act of exerting power and control, which brings this killer gratification.

Even though serial killers may fit into different categories with respect to victim characteristics and personal motivation, there are also numerous similarities that emerge across different killers.

- They tend to come from dysfunctional families where they were neglected and abused.
- Their fathers are typically absent or controlling and their mothers are usually rejecting, punishing, smothering, seductive, and/or controlling.
- Many are illegitimate or adopted and some are sons of prostitutes.
- They often abuse alcohol or drugs.
- As children and adolescents, they often develop a pattern of killing animals, especially cats.
- They show an extremely strong sex drive, and victim sexual degradation and humiliation are often a part of the killing ritual. They may have strongly violent sexual fantasies.
- They are typically preoccupied with death, blood, and violence.
- They show little guilt over their actions.
- They seldom kill their wives or children.

Knight (2006) notes that a major personality theme in nearly all serial killers is *narcissism*. Narcissists show extreme personality characteristics:

- They feel entitled to whatever they may want.
- They are very possessive, jealous, envious, and need others to admire them.
- On the outside they can act very arrogant, but inside they are insecure and fragile.
- They try to cope with reality by controlling and manipulating others, who are mere objects to them, like chess pieces, which they use to bolster their fragile sense of self.
- They feel empty, helpless, and vulnerable.

Arrigo and Griffin (2004) place great importance on the quality of parent-child relationships, particularly involving the mother, in the development of a serial killer. The narcissistic serial killer does not receive sufficient attention and love from his parents and develops feelings of inadequacy, shame, low self-esteem, and pathological narcissism. According to this model, the roots of serial killing develop in early childhood. Murderous actions are designed to compensate for inner insecurities and fears of rejection, being alone, and lack of control. When those tendencies combine with fantasies, a preoccupation with violence and death, and a huge sexual drive, the risk of serial killing increases significantly.

Infants and children attach to their caretakers in order to survive. Even if a parent-child relationship is dysfunctional, it is better than no relationship at all. Thus, infants will sacrifice their own needs and even attach to "bad" parents. The sole basis of the attachment becomes filled with anxiety because the infant fears being rejected by the bad parent. Thus, these infants grow up fearing relationships with other people, have difficulty relating to others, and become socially isolated. These tendencies are extreme in serial killers. Other people must be exploited to satisfy the killer's narcissistic needs and temporarily boost his self-esteem, thus compensating for feelings of shame and inadequacy. In a sense, the serial killer has a lot of self-hatred, and that hatred is displaced onto the victims.

Childhood abuse and rejection contribute to the evolution of a serial killer. Many experienced physical, sexual, and/or psychological abuse as children. These abuses produce feelings of powerlessness and lack of control. Killing gives them an illusion of having some control and impact on the world. When sex is involved in the serial murders, the act is not sexual per se but combines sex with power and revenge motives. Some psychologists say the serial killers are attacking the people who are responsible for their original pain and suffering. In effect, every stab in the flesh of a victim represents rage against the terror and pain experienced in childhood. Therefore some serial killers may symbolically be killing one or both of their hated parents. According to this theory, they choose victims who represent everything the killer hates about himself and his childhood.

Schlesinger (2000) believes that humiliation and shame play a large role in the personality of many serial murderers and says the origin of this shame is often the result of some sexual conflict with the mother. The backgrounds of many serial killers show a mother who was promiscuous, seductive, incestuous, and/or abusive. As a result, the killer is preoccupied with maternal sexual conduct and morality, which makes him feel ashamed of the mother. The killer then transforms this shame into rage and kills to erase painful memories from childhood. Naturally, the killing does not erase the memories, and the result is more killing. Many killing sprees are spurred by rejection from a woman. This rejection only intensifies the feelings of shame about the mother but also helps transform feelings of inadequacy and insecurity into rage directed at women.

Many serial killers show a history of torturing and/or killing animals. Psychologists feel that the killer learns quickly that these relatively helpless creatures are perfect victims that allow the killer to feel a sense of power and control. Animals give the developing serial killer an opportunity to displace aggression and feel a sense of power and control he cannot easily find in other areas of life. These killings help hide strong feelings of rejection, inadequacy, and powerlessness.

A combination of lack of love, severe physical/sexual/psychological abuse, and predisposing personality traits all help create a lethal combination that, given certain triggering events, can erupt into killing. In the case of the serial killer, the killing becomes pleasurable and difficult to stop. Unfortunately the innocent become victims because, in the mind of the killer, they symbolically represent early tormentors of rejection and abuse.

In conclusion, the backgrounds of serial killers show similarities in development of a personality pattern involving pathological narcissism. Remember, however, that although these backgrounds and traits can be warning signs of a potential adult serial killer, most individuals who grow up unloved and rejected in childhood do not become serial killers. By the same token, when a 10-year-old tortures or kills animals, those actions may signal that all is not well, but they do not guarantee the boy will be an adult serial killer. When we see warning signs and say, "There goes a future serial killer," there is the possibility of a *false positive*, which refers to a prediction that does not take place. The possibility of false positives must make us cautious in predicting someone's future behavior.

Are Serial Killers Different from Mass Murderers?

It has been 11 years since the Columbine High School mass killings in the United States, and three years since the Virginia Tech University massacre. Instances of mass murder in the United States increased noticeably during the first four months of 2009. From New York to North Carolina to Alabama and others, the number of victims killed by individuals on a shooting rampage has been high. Because these acts of violence appear to occur randomly, they tend to send shockwaves through the communities where they occur, as do serial killings. Anyone may be either a potential attacker or victim, thus generating a great deal of fear.

Tragic events like serial killings and mass murders cause us to look deeply into the dynamics of the killers' minds. When we do so, a fundamental question arises: Are the psychological dynamics of the serial killer and the mass murderer the same, or are there fundamental differences in "the psychology" of these two types of killers? There are those who argue that a murderer is a murderer, and that whether serial or mass, the killer is a sociopath (also called psychopath), and there are no significant differences between serial and mass murderers. Others, however, say there are definite differences in the two types of killers, and recognizing these differences is essential to any attempt at profiling them.

Criminologist Eric Hickey (1997) notes some clear differences in cases of mass murderers and serial killers:

- Mass murderers are usually either caught or commit suicide soon after the act. Serial killers may elude the authorities for years.
- Community reaction to a mass murder is focused, and the killer is typically seen as a deranged person who suddenly "exploded." Serial killings persist over a longer period of time and thus generate more public fear. The serial killer is seen as more tricky and clever than deranged.
- The serial killer individualizes his victims, whereas the mass murderer kills large groups of people at once.

- Mass murderers seldom commit a second mass murder. Conversely, serial killers rarely commit mass murder.
- The serial killer is usually in close proximity to victims, literally on top of them and attacking at close range with a knife, hammer, or choking device. Mass murderers maintain a distance from their victims and resort to efficient automatic weapons and even explosives that increase the body count.

Given these overt differences between serial and mass killings, do we find similar differences between the personalities and backgrounds of these killers? Do different psychological pictures emerge?

As noted earlier, serial murderers are usually men who suffer from extreme narcissism, sexual sadism, and/or antisocial personality disorder (sociopaths/psychopaths). Generally they are not psychotic. That is, they know who they are, where they are, what year it is, and so on. However, they have typically had traumatic sexual experiences while very young and have violent sexual fantasies as adults, probably as a result of these early traumas.

Serial killers show no remorse for their acts and do not have much of a value system. They generally use a weapon like a knife, hammer, or choking device to kill their victims. Prior to the murder, they usually show some warning signs in their behavior:

- Breaking and entering, but not to steal
- Engaging in unprovoked attacks and general mistreatment of women
- Expressing hatred, contempt and sometimes fear of women
- Showing a fetish for female undergarments
- Committing violence against animals (especially cats)
- Showing confusion over sexual identity
- Showing sexual inhibitions and preoccupation with rigid standards of morality

Mass murderers, also generally men, show a different personality and behavior profile.

- They are usually socially isolated and have very poor social skills.
- They are typically uncomfortable in social situations, tending to have few friends and a weak family support system.
- They are typically very angry men whose hostility has built up over a long period of time. Thus, they are carrying around a huge amount of rage.
- They show paranoid thoughts that have been with them for some time. These thoughts that "others are out to get me" strengthen their rage and make them ticking time bombs.

The mass murder takes place when some event tips the scale and the pent-up rage can no longer be held in check. Such events might be losing a job, being rejected by a wife or girlfriend, or being criticized one too many times by others. On April 4, 2009, James

Harrison of Graham, Washington, killed his five children and then himself after discovering that his wife was leaving him for another man. The case of Jiverly Wong, who killed 13 people and then himself in a rampage in Binghamton, New York, on April 3, 2009, shows how paranoid thoughts can contribute to the act. Prior to carrying out his murders, Wong wrote in a suicide note that the police were watching him and had even entered his house and touched him while he slept in his own bed.

There are important differences between serial killers and mass murderers in both the causes of their behavior and their actions prior to killing. What they do have in common, however, is a poorly developed social conscience, the ability to kill without remorse, and displacing their internal rage onto strangers and innocent victims. Both types of killers are also basically predators who plan their heinous acts in a purposeful fashion.

Can We Prevent Serial Killings and Mass Murders?

Both serial killers and mass murderers plan their actions before carrying them out. Both show definite signs of emotional distress in social interactions. The opportunity for profiling and preventing their actions seems to be present. We must recognize, however, that it is impossible to understand and predict individual human behavior in all situations.

- Genetic and biological factors (e.g., brain damage or mental illness) can be a major causes of serial killing and mass murder, and these factors are not fully understood or under our direct control.
- We have little influence over how parents establish the emotional atmosphere in the home and how they treat their children on an hour-by-hour, day-by-day basis. Children and young adults can develop disruptive, violent, and sociopathic patterns of behavior long before they come to our attention.
- We cannot prevent the domestic or job events that can push the mass murderer into action.

In spite of these problems, law enforcement officials and mental health workers can be vigilant to many warning signs, "markers," in individuals at risk for becoming killers. These markers include but are not limited to the following:

- An abnormal mother-child bond
- An absent and/or abusive father
- Receiving physical and/or sexual abuse from a parent or family member
- Torturing and/or killing cats, dogs, and other animals
- Difficulties relating to peers and general antisocial behavior during adolescence
- Violent sexual fantasies involving specific others (usually women)
- Sexual identity confusion

- Sociopathic/psychopathic patterns showing lack of guilt or remorse over actions
- Paranoid thinking that "someone is out to get me"
- Domestic problems and/or getting fired from work
- Increasing social isolation

On September 25, 1982, in Wilkes-Barre, Pennsylvania, George Banks went on a killing rampage. He murdered 13, including five of his own children and the four women who bore them. Banks was caught, tried, convicted of 12 counts of first-degree murder, and remains in jail. Just days before his killing spree, Banks was evaluated at a local counseling center. He showed clear symptoms of paranoid schizophrenia but was not hospitalized. This is the type of case that could be preventable.

One reason for studying both serial killers and mass murderers is to be able to identify them in advance—to be able to predict their behavior before it occurs. In a perfect world we would have reliable "markers" that would warn us about a person, and we could take steps to prevent the killing from occurring. Specifying these "markers" would be a part of a standard profiling protocol. Unfortunately, to profile and predict who will kill before they do so is an extremely difficult undertaking.

See also **Death Penalty; Insanity Defense; School Violence**

Further Reading

Arrigo, B. A., and A. Griffin, "Serial Murder and the Case of Aileen Wuornos: Attachment Theory, Psychopathy, and Predatory Aggression." *Behavioral Sciences and the Law,* 22 (2004): 375–393.

Bateman, A. L., and C. G. Salfati, "An Examination of Behavioral Consistency Using Individual Behaviors or Groups of Behaviors in Serial Homicide." *Behavioral Sciences and the Law.* 25 (2007): 527–544.

Douglas, J. E, and C. Munn, "Violent Crime Scene Analysis: Modus Operandi, Signature, and Staging." *FBI Law Enforcement Bulletin.* February (1992a): 1–10.

Douglas, J. E., and C. Munn, "Modus Operandi and the Signature Aspects of Violent Crime." In *Crime Classification Manual,* ed. J. Douglas et al. New York: Lexington Books, 1992b.

Hickey, E. R., *Serial Murderers and Their Victims.* New York: Wadsworth, 1997.

Knight, Z., "Some Thoughts on the Psychological Roots of the Behavior of Serial Killers as Narcissists: An Object Relations Perspective." *Social Behavior and Personality* 10 (2006): 1189–1206.

Knight, Z., "Sexually Motivated Serial Killers and the Psychology of Aggression and 'Evil' within a Contemporary Psychoanalytical Perspective." *Journal of Sexual Aggression* 13 (2007): 21–35.

Nichols, D. S., "Tell Me a Story: MMPI Responses and Personal Biography in the Case of a Serial Killer. *Journal of Personality Assessment 86* (2006): 242–262.

Ramsland, K., *Inside the Minds of Mass Murderers.* Westport, CT: Praeger, 2005.

Ramsland, K., *Inside the Minds of Serial Killers.* Westport CT: Praeger, 2006.

Schlesinger, L. B., *Serial Offenders: Current Thought, Recent Findings.* Boca Raton, FL: CRC Press, 2000.

SEX-OFFENDER REGISTRIES

Jim Thomas and Will Mingus

Since 1996, federal, state, county, and municipal legislation has required convicted sex offenders to register with law enforcement agencies and has imposed escalating restrictions on the lives of the offenders. These expanding restrictions and the growing number of registered sex offenders, nearly 705,000 in the United States as of December 2009, have led some observers to examine the unanticipated consequences of registries as harmful to ex-offenders, their families, and their communities. Recognizing the unanticipated outcomes of registries is only one of the four more prominent controversies revolving around sexual offender registries. The other three controversies pertain to issues of: defining the term *sex offender*, coping with reentry problems, and questioning whether or not registries work or are effective in keeping children safe from predators.

For example, consider this: When 16-year-old Traci Lords became an immediate porn star in 1984 in the commercially successful X-rated video *What Gets Me Hot*, she had lied about her age to get the part. If, today, you retained a copy of her early videos or viewed it in the privacy of your home or at a party, you could be convicted of child pornography. Or this: Chicago police checked a halfway house for released felons to determine whether registered sex offenders had complied with state law to provide a valid address. A man wearing a bathrobe stood up and began screaming, "I'm a murderer! I'm a murderer!" He preferred the stigma of being a killer to that of being a sex offender (Sheehan 2006). So which would a person rather be: a murderer, or a 20-year-old college male caught watching the original Traci Lords video, which under current state laws could lead to prosecution, stigma as a pedophile, and possible lifelong registration as a sex offender?

From the scarlet letter worn by the adulteress in Hawthorne's novel to the Hitlerian pink and gold stars forced on gays and Jews in Nazi Germany, societies have traditionally identified their pariahs with public symbols of stigma. In the past two decades, the United States has witnessed a similar rise in public identification and increased stigmatization of social pariahs: sex offenders. In most cases, unlike the earlier symbols that pariahs displayed on their bodies or property, the new sign is borne digitally through online registries that are easily accessible to the public worldwide across the Internet. In other cases, offenders may wear electronic monitoring devices to allow law enforcement personnel to keep tabs on them.

Background

Sex-offender registries are relatively new. California was the first state to enact tracking legislation in 1947, and only five states required convicted sex offenders to register with local law enforcement prior to 1994. Since then, in response to several highly dramatic and media-grabbing murders of children in the early 1990s, Congress passed the Jacob

Wetterling Crimes against Children Act (Bureau of Justice Assistance 2006), providing financial incentives for states to comply with federal guidelines to establish registries at state and local levels. The act was the result of the disappearance of 11-year-old Jacob Wetterling in Minnesota, who, on returning home from a convenience store with a friend, was abducted by an armed masked man.

While they were investigating his disappearance, police discovered that nearly 300 known sex offenders were living in the counties surrounding Jacob's home (Scott and Gerbasi 2003). Although police never established a link between Jacob's abductor and any convicted sex offenders, public attention became focused on sex offenders residing nearby. This opened the legislative floodgates to a subsequent deluge of registry laws. Even though it specified minimum criteria for states to follow, the act encouraged states to enact more stringent legislation and provided the model for disclosing offender information to the public.

In the same year that the Jacob Wetterling Act was passed, another high-profile case further fueled the fears of an already angered public, triggering more legislation. Seven-year-old Megan Kanka disappeared from her New Jersey neighborhood on July 29, 1994. The door-to-door search for her eventually led police to a twice-convicted sex offender who had recently moved in across the street. There had been rumors about the offender and his two housemates, but no one was aware that all three were convicted sex offenders. The offender confessed to Megan's rape and murder and led authorities to her body.

In response, New Jersey passed Megan's Law, the first major state registration legislation. The law required public disclosure of the names, photographs, and other personal information of sex offenders. In 1996, the federal Jacob Wetterling Act was amended to incorporate Megan's Law, requiring states to inform the public of sex offenders living in neighborhoods and near schools (Levenson and Cotter 2005). Although states have individual names for their registry legislation, usually named after a child victim who inspired it, they have become known collectively as "Megan's Laws." Since 1996, all states have complied with "Megan's Law" requirements; currently there are hundreds of overlapping governmental and private registries and databases containing the names and personal information of adjudicated sex offenders (Logan 2003).

To date, the primary legal challenges include the constitutionality of releasing offenders' private information to the public; the restrictions in living accommodations; and the retroactive requirement that offenders convicted and released prior to the enactment of registry laws be required to register. In general, the U.S. Supreme Court has upheld both the constitutionality of the registries and most of the provisions.

One of the most significant challenges to registries was to the requirement that offenders who had served their time, even decades prior to the enactment of registry laws, be required to register. This requirement, it was argued, violated the Constitution's ex post facto clause, whereby a law passed after the commission of an offense may not increase the punishment after the offense has occurred. However, in 2003, the U.S.

SEX OFFENDER REGISTRATION

The U.S. Supreme Court's View

In the past 10 years, sex offender registration laws have been challenged on numerous constitutional grounds. Although lower courts have on occasion upheld the challenges, no challenge has survived appeal to the U.S. Supreme Court. Two of the most significant decisions challenged constitutional issues of the ex post facto clause, double jeopardy, and deprivation of due process.

Ex Post Facto and Double Jeopardy

Ex post facto laws change the consequences of an act after it has occurred. It is unconstitutional to impose new, harsher, punishments on an offender after the fact. Double jeopardy refers to being prosecuted or punished twice for the same crime, which is also prohibited. Many sex offenders are required to register for offenses that were committed before registration laws existed. This, critics argued, violates the Constitution's protection against ex post facto laws. In addition, because registration was not a part of the original sentence, and because registration imposes new restrictions and hardships on an offender that were not part of the original sentence, challengers claimed that they were being punished twice for the same offense. Both of these claims made their way to the Court. In *Smith v. Doe* (2003), the Court upheld Alaska legislation that required previously released offenders to register, and also ruled that disseminating personal information and photographs to the public was constitutional.

In holding that the registry is a civil procedure and thus not punitive, the Court ruled that registries could be applied retroactively without triggering the protections of the ex post facto clause, which only apply to criminal proceedings. Because the registries are civil, not criminal proceedings, they do not constitute double jeopardy, or being retried for the same crime.

Due Process

A second major challenge addressed whether registries deprived offenders of due process because there is no opportunity to defend them. The Fourteenth Amendment to the Constitution guarantees that states shall not deprive citizens of life, liberty, or property without due process of law. This led to challenges on the grounds that being required to register violates an offender's right to due process. In *Connecticut Department of Public Safety v. Doe* (2002), the U.S. Supreme Court held that an offender was not entitled to due process before being placed on a sex offender registry because the only factor that determines whether or not a person is included in the registry is that he or she was convicted of an eligible sex offense. The Court ruled that the offender received the right of due process in the original conviction.

Supreme Court upheld the retroactive provision of registries in ruling that sex-offender registries are civil rather than punitive proceedings and therefore do not violate the ex post facto clause (*Smith v. Doe* 2003).

These and other rulings provided the legal basis for registries, which have led to efforts to expand their contents. In order to centralize sex offender information, in August

2006, Congress passed the Adam Walsh Child Protection and Safety Act (U.S. Public Law 109–248 2006), which created a national centralized database of sex offenders. State and local authorities continue to pass increasingly restrictive provisions on sex offenders.

In some states, such as Illinois, sex offenders who attend an institution of higher learning are required to notify the institution of their status; failure to comply risks additional felony prosecution. Residency restrictions, which create "banishment zones" that prohibit child sex offenders from living near schools, parks, daycare centers, and other places where children might congregate, have gained popularity. In some states, this limits offenders from living within up to 2,500 feet of schools, swimming pools, playgrounds, parks, school bus stops, churches, or other locations where children might congregate (Nieto and Jung 2006).

Critics have argued that these restrictions place an unjust hardship on offenders. They also have argued that, because not all sex offenders are pedophiles, violent, or predators, the restrictions are far too broad in scope, often irrelevant, often not easily enforceable, and unjust. For example, if a school bus stop is placed within the banishment zone where an offender resides, then the offender must move out of the new zone or face felony prosecution (Miller 2006). In enacting banishment zones, an increasing number of cities are requiring offenders who already reside within the zone to move, even if they own their homes. Although these laws have been challenged in federal courts in recent years, in fall 2005 the U.S. Supreme Court declined to review a challenge from the Iowa American Civil Liberties Union (ACLU), which left the laws intact and inspired other states to pass their own residency restrictions.

Other measures designed to publicly identify sex offenders have found their way into legislative agendas in a number of states. Some, such as Illinois, have begun monitoring sex offenders' movements in the community by requiring global positioning system (GPS) monitoring systems that inform authorities if a "high-risk" offender has encroaches into a restricted area. Computer monitoring can trace and record retrievable information for real-time alerts or for later review. This can lead to revocation of parole or to further felony prosecution, even if a registered offender is unaware of the banishment zone and has inadvertently entered it.

Other legislative proposals range from placing special insignia on an offender's driver's license to special pink license plates for all sex offenders (WKYC-TV 2005). In Texas, a judge ordered signs placed in sex offenders' yards, alerting the public that sex offenders are resided there (Milloy 2001). In one Illinois county, an elaborate e-mail distribution system was established to notify neighborhoods when a sex offender moved into the area. Such legislative efforts have prompted the expansion of the scope and restrictions in states and municipalities, creating what has been described as "an arms race of circle-drawing as offenders bounce from city to city" (Howley 2006).

It would seem that sex offender registration is a positive safeguard and a reasonable response to protecting our children. Who, after all, wants to put children at risk of baby rapers, child murderers, and fiends? To the public, notification laws are a necessary and proactive response to a major social problem, so the responses seem like solutions (Presser and Gunnison 1999, 299–315).

The rationale behind registering sex offenders seems hard to dispute: if we know who offenders are, we will be safe (Sheehan 2006). Given that these laws are intended to protect the public, especially children, and given the public's animosity toward sex offenders and overwhelming support of registries, why should they be controversial?

Key Controversies

There is little disagreement that the public, especially children, should be kept safe from predators. In fact, in a 2005 Gallop poll, over two-thirds of U.S. adults expressed that they were "very concerned" about predators of children (Kelly 2005). Coupled with overwhelming public and legislative support for tougher restrictions on sex offenders returning from prison to the community and an increase in the rhetoric about the dangers of sex offenders, legislators have been eager to act. There is, however, emerging evidence that sex-offender registries and corresponding restrictions on movement, residency requirements, and public stigma may be creating new problems while doing little to enhance public safety. As a result, controversies of all kinds have developed. In particular, four emerging issues demonstrate, but hardly exhaust, the increasing complexity and unanticipated outcomes of sex-offender registries.

The first issue is that of defining a sex offender, as an increasing array of offenses are subsumed in the category. The second issue involves the outcomes: Do restrictive laws do more harm than good? The third issue raises questions about how registries pose problems for offenders attempting to reenter society. The fourth issue asks: Do registries work?

What Is a Sex Offender?

Sex offender rhetoric quickly shifts the meaning of the broad term *sex offender* to the more narrow and highly pejorative label of *child molester* or *pedophile*, as if they were synonymous. They are not. Several problems cloud the definition.

First, despite attempts by politicians to demonize offenders with bombastic rhetoric (Mingus 2006), the reality is that the category of sex offenses requiring registration includes infractions ranging from minor misdemeanors to violent predatory sexual assaults. In Illinois, typical of many states, "sex offenses" can include the commonly accepted definitions, such as forcible rape and pedophilia, but can also include other serious predatory but not sex-related acts such as carjacking if a child is a passenger, kidnapping and unlawful restraint if the carjacker is not the parent, and other crimes against a minor or an adult victim that, while felonies, are not necessarily sexual in nature. Sex offenses also include other actions that can require registration but are not normally considered violent or predatory. This can include sex with a person under age

18, consensual sex between an adult and custodial staff, "indecent exposure," voyeurism if the "victim" is under 18, and "importuning" (indecent solicitation) of a person of any age. We need not condone any of these behaviors to raise the question of whether they all ought to be combined under the single label of *sex offense*.

A second problem arises in defining the term *child offender*. In some states, conviction of any crime against a child, such as child abuse, can result in the requirement to register as a sex offender. No crime against children is acceptable, but words have meanings, and without an explicit sexually predatory component to an offense, we risk casting the net far too wide and catching offenders convicted of fairly minor crimes who then must bear the burden of a spoiled identity.

A third problem with the sex offender label is that the public assumes that *sex offender* is the same as *pedophile*. This is erroneous for two reasons.

First, very few sex offenders are pedophiles, a clinical diagnosis applied to individuals who are sexually attracted to, or engage in sex with, prepubescent children, generally aged 13 years or younger ("Pedophilia" 2005). In reality, however, the overwhelming majority of victims of a sex crime are between 13 and 35, and it is family members or acquaintances who fall within a five-year age range of the victim who usually victimize juvenile victims between ages 13 and 17.

Two, by law, the term *child* broadly refers to a minor, which is any youth under age 18. Thus, a victim aged 2 and one aged 17 years and 11 months are each categorized as "children." This encompassing label also ignores the changing conceptions of childhood over the decades in which the age of consent for marriage or consensual sexual relations has increased from the early teens to the now standard age of 17 or 18 in most states.

Because age 18 is a largely arbitrary social construct reflecting contemporary social norms rather than any inherent biological or other objective standard, some critics of registries argue that they are not so much a reflection of the dangerousness of offenders but of the imposition of subtle patriarchal and gender-based conceptions, especially of young women as "childlike" and in need of protection. Few people would defend behaviors that prey on powerless victims. However, the historical context of the changing conception of childhood suggests that sex-offender registries, in many cases, go too far in criminalizing what, even two decades ago, might not have been an offense. Thus, requiring registration of offenders who committed an offense in 1980 that was not then covered under current laws strikes some critics as unjust.

A fourth problem with defining a sex offender centers on the legal protections of due process: Is a sex offender a person who has been convicted in a court of law, or can criminal proceedings be bypassed to label a person as a sex offender and require registration with subsequent restrictions? State legislators in Ohio have begun a process that would allow alleged sex offenders to be publicly identified and tracked even if they were never charged with a crime ("Sex Offenders" 2006). The proposal would allow prosecutors or alleged victims to petition a judge to have a person civilly declared a sex offender. The "offender's" name, picture, address, and other information would be placed in public files and on the Internet and subject to the same registration requirements and restrictions as a convicted offender. Although the "offender" could petition to have the name removed, once made public on the Internet, the information becomes a de facto permanent record in private archives and cached files.

Unanticipated Outcomes

The public generally feels that sex offenders "deserve what they have coming" after release. If registries harm offenders, these perpetrators should have thought of that before committing the crime. However, the consequences of registries affect others as well, including some groups that are rarely considered. Here are just a few from a substantial list.

Costs

The increasing number of registered offenders, conservatively estimated to be growing by at least 10 percent per year, adds to the burden of law enforcement agencies that, in most jurisdictions, already operate with strained budgets. Preliminary interviews that we (the present authors) conducted with law enforcement personnel suggest that larger jurisdictions may be facing staff and resource problems in processing offenders, keeping databases up to date, coordinating databases with other agencies, meeting public demand for access to registration information, and maintaining the digital infrastructure required for electronic storage and Internet access. Smaller agencies, lacking specialized personnel to process data, divert the labor of patrol officers and other staff for processing and assuring registry compliance. In jurisdictions that record 10 or fewer registrations a week, this may not be a significant hardship. Nonetheless, according to one law enforcement interviewee, it dramatically diverts staff time away from other more urgent tasks.

Although there are no reliable data for the costs of maintaining registries and some of the costs are absorbed as part of other routine clerical or patrol tasks, there appears to be a growing consensus that as the mission creep of registries expands and the list of offenders grows, law enforcement will need to comply with legislation to process offenders, enforce compliance and other registry provisions, and maintain databases.

The implementation of GPS monitoring adds another direct cost to monitoring, costing up to $10 a day, and tracking a single offender can cost up to $3,650 per year for the technology alone. As of 2006, a total of 13 states had GPS monitoring in place, six more had GPS legislation pending, and other states were considering implementation (Koch 2006).

Property Values

One irony of the registries is that while they may give the perception of increased physical security, they can have a negative economic impact on a neighborhood. Our initial interviews with realtors in a medium-sized city suggested that the presence of sex offenders living in a neighborhood could be a "deal breaker." Some studies have found that an offender living within a tenth of a mile of an offender's home can lower property values by an average of 10 to 17.4 percent (Larsen, Lowrey, and Coleman 2003; Leigh and Rockoff 2006).

Adoption

Another unanticipated consequence of registries can occur when someone is attempting to adopt a child. A few high-profile cases in which sex offenders adopted and then abused a child have led to closer scrutiny of adopters. Some adoption agencies now include routine checks for sex offending neighbors during background checks, which can complicate or prevent adoption. For example, one of our interviewees in Minnesota began adoption proceedings, but a sex offender moved into the neighborhood. The adoption agency had searched the database for sex offenders, and this then became a potential obstacle in the adoption.

Reentry

Reentry into society is one of the major hurdles that offenders face on release from prison. Sex offenders must overcome additional burdens because of the consequences of registries and the ease of public access to them. For offenders with families, repairing the emotional breaches with partners and children triggers additional family stresses from trying to explain the offense to children, regaining their respect, providing discipline and control in light of the offender's own background, and coping with the withdrawal of neighbors' families and children's school peers. In addition, because of travel restrictions and limits on associations, registered offenders are commonly unable to participate in school or church functions with their families or to engage in other routine domestic activities outside the home.

Another reentry problem lies in the residency requirements. If, on release, an offender's original residence was located within a banishment zone, the offender must move. In some cities, the banishment zones exclude up to 95 percent of available housing.

Mental health issues add special obstacles. For most sex offenders, postrelease counseling is generally a condition of release back into the community. Residency restrictions can make access to counseling services difficult, especially in locations lacking viable mass transit. Other mental health issues include the loss of self-esteem and increased insecurity resulting from the stigma and ubiquitous visibility of their spoiled identity and to constant fears of being "outed" in situations where their identity is not yet known. Because the laws affecting them constantly change, and because registration ranges from 10 years to life, there is the continual uncertainty of not knowing what new requirements or restrictions will disrupt the stability of a normal life. This makes day-to-day living tenuous and long-term planning difficult.

Do Registries Work?

To date, there have been no studies to support the claim that sex-offender registries reduce recidivism or make a community safer. Registration and notification laws have gained a tremendous level of public support, largely due to the perception that the vast majority of sex offenders will repeat their crimes (Levenson and Cotter 2005). The expectation is that these laws will protect society by curbing recidivism and making community members aware of the presence of sex offenders, thus allowing them to monitor or avoid offenders.

The belief that sex offenders have a high probability of repeating their crimes has fueled much of the hysteria surrounding registration and notification. Such perceptions are often formed on the basis of high-profile cases in which a previously convicted sex offender goes on to commit another atrocious offense. However, research has found that sexual offense recidivism rates are far lower than the public perception (Levenson and Cotter 2005). Despite claims by registry proponents that 95 percent of sex offenders will repeat their crimes, the Bureau of Justice Statistics (2003) showed the recidivism rate for sex offenders to be closer to 5 percent (Langan, Schmitt, and Durose 2003). Media and politicians highlighting the dramatic but infrequent cases have largely created the view that sex offenders are all high-risk individuals (Kelly 2005).

In short, sex-offender registries, rather than protecting society, could actually push an offender closer toward recidivism, because they hamper reentry into society and exacerbate the very issues that may have led to the original sex offense (Tewksbury 2005). Some have asked this question, for example, in the case of Phillip Garrido, who was discovered to be holding, in his California home, a woman (Jaycee Dugard) he had kidnapped as a child years before and with whom he had fathered two children despite being a registered sex offender (Cunningham 2009).

There are other concerns with the registries. For example, sex offenders can become victims of vigilante justice; persons on the registries may be there by mistake; there is a growing problem of offender compliance with registries as laws become more restrictive, thus penalizing law-abiding registrants while nonregistrants disappear; and registered names can remain indefinitely on the Internet even after being removed from official lists.

Conclusion

Some states are starting to recognize that sex-offender registries are flawed and result in costly unintended consequences. However, the current trend is for increased restrictions on offenders, harsher laws for noncompliance in registration, and expansion of the definition of a sex offense to assure that no potential predators slip through the cracks.

The escalation of registries and restrictions are fed in part by an ideology of "tough on crime," by fear, and by ignorance. There are no simple answers to complex problems,

TRUE OR FALSE?

1. Most sex offenses are committed by strangers.

False. Studies simply do not support this. Federal data show that 83.9 percent of the abuse or neglect of children was committed by a parent rather than by a stranger (SOHopeful 2005). FBI Uniform Crime Reports in 2004 found that over 80 percent of all sexual offenses are committed by someone known to the victim.

2. Most sex offenders will reoffend.

False. The Bureau of Justice Statistics did a long-term study in 2003 examining the recidivism of sex offenders released from prison in 1994. The study showed that only 5.3 percent of convicted sex offenders were reconvicted of a sex offense within three years of their release according to U.S. Bureau of Justice Statistics in 2003.

3. All sex offenders are pedophiles.

False. The psychiatric profession defines a pedophile as someone whose primary attraction is toward prepubescent children. The word pedophile is often used interchangeably with the term sex offender. Yet relatively few sex offenders are actually pedophiles. Determining the exact number is difficult, because diagnosing an individual as a pedophile would require a psychological evaluation, and few sex offenders actually undergo such an evaluation.

4. Sex-offender registries will make our communities safer.

False. There is little evidence that communities are safer as a result of sex-offender registries. In fact, experts have suggested that registries tend to give communities a false sense of security, causing residents to become less vigilant if they check the registry and find no sex offenders living near them. Summary data from FBI Uniform Crime Reports in 2004 indicate that infants and young children who are victims "are usually dependents living in the household" and not neighbors or strangers on the street. In addition, sex-offender registries can exacerbate the very issues (such as isolation, rejection, ostracism) in an offender that caused him to offend in the first place, thus increasing the chances of reoffending. The Jacob Wetterling Foundation Web site states that "sex offenders are less likely to reoffend if they live and work in an environment free of harassment, so it is very important that an offender be allowed to live peacefully." Some experts believe that sex-offender registration and notification make it nearly impossible for an offender to live peacefully in a community.

5. Killing or attempting to kill a teenager in a drive-by shooting or a fight could lead to charges as a sex offender.

True. In some states, such as Illinois, sex offenses are vaguely worded and first-degree murder of a "child" under 18 or any attempt to do so could constitute a sex offense requiring registry.

6. Adults commit most sexual offenses.

True. According to the FBI Uniform Crime Reports (2004, 332), juveniles account for about 16 percent of forcible rapes and 22 percent of sexual offenses. Adults over 25 account for about 64 percent of both forcible rapes and sexual offenses.

and policy makers are generally reluctant to appear soft on crime, especially when the welfare of children appears to be at risk.

If legislators were to approach the problem of sex offenses rationally with data-driven judgments rather than demagoguery, then a few modest proposals would be in order:

1. There should be reexamination of whether registries are needed. If, on balance, they are ineffective in solving the problems, and instead create new ones, then they should be discarded.
2. The political rhetoric underlying public discussions of sex offenders and registries should have accurately data-based descriptions of the nature of the problem, avoid the myths surrounding sex offenders, and take into account the impact of hyperbole in obscuring solutions.
3. Media should present to the public a more accurate and less inflammatory characterization of the nature of crime in general and sex offenders in particular.
4. If registries remain a requirement for sex offenders after release, then the criteria for registration should be refined. At a minimum, criteria should include recognition that not all sex offenders are pedophiles, predators, or violent; that the range of sex offenses is overly broad and nets minor offenders, including those whose offense was not sexual in nature; and that policies should distinguish between sexually dangerous persons and one-time offenders.
5. If registries make a community safer, then registries should be expanded to include high-risk offenders who pose a far greater threat to the community than sex offenders. This category would include drug users and dealers, drunk drivers, and burglars.
6. Current laws across the country are a patchwork of inconsistent requirements, definitions, and enforcement. If registries are retained, then there should be consistency such that the harsh laws of one community do not drive offenders to other communities that allow offenders more latitude.
7. Existing policies should be revised to reflect the deleterious impact of registries on families, communities, and on the offenders themselves in order to prevent creating new problems and tacit punishments borne by both nonoffenders and offenders.

8. The movement toward banishment, an ancient practice that most people in an enlightened civilization would reject, should be halted lest we create gulags for ex-offenders.

9. Policy makers should recognize that nearly all incarcerated offenders will eventually return to their communities. Reentry obstacles make adjustment and successful reintegration difficult. Rather than create problems for ex-offenders, legislators should recognize that the best way to assure public safety is to facilitate reentry and work to provide conditions that facilitate family stability, employment opportunities, and reduced costs to taxpayers resulting from all offenders' physical and mental health problems, recidivism, and long-term well-being.

Whether one supports or opposes sex-offender registries, the reality is that they raise complex issues. Those wishing to make their communities safer, protect children and adults, and promote the well-being of all community residents should recognize that this critical issue should not be driven by fear, but by a deeper understanding of the intents and outcomes of our treatment of all ex-offenders.

See also **Sexual Assault and Sexual Harassment**

Further Reading

Bureau of Justice Assistance, "Overview and History of the Jacob Wetterling Act." U.S. Department of Justice, Washington, DC. 2006. http://www.ojp.usdoj.gov/BJA/what/2a1jwacthistory.html

Cote, Suzanne, "Revisiting Megan's Law and Sex Offender Registration: Prevention or Problem?" In *Sexual Violence: Policies, Practices, and Challenges in the United States and Canada,* ed. James F. Hodgson and Debra S. Kelley. Westport, CT: Praeger, 2002.

Cunningham, Erin, "Staying Ahead of Sex Offenders: California Case Likely to Spark Legislation in 2010." *Gazette.Net* (September 18, 2009). http://www.gazette.net/stories/09182009/polinew200041_32521.shtml

Gibson, Camille, and Donna M. Vandiver, *Juvenile Sex Offenders: What the Public Needs to Know.* Westport, CT: Praeger, 2008.

Howley, Kerry, "Sending Sex Offenders into Exile." *Erogenous Zoned* (June 30, 2006). http://www.reason.com/links/links063006.shtml

Kelly, Katy, "To Protect the Innocent: Learning to Keep Sexual Predators at Bay." *U.S. News and World Report* (June 13, 2005). http://www.usnews.com/usnews/culture/articles/050613/13children.htm

Kinnear, Karen L., *Childhood Sexual Abuse: A Reference Handbook,* 2d ed. Santa Barbara, CA: ABC-CLIO, 2007.

Koch, Wendy, "More Sex Offenders Tracked by Satellite." *USA Today* (June 6, 2006). http://www.usatoday.com/tech/news/techinnovations/2006–06–06-gps-tracking_x.htm

Langan, Patrick A., Erica L. Schmitt, and Matthew R. Durose, *Recidivism of Sex Offenders Released from Prison in 1994.* Washington, DC: Bureau of Justice Statistics, 2003.

Larsen, J. E., Kenneth J. Lowrey, and J. Coleman, "The Effect of Proximity to a Registered Sex Offender's Residence on a Single-Family House Selling Price." *Appraisal Journal* (July 2003): 253–265.

Leigh, Linden, and Jonah E. Rockoff, "How Do People Respond to the Fear of Crime? Evidence from Megan's Laws and the Housing Market." Unpublished manuscript. March 2006. http://www.columbia.edu/~ll2240/megans_law_october_05.pdf

Levenson, J., and L. Cotter, "The Effects of Megan's Law on Sex Offender Reintegration." *Journal of Contemporary Criminal Justice* 21, no. 1 (2005): 49–66.

Logan, W., "Sex Offender Registration and Community Notification: Emerging Legal and Research Issues." *Annals New York Academy of Sciences* 989 (2003): 337–351.

Miller, J. Y., "Sex Offenders Told to Leave Church Areas: Lesser-Known Provision Nets Handful of Arrests." *Atlanta Journal-Constitution* (August 25, 2006).

Milloy, Ross E., "Texas Judge Orders Notices Warning of Sex Offenders." *New York Times* (May 29, 2001). http://www.nytimes.com/2001/05/29/us/texas-judge-orders-notices-warning-of-sex-offenders.html?sec=health

Mingus, Will, "The Music Man—On Salesmen and Politicians: Creating a Populism of Fear." Paper presented to the American Correctional Association, Charlotte, NC, August 12, 2006.

Nieto, Marcus, and David Jung, "The Impact of Residency Restrictions on Sex Offenders and Correctional Management Practices: A Literature Review." Sacramento, CA: California Research Bureau, 2006. http://www.ccoso.org/residencyrestrictionsimpact.pdf

"Pedophilia." *Diagnostic and Statistical Manual of Mental Disorders,* 4th ed. (DSM-4). Washington, DC: American Psychiatric Association, 2005, Sect. 302.2, 527–528.

Place, Vanessa, *The Quilt Project: Rape, Morality, Law.* New York: Other Press, 2010.

Presser, L., and E. Gunnison, "Strange Bedfellows: Is Sex Offender Notification a Form of Community Justice?" *Crime and Delinquency* 45, no. 3 (1999): 299–315.

Scott, C., and J. Gerbasi, "Sex Offender Registration and Community Notification Challenges: The Supreme Court Continues Its Trend." *Journal of American Academy of Psychiatry and the Law* 31 (2003): 494–501.

"Sex Offenders: Plan Gains to Publicly Identify Accused: Ohio Panel Backs Registry Proposal." *Toledo Blade* (August 29, 2006). http://www.toledoblade.com/apps/pbcs.dll/article?AID=/20060829/NEWS24/608290360/-1/NEWS

Sheehan, C., "Sex-Offender List Altered: State to Remove Non-Sex Crimes." *Chicago Tribune* (July 3, 2006): Metro 1.

Smith v. Doe, 538 U.S. 84 (2003).

Tewksbury, R., "Collateral Consequences of Sex Offender Registration." *Journal of Contemporary Criminal Justice* 21, no. 1 (2005): 67–81.

U.S. Public Law 109–248, 109th Congress, 27 August, 2006, Adam Walsh Child Protection and Safety Act. http://www.justice.gov/criminal/ceos/Adam%20Walsh.pdf

Winick, Bruce J., and John Q. La Fond, eds., *Protecting Society from Sexually Dangerous Offenders: Law, Justice, and Therapy.* Washington, DC: American Psychological Association, 2003.

WKYC-TV, "New Sexual Offender License Plate Bill Introduced." Cleveland, OH: WKYC Television, April 28, 2005.

Zilney, Laura J., *Perverts and Predators: The Making of Sexual Offending Laws*. Lanham, MD: Rowman & Littlefield, 2009.

Zimring, Franklin E., *An American Tragedy: Legal Responses to Adolescent Sex Offending*. Chicago: University of Chicago Press, 2004.

SEXUAL ASSAULT AND SEXUAL HARASSMENT

Kathryn Woods

The gendered nature of sexual violence is well documented in academic research, organizational and policy studies, and government documents. Viewpoints on why men are responsible for the vast majority of rapes and cases of sexual harassment, with the victims being largely women and girls, often clash in the social, political, and advocacy arenas. Battles between nature and nurture, social construction and biology, and feminism and conservatism contribute to divergent views on both the causes and the consequences of these behaviors.

Background

Whereas men are sexually assaulted by women and same-gender sexual assault does occur (for example, a man sexually assaults a man), statistics indicate that the majority of sexual violence perpetrators are men and the majority of victims are women. In fact, 90 percent of the victims of sexual assault are women and 10 percent are men, and nearly 99 percent of offenders in single-victim assaults are men (Bureau of Justice Statistics 2010). However, not all men who commit acts that meet the legal definition of sexual assault identify their behavior as such. For example, 1 in 12 male college students surveyed report engaging in acts that meet the legal definition of rape or attempted rape, but 84 percent of them report that what they did was "definitely not rape" (Warshaw 1994). The debate about the gendered nature of sexual violence exists in multiple social contexts. Some argue that it is men's nature to sexually dominate and control women. Driven by a biological need to procreate, men sexually dominate women to ensure the continuation of the species and of their own biological line. Thus, when a man is presented with a situation that imposes a barrier to reaching this goal, such as a woman who does not want to have sex, the man's biological predisposition takes the driver's seat, resulting in a disregard for the woman's wishes and leading to sexual assault. However, others argue that it is the patriarchal U.S. society and systemic oppression by men of women that explains the prevalence of men's sexual violence. In what is called a culture of violence, dominance and control are presented as positive attributes of masculinity in society. According to this argument, men's and women's socialization begins in childhood, where toughness is valued in boys and submissiveness is valued in girls. Observers and advocates point out that these messages, paired with a society where men's sexual violence is tacitly accepted, lead to rampant sexual violence with minimal consequences.

The Sexual Violence Continuum

Regardless of their ideological perspectives on sexual violence, most observers would agree that the phenomenon of sexual violence in the United States has grown into an epidemic. With statistics indicating that a rape occurs every 2.5 minutes in the United States and that one in every six women in the U.S. is a victim of rape or attempted rape (Rape, Abuse and Incest National Network 2006), sexual violence causes increasing alarm and commands increasing attention. When viewed as a systemic form of violence, sexual violence is not seen as a single act; rather, sexual violence refers to a range of behaviors commonly described as a sexual violence continuum. These behaviors include stranger rape, date/acquaintance rape, intimate partner rape, and sexual harassment as well as incest, child sexual abuse, voyeurism, and unwanted sexual touching. The concept of a sexual violence continuum is used as an explanatory model by rape crisis centers and sexual assault coalitions nationwide. Although various versions of the model use slightly different stages, they generally refer to a range of behaviors beginning with socially accepted behavior and ending with sexually violent death.

This continuum serves as a road map for exploring the many facets of sexual violence in a larger societal context.

Social Norms versus Criminalization

Although violent crimes such as stranger rape are criminalized in our society, the social norms—that is, the attitudes, behaviors, and beliefs that are considered acceptable in a society—about violence against women often contradict or undermine laws and policies. Thus, whereas institutional policies and laws may specifically denounce and sometimes criminalize a behavior, social norms may contradict this by allowing or failing to respond to certain behaviors. For example, in most states it is illegal to initiate sexual activity with someone who is asleep, as that person is unable to give consent to the activity. However, many fairy tales tell of a prince kissing a princess who is asleep as a result of a wicked spell. The kiss is the only thing that can break the spell, and it is seen as loving and romantic. In fact, many young girls wait for their "prince" to carry them off to a castle to live happily ever after. The idea, or social norm, that kissing a sleeping princess is romantic is both powerful and pervasive in U.S. culture and strongly contradicts legal definitions of nonconsensual sexual behavior. Social norms create an atmosphere in which behaviors are accepted and even socially rewarded based on responses from peers.

Imagine a situation in which a number of college-age young adults are attending a party. Most guests are drinking alcohol, there is music, and plenty of people are dancing and kissing. In this situation, there may be peer pressure for young women and men to behave in certain ways. Young men receive messages that they are supposed to "get a girl," and they receive positive peer reinforcement for initiating and maintaining intimate contact with one or more young women. In fact, the more the man encourages a woman to drink alcohol and engage in intimate behavior, the more social messages the man receives from his peers, praising him as a "stud." At the same time, the young woman receives messages that she should feel flattered by the sexual attention and that she should do as the man encourages or wants. The social norms of this situation send messages to the woman that she should not assert her own feelings or desires if it will cause a scene or embarrass the man, and the man receives messages that he should continue to push the woman, regardless of her wishes. These messages create an environment where unwanted sexual behavior can occur with little or no intervention from bystanders. This has important consequences for the way observers of rape and sexual harassment patterns assign blame and design policies and laws to address these behaviors.

Individual Belief Systems

Despite existing social norms, sexual violence can occur only when the perpetrator holds a belief system that allows him to engage in sexually intrusive behavior. These belief systems include the ideas that men have ownership or control over women, that a woman owes a man sexual behavior in exchange for some interaction (for example, "If I buy you dinner, you owe me sex"), and that men have earned or have the right to sexual activity regardless of a woman's wishes. These belief systems are reinforced by the larger societal context of systemic oppression and sexism, which sends messages about gender roles, power, and control though the media and social norms. No amount of alcohol or peer pressure can "make" a person force sexual behavior on an unwilling participant if his or her individual belief system does not already support such action to some extent. The controversy lies in people's support for or opposition to individual belief systems that view rape as consensual ("even if she says no, she means yes") and in the belief that sexual harassment is natural and simply part of a man's natural sex drive rather than an unjustifiable act of aggression toward a woman.

Rape and Sexual Assault

Although there are many legal definitions of *sexual assault* and *rape,* in general these terms refer to oral sexual contact or intercourse without consent. Whereas stranger rape is the most publicized type of rape, it is one of the least often committed. Among female victims of sexual assault, 67 percent reported they were assaulted by intimate partners, relatives, friends, or acquaintances (Catalano 2005). In addition, only 8 percent of sexual assaults involve weapons, again in contradiction to the stereotypical idea of stranger rape. This is important, because societal myths about rape and sexual assault affect offenders, victims, bystanders, and those responding to the crimes through law enforcement and social service systems. In struggling with these myths, many victims either believe that the rape was their fault or fail to identify what happened to them as rape. According to one study, only approximately 35 percent of sexual assaults were reported to the police in 2004, an increase in recent years but still a rate substantially lower than the rates for noninterpersonal crimes (Catalano 2005). Many victims choose

RAPE MYTHS AND FACTS

Myth #1: If I am careful, I will never be raped.

Fact #1: Anyone can be raped. While there are steps people can take to protect themselves, such as going out with a friend or meeting dates in a public place, it is the rapist who chooses to assault the victim. Only the rapist can prevent the crime.

Myth #2: Rape is about sexual desire.

Fact #2: Rape is about power and control. Sex becomes the weapon of humiliation, not the goal.

Myth #3: Most rapists are strangers.

Fact #3: Approximately 60 to 80 percent of rape victims know their attacker, and for women 15 to 25 years old, 70 percent of sexual assaults happen during dates (Kanel 2007).

Myth #4: Women who are drinking or wearing revealing clothes are asking to be raped.

Fact #4: No one asks to be raped, and the rapist has sole responsibility for the crime. Women should be able to wear anything they wish and drink alcohol without fear of being sexually victimized.

Myth #5: Once men get turned on, they can't stop.

Fact #5: Could he stop if his mother walked in? (Kanel 2007, 233). There is no "point of no return." Both men and women can choose to stop sexual behavior at any point, even if the result may be discomfort or embarrassment.

Adapted from Kristi Kanel, *A Guide to Crisis Intervention*, 3d ed. (Pacific Grove, CA: Brooks/ Cole, 2007).

not to report because of shame, fear, guilt, or concern about others' perceptions. The responses of varying social systems, and in particular of law enforcement, can reinforce these feelings if the victim feels blamed by first responders. On one hand, the judicial system is set up to address charges of rape, based on the societal view that rape is wrong. In practice, however, many people find it difficult to address the issue, and there is often great silence and shame experienced by victims as well as perpetrators, families, law enforcement officials, and other people involved in the process.

Sexual Harassment

Sexual harassment is even more difficult than rape to define and document legally; observers disagree as to when an act actually constitutes harassment. According to law, sexual harassment is an illegal form of sex discrimination that violates two federal

laws: Title VII of the Civil Rights Act of 1964 and Title IX of the Education Amendments of 1972. Both laws address sexism and gender discrimination; the Civil Rights
Act focuses on nondiscrimination in the workplace, while the Education Amendments focus on nondiscrimination in educational settings. As defined by the U.S.
Equal Opportunity Commission (2002), "unwelcome sexual advances, requests for
sexual favors, or other verbal or physical conduct of a sexual nature constitute sexual
harassment when submission to or rejection of this conduct explicitly or implicitly
affects an individual's employment, unreasonably interferes with an individual's work
performance or creates an intimidating, hostile or offensive work environment" (U.S.
Equal Employment Opportunity Commission 2002, 1). In an educational environment, this sexual harassment can "threaten a student's physical or emotional well-
being, influence how well a student does in school, and make it difficult for a student to
achieve his or her career goals" (U.S. Department of Education 2005, 1). There are two
types of sexual harassment as defined by law: quid pro quo and hostile environment.

Quid pro quo, which means "something for something," is a type of sexual harassment that occurs when "an employee [or student] is required to choose between submit-
ting to sexual advances or losing a tangible job [or educational] benefit" (Rubin 1995, 2).
Examples may include a boss harassing an employee, a teacher harassing a student, or
a coach harassing an athlete. In quid pro quo sexual harassment there must be a power
differential between the target and the harasser. The harasser must be able to exercise
control over the threatened job or educational benefit. Sexual harassment occurs regardless of whether the target chooses to accept the sexual behavior as long as the conduct
is unwelcome.

Hostile environment harassment is "unwelcome conduct that is so severe or pervasive
as to change the conditions of the claimant's employment [or education] and create an
intimidating, hostile, or offensive work environment" (Rubin 1995). Hostile environment harassment can include gender- or sexual orientation–based jokes or comments,
calling people by derogatory gender-related names (for example, "slut"), threats, touching of a sexual nature, offensive e-mail or Web site messages, talking about one's sexual
behaviors in front of others, spreading rumors about coworkers' or other students' sexual
performance, and negative graffiti (for example, in a bathroom stall).

In general, the standard for sexual harassment is what a "reasonable person" would
find offensive. However, a decision by a 1991 circuit court allowed for a "reasonable
woman" standard, allowing for differences in perception of offensiveness across gender
lines (Rubin 1995). Some argue that jokes, comments, and sexual innuendos are actually
compliments to women and are men's natural way of bringing their biological drive for
sexual behavior to the forefront. However, men and women often report different perspectives on whether behavior is flattering or offensive.

Additional issues related to the legal criminalization of sexual harassment and rape
concern encroachment on a person's sense of sexual safety and invasion of a person's

NORTH COUNTRY

North Country, a Hollywood film starring Academy Award winner Charlize Theron, is based on the nonfiction bestseller *Class Action*. The film and book are based on the true story of Lois Jensen, one of the first women hired to work in a northern Michigan mine in 1975. As one of a handful of female miners in the company, Jensen was subjected to repeated incidents of harassment, including derogatory language, pornographic graffiti, stalking, and physical assaults. In 1984, she decided to file a complaint against the company. Although at first other female miners were afraid to become plaintiffs in the case, eventually many of them joined Jensen. With a strong team of lawyers, they won their case in court, making this the first successful sexual harassment class action lawsuit in the United States.

space. This type of behavior may include a physical intrusion, such as "accidentally" brushing against someone in a sexual manner, but often does not involve actual touch. Sexual jokes, catcalls and whistles, leering at a sexual body part, and making sexual comments are all invasions of sexual space. Some argue that such behavior by men is actually complimentary to women, and frequently those who speak up by identifying such behavior as degrading and disrespectful are labeled as vindictive feminists, jealous, or too serious. Comments such as "Lighten up, it's a just a joke" reflect this view. Sexual assault activists argue that this type of commentary sends a message condoning harassment and also contributes to silencing bystanders who seek to intervene. According to some activists, unwanted sexual touch is the first point on the sexual violence continuum. This is a point at which gender role messages conflict with sexual safety. In most social settings, men receive positive messages with regard to engaging in such behavior in a public setting, and women are often acutely aware of the message that it is not acceptable to embarrass a man. Often, if a woman rebuffs the initial stages of sexual touching, this results in both the woman and the man being viewed negatively in a social context.

Sexual Assault Prevention: Responses to Violence against Women

Traditional sexual assault prevention programs focus on risk reduction strategies for women and girls, teaching them how to avoid situations in which sexual assault is likely to occur based on knowledge of risk factors. However, some argue that risk reduction programs inherently carry a biased view, namely that victims can prevent sexual assault if they simply learn to behave in the "right way." Therefore more recent strategies involve addressing men's socialization processes as well. Literature on engaging men in rape prevention activities focuses clearly on how essential it is to appeal to men as bystanders, not as perpetrators or potential perpetrators (Katz 2001). In order for bystanders to intervene, they must understand the dynamics and risks of sexual violence, have empathy for the devastating impact of sexual violence on victims, and have the skills and confidence to intervene. In social situations, many young people report feeling uncomfortable when they notice a woman who is the target of sexual attention that appears to be unwanted, but they also report feeling embarrassed at the reaction of their peers if they intervene (Warshaw 1994). Men's love and care for the women in their lives can be a powerful tool in building empathy. And it is men who are "embedded in peer culture" with other men and who are in the most influential position to intervene (Katz 2001, 7). Additionally, activists point out that we cannot challenge the systemic oppression of patriarchy, men's entitlement and privilege, and violence as acceptable without engaging men. According to Katz, "as empowered bystanders, men can interrupt attitudes in other men that may lead to violence. They can respond to incidents of violence or harassment before, during or after the fact. They can model healthy relationships and peaceful conflict resolution" (Katz 2001, 7). Teaching men to intervene at the earlier stages of the sexual violence continuum, especially at the social norms and individual belief systems stages, will result in preventing sexual assaults from occurring.

Conclusion

Viewed through the lens of the sexual violence continuum, it can be seen that there is a clear connection between sexism, social norms that condone violence and the transgression of sexual boundaries, gender role socialization messages to men and women, and sexual harassment, abuse, and assault. According to this model, intervention at the initial stages will prevent the later stages (sexual violence). Ultimately, though, sexual assault activists argue that sexual violence will end only when it becomes completely intolerable in society. Owing to long-held beliefs in men's innate sex drive and women's innate desire to be protected, conquered, or gazed upon, debates on how to address rape and sexual harassment will surely continue. Whereas some observers believe that the federal government should support sexual assault initiatives, others believe that only state or local governments or the private sector should be held responsible for addressing these behaviors. This reveals how difficult it is to legally address behaviors that we are socialized to see as naturally emanating from biology rather than from our social environments, although of course sexual assault activists have worked hard to change these beliefs.

See also **Domestic Violence Interventions; Sex-Offender Registries; Child Abuse (vol. 3)**

Further Reading

Bureau of Justice Statistics, *Criminal Victimization in the United States, 2007.* Washington, DC: U.S. Department of Justice, Bureau of Justice Statistics, 2010.

Bureau of Justice Statistics, *Extended Homicide Report.* FBI Uniform Crime Reports. Washington, DC: U.S. Department of Justice, Bureau of Justice Statistics, 2005.

Catalano, Shannan M., *Criminal Victimization, 2004*. Washington, DC: U.S. Department of Justice, Bureau of Justice Statistics, September 2005.

Harrell, Margaret C., and Laura Werber Castaneda, *A Compendium of Sexual Assault Research*. Santa Monica, CA: Rand, 2009.

Kanel, Kristi, *A Guide to Crisis Intervention*, 3d ed. Pacific Grove, CA: Brooks/Cole, 2007.

Katz, J., *Building a "Big Tent" Approach to Ending Men's Violence*. Report published through a grant from the Office on Violence Against Women, Office of Justice Programs. Washington, DC: U.S. Department of Justice, 2001.

Kilpatrick, Dean G., and Ron Acierno, "Mental Health Needs of Crime Victims: Epidemiology and Outcomes." *Journal of Traumatic Stress* 16, no. 2 (2003): 119–132.

Rape, Abuse and Incest National Network (RAINN), 2006. http://www.rainn.org/statistics/index.html

Rennison, Callie Marie, *Rape and Sexual Assault: Reporting to the Police and Medical Attention, 1992–2000*. Washington, DC: U.S. Department of Justice, Bureau of Justice Statistics, 2002.

Rubin, Paula N., *Civil Rights and Criminal Justice: Primer on Sexual Harassment*. National Institute of Justice: Research in Action. Washington, DC: U.S. Department of Justice, Office of Justice Programs, 1995.

Sidran Foundation, "Post-traumatic Stress Disorder Fact Sheet." 2005. http://www.sidran.org/ptsdfacts.html

U.S. Department of Education, *Sexual Harassment: It's Not Academic*. Washington, DC: U.S. Department of Education, 2005.

U.S. Equal Employment Opportunity Commission, "Facts about Sexual Harassment." 2002. http://www.eeoc.gov/facts/fs-sex.html

Warshaw, Robin, *I Never Called It Rape: The Ms. Report on Recognizing, Fighting, and Surviving Date and Acquaintance Rape*. New York: HarperCollins, 1994.

SOCIAL JUSTICE

Leila Sadeghi and Byron E. Price

The path to social justice is fundamentally controversial because it raises issues, ideological and otherwise, that question or debate notions of equity, equality, fairness, and justice itself. Advocates or proponents of "intervention" argue that because institutions and policies establish and maintain social, political, and economic inequality, they also represent the route to achieving social justice or the common good through the equalization of goods and services.

For example, the Green Party, or "leftists" more generally, declare that government must be responsive to injustice by eliminating discrimination, racism, and free-market competition. They believe that government should focus on providing all humans with "basic needs" and a "fair" market system. They further elaborate that in order to accomplish such Herculean tasks of social justice, issues of access, poverty, racism, labor division, and inadequate health care need to be addressed.

THE ACT OF SOCIAL JUSTICE

As noted by Norman Kurland in his foreword to the *Introduction to Social Justice* (1997, ii), "the 'act' of Social Justice is whatever is done in association with others to restructure our institutions and laws to advance the perfection of every person and family affected by that institution."

Opponents or supporters of "nonintervention" argue that social justice cannot be achieved through social engineering and a redistribution of goods and services for all. They argue that government should not be in the business of social intervention, as regulation and control alter at best surface issues do not in fact change the deeper-rooted issues associated with society's ills, and interfere with the "free" market system. Left to its own devices, "conservatives" contend that the free market would solve many problems of inequality because capitalism rewards innovation and hard work. This argument further holds that those disadvantaged by capitalism are unwilling to imitate Horatio Alger and that is the reason they suffer in a system that breeds abundance.

Background

Advocates of social justice are active in voicing their concerns about the unequal distribution of services and goods in society. Although labeled leftists, social justice activists seek to provide quality and equality of life services and goods by campaigning to close the gap between the rich and poor, eliminate hunger and unemployment through such means as providing health care for all, and diminish the social barriers in society that lead to these ills. Still others claim that the only means of achieving social justice would be through the redistribution of income and quasi-control of supply and demand (Ferree 1997).

It is these invisible barriers that prevent society from achieving a utopian state, where all people are treated equally in every aspect of life. Furthermore, these same barriers have been constructed by society to divide and categorize people based on a common set of characteristics, such as class, social stratification, and the division of labor. Additionally, we find that such divisions exist across all of society's institutions, including education, health care, and welfare systems to name a few. Common among these institutions are lateral levels of class stratification according to income and race.

Social justice is typically conceived in two forms, where one end of the spectrum claims that actions must be taken in order to eliminate the ills of society and the other end accepts no preconceived notions in studying those same ills. The first group claims that areas like poverty, division of labor, and homelessness are the underlying causes of social injustice. The latter group studies those areas, claims the importance of doing so, and takes a neutral position. Moreover, social justice has been based on redistributive and recognition theories toward achieving social justice.

Based on the teachings of Thomas Aquinas, the term *social justice* was coined by Luigi Taparelli, an Italian Catholic priest, in his book, published between 1840 and 1843, *Theoretical Treatise on Natural Law Based on Fact*, although others studied the components of social justice before him (Behr 2005). Thomas Aquinas (1225–1274), known as the Doctor Universalis, based his claims on natural theology, in which morality, based on religion, ought to be sought after by all people, who, under God, must adhere to their moral beliefs in doing what is right. This reflected the Christian view that under God's watch, people were to be just and moral in society. He promulgated the idea that justice should not be forced onto humankind but rather felt as the responsibility of the individual based on the rules or laws of Christian religion and the adherence to God's judgment.

Luigi Taparelli came to his theoretical interpretations by examining the levels to which society had been affected and changed by the Industrial Revolution. For one, he believed that the mass migration to the city factories, the design of the wage-laborer, and competition in the marketplace led to the injustices that later formed in society—for instance, the division of the poor and the rich, the competition for jobs and employees, and the turnover of self-employed farmers and peasants to the division of labor and class stratification. At the same time, people were disengaging themselves from the Church and the associated fear of God and engaging in immoral behaviors and manners that contributed largely to the formation of society's ills. Taparelli wanted to create a unified society and used this as his framework of study.

The late Father William J. Ferree, a second great thinker of the social justice movement, wrote "The Act of Social Justice" in 1948, characterizing social justice as a moral duty that obliged each person in society to care for the common good of all (Ferree 1997). According to Kurland, Father Ferree defined the common good as "the network of customs, laws, social organizations—that is, our institutions—that make up the social order and largely determine the quality of culture" (Ferree 1997).

FOUNDATIONS OF SOCIAL JUSTICE

Freedom of speech
Freedom of association
Freedom from racism, discrimination, and sexism
Freedom of ethnic and religious culture and liberty
Freedom from slavery
Freedom of thought
The right to equality
The right to satisfy basic human needs
The redistribution of power, wealth, and status to achieve equitable levels for all

Controversies Surrounding Social Justice

The commitment to social justice has come under attack in several key areas, such as voting, the increasing gap between the rich and the poor, racial profiling, affirmative action, disproportionate incarceration of minorities, and inequitable funding for inner-city schools. Each area mentioned has brought on its own set of unique problems and issues.

The concerns about voting centers in the 2000 presidential election, which reappeared in the 2004 presidential elections, have been heavily debated. Besides the problems with the "hanging chads," hundreds of thousands of felons from Florida were disenfranchised in the 2000 election, which tilted the elections to George W. Bush in 2000. In 2004, Ohio had similar problems and the results were the same, the election was tilted in President Bush's favor as a result of these breaches of social justice. On the other hand, advocates of disenfranchisement contend that felons should not be able to vote and that if people cannot cast a vote correctly, they do not deserve to vote.

Economic inequality has continued to grow, and the latter part of the 20th century, which has been characterized as the most economically prosperous period in U.S. history, has not reversed the gap between the rich and poor. The gap actually widened and the living standards of laborers went from bad to worse during this prosperous period. Issues such as poverty, hunger, and homelessness increased and proved extremely challenging to solve. Sadly, the gap between the rich and poor in the United States grew at the same pace as economic growth. However, proponents of capitalism assert that this inequality could be ameliorated if the poor would take advantages of the opportunities that a wealthy country such as America offers.

Racial profiling has also been a persistent problem that has mostly plagued African American males. The problem is so bad that the neologism "driving while black" has been added to the American vernacular. Furthermore, these stops have been characterized as pretextual stops; that is, the police stop minorities on minor traffic violations in hopes that they will find drugs. Critics contend that these stops are unconstitutional. Proponents of profiling assert that, since minorities are disproportionately the ones found to be in possession of drugs, it is good policing to stop them disproportionately.

Another contentious social justice issue is affirmative action, which seeks to redress inequality in employment and educational opportunity. This issue has been extremely contentious, as it concerns educational admissions and funding. The complaint against affirmative action is that it is a form of reverse discrimination and is no longer needed because we live in a color-blind society. People should not obtain an advantage because of their race. On the other hand, proponents of affirmative action aver that if schools were funded equally and racism was not a part of America's core, there would be no need for initiatives like affirmative action.

Still another contentious issue with social justice ramifications is the disproportionate incarceration of African Americans and Latinos. Compared with their presence in the population overall, critics contend that criminal justice policy is as racist as it was in the past. For instance, they point out that the prison system comprised white men only prior to the emancipation of black slaves. Once the slaves were freed, the prison system became majority black, and the same diabolical practices are prevalent today. However, if blacks commit crimes, why should they not be incarcerated more than whites? It should not matter whether they are disproportionately incarcerated if they have committed a crime, critics argue.

Finally, the debate in respect to educational funding has been just as bitter as the other debates surrounding social justice, along with the perceived inequality that permeates the American system. For example, critics consider the strategy of using property taxes to fund schools as unfair and discriminatory, especially in view of the fact that the gap between rich and poor continues to grow. A system such as this cannot be the way we fund our schools, opponents of this practice avow. But why should the wealthy be penalized for being able to fund their schools and have money diverted from their districts to poorer districts? Advocates of the current funding system contend that their rights are abridged as well when this practice occurs.

In sum, there are a plethora of social justice issues that could be discussed here, but the ones mentioned are the ones that continue to plague society currently and appear to be the most contentious ones. The issues also threaten to divide the country along the lines of race, class, and social status; that is why they are addressed here.

Legal Decisions

The Help American Vote Act of 2002 was passed to address the voting irregularities that took place in the 2000 presidential elections. The act's main focus is to "assist in the administration of Federal elections and to otherwise provide assistance with the administration of certain Federal election laws and programs, to establish minimum election administration standards for States and units of local government with responsibility for the administration of Federal elections, and for other purposes" (Help America Vote Act 2007).

The act does not address felony disenfranchisement. There have been several challenges to felony disenfranchisement, and for the most part, they have been unsuccessful. In *Richardson v. Ramirez* (1974), the "Supreme Court held that Section Two of the amendment amounted to an 'affirmative sanction' of felon disenfranchisement" (Uggen, Behrens, and Manza 2005). Since the Ramirez case, however, most lawsuits involving felony disenfranchisement have been unsuccessful. For instance, in the *Farrakhan v. Washington* (2003) disenfranchisement case, the plaintiff applied the Voting Rights Act to challenge felony disenfranchisement, but to no avail. Lately this seems to be the pattern, especially as courts have become more conservative.

On the racial profiling issue, an international human rights tribunal filed the first-ever legal challenge to racial profiling and the application was submitted to the United

Nations Human Rights Committee with the intended purpose of halting racial profiling by police. This lawsuit was filed against Spain, and on the American front the End Racial Profiling Act of 2004 still has not passed and is unlikely to pass especially since the attacks of September 11, 2001. Furthermore, racial profiling does not just occur in traffic stops; juries also are subject to racial profiling. It is alleged that African Americans are more lenient on each other and prosecutors use preemptory challenges more often on blacks than on whites.

There have been several challenges to affirmative action on many fronts, but the one making the most noise is in the area of admission policies. In the *Gratz and Hamacher /Grutter v. the Regents of the University of Michigan* lawsuit, it was alleged that the University of Michigan accords unlawful preference to minorities in the undergraduate admissions process. *Hopwood v. Texas* in 1992 brought suit against the University of Texas law school on the same basis. California has also had challenges to its admission process based on reverse discrimination claims because of affirmative action policies in its admissions process.

On the educational funding issue, Ohio, New Jersey, and Texas, to name a few, have been cited as discriminatory in the way they fund their school systems. In 1997, the Ohio Supreme Court ruled that the way Ohio funded its schools was unconstitutional. To date, nothing has been done to adhere to the court's ruling. In New Jersey, the Supreme Court ruled that Abbott districts were inadequate and unconstitutional. The Court in Abbott II and in subsequent rulings, ordered the state to assure that these children receive an adequate education through implementation of a comprehensive set of programs and reforms (*Abbott v. Burk* 1997).

As people continue to compete for scare resources and opportunities, impacted by globalization and structural adjustments to the economy, the likelihood that these controversies will be solved in the near future appears dim in some respects, but Americans are known for innovation.

Redistributive and Recognition Theories

Many argue that social justice can be achieved through the combination of the redistributive and recognition theories. Although both theories examine society's ills and injustices as problems that ought to be corrected, each theory puts forward varying strategies toward curing those ailments. The redistributive theory places emphasis on the economic framework of society as the vital factor in determining society's distribution of goods (Fraser 1998). For example, redistributive theorists argue for the need of a standard of living wage. This would increase family income, provide a better standard of life and care, and overall aid in the mobility of lower-socioeconomic-status families, thus creating a more balanced economy and society. Redistribution taken in a political sense is often based on socioeconomic status and relies on the economy to cure society's injustices. As noted by Fraser (1996), "The politics of redistribution encompasses not only class-centered orientations, such as New Deal liberalism, social democracy and socialism, but also those forms of feminism and anti-racism that look to socioeconomic transformation or reform as the remedy for gender and racial-ethnic injustice."

Although redistribution theorists view society's economic framework, recognition theorists approach the problem with a varying lens. Recognition theory essentially determines society's ailments and injustices as cultural phenomenon and evaluates them from this prism. It views culture as the determinant of social patterns, behaviors, and interpretations. One's culture often heavily influences many facets of life, including how various cultures view one another, teaches generation upon generation certain biases, attitudes, and beliefs. In order to achieve a better society by use of recognition theory, a greater emphasis must be placed on valuing various cultures and also on deconstructing some of their long-held and often destructive beliefs. Redistribution theory aims to eliminate society's existing economic structure; recognition theory aims to eliminate the existing cultural differences.

Conclusion

As politics becomes more polarized and money continues to drive the decision-making process, decisions will continue to be made from the top, which more than likely means that the wealth gap will continue to grow. Additionally, as globalization continues to restructure the economy and create more competition for wages, there will be less tolerance for programs like affirmative action and equalizing educational funding. Capitalism is in opposition to social justice, because social justice requires a commitment to providing a social safety net for the less fortunate, and that may mean that initiatives that equalize educational funding are an important component of any system committed to providing a social safety net. Moreover, redistributive theories are more likely to become unpopular as the economy contracts and competition becomes stiffer from globalization and the dollar's weakening value.

See also **African American Criminal Injustice; Class Justice; Juvenile Justice; Environmental Justice (vol. 4).**

Further Reading

Abbott v. Burk IV 149 N.J. 145, 693 A2d 417 (1997).

Adams, Maurianne et al., eds., *Readings for Diversity and Social Justice,* 2d ed. New York: Routledge, 2010.

Arrigo, B., S*ocial Justice/Criminal Justice: The Maturation of Critical Theory in Law, Crime, and Deviance.* Contemporary Issues in Crime and Justice Series. Belmont, CA: Wadsworth, 1999.

Behr, Thomas, "Luigi Taparelli and Social Justice: Rediscovering the Origins of a Hallowed Concept." *Social Justice in Context* 1 (2005): 3–16.

Brooks, Roy L., *Racial Justice in the Age of Obama.* Princeton, NJ: Princeton University Press, 2009.

D'Souza, Eugene, ed., *Crime and Social Justice: Society and Law Enforcement.* New Delhi: Commonwealth, 2002.

Ferree, William J., *Introduction to Social Justice.* Mahwah, NJ: Paulist Press, 1997.

Fraser, Nancy, "Social Justice in the Age of Identity Politics: Redistribution, Recognition, and Participation." *Tanner Lectures on Human Values.* Vol. 19. Salt Lake City: University of Utah Press, 1998.

Help America Vote Act. 2002. http://www.fec.gov/hava/haval.htm

Moore, David B., "Shame, Forgiveness, and Juvenile Justice." *Criminal Justice Ethics* 12, no. 1 (Winter/Spring 1993): 3–26.

Quinney, R., *Bearing Witness to Crime and Social Justice.* Albany: State University of New York Press, 2000.

Schwartz, Martin D., and Suzanne E. Hatty, *Controversies in Critical Criminology.* Dayton, OH: Anderson, 2003.

Soohoo, Catherine Albisa, and Martha F. Davis, eds., *Bringing Human Rights Home.* Westport, CT: Praeger, 2008.

Uggen, Christopher, Angela Behrens, and Jeff Manza, "Criminal Disenfranchisement." *Annual Review of Law and Social Science* 2 (2005): 233–254.

Welch, M., "Critical Criminology, Social Justice, and an Alternative View of Incarceration." *Critical Criminology* 7, no. 2 (September 1996): 43–58.

T

THREE-STRIKES LAWS

Rick M. Steinmann

Three-strikes laws mandate long sentences for habitual offenders. The ongoing controversy surrounding these laws revolves around those advocates who argue that long-term incarceration is the most effective way for the community to remain safe and secure; a similarly active group of opponents argues that such laws (particularly California's) are in violation of the Eighth Amendment of the U.S. Constitution because they impose "cruel and unusual" punishment.

In 1993, a parolee who had been released after serving 8 years of a 16-year sentence for kidnapping killed 12-year-old Polly Klaas. Her death received nationwide media coverage and was met with significant public outrage. Amid this atmosphere, three-strikes laws emerged. The same year as Klaas's murder, Washington state became the first state to enact a three-strikes law. One year later, by way of a statewide proposition, California did likewise. By the end of the decade, the federal government and over half the states had also instituted laws of this type. These laws followed a trend begun in the 1980s when "get tough" attitudes were evidenced by lengthier prison sentences and increased prison populations.

Under the most prevalent definition of a three-strikes law found in most states, a person who has been convicted of two prior felonies and then is charged with a new, third serious or violent offense is subject to receiving a prison sentence of from 25 years to life. The intent is to respond to repeat violent offenders in a harsh manner and to decrease the number of inmates involved in the prison's "revolving door" of entry, release, and re-entry. Three-strikes incarcerations are typically premised on the penology concepts of "incapacitation" (i.e., long-term isolation from society for selected individuals) and "deterrence" (i.e., discouraging the general public from committing criminal offenses).

This entry focuses on the California three-strikes law, as it has received the most extensive nationwide examination by both legal scholars and social science researchers. The extensive review of the California law is attributable to its extremely widespread use by California officials and also the unique language of the statute, which sets it far apart from the laws of other states.

Background

California accounts for about 90 percent of all three-strikes cases nationwide (Vitiello 2002). The impact of the law is reflected in the third-strike population in California jumping from 254 in 1994 to 7,234 in 2003, a 2,709 percent increase (Ehlers, Schiraldi, and Zeidenberg 2004). As for California's statute, it is distinctive in that "any felony," including nonviolent offenses, can constitute the third strike. See California Penal Code Ann., Section 667 (e) (2) (A) (West 1999). One 2003 study of California's three-strikes law found that for 57 percent of third strikers, the offense that triggered their 25-years-to-life in prison was a nonviolent offense. For example, it was found that over 10 times as many third strikers were serving life sentences for drug possession (672) than for second-degree murder (62) (Ehlers, Schiraldi, and Ziedenberg 2004). In fact, 360 individuals in California are serving life sentences under three strikes for shoplifting small amounts of merchandise (Chemerinsky 2004, 11–13), a result of a "wobbler offense" legal provision whereby a misdemeanor petty theft can be treated, under certain circumstances, as if it were a felony.

Inmates who contest their incarceration under three strikes, particularly California prisoners, invariably argue on appeal that the sentence is "grossly disproportionate" to the offense and hence a violation of their Eighth Amendment right to be free from "cruel and unusual" punishment. *Cruel* is generally interpreted to mean excessive, while *unusual* is typically thought to mean out of the ordinary or deviating from normal.

During the initial years following the passage of three strikes in California, the attorney general of the state and others attributed the drop in statewide crime to the implementation of three strikes. The attorney general's office reported that since the passage of three strikes, the "violent crime rate had dropped 26.9 percent" (Vitiello 2002). Also, anecdotal comments have been made relative to the perceived effectiveness of the law.

For example, a two-strikes parolee stated that "he's flipped 100 percent…that the law has scared him… and that it will keep him working hard and keep his attitude adjusted." A prosecutor stated, "We're getting some very bad people, and instead of them doing life on the installment plan, they're just going away" (Peck 2004, 221). Additionally, a former attorney general for the state reported that "in the last year before three strikes took effect, 1994, 226 more paroled felons chose to move to California than move away from it," whereas "after the law took effect, in 1995, 1335 more paroled felons chose to move away from California than move to it" (Peck 2004, 222). In other words, California's three-strikes law has persuaded prospective third strikers to avoid the state and seek refuge in states whose laws may be perceived as being not quite so harsh.

Opponents of three-strike laws contend that there are many reasons to question the propriety and effectiveness of such laws, particularly California's law. For one, the question of whether three strikes has in fact been an actual cause of the decrease in California crime rates has been addressed in a number of studies. One study found that the California law did not reduce crime below the level that would have been expected considering the prevailing downward trend that had begun before the passage of the law (Stolzenberg and D'Alessio 1997). In other words, the nationwide decrease in crime beginning around 1992 and continuing throughout the 1990s was most likely caused by factors other than three strikes. Such factors commonly advanced include the downturn in the crack cocaine market, community policing measures, an improved economy, gun intervention programs, and a smaller population of people in the so-called crime-prone age range, generally considered to be between the ages of 15 and 25.

The Justice Policy Institute in a 2004 report compared the six California counties that used three strikes most heavily with the six counties that used the law less frequently to see if there were differences in the crime rates. They found that "counties that used the three strikes at a higher rate did not experience greater reductions in crime than counties that used the law less frequently" (Ehlers, Schiraldi, and Ziedenberg 2004, 15). In fact, "the six large counties using three strikes least frequently had a decline in violent crime that was 22.5 percent greater than was experienced by the six large counties using three strikes the most frequently" (Ehlers, Schiraldi, and Ziedenberg 2004, 17).

A 1998 study looked at the impact of three strikes by comparing the crime rates in states with such a law with those in states without such a law. The findings demonstrated that "[s]tates with three-strikes laws do not appear to have experienced faster declines in crime since those laws were implemented, than have states without such laws" (Greenwood et al. 1998). The Justice Policy Institute's more recent 2004 study compared New York (a non–three-strikes state) with California and found that California's 2002 crime rates were much higher than New York's, even though California enacted its three-strikes law eight years earlier (Ehlers, Schiraldi, and Ziedenberg 2004, 20). An earlier 1997 Justice Policy study compared the crime rate in New York City with that in Los Angeles and determined that New York City had experienced much lower levels of crime (Ambrosio and Schiraldi 1997).

The Justice Policy Institute examined the question of three-strikes laws' disproportionate impact on blacks and Latinos and determined that the "African-American incarceration rate for third strikes is 12 times higher than the third strike incarceration rate for whites" and that the "Latino incarceration rate for a third strike is 45 percent higher than the third strike incarceration rate for whites" (Ehlers, Schiraldi, and Ziedenberg 2004, 11).

The typical third-strike offender enters a California prison in his mid-thirties, whereas the "crime-prone" age range is generally considered to be between the years of 15 and 25, or perhaps to age 30. Some who question the propriety of three-strikes measures suggest that the incarcerated offender has essentially reached the point of "ageing out" of crime upon entry into prison for a third strike. Based on the premise that three strikes was initiated to take the worst and most violent offenders off the streets by selectively incapacitating them and deterring others, a study was conducted examining California crime statistics for those offenders over the age of 30. The researchers, comparing crime data that predated the implementation of three strikes with data obtained after implementation (pre–post comparison study) found that the "over 30 age group—those most subject to the three strikes law—was the only group to display an increase in violent offenses and total felony arrests during the post-three strike period. Therefore, the age group that should have been the most affected by three strikes under the deterrent or selective incapacitation theories showed no deterrent or selective incapacitation effect" (Males and Macallair 1999, 67).

In addition to the clearly enhanced incarceration costs incurred with three strikes, particularly as it pertains to older inmates' medical needs, the issue of the fiscal impact on the court system in California has been similarly examined. The Justice Policy Institute found that three strikes resulted in increased judicial workloads, the shifting of resources from civil to criminal cases, and a significantly increased number of cases going to full trial rather than being plea-bargained (Ehlers, Schiraldi, and Ziedenberg 2004, 28). The thinking among those facing a third-strike conviction is that they have nothing to lose by demanding a full trial, as the advantages of traditional plea bargaining may not be an option provided to them.

BUDGET EXPENDITURES FOR THREE-STRIKES LAWS

Los Angeles County purportedly expended $64 million in added trial and jail costs during the first year three-strikes was initiated and more than $200 million by 1998.* Prisoners added to the California prison system "under three strikes between 1994 and 2003 have been calculated to cost or will cost taxpayers $8.1 billion in prison or jail expenditures...$4.7 billion in added costs are the result of longer terms for non-violent offenses."**

*Mark Gladstone, "County Asks State to Pay for 3-Strikes Costs." *Los Angeles Times* (March 27, 1998): B10.
**Scott Ehlers, Vincent Schiraldi, and Jason Ziedenberg, "Still Striking Out: Ten Years of California's Three Strikes." *Justice Policy Institute Policy Report*, March 2004, 1–34.

Key Legal Decisions

The Eighth Amendment's "cruel and unusual punishment" clause has been the subject of extensive appellate court examination relative to methods of punishment, specifically the death penalty. However, the question of if and when a lengthy incarceration can be in violation of this clause has received less judicial appellate oversight.

In the 1910 U.S. Supreme Court case of *U.S. v. Weems*, the issue of the "proportionality" principle relative to punishment was addressed. The Court stated that "it is a precept of justice that punishment for crime should be graduated and proportioned to offense" (*U.S. v. Weems*1910). The thinking behind "proportionality" review is that the courts act as a check on the individual states' power to impose criminal sentences. In practice, however, federal appellate courts have been generally reluctant to review sentences imposed by the individual states. This resistance to such review has received the continued endorsement of the U.S. Supreme Court, as exemplified in the 1982 case of *Hutto v. Davis* (1982), where the Court, in effect, cautioned lower federal courts to be hesitant in reviewing individual state-imposed sentences. Further, it advised them that if such review is granted, actual successful challenges to proportionality review should be "exceedingly rare."

Most recently the U.S. Supreme Court has taken up the issue of sentence "proportionality" review in the landmark 2003 companion cases of *Ewing v. California* (2003) and *Lockyer v. Andrade* (2003). Both cases specifically addressed California's three-strikes law and in both cases the U.S. Supreme Court upheld the constitutionality of the law in close 5–4 decisions, holding that the "cruel and unusual punishment" clause of the Eighth Amendment had not been violated.

In *Ewing*, the third strike involved Gary Ewing's stealing of three golf clubs worth $1,200. He previously had been convicted of four other felonies and eight misdemeanor offenses. His sentence was life in prison with no possibility of parole for 25 years. In *Lockyer*, Leandro Andrade, within a two-week span, first stole five videotapes worth $84.70 and then four videotapes worth $68.82. He was subject to California's so-called "wobbler" offense provision, whereby petty offenses can be elevated to felony status if the individual has prior offenses. Andrade received a sentence of 50 years to life.

The U.S. Supreme Court in both *Ewing* and *Lockyer* used a four-part test in addressing proportionality in sentencing. The test was based on the concurring opinion of Justice Kennedy in the 1991 case of *Harmelin v. Michigan*, where he argued for the establishment of four proportionality principles in reviewing a case (*Harmelin v. Michigan* 1991). After engaging in such review, the Court in *Ewing*, although acknowledging that California's three-strikes law has "sparked controversy" and that critics have doubted the "law's wisdom, cost-efficiency, and effectiveness in reaching its goals," nonetheless stated, "We do not sit as a superlegislature to second-guess these policy choices" (*Ewing v. California* 2003, at 27–28).

"Sentence proportionality review" is guided by the recognition of four principles:

1. The setting of the lengths of prison terms had its primacy in the legislative branch.
2. The Eighth Amendment does not mandate adoption of any one penological system.
3. Benefits of the federal system of government are recognized.
4. Proportionality review must be guided by objective factors.

Source: James J. Brennan, "The Supreme Court's Excessive Deference to Legislative Bodies under Eighth Amendment Sentencing Review." *Journal of Criminal Law and Criminology* 94 (2004): 551–586.

The Court, with Justice O'Connor writing the majority opinions in both *Ewing* and *Lockyer,* upheld the constitutionality of the statute by relying on both California's "public safety interests" and California's right to impose "life sentences on repeat offenders."

The four Justices who dissented in *Ewing* and *Lockyer* argued that the Eighth Amendment clearly forbids, given prior precedent, prison terms that meet the threshold requirement of being "grossly disproportionate." The dissenting justices clearly felt, based on the case facts, that the standard of "gross disproportionality" had been met and that the sentences were unjust (538 U.S., at 35–36).

Based on prior precedent, the question of what is grossly disproportionate currently appears to turn, at least in part, on whether an incarcerated person is theoretically eligible for parole at some point in time or whether a "true" life sentence has been imposed. If the sentence is indeed a "true" life sentence, the Supreme Court may be more inclined to consider it unconstitutional if it is indeed grossly disproportionate, whereas a grossly disproportionate sentence that nonetheless provides for the possibility of parole will not be found unconstitutional (compare *Solem v. Helm* 1983 with *Rummel v. Estelle* 1980).

Some California prosecutors and trial court judges, even in counties that generally invoke three strikes, have softened the impact of the law in the exercise of their legal discretion. Prosecutors sometimes move to dismiss or strike a prior felony conviction in the furtherance of justice. (See California Penal Code Ann., section 667(f) [2]).

Judges as well have latitude in whether to invoke three strikes and can also reduce felonies to misdemeanors. Thus, the three-strike law has not been applied with full implementation and is on occasion circumvented by criminal justice officials. Additionally, the passage by California voters in the year 2000 of Proposition 36—the Substance Abuse and Crime Prevention Act—has to a degree lessened the number of new individuals being incarcerated under the three-strikes law. The law mandates that some drug possession offenders, including three-strikes eligible offenders, may be eligible for drug treatment instead of being incarcerated.

Conclusion

Three-strikes laws are based, at least in part, on the concepts of "selective incapacitation" and "general deterrence." The issue of concern here has been whether the laws actually incapacitate those offenders who are the most violent and who are considered to be strongly inclined toward repeating their offenses if they are not incarcerated for 25 years to life. As discussed earlier in this entry, research focusing on the state of California disputes whether incarcerating individuals, typically in their mid-thirties, for a third-strike nonviolent offense effectively reduces subsequent crime. The argument is that inmates in their mid-thirties are at the point of "ageing out" of crime and therefore will simply cost the prison system untold dollars as their health takes a downturn in later years. As to deterrence, research shows that states without three-strikes laws actually experience lower crime rates. This is the case even within California in counties that rarely if ever use three strikes, which likewise have lower crime rates than those counties that regularly use three strikes. In the future, proponents of three-strikes laws may contend that the laws simply serve the purpose of retribution and therefore abandon the "selective incapacitation" and "general deterrence" arguments.

The role politicians play in supporting three-strikes laws may be altered in the future. In the 1990s politicians provided widespread support for such laws; to do otherwise might have subjected them to political defeat at election time. However, given the expenses incurred in California and nationwide relating to three strikes, politicians may now be more inclined to seek alternative, less expensive ways to control crime. Currently, the money used to fund the California three-strikes initiative is money that might otherwise be available to subsidize other state services, including higher education, the park system, road construction/repair, social services, and the state highway patrol.

The Center for the Study of Media and Public Affairs reported in 1994 that "crime stories on national network television had doubled from the previous year and murder stories had tripled." (Mauer 1999, 15). This media attention actually occurred during a period when nationwide crime was decreasing; yet the question of whether it served in

SHOULD LEGISLATIVE "SUNSET PROVISIONS" APPLY TO THREE-STRIKES LAWS?

Legislative bodies that enact three-strikes laws may wish to establish "sunset provisions," in which the law is set to expire at a future date, subject to review of its impact and consideration as to the merit of continuing to have such a law as it is then written. Or they may perhaps weigh whether the law should be amended in part or perhaps even repealed. This type of process would allow legislative officials to examine any scholarly research that has been conducted on the law and then be in a position to make sound public policy judgments on the future viability of the law.

part to spur on nationwide three-strike initiatives is open to debate. If the media do significantly influence the thinking of policy makers and the public alike, the media could, in the future, similarly influence public policy decisions concerning the continuation of three-strikes policies or instead alternative less costly measures to decrease crime.

In the future, more research should be conducted into the disparate impact on blacks and Latinos relative to the application of three-strike measures. If prosecutors and trial court judges are perceived as applying the law in an inequitable fashion, justice is not served. Witnesses may question the fairness of the proceedings and be reluctant to testify, while juries may engage in jury nullification (acquitting a defendant who is otherwise legally guilty) when confronted with what appears to be selective prosecution based on race or ethnicity.

The U.S. Supreme Court will want, in future decisions, to clarify its meaning of "gross disproportionality," so that three-strikes prisoners can have more guidance in preparing their cases for appeal. Currently, the law appears somewhat unclear, and given the nature of the sentence, typically 25 years to life, an argument can be made that more thorough explanation would be advantageous. One legal scholar asserts that "The Court needs to assert a more active role in protecting an individual's Eighth Amendment guarantee from excessive prison sentence" (Brennan 2004).

In the future, the criminal justice officials most closely connected to the daily operation of three-strike provisions, namely trial court judges, prosecutors, and criminal defense counsel—may play a more substantial role in influencing California's three-strikes law. A research study examined California "courtroom workgroups" through the use of semistructured interviews and questionnaires. The researchers determined that courtroom members most often recommended that the three-strikes law be changed so that the third-strike charge should pertain only to a "serious or violent felony" (Harris and Jesilow 2000).

Whether the current language of the California three-strikes statute will remain the same or be amended in order to eliminate nonviolent offenses and the escalation of misdemeanor offenses to the status of felonies is clearly unknown at present. What is known is that the general public, politicians, criminal justice practitioners, and researchers will continue to examine whether three-strikes laws are an effective mechanism to reduce crime committed by repeat offenders.

See also **Alternative Treatments for Criminal Offenders; Cruel and Unusual Punishment; Prison Construction; War on Drugs**

Legal Citations

Ewing v. California, 538 U.S. 11 (2003).

Harmelin v. Michigan, 501 U.S. 957 (1991).

Hutto v. Davis, 454 U.S. 370 (1982).

Lockyer v. Andrade, 538 U.S. 63 (2003).

U.S. v. Weems, 217 U.S. 349, 347 (1910).

Solem v. Helm, 463 U.S. 277 (1983).

Rummel v. Estelle, 445 U.S. 263 (1980).

Further Reading

Ambrosio, Tara-Jen, and Vincent Schiraldi, *Striking Out: The Crime Control Impact of Three Strikes Laws.* Washington, DC: Policy Institute, 1997.

Brennan, James J., "The Supreme Court's Excessive Deference to Legislative Bodies under Eighth Amendment Sentencing Review." *Journal of Criminal Law and Criminology* 94 (2004): 551–586.

Chemerinsky, Erwin, "Life in Prison for Shoplifting: Cruel and Unusual Punishment." *Human Rights: Journal of the Section of Individual Rights and Responsibilities* 31 (Winter 2004): 11–13.

Clark, John, James Austin, and Henry D. Alan, *Three Strikes and You're Out: A Review of State Legislation.* Washington, DC: U.S. Department of Justice, 1997.

Domanick, Joe, *Cruel Justice: Three Strikes and the Politics of Crime in America's Golden State.* Berkeley: University of California Press, 2004.

Ehlers, Scott, Vincent Schiraldi, and Jason Ziedenberg, "Still Striking Out: Ten Years of California's Three Strikes." *Justice Policy Institute Policy Report.* March 2004.

Greenwood, Peter, et al., *Three Strikes Revisited: An Early Assessment of Implementation and Impact of Strike Laws.* Santa Monica, CA: Rand, 1998.

Harris, John C., and Paul Jesilow, "It's Not the Old Ball Game: Three Strikes and the Courtroom Workgroup." *Justice Quarterly* 17 (2000): 185–203.

Johnson, J. L., and M. A. Saint-Germain, "Officer Down: Implications of Three-Strikes for Public Safety." *Criminal Justice Policy Review* 16 (2005): 443–460.

Males, Mike, and Dan Macallair, "Striking Out: The Failure of California's Three Strikes and You're Out Law." *Stanford Law and Policy Review* 11 (Winter 1999): 65–74.

Mauer, Mark, "Why Are Tough on Crime Policies So Popular?" *Stanford Law and Policy Review* 11 (Winter 1999): 9–21.

Peck, Robert C., "Ewing v. California: Upholding California's Three Strikes Laws." *Pepperdine Law Review* 32 (2004): 191–225.

Stolzenberg, Lisa, and Stewart D'Alessio, "Three Strikes and You're Out: The Impact of California's New Law on Serious Crime Rates." *Crime and Delinquency* 43 (1997): 457–469.

Turner, Susan, et al., "The Impact of Truth-in-Sentencing and Three Strikes Litigation: Prison Populations, State Budgets, and Crime Rates." *Stanford Law and Policy Review* 11 (1999): 75–91.

Vitiello, Michael, "Three Strikes: Can We Return to Rationality?" *Journal of Criminal Law and Criminology* 87 (1997): 395–481.

Vitiello, Michael, "Three Strikes Law: A Real or Imagined Deterrent to Crime?" *Human Rights: Journal of the Section of Individual Rights and Responsibilities* 29 (Spring 2002): 3–5.

Worrall, John L., "The Effect of Three-Strikes Legislation on Serious Crime in California." *Journal of Criminal Justice* 32 (2004): 283–296.

W

WAR ON DRUGS

Lisa Anne Zilney

The War on Drugs in the United States is controversial, in part because it is based on an ever-changing cultural reaction to a substance rather than to an actual threat of individual or social harm. Public perceptions of drugs and alcohol are socially constructed and subject to change based on many factors, perhaps primarily based on the intensity of media campaigns detailing community devastation at the hands of drugs addicts and drug dealers and political pressure to once and for all win the war against drugs. Although the boundary between legal and illegal substances is arbitrary, the United States has spent decades waging this war. It involves a growing prison–industrial complex; a series of "get tough" measures; an almost continual barrage of drug-war rhetoric; and discriminatory treatment based on class, race, and gender. The cost of the War on Drugs has been violence, crime, corruption, devastation of social bonds and the destruction of inner-city communities, and the exponential growth of the number of minorities and women incarcerated. Only after nearly 40 years of conducting this war did the United States government, under President Barack Obama, shift its efforts away from heavy-handed enforcement of drug laws and toward recognition of the public health aspects of the problem, placing greater emphasis on drug-use prevention and treatment (Hananel 2010).

Background

During colonial times, the growth of hemp was required by townships because it was used for a wide variety of purposes, including the production of textiles and paper. The first prohibitionist laws in the United States were passed in the 19th century, when state and local ordinances were enacted based on the belief that minority individuals were corrupting the moral stature of white American women. High drug-addiction levels during this period were primarily a result of the liberal use of narcotics, for which accurate education was unavailable. Narcotics were viewed as a socially accepted cure-all, and the addictive nature of these substances remained unknown. To illustrate, cocaine was an ingredient in Coca-Cola from 1886 to 1900, and Bayer sold heroin over the counter in 1898 (Gray 2001, 20–21).

One of the first laws to address illicit substances was the Pure Food and Drug Act, passed in 1906, which required all medications to contain accurate labeling of contents. This act was a significant contribution to the rapid decline in the use of narcotics as society became aware of the potential side effects of such substances. Shortly thereafter the Harrison Act, in combination with *Webb v. United States,* prohibited physicians from assisting addicts through the prescription of drugs to alleviate the symptoms associated with narcotics withdrawal. As such, many addicted individuals sought out the black market and contaminated drugs to temper their withdrawal. This era marked the beginning of drug prohibition (Gray 2001, 21–22).

Moral crusaders worked to lobby governmental officials for strict legislation against alcohol and other drugs. The result was prohibition of alcohol from 1920 until 1933. This caused widespread crime and violence, a substantial increase in the law enforcement budget, and a significant rise in the number of individuals incarcerated for alcohol-related offenses. The 1920s also saw the demonization of marijuana, with movies such as *Reefer Madness* conveying to the American public that "one puff of pot can lead clean-cut teenagers down the road to insanity, criminality, and death" (Gray 2001, 24). The Marijuana Tax Act was passed shortly after the end of Prohibition in 1937, recognizing the medical usefulness of marijuana and permitting physicians and authorized others to dispense the drug provided that a licensing fee was paid. The tax, however, for an unlicensed transaction, was so steep as to dissuade the wide-scale use of marijuana for medical purposes (Gray 2001, 23–26). Attitudes toward marijuana, or at least toward its potential uses, changed briefly during World War II, when the government initiated an effort to encourage the use of domestic hemp for industrial purposes. After the end of the war, hemp once again became a "prohibited substance without any practical usages of any kind" (Gray 2001, 26). With the tide turned back toward prohibition, the plethora of get-tough laws began.

Key Moments/Events

Politicians have garnered public support and political benefit from the passage of get-tough laws that, for the most part, consider all illegal substances in one broad category. Both the Boggs Act in 1951 and the Narcotic Control Act in 1956 paved the way for increasingly strict sentences for drug offenses. This was followed in 1961 by ratification of the Single Convention of Narcotic Drugs treaty. Richard Nixon, who expanded antidrug efforts to disrupt the importation of drugs and increase interdiction, initiated the officially declared War on Drugs. The federal budget for drug prevention and law enforcement increased from $150.2 million in 1971 to $654.8 million in 1973 (Inciardi 2008, 188).

Although Nixon's drug war included moderate financial support for treatment programs, this was dismantled with Ronald Reagan's redeclaration of the War on Drugs. Nancy Reagan popularized the "Just Say No" campaign, and abstinence rather than treatment became the focus. Such campaigns increased public support for antidrug efforts, and in 1984 the Comprehensive Crime Control Act was passed, which served to increase bail and sentences, as well as to increase federal authority to seize the assets of individuals convicted of felony drug offenses. This was followed closely by the Anti–Drug Abuse Act of 1986, which enacted mandatory minimum sentences for persons found guilty of simple possession, doubled penalties for the deliberate involvement of juveniles, and mandatory life sentences for individuals found guilty of conducting a continuing criminal enterprise involving drugs. This act also made the distribution of illegal substances within 1,000 feet of a school a federal offense. In addition, the Anti–Drug Abuse Act required an annual presidential evaluation of countries producing or transporting drugs and the labeling of cooperating countries as antidrug allies in the War on Drugs. Unless granted a waiver by the president, countries that failed to cooperate with the American drug war were threatened with possible trade sanctions and the loss of foreign aid; in addition, the United States would oppose loans for these countries from international lending institutions (Gray 2001, 27).

In 1988 the Anti–Drug Abuse Act was further expanded to include as federal offenses the distribution of drugs within 100 feet of a park, youth center, playground, swimming pool, or video arcade. In 1994 the Crime Bill enacted criminal enterprise statutes resulting in mandatory sentences ranging from 20 years to life; it also indicated the death penalty as a sentence for some drug-selling offenses. All of these get-tough measures served to dramatically increase the number of individuals incarcerated and fueled the growth of the prison–industrial complex. Along with harsher sentences for drug offenses, legislation also affected an offender's ability to successfully reenter the community after serving time. Although there are no disqualifications for offenses like rape or manslaughter, in 1998 the Higher Education Act disqualified individuals who had been convicted of marijuana possession from receiving federal aid to attend college (Gray 2001, 27–28).

The current American political system rewards politicians who approach crime with a get-tough approach, and this fuels the fire of ever-increasing spending on the prison–industrial complex. The Executive Summary for 2010 of the ONDCP (Office of National Drug Control Policy 2009) indicates a 2009 federal budget of $14.8 billion for reducing illegal drug use, an increase of $1.1 billion from 2008. This is in addition to the

TIMELINE OF DRUG-RELATED LAWS AND POLICIES IN THE UNITED STATES

1906	Pure Food and Drug Act
1914	Harrison Narcotic Act
1937	Marijuana Tax Act
1951	Boggs act
1956	Narcotic Control Act
1961	Single Convention of Narcotic Drugs
1966	Narcotics Addict Rehabilitation Act
1968	Mental Health Centers Act
1970	Comprehensive Drug Abuse Prevention and Control Act
1970	Drug Abuse Education Act
1970	Racketeer-Influenced and Corrupt Organizations Act
1973	New York Rockefeller Drug Laws
1974	Narcotic Addict Treatment Act
1979	Model Drug Paraphernalia Act
1979	Marijuana section of Rockefeller Drug Laws repealed
1984	Comprehensive Crime Control Act
1984	Comprehensive Forfeiture Act
1986	Anti–Drug Abuse Act
1986	Mandatory Minimum Laws
1988	Anti–Drug Abuse Act (expanded)
1990	Crime Control Act
1994	Crime Bill
1994	First "Three-Strikes" Law in California
1996	Proposition 215 in California (medical marijuana)
1998	Higher Education Act
2000	Substance Abuse and Crime Prevention Act (California)
2010	National drug policy shifts away from the War on Drugs and toward recognition of the public health aspects of the problem

approximately $30 billion total state budgets, bringing spending for the War on Drugs to approximately $45 billion per year. The ONDCP budget, however, does not appear to fall in line with its stated priorities, which are as follows: priority I, substance abuse prevention; priority II, substance abuse treatment; priority III, domestic law enforcement; and priority IV, interdiction and international counterdrug support. Just over $5 billion in 2010, reduced slightly from 2009, has been devoted to priorities I and II combined. The remaining two thirds of the budget will be dedicated to law enforcement and disrupting the market through the use of programs such as Southwest Border Enforcement, Organized Crime and Drug Enforcement, Immigration and Customs Enforcement, support of the Drug Enforcement Administration, and interdiction programs focused on Mexico, Colombia, and Afghanistan (Office of National Drug Control Policy 2009).

Aside from the economics of the prison–industrial complex at the state and federal levels, the number of arrests for drug offenses more than tripled from 580,900 in 1980 to 1,846,400 in 2005. Governmental studies reveal that over half of those imprisoned for federal drug offenses are street-level dealers or transporters, about one third are mid-level dealers, and approximately 11 percent are high-level dealers (Federal Bureau of Investigation 2000). On the state level, 58 percent of drug offenders have no history of either violence or high-level drug activity, and one third have been convicted only of a drug-related crime (King and Mauer 2002).

In addition to the expanding prison population, it is also important to recognize the types of offenses for which individuals are receiving lengthy prison terms. During the period from 1990 to 2002 there was an increase in drug arrests of 450,000 individuals. Of these arrests, 82 percent were for marijuana charges, and 79 percent of marijuana offenses were strictly for possession. These numbers represent an increase in marijuana arrests of 113 percent during this period, while overall arrests decreased by 3 percent. During this period, the arrest of offenders using drugs other than marijuana increased by only 10 percent. These results indicate that nearly half of the drug arrests each year involve marijuana, with a mere 6 percent resulting in felony convictions. To pursue such vigorous incarceration policies toward marijuana, the United States spends an estimated $4 billion annually on arrest, prosecution, and incarceration (King and Mauer 2005; Mauer and King 2007).

Research indicates that the increases in arrest do not correspond to an increase in the use of illegal substances. Furthermore, the shifting of law enforcement resources to a focus on marijuana is not in line with any substantiated decrease in the use of other drugs. Therefore the dramatic increase in marijuana arrest rates can only be understood as the result of selective law enforcement decisions. Such enforcement decisions have varied impacts on the lower class and racial minorities as well as on the female population.

Racial Discrimination

Race is intimately connected with the consequences of the War on Drugs. An example of the intersection of class and racial discrimination with regard to drug laws involves New York's Rockefeller Drug Laws, among the harshest in the nation, which were enacted in 1973. These laws created mandatory minimum sentencing requirements intended to crack down on high-level drug offenders. Sentencing under these laws was based entirely on the quantity of drugs sold or possessed, with no consideration of the offender's circumstances or role in the drug industry. What resulted was that many offenders sentenced under these laws were punished more severely than individuals convicted of rape or manslaughter.

The Rockefeller Drug Laws greatly impacted minority communities. New York's population is 23.2 percent African American or Latino; however, these groups comprise 93 percent of those incarcerated for drug felonies. Between 1990 and 2002, New York City experienced an 882 percent increase in arrests for marijuana, including a 2,461 percent increase in arrests for marijuana possession. Although African Americans represent approximately 14 percent of marijuana users in New York City, they represent 30 percent of those arrested for marijuana violations (King and Mauer 2005). The Rockefeller laws were somewhat tempered by the 2004 Drug Law Reform Act, which created a determinate system of sentencing and reduced mandatory minimum sentences for nonviolent felony drug offenses (Real Reform 2006). However, this pattern of discrimination occurs in many states. For example, in Maryland between 1996 and 2001, of all African American offenders, 64 percent were sentenced on drug violations, and an astounding 81 percent of individuals sentenced for drug offenses were African American (Office of National Drug Control Policy 2009).

An overwhelming amount of scholarly research indicates that racial minorities do not partake in the use of drugs with any more frequency than do whites. Nevertheless, the coexistence of race and a lower-class position leaves many minorities more visible to law enforcement, leading to the misperception of higher levels of drug involvement among these groups (Riley 1997). This results in disproportionate arrest and prosecution. Of all drug prisoners in state facilities, 45 percent are African American and 20 percent Hispanic. At the same time, there has been a slow but steady increase in the number of white drug offenders (29 percent in 2005, compared with 20 percent in 1999) incarcerated in state prisons (Mauer 2009).

Gender Discrimination

Gender discrimination is another adverse consequence of get-tough drug legislation. The criminalization of women's involvement in the War on Drugs depends on the notion that female offenders have transgressed their appropriate gender roles in society. Women's involvement in the drug trade can frequently be attributed to economics as opposed to personal addiction. The feminization of poverty has resulted in women seeking alternative sources of income as decoys or drug couriers (mules) who import or transport drugs. The risks of this employment "choice" are high, often resulting in mandatory minimum sentences for women for whom this is their first offense.

In the late 1980s, the media-driven crack baby epidemic led the public to believe that children born to crack-addicted mothers would face educational and social obstacles that were insurmountable. This scenario fueled gender and racial discrimination in the War on Drugs, as an overwhelming majority of mothers portrayed in the media to have given birth to crack babies belonged to a racial or ethnic minority. The impression that this was an epidemic resulted in the passage of laws that criminalized drug use during pregnancy. Such a legal response, however, dissuaded some women from seeking prenatal care and drug treatment. In addition, maternal drug abuse laws were enforced primarily on minority women: African American and Latino women represented approximately 80 percent of those subject to prosecution. Although research from the National Institute of Drug Abuse has indicated that early medical reports regarding the long-term effects of being born crack-addicted were overstated, the stereotype of the drug-abusing African American or Latino mother remains in the eyes of many Americans (Inciardi 2008, 158–162).

At the close of 1999, more than 80 percent of the women in prison for drug offenses were sentenced using mandatory minimum sentencing laws, and approximately 70 percent of those women were mothers (Bush-Baskette 2000, 924). This has significant and adverse effects for the children's emotional and psychological well-being as well as effects on those individuals who assume guardianship responsibilities of the children and financial costs of supervising children of women who are incarcerated. Perhaps most notably, the psychological impact on the children remains for many years and disrupts their developmental maturity.

The Intersections of Discrimination

When the widespread search for drugs began, drugs were overwhelmingly found where law enforcement exerted its primary search efforts: in low-income, minority neighborhoods where use and dealing are most visible. Although crack is the least used illicit substance, the War on Drugs specifically targeted the possession and sale of crack cocaine by lower-class and minority individuals. Because minorities are overrepresented among the poor, the case of laws regarding crack cocaine versus powder cocaine is illustrative of the intersections of discrimination by class and race.

The wide discrepancy in federally mandated sentences for crack cocaine versus powder cocaine illustrates a class and racial bias in the criminal justice system. Minorities are primarily prosecuted for crack offenses, while whites are primarily prosecuted for powder cocaine offenses (Bush-Baskette 2000, 924). Although the sentencing discrepancy between crack cocaine and powder cocaine offenses has closed slightly in recent years, initially the laws specified that 5 grams of crack cocaine would earn an offender the same five-year mandatory minimum sentence as 500 grams of powder cocaine. This sentencing gap was significant in creating the current disproportion in minority confinement, as an overwhelming percentage of those sentenced for crack cocaine offenses were minority individuals. Conversely, approximately two thirds of those charged with powder cocaine offenses were white. Statistics such as these illustrate the disproportionate arrest and confinement of overwhelmingly lower-class minorities despite research by the Department on Health and Human Services reporting that less than 1 percent of young African Americans had used crack cocaine in their lifetimes, compared with 4.5 percent of whites (Barak, Leighton, and Flavin 2007, 133–135).

In an analysis of discrimination in the War on Drugs, it becomes evident that race and class are inextricably intertwined, because racial minorities are disproportionately represented among the poor. Increased social control of this group of individuals has been accomplished through the use of drug-related laws that are enforced with vigor in low-income, minority neighborhoods. Although drug laws may on their face appear equal and not discriminatory in intent, the consequences of applying get-tough legislation in fighting the War on Drugs has been the unprecedented incarceration of the poor and minorities as well as a significant increase in the number of women under the control of the criminal justice system. Assumptions based on race, class, and gender stereotypes have created and perpetuated moral panics that fuel support for the drug war.

Conclusion

When politicians and the mainstream media discuss all drug alternatives under one umbrella termed "legalization," the public becomes frightened of sacrificing communities to the adverse consequences of drug abuse and addition. There are numerous alternatives to the War on Drugs, however, such as decriminalization, regulated distribution, and harm reduction strategies, including many varieties of drug treatment programs. A bridge between the criminal justice system and the drug treatment community is the Treatment Alternatives to Street Crime (TASC) network. This program uses drug treatment as an alternative or supplement to a criminal justice penalty for a drug offense. Research on programs like TASC offers support for the harm reduction role this initiative plays in interrupting involvement in drug use and criminal activity (Inciardi 2008, 307). Such programs began the movement toward drug courts, which stress accountability, close monitoring, and treatment.

Studies examining the success of drug court programs throughout the 1990s reveal that such programs contribute to a significant reduction in recidivism. Research reveals that recidivism rates for participants range from 5 percent to 28 percent; however, recidivism rates are approximately 50 percent for defendants not participating in drug court initiatives. In addition, such programs substantially lower the self-reported drug use rates for participants (Drug Court Clearinghouse and Technical Assistance Project 1999; *Drug Courts: The Second Decade* 2006). In recent years, states such as Arizona and California have approved initiatives that mandate first- or second-time drug offenders be sentenced to probation and treatment as opposed to incarceration. A review of this program in Arizona by the state Supreme Court concluded that the rate of compliance was 62 percent as of 1999 and such initiatives saved the state $6.7 million in prison expenditures (Arizona Drug Treatment and Education Fund 2001, 364).

In light of the financial savings of many alternative initiatives and the documented success of such programs, the Obama administration has concluded that there are strong economic incentives to scale back and retool the War on Drugs. Current drug policies disproportionately affect lower-class, minority individuals, discriminate against women, and do little to reduce drug use or encourage treatment for addicted individuals and their families. Government officials now hope that by emphasizing the latter and by stressing community-based antidrug programs, better results can be achieved and a more sustainable balance might be reached between law enforcement requirements and the furtherance of public health (Hananel 2010).

See also **Drug Trafficking and Narco-Terrorism; Prison Construction; Racial, National Origin, and Religion Profiling; Three-Strikes Laws; Addiction and Family (vol. 3); Drugs (vol. 3); Medical Marijuana (vol. 4)**

Further Reading

Arizona Drug Treatment and Education Fund, "Annual Report November 2001." *Federal Sentencing Reporter* 14 (2001): 364.

Barak, Gregg, Paul Leighton, and Jeanne Flavin, *Class, Race, Gender, and Crime*, 2d ed. Lanham, MD: Rowman & Littlefield, 2007.

Benavie, Arthur, *Drugs: America's Holy War.* New York: Routledge, 2009.

Bush-Baskette, Stephanie, "The War On Drugs and the Incarceration of Mothers." *Journal of Drug Issues* 30 (2000): 924.

Campbell, Howard, *Drug War Zone: Frontline Dispatches from the Streets of El Paso and Juárez.* Austin: University of Texas Press, 2009.

Campbell, Nancy D., *Using Women: Gender, Drug Policy, and Social Justice.* New York: Routledge, 2000.

Drug Court Clearinghouse and Technical Assistance Project, *Looking at a Decade of Drug Courts,* 1999. http://www1.spa.american.edu/justice/documents/2049.pdf

Drug Courts: The Second Decade, 2006. http://www1.spa.american.edu/justice/documents/207.pdf

Federal Bureau of Investigation, *Crime in the United States: Uniform Crime Report 2000.* http://www.fbi.gov/ucr/00cius.htm

Fish, Jefferson M., ed., *Drugs and Society: U.S. Public Policy.* Lanham, MD: Rowman & Littlefield, 2006.

Gray, James P., *Why Our Drug Laws Have Failed and What We Can Do about It.* Philadelphia: Temple University Press, 2001.

Hananel, Sam, "Obama Shifts Strategy away from War on Drugs." *Boston Globe* (May 12, 2010).

Inciardi, James A., *The War on Drugs IV: The Continuing Saga of the Mysteries and Miseries of Intoxication, Addiction, Crime, and Public Policy.* Boston: Allyn and Bacon, 2008.

Jenkins, Philip, *Synthetic Panics: The Symbolic Politics of Designer Drugs.* New York: New York University Press, 1999.

King, Ryan S., and Marc Mauer, *Distorted Priorities: Drug Offenders in State Prisons,* Washington, DC: Sentencing Project, 2002. http://www.sentencingproject.org/doc/publications/dp_distortedpriorities.pdf

King, Ryan S., and Marc Mauer, *The War on Marijuana: The Transformation of the War on Drugs in the 1990s.* 2005. http://www.sentencingproject.org/doc/publications/dp_waronmarijuana.pdf

MacDoun, Robert J., and Peter Reuter, *Drug War Heresies: Learning from Other Vices, Times, and Places.* Cambridge, UK: Cambridge University Press, 2001.

Mares, David R., *Drug Wars and Coffeehouses: The Political Economy of the International Drug Trade.* Washington, DC: CQ Press, 2006.

Mauer, Marc, *The Changing Racial Dynamics of the War on Drugs,* 2009. http://www.sentencing project.org/doc/dp_raceanddrugs.pdf

Mauer, Marc, and Ryan S. King, *A 25-year Quagmire: The War on Drugs and Its Impact on American Society,* 2007. http://www.sentencingproject.org/doc/publications/dp_25yearquagmire.pdf

Office of National Drug Control Policy, 2009. http://www.whitehousedrugpolicy.gov/publica tions/policy/10budget/exec_summ.pdf

Provine, Doris Marie, *Unequal Under Law: Race in the War on Drugs.* Chicago: University of Chicago Press, 2007.

Real Reform, "Rockefeller Drug Law Reform." 2006. http://www.drugpolicy.org/docUploads/ RDLFactSheet_May06.pdf

Riley, K. Jack, "Crack, Powder Cocaine, and Heroin: Drug Purchase and Use Patterns in Six U.S. Cities." December 1997. http://www.ojp.usdoj.gov/nij/pubs-sum/167265.htm

Sadofsky Baggins, David, *Drug Hate and the Corruption of American Justice.* Westport, CT: Praeger, 1998.

Bibliography

Problems and Policies

Abele, Robert P., *A User's Guide to the USA Patriot Act and Beyond.* Lanham, MD: University Press of America, 2005.

Arrigo, B., *Social Justice/Criminal Justice: The Maturation of Critical Theory in Law, Crime, and Deviance.* Contemporary Issues in Crime and Justice Series. Belmont, CA: Wadsworth, 1999.

Barak, Gregg, Paul Leighton, and Jeanne Flavin, *Class, Race, Gender, and Crime: The Social Realities of Justice in America,* 3d ed. Lanham, MD: Rowman & Littlefield, 2010.

Barkun, Michael, *Religion and the Racist Right: The Origins of the Christian Identity Movement.* Chapel Hill: University of North Carolina Press, 1996.

Belknap, Joanne, *The Invisible Woman: Gender, Crime, and Justice,* 3d ed. Belmont, CA: Wadsworth, 2006.

Biegelman, Martin T., *Identity Theft Handbook: Detection, Prevention, and Security.* Hoboken, NJ: Wiley, 2009.

Bohm, Robert M., *Primer on Crime and Delinquency Theory,* 2d ed. Belmont, CA: Wadsworth, 2001.

Brasch, Walter M., *America's Unpatriotic Acts: The Federal Government's Violation of Constitutional and Civil Rights.* New York: Peter Lang, 2005.

Brenner, Susan W., *Cybercrime: Criminal Threats from Cyberspace.* Santa Barbara, CA: Praeger, 2010.

Brooks, Roy L., *Racial Justice in the Age of Obama.* Princeton, NJ: Princeton University Press, 2009.

Burbick, Joan, *Gun Show Nation: Gun Culture and American Democracy.* New York: New Press, 2006.

Buzawa, Eve S., and Carl G. Buzawa, *Domestic Violence: The Criminal Justice Response,* 3d ed. Newbury Park, CA: Sage, 2002.

Carruth, Bruce, et al., *Assessment and Treatment of the DWI Offender.* New York: Routledge, 2002.

Coleman, James, *The Criminal Elite.* New York: St. Martin's Press, 1985.

Cook, Philip J., and Jens Ludwig, *Gun Violence: The Real Costs*. New York: Oxford University Press, 2000.

Crews, G. A., and M. R. Counts, *The Evolution of School Disturbance in America: Colonial Times to Modern Day*. Westport, CT: Praeger, 1997.

Crooker, Constance E., *Gun Control and Gun Rights*. Westport, CT: Greenwood Press, 2003.

Cullen, David, *Columbine*. New York: Twelve, 2009.

D'Souza, Eugene, ed., *Crime and Social Justice: Society and Law Enforcement*. New Delhi: Commonwealth, 2002.

Davis, Richard L., *Domestic Violence: Intervention, Prevention, Policies, and Solutions*. Boca Raton, FL: CRC Press, 2008.

Decker, S., and B. Van Winkle, *Life in the Gang*. New York: Cambridge University Press, 1996.

Delaney, Tim, *American Street Gangs*. Upper Saddle River, NJ: Prentice Hall, 2006.

Doherty, Brian, *Gun Control on Trial: Inside the Supreme Court Battle over the Second Amendment*. Washington, DC: Cato Institute, 2009.

Eatwell, Roger, *Fascism and the Extreme Right*. London: Routledge, 2009.

Foerstel, Herbert N., *The Patriot Act: A Documentary and Reference Guide*. Westport, CT: Greenwood Press, 2008.

Frank, Nancy K., and Michael J. Lynch, *Corporate Crime, Corporate Violence: A Primer*. Albany, NY: Harrow and Heston, 1992.

Friedrichs, David O., *Trusted Criminals: White Collar Crime in Contemporary Society*. Belmont, CA: Wadsworth, 1996.

Furnell, S., *Cybercrime: Vandalizing the Information Society*. Boston: Addison Wesley, 2002.

Gerler, E. R. Jr., ed., *Handbook of School Violence*. Binghamton, NY: Haworth Press, 2004.

Gibson, Camille, and Donna M. Vandiver, *Juvenile Sex Offenders: What the Public Needs to Know*. Westport, CT: Praeger, 2008.

Gitlow, Abraham L., *Corruption in Corporate America: Who Is Responsible? Who Will Protect the Public Interest?* Lanham, MD: University Press of America, 2007.

Goldstein, Arnold P., *Delinquent Gangs: A Psychological Perspective*. Champaign, IL: Research Press, 1991.

Gosselin, Denise Kindshi, *Heavy Hands: An Introduction to the Crimes of Family Violence*, 3d ed. Upper Saddle River, NJ: Prentice Hall, 2004.

Hartmann, Thom, *Unequal Protection: The Rise of Corporate Dominance and the Theft of Human Rights*. New York: Rodale Press, 2002.

Hemenway, David, *Private Guns, Public Health*. Ann Arbor: University of Michigan Press, 2006.

Hewitt, Christopher, *Political Violence and Terrorism in America: A Chronology*. Westport, CT: Praeger, 2005.

Hewitt, Christopher, *Understanding Terrorism in American: From the Klan to al Qaeda*. London: Routledge, 2002.

Hickey, E. R., *Serial Murderers and Their Victims*. New York: Wadsworth, 1997.

Hoffman, Sandra K., *Identity Theft: A Reference Handbook*. Santa Barbara, CA: ABC-CLIO, 2010.

Jacobs, James, *Drunk Driving: An American Dilemma*. Chicago: University of Chicago Press, 1992.

Juergensmeyer, Mark, *Terror in the Mind of God: The Global Rise of Religious Violence*, 3d ed. Berkeley: University of California Press, 2003.

Kappeler, V., M. Blumberg, and G. Potter, *The Mythology of Crime and Criminal Justice.* Prospect Heights, IL: Waveland Press, 2000.

Karch, Steven B., *Workplace Drug Testing.* Boca Raton, FL: CRC Press, 2007.

Kinnear, Karen L., *Childhood Sexual Abuse: A Reference Handbook,* 2d ed. Santa Barbara, CA: ABC-CLIO, 2007.

Kleck, Gary, *Point Blank: Guns and Violence in America.* New York: Aldine De Gruyter, 1991.

Klein, Malcolm, *The American Street Gang: Its Nature, Prevalence, and Control.* New York: Oxford University Press, 1995.

Lebrun, Marcel, *Books, Blackboards, and Bullets: School Shootings and Violence in America.* Lanham, MD: Rowman & Littlefield, 2009.

Logan, T. K., *Partner Stalking: How Women Respond, Cope, and Survive.* New York: Springer, 2006.

Lott, John R. Jr., *More Guns, Less Crime: Understanding Crime and Gun-Control Laws,* 2d ed. Chicago: University of Chicago Press, 2000.

Ludwig, Jens, and Philip J. Cook, *Evaluating Gun Policy: Effects on Crime and Violence.* Washington, DC: Brookings Institution Press, 2003.

McClurg, Andrew, David B. Kopel, and Brannon Denning, eds., *Gun Control and Gun Rights: A Reader and Guide.* New York: New York University Press, 2002.

Melzer, Scott, *Gun Crusaders: The NRA's Culture War.* New York: New York University Press, 2009.

Michael, George, *Confronting Right-Wing Extremism and Terrorism in the USA.* London: Routledge, 2003.

Mullen, P. E., M. Pathé, and R. Purcell, *Stalkers and Their Victims,* 2d ed. Cambridge, UK: Cambridge University Press, 2009.

Mulloy, D. J., *American Extremism: History, Politics and the Militia Movement.* London: Routledge, 2008.

Murray, Thomas R., *Violence in America's Schools: Understanding, Prevention, and Responses.* Westport, CT: Praeger, 2006.

Olweus, D., *Bullying at School: What We Know and What We Can Do.* London: Blackwell, 1993.

Pious, Richard M., *The War on Terror and the Rule of Law.* Los Angeles: Roxbury, 2006.

Place, Vanessa, *The Quilt Project: Rape, Morality, Law.* New York: Other Press, 2010.

Quinney, R., *Bearing Witness to Crime and Social Justice* Albany: State University of New York Press, 2000.

Ramsland, K., *Inside the Minds of Serial Killers.* Westport CT: Praeger, 2006.

Reiman, Jeffrey, *The Rich Get Richer and the Poor Get Prison,* 8th ed. Boston: Allyn and Bacon, 2007.

Roberts, Albert R. ed., *Handbook of Domestic Violence Intervention Strategies: Policies, Programs, and Legal Remedies.* New York: Oxford University Press, 2002.

Rosoff, Stephen M., Henry N. Pontell, and Robert H. Tillman, *Profit without Honor: White-Collar Crime and the Looting of America.* Upper Saddle River, NJ: Prentice Hall, 2007.

Ross, H. Laurence, *Confronting Drunk Driving: Social Policy for Saving Lives.* New Haven, CT: Yale University Press, 1994.

Sawvel, Patty Jo, *Student Drug Testing.* Boston: Cengage Gale, 2006.

Schell, B. H., and C. Martin, *Cybercrime.* Santa Barbara, CA: ABC-CLIO, 2004.

Schell, B. H., J. L. Dodge, and S. S. Moutsatsos, *The Hacking of America: Who's Doing It, Why, and How.* Westport, CT: Quorum Books, 2002.

Schlesinger, L. B., *Serial Offenders: Current Thought, Recent Findings.* Boca Raton, FL: CRC Press, 2000.

Schulhofer, Stephen J., *Rethinking the Patriot Act: Keeping America Safe and Free.* New York: Century Foundation, 2005.

Schwartz, Martin D., and Suzanne E. Hatty, *Controversies in Critical Criminology.* Dayton, OH: Anderson, 2003.

Sheldon, Randall G., *Controlling the Dangerous Classes: A History of Criminal Justice in America,* 2d ed. Boston: Allyn and Bacon, 2007.

Simon, David, *Elite Deviance,* 9th ed. Boston: Allyn and Bacon, 2007.

Smith, Norris, and Lynn M. Messina, *Homeland Security.* New York: H. W. Wilson, 2004.

Spergel, Irving A., *The Youth Gang Problem: A Community Approach.* New York: Oxford University Press, 1995.

Spitzer, Robert J., *Gun Control: A Documentary and Reference Guide.* Westport, CT: Greenwood Press, 2009.

Taylor, Carl S., *Dangerous Society.* East Lansing: Michigan State University Press, 1990.

Thornton, William E., and Lydia Voight, *Delinquency and Justice,* 3d ed. New York: McGraw-Hill, 1992.

Walker, Samuel, Cassia Spohn, and Miriam DeLone, *The Color of Justice: Race, Ethnicity, and Crime in America.* Boston: Wadsworth, 2006.

Warshaw, Robin, *I Never Called It Rape: The Ms. Report on Recognizing, Fighting, and Surviving Date and Acquaintance Rape.* New York: HarperCollins, 1994.

Wellford, Charles, John V. Pepper, and Carol V. Petrie, eds., *Firearms and Violence: A Critical Reader.* Washington, DC: National Academies Press, 2005.

Winick, Bruce J., and John Q. La Fond, eds., *Protecting Society from Sexually Dangerous Offenders: Law, Justice, and Therapy.* Washington, DC: American Psychological Association, 2003.

Woody, Robert Henley, *Search and Seizure: The Fourth Amendment for Law Enforcement Officers.* Springfield, IL: Charles C. Thomas, 2006.

Zilney, Laura J., *Perverts and Predators: The Making of Sexual Offending Laws.* Lanham, MD: Rowman & Littlefield, 2009.

Zimring, Franklin E., *An American Tragedy: Legal Responses to Adolescent Sex Offending.* Chicago: University of Chicago Press, 2004.

Courtroom and Sentencing Issues

Aronson, Jay D., *Genetic Witness: Science, Law, and Controversy in the Making of DNA Profiling.* New Brunswick, NJ: Rutgers University Press, 2007.

Barak, Gregg, Paul Leighton, and Jeanne Flavin, *Class, Race, Gender, and Crime: The Social Realities of Justice in America.* Lanham, MD: Rowman & Littlefield, 2007.

Braswell, Michael C., Belinda R. McCarthy, and Bernard J. McCarthy, *Justice, Crime and Ethics,* 6th ed. Cincinnati, OH: Anderson, 2006.

Bronstein, Daniel A., *Law and the Expert Witness,* 3d ed. Boca Raton, FL: CRC Press, 2007.

Candilis, Philip J., Robert Weinstock, and Richard Martinez, *Forensic Ethics and the Expert Witness.* New York: Springer, 2007.

Clark, George Woody, *Justice and Science: Trials and Triumphs of DNA Evidence.* New Brunswick, NJ: Rutgers University Press, 2008.

Clark, John, James Austin, and Henry D. Alan, *Three Strikes and You're Out: A Review of State Legislation.* Washington, DC: U.S. Department of Justice, 1997.

Cohen, Stanley, *The Wrong Men: America's Epidemic of Wrongful Death Row Convictions.* New York: Carroll & Graf, 2003.

Cohn, Marjorie, and David Dow, *Cameras in the Courtroom: Television and the Pursuit of Justice.* New York: Rowman & Littlefield, 2002.

Cutler, Brian, and Margaret Bull Kovera, *Evaluating Eyewitness Identification.* New York: Oxford University Press, 2010.

Domanick, Joe, *Cruel Justice: Three Strikes and the Politics of Crime in America's Golden State.* Berkeley: University of California Press, 2004.

Doyle, James M., *True Witness: Cops, Courts, Science, and the Battle against Misidentification.* New York: Palgrave Macmillan, 2005.

Erickson, Patricia E., *Crime, Punishment, and Mental Illness: Law and the Behavioral Sciences in Conflict.* New Brunswick, NJ: Rutgers University Press, 2008.

Ewing, Charles Patrick, *Insanity: Murder, Madness, and the Law.* New York: Oxford University Press, 2008.

Fisher, Jim, *Forensics under Fire: Are Bad Science and Dueling Experts Corrupting Criminal Justice?* New Brunswick, NJ: Rutgers University Press, 2008.

Flew, Anthony, *Crime, Punishment, and Disease.* New Brunswick, NJ: Transaction, 2002.

Forst, Brian, *Errors of Justice: Nature, Sources, and Remedies.* New York: Cambridge University Press, 2004.

Friedman, Lawrence, *Crime and Punishment in American History.* New York: Basic Books, 1993.

Goldfarb, Ronald L., *TV or Not TV: Television, Justice, and the Courts.* New York: New York University Press, 2000.

Grisham, John, *The Innocent Man: Murder and Injustice in a Small Town.* New York: Doubleday, 2006.

Harris, Rebecca C., *Black Robes, White Coats: The Puzzle of Judicial Policymaking and Scientific Evidence.* New Brunswick, NJ: Rutgers University Press, 2008.

Kennedy, Randall, *Race, Crime and the Law.* New York: Pantheon, 1997.

Lazer, David, ed., *DNA and the Criminal Justice System: The Technology of Justice.* Cambridge, MA: MIT Press, 2004.

Lee, Henry C., and Frank Tirnady, *Blood Evidence: How DNA is Revolutionizing the Way We Solve Crimes.* Cambridge, MA: Perseus, 2003.

Loftus, Elizabeth F., *Eyewitness Testimony.* Cambridge, MA: Harvard University Press, 1996.

Lynch, Michael, et al., *Truth Machine: The Contentious History of DNA Fingerprinting.* Chicago: University of Chicago Press, 2009.

Lytle, Leslie, *Execution's Doorstep: True Stories of the Innocent and Near Damned.* Boston: Northeastern University Press, 2008.

Mann, Coramae, Marjorie S. Zatz, and Nancy Rodriguez, eds., *Images of Color, Images of Crime: A Reader.* New York: Oxford University Press, 2006.

Mauer, Marc, and Ryan S. King, *Uneven Justice: State Rates of Incarceration by Race and Ethnicity.* Washington, DC: Sentencing Project, 2007.

Meyer, Carl, *Expert Witnessing: Explaining and Understanding Science.* Boca Raton, FL: CRC Press, 1999.

Miller, Jerome G., *Search and Destroy: African-American Males in the Criminal Justice System.* New York: Cambridge University Press, 1996.

Muhammad, Khalil Gibran, *The Condemnation of Blackness: Race, Crime, and the Making of Modern Urban America.* Cambridge, MA: Harvard University Press, 2010.

Muraskin, Roslyn, and Albert R. Roberts, *Visions for Change: Crime and Justice in the 21st Century,* 5th ed. Upper Saddle River, NJ: Prentice Hall, 2008.

Provine, Doris Marie, *Unequal under Law: Race in the War on Drugs.* Chicago: University of Chicago Press, 2007.

Rhode, Deborah L., *Access to Justice.* New York: Oxford University Press, 2004.

Robinson, Matthew B., *Justice Blind? Ideals and Realities of American Criminal Justice,* 3d ed. Upper Saddle River, NJ: Prentice Hall, 2008.

Robinson, Paul H., and Michael T. Cahill, *Law Without Justice: Why Criminal Law Doesn't Give People What They Deserve.* New York: Oxford University Press, 2006.

Rossmo, D. Kim, *Criminal Investigative Failures.* Boca Raton, FL: CRC Press, 2008.

Rudin, Norah, and Keith Inman, *An Introduction to Forensic DNA Analysis,* 2d ed. Boca Raton, FL: CRC Press, 2001.

Russell-Brown, Katheryn, *The Color of Crime,* 2d ed. New York: New York University Press, 2008.

Sales, Bruce Dennis, *Experts in Court: Reconciling Law, Science, and Professional Knowledge.* Washington, DC: American Psychological Association, 2005.

Sporer, Siegfried Ludwig, Roy S. Malpass, and Guenter Koehnken, eds., *Psychological Issues in Eyewitness Identification.* Mahwah, NJ: Erlbaum, 1996.

Tonry, Michael, *Malign Neglect: Race, Crime, and Punishment in America.* New York: Oxford University Press, 1995.

Torrey, E. Fuller, *The Insanity Defense: How America's Failure to Treat the Seriously Mental Ill Endangers Its Citizens.* New York: Norton, 2008.

Walker, Samuel, Cassia Spohn, and Miriam DeLone, *The Color of Justice: Race, Ethnicity and Crime in America,* 4th ed. Belmont, CA: Wadsworth, 2006.

Weiss, Michael Scott, *Public Defenders: Pragmatic and Political Motivations to Represent the Indigent.* New York: LFB Scholarly Publishing, 2004.

Westervelt, Saundra D., and John A. Humphrey, eds., *Wrongly Convicted: Perspectives on Failed Justice.* Newark, NJ: Rutgers University Press, 2001.

Wice, Paul B., *Public Defenders and the American Justice System.* Westport, CT: Praeger, 2005.

Policing

Alpert, Geoffrey P., and Roger G. Dunham, *Understanding Police Use of Force: Officers, Suspects, and Reciprocity.* Cambridge, UK: Cambridge University Press, 2004.

Bloom, Robert M., *Searches, Seizures, and Warrants: A Reference Guide to the United States Constitution.* Westport, CT: Praeger, 2003.

Bodenhamer, David J., *Our Rights.* New York: Oxford University Press, 2007.

Bolton, Kenneth, and Joe R. Feagin, *Black in Blue: African-American Police Officers and Racism.* New York: Routledge, 2004.

Burris, John L., and Catherine Whitney, *Blue vs. Black: Let's End the Conflict between Cops and Minorities.* New York: St. Martin's Griffin, 1999.

Carmen, Alejandro del, *Racial Profiling in America*. Upper Saddle River, NJ: Pearson/Prentice Hall, 2008.

Chevigny, Paul, *Edge of the Knife: Police Violence in the Americas*. New York: New Press, 1995.

Dershowitz, Alan M., *Shouting Fire: Civil Liberties in a Turbulent Age*. Boston: Little, Brown, 2002.

Ferdico, John, *Criminal Procedure for the Criminal Justice Professional*, 10th ed. Belmont, CA: Thomson Wadsworth, 2008.

Georges-Abeyie, D., *The Criminal Justice System and Blacks*. New York: Clark Boardman, 1984.

Glover, Karen S., *Racial Profiling: Research, Racism, and Resistance*. Lanham, MD: Rowman & Littlefield, 2009.

Harcourt, Bernard E., *Against Prediction: Profiling, Policing, and Punishing in an Actuarial Age*. Chicago: University of Chicago Press, 2007.

Harris, David A., *Profiles in Injustice: Why Racial Profiling Won't Work*. New York: Free Press, 2002.

Holmes, Malcolm D., *Race and Police Brutality: Roots of an Urban Dilemma*. Albany: State University of New York Press, 2008.

Human Rights Watch, *Shielded from Justice: Police Brutality and Accountability in the United States*. New York: Human Rights Watch, 1998.

Ingram, Jefferson L., *Criminal Procedure, Theory and Practice*, 2d ed. Upper Saddle River, NJ: Pearson/Prentice Hall, 2008.

Ivers, Greg, and Kevin T. McGuire, *Creating Constitutional Change: Clashes over Power and Liberty in the Supreme Court*. Charlottesville: University of Virginia Press, 2004.

Ivkovic, Sanja Kutnjak, *Fallen Blue Knights: Controlling Police Corruption*. New York: Oxford University Press, 2005.

Krivo, Lauren J., and Ruth D. Peterson, *Race, Crime, and Justice: Contexts and Complexities*. Thousand Oaks, CA: Sage, 2009.

Levitt, Leonard, *NYPD Confidential: Power and Corruption in the Country's Greatest Police Force*. New York: Thomas Dunne Books, 2009.

Moore, Robert, *Search and Seizure of Digital Evidence*. New York: LFB Scholarly Publishing, 2005.

Muhammad, Khalil Gibran, *The Condemnation of Blackness: Race, Crime, and the Making of Urban America*. Cambridge, MA: Harvard University Press, 2010.

Nelson, Jill, *Police Brutality: An Anthology*. New York: W. W. Norton, 2001.

Prenzler, Tim, *Police Corruption: Preventing Misconduct and Maintaining Integrity*. Boca Raton, FL: CRC Press, 2009.

Roberg, Roy, Kenneth Novack, and Gary Cordner, *Police and Society*. New York: Oxford University Press, 2008.

Skolnick, Jerome, and James J. Fyfe, *Above the Law: Police Practices and Procedures*. New York: Free Press/Macmillan, 1993.

Stuart, Gary L., *Miranda: The Story of America's Right to Remain Silent*. Tucson: University of Arizona Press, 2004.

Walker, Samuel, *The New World of Police Accountability*. Thousand Oaks, CA: Sage, 2005.

Weitzer, Ronald, and Steven A. Tuch, *Race and Policing in America: Conflict and Reform*. New York: Cambridge University Press, 2006.

White, Welsh S., *Miranda's Waning Protections*. Ann Arbor: University of Michigan Press, 2001.

Williams, Kristian, *Our Enemies in Blue: Police and Power in America*. Cambridge, MA: South End Press, 2007.

Withrow, Brian L., *Racial Profiling: From Rhetoric to Reason*. Upper Saddle River, NJ: Pearson/Prentice Hall, 2006.

Immigration, Smuggling, and Border Security

Andreas, Peter, *Border Games: Policing the U.S.-Mexico Divide,* 2d ed. Ithaca, NY: Cornell University Press, 2009;

Bales, Kevin, *Disposable People: New Slavery in the Global Economy*. Berkeley: University of California Press, 2004.

Batstone, David, *Not for Sale: The Return of the Global Slave Trade, and How We Can Fight It*. New York: HarperOne, 2007.

Benavie, Arthur, *Drugs: America's Holy War*. New York: Routledge, 2009.

Brotherton, David C., and Philip Kretsedemas, eds., *Keeping Out the Other: A Critical Introduction to Immigration Enforcement Today*. New York: Columbia University Press, 2008.

Buchanan, Patrick, *State of Emergency: The Third World Invasion and Conquest of America*. New York: Thomas Dunn Books/St. Martin's Press, 2006.

Campbell, Howard, *Drug War Zone: Frontline Dispatches from the Streets of El Paso and Juárez*. Austin: University of Texas Press, 2009.

Campbell, Howard, *Drug War Zone: Frontline Dispatches from the Streets of El Paso and Juárez*. Austin: University of Texas Press, 2009.

Chomsky, Aviva, *They Take Our Jobs! and 20 Other Myths about Immigration*. Boston: Beacon Press, 2007.

Cieslik, Thomas, David Felsen, and Akis Kalaitizidis, eds., *Immigration: A Documentary and Reference Guide*. Westport, CT: Greenwood Press, 2009.

Daniels, Roger, *Coming to America: A History of Immigration and Ethnicity in American Life,* 2d ed. New York: Harper Perennial, 2002.

DeStefano, Anthony M., *The War on Human Trafficking: U.S. Policy Assessed*. New Brunswick, NJ: Rutgers University Press, 2007.

Dougherty, Jon E., *Illegals: The Imminent Threat Posed by Our Unsecured U.S.-Mexico Border*. Nashville, TN: WND Books, 2004.

Edberg, Mark Cameron, *El Narcotrafficante: Narcocorridos and the Creation of a Cultural Persona on the U.S.-Mexico Border*. Austin: University of Texas Press, 2004.

Fish, Jefferson M., ed., *Drugs and Society: U.S. Public Policy*. Lanham, MD: Rowman & Littlefield, 2006.

Gaynor, Tim, *Midnight on the Line: The Secret Life of the U.S.-Mexico Border*. New York: Thomas Dunne Books, 2009.

Gray, James P., *Why Our Drug Laws Have Failed and What We Can Do about It*. Philadelphia: Temple University Press, 2001.

Inciardi, James A., *The War on Drugs IV: The Continuing Saga of the Mysteries and Miseries of Intoxication, Addiction, Crime, and Public Policy*. Boston: Allyn and Bacon, 2008.

Johnson, Kevin R., *Opening the Floodgates: Why America Needs to Rethink Its Borders and Immigration Laws*. New York: New York University Press, 2007.

Kenney, Michael, *From Pablo to Osama: Trafficking and Terrorist Networks, Government Bureaucracies and Competitive Adaptation.* Philadelphia: University of Pennsylvania Press, 2007.

Kyle, David, and Rey Koslowski, eds., *Global Human Smuggling: Comparative Perspectives.* Baltimore: Johns Hopkins University Press, 2001.

MacDoun, Robert J., and Peter Reuter, *Drug War Heresies: Learning from Other Vices, Times, and Places.* Cambridge, UK: Cambridge University Press, 2001.

Mares, David R., *Drug Wars and Coffeehouses: The Political Economy of the International Drug Trade.* Washington, DC: CQ Press, 2006.

Martin, Philip L., *Importing Poverty? Immigration and the Changing Face of Rural America.* New Haven: Yale University Press, 2009.

Mills, Nicolaus, *Arguing Immigration: The Debate over the Changing Face of America.* New York: Touchstone, 2007.

Newton, Lina, *Illegal, Alien, or Immigrant: The Politics of Immigration Reform.* New York: New York University Press, 2008.

Ngai, Mai, *Impossible Subjects: Illegal Aliens and the Making of Modern America.* Princeton, NJ: Princeton University Press, 2004.

Payan, Tony, *The Three U.S.-Mexico Border Wars: Drugs, Immigration and Homeland Security.* Westport, CT: Praeger Security International/Greenwood, 2006.

Provine, Doris Marie, *Unequal Under Law: Race in the War on Drugs.* Chicago: University of Chicago Press, 2007.

Richardson, Chad, *On the Edge of the Law: Culture, Labor and Deviance on the South Texas Border.* Austin: University of Texas Press, 2006.

Romero, Fernando, *Hyperborder: The Contemporary U.S.-Mexico Border and Its Future.* New York: Princeton Architectural Press, 2008.

Sadofsky Baggins, David, *Drug Hate and the Corruption of American Justice.* Westport, CT: Praeger, 1998.

Skinner, E. Benjamin, *A Crime So Monstrous: Face-to-Face with Modern-Day Slavery.* New York: Free Press, 2009.

Swain, Carol M., ed., *Debating Immigration.* New York: Cambridge University Press, 2007.

Takaki, Ronald, *A Different Mirror: A History of Multicultural America,* rev. ed. Boston: Back Bay Books, 2008.

Velasco, Jose Luis, *Insurgency, Authoritarianism and Drug Trafficking in Mexico's "Democratization."* New York: Routledge, 2005.

Zhang, Sheldon X., *Smuggling and Trafficking in Human Beings: All Roads Lead to the United States.* Westport, CT: Praeger, 2007.

Prison and Other Punishments

Acker, James R., Robert M. Bohm, and Charles S. Lanier, eds., *America's Experiment with Capital Punishment: Reflections on the Past, Present and Future of the Ultimate Penal Sanction,* 2d ed. Durham, NC: Carolina Academic Press, 2003.

Allen, Harry E., ed., *Repairing Communities through Restorative Justice.* Lanham, MD: American Correctional Association, 2002.

Anderson, David, *Sensible Justice: Alternative to Prison.* New York: New Press, 1998.

Bakken, Gordon Morris, *Invitation to an Execution: A History of the Death Penalty in the United States.* Albuquerque: University of New Mexico Press, 2010.

Banner, Stuart, *The Death Penalty: An American History.* Cambridge, MA: Harvard University Press, 2002.

Bedau, Hugo, and Paul Cassell, eds., *Debating the Death Penalty: Should America Have Capital Punishment?* New York: Oxford University Press, 2004.

Begg, Moazzam, with Victoria Brittain, *Enemy Combatant: A British Muslim's Journey to Guantanamo and Back.* London: Free Press, 2006.

Bohm, Robert M., *Deathquest III: An Introduction to the Theory and Practice of Capital Punishment in the United States,* 3d ed. Cincinnati, OH: Anderson, 2007.

Bruton, James H., *The Big House: Life inside a Supermax Security Prison.* Saint Paul, MN: Voyageur Press, 2004.

Caputo, Gail A., *Intermediate Sanctions in Corrections.* Denton: University of North Texas Press, 2004.

Clear, Todd R., and David R. Karp, *The Community Justice Ideal: Promoting Safety and Achieving Justice.* Boulder, CO: Westview, 1999.

Cusac, Anne-Marie, *Cruel and Unusual: The Culture of Punishment in America.* New Haven, CT: Yale University Press, 2009.

Evans, Kimberly Masters, *Capital Punishment: Cruel and Unusual?* Detroit: Gale, 2008.

Fleisher, Mark S., and Jessica L. Krienert, *The Myth of Prison Rape: Sexual Culture in American Prisons.* Lanham, MD: Rowman & Littlefield, 2009.

Frost, Natasha, *The Punitive State: Crime, Punishment, and Imprisonment across the United States.* New York: LFB Scholarly Publishing, 2006.

Gaes, G. G., and A. L. Goldberg, *Prison Rape: A Critical Review of the Literature.* Washington, DC: National Institute of Justice, 2004.

Gottschalk, Marie, *The Prison and the Gallows: The Politics of Mass Incarceration in America.* New York: Cambridge University Press, 2006.

Hafetz, Jonathan, and Mark Denbeaux, eds., *The Guantanamo Lawyers: Inside a Prison Outside the Law.* New York: New York University Press, 2009.

Hallet, Michael A., *Private Prisons in America: A Critical Race Perspective.* Urbana: University of Illinois Press, 2006.

Haney, Craig, *Death by Design: Capital Punishment as a Social Psychological System.* New York: Oxford University Press, 2005.

Hensley, Christopher, ed., *Prison Sex: Practice and Policy.* Boulder, CO: Lynne Rienner, 2002.

Jacobson, Michael, *Downsizing Prisons: How to Reduce Crime and End Mass Incarceration.* New York: New York University Press, 2005.

Jarvis, Brian, *Cruel and Unusual: Punishment and U.S. Culture.* London: Pluto Press, 2005.

Kuznel, Regina G., *Criminal Intimacy: Prison and the Uneven History of Modern American Sexuality.* Chicago: University of Chicago Press, 2008.

Lynch, Mona, *Sunbelt Justice: Arizona and the Transformation of American Punishment.* Stanford, CA: Stanford Law Books, 2010.

May, John P., and Khilid R. Pitts, eds., *Building Violence: How America's Rush to Incarcerate Creates More Violence.* Thousand Oaks, CA: Sage, 2000.

McShane, Marilyn D., *Prisons in America*. New York: LFB Scholarly Publishing, 2008.

Melusky, Joseph Anthony, *Cruel and Unusual Punishment: Rights and Liberties under the Law*. Santa Barbara, CA: ABC-CLIO, 2003.

Neal, Donice, ed., *Supermax Prisons: Beyond the Rock*. Lanham, MD: American Correctional Association, 2002.

Pratt, Travis C., *Addicted to Incarceration: Corrections Policy and the Politics of Misinformation in the United States*. Los Angeles: Sage, 2009.

Rhodes, Lorna A., *Total Confinement: Madness and Reason in the Maximum Security Prison*. Berkeley, CA: University of California Press, 2004.

Riveland, Chase, *Supermax Prison: Overview and General Considerations*. Longmont, CO: National Institute of Corrections, 1998.

Selman, Donna, and Paul Leighton, *Punishment for Sale: Private Prisons, Big Business, and the Incarceration Binge*. Lanham, MD: Rowman & Littlefield, 2010.

Shalev, Sharon, *Supermax: Controlling Risk through Solitary Confinement*. Uffculme, UK: Willan, 2009.

Sundby, Scott E., *A Life and Death Decision: A Jury Weighs the Death Penalty*. New York: Palgrave Macmillan, 2007.

Tucker, Susan, and Eric Cadora, *Ideas for an Open Society: Justice Reinvestment*. New York: Open Society Institute, 2003.

Useem, Bert, and Anne Morrison Piehl, *Prison State: The Challenge of Mass Incarceration*. New York: Cambridge University Press, 2008.

Vass, Anthony A., *Alternatives to Prison: Punishment Custody and the Community*. Newbury Park, CA: Sage, 1990.

Whitman, James Q., *Harsh Justice: Criminal Punishment and the Widening Divide between America and Europe*. New York: Oxford University Press, 2003.

About the Editor and Contributors

Editor

Michael Shally-Jensen is former editor-in-chief of the *Encyclopedia Americana*, executive editor of the *Encyclopedia of American Studies*, and editor of numerous other books and reference publications. He received his Ph.D. in cultural anthropology from Princeton University, having specialized in aspects of American culture and society. He lives in Amherst, Massachusetts.

Contributors

Gregg Barak is a professor of criminology and criminal justice at Eastern Michigan University and a former visiting distinguished professor and scholar in the College of Justice and Safety at Eastern Kentucky University. Barak has more than 100 publications, including more than 15 books. His most recent title is *Criminology: An Integrated Approach* (2009).

Christopher Bickel is an assistant professor of sociology at California Polytechnic State University, San Luis Obispo. He specializes in criminal justice with an emphasis on juvenile justice. He is currently the director of the "Continuation to College" program at a local continuation school.

Robert M. Bohm is a professor of criminal justice and legal studies at the University of Central Florida. Among his most recent publications are *Introduction to Criminal Justice*, 5th ed. (McGraw-Hill, 2008) and *Deathquest III: An Introduction to the Theory and Practice of Capital Punishment in the United States*, 3rd ed. (2007). He is a past president and fellow of the Academy of Criminal Justice Sciences.

Charles I. Brooks is professor and chair of the Department of Psychology, King's College, Wilkes-Barre, Pennsylvania. He received his masters in psychology from Wake Forest University and his doctorate in experimental psychology from Syracuse University. He has taught at King's College since 1975 and was designated a distinguished service professor in 1993. He has authored or coauthored more than 40 scholarly publications in psychology.

Michael A. Church is associate professor of psychology at King's College in Wilkes-Barre, Pennsylvania. He received his masters and doctoral degrees in psychology from the University of Miami. He has taught at King's College since 1976 and has been a licensed clinical psychologist with a private practice since 1980. He is a member of the Council of National Register of Health Service Providers in Psychology.

Marilyn Corsianos is an associate professor of criminology and sociology at Eastern Michigan University. She has published a number of articles dealing with policing, social justice, and gender issues and is the coeditor of *Interrogating Social Justice: Politics, Culture and Identity* (CSP, 1999). She is also the author of the book, *Policing and Gendered Justice: Examining the Possibilities* (UTP, 2009). She teaches a number of courses in both criminology and sociology at both the graduate and undergraduate level and has presented at local, national, and international professional conferences.

Allison M. Cotton is an associate professor of criminology at the Metropolitan State College of Denver in Colorado. She received a master's degree in sociology from Howard University in Washington, D.C., and a Ph.D. in sociology from the University of Colorado at Boulder. Her research interests include issues of race and gender and portrayal of crime and criminals in the media. She is the author of *Effigy: Images of Capital Defendants* (2008).

Annie Fukushima is a Ph.D. candidate in ethnic studies with an emphasis on gender, women, and sexuality at the University of California, Berkeley. As a scholar activist, Fukushima founded an arts and awareness initiative called Students & Artists Fighting to End Human Slavery. Her scholarly work also includes her collaboration with various academic working groups and organizations from grassroots to nonprofit.

Venessa Garcia is an assistant professor of criminal justice at Kean University in Union, NJ. She received her Masters degree and Ph.D. in sociology from the State University of New York University at Buffalo. Her teaching and research interests focus on women and criminal justice, police culture, and portrayals of crime and victims in the media. She is the coauthor (with Janice Clifford) of *Female Victims of Crime* (2008).

Jo-Ann Della Giustina teaches in the sociology and government departments at John Jay College. She earned an M.A. in interdisciplinary arts education from Columbia College Chicago, and a J.D. from Chicago-Kent College of Law. Currently, she is a doctoral candidate in the Criminal Justice program at the City University of New York Graduate

Center. Her areas of research interest include women and crime, domestic violence, community issues, and media and the law.

Karen S. Glover is an assistant professor in the Criminology and Justice Studies program at California State University San Marcos, where she teaches courses in critical criminology and race studies. She received her Ph.D. from Texas A&M University. Her research interests include racialization and criminalization processes in the criminal justice system. Among her publications is the book *Racial Profiling: Research, Racism, and Resistance* (2009).

Richard D. Hartley is an assistant professor in the Department of Criminal Justice at the University of Texas at San Antonio. He holds a Ph.D. from the School of Criminology and Criminal Justice at the University of Nebraska at Omaha. He teaches courses relating to criminal courts and the administration of justice as well as research methods and statistics. His research interests include prosecutorial and judicial discretion, race/ethnicity and crime, and quantitative methods. Some of his recent and forthcoming publications appear in *Aggression and Violent Behavior, Crime and Delinquency, Criminal Justice Review, Journal of Criminal Justice,* and *Journal of Pediatrics.*

Jessica S. Henry is an assistant professor at Montclair State University, where she teaches in the Department of Justice Studies. She received her J.D. from New York University School of Law. Her primary research areas are criminal law and procedure, prisoner reentry, and hate crimes.

Li-Ching Hung teaches at the Overseas Institute of Technology in Taijung, Taiwan. She earned her Ph.D. in education at Mississippi State University and is working toward a second doctorate in counselor education. She has more than 40 publications, including (with Cary Stacy Smith), *The Patriot Act* (2010).

Jonathan Kremser joined the faculty of criminal justice at Kutztown University of Pennsylvania in 2003. His previous research interests have focused on secondary school violence and disciplinary policies in Ontario, Canada. His current academic and research interests include school safety initiatives and legislation, street-level interventions targeting young offenders, urban crime prevention, and critical theory. He has presented papers on school discipline policy and urban crime control at several major conferences in the United States and Canada.

Paul Leighton is a professor in the Department of Sociology, Anthropology and Criminology at Eastern Michigan University. His research interests include violence, white collar crime, criminal justice policy, and punishment. Along with Jeffrey Reiman, he edited *Criminal Justice Ethics* (Prentice Hall, 2001) and he coauthored—with Gregg Barak and Jeanne Flavin—*Class, Race, Gender and Crime* (2007). He has been the North American editor of *Critical Criminology: An International Journal* and the American

Society of Criminology's Division on Critical Criminology named him Critical Criminologist of the Year in 2001. He is founder and webmaster of StopViolence.com, a collection of information about violence prevention.

Keith G. Logan is a former federal law enforcement officer, having served with the U.S. Drug Enforcement Administration, the U.S. Environmental Protection Agency, and the U.S. Nuclear Regulatory Commission. He was a special assistant U.S. attorney for the District of Columbia and the Eastern District of Virginia, where he is presently admitted to practice law, in addition to the U.S. Supreme Court. He is a former U.S. Army Reserve Officer, Major, Military Police Corps, as well as a consultant specializing in the investigation of whistleblower retaliation allegations and Equal Economic Opportunity (EEO) concerns. He has been a visiting instructor on the U.S. Criminal Justice system at the Diplomatic Academy in Moscow, Russia.

Catherine D. Marcum is an assistant professor of justice studies in the Political Science Department at Georgia Southern University. She received her Ph.D. in criminology from Indiana University of Pennsylvania. Her most recent work appears in *Deviant Behavior, Criminal Justice Studies, International Journal of Cyber Criminology,* and *Journal of Child Sexual Abuse.*

Will Mingus is a counselor for sex offenders in Chicago and is pursuing an advanced degree in sociology at the University of Illinois at Chicago. His current research focuses on how sex offender registries create unanticipated reentry problems for offenders that hamper successful reintegration into their communities.

Matthew Muraskin is an attorney, former head of the Nassau County Legal Aid Society, and coauthor (with Roslyn Muraskin) of *Morality and the Law* (2000).

Roslyn Muraskin is a professor of criminal justice at the C.W. Post Campus of Long Island University. Among her many published works are *Key Correctional Issues,* 2d ed. (2009), *It's a Crime: Women and Justice,* 4th ed. (2006), and (with Shelly Domash) *Crime and the Media* (2006). She is the editor of the journal *Criminal Justice Studies.*

Matt Nobles is an assistant professor in the Criminal Justice program at Washington State University. He received his doctorate in criminology from the University of Florida. His areas of interest include violent and interpersonal crime, guns and gun policy, and communities and crime.

Leanne R. Owen is an associate professor of criminal justice in the School of Arts and Sciences at Holy Family University in Philadelphia, where she also serves as program director for the Criminal Justice Graduate Program. She earned her master's and doctorate in comparative criminology and criminal justice from the University of Wales, Bangor. Her research interests include prosecutorial discretion and juvenile delinquency.

Alexander W. Pisciotta is a professor of criminal justice and chair of the Criminal Justice department at Kutztown University of Pennsylvania. He has written numerous articles appearing in criminal justice, criminology, and law journals, and is author of the book *Benevolent Repression: Social Control and the American Reformatory-Prison Movement* (1996).

Byron E. Price is an assistant professor of public administration at Rutgers University–Newark. He is the associate director of the National Center for Public Productivity, Rutgers University–Newark, editor-in-chief of the *Journal of Public Management and Social Policy,* and case study editor for *Public Productivity and Management Review.* His current research agenda includes constitutional implications of public and private arrangements, prison privatization, e-governance, performance measurement, and education reform.

Rebecca Romo is a graduate student at the University of California–Santa Barbara. Her particular interests rest in the Northern (Norteño) and Southern (Sureño) California Chicana/o gangs and the interethnic relations between blacks and Chicanas/os in the United States. Rebecca is currently involved in multiple social justice campaigns.

Jeffrey Ian Ross is an associate professor in the Division of Criminology, Criminal Justice and Social Policy, and a fellow of the Center for International and Comparative Law at the University of Baltimore. He has researched, written, and lectured on national security, political violence, political crime, violent crime, corrections, and policing for over two decades. Ross's work has appeared in many academic journals and books as well as popular outlets. He is the author, coauthor, editor, and coeditor of 13 books including most recently *Beyond Bars: Rejoining Society after Prison* (2009).

Tawandra L. Rowell is a postdoctoral fellow at the HIV Center for Clinical and Behavioral Studies at the New York Psychiatric Institute and Columbia University. She received her doctorate in Social Welfare from the University of Pennsylvania. Rowell is interested in the role of incarceration, substance abuse, and sexual behavior in HIV acquisition and transmission among African American men.

Leila Sadeghi is an assistant professor and senior research associate with the Center for Executive Leadership in Government at Rutgers University. Her research and teaching interests focus on social media for government, privatization, and criminal justice policy. She has published several book chapters, articles, and reports on these topics and she has designed and hosted training sessions for public officials in these areas.

Claudia San Miguel is an assistant professor and director of the Criminal Justice Program at Texas A&M International University. She received her Ph.D. in criminal justice from Sam Houston University. She is co–guest editor of *The Journal of Social and*

Ecological Boundaries (JSEB) Special Issue: Immigration: Crime, Victimization and Media Representation. She has published in the *Criminal Justice Review, JSEB.*

Xuan Santos is a graduate student at the University of California-Santa Barbara. His research interests focuses on the informal labor market and the underground economy of immigrants in the United States, and the intersection of antigang and anti-immigrant public policy. He is a community activist and advocate for gang and immigrant rights reform.

Bernadette H. Schell is a professor of business and information technology at the University of Ontario Institute of Technology, Oshawa, Ontario. Her published works include (with John L. Dodge) *The Hacking of America: Who's Doing It and Why* (Praeger, 2002) and (with Clemens Martin) *Cybercrime: A Reference Handbook* (ABC-CLIO, 2004).

Julia Selman-Ayetey is a lecturer in criminology at Anglia Ruskin University in Cambridge, U.K. She is particularly interested in the legislative framework governing the use of DNA in criminal justice systems and its impact on civil liberties and human rights. She is a member of the National DNA Database Ethics Group which advises the British Home Office and has contributed to a number of edited books on the forensic use of DNA.

Donna Selman-Killingbeck received her doctorate from Western Michigan University and is currently an assistant professor in the department of sociology, anthropology, and criminology at Eastern Michigan University. Her research interests include prison privatization, restorative justice, and community justice.

William L. Shulman is an associate professor of criminal justice at Middle Tennessee State University. Prior to teaching at Middle, in 1990 he served as an assistant public defender, a senior assistant public defender, and the elected public defender for Nashville, Tennessee, from 1980 to 1990. He obtained his J.D. from the University of Tennessee College of Law.

Cary Stacy Smith is a Ph.D. candidate in psychology at Mississippi State University. He has authored or coauthored numerous publications, including most recently (with Li-Ching Hung) *The Patriot Act* (2010).

Daniel L. Smith-Christopher is a professor of theological studies and director of peace studies at Loyola Marymount University. He appears regularly on television as a consultant and scholarly commentator on documentaries broadcast by A&E, Discovery, the History Channel, The National Geographic Network, and PBS (Public Broadcasting System), and is the author of numerous works of scholarship.

Rick M. Steinmann received his master's in criminal justice from Youngstown State University and a law degree from Hamline University School of Law. He has fieldwork experience in juvenile justice, corrections, policing, and within the court system. He has taught criminal justice courses full-time at the university level for 24 years and his research interests generally pertain to how various legal issues impact on the criminal justice system.

Angela Taylor is an assistant professor of criminal justice at Fayetteville State University. She received her M.A. and Ph.D. degrees in criminal justice from Rutgers University. Her research areas are violence, drugs–crime linkages, drug use measurement, and health disparities and crime.

Jim Thomas is professor emeritus at Northern Illinois University, where he specializes in research on prison culture, research ethics, and computer crime. He has been active in prison monitoring and reform and prisoner education for over 25 years and is currently exploring the impact of faith-based initiatives in prison programming. His most recent publications include self-injury among women prisoners and Nigerian e-mail scams. He is also completing a volume on ethnographic research methods and adaptation to prison culture.

E. Andreas Tomaszewski is on the Justice Studies faculty of Mount Royal University, Calgary, Alberta, Canada. A native of Germany, he obtained an M.A. in Canadian studies and a Ph.D. in sociology from Carleton University in Ottawa. His research interests focus on the sociology of crime and deviance, with a special interest in social control, as well as social justice issues. He has published on Aboriginal justice issues, violence against women, street crime, drugs, transnational crime, and social justice pedagogy.

Judith Ann Warner is a professor of sociology and criminal justice at Texas A&M International University (TAMIU). In 2008, she received the Distance Educator of the Year award, and in 1991 she received the Scholar of the Year award from TAMIU. She is co-editor of the *Journal of Social and Ecological Boundaries* and has published in the areas of immigration, homeland security, and domestic violence. Her research interests include immigration, homeland security, and the intersection of race, class, and gender.

Dianne Williams is a lecturer at North Carolina Agricultural & Technical State University. She is a certified Social & Behavioral Research Investigator and a certified Criminal Justice Specialist. Her research interests include minority issues in criminal justice, capital punishment, and media influence in criminal justice. She is the author of *Race, Ethnicity, and the Criminal Justice System* (2010).

Jessica Williams attends Loyola Law School in New Orleans, having graduated summa cum laude from North Carolina Agricultural and Technical State University with a double bachelor's degree in psychology and criminal justice.

Kathryn Woods is assistant director of the Office of Women's Programs and Studies at Colorado State University, Fort Collins. She received her M.S.W. from Arizona State University.

Lisa Anne Zilney is an assistant professor of justice studies at Montclair State University in New Jersey. She earned her M.S. in criminal justice from Eastern Kentucky University, and her Ph.D. in sociology from the University of Tennessee. Her research interests revolve around issues of social justice, including family violence, drugs and society, environmental inequities, and sexual offenses and offenders.

Index

"driving while black," 358, 589, 631, 633, 637, 712
eating disorders, 939–940
elder care issues, 952
equal opportunity, 1301
gang memberships, 991
glass ceiling and, 124–127
HIV/AIDS, 1478
incarceration rates, 358, 604
medical treatment, 1320, 1337
parental corporal punishment, 855
pollution, 1352, 1383–1389, 1493–1494
poverty/public assistance, 1106
poverty rates, 270
punch-card voting, 1658
racial disparity, 1385–1387
and standardized testing, 1160
students, 875, 879–880
and teenage pregnancy, 1194
transportation dangers, 1643
voting data, 1034
See also Minorities, racial and ethnic
AgBioWorld Foundation, 1453
Aging out of foster care, 976
Agricultural concerns
biotechnology, **1293–1297**
genetically modified foods, 1296–1297
hog farms, 1505
by organic farmers, 1454
plant engineering, 1451–1452
ranching/ranchers, 1411, 1631, 1678–1679
soil erosion, 1534
stock grazing, **1630–1633**
"super weeds," 1297
sustainability, 1500
See also Industrial agriculture; Industrial feeding operations; Logging; Pesticides; U.S. Department of Agriculture
Agricultural Jobs, Opportunity, Benefits and Security Act (AgJOBS) bill, 1036
Agricultural subsidies, 140, 141–144
Ahrons, Constance, 882, 889
See also Divorce
Aid to Families with Dependent Children (AFDC), 264, 929, 973, 1028, 1108–1109
See also Poverty and public assistance
AIG (American International Group), 19, 101
Ain't I a Woman: Black Women and Feminism (Hooks), 783
Air America network, 1147
Air cargo security, 1267–1268
Air pollution, **1255–1261**
and acid rain, 1237–1245

in Arvin, California, 1260
defined, 1258–1259
indoor, 1259–1260, 1319
and oil drilling, 1579–1580
ozone, 1257
and public health, 1256–1258
quality of, 1256
state of, 1258
and transportation issues, 1644–1646
See also Incineration; Transportation
Airport/aviation security, 298, **1262–1271**
for air cargo, 1267–1268
aircraft surveillance technology, 1635–1636
and general aviation, 1268–1269
in-flight security, 1266–1267
passenger/baggage screening, 1263–1264
prescreening/behavior observation, 1264
responsibility for, 1262–1263, 1265–1266
shoulder-fired missiles, 1267
Airport Watch program, 1268
Alaskan North Slope, 1577–1579
Alcohol/alcohol abuse, 768
binge drinking, 208
blood alcohol limits, 475
Breathalyzer testing, 475
child abuse and, 826, 827
DWI and drug testing, 473–478
mental illness and, 1058
See also Marketing of alcohol and tobacco
Algae, 1286–1287, 1290, 1580, 1595, 1667
ALI (American Law Institute), 545
ALI-*Brawner* test, 545
Allergies
and GMOs, 1297, 1454, 1460–1461
from pests, 1596
from pollution, 1238, 1256, 1318–1320
to vaccines, 1653
Alliance for the Prudent Use of Antibiotics, 1425
Alternative fuel technologies, 1282, 1286
See also Fossil fuels
Alternative treatments for criminal offenders. *See* Criminal offenders, alternative treatments
Aluminum toxicity, **1238–1239**, 1258, 1524
Alzheimer's disease, 1058
Amazon.com, 1, 1516–1517
American Academy of Matrimonial Lawyers, 882
American Academy of Pediatrics (AAP), 998
American Anti-Doping Agency, 1168
American Association of Retired Persons (AARP), 194–195

Black hat hackers, 421
Black Power movement, 551
BlackBerry (device), 179
Blake, Paul, 1418
Blood alcohol limits, 475
Blow, Susan, 932
Board of Education v. Earls (2002), 474, 477
Bobo doll studies (media violence study), 1205–1206
Body image. *See* Self-injury (and body image)
Body mass index (BMI), 1569, 1571
Body searches, 674–675
Boggs Act (1951), 728, 924
Bomb squad robots, 1607–1608
Bonding and control theory (of gangs), 989
Bonds, Barry, 1168
Bonds, government. *See* Treasury securities
Books Not Bars, 558–559
Bookstores, 581–582
Boot camp (criminal justice), 370–371
Borchard, Edwin, 574
Border fence, **378–386**
  drug trafficking effects, 464
  installation of, 379–380
  opposition to, 384–386
  support for, 381–384
Border Patrol, U.S. (USBP)
  border fence and, 379–381
  creation of, 535
  drug trafficking and, 464
  national origin profiling, 638–640
  Operation Wetback, 637
  role of, 539
Border Tunnel Prevention Act (2006), 385
Born-Again Christians and divorce, 887
Born to Buy (Schor), 217
Botnets (Internet), 425
Bovine growth hormone (BGH), 1426–1427
Bovine spongiform encephalopathy (BSE), 1273, 1422
Box, Stephen , 394
Boycott Anorexic Marketing group, 941–942
Boyer, Herb, 1441, 1452
Boyle, Greg, 502
Boylston, Zabdiel, 1394
BP-Deepwater Horizon rig disaster (2010), 237, 245, 305–306, 410, 1282, 1428, 1523, 1578, 1580–1581, 1585, 1616
Brace, Charles Loring, 973
Bracero Program, 535
Bradford, William , 430
Bradley v. State (1824), 451
Brady Campaign (gun control), 507

Brady Handgun Violence Protection Act (1993), 508
Brain cancer, 1324–1327
Brain drain, 118
Branch Davidian movement, 655
Branch v. Texas (1972), 434
Brands (products)
  differentiation, 208
  recognition/loyalty, 217–218
Brawner test, 545
Breast cancer, 1308, 1310, 1386, 1406, 1427, 1484, 1559
Breathalyzer testing, 475
Breazeal, Cynthia, 1611
Bridge infrastructure, 1252
Bronchitis, 1256, 1321, 1384
Brown, Janice, 501
Brown, Louise, 1602
Brown, Michael, 14
Brown v. Board of Education (1954), 362, 873–876, 1030, 1075, 1076, 1133
Brown v. City of Oneonta (2000), 638
Brown v. Mississippi (1936), 568
Brownsfields Development policy, **1298–1305**
  beginnings of, 1298–1299
  and biofuel industry, 1304–1305
  clean-up campaigns, 1302–1303
  and environmentalism, 1300
  recent developments with, 1299–1300
  Superfund sites, 1300–1301
  urban environments, 1301–1302
Brumberg, Joan, 936–937, 1571
Buchanan, Patrick, 381–382
Buck, Carrie, 1404
Buck, Linda, 1014
Buckley v. Valeo (1976), 84, 89
Buddhists, 1121
Bulger, James Patrick, 1636
Bulimia nervosa, 937
Bullying, 664
Burden of proof
  in insanity defense, 545–546
  for juveniles in criminal court, 564
Bureau of Alcohol, Tobacco and Firearms (ATF), 508, 655
Bureau of Consumer Financial Protection, 107
Bureau of Indian Affairs, 1060
Bureau of Labor Statistics (BLS), 323
Bureau of Land Management (BLM), 1409, 1583
Burke, Alan, 1152
Burnet, Frank MacFarlane, 1509